Microprocessor System Design Concepts

OTHER BOOKS OF INTEREST

S. I. AHMAD and K. T. FUNG
Introduction to Computer Design and Implementation

MICHAEL ANDREWS
Principles of Firmware Engineering in Microprogram Control

J. E. ARSENAULT and J. A. ROBERTS
Reliability and Maintainability of Electronic Systems

JEAN-LOUP BAER
Computer Systems Architecture

JEAN-LOUP BAER and H. T. KUNG, Editors
Journal of VLSI and Computer Systems

MELVIN A. BREUER
Digital System Design Automation: Languages, Simulation,
and Data Base

MELVIN A. BREUER and ARTHUR D. FRIEDMAN
Diagnosis and Reliable Design of Digital Systems

RANDAL BRYANT, Editor
Proceedings of the Third Caltech Conference on VLSI

LUBOMIR BIC
MICOS: A Microprogrammable Computer Simulator

ERIK L. DAGLESS and DAVID ASPINALL
Introduction to Microcomputers

R. MICHAEL HORD
The Illiac IV: The First Supercomputer

H. T. KUNG, GUY STEELE, and ROBERT SPROULL, Editors
VLSI Systems and Computations

HAROLD LAWSON
Understanding Computer Systems

J. PAUL ROTH
Computer Logic, Testing, and Verification

IVAN TOMEK
Introduction to Computer Organization

JEFFREY D. ULLMAN
Computational Aspects of VLSI

R. MICHAEL HORD
Illiac IV: The First Supercomputer

Microprocessor System Design Concepts

NIKITAS A. ALEXANDRIDIS

National Technical University of Greece

COMPUTER SCIENCE PRESS

Computer Science Press
11 Taft Court
Rockville, Maryland 20850

    2   3   4   5   6   Printing   Year   89   88   87   86   85   84

Library of Congress Cataloging in Publication Data

Alexandridis, Nikitas A., 1943–
    Microprocessor system design concepts.

    Bibliography: p.
    Includes index.
    1. Microprocessors. 2. Computer architecture.
3. Computer engineering. I. Title.
QA6.5.A369 1984   621.3819'58   82-18189
ISBN 0-914894-66-8

To my wife, Aimy

CONTENTS

Preface

Digital systems and computers by now have entered all sectors of our everyday life, and the number of their applications is increasing rapidly.

With the appearance of *minicomputers* in the mid-1960s, the applications spectrum in which computers could be used widened significantly. In a number of industrial installations, minicomputers were placed in functioning systems in order to automate and optimize the plants' operation. Nevertheless, there were many situations for which minicomputers did not constitute a satisfactory solution, primarily because they were expensive and bulky. In those cases, control of the installation was still done by a digital system implemented with "random" logic. The basic electronic components of such "hardwired" systems were logic gates, flip-flops, and medium scale integration (MSI) devices such as counters, multiplexers, etc. Because of the inflexibility and high cost of manufacturing such digital systems, however, this method was used primarily for simple constructions or special-purpose designs.

With the introduction of the *microprocessor* in the early 1970s, a new dimension was provided for digital systems designers and engineers. This device was cheaper, smaller, required less power, and its programmability led to a more flexible design. New, "microprocessor-based systems" appeared. The applications spectrum in which computers could be used widened even further.

Since their first emergence, microprocessors have expanded in number, power, and diversity at an explosive rate. In recent years, quite a few advances have taken place which have been highlighted by the appearance of powerful 16- and 32-bit microprocessors. Very large scale integration (VLSI) technology has advanced to the point of supporting more features on a single chip, and thus eliminating limitations imposed on earlier generations of microprocessors, such as few internal registers, limited data-path widths and instruction set power, inadequate address spaces, and slow computational speeds.

At least as important as technology is the fact that many architectural sophistications are found in today's microprocessors. Most of them are old, powerful features previously found only in larger computers, but which migrated down to the microprocessor level. These include such features as instruction look-ahead and pipelining, multi-level priority interrupt structures, dynamic storage allocation capability, large address spaces, and hardware-supplied mechanisms for implementing virtual memory and multiprocessing systems.

Microprocessors can be programmed for a wide variety of tasks. At the low end of the applications spectrum, they can be programmed to replace hardwired or random-logic designs that require a large number of digital integrated circuits (ICs). At the high end, as new and more powerful microprocessors appear and are combined with memory, input/output devices and advanced software, they open vast new areas of applications where minicomputers and larger machines are not economically feasible.

Microprocessors force design engineers to learn new skills. The modern engineer must be a good computer programmer, since the design of digital systems today involves microprocessor programming, and often at the assembly language level. The designer, therefore, must be familiar with both systems and applications programming, since he or she often has to develop the software. Furthermore, the designer should understand not only how each individual system module is designed and operating, but also the set of signals issued on the system buses to coordinate and synchronize the operation of all these modules together in a completely working system. This means that the designer must be knowledgeable of digital systems organization and computer architecture, as well as proficient with the various methods and techniques used to interface a microprocessor system with external devices and other systems. Finally, he or she must have a fundamental working knowledge of hardware, software, and firmware integration.

This book is intended primarily for engineers and designers of microprocessor-based systems, software writers, and potential users of such systems. In that sense it covers architecture, system design concepts, and software. I have avoided reproducing extensive information on manufacturers' data which is widely available in the literature, but which quickly becomes dated. I have chosen a unified approach in presenting material on 8-, 16-, and 32-bit microprocessors, and in giving the basic principles and design methodology in an attempt to make this an educational book that will stand the test of time. Extensive reference is made throughout the book to the standardization effort carried out by the IEEE Society regarding floating-point arithmetic, microprocessor assembly language, and microcomputer system buses. As such, this book can be used in upper undergraduate or lower graduate courses in both electrical engineering and computer science faculties. The background required for the reader includes digital electronics, logic design of digital systems, assembly language programming, and an introductory exposure to computer organization and systems programming fundamentals. Extensive relative background references are provided at the end of each chapter.

The Introduction, chapter 1, outlines briefly the impressive advances in semiconductor technology that made possible the development of these powerful microprocessor chips, and the limitations and impacts technology will have on future systems. It defines microprocessors and microcomputers, traces their evolution, lists their present capabilities, and gives a quick overview of the topics treated in more detail in subsequent chapters of the book.

Chapter 2 reviews some background material on arithmetic systems, number representations, radix conversions, and coding used to represent digital information and ensure its reliable transmission.

The 8-bit microprocessors provide internal hardware for additions and subtractions only, and the 16-bit microprocessors include hardware multiply and divide facilities, whereas floating-point hardware has appeared exclusively in the recent 32-bit microprocessors. When a microprocessor does not provide appropriate hardware, arithmetic operations have to be programmed by the user. Procedures for carrying out binary and decimal arithmetic operations are given in chapter 3. The chapter covers microprocessor arithmetic on both fixed-point and floating-point numbers; for the latter, major emphasis is placed on the proposed IEEE standard.

Chapter 4 focuses mainly on the internal architecture and operation of the major component of the system, the microprocessor CPU. The first part of the chapter presents the major features and characteristics of the microprocessor, its basic architectural components and internal organization, and explains the steps involved in executing a program. The microprocessor CPU executes each instruction by initiating a number of "machine cycles," which are further subdivided into "states," corresponding to the fundamental units of processing activity. Common CPU operations executed by most microprocessors are outlined, and a brief discussion is given regarding other special operating modes not found in all microprocessors. The last part of the chapter describes the instruction look-ahead and pipeline features implemented in more recent 16- and 32-bit microprocessors.

The buses covered in chapter 5 constitute a major design component of any microprocessor system. A bus is the physical interconnecting link among all modules that make up a system, and the means through which these modules exchange information and communicate with each other. All control signals necessary to coordinate and synchronize the operation of the system modules travel over this bus. A distinction is made between the local "CPU bus" and the global "system bus" (again, for the latter, the IEEE proposed 796 system bus standard is used), and alternative bus organizations and possible microprocessor system configurations are presented. The chapter analyzes the subset of the bus signals required to interconnect the microprocessor CPU with the memory subsystem, explains the operation of both CPU and system buses, and presents the bus timing diagrams for a number of representative microprocessors.

The book examines next each of the remaining components of a working microprocessor system. Since, for large system configurations (systems that contain two or more printed circuit boards) the memory subsystem is connected to the system rather than the CPU bus, the first part of chapter 6 covers the CPU interface circuitry required to convert the CPU bus signals to the non-multiplexed signals of the system bus. The remainder of the chapter presents the design and operation of the memory subsystem.

Before continuing with the design of the I/O subsystem, chapter 7 examines some software and programming issues. The various software components usually provided to the user are presented, microprocessor programming in machine and assembly language is discussed (with special mention of the IEEE proposed microprocessor assembly language standard), and the chapter concludes with a detailed description of the addressing modes and structures found in microprocessors.

The discussion of input/output and I/O subsystem design starts with chapter 8. This chapter analyzes the program-driven I/O operation (both the accumulator I/O and the memory-mapped I/O techniques are covered), gives a number of illustrative examples, and presents the design of the I/O subsystem using MSI and LSI devices.

Chapter 9 continues further on the input/output topic, covering the interrupt-driven I/O and DMA-I/O methods. For the interrupt-driven I/O, the interrupt signals on both CPU and system buses are presented, the necessary interrupt interface control logic is analyzed, and the way the CPU responds to such interrupt request signals from peripheral devices is described. The ways in which interrupts are treated by specific representative 8- and 16-bit microprocessors are also presented. Finally, both single-line and multi-line interrupt configurations are discussed, and the discussion is supported by a number of examples. For the DMA-I/O, the necessary bus signals are presented, and various methods of executing the DMA transfer are outlined. Since recent microprocessors dedicate the whole I/O operation to separate, independent "I/O processors," this leads to the multiprocessor configurations discussed in the last part of this chapter. The bus exchange signals required to support multiprocessing are presented, along with bus arbitration techniques and both serial and parallel priority resolution mechanisms. Capabilities of representative 16-bit microprocessors to support multiprocessor configurations are also outlined.

Chapter 10 covers the segmentation and memory management mechanisms found in recent 16- and 32-bit microprocessors. The first part of the chapter presents some useful definitions and background material on the way memory is "logically" organized and on techniques for mapping the logical address space to physical address space. The second part of the chapter describes the mechanisms available in representative new microprocessors for supporting segmentation and efficient management of these large address spaces. These mechanisms are of interest not only to the systems architect and software engineer but also to the applications programmer, since they have an explicit effect on how he or she writes programs.

Chapter 11 focuses on multi-chip, bipolar microprocessors with bit-sliced architectures. It gives the design philosophy, discusses system configurations, and presents the internal organization of the bit-sliced devices used for such designs. Also described is the microprogrammability aspect of these systems, which provides increased system capability and flexibility for applications having unique requirements that cannot be satisfied by conventional MOS microprocessors.

Finally, the Appendices of this book provide more detailed information on specific 8-, 16-, and 32-bit microprocessors. Whenever these microprocessors are discussed in the main text of the book, the reader is urged to refer to the respective material given in the Appendices.

I started writing this book in mid-1980 at the National Technical University of Athens, but it was not until the spring of 1983 that I completed the last stages of this project, while on a six-month sabbatical leave at the Computer Science Department of U.C.L.A.

I would like to thank Arthur Friedman for the reviews and useful suggestions he provided on the preliminary manuscript and Jan Thompson for her fine grammatical copy editing.

I would like to express my gratitude to my wife, Aimy, for her encouragement, understanding, and the great patience she showed when family affairs had to be sacrificed during the long, tedious preparation period of this book.

Nikitas A. Alexandridis
Athens, Greece

Chapter 1

SEMICONDUCTOR TECHNOLOGY, MICROPROCESSOR CPUs, AND MICROPROCESSOR SYSTEM CONCEPTS

1.1 INTRODUCTION

This chapter outlines briefly the advances and state of the art of semiconductor technology, defines microprocessors and microcomputers (or microprocessor systems), presents the microprocessor evolution and present capabilities, and gives a brief overview of the topics to be treated in more detail in subsequent chapters of the book.

When the third generation circuits of *medium scale integration* (MSI) appeared, designers moved away from the classical methods of designing hardware systems, for which the basic elements used were *small scale integration* (SSI) circuits (e.g., gates, flip-flops, etc.), and in which the main goal of optimizing the design was to (mathematically) minimize the total number of gates or flip-flops required. With those MSI devices, the design criteria had changed. The cost of individual devices, or the minimum number of devices, did not constitute significant design factors any more. The new parameter entering the logic design methodology was the "gate-to-pin ratio." This ratio represents the number of logic elements contained in the MSI device, with respect to the number of I/O pins provided for interfacing with other devices. The greater the number of logic elements the MSI device contains, the more the interconnections of these elements will be internal to the device, thus reducing the number of external interface pins required. The basic goal of designing with MSI was to convert the problem properly, and adjust the application to the already existing standard MSI devices [4].

The continuous evolution of *metal oxide semiconductor* (MOS) technology[1] resulted in the next generation devices of *large scale integration* (LSI). The packing density—given as the number of MOS transistors contained—of these "LSI-on-chip" devices increased dramatically. At the same time, their cost decreased equally spectacularly. One could buy more than 1024 flip-flops in the form of a *random access memory* (RAM) for less than the cost of a single flip-flop a few years earlier. The same holds for the *read only memories* (ROMs) (equivalent to hundreds of gates) which were used to replace hard-wired combinational networks. Memory and hardwired logic became equivalent, in the sense that hardware elements could be replaced with bits in memory. This resulted in more flexible designs, since changes in the circuit simply meant modifying bits in memory. The classical design with random logic was replaced by programming! In the early 1970s a "universal," programmable logic device, actually a CPU-on-a-chip, was manufactured. This device was the *microprocessor*, which substantially replaced previous methods of designing digital systems. The double advantage it provides is using an IC of the highest possible complexity, which is also user-programmable.

The microprocessor-based or programmable implementation presents several advantages over hardwired implementations:

(a)   Reduced system implementation costs: Since the cost of a system is proportional to the number of ICs used for it, reducing the number of ICs through the use of LSI components and microprocessors reduces the overall cost of the system.

(b)   Reduced system implementation time: The use of microprocessors reduces the system implementation time, since: (1) the design and evaluation become easier, (2) the smaller number of ICs and the smaller size of the system under construction make working with it easier, and (3) the number of drawings and amount of documentation required are generally reduced.

(c)   Increased flexibility: The system under construction becomes more flexible, since expansions, improvements, and modifications to it can—in most cases—be achieved easily by changing a program, or replacing the ROM that contains it. Higher generality is also achieved, since the microprocessor constitutes a multipurpose raw material that can be used in the design of a number of different products.

---

[1]MOS technology includes NMOS (negative MOS), PMOS (positive MOS), CMOS (complementary MOS), HMOS (high-density MOS), and FAMOS (floating-gate avalance-injection MOS).

(d)   Increased reliability of the final product: The reliability of a micro-processor-based system is at least ten times higher than that of a hardwired implementation. In a digital system, most faults appear at the interconnecting points among its various logic devices; therefore, the interconnections contribute mainly to the unreliability of the system. On the other hand, one microprocessor can replace a large number of such logic devices, which means that it also eliminates all their interconnections. Thus, using a microprocessor reduces the total number of interconnections required for the system, which in turn increases the final product's reliability and reduces its maintenance requirements.

A few years later, as the next step of evolution, *very large-scale integration* (VLSI) circuits were introduced. As with MSI and LSI, the appearance of VLSI circuits again changed the design criteria. The number of devices packed on the VLSI chip was no longer an appropriate measure for the cost of a VLSI circuit. Instead, important parameters were the amount of power dissipated and the area of silicon used [11]. By the end of the 1970s, VLSI technology helped the manufacture of complex and powerful 16- and 32-bit microprocessors. The architectural sophistication and processing capabilities offered by these devices allowed the design of advanced microcomputers. This microprocessor-based system can now be used as a conventional computer that strongly competes with, and often replaces, larger minicomputers in a number of applications.

Section 1.2 summarizes the advances and recent developments in digital semiconductor technology. Although technology has already entered the VLSI era, it is still far from a practical limit, and technological acceleration will thus continue beyond this decade. The tremendous impact this will have upon future microprocessors and systems architectures, and the serious challenges it will present to the designers and engineers of the 1980s are also outlined in this section. The basic concepts and definitions of microprocessors and microcomputers are presented in section 1.3. The section also outlines the evolution of microprocessors, presents the basic characteristics and capabilities of several microprocessor generations, and lists a number of representative devices. Since the microprocessor corresponds only to a central processing unit (CPU), however, additional modules are also required to form a complete functioning system, such as memory and input/output modules, buses to link these modules together, and the necessary systems and application software. Such system concepts are overviewed in section 1.4. Finally, the chapter concludes by listing the advantages and disadvantages of microprocessors.

1.2   ADVANCES AND IMPACTS OF SEMICONDUCTOR TECHNOLOGY

The development of microprocessors and microcomputers was primarily a result of the impressive advances in semiconductor technology. Therefore, in order to appreciate the microprocessor evolution during the 1970s, understand current developments, and realize future limitations, one has to pay attention to these semiconductor advances.

Very large scale integration technology continuously provides higher component densities, circuit complexity, and switching speeds, while considerably reducing cost and power consumption in both processors and main memory units.

1.2.1   Rate of Change

During the past two decades, the developments in both semiconductor components and digital systems have improved both processing speed and cost per unit of work more than 1000-fold. For main memory units, the cost is being cut approximately in half every three years, access times are being reduced exponentially by about an order of magnitude every five years, while the density increases by a factor of 4 every four years. For processing modules, the cost decreases every year by approximately twenty-five percent, while microprocessor operating clock frequencies increase exponentially. At the same time, their component count per module almost doubles every twelve to eighteen months, primarily because of the following approximately equally contributing factors [18]: the increase in chip area, the decrease in minimum physical dimensions of components, and the contributions made by the invention of new structures and/or circuit cleverness. Although this complexity of circuits put onto a single chip has an exponential growth rate, the growth on the number of pins that can be accommodated per chip is at best linear.

Big 256K bits/chip MOS dynamic *random-access memories* (RAMs) and sub-20-nanosecond CMOS memories appeared early in the 1980s, and now work is being carried out in manufacturing the 512K-bit RAM. In microprocessors, word length has increased to thirty-two bits, operating clock frequency has reached 32 MHz, and chip density has increased to contain more than 450,000 transistors (the equivalent of more than 100,000 gates), while at the same time, power dissipation has been reduced to less than 2.5 watts. Single chips containing a million transistors will become available in the mid-1980s.

Although progress in component technology has been spectacular, it is actually the result of a steady evolution along a broad front of disciplines and techniques. Some of the most important advances in related disciplines that helped these new developments are given next [5].

Semiconductor Component Technology

- *Materials:* There has been a continuous increase in wafer sizes, from the 2-inch diameter in 1960, to 4-inch in 1977, and 5-inch diameter in the early 1980s. At the same time, the chip size increased from 0.5 mm^2 in the early 1960s, to 5.1 mm^2 (200 mils^2) for LSI technology, to 6.1 mm^2 (250 mils^2) for VLSI technology, to 25.5mm^2 (1000 mils^2) expected in a few years. There is also an increasing interest in gallium arsenide as the semiconductor material rather than silicon, superconductor technology material, and Josephson circuits.
- *Processes:* Advances in fabrication processes have caused reductions in line widths. The practical limit of 1.5 μm (micrometers) for the optical processes was already reached in the late 1970s. The new E-beam technologies present a practical limit of 0.25 μm, while X-ray lithography has a typical line width of 0.1–0.5 μm. E-beam and X-ray equipment should become available by the mid-1980s. Chemical processes for etching will give way to dry etching and ion implantation. Resolution of lines and spaces and accuracy of registration between one patterned layer and another are important to reducing overall circuit size.
- *Productivity:* (Defined as the number of good chips per wafer.) Advances here have made devices smaller and wafers larger, while at the same time imperfections were minimized, chip reliability was improved, and cost was reduced.

Logic Circuit Technology

- *Speed-power product:* Increasing the switching speed of the basic logic gate is directly related to power consumption requirements. The range of switching speeds and respective power consumptions per gate are: from 10^{-6} sec (10^{-4} watts) to more than 10^{-7} sec (10^{-3} watts) for PMOS logic; from less than 10^{-7} sec (less than 10^{-4} watts) to almost 10^{-8} sec (10^{-2} watts) for NMOS logic; from 10^{-8} sec (10^{-3} watts) to 10^{-9} sec (almost 10^{-1} watts) for TTL logic.
- *Densities:* Improvements in field effect transistor (FET) technology resulted in higher semiconductor chip complexity, from 100 transistors/chip in 1960, to 5,000 transistors/chip in 1970, to over 100,000 transistors/chip in 1980, to the current almost half million transistors/chip.
- *Physical size:* Taking the 1955 tube as the unit of measurement, the improvements in relative volumes present a reduction of 1/10 by 1965, of 1/12.5 by 1970, of 1/40 by 1975, and of 1/500 by 1980.

Memory Technology

- *Densities:* The improvements in memory device integration have been more pronounced than those in logic. Aside from factors that are common with logic, this is primarily a result of the "regularity" of interconnections inherent in memory devices, the reduction of active components/cell from six to one, and the implementation of the single-transistor cell with double-polysilicon and scaled-NMOS techniques. From the 1K bits/chip in the early 1970s, main memory integration moved to 4K bits/chip by the mid-1970s, to 16K bits/chip by the late 1970s, to 64K bits/chip by 1980, to 256K bits/chip by the early 1980s.

- *Physical size:* Compared to 1953's drum, the improvements in relative volume present a reduction of 1/4 in 1959's core, 1/50 in 1971's bipolar, and 1/6000 in 1979's FET.

- *Storage process technology:* Bipolar and MOS are the primary technologies used to manufacture microprocessor main memories. There are, however, newer memory types, referred to as "solid-state mass storage,"—the bubble, charge-coupled device (CCD) memories, and electron beam addressed memories (EBAMs)—which can be used to fill the cost/performance gap that exists between technologies used for main memory and those used for backing or direct access storage (such as disks or floppies). Newer systems will mix such technologies at various levels of the storage hierarchy. Magnetic bubble memories (MBMs) have faster access times than mechanical peripheral devices, lower power requirements, higher reliability, and are non-volatile. MBMs are available with capacities of 256K bits/chip (7 msec access time) and 1M bits/chip (40 msec access time), expandable in smaller increments, while 10-megabit chips are being experimented with in the laboratory. CCD memories promise to fill the cost/performance gap between semiconductor RAMs and bubble memories. CCDs are volatile semiconductor storage devices also incremented in modular forms of 16K, 64K (400 μsec access time), and 256K bits/chip. Some of their projected applications are in replacing fixed-head disks, main memory, and disk caches. Finally, EBAM chips have a cost/performance somewhere between CCD and MOS memories, and have already achieved densities of 22M bits. Figure 1.1 shows projected memory technology developments.

Geometries and Packaging

- *Performance:* There have been significant advances in reducing the delay time per stage, from the few hundred nsec/stage delay in 1955, to 3 nsec/stage in 1978, to approximately 1 nsec/stage in 1980, mainly as a result of progress in photolithography. Further scaling to 2 μm is expected

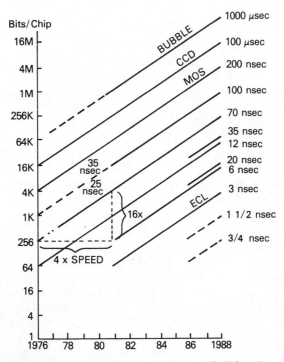

Figure 1.1 Projections for memory technology develoments, *G. Haley, "Interpreting the Needs of Computer Architects,"* Infotech State of the Art Report on Microelectronics, © *1980, p. 118* [11]. *Reprinted by permission of G.Haley, Manchester, England.*

to result in 0.5 to 1 nsec gate delays with a 0.1 pJ speed-power product. In general, the delay may be decreased by applying more power to the circuit. If it is desired to obtain an equivalent delay at lower power, then the physical size of the circuit will have to be reduced by utilizing smaller geometries in the component design and manufacture.

- *Power:* Significant progress has also been achieved in reducing the required power consumption per circuit from 3 mW/gate in 1976 to 0.5 mW/gate in 1980. Correspondingly, the speed-power product was reduced from 18 pJ in 1976 to 0.5 pJ in the early 1980s, and 0.1 pJ is planned for the coming years. Power dissipation, however, is still a major impediment to both bipolar and NMOS circuit designs. Power dissipation and power distribution characteristics are related to packaging density [24]. Power dissipation limits the number of transistors that can be put onto a single chip of silicon. To increase density, proper distribution of power in time and space is required.

- *Packaging:* Finally, the advances in packaging also have been significant. The chip improvements have reduced the packaging requirements and made their placement on printed circuit boards easier. The recent alternative to the 32- and 64-pin dual-in-line packages (DIPs), the quad-in-line package (QUIP), takes only half as much space on a board as equivalent DIPs. At the same time, however, while the ratio of the number of circuits on the chip to the number of its I/O connections is improved, this also imposes more critical demands on the power dissipation system. High chip densities with a fast circuit result in higher power dissipation for the chip, and force an appropriate spacing of the chips on the printed circuit board for cooling purposes. Closer spacing on the board can be implemented by lowering the chip density in order to reduce the chip power dissipation (or, alternatively, lower the circuit power while maintaining chip density).

1.2.2   VLSI: Practical Limits and Impacts

VLSI is viewed as providing more components per chip, costing less, and combining larger functional modules on a single chip [24]. A *definition of VLSI* would include the following [10,12]: micron and submicron design rules; large chips (over 6x6 mm) containing active devices of more than 50K; and memory chips with more than 64K bits. The first signs of the VLSI era appeared with the introduction of the 64K-bit dynamic RAM (5v supply voltage, access time around 100 nsec, cycle time 200–250 nsec, and power dissipation 150 mW) and the 16-bit single-chip microprocessors (containing almost 70K transistors on a chip of 265x265 mils, operating at clock speeds of over 5 MHz, and having speed-power products of less than 2 pJ). Today, dynamic RAMs of 256K bits/chip (access time around 160 nsec, and power dissipation of about 150 mW at 400 nsec cycle time) and 32-bit microprocessors (containing more than 100,000 transistors and operating from 10 MHz clocks) are commercially available.

The previously mentioned progress cannot continue forever. The *practical limits* for MOS technology suggest [8]: a circuit using CMOS technology, operating at a supply voltage of 400 mV, having a minimum line width of around 0.1 μm, dissipating 1 watt at an operating frequency of 100 MHz, having a chip size of about 5×5 cm, and having a complexity of 100M gates! Since we are still far from a practical limit, technological acceleration will continue beyond this decade.

The VLSI semiconductor era will have profound impacts in many related areas. It is not merely that the straight projection from past to future will continue to make quantitative computation smaller, faster, and cheaper, but, even more important, that VLSI promises to offer that quantum jump in capabilities which, when properly handled by scientists and designers, may lead to the long-needed changes in computational philosophy, system architecture and organization, and machine intelligence, thus making better the qualitative rather than the quantitative computation.

The effort to achieve such ambitious goals has spurred an international competition. In the United States, the Department of Defense has initiated a program to speed development of VLSI circuits for impending weapon systems, termed *very high-speed integration* (VHSI). Similarly, in Japan an industry-wide, government-sponsored VLSI program has already started (the Fifth Generation Computer Systems). In Europe, the European Economic Community is launching a long lead time research and development effort, termed "european strategic program of research and development in information technologies (ESPRIT)."

Out of the many possible areas, the following are distinguished, in that the effects and impacts of VLSI will be quite significant on them.

Effects on Machine Architecture and Software

Advances in semiconductor technology have contributed to an accelerating rate of progress in computer capability. Improvements in high-performance machines, however, have come about by combining semiconductor advances with those in machine design and architecture. The advanced capabilities of devices lead to new approaches in system architecture, machine organization, and function. Better theories for physical packaging and interconnection of computer modules are urgently needed. The traditional design techniques are presently being strongly questioned [25]. The efforts and trends from now on should be not so much in improving the von Neumann-based organizations for handling the large, complex problems, as in developing new techniques for decomposing these problems into simpler ones, in order to take proper advantage of these sophisticated hardware resources [15,23,25]. New architectural concepts are required for distributed, interconnected, multiprocessor configurations (pipeline, array, and independent processors) [16,27,29]. Redundancy and fault-tolerance may also be added in newer configurations (e.g., redundant modules with majority voting) to improve overall system reliability.

At the same time, related software concepts will also have to change. The previous limitations of systems (such as small memories, single, expensive CPUs, slow secondary memories) that drove the respective software developments, do not exist anymore. In the light of newer hardware developments, the role of software will probably change, thus affecting both systems designers and users. For the systems designers, the software will be used to control system configurations and data link interconnections in dynamically reconfigurable architectures and redefinable hardware functions. For the programmer, his task should become easier through the introduction of directly executable higher-level languages requiring no separate compilation step. The design of more advanced system/user interfaces (both in hardware and very high-level languages (VHLL)) will allow the "user" to define his or her problem directly to the system. The appropriate internal reconfiguration and allocation of system resources to fit the specific problem better, will be transparent to the user.

The approach to this end should follow a slow, consistent, and determined methodology. This transition must be systematic to minimize industry and market reaction and give time for all involved parties (education, industry, programmers, designers, and users) to adapt to it properly.

Impact on Microprocessor Systems

VLSI technology is influencing microprocessors and low-end minicomputers more rapidly than it is influencing high-end minicomputers or mainframe machines. This is primarily a result of the high volume of IC manufacturing and the relatively low production volumes of high-end machines. As already mentioned, memory systems are benefiting even more rapidly than microprocessors from progress in semiconductor technology.

With the new generation of VLSI circuits, it is not unreasonable to foresee single-chip microcomputers with as much as 256K bits of on-chip electrically erasable memory being used as the building blocks to configure more advanced computing systems. The architectural revolution in microprocessors that VLSI suggests has not taken place yet. Instead, what we have seen, in an evolutionary manner, is a repetition of the larger computer's history. Mainframe computer concepts and features, such as overlapped operations, cycle stealing, pipelining, floating-point hardware, virtual memory with dynamic allocation and real-time-driven interrupt mechanisms, have all migrated to minicomputers, and finally, toward the smaller microprocessors. The same has happened with software, in that high-level languages, design languages, compilers, position-independent code, and re-entrant programming are also being handled by today's more advanced microprocessors.

Instead of developing more sophisticated, larger word-length microprocessors, parallel architectures (already appearing in networks of microprocessors and controllers) may prove to be what can best take advantage of VLSI. Similarly, modular software operating systems will have to be generated to support the parallel architecture approach, and methods must be devised for exploiting parallelism in the work load. Along with the standard hardware module, standard firmware in the form of fully debugged ROM-resident subprograms (of 4K to 8K bytes long) may become available from semiconductor manufacturers to enable users to split programming tasks into small, manageable, modules [22].

Effects on Digital Test Technology

The introduction of more complex, operationally faster VLSI chips increases testing problems. The costs of classical testing methods tend to increase geometrically as the circuit complexity increases [24]. Testing, instead of being an after-the-fact activity, must now move into the design level. The design and testing of VLSI devices requires computers for data handling and decision-making, new techniques for measuring, and greater investments in testing equipment. At the same time, better algorithms are needed with self-testing capabilities to improve diagnostic resolution, and their implementation will present analogous software and programming difficulties [7,28].

Impact on Applications

Recent developments allow more main memory capacity for mainframe-type computer applications. We are seeing more extensive use of computer systems, highlighted by the "personal" computers. Advances in digital communication and reduction of hardware costs allow intelligence to be distributed close to where it is needed. Data base machines and software testing machines are two other application areas that can benefit from advances in the semiconductor technology.

1.2.3 Challenges that Must be Met

In order for the goals mentioned in the previous section to reach a satisfactory, user-acceptable level, there are certain challenges that must be met, including the following:

(a) Industry will have to develop better computer-aided design tools and techniques than those currently available. This also means more software problems and expensive installation investments.

(b) New fabrication technologies need to be developed (e.g., E-beam, X-ray lithography, etc.).

(c) There is a need to scale down the standard 5v TTL voltage level currently used for MOS devices (probably to 3 or 1.5v), and reduce the power dissipation/gate to the microwatt level in order to achieve the high densities and reduce internal gate speeds below 1 nsec [6].

(d) Increases in the effectiveness and probably in the number of I/O pins per chip (presently limited to sixty-four pins) are required as well. This may also mean shifting to other interface voltage standards that will make it easier to achieve higher frequencies (e.g., through fiber optics), and eliminate the need for time multiplexing the signals on the I/O pins.

(e) There are also a number of design problems that must be solved such as:

  • Determining the most cost-effective method of dynamically allocating
    tasks among different resources.
  • In a multi-user environment, resolving issues dealing with how the
    network is to be dynamically distributed among users.
  • Developing better theories, since relevant design problems are shifting
    from the modules themselves to the interconnections and module-to-
    module communications.

(f) In order to maximize the efficient exploitation of these powerful proces-
    sors and memories, engineers should be provided with new, greatly
    enhanced design tools adequate to deal with their complexity [7,17]:

  • New functional decomposition and design theories and techniques are
    needed.
  • Similar techniques are also required at the physical design level,
    including better layout strategies.
  • Better procedures should be invented to ensure system testability
    (self-testing through microdiagnosis) and measurement.
  • Ways and means must be devised for measuring and maintaining data
    integrity.

(g) As hardware becomes less expensive, the tradeoff between hardware and
    software requires new analysis.
(h) With the rapid advances in semiconductor technology and the appear-
    ance of VLSI, the real challenge will be what to do with all the powerful
    and complex ICs. A serious question is whether industry is ready and able
    to define the products of the future that will employ these VLSI chips
    effectively [19,3].

1.3 MICROPROCESSORS AND MICROCOMPUTERS

1.3.1 Basic Concepts and Definitions

Microprocessor

There are quite a few, sometimes completely different, definitions for microprocessors and microcomputers. In simple terms, the microprocessor is a
program-controlled device, which fetches (from memory), decodes, and executes instructions. In other words, it is a central processing unit (CPU), similar
to those found in any computer system, but with the distinction that it is
manufactured out of LSI and VLSI technologies. Most microprocessors are
single-chip devices, although some—especially in the recent 32-bit category—
are manufactured on more than one chip. The microprocessor module com-

municates with the memory and I/O modules of a system by sending addresses to them and sending or receiving data from them. Therefore, a microprocessor has both data handling components and control components. Although the details of the microprocessor architecture will be given in chapter 4, a brief outline of these components is presented here.

- *Data handling components* include: an accumulator (used for arithmetic/ logic operands and results, and for input/output operations), general-purpose registers (used to hold operands and intermediate results), addressing registers (used during memory access to hold addresses, index values, and stack and base pointers), relocation or segment registers (found in the new 16- and 32-bit microprocessors), an arithmetic logic unit (ALU) (to execute the arithmetic/logic operations), and flags (referring to the ALU result and the state of the CPU).
- *Control components* include: a program counter (pointing to the next instruction address), an instruction register (containing the operation code of the current instruction), some type of instruction queue (found in the new 16- and 32-bit microprocessors) for prefetching and holding a number of instruction bytes, data and address buffers (to latch data and addresses and to drive other external circuits), decoding circuitry (to decode the operation code and determine the control signals that must be issued for the instruction execution), and timing and control circuitry (driven by basic clock pulses and providing internal and external control and timing signals to facilitate data movements).

Microcomputer (or Microprocessor System)

For our purposes, we will use the classical definition, in which a microcomputer is a computer that has as its CPU an LSI/VLSI microprocessor, and includes program (usually ROM) and data (usually RAM) memory modules, a clock chip,[2] I/O interface devices,[3] may include some other special purpose modules, and has the general diagram of Figure 1.2. There may be one or more functionally separate *buses*[4] linking the various microcomputer modules. The

---

[2]Most recent microprocessors have an on-chip clock generator (triggered by an external crystal or RC network).

[3]The terms "device" or "module" will be used interchangeably throughout this book to denote any product properly connected to—and communicating information via—the bus.

[4]The "bus" is a communication path (usually a set of lines) used to transfer information (such as instructions, data, addresses, or control signals) between the modules that make up the system.

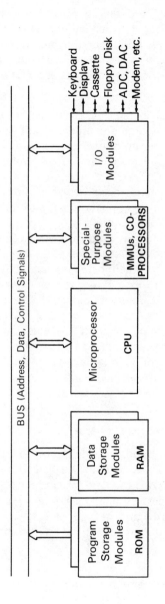

Figure 1.2 General block diagram of a microprocessor system.

terms "microprocessor system," or "microprocessor-based system" will also be used in this book as synonymous with microcomputer.

Continuing advances in VLSI, however, result in combining not only technologies, but also functions on a single chip. This leads to a "system-on-a-chip" or "microcomputer-on-a-chip," which besides the CPU, also contains many other support functions on the same chip, such as memory (RAM/ROM), counters/timers, and I/O ports (serial/parallel). Examples of such devices include the Motorola 6801, the Zilog Z8, the Intel 8051, and the Texas Instruments TMS 9940.

1.3.2 Microprocessor Evolution

The evolution of microprocessors has been very rapid, and the plethora of microprocessor applications, spectacular. In 1968 VIATRON surprised the world when it announced that it would manufacture a very inexpensive microcomputer,[5] and in 1969 General Electric had already manufactured a programmable LSI chip.[6] Nevertheless, the history of microprocessors does not begin until the end of 1970, when Intel Corporation started selling its first microprocessor, the Intel 4004. This 4-bit device had been placed completely on a single chip of PMOS technology, and constituted the first generation of microprocessors.

The design of the microprocessor was an accidental by-product of the general effort to manufacture semiconductor memories of MOS-LSI technology. By the end of the 1960–70 decade, it was already obvious that a technology was needed which would allow the placing of thousands of transistors on a single chip. However, it was not yet completely clear which functions could really use so many devices effectively. Memories were of course one such function. With the design and manufacture of such semiconductor memories, an equally complex processor was also required, which would not only be able to use them effectively, but would also make memory sales easier. Thus, the microprocessor was born.

Appearing three decades after the first electronic computers, the microprocessor benefited very much by the experience already acquired in the organization and architecture of larger computers. Many advanced concepts and

---

[5] In the heart of this microcomputer there was to be an 8-bit microprocessor, to form the microcomputer's CPU. This design, however, was never realized.

[6] An 8-bit basic logic unit or BLU, which could be used in the manufacture of a wide variety of terminals. All terminals would include the same unit, each terminal having its own individual program.

architectural characteristics, seldom met even in the much larger and more expensive computers of a few years ago, now constitute a basic part of almost all microprocessors (such as the stack, direct memory access (DMA) channel, vectored interrupts, etc.).

First-Generation Microprocessors

Many difficulties had to be overcome for the manufacture of the first micro-processors. Although the packing density of the elements had reached a satisfactory degree of integration, both for the microprocessor (CPU) and memories (RAM, ROM), the interconnection of these elements presented the following two basic problems: (1) problems relating to connections inside the CPU, where the microprocessor had to be constructed in such a way that internal connections should occupy the smallest possible area on the chip, and (2) problems relating to external interconnections between the microproces-sor and other modules of the system, mainly as a result of the fact that the first chips usually provided only sixteen pins for those interconnections. A solu-tion to both problems was given by the use of bidirectional and multiplexed buses.

To form a working system, however, additional external support circuits were now required to handle these multiplexed data and address buses. The number of these additional circuits could be as high as thirty ICs. For example, one of the first-generation microcomputers, the Intel MCS-4, was using four of the microprocessor pins in order to: (1) transmit to memory 12-bit addresses, (2) receive from memory 8-bit instructions, and (3) transmit and receive 4-bit data words over a 4-bit wide bus. To achieve an effective synchronization of all these operations, the Intel MCS-4 was using a signifi-cant number of external support circuits, such as memory access registers, memory address decoders, ICs for handling the information on the bus and synchronizing their transfer, and timing circuits.

The most widely used technology for the first-generation microprocessors was PMOS, the chips usually provided sixteen pins, and the microprocessor systems exhibited unibus architectures. Some representative first-generation microprocessors and microcomputers are given in Table 1.1. They are usually used in simple industrial applications, consumer equipment, and low-end special-purpose applications.

Second-Generation Microprocessors

The second-generation microprocessors appeared in 1973, and were manufac-tured in NMOS technology. Characteristics of second-generation micropro-cessors were: larger chips (size 170×200 mils) with forty pins, more on-chip decoded timing signals, the ability to address both larger memory spaces (64K

Table 1.1 Representative first-generation microprocessors and microcomputers.

	Microprocessors	Microcomputers
4 bits	•INTEL 4004 & 4040 •FAIRCHILD PPS-25 •NATIONAL IMP-4 (GPC/P) •ROCKWELL PPS-4 (P/N 10660) •MICROSYSTEMS INTL. MC-1	•INTEL MCS-4 & MCS-40 •FAIRCHILD PPS-25 •NATIONAL IMP-4 •ROCKWELL PPS-4 •MICROSYSTEMS INTL. MC-1 •AMI CK 114
8 bits	•INTEL 8008 •NATIONAL IMP-8 •ROCKWELL PPS-8 (10806) •AMI 7200 •MOSTEK 5065	•INTEL MCS-8 •NATIONAL IMP-8 •ROCKWELL PPS-8 •AMI 7200 •DEC MPS
16 bits	•NATIONAL IMP/16 •NATIONAL PACE	•NATIONAL IMP-16 •NATIONAL PACE

bytes) and more I/O ports (256 input ports and 256 output ports), faster operation, more powerful instruction sets, a greater number of levels of subroutine nesting (sixteen or more), and better interrupt handling capabilities (eight levels of vectored interrupts). Their basic electronic components were of smaller size (densities of 4K–5K transistors/chip), faster (gate delays of about 15 nsec), and dissipated less power (power-speed product of around 40 pJ). The cycle time was reduced to half, and the time required to execute an instruction was between 1.3 and 9 μsec. Since memory devices had at that time almost equal speeds, the manufacture of faster and more expensive microprocessors was not judged to be economically justifiable. Since these microprocessor chips had forty pins, they allowed separate buses for the data and the addresses. Therefore, multiplexing between data and address was not required, and most of the support circuits were eliminated, thus reducing the IC packages for external connections. For those applications needing low power consumption, the CMOS technology, which required power on the order of μwatt/chip, was used (for the NMOS, power was on the order of few mwatts/chip). More recent products of the second-generation microprocessors have reduced the power supply requirements to just a single +5v supply, and have placed the clock generator on the same microprocessor chip now needing only an external crystal or resistor capacitor (RC) network (e.g., Intel 8085, Zilog Z80).

Table 1.2 gives some representative second-generation microprocessors and microcomputers. These devices have a larger applications spectrum that includes: more complex industrial controllers; process control and data acquisition systems; instrumentation; peripheral equipment and intelligent terminals; military applications; communications; etc.

Table 1.2 Representative second-generation microprocessors and microcomputers.

	Microprocessors	Microcomputers
8 bits	•INTEL 8080/8085 •FAIRCHILD F-8 • MOTOROLA M6800/6809 •NATIONAL CMP-8 •RCA COSMAC •MOS Tech. 6500 •SIGNETICS 2650 •ZILOG Z80	•INTEL MCS-80 •MOTOROLA MC6800/6809 •GENERAL AUTOMATION LSI 12/16 •SIGNETICS PC 3000 •ZILOG Z80
12 bits	•INTERSIL 6100 (CMOS) •TOSHIBA TLCS-12	•INTERSIL CMOS-12
16 bits	•TI TMS 9900 •DEC (W.D. MCP-1600) •GENERAL INSTRUMENT CP1600 •DATA GENERAL μN601	•TI MODEL 990/4 •DEC LSI-11 •GENERAL INSTRUMENT 1600 •GENERAL AUTOMATION LSI 16 •DATA GENERAL microNOVA

Bit-sliced Microprocessors

Soon after the second-generation microprocessors appeared, another type of microprocessor, the bit-sliced microprocessor, manufactured mainly with TTL bipolar technology, was also introduced [1,20]. However, because TTL technology required higher power dissipation, it had not been possible to manufacture one full microprocessor on only one chip. Instead, several similar chips—each one corresponding to a register arithmetic logic unit (RALU) or CPU slice (of two or four bits) of the microprocessor—could be used in parallel to form a complete microprocessor having the desired word length. The operation of these "CPU slices" was controlled by a micropro- gram residing in a control store on a separate control chip. Microinstructions in the control store were fetched under the control of another chip called the "control store sequencer." Representative times for the microinstructions were 100–200 nsec, while the time required for the execution of a normal machine language instruction was on the order of 1 μsec. Although the microprocessor and the RAM or ROM memories were manufactured using bipolar technology, cheaper MOS technologies were utilized for peripheral mass storage memory.

The use of bipolar technology results in very high speeds. Microprocessors have very strong processing capabilities (they are user-microprogrammable, and slices can be cascaded to handle any word lengths), and flexible architec- ture with large memory handling capabilities. However, they are difficult to use and program, and have limited software support and I/O supporting devices.

Some proper applications for these bit-sliced devices are: sophisticated microcontrollers; emulation of existing minis; high-performance applications requiring large word lengths, high speed, and flexible architecture; scientific processing (such as Kalman filtering); etc. Bit-sliced microprocessors are treated in more detail in chapter 11.

Third-Generation (16-bit) Microprocessors

The third generation started in 1978 with the introduction of the single-chip 16-bit Intel 8086 microprocessor. This generation includes primarily the newer 16-bit microprocessors, such as: the Intel 8086 (Intel's new nomenclature for it is APX 86), the Zilog Z8000, the Motorola 68000, the National NS16016, and the Texas Instruments TMS 99000 series.

These new 16-bit microprocessors achieve enhanced performance relative to the 8-bit microprocessors. They represent a significantly more complex breed than the previous generation of 16-bit microprocessors, and include quite a few sophisticated features. HMOS technology is used to manufacture the microprocessor chip, which now has forty, forty-eight, or sixty-four pins. These new devices display very high speeds (clock frequencies from 4 to 10 MHz) and very strong processing capabilities (full minicomputer instruction sets), are easier to program, and allow for dynamically relocatable programs. Internally, they have increased the number and width of registers, and include multiply/divide arithmetic hardware. Almost all of them (except, perhaps, the Z8000) are microprogrammed. Memory accessing capability has increased to very large physical memory spaces (from 1M to 16M bytes) through a variety of flexible and powerful addressing modes, and these microprocessors have incorporated segmented (logical) addresses and virtual memory features. Virtual memory space has increased to 48M bytes. The interrupt handling capabilities have also become more powerful, the I/O has become more flexible, and most of these new 16-bit microprocessors provide "privileged" instructions and both "user" and "supervisor" modes of operation.

The third-generation devices may now be used in business and data processing applications, sophisticated real-time control, advanced communications, distributed processing networks, etc.

Fourth-Generation (32-bit) Microprocessors

The fourth generation was introduced in 1981 with the appearance of the 3-chip, 32-bit Intel APX 432 processing system. (The early version of the Motorola 68000, which incorporated features to handle 32-bit quantities, may be considered the "bridge" between third- and fourth-generation microprocessors). Other 32-bit microprocessors of this generation include the Bell Labs single-chip Bellmac-32, a 32-bit microprocessor from Hewlett-Packard, the

National NS16032, the Texas Instruments 99000, and the latest version of the Motorola 68000.

All of them have taken full advantage of the latest technology to integrate more devices per chip. The three-chip set APX 432 uses 64-pin chips, comes in QUIPs (quad-in-line packages), and packs about a quarter of a million transistors. The HMOS process is used, and the most complex of the three chips contains more than 100,000 transistors, laid out according to 3.5-μm design rules. Each chip dissipates less than 2.5 watts of power from a single 5-volt supply. Hewlett-Packard uses the NMOS 3 process, with a minimum size of 1.5 μm for line widths and 1 μm for spaces, achieved through the use of E-beam lithography. The component integration reaches the 450,000 transistors per chip. The clock operating frequencies for fourth-generation microprocessors range from 8 MHz to 32 MHz.

These 32-bit microprocessors have increased sophistications that compete strongly with mainframes. Virtual memory address spaces of up to 2^{40} bytes are supported, while the physical address space manipulated is 2^{24} bytes. All 32-bit microprocessors have incorporated floating-point hardware, and support an increased number of addressing modes (e.g., for scalar, vector, and record elements). Most of these VLSI chips have included self-testing routines kept in microstore, and their design separates fetch-and-decode as well as execution units (either on the same microprocessor chip or on two separate chips). Privilege levels also exist to isolate system and user software, while basic software routines have been microcoded on the CPU silicon. Also, more efficient multiprocessor system configurations are supported. For example, in the APX 432, processors can be added to or deleted from a system without software modification. Finally, a new bus structure has been introduced in the APX 432, in which communication among the system's modules is done via packeted messages through an appropriate interconnect protocol.

These fourth-generation devices now can be used for general-purpose computation in applications requiring mainframe-type computing power. Other uses include office information equipment, distributed data-processing systems, and multi-user, multi-function, environments.

1.3.3 Present Capabilities

Thus, we are witnessing a steady increase in microprocessor capabilities supported by: (1) semiconductor technology advances which reduce basic component size and power dissipation, and increase the number of pins per chip and operating speeds; (2) architectural advances which increase word length and throughput and external accessible address spaces.

Figure 1.3 summarizes the evolution in some of the most important characteristics of microprocessors [3,26].

Characteristic	1972	1974	Early 1978	Late 1978	1979	1981
Type: 1. Representative μP	i8008	i8080 (M6809/Z80)	i8086	Z8000	M68000	APX 432
CPU: 2. Word Length (Bits)	8	8 (some 16)	All 16 and 8	16 and 32	16 and 32	32
3. Clock Speed (MHz)	0.5–0.8	2–3	5–8	4–10	8	8
4. General Register File	7 (8 bits)	7 (8 bits)	8 (16 bits)	16 (16 bits)	16 (32 bits)	16 (32 bits) in 43202
Memory: 5. Physical Address Space (Bytes)	16K	64K	1M	8M	16M	16M
6. Segments	—	—	4 (Fixed size 64K bytes)	64/MMU (Variable size up to 64K bytes)	64/MMU (Variable size up to 64K bytes)	2^{24} of 2^{16} bytes/segment
Physical Characteristics: 7. Process	PMOS	PMOS/NMOS	Scaled NMOS	Scaled NMOS	Scaled NMOS	H MOS
8. Transistors/Chip	2K	4.5K	20K	17.5K	68K	100K
9. Chip Size (mils)	—	170 x 200	225 x 225	238 x 256	265 x 265	
10. Gate-Delay (nsec)	30	15	3	1–10	1–10	1–10
11. Speed-Power Product (pJ)	100	40	2	3–5	1	(power: 2.5 watts/chip)

Figure 1.3 Evolution of major microprocessor characteristics. *R. Sugarman, "Computers: Our Microuniverse Expands,"* IEEE Spectrum, *January 1979, p. 33 © 1979 IEEE, New York.*

With the 16- and 32-bit microprocessors we are presently seeing improved capabilities and advanced architectural features. Here is a brief glimpse at some of them:

(a) Generally, there has been increased architectural sophistication.

(b) User/supervisor modes: Most new microprocessors allow both user and supervisor modes through privileged instructions for I/O and processor control register handling.

(c) Multiprogramming capabilities: Most new microprocessors provide mechanisms for memory space protection among concurrently running programs. Resident operating systems are expected with resource allocation features and the ability to control I/O flow among these concurrent programs.

(d) Instruction sets: The new instruction sets are designed for array and repetitive operations, and include more powerful instructions (super instructions, STRING, MOVE, etc.,) with various addressing mode capabilities.

(e) Internal registers: A larger number of registers are provided to the programmer with more internal stacks.

(f) Program relocation: The new microprocessors have the sophistication to permit position-independent coding and dynamically relocatable programs.

(g) Memory management: The new devices also possess memory management hardware and protection features, for example:

Intel 8086:   Has no protection mode for memory management, divides the 1M-byte address space into 64K-byte segments, with the memory management mechanism placed on the CPU chip.

Zilog Z8000:   Has several protection modes for memory management, and its memory management mechanism is implemented on a separate chip called MMU (memory management unit).

Motorola 68000:   Also has several memory protection modes, and its memory management mechanism is again placed on a separate chip called memory management controller.

Intel APX432:   Has both segment-specific protection as well as user-specific protection, and its two-level mapping mechanism is implemented on a separate chip, the APX 43202 execution unit.

(h) Increased address space: The address space recently has been increased much more than the previously existing 64K bytes. The 8086 can directly access up to 1M bytes of memory in segmented mode. The Z8000 provides two CPU versions: the 40-pin version directly accesses the normal 64K-byte space, while the 48-pin version directly accesses an 8M-byte space in segmented mode. (The maximum physical main memory for the segmented Z8000 can be as large as 16M bytes). The 68000 directly accesses up to 16M bytes of physical space without a separate memory management device. And the APX 432 can access a logical address space of up to 2^{40} bytes, and support a physical address space of up to 2^{24} bytes.

(i) Instruction prefetching: The new 16-bit chips have included some kind of instruction look-ahead to increase system throughput. The 8086 prefetches instructions into an internal 6-byte first-in-first-out (FIFO) queue, the Z8000 has a one-instruction look-ahead capability, while the 68000 interleaves instructions through three separate internal ALUs. The new 32-bit entries have independent units, either on the same or on two separate chips: one to optimize the fetching and storing of upcoming instructions in a queue, and the other for executing them. Multi-stage pipelining is used to overlap the fetching, decoding, and execution portions of a number of instructions simultaneously.

(j) Interrupts: Most of the new chips have increased capabilities of handling exceptional conditions. These exceptional conditions include both external multi-level vectored interrupts and internal software traps.

(k) Arithmetic and data handling: The 16-bit microprocessors can handle 8- and 16-bit data; the Z8000 and 68000 can also handle 32-bit arithmetic operations. All possess internal multiply/divide hardware. The 32-bit microprocessors can handle larger data types, and include floating-point hardware.

(l) Multiprocessor configuration: All recent 16- and 32-bit microprocessors contain both hardware and software features to support multiprocessor system organizations, and facilitate distributed network configurations.

1.4 MICROPROCESSOR SYSTEM CONCEPTS

As shown in Figure 1.2, the microprocessor is just one of the many modules required to form a working microprocessor system. By itself, the microprocessor can do almost nothing. The additional modules required include various types of memories to hold information, and input/output or interface modules to transfer data in serial or parallel fashion between the microprocessor system and peripheral devices. Furthermore, all these modules must be suitably interconnected to communicate and exchange information with each other; this is accomplished through the use of information "buses."

1.4.1 Memory Modules

Whenever we refer to memory modules, we will mean main memory that is implemented on external, separate chips, and not the memory which may be incorporated on the same microprocessor CPU chip. These memory modules are used for two things: to hold instruction sequences (programs), and to store data. Functionally, the various types of storage modules are categorized as follows: random access memory (RAM), nonvolatile memories (read only memory or ROM, and its several variations), programmable logic arrays (PLA), content addressable memory (CAM), shift registers, and first-in-first-out (FIFO) memories. Another classification scheme used for semiconductor memories categorizes process technology into: bipolar, MOS, CCD, and the bubble technologies mentioned earlier. A brief discussion is given below, on the first two categories of RAM and ROM memories, which are usually used for the microcomputer's main storage.

Random Access Memory (RAM)

RAM memory (or read/write, or alterable memory) has the main characteristic that any memory location can be reached or accessed at random, and information can either be read from it or written into it. Therefore, RAM memories may be used for either program or data storage. Their main disadvantage is their volatility, i.e., all stored information is lost when power is switched off, and the information must therefore be reloaded after every power-on. RAM chips are manufactured using bipolar or MOS technology.

Bipolar RAMS

Compared to the MOS RAMs, bipolar memories are faster, but have smaller densities, are more expensive, and consume more power. The most common types of bipolar RAMS are TTL or ECL, and their applications are mainly in high-speed, writable control stores, buffers, caches, and scratchpad memories [13].

MOS RAMS

Although MOS RAMs were initially slower than bipolar, their evolution has been more rapid, and MOS RAMs exist today that have access times which overlap those of bipolar RAMs. The basic advantages of MOS RAMs are:

- They are quite fast, and the decoding circuits are placed on the same memory chip. They are manufactured using PMOS or NMOS technology. NMOS RAMs are faster, and memory speed may be increased even more by placing the decoding circuits outside the memory chip.
- They have small power consumption.
- They have great densities.
- Full compatibility exists between the memory storage cells and their supporting circuits (such as decoders, sense amplifiers, etc.).
- A great variety of MOS RAM memories exist, with different configurations, speeds, and capacities.

MOS RAMs exist in static and dynamic form. *Static* MOS RAMs hold stored data as long as power is being applied. Each memory cell is a bistable flip-flop that stores information. No special clock pulses are required to refresh their contents, and these RAMs are more immune to noise than dynamic RAMs. New high-speed static MOS RAMs are expected to replace bipolar TTL RAMs soon in a number of applications. On the other hand, *dynamic* MOS RAMs are cheaper, have greater densities, and require less standby power. However, information in the dynamic RAM is usually stored as an electrical charge on a capacitor of single transistor cell, which only provides for temporary storage of data (in the order of msecs). Therefore, these RAMs require special circuits and high-voltage clock pulses to refresh memory periodically (about once every 2 msec). This periodic refresh requirement makes dynamic memories slower than static memories.

As far as microprocessor systems go, for memory capacities of up to 4K words it is economically preferable to use static MOS RAMs. For larger capacities, however, dynamic MOS RAMs are preferable. CMOS RAMs also exist, but their difference from dynamic MOS RAMs, at least as far as their power consumption is concerned, is not very big.

Nonvolatile Memories

In quite a few microprocessor applications it is desirable to have the basic software and application programs stored permanently in memory, so that they are not lost when power is removed and do not need to be reloaded each time the system is powered on. Such nonvolatile storage is achieved by using read only memories (ROMs) and their recent alternatives.

ROM

The basic type of permanent storage memory is the ROM, also called "masked ROM," which permits only reading of its contents and not writing new information into it. Technologies used for ROM manufacture include: bipolar (TTL) and MOS (PMOS, NMOS, CMOS, and FAMOS). ROM memories are "programmed" initially during manufacture, by using special "masks." They are usually used for the permanent storage of programs for those applications that function by always executing the same unchanged program. They are very fast, having small access times (35-1200 nsec).

Besides the permanent storage of the system programs, some other applications of ROM memories include:

● Controlling stores in microprogrammed systems to hold the microinstructions that define the control signals and the way of executing the system's instructions.

- Replacing combinational and sequential random logic implementations (because their speed approaches that of semiconductor gates).
- Many common applications, such as, for example, generating and displaying characters on cathode ray tube (CRT) displays, code conversion, terminal device control, etc.
- Effective emulation of other machines by microprocessors, using the firmware approach with ROMs.

Of course, the characteristic that the ROM contents are not modifiable requires that the program to be stored (burned) in ROM be "perfect."

Another conceivable step may be the construction of a "ROM library" for microprocessors. Such a library may contain special application programs, such as multiply and divide programs, keyboard or CRT scanning programs, code conversion programs, and other useful routines, with each program placed on a separate ROM chip. We can then elect to use those ready ROM chips that contain the programs needed for our specific application (or construction).

A recent use of ROM memory has been to implement operating system microcoded routines in what the 32-bit Intel APX 432 calls "the silicon operating system."

PROM

The above-mentioned mask-programmed ROM memory is considered practical only when it is to be used in at least 100–300 similar systems (all ROMs programmed using the same mask).

A variation of ROM is the "programmable ROM," (PROM) or "write once memory." The time required to write a program in a PROM permanently varies from milliseconds to seconds. PROM memories can be programmed by the customer only once, and are usually manufactured in bipolar technology. The preparation of the data to be written in PROM is usually given (as is done for ROMs) in the form of truth tables or their equivalents, for example, specially prepared paper tapes, punched cards, etc. A useful device for programming PROMs is the "PROM programmer."

The basic advantage that PROMs have over ROMs is that they do away with the expense of manufacturing the mask. On the other hand, however, PROMs are more expensive (about ten times the cost per bit of that of ROMs). With PROMs, a quick turnaround is accomplished during the system development phase. Low costs are achieved for small system volume productions (less than 100-200). Each PROM usually has a pin compatible counterpart in the form of ROM. However, correcting errors is again not possible with PROMs.

EPROM

The last disadvantage of PROMs can be alleviated by using another type of ROM: the erasable PROM (EPROM). These memories are programmable more than once. Their basic difference from RAM memories is that their write time is much longer. The contents of an EPROM memory can be erased by exposing the memory to ultraviolet light (for a period of approximately 10-25 minutes), and the memory can then be programmed again. The most attractive technology for manufacturing PROMs is the FAMOS, primarily because of its high speed, low cost, and small size.

EPROM memories are widely used for prototype constructions and small quantity systems, because they allow for corrections of software errors without having to throw away a non-satisfactory chip. Each EPROM also has its counterpart in ROM form. EPROMs are more expensive and slower than bipolar PROMs.

EEPROM

The electrically erasable PROM is a type of PROM which can have selected parts of its memory electrically changed (i.e., erased and re-written). Electrical erasability implies the potential for programming the device without removing it from the circuit (as is usually done with EPROMs) and without the need for ultraviolet lamps. There are two types of EEPROMs: (1) metal nitride oxide semiconductors (MNOS EEPROMs), also called *EAROMs* (electrically alterable ROMs), and (2) floating-gate EEPROMs, also called *EEROMs*. Of the two, the EAROMs are most commonly used. The memory parts can be erased in 5-10 msec and re-written at the rate of 250 μsec to 1 msec per word. Erasing and writing require threshold voltages of 5-8v DC. These electrically erasable PROMs, however, are generally too slow to be used as main memories in the final product, and, at present, are rather expensive.

In one design of a microcomputer system, memories for storing the programs are used in an evolutionary manner, starting first with RAM, then using EPROM, then PROM, and finally, ROM. Thus, at the beginning, after the software has been written and properly debugged using a RAM memory, the programs are then placed into an EPROM memory for the evaluation and quality control of the prototype. If the prototype's throughput and performance are satisfactory, the programs are then usually transferred to the PROM memory in order to reduce the manufacture cost during the production of the first systems. The next step is to place the programs into ROM memory, if the anticipated production volume is sufficiently large to justify the expense of manufacturing the mask required for writing into ROMs. If the production volume is low, then the final means for nonvolatile storing of the programs is usually the PROM memory. The details of designing the memory system are given in chapter 6.

1.4.2   I/O Modules

Interfacing and software are the most tedious and difficult parts of the microprocessor system design. To connect external devices to the micropro-cessor, two facilities are required: I/O ports and interface circuitry. The interface circuitry converts voltages and currents from the outside world into digital form (e.g., by an A/D converter), to be presented at the input ports of the microporcessor system; inversely, it converts digital signals at the output ports of the microprocessor system to voltages and currents (e.g., by a seven-segment display driver) required by the external devices. Input and output signals in digital form are sensed by the microcomputer input ports or actuated by its output ports, respectively.

The microprocessor communicates with a peripheral device through one or more I/O ports. All I/O ports share the bidirectional data bus of the microp-rocessor system, and at the time data is being transferred (in either direction) between the microprocessor system and a peripheral device, only one port is allowed access to the data bus. The selection of the appropriate port is done by the microprocessor itself, and the direction of the data transfer is determined by proper control signals issued from the microprocessor CPU. In its simplest implementation, a parallel input port may be a register made up of three-state buffers, while a parallel output port may be a register made up of D-latches. LSI interface chips also exist to interconnect easily to the microprocessor system buses, and enable the designer to build complex interfaces with relative ease. Examples of LSI interface chips include keyboard encoders, priority encoders, universal asynchronous receivers/transmitters (UARTs), drivers for alphanumeric displays, seven-segment display drivers, etc. Chapter 8 covers all the details for accessing I/O ports, generating the appropriate control signals, and implementing the I/O interface system using SSI, MSI, and LSI devices.

I/O modules may also involve higher-complexity interface devices such as direct memory access (DMA) controllers, providing a number of DMA channels to interconnect peripheral devices. DMA controllers allow direct communication between peripheral devices and the system's main memory with no intervention of the microprocessor CPU in the data transfer path. Finally, "I/O processors" may also be used in the interface system, removing another level of control from the CPU. They contain a number of DMA channels, have processor-like capabilities executing their own instruction sets, and operate independent of the microprocessor CPU. Input/output operations through interrupt signals, DMA controllers, I/O processors, and multiprocessor configurations are discussed in detail in chapter 9.

1.4.3 Memory Management Units (MMUs)

Another type of module found in the 16- and 32-bit microcomputer systems is the memory management unit (MMU), implemented in one or more separate chips.

Memory management is usually required to prevent problems that result when multiple tasks within a given application contend for limited physical memory, or when users share common data or employ common programs. An MMU, aided by system programs, provides a technique for handling a larger addressing space in a flexible fashion, on behalf of the user. It does this by subdividing the total address space into variable length segments, defining logical addresses, and transforming them into physical addresses. This *address translation* performed by the MMU also facilitates segment relocatability (transparent to the user software), and protection for memory segments, very useful features for high-level languages and advanced operating systems (with multiprogramming and time-sharing capability). *Segment relocatability* makes user software addresses independent of physical memory addresses, thus freeing the user from specifying where information is actually stored in physical memory. Memory (or segment) *protection* and *management* prevent illegal uses of logical segments by having the MMU check a number of attributes, some of which include: differentiation between user and supervisor status of the segment, size of the segment, class of ownership (i.e., which tasks are permitted access to a segment), mode of accessing (i.e, read-only from a write-protected code or data zone, read/write, or execute only), etc.

A memory management unit usually functions as an I/O peripheral which can be manipulated (i.e., given the attributes of each segment, have its segment registers updated with new values, etc.) in supervisor mode by special privileged I/O instructions. The segmentation and memory management mechanisms are discussed in chapter 10.

1.4.4 Special-Purpose Modules

More complex microprocessor systems can be configured also by incorporating additional special-purpose support modules. These can be as simple as a bus controller (an IC that provides command and control timing generation as well as a bipolar drive capability), or as complex as another processor. These modules are compatible and easily interfaceable with the microprocessor CPU, and—acting like satellite processors—they free it from complex tasks that formerly required considerable CPU time. By themselves they can be quite complex processors with an instruction set of their own, supported by the enhanced instruction set of the newer, powerful CPUs. Typical functions that can be allocated to these external co-processors include: I/O processing to minimize I/O overhead, math functions, floating-point arithmetic, database search and maintenance operations, network interfaces, graphics-support operations, etc.

1.4.5   Buses

The microprocessor system buses are communications pathways, linking together the various modules of the system. The bus of Figure 1.2 is usually subdivided into three functionally separate buses: the data bus, the address bus, and the control bus. The data bus is used to transfer data, and it is usually as wide as the basic word length of the microprocessor. Thus, the 8-bit microprocessors (Intel 8085, Motorola 6800, Zilog Z80) employ 8-bit wide data buses, and the 16-bit microprocessors (Intel 8086, Motorola 68000, Zilog Z8000) employ 16-bit wide data buses. The address bus is used to transfer memory addresses (to select a memory location) or device numbers (to select an I/O port). For the 8-bit microprocessors the address bus is usually sixteen bits wide in order to accommodate a 64K-byte direct memory address space. The newer 16-bit microprocessors have wider address buses, thus allowing access to a larger memory space. Finally, system-wide control and timing signals are required to synchronize the operation of the separate and different modules of the system, and facilitate their intercommunication activities over the buses. Such control signals may include those that initiate or start a transfer and specify the direction of the transfer, notify the CPU that memory or I/O is not yet finished, notify all modules that CPU has halted, etc.

Usually the microprocessor CPU is in control of these buses. The timing of events on the buses is very important. Knowing the system state at all times, the microprocessor provides all other modules of the system with properly timed control signals that inform them as to the state of the CPU and what information is on the bus at all times. The control, operation, and signals of these buses are treated in chapter 5, along with other system concepts.

1.4.6   Programming and Software

Although software is mentioned last, its importance cannot be overestimated; software is a critical, expensive element in microprocessor system design. To use the microprocessor effectively, the designer must have a very strong understanding of software, in addition to topics such as hardware design, interfacing, system architecture, etc.

Independent of the specific language and machine to be used, software design is a very important step which must precede that of code writing (i.e., carrying out the actual programming). The basic steps of designing any system are also followed here in designing the software; they are:

- Understand user needs.
- Analyze the problem.
- Partition it into manageable-sized functional modules.
- Identify module interfaces and formulate the software specifications.
- Develop the algorithms and methods to be followed for each functional module.
- Construct the corresponding flowcharts.

When this software design phase is finished, one must: (1) decide upon the machine and language to be used; (2) code, execute, and debug the programs; and, (3) produce the required documentation of the finished work. It must also be remembered that this is an iterative process with subiterations within each step, usually requiring several tries before it is complete and correct. This last item of producing completely error-free software is a critical factor in microprocessor system designs, since programs may be committed to ROMs.

To ease the system development effort, a number of software tools are usually provided to the user to develop application programs. Some of these *software tools* are listed below:

- *System monitors:* Small programs that give the designer some way to load programs in memory, execute them, and monitor their performance (for example, by displaying the contents of memory or of CPU registers).
- *Text editors:* Used to create and modify source programs (for example, by deleting old text, inserting new text into old text, etc.).
- *Assemblers:* Utility programs which translate a program written in symbolic assembly language into binary code (machine language), which is executable by the microcomputer. Macroassemblers allow the use of macros when one is developing the application programs.
- *Compilers/interpreters:* Used to convert higher-level language source programs (e.g., BASIC, FORTRAN, Pascal, COBOL, APL, PLZ, PL/M, etc.) into machine language instructions. Compilers translate the entire source program at once to produce the entire object code, while interpreters translate each statement as it is encountered during program execution.
- *Loaders:* Programs to position machine language instructions and data into appropriate memory locations.
- *Utility programs:* Used to perform data conversion, file transfer tasks and mathematical subroutines, etc.
- *Simulators:* Used to simulate microprocessor operation by receiving as input the object code from assembler output.
- *Cross-software:* Such as cross-assemblers and cross-compilers that execute on larger computers.

Every day newer and more sophisticated high-level languages are continuously being developed to ease the task of the computer user and programmer. However, there still is and always will be a need for programming in assembly language, especially by the system designer and user of the smaller, low-end, microcomputers. As if programming at this lower level does not in itself present enough difficulties, a serious hindrance to the wider use of microprocessor assembly languages and to their becoming more machine-independent is the fact that each microprocessor manufacturer uses its own instruction set and mnemonics. Thus, it is difficult for a person whose experience was obtained on one microprocessor to understand the code developed for a different microprocessor.

Faced with such a large proliferation of mnemonic codes, inconsistent and conflicting use of operands, and varying definitions of address modes, the IEEE Computer Society is now trying to consolidate existing microprocessor assembly language features, and propose a standard for establishing assembly language conventions for present and future microprocessors (IEEE Task P694/011) [9]. This IEEE standard, as well as microcomputer software and assembly language programming aspects, are discussed further in chapter 7.

1.5 CONCLUSIONS

To recapitulate, then, microprocessors offer the following advantages and disadvantages:

Advantages:
• They combine the advantages of high density with small power consumption.
• The size and cost of the final product are reduced, while its capabilities and flexibility are increased.
• At the low end of the applications spectrum, microprocessors replace inflexible hardwired implementations, while at the high end, they replace expensive minicomputers.

Disadvantages:
• Compared to most minicomputers, microcomputers usually have smaller speed and instruction lengths, restricted ways of accessing memory, fewer internal registers, and less powerful interrupt capabilities and instruction repertoires. Software, customer support, and documentation for microcomputers are not as good.

With the appearance of new, powerful 16- and 32-bit microprocessors, however, most of these disadvantages have either been completely eliminated or minimized significantly.

With the dramatic decreases in hardware cost and the increases in hardware's computational capabilities, the trade-off between hardware and software may require a new analysis. Software today is replacing hardware because memory costs decline, and because it introduces more flexibility. The traversing of the circle may continue until the point is reached again at which firmware or hardware will replace common applications and system software.

These technological advances will give the impetus for a new creativity, which will involve a complete rethinking of computer and system architecture and functioning, and will focus more on qualitative than quantitative computation, with the emphasis primarily on making simpler the "user's" function.

REFERENCES AND BIBLIOGRAPHY

[1] Alexandridis, N.A., "Bit-sliced Microprocessor Architecture," *Computer*, June 1978, pp. 56–80.

[2] Alexandridis, N.A. "Microprocessor Systems—Architecture and Engineering," *Infotech State of the Art Report on Microelectronics*, Pergamon Infotech, series 8, no. 2, 1980, pp. 1–41.

[3] Allan, R., "VLSI: Scoping its Future," *IEEE Spectrum*, April 1979, pp. 30–37.

[4] Blakeslee, T.R., *Digital Design with Standard MSI & LSI*, New York: John Wiley & Sons, Inc., 1975.

[5] Bloch, E. and D. Galage, "Component Progress: Its Effect on High-Speed Computer Architecture and Machine Organization," *Computer*, April 1978, pp. 64–76.

[6] Caswell, H.L., et al, "Basic Technology," *Computer*, September 1978, pp. 10–19.

[7] Eichelberger, E.B., "Computer Technology Testing in the '80s," *Proceedings of the Conference on Computing in the 1980s*, Portland, OR, Long Beach, CA: (IEEE Computer Society, 1978 pp. 210–12.

[8] Faggin, F., "How VLSI Impacts Computer Architecture," *IEEE Spectrum*, May 1978, pp. 28–31.

[9] Fischer, W.P., "Microprocessor Assembly Language Draft Standard," *Computer*, December 1979, pp. 96–109.

[10] Gossen, R.N., Jr., "The 64K-bit RAM: A Prelude to VLSI," *IEEE Spectrum*, March 1979, pp. 42–45.

[11] Haley, G., "Interpreting the Needs of Computer Architects," *Infotech State of the Art Report on Microelectronics*, Pergamon Infotech, series 8, no. 2, 1980, pp 113–32.

[12] Heilmeier, G.H.,"Needed: a 'Miracle Slice' for VLSI Fabrication," *IEEE Spectrum*, March 1979, pp. 45-47.

[13] Hnatek, E.R., "Semiconductor Memory Update," Parts 1-3, *Computer Design*, December 1979 (pp. 67-77), January 1980 (pp. 119-31).

[14] Kartashev, S.I. and S.P. Kartashev, "Dynamic Architectures: Problems and Solutions," *Computer*, July 1978, pp. 26-40.

[15] Kartashev, S.I. and S.P. Kartashev, "LSI Modular Computers, Systems, and Networks," *Computer*, July 1978, pp. 7-15.

[16] Liebowitz, B.H., "Multiple Processor Minicomputer Systems—Part I: Design Concepts," *Computer Design*, October, 1978, pp. 87-95.

[17] Losleben, P., "Utilizing Semiconductor Technology of the '80s—A Design Problem." *Proceedings of the Conference on Computing in the 1980s*, Portland, OR, Long Beach, CA: IEEE Computer Society, 1978 pp. 237-43.

[18] Moore, G.E., "Digest of Papers," *International Electronic Devices Meeting*, Washington, D.C., New York: IEEE Press, 1975, p. 11.

[19] Moore, G.E., "VLSI: Some Fundamental Challenges," *IEEE Spectrum*, April 1979, pp. 30-37.

[20] Nemec, J., et. al., "A Primer on Bit-Sliced Microprocessors," *Electronic Design*, 3, February 1, 1977, pp. 52-60.

[21] Patterson, D.A. and C.H. Sequin, "Design Considerations for Single-Chip Computers of the Future," *IEEE Transactions on Computers*, vol. C-29, no. 2, February 1980, pp. 108-16.

[22] Queyssac, D., "Projecting VLSI's Impact on Microprocessors," *IEEE Spectrum*, May 1979, pp. 38-41.

[23] Siewiorek, D.P., et al, "The Use of LSI Modules in Computer Structures: Trends and Limitations," *Computer*, July 1978, pp. 16-25.

[24] Slana, M.F., "Computer Elements for the '80s," *Computer*, April 1979, pp. 98-102.

[25] Smith, S. and E.R. Garen, "The Impact of VLSI upon Computer Architecture," *Computer Design*, October 1978, pp. 200-204.

[26] Sugarman, R., "Computers: Our Microuniverse Expands," *IEEE Spectrum*, January 1979, pp. 32-37.

[27] Sutherland, I.E. and C.A. Mead, "Microelectronics and Computer Science," *Scientific American*, September 1977, pp. 210-28.

[28] Torrero, E.A., "VLSI and Other Solid-State Devices," *IEEE Spectrum*, January 1979, pp. 43-47.

[29] Wiessberger, A.J., "Analysis of Multiple-Microprocessor System Architectures," *Computer Design*, June 1977, pp. 151-63.

Chapter 2

ARITHMETIC SYSTEMS AND CODES

2.1 INTRODUCTION

This chapter reviews background material on arithmetic systems and codes. The section on arithmetic systems covers radix conventions, methods of converting from one radix system to another, and the three basic ways of representing numeric information within a processing system (sign and magnitude, radix complement, and digit complement), and reviews some useful rules needed for handling such information. The section on codes covers number codes (weighted and non-weighted) for representing numerical data, codes used for error detection and correction purposes, and character codes used to represent alphanumeric characters and special symbols.

2.2 ARITHMETIC SYSTEMS

Every computing system handles two basic types of information: instructions and data. Each *instruction* consists of at least an "operation code" field and an "operand" or "address" field, and it may also have some other smaller, special-purpose fields. The instruction format varies from one microprocessor to the next, and will be discussed in more detail in later chapters of this book. *Data* information may represent "arithmetic," "non-arithmetic," or "character" information.

Although the smallest possible unit of information is the single *bit*, a number of such bits are usually grouped together to form larger information units. The various ways of grouping these bits have been given specific names. The most common is the *character* or *byte*, used to represent a numeric digit, a letter, or some other special symbol of the alphabet. Although various lengths exist for the byte, the one most commonly used is the 8-bit byte. Another name for an information unit is the *word*, which for microprocessor systems, may be four bits long, eight bits long (a byte), sixteen bits long (a word), or an integer multiple of the byte.

The type, length, and internal structure of data representation vary from one system to another, and are usually determined by the specific operation for which the data are to be used. There are three principal categories of operations:

(a) Operations using "arithmetic" data, classified as:
  • either fixed-point arithmetic operations,
  • or floating-point arithmetic operations.
  Arithmetic operations are covered in the next chapter.
(b) Operations using "logical" data. Logical data have a simple structure composed of a string of bits, and the data length usually equals the length of the microprocessor word. Each bit has a separate and distinct meaning, in contrast to the arithmetic data, in which all the bits together define the value of the data.
(c) Operations using "alphanumeric characters," in which each numeric digit, letter, or special symbol of the alphabet is coded into binary form through one of the character codes (to be considered in section 2.4.)

Even more important than the internal structure, the lengths of information units influence considerably the means of storage in memory, the speed of processing by the system, and the system's I/O speed. Mentioned below are some of the most important factors that determine the length of an information unit:

(a) The density for storing information in memory. Given a memory size, the larger the length of the information unit, the smaller the total number of information units which can be stored in memory.
(b) The effectiveness of storing information in memory. This is related to whether the memory has bit, byte, or word organization, as well as to the method used for accessing memory.
(c) The number of bits in the information unit. This impacts the system's processing and I/O speeds. For a given width of the data transfer path and the data processing circuitry, the smaller the information unit, the larger the number of information units the system can process simultaneously.
(d) The range of the numbers (i.e., the extreme values the numbers may assume) the system is being asked to handle.
(e) The precision the processing system must have, i.e., the number of bits required for a series of computations, so that the final result will have the desired significance.
(f) The memory size (or capacity). This directly influences the length of the address field in an instruction.
(g) The number of instruction types in the system. This directly influences the length of the operation code in the instruction.

(h) The number of different fields in the instruction.
(i) The number of processor internal registers. This influences the length of the instruction.
(j) The arithmetic system used, i.e., radix 2, 16, etc.
(k) Special condition bits contained within the instruction.

2.2.1 Radix and Radix Conversion

Generally, arithmetic information is represented within the processor as a vector of some fixed length μ. For example, the number X is given in the vector form

$$(X)_r = (X_{n-1}X_{n-2} \ldots X_i \ldots X_0.X_{-1}X_{-2} \ldots X_{-m})_r, \qquad (2.1)$$

where r is an integer greater than 1, representing the *radix* or *base* of the arithmetic system being used, and where the value of each digit X_i is in the range $0 \leq X_i \leq r - 1$. Each X_i is called the "ith component" of the vector. The *length* μ of the above vector (2.1) equals $\mu = n + m$.

Numbers to be represented may be either positive or negative. In one representation, the first digit X_{n-1} of vector (2.1) is used to represent the sign (usually $X_{n-1} = 0$ for positive numbers and $X_{n-1} = r - 1$ for negative numbers), and the remaining digits $X_{n-2}X_{n-3} \ldots X_{-m}$ to represent the magnitude of the number, i.e., its absolute value. This representation is called *sign and magnitude* representation. Two other ways of representing positive and negative numbers are : the *radix complement* and the *digit complement* representations. The magnitude of the number (2.1) is symbolized as $|X$ and is given by the vector

$$(|X)_r = (X_{n-2}X_{n-3} \ldots X_0.X_{-1}X_{-2} \ldots X_{-m})_r, \qquad (2.2)$$

where the leftmost component X_{n-2} is its *most significant digit* and the rightmost component X_{-m} is its *least significant digit*. The part of the number falling to the left of the radix point and consisting of the digits $X_{n-2}X_{n-3} \ldots X_0$ is the *integer* part of the number, while the part to the right of the radix point and consisting of the digits $X_{-1}X_{-2} \ldots X_{-m}$ is the *fraction* part of the number.

Binary, Octal, and Hexadecimal Numbers

In the binary ($r = 2$) system, each digit X_i of the number is called a *bit*, and takes the value 0 or 1. The respective position weights are—from right to left—1, 2, 4, 8, 16, $\ldots$, 2^k.

Since the binary system has the disadvantage that the numbers become quite long and difficult to handle, two other equivalent representations are frequently used, *octal* and *hexadecimal*. Figure 2.1a shows the equivalence between octal digits and their respective binary representations, while Figure

2.1b shows the equivalence between hexadecimal digits and their respective binary representations. Each octal digit is represented by exactly three bits (since the radix 8 is the third power of 2), while each hexadecimal digit is represented by exactly four bits (since the radix 16 is the fourth power of 2).

Octal Digit

0	1	2	3	4	5	6	7

Equivalent Binary Representation

000	001	010	011	100	101	110	111

(a) The binary equivalent of each octal digit.

Hexadecimal Digit

0	1	2	3	4	5	6	7	8	9	A	B	C	D	E	F

Equivalent Binary Representation

0000	0001	0010	0011	0100	0101	0110	0111	1000	1001	1010	1011	1100	1101	1110	1111

(b) The binary equivalent of each hexadecimal digit.

Figure 2.1 Relationships between binary, octal, and hexadecimal digits.

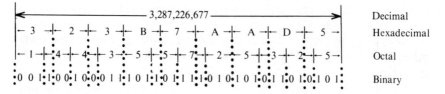

Figure 2.2 The octal, hexadecimal, and decimal equivalents of a 36-bit binary vector.

Conversion between binary and octal, or hexadecimal numbers is quite straightforward. Figure 2.2 shows a 36-bit vector that may be considered as a 36-bit binary number, a 12-digit octal number, or a 9-digit hexadecimal number. No matter what its representation, its decimal value is 3,287,226.677. Therefore:

$$(3,287,226.677)_{10} = (323B7A.AD5)_{16} = (14435572.5325)_8 =$$
$$= (001100100011101101111010.101011010101)_2$$

Radix Conversion

Radix conversion from one arithmetic system to another is done separately for the integer and fraction parts of the number. Let us assume the following number N of radix r,

$(N)_r = (I)_r.(F)_r = $ (Integer part)$_r$.(Fraction part)$_r$.
$$= d_{n-2}d_{n-3} \ldots d_0.d_{-1}d_{-2} \ldots d_{-m} \qquad (2.3)$$

which we want to convert into a number N' with respect to a new radix g. Let the general form of this new number be:

$(N')_g = (I')_g.(F')_g = $ (New integer part)$_g$.(New fraction part)$_g$
$$= b_{u-2}b_{u-3} \ldots b_0.b_{-1}b_{-2} \ldots b_{-j}. \qquad (2.4)$$

Conversion of Integers

Here we want to convert the integer part $(I)_r = d_{n-2}d_{n-3} \ldots d_0$ of Equation (2.3) into the respective integer part $(I')_g = b_{u-2}b_{u-3} \ldots b_0$ of the *new* number of Equation (2.4). The conversion is based upon the observation that we wish to have the following relationship:

$$[(I)_r]_{10} = b_{u-2} \times g^{u-2} + \ldots + b_1 \times g^1 + b_0 , \qquad (2.5)$$

where $[(I)_r]_{10}$ is the decimal value[1] of $(I)_r$. The above expression (2.5) may also be written as

$$I = g \times Q_1 + b_0 , \text{ where } 0 \le b_0 < g , \qquad (2.6)$$

and where

$$Q_1 = b_{u-2} \times g^{u-3} + \ldots + b_2 \times g^1 + b_1 \times g^0 . \qquad (2.7)$$

In other words, we wish to end up with a relationship, such that, the initial number $(I)_r = d_{n-2} \ldots d_0$ equals the product of the new radix g times the Q_1 given from Equation (2.7), plus some constant b_0. Since, however, this is the familiar definition of the division operation, if we divide $(I)_r$ by the new radix g, then we will get the quotient Q_1 and the remainder b_0. Therefore, the conversion of integer $(I)_r$ into integer $(I')_g$ may be accomplished by the following procedure of repeated division:

Procedure 2.1   (Conversion of Integers)

(1) Divide the original number $(I)_r = d_{n-2} \ldots d_1 d_0$ by the *new* radix g and obtain an integer quotient Q_1 and a remainder b_0.
(2) The quotient Q_1 may also be represented as the product of radix g times a new Q_2, plus some constant b_1, i.e.,

$$Q_1 = g \times Q_2 + b_1 , \qquad (2.8)$$

---

[1]For binary numbers where $r = 2$, this lower subscript r will be omitted and the decimal value of a binary vector X will be denoted as $(X)_{10}$.

where

$$Q_2 = b_{u-2} \times g^{u-4} + \ldots + b_3 \times g^1 + b_2 \times g^0 . \qquad (2.9)$$

Divide Q_1 by the new radix g and obtain a new integer quotient Q_2 and a new remainder b_1.

The above two-step procedure is continued, until, during some step i, a quotient Q_i is found, such that $Q_i = 0$. The various remainders produced from the above divisions represent the new integer number $(I')_g = b_{u-2}b_{u-3} \ldots b_1 b_0$, with the result b produced least significant position first.

Conversion of Fractions

We now consider the conversion of the fraction part $(F)_r = 0 . d_{-1}d_{-2}\ldots d_{-m}$ of Equation (2.3) into the respective fraction part $(F') = 0 . b_{-1}b_{-2} \ldots b_{-j}$ of Equation (2.4).

In the converting of fractions, a situation may arise in which a fraction consisting of a finite number of digits may contain an infinite number of digits when converted into a new radix. Consequently, the fraction conversion algorithm usually continues to a prespecified number of positions j. This j depends upon the accuracy desired in the result.

Keeping this in mind, we observe that in fraction conversions, we wish to have the following relationship:

$$[(F)_r]_{10} = b_{-1} \times g^{-1} + b_{-2} \times g^{-2} + b_{-3} + g^{-3} + \ldots + b_{-j} \times g^{-j} , (2.10)$$

where $[(F)_r]_{10}$ is the decimal value of $(F)_r$.

Thus, this leads to the following procedure of repeated multiplication:

Procedure 2.2   (Conversion of Fractions)

(1) Multiply the original fraction F with the *new* radix g, to obtain:

$$g \times F = b_{-1} + b_{-2} \times g^{-1} + \ldots + b_{-j} \times g^{-j+1} = b_{-1} + P_1 , \quad (2.11)$$

$$\text{where } P_1 < 1 \text{ and } 0 \le b_{-1} \le g - 1 .$$

(2) Multiply P_1 with the *new* radix g, to obtain:

$$g \times P_1 = b_{-2} + b_{-3} \times g^{-1} + \ldots + b_{-j} \times g^{-j+2} = b_{-2} + P_2 . \, (2.12)$$

Continuing in a similar manner, we end up with the relationship:

$$g \times P_{j-1} = b_{-j} + P_j , \qquad (2.13)$$

where $g^{-j} \times P_j \le \epsilon$ and ϵ is the largest acceptable error during this approximate conversion. If $P_j = 0$, then the fraction conversion is absolutely exact (without an approximation error).

2.2.2 Number Representation

The complexity of the arithmetic algorithms depends upon the specific method used by the processor for representing numbers. In general, every number is given in the vector form of Equation (2.1), where, if $X_{n-1} = 0$, then the number is considered positive, and if $X_{n-1} = r - 1$, then the number is considered negative.

There are three basic ways of representing positive and negative numbers: the sign and magnitude, the radix complement, and the digit complement representations.

Sign and Magnitude (S&M) Representation

Here, the leftmost digit X_{n-1} of the number represents its sign, while the remaining digits $X_{n-2} \ldots X_{-m}$ represent its magnitude. Therefore, the decimal value of the number is given by the expression:

$$(X_r)_{10} = \sum_{i=-m}^{n-2} X_i \times r^i \text{, if } X_{n-1} = 0 \text{ (positive number)}$$

and

$$(X_r)_{10} = -\sum_{i=-m}^{n-2} X_i \times r^i \text{, if } X_{n-1} = r-1 \text{ (negative number).}$$

(2.14)

If the radix r is an even number, then the above expression (2.14) reduces to:

$$(X_r)_{10} = (-1)^{X_{n-1}} \times \sum_{i=-m}^{n-2} X_i \times r^i.$$

(2.15)

The *range* of these values is

$$-(r^{n-1} - r^{-m}) \leq (X_r)_{10} \leq (r^{n-1} - r^{-m}),$$

(2.16)

where the *largest* possible number is represented by the $(n + m)$-digit vector $[0 \ (r - 1) \ (r - 1)\ldots(r - 1)]$ and the *smallest* possible number by the $(n + m)$-digit vector $[(r - 1) \ (r - 1)\ldots(r - 1)]$. The S&M representation has the peculiarity that there are two expressions for the number 0:

$$+0 \text{ represented by } (0 \ 0 \ 0\ldots0)$$

and

$$-0 \text{ represented by } [(r - 1) \ 0 \ 0 \ 0\ldots0] \ .$$

Complement Notation

Let θ be the maximum positive value of number X. Given the unsigned integer numbers λ, X, and $\overline{X}$, we say that "$\overline{X}$ is the *complement* of X with respect to λ" if the following relationship holds:

$$X + \overline{X} = \lambda . \tag{2.17}$$

Every integer X falling in the region $[0,\theta]$ will have a distinct and unique complement $\overline{X}$, if all these $\overline{X}$ fall outside the region of X. This condition is satisfied if the restriction $\lambda - \theta > \theta$ is valid, which gives the following condition for the modulus λ:

$$\lambda > 2 \times \theta . \tag{2.18}$$

In the complement system, the integers X $(0 \le X \le \theta)$ represent the *true form* of the numbers, while the integers $\overline{X} = \lambda - X$ (whose real value is greater than θ) represent the *complement form of X with respect to λ, or λ's complement*. Therefore, the positive number $+X$ is represented in the complement system by the unsigned true form X, while its negative $-X$ is represented by the complement of X with respect to λ, in other words, by the unsigned number $\overline{X} = \lambda - X$ (Equation 2.17). Given the vector

$$(X)_r = (X_{n-2}X_{n-3} \dots X_1 X_0 . X_{-1}X_{-2} \dots X_{-m}), \tag{2.19}$$

its maximum possible *magnitude* has the form

$$(|X_{max}|)_r = [(r-1)_{n-2}(r-1)_{n-3} \dots (r-1)_0 . (r-1)_{-1} \dots (r-1)_{-m}], \tag{2.20}$$

$$n-1+m \text{ digits}$$

and its decimal value is

$$[(|X_{max}|)_r]_{10} = \theta = r^{n-1} - r^{-m} .$$

In order to satisfy the condition (2.18) for the above vector X, the modulus λ must be chosen so that $\lambda > 2 \times (r^{n-1} - r^{-m})$. The two most common and practical values for this modulus λ are: $\lambda_r = r^n$ and $\lambda_d = r^n - r^{-m}$. These two different moduli define two different representations: the radix complement and the digit complement representations.

Radix Complement (or r's Complement)[2]

In this representation, the modulus λ used is given by

$$\lambda_r = r^n , \tag{2.21}$$

---

[2]This is also called "range complement representation."

where n is the number of integer digits in Equation (2.1) including the sign-digit. For decimal numbers ($r = 10$) this system is called the "10's complement system," while for binary numbers ($r = 2$) this system is called the "2's complement system."

The negative number $-X$ corresponds to the r's complement of X, symbolized by $\bar{X}$, and is given by the vector difference

$$\bar{X} = \lambda_r - X = r^n - X, \tag{2.22}$$

where, for the general case of the mixed numbers of Equation (2.1), the modulus λ_r has the vector form:

$$\lambda_r = r^n = \underbrace{(1\ 0\ 0\ldots 0)}_{n+\ 1+m\ \text{digits.}} \tag{2.23}$$

The decimal value of the number X of Equation (2.1) is now given by:

$$(X_r)_{10} = \begin{cases} \displaystyle\sum_{i=-m}^{n-2} X_i \times r^i, & \text{if } X_{n-1} = 0 \text{ (positive number)} \\[2em] \displaystyle -r^{n-1} + \sum_{i=-m}^{n-2} X_i \times r^i, & \text{if } X_{n-1} = r - 1 \text{ (negative number)} \end{cases} \tag{2.24}$$

The *range* of these values is

$$-r^{n-1} \leq (X_r)_{10} \leq (r^{n-1} - r^{-m}), \tag{2.25}$$

where the *largest* possible number is represented by the $(n + m)$-digit vector $[0\,(r - 1)\,(r - 1)\ldots(r - 1)]$, and the *smallest* possible number by the $(n + m)$-digit vector $[(r - 1)\,0\,0\ldots 0]$. The r's complement system has the peculiar-ity that this smallest possible number and its r's complement are the same. In the r's complement system there is only one representation for 0: $(0\ 0\ 0\ldots 0)$.

Digit Complement [or ($r - 1$)'s Complement][3]

In this representation, the modulus λ used is given by

$$\lambda_d = r^n - r^{-m}, \tag{2.26}$$

where n is the number of integer digits in Equation (2.1) including the sign-digit and m is the number of fraction digits in (2.1). For integer numbers where $m = 0$, the above modulus λ_d becomes

$$\lambda_d = r^n - 1. \tag{2.27}$$

---

[3]This is also called "diminished radix complement representation."

For decimal numbers $(r = 10)$ this system is called the "9's complement system," while for binary numbers $(r = 2)$, this system is called the "1's complement system."

The negative number $-X$ corresponds to the $(r-1)$'s complement of X, is again symbolized by $\overline{X}$, and is given by the vector difference

$$\overline{X} = \lambda_d - X = (r^n - r^{-m}) - X , \qquad (2.28)$$

where, for the general case of the mixed numbers of Equation (2.1), the modulus λ_d has the form:

$$\lambda_d = r^n - r^{-m} = \underbrace{[(r - 1)\ (r - 1)\ldots(r - 1)]}_{n+m \text{ digits}}. \qquad (2.29)$$

The decimal value of the number X of Equation (2.1) is given by:

$$(X_r)_{10} = \begin{cases} \displaystyle\sum_{i=-m}^{n-2} X_i \times r^i , & \text{if } X_{n-1} = 0 \text{ (positive number)} \\[2em] -(r^{n-1} - r^{-m}) + \displaystyle\sum_{i=-m}^{n-2} X_i \times r^i , & \text{if } X_{n-1} = r - 1 \text{ (negative number)} \end{cases} \qquad (2.30)$$

The *range* of these values is

$$-(r^{n-1} - r^{-m}) \le (X_r)_{10} \le (r^{n-1} - r^{-m}) , \qquad (2.31)$$

where the *largest* possible number is represented by the $(n + m)$-digit vector $[0\ (r - 1)\ (r - 1)\ldots(r - 1)]$ and the smallest possible number by the $(n + m)$-digit vector $[(r - 1)\ 0\ 0\ldots0]$. The $(r - 1)$'s complement system has the peculiarity that there are two representations for 0:

$$+0 \text{ represented by } (0\ 0\ 0\ldots0)$$

and

$$-0 \text{ represented by } [(r - 1)\ (r - 1)\ldots(r - 1)].$$

2.2.3 Some Useful Rules

Arithmetic Shifts

Arithmetic operations quite often require the execution of left and right shifts on the operands and/or the results. These shifting operations are governed by basic rules that differ, depending upon the specific system used for representing numbers.

Let us assume that the initial number is given as

$$X = X_{n-1}X_{n-2}\ldots X_1X_0 \, ,$$

and that the result of the shifting operation is given as

$$X' = X'_{n-1}X'_{n-2}\ldots X'_1X'_0 \, .$$

When shifting *positive numbers*, the following rules apply for all three systems of representing numbers, i.e., S&M, r's complement, and $(r-1)$'s complement.

(a) Shifting a positive number *right* by one position:

$X'_{n-1} = X_{n-1} = 0$ (the sign-digit does not change)

$X'_{n-2} = 0$ (the digit to the right of the sign-digit takes on the value 0)

$X'_i \;\;\;= X_{i+1} \, ,$ for $i = 0,1,\ldots,n-3$.

    The digit X_0 is (usually) lost.

(b) Shifting a positive number *left* by one position:

$X'_{n-1} = X_{n-1} = 0$ (the sign-digit does not change)

$X'_0 \;\;\;= 0$ (a 0 is inserted to the right)

$X'_i \;\;\;= X_{i-1} \, ,$ for $i = 1,2,\ldots,n-2$.

    The digit X_{n-2} is (usually) lost.

The above (a) and (b) can be generalized easily for positive number shifts of more than one position.

The shifting rules for *negative numbers*, however, differ. All negative numbers have a sign-digit of $X_{n-1} = r-1$. After the shifting operation (left or right) of the number by one position, the sign-digit continues to equal $X'_{n-1} = X_{n-1} = r-1$, i.e., the number continues to remain negative. The remaining digits—for shifts by one position—are given according to the rules listed in Table 2.1.

Table 2.1 Arithmetic shifting rules for negative numbers (shifting by one position).

Shifting	The new values of the digits		
	S&M	$(r-1)$'s Complement	r's Complement
Right	$X'_{n-2} = 0$ $X'_i = X_{i+1}$, for $i = 0,1,\ldots,n-3$	$X'_{n-2} = r-1$ $X'_i = X_{i+1}$, for $i = 0,1,\ldots,n-3$	$X'_{n-2} = r-1$ $X'_i = X_{i+1}$, for $i = 0,1,\ldots,n-3$
Left	$X'_0 = 0$ $X'_i = X_{i-1}$, for $i = 1,2,\ldots,n-2$	$X'_0 = r-1$ $X'_i = X_{i-1}$, for $i = 1,2,\ldots,n-2$	$X'_0 = 0$ $X'_i = X_{i-1}$, for $i = 1,2,\ldots,n-2$

The above cases can be generalized easily for right and left shifts of negative numbers by more than one position.

Range Extension

We will see in the next chapter that fixed-point operations quite often require one or both operands to be extended. This must be done before executing the specific arithmetic operation, in order to avoid overflow situations. For example, we often assume that addition and subtraction are performed between two equal-length operands. If their number of digits differ initially, then the need arises to extend the shorter operand "properly" to the left, without changing its decimal value. "Properly" means that the following range extension procedures must be applied:

Procedure 2.3   (Increasing the Length of Numbers in S&M Representation)

> The length of a number X (positive or negative) in S&M representation is increased by p digits by inserting p 0's (zeros) between the digits X_{n-1} and X_{n-2} of the number (i.e., to the left of the number's magnitude).

The length of a number X in complement representation (both radix and digit complements) can be increased by p digits with the following procedure:

Procedure 2.4   (Increasing the Length of Numbers in Complement Representation)

> If X is a positive number, then attach p 0's (zeros) to the left end of X;
> If X is a negative number, then attach p digits of value $r - 1$ to the left end of X.

In other words, for either positive or negative numbers, the sign-digit is repeated p times.

The decimal value of a number that has been range extended by either of the above procedures does not change.

2.3   NUMBER CODES

Coding, as applied to microprocessors, is the scheme through which a given quantity or symbol is expressed in binary form. In this chapter we are distinguishing between two general categories of codes: *number codes*, having to do with the binary representation of numerical information, and *character codes*, having to do with the binary representation of numeric and alphabetic characters, and other common symbols. This section covers binary number codes.

A variety of such codes exist. Within the processing system, various methods for representing information are usually used, each method based upon a different coding scheme. Besides internal operations on this information, the processor must also communicate and exchange information with human operators or with other peripheral units or systems, each of which may utilize a coding scheme different from the one used internally by the processor. Therefore, quite frequently it is necessary to perform code conversions from one coded form into a different code.

2.3.1 Weighted Codes

In the weighted codes, each bit position carries a corresponding weight. The decimal value of such a coded number is found by summing the products of the individual bits times their respective weights. In other words, if $b_3 b_2 b_1 b_0$ is a given 4-bit combination, then the decimal value of this number is given by

$$(N)_{10} = w_3 \times b_3 + w_2 \times b_2 + w_1 \times b_1 + w_0 \times b_0 = \sum_{i=0}^{i=3} b_i \times 2^i , \qquad (2.32)$$

where w_i is the weight in position i.

Binary-coded Decimal (BCD) Code

The BCD is the most commonly used code for representing decimal numbers in binary form. In this code, each digit of the decimal number is represented by its binary equivalent. Four bits are used to represent the ten decimal digits 0–9. Since four bits can represent 2^4 different states, there are six 4-bit numbers (the 1010, 1011, 1100, 1101, 1110, 1111) that are "forbidden" combinations in the BCD code.

The weights of the BCD code are 8-4-2-1 (i.e., increasing powers of 2). The second column of Table 2.2 gives the BCD equivalent of the ten decimal digits.

Excess-3 Code

The excess-3 code (sometimes referred to as "biased weighted code") is derived from the 8-4-2-1 BCD code by adding 3 to each coded number, as shown in the third column of Table 2.2. The excess-3 code is sometimes used instead of the BCD code, because it possesses some advantages in certain arithmetic operations. For example, that the 9's complement can be performed by complementation (changing all 0's to 1's, and all 1's to 0's) reduces the operation of subtraction into complementing the subtrahend and then performing the addition with the minuend.

Table 2.2 Various 4-bit weighted codes. Z. *Kohavi,* Switching and Finite Automata Theory, © *1970, pp. 11-12. Adapted by permission of McGraw-Hill, New York.*

Decimal Digit	8-4-2-1 BCD	Excess-3 Code	2-4-2-1	7-4-2-1	8-4-(−2)-(−1)
0	0000	0011	0000	0000	0000
1	0001	0100	0001	0001	0111
2	0010	0101	0010	0010	0110
3	0011	0110	0011	0011	0101
4	0100	0111	0100	0100	0100
5	0101	1000	1011	0101	1011
6	0110	1001	1100	0110	1010
7	0111	1010	1101	1000	1001
8	1000	1011	1110	1001	1000
9	1001	1100	1111	1010	1111

Other Weighted Codes

Table 2.2 above lists three other weighted codes, in which two different bit positions may carry the same weight or in which some of the weights may also be negative. In these weighted codes, the representation of a decimal digit is not always unique (for example, in the 2-4-2-1 code, digit 7 may be represented as either 1101 or 0111). By choosing the specific representations in the way listed in Table 2.2, codes are formed that have the property of being "self-complementing." A code is self-complementing when the new combination that results from changing all 0's to 1's and 1's to 0's represents the 9's complement of the original combination. Such codes are, for example, the excess-3 code, the 2-4-2-1 code, and the 8-4-(−2)-(−1) code. It can be proved, moreover, that a necessary condition for a weighted code to be self-complementing is that the sum of its weights be equal to 9.

2.3.2 The Gray Code

Non-weighted codes are also often used, for example, the Gray code. The Gray code is a *unit-distance* code, i.e., a code in which only one bit changes between the representations of two consecutive numbers. Although these codes are not well-suited for arithmetic operations, their unit-distance property makes them very suitable for I/O devices (e.g., shaft-encoders, analog-to-digital converters, linear displacement encoders, etc.), and for situations where erroneous or ambiguous results may be produced during those transitions in which more than one bit of the code is changing.

The n-bit Gray code belongs to the general class of "reflected codes," which are unit-distance codes. For example, the 3-bit Gray code is formed by taking the mirror image of the 2-bit Gray code, the 4-bit Gray code is formed by taking the mirror image of the 3-bit Gray code, etc., as shown in Table 2.3.

Table 2.3 Forming the n-bit Gray code as a mirror image of the $(n-1)$-bit Gray code. *From* [6], *p. 14. Adapted by permission of McGraw-Hill, New York.*

Gray Codes		
2-Bit	3-Bit	4-Bit
00	0 00	0 000
01	0 01	0 001
11	0 11	0 011
10	0 10↑	0 010
	1 10↓	0 110
	1 11	0 111
	1 01	0 101
	1 00	0 100↑
		1 100↓
		1 101
		1 111
		1 110
		1 010
		1 011
		1 001
		1 000

The conversion procedure between Gray and binary codes is very simple. For example, let $b = (b_{n-1}b_{n-2}b_{n-3}\ldots b_2b_1b_0)$ be the binary representation of a number, and $g = (g_{n-1}g_{n-2}g_{n-3}\ldots g_2g_1g_0)$ the number's representation in Gray code. Then converting from binary to Gray code is done according to the following procedure:

Procedure 2.5   (Converting Binary to Gray)

$$g_{n-1} = b_{n-1}$$
$$g_{n-2} = b_{n-1} \oplus b_{n-2}$$
$$g_{n-3} = b_{n-2} \oplus b_{n-3} ,$$

or in general:

$$g_{n-1} = b_{n-1}$$
$$g_i = b_{i+1} \oplus b_i, \ 0 \le i \le n-2 ,$$

where the symbol $\oplus$ means "modulo-2 addition" or the "exclusive-OR" operation.

For example, the Gray code representation of the binary number 101011 is 111110 and is found as follows:

$$
\begin{array}{cccccc}
b_5 & b_4 & b_3 & b_2 & b_1 & b_0 \\
1 & 0 & 1 & 0 & 1 & 1
\end{array}
$$

$$
\begin{array}{cccccc}
1 & 1 & 1 & 1 & 1 & 0 \\
g_5 & g_4 & g_3 & g_2 & g_1 & g_0
\end{array}
$$

Conversion from Gray code to binary is done according to the following procedure:

Procedure 2.6 (Converting Gray to Binary)

$$b_{n-1} = g_{n-1}$$
$$b_{n-2} = g_{n-1} \oplus g_{n-2}$$
$$b_{n-3} = g_{n-1} \oplus g_{n-2} \oplus g_{n-3}$$

or general:

$$b_i = \sum_{j=i}^{n-1} g_i , \quad 0 \leq i \leq n - 1,$$

where the symbol $\sum$ represents "modulo-2 sum."

In other words, we start from the most significant bit moving toward the least significant bit, and set $b_i = g_i$ when the number of 1's preceding the g_i bit is an even number (including 0), or set $b_i = \overline{g_i}$ (the inverse of g_i) when the number of 1's preceding the g_i bit is an odd number.

2.3.3 Error-detecting and Correcting Codes

The codes mentioned so far, although satisfactory for representing decimal digits, are quite sensitive to errors that may appear during data transmission or during the execution of arithmetic/logic operations. There is always a possibility for the appearance of a "single-bit error" (i.e., an error in one bit position of the digital information). The increased demands for reliability of digital processing systems necessitate the use of "error-checking or correcting codes," which have the ability of detecting and/or correcting errors. Such codes usually contain two kinds of digits: information or message digits, and check digits. Since the probability for the simultaneous appearance of two or more errors is much smaller than that for single errors, attention is frequently forced on detecting and correcting only single-bit errors.

The choice of the most suitable error-checking code is based upon the following criteria:

(a) Ability to check both the transmission of information and the arithmetic/ logic operations.
(b) Minimizing the number of bits, so that the requirements for electronic circuitry (cost) and transmission time (bandwidth) are also minimized.
(c) Minimizing errors during the digitization of analog quantities.
(d) Ability to identify errors so that they may be corrected.

The above criteria are, of course, conflicting, and consequently, a compromise must be made. For example, information theory tells us that it is always possible to inject enough redundancy in a message so as to minimize the probability of the appearance of errors. Adding redundancy, however, reduces the effective speed for transmitting messages.

A very useful concept related to error-detecting and correcting codes is that of *distance*. The distance between two binary numbers equals the number of positions in which these representations differ from each other. For example, the distance between the two representations 1010 and 1011 is 1, since they differ in only one position (the rightmost position). Similarly, the distance between 111 and 100 is 2, while the distance between 1111 and 0000 is 4.

In the general case, let us consider the two n-bit code words or messages:

$$X = (X_{n-1}X_{n-2}\ldots X_i \ldots X_1 X_0)$$

and

$$Y = (Y_{n-1}Y_{n-2}\ldots Y_i \ldots Y_1 Y_0).$$

Let the symbol $|w|$ represent the number of 1's in a message w. Then the distance between these two messages X and Y is defined as:

$$D(X, Y) = |X \oplus Y|$$

Figure 2.3a shows a 3-dimensional cube (a 3-cube), each vertex of which represents a 3-bit code word. The code words are assigned to vertices, in such a way that two neighboring vertices of the cube correspond to two code words of distance 1. Coding of information in this way, where all of the 2^n vertices of the n-cube have been assigned, presents no redundancy. If, however, fewer vertices are used, then one can utilize the non-valid or non-assigned vertices for the purpose of detecting the appearance of errors. If the vertices are chosen in such a way that a single error converts a valid code word into a non-valid one (i.e., a code word corresponding to a non-assigned vertex), then the code so formed has the ability of at least detecting a single-bit error. The general rule applied is that, in order to form an n-digit *single-error-detecting code*, code words should be assigned to no more than half of the 2^n vertices of the cube. Furthermore, the specific assignments of code words should be done in such a way that, in order for one valid code word to be changed into another valid code word, at least two of its bits must be changed. Thus, if the "minimum distance" of a code is defined as the smallest number of bits in which any two combinations of the code differ from each other, then this code is a single-error-detecting code only if it is a code of minimum distance 2 or more. Such a code can be formed, for example, by using the combinations 001, 010, 100, and 111 of Figure 2.3a, since an error in one bit of any of these combinations will result in a new combination not present in the code, i.e., a non-valid code word. In the case of 4-bit codes, the above minimum distance 2 restriction implies that only eight of the possible $2^4 = 16$ combinations are allowed. Thus, for example, to form an error-detecting code that covers the ten decimal digits, four bits will not be sufficient, and therefore, five bits are required.

Furthermore, if the combinations used for the code are such that each non-valid combination that results from the appearance of a single error is closer to its originating combination (vertex) than to any other combination (vertex) of the code, then this code is also a *single-error-correcting code*. Consider, for example, the 3-cube of Figure 2.3b. In this case, a single-error-correcting code may be formed by using only the vertices shown in heavy circles, i.e., combinations 000 and 111 only. If a single error appears in the first combination, the combination will become 010, 001, or 100. If a single error appears in the second combination, the combination will become 101, or 110, or 011. In each case, the resulting non-valid combination is unique. Moreover, each such non-valid combination is distance 1 from the respective valid combination from which it originated. For these previous six non-valid combinations, three of them are closer to the first valid combination, 000, while the other three are closer to the second combination, 111. Therefore, this criterion can now be used for correcting the detected error. The two combinations 000 and 111 form a single-error-correcting code, whose minimum distance is 3. The general rule applied is that, in order to form an n-digit code for correcting up to k errors, the combinations should be so chosen on the n-dimensional cube that each combination differs from every other by a

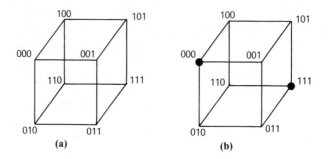

Figure 2.3 (a) A 3-cube. (b) The allowed vertices (drawn in heavy circles) that form a single-error-correcting code.

distance of at least $2k + 1$, where k is a constant. If the minimum distance among the combinations of a code is $2k$ (i.e., an even number), then this code can detect up to $2k - 1$ errors, or it can detect up to k errors *and simultaneously* correct up to $k - 1$ errors. For example, codes of minimum distance 4, allow either for the detection of up to triple errors, or the detection of up to double errors, *and simultaneously*, the correction of single errors.

Error-detecting Codes

Odd and Even Parity Error Detecting

The most widely used single-error-detecting code is the odd/even parity code, in which one check bit is added to every code word. For the odd/even parity check, the additional bit is chosen so that the sum of all 1's in the code word, including this check bit, is odd/even. If this parity check bit is denoted as p, then this condition can be expressed in the form of a modulo-2 sum as follows:

for odd parity: $\quad X_{n-1} \oplus X_{n-2} \oplus X_{n-3} \oplus \ldots \oplus X_1 \oplus X_0 \oplus p = 1$, (2.33)

for even parity: $\quad X_{n-1} \oplus X_{n-2} \oplus X_{n-3} \oplus \ldots \oplus X_1 \oplus X_0 \oplus p = 0$. (2.34)

It can also be shown (since $p \oplus p = 0$ and $1 \oplus 1 = 0$) that

$$p(\text{odd}) = X_{n-1} \oplus X_{n-2} \oplus X_{n-3} \oplus \ldots \oplus X_1 \oplus X_0 \oplus 1 \qquad (2.35)$$

and

$$p(\text{even}) = X_{n-1} \oplus X_{n-2} \oplus X_{n-3} \oplus \ldots \oplus X_1 \oplus X_0 . \qquad (2.36)$$

Table 2.4 shows the 4-bit BCD code words with the added odd and even parity bit.

Table 2.4 The BCD code with odd and even parity.

Decimal Digit	Odd Parity BCD Code p 8 4 2 1	Even Parity BCD Code p 8 4 2 1
0	1 0 0 0 0	0 0 0 0 0
1	0 0 0 0 1	1 0 0 0 1
2	0 0 0 1 0	1 0 0 1 0
3	1 0 0 1 1	0 0 0 1 1
4	0 0 1 0 0	1 0 1 0 0
5	1 0 1 0 1	0 0 1 0 1
6	1 0 1 1 0	0 0 1 1 0
7	0 0 1 1 1	1 0 1 1 1
8	0 1 0 0 0	1 1 0 0 0
9	1 1 0 0 1	0 1 0 0 1

Other Error-detecting Codes

Two other codes used for error detection are the 2-out-of-5 code and the 2-out-of-7 code shown in Table 2.5.

Table 2.5   The 2-out-of-5 and 2-out-of-7 error-detecting codes.

		2-out-of-5 Code	2-out-of-7 Code
Decimal Digit	Added Bit	Weights 7 4 2 1	Weights 5 0 4 3 2 1 0
0	0	1 1 0 0	0 1 0 0 0 0 1
1	1	0 0 0 1	0 1 0 0 0 1 0
2	1	0 0 1 0	0 1 0 0 1 0 0
3	0	0 0 1 1	0 1 0 1 0 0 0
4	1	0 1 0 0	0 1 1 0 0 0 0
5	0	0 1 0 1	1 0 0 0 0 0 1
6	0	0 1 1 0	1 0 0 0 0 1 0
7	1	1 0 0 0	1 0 0 0 1 0 0
8	0	1 0 0 1	1 0 0 1 0 0 0
9	0	1 0 1 0	1 0 1 0 0 0 0

The 2-out-of-5 code utilizes five bits in such a way that the appearance of a single error yields a non-valid code word. Each 5-bit code word contains exactly two 1's. A single error 1-to-0 or 0-to-1 results in a new word which will not contain exactly two 1's. The hardware implementation is quite simple. This code can detect all single errors, but can detect only those double errors that generate non-valid code words (i.e., it can detect only forty percent of the double errors). The 2-out-of-5 code cannot correct detected errors.

In the 2-out-of-7 code, there are two groups of binary numbers: one group of two bits and the other group of five bits. Each group contains exactly one 1, and this code can detect only single errors.

Error-correcting Codes

Block Parity Error-correcting Codes

The parity check discussed previously required the addition of an extra bit to each code word. This is also called "horizontal" parity checking. If, however, the code words of a longer message are arranged in an array of n rows and m columns, then, besides the horizontal parity bit added to each row, another "vertical" parity bit may also be added to each column. In Figure 2.4, odd horizontal and vertical parity bits have been used. These horizontal and vertical parity bits are also checked at the intersection of the parity row and column.

Symbols	BCD Code Word	Horizontal Parity Bits ↙ (Odd)
8	1 0 0 0	0
9	1 0 0 1	1
6	0 1 1 0	1
4	0 1 0 0	0
2	0 0 1 0	0
7	0 1 1 1	0
Vertical→ Parity Bits (Odd)	1 0 0 1	1

Figure 2.4 Block parity error-correcting code.

If a single error appears in a code word, then it can be detected either from its horizontal parity bit or from its vertical parity bit. These two checks, however, taken together, indicate the location of the faulty bit (at the intersection of the respective row and column), and thus, a correction can be performed on this corrupted bit. Therefore, this code provides the capability for single error detection and correction, and is widely used in magnetic tapes and other computer peripherals.

Hamming Code

One of the most important single-error-detecting and correcting codes is the Hamming code. This code is a distance-3 code that can also detect double errors.

The Hamming code is formed by first determining the number of check bits required. In each binary message of n information bits ($M_n M_{n-1} \ldots M_1$) to be transmitted, k check bits ($C_k C_{k-1} \ldots C_1$) are added for checking even (or odd) parity. Thus, a composite or "coded message" of $n + k$ bits is formed. The check bits C_i ($i = 1, 2, \ldots, k$) occupy specific positions in the coded ($n+k$)-bit message. These positions are $1, 2, 4, 8, \ldots, 2^{k-1}$, i.e., positions that are integer powers of 2. The value of each C_i is determined by checking the parity of specific locations in the original message M as shown in Table 2.6. Thus, the check bit C_1 checks all odd positions $1, 3, 5, 7, \ldots$; the check bit C_2 checks the pair sets of positions $\{(2,3), (6,7), (10,11), \ldots\}$; the check bit C_3 checks quadruple sets of positions; etc.

The number of check bits required for a given message length is given in Table 2.7. For example, if the original message is a BCD code word, where $n = 4$, then $k = 3$ parity checks bits must be added in positions 1, 2, and 4. Thus, the transmitted Hamming code message will be seven bits long, as shown in Table 2.8 for the ten BCD code words, assuming even parity.

Table 2.6 The message bits that are examined by each C_i and p_i.

	At the Transmitting End		At the Receiving End
Check Bits C_i	The bit locations checked in the original message M	Position Number Bits p_i	The bit locations examined of the received coded message M'
C_1	$(M_1),(M_3),(M_5),(M_7),(M_9),\ldots$	p_1	$(M'_1),(M'_3),(M'_5),(M'_7),(M'_9),\ldots$
C_2	$(M_2,M_3),(M_6,M_7),(M_{10},M_{11}),(M_{14},M_{15}),\ldots$	p_2	$(M'_2,M'_3),(M'_6,M'_7),(M'_{10},M'_{11}),(M'_{14},M'_{15}),\ldots$
C_3	$(M_4,M_5,M_6,M_7),(M_{12},M_{13},M_{14},M_{15}),\ldots$	p_3	$(M'_4,M'_5,M'_6,M'_7),(M'_{12},M'_{13},M'_{14},M'_{15}),\ldots$
C_4	$(M_8,M_9,M_{10},M_{11},M_{12},M_{13},M_{14},M_{15}),\ldots$	p_4	$(M'_8,M'_9,M'_{10},M'_{11},M'_{12},M'_{13},M'_{14},M'_{15}),\ldots$

Table 2.7 Hamming code: Number of check bits required for a given code word length.

Number of Information Bits in Code Word M	Minimum Number of Check Bits C	Total Length of Coded Message $M' = M + C$
2	2	3
2–4	3	5–7
5–11	4	9–15
12–26	5	16–31
27–54	6	32–63

Table 2.8 BCD representation using even parity Hamming code.

	Positions:	7	6	5	4	3	2	1
Decimal Digit	BCD Positions: Check Bits:	M_4	M_3	M_2	C_3	M_1	C_2	C_1
0		0	0	0	0	0	0	0
1		0	0	0	0	1	1	1
2		0	0	1	1	0	0	1
3		0	0	1	1	1	1	0
4		0	1	0	1	0	1	0
5		0	1	0	1	1	0	1
6		0	1	1	0	0	1	1
7		0	1	1	0	1	0	0
8		1	0	0	1	0	1	1
9		1	0	0	1	1	0	0

At the receiving end now, the same parity checking (this time the various C_i's are also examined) is applied to the received coded message M'. A "checking number" or "position number" $P = p_k p_{k-1} \ldots p_2 p_1$ is formed, such that, if no error is detected then P will equal 0. If, however, a single-bit error is detected, then the decimal value of P will correspond to the position of the received message where the error occurred.

If this number P is to specify the position where an error appeared, then the various position number bits p_j must check specific positions in the received message M'. If an error appears in an odd position—1,3,5,7,9,11,...—of the received message, then the least significant bit p_1 of the position number P must equal 1. If the coding was done so that in each Hamming code message all odd positions 1,3,5,7,9,11,... have even parity, then a single error in one of these positions will form an odd parity. In this case, the least significant bit p_1 of the position number will take the value of 1. If no error appears in these positions, then the parity check will show even parity and p_1 will take the value of 0. Similarly, the appearance of a single error in one of the positions 2,3,6,7,10,11,... will indicate $p_2 = 1$, otherwise $p_2 = 0$, etc. Table 2.6 shows the specific positions of the received message M' examined by the respective p_j's. With k such position number bits, 2^k different position numbers P may be formed, where $2^k \geq n + k + 1$. If, for example, the position number in the BCD messages using the Hamming code of Table 2.8 is $P = p_3 p_2 p_1 = 110$, this signifies the appearance of an error in position M'_6 of the received message, which in turn can then be corrected. If $P = 0$, this implies that the message was received correctly.

In general, to check for the correct reception of a Hamming code message with even parity, one must compute for each j the modulo-2 sum

$$p_j = \sum M'_j, \tag{2.37}$$

where M'_j are the respective position bits of the received message M' to which this check p_j is applied. If no error exists in these M'_j bits, then $p_j = 0$, otherwise $p_j = 1$. This procedure repeats for all $j = 1,2,3,...$

Example 2.1
Apply a Hamming code to the 6-bit message 101011, using even parity.

(1) Using the Hamming Code

The initial message is $M_6 M_5 ... M_1 = 101011$. Since $n = 6$, it requires $k = 4$ ($C_4 C_3 C_2 C_1$) check bits, and it will thus be converted into a 10-bit Hamming code message. These $C_4 C_3 C_2 C_1$ check bits are placed in positions 8,4,2,1 of the message, respectively. Therefore, the coding shown in Figure 2.5 results.

Positions:	10	9	8	7	6	5	4	3	2	1
Original Message Bit Positions:	M_6	M_5		M_4	M_3	M_2		M_1		
Even Parity Check Bit Positions:			C_4				C_3		C_2	C_1
Original Message M:	1	0		1	0	1		1		
$C_1 = M_3 \oplus M_5 \oplus M_7 = 1$:	1	0		1	0	1		1		1
$C_2 = M_2 \oplus M_3 \oplus M_6 \oplus M_7 \oplus M_{10} = 1$:	1	0		1	0	1		1	1	1
$C_3 = M_4 \oplus M_5 \oplus M_6 \oplus M_7 = 0$:	1	0		1	0	1	0	1	1	1
$C_4 = M_8 \oplus M_9 \oplus M_{10} = 1$:	1	0	1	1	0	1	0	1	1	1
The Hamming code message M':	1	0	1	1	0	1	0	1	1	1

Figure 2.5 Using the Hamming code with the 6-bit message 101011 (even parity).

(2) Checking the Received Message

Assume that the received message M′ has an error in position 6, i.e., instead of being correctly received as 1011010111, it has been received as 1011110111. Perform the examination of the received message:

$$p_1 = M'_1 \oplus M'_3 \oplus M'_5 \oplus M'_7 \oplus M'_9 = 0$$
$$p_2 = M'_2 \oplus M'_3 \oplus M'_6 \oplus M'_7 \oplus M'_{10} = 1$$
$$p_3 = M'_4 \oplus M'_5 \oplus M'_6 \oplus M'_7 = 1$$
$$p_4 = M'_8 \oplus M'_9 \oplus M'_{10} = 0$$

The position number thus formed is $P = p_4 p_3 p_2 p_1 = 0110$. Its decimal value is 6, which indicates that an error exists in position 6 of the received message. This error can be corrected by changing bit M'_6 from 1 to 0.

2.4 CHARACTER CODES

The various codes covered in section 2.3 are used mainly to represent numerical data, i.e., numbers. Like larger computers, however, microprocessors also handle alphabetic data (letters) and special characters (such as punctuation and special symbols), in addition to numbers. Codes used to represent such characters are called "alphanumeric codes."

2.4.1 The 6-bit BCD Code

The 6-bit BCD code uses six bits to represent alphanumeric characters internally. An additional parity bit is used for error detection. With six bits, $2^6 = 64$ different characters can be represented, each character having the format given in Figure 2.6. Figure 2.7 gives the full 6-bit BCD code.

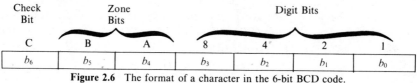

Figure 2.6 The format of a character in the 6-bit BCD code.

2.4.2 The Standard ASCII Code

The American Standard Code for Information Interchange (ASCII) shown in Figure 2.8 is the standard code used today by all microprocessors, computer peripherals, and data communication equipment. This is also the code generated by most keyboards and teletypes. Quite often, an additional bit (b_8) is incorporated as an (even or odd) parity bit. Thus, the full ASCII is normally used as an 8-bit word.

Left panel

Character 1	Character 2	Card Punches	C	B	A	8	4	2	1
b		No Punches	C						
.	)	12-3-8		B	A	8		2	1
[		12-4-8	C	B	A	8	4		
∨		12-5-8		B	A	8	4		1
≠		12-6-8		B	A	8	4	2	
&	+	12-7-8	C	B	A	8	4	2	1
$		12	C	B	A				
*		11-3-8	C	B		8		2	1
]		11-4-8		B		8	4		
;		11-5-8	C	B		8	4		1
Δ		11-6-8	C	B		8	4	2	
			11-7-8		B		8	4	2	1
/		11		B					
.		0-1	C		A				1
%	(	0-3-8	C		A	8		2	1
/		0-4-8			A	8	4		
≢		0-5-8	C		A	8	4		1
b		0-6-8	C		A	8	4	2	
#	=	0-7-8			A	8	4	2	1
@		2-8	C			8		2	
⌐	∨	3-8				8		2	1
√		4-8	C			8	4		
?		5-8				8	4		1
A		6-8				8	4	2	
B		7-8	C			8	4	2	1
C		12-0	C	B	A	8		2	
D		12-1		B	A				1
E		12-2		B	A			2	
F		12-3	C	B	A			2	1
			12-4		B	A		4		
			12-5	C	B	A		4		1
			12-6	C	B	A		4	2	

Right panel

Character	Card Punches	C	B	A	8	4	2	1
G	12-7		B	A		4	2	1
H	12-8		B	A	8			
I	12-9	C	B	A	8			1
!	11-0	C	B		8		2	
J	11-1	C	B					1
K	11-2	C	B				2	
L	11-3		B				2	1
M	11-4	C	B			4		
N	11-5		B			4		1
O	11-6		B			4	2	
P	11-7	C	B			4	2	1
Q	11-8	C	B		8			
R	11-9		B		8			1
‡	0-2-8			A	8		2	
S	0-2	C		A			2	
T	0-3			A			2	1
U	0-4	C		A		4		
V	0-5			A		4		1
W	0-6			A		4	2	
X	0-7	C		A		4	2	1
Y	0-8	C		A	8			
Z	0-9			A	8			1
0	0	C			8		2	
1	1							1
2	2						2	
3	3	C					2	1
4	4					4		
5	5	C				4		1
6	6	C				4	2	
7	7					4	2	1
8	8				8			
9	9	C			8			1

Figure 2.7 The full 6-bit BCD code. *T. C. Bartee, Digital Computer Fundamentals, 2d. ed., © 1966, p. 334. Reprinted by permission of McGraw-Hill, New York.*

With the seven bits available, there are $2^7 = 128$ possible different codes shown in Figure 2.8. These may be grouped into four groups of thirty-two characters each, and, depending upon the system complexity, one may or may not use all four of these 32-character groups.

BIT NUMBERS	b_7 b_6 b_5	0 0 0	0 0 1	0 1 0	0 1 1	1 0 0	1 0 1	1 1 0	1 1 1
$b_4\ b_3\ b_2\ b_1$ ↓ ↓ ↓ ↓		0	1	2	3	4	5	6	7
0 0 0 0	0	NUL	DLE	SP	0	@	P	′	p
0 0 0 0	1	SOH	DC1	!	1	A	Q	a	q
0 0 1 0	2	STX	DC2	″	2	B	R	b	r
0 0 1 1	3	ETX	DC3	£	3	C	S	c	s
0 1 0 0	4	EOT	DC4	$	4	D	T	d	t
0 1 0 1	5	ENO	NAK	%	5	E	U	e	u
0 1 1 0	6	ACK	SYN	&	6	F	V	f	v
0 1 1 1	7	BEL	ETB	′	7	G	W	g	w
1 0 0 0	8	BS	CAN	(	8	H	X	h	x
1 0 0 1	9	HT	EM	)	9	I	Y	i	y
1 0 1 0	10	LF	SUB	*	:	J	Z	j	z
1 0 1 1	11	VT	ESC	+	;	K	[	k	{
1 1 0 0	12	FF	FS	,	≦	L	\	l	‖
1 1 0 1	13	CR	GS	—	<	M	]	m	}
1 1 1 0	14	SO	RS	.	>	N	≙	n	~
1 1 1 1	15	SI	US	/	?	O	—	o	DEL

| | 1 | 2 | 3 | 4 |

- Lowercase Alphabet
- Infrequent Punctuation
ASCII-6 Subset
- Uppercase Alphabet
- Numbers
- Frequent Punctuation
- Machine Commands
- Control Functions

Figure 2.8 The American Standard Code for Information Interchange (ASCII). *Carol Anne Ogdin,* Software Design for Microcomputers, © *1978, p. 22. Adapted by permisson of Prentice-Hall, Inc., Englewood Cliff, NJ.*

The two middle groups 2 and 3 of Figure 2.8 make up the ASCII-6 subset (b_6 to b_1), which represents $2^6 = 64$ different characters, i.e., the uppercase alphabet, the numbers, and some frequently used punctuation symbols. In the ASCII-6 subset, the numbers are represented in BCD with two additional 1's "hardwired" in front. Also, given a character in the ASCII-6 format, one can represent it with seven bits, by setting the seventh bit equal to the complement (the inverse) of the sixth bit.

The first 32-character Group 1 in ASCII corresponds to the machine commands or control functions, shown in Figure 2.9. The machine commands or control functions, which always have both bits 6 and 7 equal to 0, usually are not printed or displayed on a screen; instead, they provide control functions of the support circuitry.

Finally, the two rightmost columns of the ASCII code of Figure 2.8 (Group 4) correspond to the lowercase alphabet and some infrequent punctuation symbols, identified by their sixth and seventh bits always being 1.

NUL	NULL	DLE	DATA LINK ESCAPE
SOH	START OF HEADING	DC1	DEVICE CONTROL 1
STX	START OF TEXT	DC2	DEVICE CONTROL 2
ETX	END OF TEXT	DC3	DEVICE CONTROL 3
EOT	END OF TRANSMISSION	DC4	DEVICE CONTROL 4
ENQ	ENQUIRY	NAK	NEGATIVE ACKNOWLEDGE
ACK	ACKNOWLEDGE	SYN	SYNCHRONOUS IDLE
BEL	BELL	ETB	END OF TRANSMISSION BLOCK
BS	BACKSPACE	CAN	CANCEL
HT	HORIZONTAL TAB	EM	END OF MEDIUM
LF	LINE FEED	SUB	SUBSTITUTE
VT	VERTICAL TAB	ESC	ESCAPE
FF	FORM FEED	FS	FILE SEPARATOR
CR	CARRIAGE RETURN	GS	GROUP SEPARATOR
SO	SHIFT OUT	RS	RECORD SEPARATOR
SI	SHIFT IN	US	UNIT SEPARATOR

Figure 2.9 Explanation of the ASCII machine commands or control functions. *Andrew S. Tanenbaum,* Structured Computer Organization, © *1976, p. 35. Reprinted by permission of Prentice-Hall, Inc., Englewood Cliffs, NJ.*

EXERCISES

2.1 Convert the following numbers into binary form:

(a) 17.362_8
(b) 123.456_{10}
(c) $1ABC.F_{16}$

2.2 Give the BCD representation in 9's complement notation of the number -347.62_{10}.

2.3 Convert the following decimal numbers to their equivalent octal and hexadecimal representations:

(a) 34.72_{10}
(b) 1347.69_{10}

2.4 What is the largest integer that can be placed in a register of three hexadecimal digits?

2.5 Convert the following decimal fractions into hexadecimal numbers (with $j = 3$) :

(a) $3/8$
(b) $71/64$
(c) $1/3$
(d) $4/5$

2.6 Express the numbers -6, 17, and -23 in sign and magnitude notation, and in 1's and 2's complement notation, in a processor that uses words of six bits to represent integers.

2.7 Give the flowchart for converting a number with respect to radix b into a number with respect to radix d, where b and d are integers greater than 1.

2.8 Give all possible representations for 0 (zero) using an N-bit number representation in 1's complement notation. Using an N-bit number in 2's complement notation. Using an N-bit number in sign and magnitude notation.

2.9 Prove that the correct rule for doubling a number in 1's complement notation is the left circular shift by one.

2.10 Find the Gray code representations of the following positional binary numbers:

(a) 101110101_2
(b) 11101111_2
(c) 1111111_2

2.11 Repeat Example 2.1 from the text using odd parity.

REFERENCES AND BIBLIOGRAPHY

[1]   Avizienis, A., *Information Processing Systems*, (Class Notes), Los Angeles, CA: Computer Science Department, UCLA, 1968.

[2]   Bartee, T.C., *Digital Computer Fundamentals*, 2d ed., New York: McGraw-Hill, 1966.

[3]   Brown, D.T., "Error Detecting and Correcting Binary Codes for Arithmetic Operations," *IRE Transactions on Electronic Computers*, September 1960, pp. 333–37.

[4]   Buchholz, W., *Planning a Computer System: Project Stretch*, New York: McGraw-Hill, 1962.

[5]   Flores, I., *The Logic of Computer Arithmetic*, Englewood Cliffs, NJ: Prentice-Hall, Inc., 1963.

[6]   Kohavi, Z., *Switching and Finite Automata Theory*, New York: McGraw-Hill, 1970.

[7]   Tanenbaum, A.S., *Structured Computer Organization*, Englewood Cliffs, NJ: Prentice-Hall, Inc., 1976.

[8]   Ogdin, C.A., *Software Design for Microcomputers*, Englewood Cliffs, NJ: Prentice-Hall, Inc., 1978.

[9]   Tocci, R.J., *Digital Systems, Principles and Applications*, Englewood Cliffs, NJ: Prentice-Hall, Inc., 1977.

Chapter 3

MICROPROCESSOR ARITHMETIC

3.1 INTRODUCTION

This chapter covers both fixed-point and floating-point arithmetic, with binary numbers in S&M, 1's complement, and 2's complement notations.

Fixed-point numbers are usually used in problems in which the analysis of the magnitude of the variables involved is rather simple or in which the range of the numbers dealt with is predictable. In fixed-point numbers the position of the radix point is assumed to be fixed. Furthermore, fixed-point arithmetic data can be either binary numbers or decimal numbers properly coded into a binary form. In binary arithmetic, the fixed-point numbers have a simple internal structure, and their length remains constant, and usually equals the word length of the processor. In decimal arithmetic, the numerical data appear as a string of decimal digits, each digit encoded separately in some binary form, and the length of the data is variable depending upon the number of decimal digits. One of the major problems that the fixed-point notation presents is the limited range of the numbers, and thus, the programmer is required to perform scaling.

Floating-point numbers are usually used for scientific computations. Floating-point arithmetic frees the programmer from the difficult task of performing a magnitude analysis on a problem's variables. Each floating-point number is given as a pair (e, f), composed of the "exponent" e and the "mantissa" or "fraction" f, and representing the number $f \times r^e$. In most 8- and 16-bit microprocessors, floating-point operations are performed through appropriate software routines, whereas, in the new 32-bit microprocessors, they are executed by internal hardware. The use of floating-point notation extends the range of the numbers that the processor can handle, and facilitates automatic scaling operations. In this chapter more emphasis is placed on the discussion of the proposed IEEE standard for binary floating-point arithmetic [7, 11].

3.2 FIXED-POINT ARITHMETIC

3.2.1 Introductory Remarks

Most of the microprocessors presently available have only fixed-point hardware capabilities.

In the fixed-point notation, a number is represented by a fixed number of digits, in which the number's radix point is assumed to be in a fixed position. Number data used in fixed-point arithmetic may be either straight binary (binary arithmetic), or they may have an inner structure of digits individually encoded in binary form (decimal arithmetic). *Binary* numbers always have homogeneous internal structures of fixed length. *Decimal* numbers may be either signed or unsigned numbers in memory. For unsigned decimal numbers, the sign digit is omitted and the numbers are assumed to be positive. This unsigned mode of decimal arithmetic is convenient, since in many data processing applications numerical data are frequently inherently positive, and therefore, significant storage space can be saved by omitting sign bits. Decimal numbers may have variable lengths (usually up to 256 bytes).

In binary or decimal fixed-point operations, the arithmetic performed may be either integer or fraction, depending upon the assumed position of the radix point. In *integer arithmetic*, a radix point is assumed to be at the extreme right, and thus, all results are lined up at the right end of the registers. In *fraction arithmetic*, the apparent radix point is assumed to be at the left, and therefore, all results are lined up at the left end of the registers regardless of length. In both integer and fraction arithmetic the operations produce the same result digits, regardless of where the radix point is. The discussion in this section assumes binary integer operands.

Although most microprocessors today use 2's complement (radix complement) notation for representing numbers, the microprocessor-based system designer is often required to handle sign and magnitude (S&M) representations as well. For example, data from an analog to digital converter are often in S&M notation; floating-point numbers also use the S&M notation. For completeness, arithmetic operations are covered here in both S&M and complement notations.

There are two basic problems that fixed-point arithmetic may present: the range and the precision of numbers.

Range and Scaling

The *range* of numbers is given by the extreme values that the numbers may assume. With n digits in radix r, all numbers are considered less than or equal to r^B in absolute value, where B is an integer. If $B = n - 1$, then the quantity represented is an integer (the nth digit represents the sign). This B is sometimes called the *binary scale factor*. It may be either implicit (i.e., existing only in the mind of the programmer, and thus obliging him or her to use some method for keeping an external record of the position of the radix point), or it may be explicit (i.e., appearing explicitly in the computer memory, and thus obliging the programmer to write separate programs designed to keep a record of the position of the radix point, or to modify the binary scale factor when necessary).

With this convention then, there are different values for the following binary number stored in memory as:

$$\boxed{0\ |1010110\ }$$

For $B = 0$, the value of this number is $+0.101011$.
For $B = 1$, the value of this number is $+1.01011$.
For $B = 7$, the value of this number is $+1010110$.
For $B = 8$, the value of this number is $+10101100$ (i.e., an extra 0 is added to the right).
For $B = -3$, the value of this number is $+0.000101011$ (i.e., three extra 0's are added between the sign and the most significant bit of the number).

Normally, the binary scale factor is chosen so that there are no leading zeros in memory (or leading ones, if the number is negative and in complement form).

The usual convention used is $B = 0$ for binary fraction fixed-point arithmetic and $B = n - 1$ for binary integer fixed-point arithmetic. With this convention, all numbers in fraction arithmetic are considered less than or equal to 1 in absolute value. Therefore, a 2's complement processor cannot contain a $+1$, but it can hold a -1. In integer arithmetic, all 8-bit numbers are considered less than or equal to 2^7 in absolute value. In either type of arithmetic, larger or smaller numbers can be represented by moving the implicit radix point (i.e., modifying B appropriately). The range of discrete values, however, still remains constant. A range which is too small will cause frequent overflow (or underflow).

The problem of range is usually handled by a technique called *scaling*. Scaling is not always easily done, and, for sophisticated calculations, complex and deeper analysis of the problem is usually required. Scaling can be applied to a problem or its arithmetic (the variables) [5]. In order for a problem to be scaled, it must be transformed into a problem that falls within the number range. Scaling of the arithmetic requires that the programmer maintain a running account of the magnitudes of the variables throughout the problem. Thus, a considerable mathematical analysis of the problem may be required, as well as a need to handle properly the "significance" problem introduced [1,6].

Fortunately, there are some well-defined rules for scaling the arithmetic operations which ease the programmer's effort. The binary scale factor of the numbers at every step in the calculation must be considered. All numbers involved usually share a common binary scale factor B, with the added condition that no number or result of an arithmetic operation can be as large as r^B in magnitude. The scaling rules for fixed-point arithmetic operations are as follows [13]:

(a) For binary addition (subtraction), the binary scale factor of the addend (subtrahend) must equal that of the augend (minuend).
(b) For binary multiplication, the binary scale factor of the product must equal the sum of the binary scale factors of the multiplicand and the multiplier.
(c) For binary division, the binary scale factor of the quotient must be equal to the difference of the binary scale factors of the dividend and the divisor. The divisor must be greater in magnitude than the dividend as they are positioned in the registers.

In order to prevent overflow, the condition is required that no number or result of an arithmetic operation can be as large as r^B in magnitude. This condition can be satisfied by properly performing range extension to the numbers used in the arithmetic operation, as described in section 2.2.3 of chapter 2. For example, when the two numbers $+35_{10}$ ($=0100011)_2$ and $+41_{10}$ ($=0101001)_2$—both have the same scale factor $B = 6$ (since they are smaller than $2^6 = 64$ in magnitude)—are added, the correct sum should be $+76_{10}$ ($=01001100)_2$, which requires a minimum binary scale factor of $B = 7$ (since the sum is greater than $2^6 = 64$ but smaller than $2^7 = 128$ in magnitude). To avoid the overflow condition from such an operation, both numbers should have been range-extended first with $B = 7$, to become $+35_{10} = (00100011)_2$ and $41_{10} = (00101001)_2$, and then added, to give a same-scale factor ($B = 7$) result of $+76_{10} = (01001100)_2$.

Most microprocessors have an overflow flag that can be tested by the programmer to determine whether or not an overflow has occurred in the operation.

Precision

Another major problem besides overflow is possible loss of precision. The precision of a system is a function of its fixed word length. For a given length of n bits, numbers can be represented with a maximum error of $2^{(B-n+1)}/2$. To maximize precision, appropriate binary scale factors must be used in order that the numbers do not have leading 0's (or leading 1's if they are negative and in complementary form). Such numbers are sometimes called *normalized*.

Even with this precaution, however, the word length of the microprocessor may not be adequate for a particular calculation. In such cases, the sole recourse is *multiple-precision arithmetic*, in which more than one word is used to represent a single number. Multiple-precision arithmetic, though, is slower than corresponding single-precision arithmetic, wastes memory storage, and complicates the programming effort.

3.2.2   Arithmetic in S&M Notation

This section covers the four arithmetic operations—addition, subtraction, multiplication, and division—in the S&M representation. With this representation, a binary integer number is given as

$$x = (x_{n-1}x_{n-2} \ldots x_1 x_0)_2 = (x_{n-1}, mx)_2 , \qquad (3.1)$$

where the first bit x_{n-1} corresponds to the sign of the number ($x_{n-1} = 0$ for positive numbers and $x_{n-1} = 1$ for negative numbers), and the remaining bits $x_{n-2}x_{n-3} \ldots x_0$ represent the number's magnitude mx. The number's decimal value is given by the general expression (2.14) of chapter 2, with $r = 2$.

Addition in S&M

Addition in S&M is performed by adding the $(n - 1)$-bit magnitudes of the two numbers x and y (i.e., the sign bit does not enter into the operation) to get the $(n - 1)$-bit magnitude sum

$$ms = mx + my . \qquad (3.2)$$

During this addition operation, care must always be taken (e.g., by properly extending the length of the operands) to ensure that the correct final magnitude result will also have a length of $(n - 1)$ bits. If the addition of two $(n - 1)$-bit magnitudes yields a result of length larger than $(n - 1)$, then an overflow situation results.

In S&M addition, one must distinguish between the following two cases: (1) that in which the two numbers have the same sign (i.e., $x_{n-1} = y_{n-1}$), or (2) that in which the two numbers have different signs (i.e., $x_{n-1} \neq y_{n-1}$).

Same Signs

The two $(n - 1)$-bit magnitudes are added to get a "temporary" magnitude result[1] $ms*$

$$ms* = mx + my . \qquad (3.3)$$

---

[1] We introduce here the notion of a "temporary" result, symbolized as a variable with an asterisk, which we will need later in this section.

Since the signs of the two numbers are equal (i.e., $x_{n-1} = y_{n-1}$), the sign s_{n-1} of the final sum s will be given by

$$s_{n-1} = x_{n-1} = y_{n-1} \ . \tag{3.4}$$

In this case no correction is required on the temporary magnitude result ms^*, which, therefore, equals the correct final result magnitude ms. Thus, the final sum is

$$s = (s_{n-1}, ms) = (s_{n-1}, ms^*) = [s_{n-1}, (mx + my)]. \tag{3.5}$$

An overflow may result when two same-sign numbers are added, if the addition (3.3) of the two magnitudes generates a carry bit from position $n-2$ (i.e., from the most significant position of the temporary magnitude) which has the value:

$$c^*_{n-1} = 1 \ . \tag{3.6}$$

Different Signs (General Case)

The sign of the sum of two differently signed numbers in S&M notation depends upon the value of the two numbers as follows:

If $(x)_{10} > (y)_{10}$, then: $s_{n-1} = x_{n-1}$ and $ms = mx - my.$ $\qquad$ (3.7)

If $(x)_{10} < (y)_{10}$, then: $s_{n-1} = y_{n-1}$ and $ms = my - mx.$ $\qquad$ (3.8)

If $(x)_{10} = (y)_{10}$, then: $s_{n-1} = 0$ and $ms = 0.$ $\qquad$ (3.9)

Overflow cannot occur when two differently signed numbers are added.

Different Signs (As Carried Out in the Computer)

The above algorithms (3.7–3.9), represent the way humans carry out the addition operation when two numbers have different signs. Of course, humans can very easily and quickly estimate which of the two numbers being added has the larger value. Digital processors, however, do not in general include circuitry that can give a quick estimate of these values. Therefore, the addition of two differently signed numbers (i.e., $x_{n-1} \neq y_{n-1}$) in S&M notation, is carried out by the computer in a slightly different manner, by the following two-step procedure:

Procedure 3.1 (Adding Two Differently Signed Numbers in S&M Notation)

(1) The 1's complement of the magnitude of the second number y (the $\overline{my}$) is computed, and then added to mx to generate

$$ms^* = mx + \overline{my} \ ,$$

where ms^* is the magnitude of the temporary result s^*.

(2) After computing this temporary result, the carry bit c^*_{n-1} (generated during the above magnitude addition from the most significant position $n - 2$) is examined:

- If $c^*_{n-1} = 1$, then this carry bit is added to the least significant bit of the temporary ms^*, forms the correct final ms, and its sign s_{n-1} is set to $s_{n-1} = x_{n-1}$.
- If $c^*_{n-1} = 0$, then the correct magnitude of the final result is given as $ms'\overline{ms}^*$ (the 1's complement of ms^*), and its sign s_{n-1} is set to $s_{n-1} = x_{n-1}$ (the inverse of x_{n-1}).

Note: If $ms = 0$, then $s_{n-1} = 0$.

Example 3.1

Consider the case in which $x_{n-1} = y_{n-1} = 0$. Let $x = (0010101)_2 = (+21)_{10}$ and $y = (0011101)_2 = (+29)_{10}$ in S&M notation. Compute $s = x + y$.

Solution:

The two magnitudes are added together:

$$
\begin{aligned}
& (010101)_2 = (21)_{10} \\
+\ & (011101)_2 = (29)_{10} \\
\hline
ms^* =\ & (110010)_2 = (50)_{10} \\
c^*_6 =\ & 0
\end{aligned}
$$

The sign of the result is $s_6 = x_6 = y_6 = 0$, and the final sum is given as:

$$s = (s_6, ms) = (s_6, ms^*) = (0110010)_2 = (+50)_{10}.$$

Example 3.2

Consider the case in which $x_{n-1} = y_{n-1} = 0$ and the operation generates an overflow. Let $x = (0110101)_2 = (+53)_{10}$ and $y = (0111101)_2 = (+61)_{10}$ in S&M notation. Compute $s = x + y$.

Solution:

The two magnitudes are added together:

$$
\begin{aligned}
& (110101)_2 = (53)_{10} \\
+\ & (111101)_2 = (61)_{10} \\
\hline
ms^* =\ & (110010)_2 = (114)_{10} \\
c^*_6 =\ & 1
\end{aligned}
$$

Since $c^*_6 = 1$, an overflow situation exists, and therefore, there is an erroneous result. The correct result would have been found if the lengths of the two numbers were first extended (without modifying their decimal values), and then two magnitudes added as shown below:

$$\text{Extended magnitude of } x: (0110101)_2 = (53)_{10}$$
$$+$$
$$\text{Extended magnitude of } y: (0111101)_2 = (61)_{10}$$
$$ms^* = (1110010)_2 = (114)_{10}$$
$$c^*_7 = 0$$

The sign of this result is $s_7 = x_7 = y_7 = 0$, and the final sum is given as:

$$s = (01110010)_2 = (+114)_{10} .$$

Example 3.3

In the addition of differently signed numbers, as executed by the computer, let $x = (101101)_2 = (-13)_{10}$ and $y = (001011)_2 = (+11)_{10}$ in S&M notation. Execute the addition operation $s = x + y$ as done by the computer:

Solution:

Through the application of Procedure 3.1:

$$\overline{my} = (10100)_2 .$$

The two magnitudes are added together:

$$mx = (01101)_2$$
$$+ \ \overline{my} = (10100)_2$$
$$\dot{1}\vdots 00001 = ms^*$$
$$+ \quad \cdots\!\!\blacktriangleright 1 \quad (c^*_5 = 1 \text{ is added to the least}$$
$$\text{significant bit of } ms^*)$$
$$00010 = ms$$

The sign of the result is $s_5 = x_5 = 1$, and so the final correct result of the addition is given as:

$$s = (s_5, ms) = (x_5, ms) = (100010)_2 = (-2)_{10} .$$

Subtraction in S&M

The subtraction operation between two numbers in S&M notation is done simply by changing the sign of the second number and then performing the addition operation, as described above. Thus, the result of the subtraction $x-y$ is given by:

$$d = x + (-y) . \qquad (3.10)$$

An overflow may occur if $x_{n-1} \neq y_{n-1}$ and $c_{n-1} = 1$.

Example 3.4:

Let $x = (0010101)_2 = (+21)_{10}$ and $y = (0001111)_2 = (+15)_{10}$ in S&M notation. Execute the subtraction $d = x - y$, as done by the computer.

Solution:

The sign of y is changed to give $-y = (1001111)_2 = (-15)_{10}$. Now, since this is a case in which $x_{n-1} \neq y_{n-1}$, the addition Procedure 3.1 must be applied. Thus, the 1's complement of this second number's magnitude $-y$ is computed to get:

$$\overline{m(-y)} = 110000 .$$

The two magnitudes are added together:

$$
\begin{aligned}
& mx = (010101)_2 \\
+\ & \overline{m(-y)} = (110000)_2 \\
\hline
ms^* = md^* =\ & \boxed{1} (000101) \\
+\ & \cdots\cdots\!\blacktriangleright 1 \\
\hline
& (000110) = md
\end{aligned}
$$

The final sign is $d_6 = x_6 = 0$, and therefore, the final result is:

$$d = (d_6, md) = (x_6, md) = (0000110)_2 = (+6)_{10} .$$

Logical Expressions for the Addition/Subtraction Operations

Using logical functions, where ADD $= 1$ denotes addition, SUB $= 1$ denotes subtraction, $\oplus$ denotes modulo-2 addition and $\odot$ denotes the complement of modulo-2 addition, the algorithms for the S&M notation can be expressed as follows:

Procedure 3.2

If the following logical expression holds:

$$\text{ADD} \times \underbrace{(x_{n-1} \odot y_{n-1})}_{\substack{\text{same} \\ \text{signs}}} + \text{SUB} \times \underbrace{(x_{n-1} \oplus y_{n-1})}_{\substack{\text{different} \\ \text{signs}}} = 1,$$

then, add the magnitudes of x and y and set

$$s_{n-1} = x_{n-1}.$$

Procedure 3.3

If the following logical expression holds:

$$\underbrace{\text{ADD} \times (x_{n-1} \oplus y_{n-1})}_{\substack{\text{different} \\ \text{signs}}} + \underbrace{\text{SUB} \times (x_{n-1} \odot y_{n-1})}_{\substack{\text{same} \\ \text{signs}}} = 1,$$

then, to the magnitude of x add the 1's complement of y to get the temporary result ms^*. Further:

(1) If $c^*_{n-1} = 1$, add c^*_{n-1} to the least significant bit of ms^* to find the correct final result ms, and set $s_{n-1} = x_{n-1}$.

(2) If $c^*_{n-1} = 0$, then compute the 1's complement of the temporary result ms^*, symbolized by $\overline{ms^*}$, to find the correct final result ms, and set $s_{n-1} = \overline{x}_{n-1}$.

Procedure 3.4   (Identification of an Overflow Situation)

An overflow is identified if the following logical expression holds:

$$c^*_{n-1} \times [\text{ADD} \times (x_{n-1} \odot y_{n-1}) + \text{SUB} \times (x_{n-1} \oplus y_{n-1}) = 1,$$

where c^*_{n-1} is the carry generated from position $n-2$ during the addition of the two magnitudes.

Multiplication in S&M

Let x be the n-bit integer multiplicand and y the n-bit integer multiplier in S&M notation. Their multiplication is carried out using their respective $(n-1)$-bit magnitudes mx and my to form the magnitude product mp of the final product p. The sign of the final product depends upon the signs of the two numbers x and y. The procedure followed for the S&M multiplication is:

Procedure 3.5   (Multiplication in S&M Notation)

(1) For each y_i, $0 \leq i \leq n - 2$,[2] form the respective intermediate vector $p^{(i)}$ which equals $mx \times y_i$ shifted left by i positions. In other words, form all vectors

$$p^{(i)} = mx \times y_i \times 2^i \tag{3.11}$$

for $i = 0,1,2,\dots,n - 2$.

---

[2]If the multiplier y is k bits long, then this i ranges from 0 to $k - 2$.

The decimal value of each such vector is given by

$$(p^{(i)})_{10} = \left(\sum_{j=0}^{n-2} x_j \times 2^j \right) \times y_i \times 2^i = \sum_{j=0}^{n-2} (x_j \times y_i) \times 2^{j+i}. \qquad (3.12)$$

(2) Add all these intermediate vectors[3] to get the magnitude mp of the final product p. This magnitude is extended to the left with 0's, so that its total number of bits equals the sum of the number of bits of the multiplicand and the multiplier minus 1.

(3) The sign bit sp of the final product p is computed using the signs of the multiplicand and multiplier as follows:

If $x_{n-1} = y_{n-1}$, then the sign of the final product is $sp = 0$.
If $x_{n-1} \neq y_{n-1}$, then the sign of the final product is $sp = 1$.

This may also be expressed by the logic operation:

$$sp = x_{n-1} \oplus y_{n-1}. \qquad (3.13)$$

Example 3.5

Let $x = (0101101)_2$ and $y = (0101)_2$ in S&M notation. Compute the product $p = x \times y$.

Solution:

$$
\begin{array}{r}
\times \quad mx = (101101)_2 \\
my = \quad\quad (101)_2 = (y_2 y_1 y_0)
\end{array}
$$

$$
\begin{array}{ll}
101101 & \text{represents } mx \times y_0 \times 2^0 \\
000000- & \text{represents } mx \times y_1 \times 2^1 \\
+ \quad 101101-- & \text{represents } mx \times y_2 \times 2^2 \\
\hline
(11100001)_2 &
\end{array}
$$

The magnitude of the product is extended to the left with two 0's to get:

$$mp = (0011100001)_2.$$

The sign of final product is:

$$sp = x_6 \oplus y_6 = 0 \oplus 0 = 0.$$

Thus, the final product is:

$$p = (sp, mp) = (00011100001)_2.$$

---

[3]The additions can be done iteratively by accumulating all properly shifted vectors.

Division in S&M

Given the dividend x and the divisor $y \neq 0$, where $|x| \geq |y|$ then the division operation yields a quotient q (of, say, k bits) and a remainder t, such that:

$$x = (q \times y) + t \text{ with } 0 \leq |t| \leq |x|$$

$$\text{and sign } t = \text{sign } x. \tag{3.14}$$

Like multiplication, the division operation is carried out using the magnitudes of the dividend mx and the divisor my. The division algorithm generates the quotient-vector q, bit by bit, through the computation of a series of *partial remainders*.

The value of the final remainder is $t = mx - q \times my$. If the absolute value of the quotient is expressed as

$$q = \sum_{j=0}^{k-1} q_j \times 2^j \quad ,$$

then the value t of the remainder is given by:

$$t = mx - \sum_{j=0}^{k-1} my \times q_j \times 2^j .$$

The first step of the first partial remainder $t^{(1)}$ is given from the expression

$$t^{(1)} = mx - (q_{k-1} \times my) \times 2^{k-1}, \tag{3.15}$$

and this step is repeated k times, to compute the k bits of the quotient $q = q_{k-1}q_{k-2}\ldots q_0$.

Consequently, for each step i, the division algorithm of the two magnitudes is given by the recursive formula:

$$t^{(i)} = t^{(i-1)} - (q_{(k-1)-i} \times 2^{(k-1)-i}),$$

where

$$t^{(-1)} = mx \tag{3.16}$$

is the dividend, and

$$t^{(k-1)} = t$$

is the final remainder.

Since $q_{(k-1)-i}$ is either 0 or 1, the above algorithm (3.16) is expressed as:

$$t^{(i)} = t^{(i-1)} - my \times 2^{(k-1)-i}, \text{ if } q_{(k-1)-i} = 1$$

or $$\tag{3.17}$$

$$t^{(i)} = t^{(i-1)}, \text{ if } q_{(k-1)-i} = 0.$$

Since the value if each $q_{(k-1)-i}$ is not known in advance, the processor executes the following procedure, for each step i $(i = 0,1,\ldots,k-1)$:

Procedure 3.6 *(Division in S&M Notation)*

(1) Start with $q_{(k-1)-i} = 1$, and compute the temporary partial remainder $t^{(i)}$:

$$t^{(i)} = t^{(i-1)} - my \times 2^{(k-1)-i} \tag{3.18}$$

(2) This $t^{(i)}$ is examined to determine what will finally be the correct values for $q_{(k-1)-i}$ and $t^{(i)}$, as follows:

- The value $q_{(k-1)-i} = $ M 1 used initially is correct, and the temporary $t^{(i)}$ obtained from Equation (3.18) is the correct $t^{(i)}$, if the value of this $t^{(i)}$ is $t^{(i)} \geq 0$.
- However, if the temporary $t^{(i)}$ obtained from Equation (3.18) has a value of $t^{(i)} < 0^4$, then the correct value of bit $q_{(k-1)-i}$ is 0, and the correct partial remainder $t^{(i)}$ is given from $t^{(i)} = t^{(i-1)}$.

This method is called the "restoring division" method, since every previous remainder $t^{(i-1)}$ replaces the $t^{(i)}$ of the present step, if the partial remainder $t^{(i)}$ obtained from (3.18) has a negative value (i.e., the correct partial remainder is being restored).

The correct sign for the result is again appended to the magnitude, following a rule similar to that of Equation (3.13).

Example 3.6

Let $x = (00010110)_2$, $y = (00101)_2$, and $k = 5$. Perform the division in S&M notation.

Solution:

The two magnitudes are divided as follows:

$$
\begin{array}{r}
01001 = q = (q_4 q_3 q_2 q_1 q_0) \\
\hline
\end{array}
$$

$my = 0101 \bigg/ \quad$ 00101110 ⌐ $= t^{(-1)} = mx$

(1) $i = 0,$ subtract[5]: $\quad \underline{0101----}$ │ Represents $my \times 2^4$.

$t^{(0)} = \quad$ ~~11011110~~ │ Rejected as negative. Thus, $q_4 = 0$.

$t^{(0)} = t^{(-1)} = \quad$ 00101110 ◄ $t^{(-1)}$ is restored.

---

[4]A negative result is obtained if a larger magnitude is subtracted from a smaller magnitude.

[5]Note that the computer performs this subtraction using the subtraction algorithm described previously (see Equation 3.10)

(2) $i = 1$,   subtract: 0101 ---   Represents $my \times 2^3$.

            $t^{(1)} =$ 00000110 Saved. Thus, $q_3 = 1$.

(3) $i = 2$,   subtract: 0101 --   Represents $my \times 2^2$.

                            11110010   Rejected as negative. Thus, $q_2 = 0$.

            $t^{(2)} = t^{(1)} =$ 00000110 $t^{(1)}$ is restored.

(4) $i = 3$,   subtract: 0101-   Represents $my \times 2^1$.

                            11111100   Rejected as negative. Thus $q_1 = 0$.

            $t^{(3)} = t^{(2)} =$ 00000110 $t^{(2)}$ is restored.

(5) $i = 4$,   subtract: 0101   Represents $my \times 2^0$.

            $t^{(4)} =$ 00000001   Saved. Thus, $q_0 = 1$.

The sign of the final quotient is $q_5 = 0$. Thus, the final answers are:
quotient: $(q_5 q_4 q_3 q_2 q_1 q_0) = (001001)_2$, remainder $t^{(4)} = (00000001)_2$.

3.2.3   Arithmetic in Complement Notation

This section covers the four basic arithmetic operations in the complement
representation of negative numbers.

Addition

The addition of two n-bit numbers x and y in complement notation will yield
the correct result if, after the addition, the sum is taken modulo-λ, i.e.:

$$s = \lambda|(x + y), \tag{3.19}$$

where, for 1's complement $\lambda_d = 2^n - 1$ is used, while for 2's complement $\lambda_r = 2^n$
is used.

Inside the processor, all n bits of the two numbers x and y are added
together (the sign bit is now participating in the operation), giving a temporary result $s^* = (x + y)$. The final sum is then formed by

$$s = \lambda|s^*. \tag{3.20}$$

Two possibilities exist for the temporary result s^*:

(a) $|s^*| < |\lambda|$: This situation arises when the carry bit coming out from
    position $n - 1$ of the temporary result has the value $s^*_n = 0$. In this case,
    the above Equation (3.20) becomes

$$s = s^*. \tag{3.21}$$

In other words, the computed temporary result is the correct final sum.

(b) $|s^*| \geq |\lambda|$: This situation arises when the carry bit out from position $n-1$ of the temporary result has the value $s_n^* = 1$. In this case the above Equation (3.20) becomes

$$s = s^* - \lambda. \qquad (3.22)$$

For binary integers, vector λ has the following forms:

For 2's complements: $\lambda_r = 2^n = [\underbrace{1000\ldots00}_{n+1 \text{ terms}}] \qquad (3.23)$

For 1's complements: $\lambda_d = 2^n-1 = [\underbrace{111\ldots11}_{n \text{ terms}}] \qquad (3.24)$

Therefore, for 2's complement addition, the correct final sum s is found by disregarding this carry bit s^*_n of the temporary result; for 1's complement addition, the correct final sum s is found by subtracting 1 from each bit of the temporary result s^*, or by end-around-adding $s^*_n = 1$ to the least significant bit of the temporary result s^*.

Thus, addition in complement notation is done according to the following procedure:

Procedure 3.7   (Addition in Complement Notation)

(1)   Add together all bits of the two numbers, including the sign bit.
(2)   If the carry bit is $s^*_n = 1$, then:

- In 2's complement notation, disregard it.
- In 1's complement notation, end-around-add it to the least significant bit of the temporary result.

The 2's complement notation has only one 0, the "positive zero," but it has the peculiarity that the number represented by the vector $(1000\ldots0)$ and equaling $\lambda_r/2$ does not have a complement (or, rather, this number and its complement are the same). Such a number may result from the addition of two negative numbers.

On the other hand, 1's complement notation exhibits the peculiarity that it has a "negative zero," represented as $(111\ldots1)$. All 0 results of the addition operation are "negative zeros." A "positive zero" results only when two "positive zeros" are added.

The overflow conditions for the addition operation are as follows:
(1)   In 2's complement notation, the overflow is given by the logical expression

$$x_{n-1} \times y_{n-1} \times \bar{c}^*_{n-1} + \bar{x}_{n-1} \times \bar{y}_{n-1} \times c^*_{n-1} = 1, \qquad (3.25)$$

where c^*_{n-1} is the carry bit out from position $n-2$ of the *temporary* result s^*. This means that an overflow appears when two positive numbers are added and $c^*_{n-1} = 1$, or when two negative numbers are added and $c^*_{n-1} = 0$.

(2) In 1's complement notation, the overflow is given by the logical expression

$$x_{n-1} \times y_{n-1} \times \bar{s}_{n-1} + \bar{x}_{n-1} \times \bar{y}_{n-1} \times s_{n-1} = 1, \qquad (3.26)$$

where s_{n-1} is the sign bit of the *final* sum (i.e., after $c^*_n = 1$ has been end-around-added). This means that an overflow appears when two positive numbers are added and $s_{n-1} = 1$, or when two negative numbers are added and $s_{n-1} = 0$.

Example 3.7

Given $x = (001101)_2$ and $y = (001011)_2$ in 2's complement notation, compute $s = x + y$.

Solution:

$$
\begin{aligned}
x &= (001101)_2 &= (+13)_{10} \\
+ \; y &= (001011)_2 &= (+11)_{10} \\
\hline
s = s^* &= (011000)_2 & (+24)_{10} \\
c^*_{n-1} &= 1
\end{aligned}
$$

Example 3.8

Given $x = (110010)_2$ and $y = (110100)_2$ in 2's complement notation, compute $s = x + y$.

Solution:

$$
\begin{aligned}
x &= (110010)_2 &= (-14)_{10} \\
+ \; y &= (110100)_2 &= (-12)_{10} \\
\hline
s^* &= (100110)_2 &= (-26)_{10} \\
& \quad \text{— disregard } c^*_6 \\
s &= (100110)_2
\end{aligned}
$$

Subtraction

The subtraction $x - y$ in complement notation is done according to the following procedure:

Procedure 3.8   (Subtraction in Complement Notation)

(1) Find the complement of y, denoted as $\bar{y}$.

(2) Add $\bar{y}$ to x, modulo λ, according to Procedure 3.7.

For 2's complement subtraction the difference is given as:

$$d = x - y = x + (-y) = x + (-\lambda_r + \lambda_r - y) = x - \lambda_r + \bar{y}$$
$$= (x + \bar{y}) - \lambda_r = \lambda_r \mid (x + \bar{y}) \tag{3.27}$$

For 1's complement subtraction the difference is given as:

$$d = x - y = x + (-y) = x + (-\lambda_d + \lambda_d - y) = x - \lambda_d + \bar{y}$$
$$= (x + \bar{y}) - \lambda_d = \lambda_d \mid (x + \bar{y}) \tag{3.28}$$

The overflow conditions for the subtraction operations are as follows:

(1) In 2's complement notation, the overflow is given by the logical expression

$$\bar{x}_{n-1} \times y_{n-1} \times c^*_{n-1} + x_{n-1} \times \bar{y}_{n-1} \times \bar{c}^*_{n-1} = 1, \tag{3.29}$$

where c^*_{n-1} is the carry bit out from position $n-2$ of the *temporary* result s^*. This means that an overflow appears when a negative number is subtracted from a positive number and $c^*_{n-1} = 1$, or when a positive number is subtracted from a negative number and $c^*_{n-1} = 0$.

(2) In 1's complement notation, the overflow is given by the logical expression

$$\bar{x}_{n-1} \times y_{n-1} \times d_{n-1} + x_{n-1} \times \bar{y}_{n-1} \times \bar{d}_{n-1} = 1, \tag{3.30}$$

where d_{n-1} is the sign bit of the *final* difference (i.e., after $d^*_n = 1$ has been end-around-added). This means that an overflow appears when a negative number is subtracted from a positive number and $d_{n-1} = 1$, or when a positive number is subtracted from a negative number and $d_{n-1} = 0$.

Example 3.9

Given $x = (0101)_2$ and $y = (0010)_2$ in 2's complement notation, compute the difference $d = x - y$.

Solution:

$$+ \quad \begin{array}{l} x = (0101)_2 \\ \bar{y} = (1110)_2 \end{array}$$

$$(0011)_2 = s^*$$
$$\text{disregard } c^*_4$$
$$(0011)_2 = d$$

Example 3.10

Given $x = (001011)_2$, which equals $(+11)_{10}$, and $y = (001101)_2$, which equals $(+13)_{10}$ in 2's complement notation, compute the difference $d = x - y$.

Solution:

$$+\frac{\begin{array}{l} x = (001011)_2 \\ \overline{y} = (110011)_2 \end{array}}{(111110)_2 = s^* = d \text{ which equals } (-2)_{10}}$$

Example 3.11

Given $x = (01011)_2$, which equals $(+11)_{10}$, and $y = (10011)_2$, which equals $(-13)_{10}$ in 2's complement notation, compute the difference $d = x - y$.

Solution:

$$+\frac{\begin{array}{l} x = (01011)_2 \\ \overline{y} = (01101)_2 \end{array}}{(11000)_2 = s^*}$$
$$c^*_{n-1} = c^*_4 = 1$$

Here an overflow situation arises (and therefore, an erroneous result), since $x_4 = 0$, $y_4 = 1$, and $c^*_{n-1} = c^*_4 = 1$. To find the correct result, the length of the two numbers x and y must first be extended, as follows: the two numbers become $x = (001011)_2$, which equals $(+11)_{10}$, and $y = (110011)_2$, which equals $(-13)_{10}$. Then:

$$+\frac{\begin{array}{l} x = (001011)_2 \\ \overline{y} = (001101)_2 \end{array}}{(011000)_2 = s^* = d}$$
$$c^*_{n-1} = c^*_5 = 10,$$

which equals the correct result of the subtraction: $(+24)_{10}$.

Multiplication

Various methods exist for performing the multiplication operation. Presented here are the "Robertson's second method [16]" and "Booth's method [8]".

The multiplication operation is given as

$$p = x \times y, \tag{3.31}$$

where x is the multiplicand, y is the multiplier, and p is the final product. Multiplication is generally executed as a series of partial additions and shifts, and the length of the final product equals the sum of the lengths of x and y.

Robertson's Second Method

The multiplication algorithm in complement notation differs, depending upon whether the multiplier is positive or negative.

Procedure 3.9   (Robertson's Multiplication, Positive Multiplier)

(1) Examine step-by-step the multiplier bits from right to left.

(2) At each step i of the operation the following possible situations occur:

- If the examined bit is 0, then add 0's to the previous intermediate product $p^{(i-1)}$.
- If the examined bit is 1, perform a one position left arithmetic shift [6] on the multiplicand x, and then add it to the previous intermediate product $p^{(i-1)}$.

Example 3.12

Let $x = (1101101)_2$ and $y = (0110)_2$ in 1's complement notation. Compute the product $p = x \times y$.

Solution:

$$
\begin{array}{rlr}
\times \quad x = (1101101)_2 = & & (-18)_{10} \\
y = \quad (0110)_2 = (y_3y_2y_1y_0)_2 & & = (+6)_{10} \\
\hline
0000000 = p^{(0)} & & (-108)_{10} \\
+ \; 0000000 = x \times y_0 \times 2^0 & & \\
\hline
0000000 = p^{(1)} & & \\
+ \; 1101101 = x \times y_1 \times 2^1 & & \text{(According to the} \\
\hline
11011011 = p^{(2)} & & \text{rules for left shifts)} \\
+ \; 1101101 = x \times y_2 \times 2^2 & & \\
\hline
110010010 & & \\
+ \qquad\qquad 1 & & \\
\hline
110010011 = p^{(3)} & & \\
+0000000\text{---} = x \times y_3 \times 2^3 & & \\
\hline
1110010011 = p^{(4)} = p & &
\end{array}
$$

(Increasing the length of the numbers)

Procedure 3.10   (Robertson's Multiplication, Negative Multiplier)

(1) Generate the complement of the multiplier.

---

[6]Section 2.2.3 of chapter 2.

(2) Examine step-by-step the bits of this complement from right to left.

(3) At each step i of the operation the following situations are possible:

- If the examined bit is 0, then add 0's to the previous intermediate product $p^{(i-1)}$.
- If the examined bit is 1, generate the complement of the multiplicand, perform a one position left arithmetic shift on it, and then add it to the previous intermediate product $p^{(i-1)}$.

This procedure does not hold when in the 2's complement notation the value of the multiplier equals $2^n - 1$.

Example 3.13

Given $x = (0101101)_2$ and $y = (1010)_2$ in 2's complement notation, compute the product $p = x \times y$.

Solution:

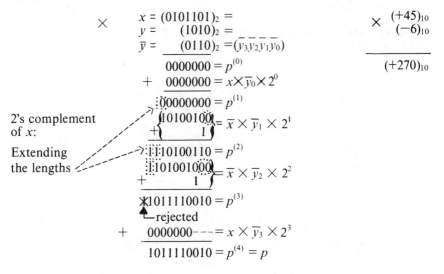

Booth's Method

Booth's method is used for multiplying two binary numbers in 2's complement notation without requiring the examination of the multiplier's sign. This method leads to the construction of a multiplier unit operating under the same algorithm, irrespective of the multiplicand and multiplier signs. The procedure is as follows:

Procedure 3.11   (Booth's Multiplication)

(1) Let register A contain 0's, register B hold the multiplicand, and register C hold the multiplier.
(2) Examine the multiplier bits in pairs, from right to left. For 0 to 1 transitions, the multiplier is subtracted from register A (the result is placed back into A). For transitions from 1 to 0, the multiplier is added to register A (the result is placed back into A). When there are no transitions (i.e., 0 to 0 or 1 to 1), then the contents of A do not change.
(3) The contents of A and C are shifted arithmetically one position to the right.
(4) The above steps (2) and (3) are repeated for all bits of the multiplier.

Comments:

• When the least significant bit of the multiplier is examined, $C_{-1} = 0$ is used as the initial (rightmost) comparison bit.
• No right shift is required after the last operation.
• The final product is contained in both registers A and C.

Booth's method of multiplication is given in Table 3.1 and in Figure 3.1 in flowchart form.

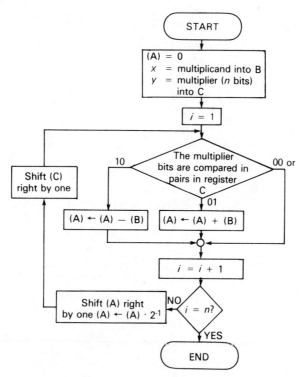

Figure 3.1   The flowchart for multiplying two binary numbers in 2's complement notation using Booth's method.

Table 3.1 Booth's multiplication method.

The Multiplier Examined Bits in Register C C_{i+1} C_i	Action	Comments
00	$(A,C) \leftarrow (A,C) \times 2^{-1}$	Shift (A) and (C) right one.
01	$(A) \leftarrow (A) + (B)$ and then $(A,C) \leftarrow (A,C) \times 2^{-1}$	Add (A) and (B), and then shift (A) and (C) right one.
10	$(A) \leftarrow (A) - (B)$ and then $(A,C) \leftarrow (A,C) \times 2^{-1}$	Subtract (B) from (A), and then shift (A) and (C) right one.
11	$(A,C) \leftarrow (A,C) \times 2^{-1}$	Shift (A) and (C) right one.

Example 3.14

Given $x = (0101101)_2$ and $y = (1010)_2$ in 2's complement notation, compute the product $p = x \times y$ with Booth's method.

Solution:

$$
\begin{array}{rll}
\times \quad x = (0101101)_2 = (B) & = (+45)_{10} \\
y = \quad\quad (1010)_2 = (C) = (C_3 C_2 C_1 C_0) & = (-6)_{10} \\
\hline
p^{(0)} = (A) = 0000000 & (-270)_{10}
\end{array}
$$

$C_0 C_{-1} = 00$ $\quad p^{(1)} = \overset{\cdot\cdot}{0}000000\ 0 \quad (A,C) \leftarrow (A,C) \times 2^{-1}$

$C_1 C_0 = 10$ $\qquad\qquad\quad \left.\begin{array}{r} 1010010 \\ + \qquad\quad 1 \end{array}\right\}$ 2's complement of (B)

$\qquad\qquad\qquad\quad \overline{1010011\ 0}$

$\qquad\qquad p^{(2)} = \overset{\cdot\cdot}{1}101001\ 10 \quad (A,C) \leftarrow (A,C) \times 2^{-1}$

$C_2 C_1 = 01$ $\qquad\qquad + \ 0101101 \qquad\quad \textbf{(B)}$

$\qquad\qquad\quad \overline{\diagup 0010110\ 10} \quad (A) \leftarrow (A) + (B)$

$\qquad\qquad\quad \overset{\blacktriangle}{\underline{\quad}}\!\!\text{— disregard}$

$\qquad\qquad p^{(3)} = \quad 001011\ 010 \quad (A,C) \leftarrow (A,C) \times 2^{-1}$

$C_3 C_2 = 10$ $\qquad\qquad\quad \left.\begin{array}{r} 1010010 \\ + \qquad\quad 1 \end{array}\right\}$ 2's complement of **(B)**

$\qquad\qquad\quad \overline{1011110\ 010} \quad (A) \leftarrow (A) - (B)$

$\qquad p^{(4)} = p = \underline{\underbrace{101111}_{(A)}\ \underbrace{0010}_{(C)}} \quad (A,C) \leftarrow (A,C) \times 2^{-1}$

Division

The division operation is executed as a series of subtractions and shifts. The following symbols are used: x is the dividend, $y \neq 0$ is the divisor, q is the k-bit quotient, and t is the remainder. The "restoring division" method is presented here for dividing binary integers in 2's complement notation. The procedure is as follows:

Procedure 3.12   (Restoring Division in Complement Notation)

(1) If, at step i, the previous partial remainder $t^{(i-1)}$ and the divisor y have same (different) signs, then the divisor y is subtracted from (added to) $t^{(i-1)}$.

(2) The above operation described in (1) is successful if the signs of $t^{(i-1)}$ and $t^{(i)}$ (i.e., of the previous and of the present partial remainders) are the same. Therefore:

 • If the operation is successful or $t^{(i)} = 0$, then the temporary quotient bit is $q^*_{(k-1)-i} = 1$, where k is the total number of quotient bits to be computed.

 • If the operation is unsuccessful and $t^{(i)} \neq 0$, then the result $t^{(i)}$ is rejected, and $q^*_{(k-1)-i} = 0$.

(3) Following each operation (successful or not), the divisor y is shifted right by one position.

(4) The temporary quotient q^* is the correct result of the division, (i.e., the final quotient q), if the initial dividend x and the divisor y have the same sign. If their signs differ, then the correct quotient q of the division is found by forming the 2's complement of the computed temporary quotient q^* (i.e., $q = \overline{q}^*$).

Example 3.15

Given $x = (11101101110)_2$ and $y = (001101)_2$ in 2's complement notation, execute the division operation, with $k = 6$.

Solution:

$$
\begin{array}{r}
110101 \doteq q \\
y = 001101 \, / \, \overline{11101101110} \\
+ \quad 00110100000 \\
\end{array}
$$

(1) $i = 0$. Add $y \times 2^5$

$t^{(0)} = \cancel{1}00100001110$ Different signs. Rejected.

$\qquad\qquad$ —disregard   Thus, $q^*_5 = 0$.

$t^{(0)} = t^{(-1)} = \quad 11101101110$

$110101 \doteq q = (q_5 q_4 q_3 q_2 q_1 q_0)$

$= x = t^{(-1)}$

(2) $i = 1$. Add $y \times 2^4$ $+$ $\dot{0}0011010000$ Right shift of y, by 1 position.

$$t^{(1)} = \cancel{X00000111110}$$
<u>disregard</u>   Different signs. Rejected. Thus, $q*_4 = 0$.

$t^{(1)} = t^{(0)} = 11101101110$

(3) $i = 2$. Add $y \times 2^3$ $+$ $\dot{0}0001101000$ Right shift of y, by 2 positions.

$$t^{(2)} = 11111010110$$ Same signs. Thus, $q*_3 = 1$.

(4) $i = 3$. Add $y \times 2^2$ $+$ $\dot{0}0\dot{0}000110100$ Right shift of y, by 3 positions.

$$t^{(3)} = \cancel{X00000001010}$$
<u>disregard</u>   Different signs. Rejected. Thus $q*_2 = 0$.

$t^{(3)} = t^{(2)} = 11111010110$

(5) $i = 4$. Add $y \times 2^1$ $+$ $\dot{0}0\dot{0}0\dot{0}0011010$ Right shift of y, by 4 positions.

$$t^{(4)} = 11111110000$$ Same signs. Thus, $q*_1 = 1$.

(6) $i = 5$. Add $y \times 2^0$ $+$ $\dot{0}0\dot{0}0\dot{0}0001101$ Right shift of y, by 5 positions.

$$t^{(5)} = 11111111101$$ Same signs. Thus, $q*_0 = 1$.

Since the initial x and y have different signs:

$$t = t^{(5)} = (11111111101)_2 = (-3)_{10} \text{ and } q = \overline{q}* = (110101)_2 = (-11)_{10}$$

Note: The $q* = (q_5 q_4 q_3 q_2 q_1 q_0)$ is the temporary quotient being formed.

3.3 DECIMAL (BCD) ARITHMETIC

3.3.1 Introduction

Although all digital systems use some form of binary numbers for their internal operations, the external world is decimal in nature. Since most people are only familiar with decimal numbers, their interaction with digital machines must be in decimal form. Thus, numerical inputs into such machines—for example, by pressing one of ten digit keys of a calculator-type keyboard, through a teletype keyboard, etc.—are in decimal form. Similarly, numerical outputs from these machines—for example, on a teletype printer, a 7-segment display, etc.—are also in decimal form. This means that there is a constant need for performing conversions between the decimal and binary systems. Since decimal operations are complex, more awkward, and slower than binary operations, the binary numbers are preferred for sophisticated applications, and hardware or software routines are utilized by larger systems to do the conversions.

In many calculator-type and microprocessor applications, however, the internal operations to be performed involve rather simple arithmetic operations. In these cases, constant conversion between decimal and binary can become long for large numbers, inefficient, and slow, and it is preferable to work directly in decimal. These decimal numbers can be represented (encoded) internally under various forms, such as in excess-3 code, in Gray code, in BCD form, etc. The BCD is the most commonly used code for internal representation, and most calculators and microprocessors have the appropriate hardware and software to facilitate arithmetic operations in BCD. In the BCD code, converting to and from decimal is relatively easy, and it involves rather simple hardware structures.

3.3.2   Decimal Addition/Subtraction

The decimal operations are carried out either between two signed numbers or between two unsigned numbers. For unsigned data, the sign digit is simply omitted in memory to save space. Unsigned numbers are treated arithmetically as if they were positive numbers. Situations, however, do arise that require the representation of negative decimal numbers, as, for example, in representing the result of subtracting a larger positive number from a smaller positive number. The simplest way of assigning a value to the sign digit is $0_{10} = 0000_{2BCD}$ for the positive numbers, and $9_{10} = 1001_{2BCD}$ for the negative numbers. With such an assignment, the familiar check is still valid, in that, if the most significant bit of the BCD number is 0, then the decimal number is positive; otherwise, the number is negative.

The way decimal additions or subtractions are performed again depends upon the specific representation used for (basically the negative) decimal numbers.

Decimal addition and subtraction in S&M notation are performed in a way similar to that discussed for the binary numbers in section 3.2.2, but with the difference that, instead of the 1's complement, the 9's complement is now used.

Decimal addition and subtraction in complement notation are done similarly to addition and subtraction in binary numbers described in section 3.2.3. However, the 9's complement is now used instead of the 1's complement, and the 10's complement instead of the 2's complement.

Although the rules for decimal addition and subtraction are similar to those for binary operations, the BCD operations may require some corrections to the individual BCD digits of the calculated result. This happens because the sum of two BCD digits may give a result greater than 9 ($= 1001)_2$, which cannot be represented as an allowable 4-bit BCD digit.

Consider, for example, the decimal addition between the two numbers 0698 and 0786, where both are given in BCD representation. Carrying out the normal binary addition between the two numbers gives:

```
                          1 (Intermediate Carry)
   0698        0000   0110  ·.  1001    1000 ) Binary
+  0786      + 0000   0111  :  1000    0110 ∫ Addition
  ─────        ──────────────────────────────
   1484        0000   1110 :1:0001    1110
```

Consequently, it is observed that an erroneous BCD result is obtained, because: (1) each of the second and fourth digits is a number greater than 9 (and therefore a "forbidden" BCD digit), and (2) the third digit of the result is also in error.

In order to find the correct result of a decimal addition, a correction of one or more of the digits in the above sum may be required. Corrections are performed on each digit of the binary addition result, starting from the least position and moving to the left, according to the following procedure:

Procedure 3.13   (BCD Corrections)

(1) If the 4-bit digit of the result of the binary addition is equal to or smaller than 9 ($= 1001)_2$, then this is a correct BCD digit and no correction is required.

(2) If the 4-bit digit of the result of the binary addition is greater than 9 ($= 1001)_2$, or if an intermediate carry appears (the auxiliary carry generated every four bits,[7] then, the correct result in this position will be found by adding the constant 6 ($= 0110)_2$.[8]

In the above example, therefore, the following corrections are applied to the binary addition:

```
                    1
   0698    0000   0110 : 1001    1000 ) Binary
+  0786 +  0000   0111 : 1000    0110 ∫ Addition       Decimal
  ─────    ──────────────────────────────
   1484      1           1                             BCD
           0000   1110:1:0001   : 1110                 Addition
                  0110  0110    : 0110  ← Corrections
           ──────────────────────────────
           0001  1 0100   1000  :1:0100
```

---

[7]Generated when the sum of the two digits (plus a possible carry) is greater than 9 and equal to or smaller than 19 ($= 10011_2$).

[8]Most 8-bit microprocessors provide an instruction such as DAA (decimal adjust after addition or decimal adjust accumulator) to perform this correction in software.

Thus, the final correct BCD result is:

0001	0100	1000	0100
1	4	8	4

Example 3.16

Subtract the decimal $(0326)_{10}$ from $(0736)_{10}$, encoded in BCD format. Perform this subtraction operation in both 9's complement and 10's complement notation.

Solution:

$$(0736) = (0000011100110110)_{BCD}$$

and

$$(0326)_{10} = (0000001100100110)_{BCD}$$

(1) Subtraction in 9's complement notation is performed by adding the 9's complement of the second number, which is: $(9673)_{10} = (1001011001110100)_{BCD}$.
   We have:

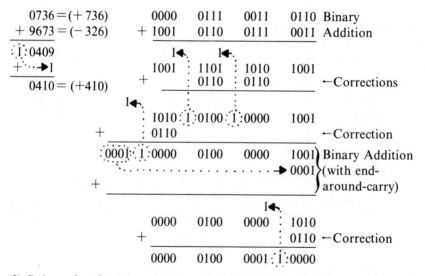

(2) Subtraction in 10's complement notation is performed by adding the 10's complement of the second number, which is: $(9674)_{10} = (1001011001110100)_{BCD}$.

We have:

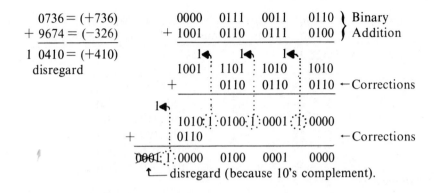

```
  0736 = (+736)         0000   0111   0011   0110 ⎫ Binary
+ 9674 = (−326)       + 1001   0110   0111   0100 ⎭ Addition
  1 0410 = (+410)        1◄     1◄     1◄
  disregard             1001 ┊ 1101 ┊ 1010 ┊ 1010
                        +    ┊ 0110 ┊ 0110 ┊ 0110  ←Corrections
                   1◄
                    ┊ 1010:1:0100:1:0001:1:0000
                +   ┊ 0110                         ←Corrections
                  0001:1:0000   0100   0001   0000
                  └─ disregard (because 10's complement).
```

3.3.3   Decimal Multiplication

For decimal multiplication, the same rules apply as those mentioned in the previous section, 3.2, for binary multiplication. However, in general, the decimal multiplication between two BCD numbers is more complicated than binary multiplication. Whereas, in binary multiplication either a shift, or addition of the multiplicand and then a shift is performed (depending on whether the multiplier bit examined is 1 or 0, respectively), in decimal multiplication, one of ten different possible products of the multiplicand times one of the digits 0 to 9 may be added, and then a shift performed.

Decimal multiplication and division are not usually built into the microprocessor directly; instead these operations are perfomed via standard software subroutines.

The decimal multiplication between two BCD numbers in S&M notation is relatively simple, and rather similar to the respective binary multiplication described in section 3.2.2. The final product is positive whenever two numbers of the same sign are multiplied; otherwise it is negative. The decimal multiplication between two BCD numbers in complement notation, however, is best performed by first converting them into sign and magnitude notation and then multiplying.

Covered below is the decimal multiplication between two BCD numbers in sign and magnitude notation. As in decimal addition, the decimal multiplication of two BCD digits may require some corrections. The difference is that the product of two BCD digits may now have a value greater than 19 (= $10011)_2$. Consequently, these corrections involve the addition of a binary number, whose value depends upon the value of the product of the two respective BCD digits, as follows:

The value of the product (p) between two decimal digits.	The binary number that must be added as correction.
$9 < p \leq 19$	$0110 = (6)_{10}$
$19 < p \leq 29$	$01100 = (12)_{10}$
$29 < p \leq 39$	$010010 = (18)_{10}$
$39 < p \leq 49$	$011000 = (24)_{10}$
$49 < p \leq 59$	$011110 = (30)_{10}$
$59 < p \leq 69$	$0100100 = (36)_{10}$
$69 < p \leq 79$	$0101010 = (42)_{10}$
$79 < p \leq 89$	$0110000 = (48)_{10}$

Example 3.17

Multiply the two decimal numbers $(04763)_{10}$ and $(091)_{10}$ in BCD format, and S&M notation.

Solution:

$$
\begin{array}{r}
04763 \\
\times\ \ 091 \\
\hline
4763 \\
+\ \ 42867 \\
\hline
0433433
\end{array}
\quad
\begin{array}{l}
= (0000\ 0100\ 0111\ 0110\ 0011)_{BCD} \\
= (0000\ 1001\ 0001)_{BCD}
\end{array}
$$

(1) Multiplying the $(0100011101100011)_{BCD}$ by the $(0001)_{BCD}$ gives the following result:

$$p^{(1)} = (0100\ 0111\ 0110\ 0011)_{BCD}$$

(2) Multiplying the $(0100011101100011)_{BCD}$ by the $(1001)_{BCD}$ gives the following result:

```
      0100      0111      0110      0011
    ×                               1001
    ─────────────────────────────────────
      0100      0111      0110      0011
      0000      0000      0000      0000
      0000      0000      0000      0000
  +   0100      0111      0110      0011
```

```
 0011◄    0110◄    0101◄    0010◄
     :0100100  :0111111  :0110110  :0011011
 +   :0010010  :0100100  :0011110  : 001100   ←Corrections
 ─────────────────────────────────────────────
     1◄
 0011 :011:1100  :1101000 :01010110 :00100111
 +    :      0110                            ←Corrections
 ─────────────────────────────────────────────
 0100  :.1:0010   1000      0110      0111
```

The result is:

$$p^{(2)} = (0100\ 0010\ 1000\ 0110\ 0111)_{BCD}.$$

(3) Add the two partial products $p^{(1)}$ and $p^{(2)}$ to get:

		0100	0111	0110	0011	$= p^{(1)}$
+ 0100	0010	1000	0110	0111		$= p^{(2)} \times 10^1$

		1←	1←	1←		
0100	0010	1100	1101	1101	0011	
+		0110	0110	0110		←Corrections
0100	0011	1:0011	1:0100	1:0011	0011	

Therefore, the final product is given as:

$$p = (0100\ 0011\ 0011\ 0100\ 0011\ 0011)_{BCD} = (433433)_{10}.$$

3.3.4 Decimal Division

As in the binary case, there are various methods of dividing two decimal numbers. The method usually used is the "restoring method for decimal division," which is similar to that described in section 3.2.3. The final quotient is positive when two numbers with similar signs are divided, otherwise it is negative. However, this division of BCD numbers becomes more complicated, because corrections are again required which are analogous to those for the decimal multiplication.

3.4 FLOATING-POINT ARITHMETIC

Because of the narrow data paths and slow execution speeds, floating-point arithmetic was not widely used in microprocessors, and when needed, it was usually carried out in software. However, with the appearance of newer 16- and 32-bit microprocessors, floating-point arithmetic is now becoming an attractive alternative for serious scientific and engineering microprocessor applications. Compared to fixed-point, floating-point notation offers automatic scaling and extends the range of numbers that the microprocessor can handle.

Realizing this importance, and trying to assure a uniform floating-point software environment for programmers, the IEEE Society has proposed a standard (the Draft 8.0 of IEEE Task P754) for binary floating-point arithmetic [7,11]. It may be implemented entirely in hardware, software, or any combination of the two.[9] This standard specifies floating-point number formats, the results of floating-point operations, conversions between integers and floating-point numbers, conversions between different floating-point formats, etc. Most of the discussion that follows uses the terminology and definitions proposed by the IEEE standard.

3.4.1 Definitions

Floating-Point Numbers

A binary floating-point number is represented as a bit string characterized by three components: a sign, a signed integer exponent, and a significand. The *sign bit*, denoted by s, identifies positive (when $s = 0$) or negative (when $s = 1$) floating-point numbers. The *exponent*, denoted by e, signifies the power to which 2 is raised in determining the magnitude of the represented number. The *significand*, denoted by "$l.f$," consists of an explicit or implicit leading bit l to the left of its binary point, and a fraction field f to the right of the binary point. This fraction communicates the precision of the number. The more significand bits the fraction contains, the better the precision in representing a number. Similarly, the more bits in the exponent, the wider the dynamic range of numbers being represented. Therefore, the exponent sets off the range, while the fraction notes the exact value of the number within that range.

Normalized, Unnormalized, and Denormalized Numbers

Given here are the definitions proposed by the IEEE standard for floating-point numbers.

Normalized Numbers

For a given length of the fraction f, the greatest accuracy is achieved if the leading significand bit is $l = 1$ (the only exception to this is the number 0). The operation of removing all leading 0's by shifting the significand left (until the leading significand bit becomes 1) and decrementing the exponent accordingly, is called normalization. Thus, any nonzero real number may be expressed in "normalized floating-point" form as

$$\pm 2^e \times (1.f), \tag{3.32}$$

where the significand field (1.f) satisfies $1 \leq (1.f) \leq 2$.

---

[9]The 32-bit Intel APX 432 microprocessor has inplemented this IEEE floating-point arithmetic standard internally in hardware.

Unnormalized Numbers

A number whose leading significand bit, whether implicit or explicit, is 0 is an unnormalized number. Unnormalizing of an operand may be required before an add/subtract operation if the exponents of the two operands X and Y are not equal. In such a case, the binary points of X and Y are aligned by unnormalizing the operand with the smaller exponent (i.e., shifting its significand to the right and incrementing its exponent) until the two exponents become equal. This right shifting in general may be done up to n positions, where n is the number of bits in the significand. If this right shift is of more than n places, then the two operands are considered incommensurate, and the result usually takes the value of the operand with the larger exponent (with suitable sign manipulation).

Denormalized Numbers

The result of a floating-point operation is delivered to a "destination," which may either be explicitly designated by the user or implicitly supplied by the system. The destination format (regardless of the rounding precision control to be discussed later) shall be at least as wide as the operands' format. The result may also be denormalized. To denormalize a binary floating-point result, its significand is shifted to the right while its exponent is incremented until it reaches that of the smallest normalized number representable in the destination.[10] Denormalization on the result is performed before rounding.

Biased Exponent

The exponent of a binary floating-point number may be either a "signed" exponent or a "biased" exponent.

A "signed" exponent may be represented in 2's complement or in S&M notation. For example, consider an 8-bit exponent. In 2's complement representation, the minimum exponent is given as $10000000 = -2^7 = -128$ and the maximum exponent is given as $01111111 = +(2^7 - 1) = +127$. Such a system, therefore, will accommodate binary floating-point numbers within the approximate range of $2^{\pm 127}$, which corresponds to a decimal range of approximately $10^{\pm 38}$. Similarly, if the S&M representation is used, the minimum exponent is

---

[10]These definitions of *unnormalized* and *denormalized* numbers are used here in their traditional sense, that is, denormalized numbers are simply those unnormalized numbers whose exponent is the format's minimum. However, Draft 8.0 of the IEEE standard [15], restricts the word *unnormalized* to apply only to numbers whose leading significand bit is 0 but which are not denormalized.

given as $11111111 = -(2^7 - 1) = -127$, and the maximum as $01111111 = +(2^7 - 1) = +127$, thus resulting in approximately the same range as before.

The standard representation, however, is the "biased" exponent; some appropriate integer constant, called the "bias," is added to all exponents in order to keep them always positive. This bias usually equals $2^{k-1} - 1$, where k is the number of bits in the binary exponent. The binary representation of this bias is $0111\ldots11$, a total of k bits. Under this representation, a k-bit binary exponent ranging from $-(2^{k-1} - 1)$ to $+(2^{k-1} + 1)$, will now be expressed as a positive biased number e. The actual value of the exponent is found by the subtraction $e-\text{bias}$. The minimum biased exponent is $e_{min} = 0$, represented as $000\ldots00$; the maximum biased exponent is $e_{max} = 2^k - 1$, represented as $111\ldots11$. These two extreme values, $e_{min} = 0$ and $e_{max} = 2^k - 1$, are reserved to designate special operands; one of them, the "normal zero," is represented by $e = (l.f) = 0$.

For single-precision floating-point, the IEEE standard suggests that a normalized nonzero number X has the form

$$X = (-1)^s \times 2^{e-127} \times (1.f), \tag{3.33}$$

where

$s = $ sign bit

$e = $ 8-bit exponent biased by 127. (Range of e is from $e_{min} + 1$ to $e_{max}-1$)

$f = X$'s 23-bit fraction, which, together with an implicit leading 1, yields the significand part $1.f$.

These numbers can range in magnitude between $2^{-126} \times 1.000\ldots00$ and $2^{127} \times 1.111\ldots11$, inclusive. Given below are some examples of such normalized floating-point representations:

Unpacked Format 24 Bits	Packed 32-Bit Single-Precision Format
$2^0 \times 1.000\ldots00$	3F800000
$2^{-1} \times 1.000\ldots00$	3F000000
$2^{-1} \times 1.111\ldots00$	3F7FFFFF
$2^1 \times 1.000\ldots00$	40000000
$2^2 \times 1.000\ldots00$	40800000
$2^{-23} \times 1.000\ldots00$	34000000
$2^{-126} \times 1.000\ldots00$	00800000
$2^{127} \times 1.111\ldots00$	007FFFFF

3.4.2 Floating-Point Formats

Presented here are a number of existing microprocessor floating-point formats, as well as the formats suggested by the IEEE standard. In all cases, the basic format sizes for floating-point numbers are thirty-two bits (single format, for single-precision operations) and sixty-four bits (double format, for double-precision operations).

American National Standards Institute (ANSI) FORTRAN

The ANSI FORTRAN format for a microprocessor single-precision floating-point number is shown in Figure 3.2a. It consists of a sign bit s which is the sign of the fraction (thus the fraction is represented in S&M notation), a 7-bit exponent, and a 24-bit fraction magnitude. The fraction represents a "normalized" number (where "normalized" is defined as a fraction whose most significant bit is nonzero, unless the number itself is 0, in which case all thirty-two bits are 0) with the binary point assumed to be to the left of its most significant bit [10]. An additional "guard byte" (to be explained later) is attached to the right of the 24-bit fraction, temporarily creating a 32-bit fraction to be used internally during arithmetic operations. The exponent is biased by 64; a 0 exponent is represented by $e = 1000000$, the minimum exponent by $e_{min} = 0000000$, and the maximum exponent by $e_{max} = 1111111$. The radix of the floating-point number is $r = 16$, allowing this format to represent numbers within the approximate range of $16^{\pm 63}$, which corresponds to the decimal range of approximately $10^{\pm 77}$.

Digital Equipment Corporation (DEC) and Hewlett-Packard (H-P)

The two companies, DEC and H-P, have implemented a binary floating-point format in their BASIC interpreters (Figure 3.3). The fraction is again in S&M notation, with its sign kept in the most significant bit location of the 32-bit number. The magnitude of the fraction consists of twenty-three bits plus a "hidden" or "implicit" bit, which is always 1 for nonzero normalized numbers, and is thus not explicitly represented in the format. An 8-bit "guard byte" is used in all internal operations performed on 32-bit fractions. The hidden bit also participates in these calculations, and must therefore be explicitly represented. The exponent is binary, biased by 128. The floating-point radix is $r = 2$, allowing this format to represent numbers in the approximate range of 2^{+127} or approximately $10^{\pm 38}$. Thus, the maximum exponent is represented by the largest number 11111111, the minimum exponent by the smallest nonzero number 00000001, and an exponent of 0 is represented by 10000000, while the number 0 in the exponent is reserved to indicate a 0 fraction. Given below are examples of normalized binary floating-point representations (the implicit leading 1 is now shown explicitly) for various decimal numbers [10].

Decimal Number	Binary Floating-Point Number
	s e f
0	0 00000000 0......0
−1	1 10000001 0......0
+1	0 10000001 0......0
−0.50	1 10000000 0......0
+0.50	0 10000000 0......0
+6.00	0 10000011 10.....0
+100.00	0 10000111 10010 .0
-1×2^{-128}	1 00000001 0......0
$+1 \times 2^{-128}$	0 00000001 0......0
$-1 \times 2^{+126}$	1 11111111 0......0
$+1 \times 2^{+126}$	0 11111111 0......0

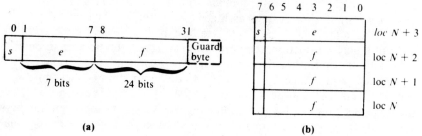

(a)   (b)

s: sign of fraction

e: 7-bit exponent biased by 64

f: 24-bit fraction

floating-point radix: $r = 16$

Figure 3.2 **(a)** The ANSI FORTRAN floating-point format with the guard byte; **(b)** an arrangement for storing the floating-point number in memory (the guard byte is not stored). *Adapted from "Floating-Point Arithmetic," by B. Hashizume, appearing in the November 1977 issue of* BYTE *magazine. Copyright © 1977 Byte Publications, Inc. Adapted with the permission of Byte Publications, Inc.* [10].

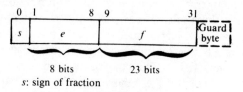

s: sign of fraction

e: 8-bit exponent biased by 128

f: 23-bit fraction (plus an implicit leading 1)

floating-point radix: $r = 2$

Figure 3.3 The DEC and H-P BASIC interpreters floating-point format with the guard byte. [10]

Motorola

The Motorola floating-point number representation has the format of Figure 3.2a [4]. However, the 7-bit exponent is now represented in signed 2's complement notation, and the floating-point radix is $r = 2$, thus allowing this format to represent numbers within the approximate range of 2^{+63} or, approximately, 10^{+19}.

Intel

The floating-point number representation used by Intel for single- and double-precision has the same format as that proposed by the IEEE standard, discussed next [14].

IEEE Standard

The IEEE standard categorizes four floating-point formats in two groups: "basic" and "extended," each of which has two widths, single and double. Discussed below are the two widths of the "basic" formats, single-precision and double-precision.

Single-Precision Format

Single-precision floating-point numbers are 32-bit quantities having the format shown in Figure 3.4a. This is the bit string for representing the number in storage. The value v of this number is as follows:

- If $e = 255$ and $f \neq 0$, then $v = $ NaN (Not-a-Number).
- If $e = 255$ and $f \neq 0$, then $v = (-1)^s \times \infty$
- If $0 < e < 255$,   then $v = (-1)^s \times 2^{-127} \times (1.f)$.
- If $e = 0$ and $f \neq 0$, then $v = (-1)^s \times 2^{-126} \times (0.f)$.
- If $e = 0$ and $f = 0$, then $v = (-1)^s \times 0$ (zero).

Double-Precision Format

Double-precision floating-point numbers are 64-bit quantities having the format shown in Figure 3.4b. This is the bit string for representing the number in storage. The value v of this number is as follows:

- If $e = 2047$ and $f \neq 0$, then $v = $ NaN (Not-a-Number).
- If $e = 2047$ and $f = 0$, then $v = (-1)^s \times \infty$
- If $0 < e < 2047$,   then $v = (-1)^s \times 2^{e-1023} \times (1.f)$.
- If $e = 0$ and $f \neq 0$, then $v = (-1)^s \times 2^{-1022} \times (0.f)$.
- If $e = 0$ and $f = 0$, then $v = (-1)^s \times 0$ (zero).

Finally, when floating-point numbers are used internally in arithmetic operations, three additional bits, the guard bit (G), the round bit (R), and the sticky bit (S), are appended to the right, and another bit, the overflow bit (V), is attached to the left of the most significant bit of the fraction; thus, preliminary numeric results may be viewed, as in Figure 3.4c.

3.4.3   Floating-Point Arithmetic Operations

The IEEE standard provides for the following operations: add, subtract, multiply, divide, square root, remainder, floating-point format conversions, conversions between floating-point and integers, binary ↔ decimal conversions, and comparisons. We discuss here only the first four arithmetic floating-point operations.

The usual type of arithmetic operations are those performed on unnormalized operands. The IEEE standard calls this the *warning mode*. The standard also allows an optional *normalized mode*, in which all results are computed as though all denormalized operands had first been normalized. The algorithms for unnormalized and normalized operands are essentially the same. (The only unnormalized result possible with normalized operands is a denormalized number on underflow). In a system that offers both, the IEEE standard suggests the warning mode to be the default.

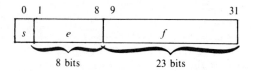

s: sign of fraction
e: 8-bit exponent biased by 127 ($e_{min} = 0$, $e_{max} = 255$). Range of e from ($e_{min}+1$) to ($e_{max}-1$)
f: 23-bit fraction (plus an implicit leading 1)
floating-point radix $r = 2$
Representation of normalized numbers: $(-1)^s \times 2^{e-127} \times (1.f)$, if $0 < e < 255$.

(a)   IEEE single-precision format.

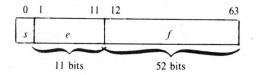

s: sign of fraction
e: 11-bit exponent biased by 1023 ($e_{min} = 0$, $e_{max} = 2047$). Range of e from ($e_{min}+1$) to ($e_{max}-1$)
f: 52-bit fraction (plus an implicit leading 1)
floating-point radix: $r = 2$
Representation of normalized numbers: $(-1)^s \times 2^{e-1023} \times (1.f)$, if $0 < e < 2047$.

(b)   IEEE double-precision format.

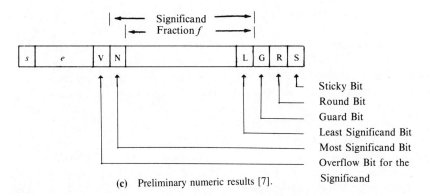

(c)   Preliminary numeric results [7].

Figure 3.4   The IEEE standard basic formats. *Parts* **(a)** *and* **(b)** *from IEEE Task P754, Draft 8.0, "A Proposed Standard for Binary Floating-Point Arithmetic,"* Computer, *March 1981, p. 55.* © *IEEE, New York.*

To perform the arithmetic operations on floating-point numbers stored in either of the two forms shown in Figures 3.4a and 3.4b, the system will generally unpack the bit strings into their component fields s, e, and f. Moreover, the leading significand bit will be made explicit, and perhaps the bias will be removed from the exponent. In arithmetic operations, therefore, there are two parts in each of the basic operations: the significand calculation and the exponent calculation, both done in fixed-point. Depending upon the specific representation used, the arithmetic operations will follow the rules of fixed-point arithmetic discussed in section 3.2.

In the operations discussed below, the fractions are given in S&M notation, and exponents are biased. In the examples, it is assumed that only valid, nonzero normalized operands are used.

Addition/Subtraction

Addition and subtraction are treated together because their algorithms are similar. The numbers used are in their unpacked format. The procedure is as follows:

Procedure 3.14   (Floating-Point Addition/Subtraction)

(1)   Normalize any denormalized operands.
(2)   Compare the two exponents, and:
   • If equal, proceed to either step (3a) or (3b), depending upon the operation.
   • If unequal, unnormalize the operand with the smaller exponent until the exponents are equal. During this process, the extra G, R, and S

positions are used. The S bit is the logical OR of all bits to the right of R.

The exponent comparison and the shifting of the operand follow the respective rules, depending upon the specific representation used.

At the end of this step the binary points of the two numbers are aligned.

(3a) Addition of magnitudes: Add the two magnitudes to obtain the preliminary result Z, which has the form shown in Figure 3.4c. If the overflow bit is $V = 1$, then right-shift one bit the magnitude of the result and increment the exponent. During the shift, R is ORed into S.

(3b) Subtraction of magnitudes: Subtract the two magnitudes to obtain the preliminary result Z, which has the form shown in Figure 3.4c. Normalize the result, i.e, left-shift the significand and the guard bit G while decrementing the exponent until $N = 1$. The sticky bit S need not participate in the left shifts; 0 or S may be shifted into round bit R from the right.

(4) Round the result (according to the procedures to be discussed later in this chapter). Check for overflow (which may require another right-shift of the result) and other floating-point exceptions.

There exist the following special cases:

(a) Z is $+0$ if both operands are $+0$.
(b) Z is -0 is both operands are -0.
(c) $Z = X$ if X extremely large (close to $\pm\infty$).
(d) $Z = Y$ if Y extremely large (close to $\pm\infty$).

Example 3.18

Add the two floating-point numbers whose packed 32-bit single formats are $X = 40000000$ and $Y = 34000000$.

Solution:

Packed Format	Unpacked Format 24 Bits
$X = 40000000$	$2^1 \times 1.000\ldots00$
$+$	
$Y = 34000000$	$2^{-23} \times 1.000\ldots00$

step (1): Unnormalize Y to get: $2^1 \times 0.000\ldots10\,\boxed{0}\boxed{0}\boxed{0}$.
step (2): Add the two magnitudes:

$$
\begin{array}{r}
1.000\ldots\ 00 \\
+ \\
0.000\ldots\ 10\boxed{0}\boxed{0}\boxed{0} \\
\hline
Z = 2^1 \times \boxed{0}\,1.000\ldots\ 10\boxed{0}\boxed{0}\boxed{0}
\end{array}
$$

Since V = 0, this is the correct result whose packed 32-bit single format is: 40000002.

Example 3.19

Add the two floating-point numbers whose packed 32-bit single formats are X = 40000000 and Y = 40000000.

Solution:

Packed Format	Unpacked Format 24 Bits
X = 40000000	$2^1 \times 1.000\ldots00$
+	
Y = 40000000	$2^1 \times 1.000\ldots00$

step (1): Exponents are equal.
step (2): Add the two significands:

$$1.000\ldots00$$
$$+$$
$$1.000\ldots00$$

$$Z = 2^1 \times \boxed{1}\,0.000\ldots00\,\boxed{0}\boxed{0}\boxed{0}.$$

Since V = 1, right-shift one bit to obtain:

$$Z = 2^2 \times \boxed{0}\ 1.000\ldots00\ \boxed{0}\boxed{0}\boxed{0}.$$

The packed 32-bit single format of the result is: 40800000

Example 3.20

Subtract the two floating-point numbers whose packed 32-bit single formats are X = 3F800000 and Y = 3F7FFFFF.

Solution:

Packed Format	Unpacked Format 24 Bits
X = 3F800000	$2^0 \times 1.000\ldots00$
−	
Y = 3F7FFFFF	$2^{-1} \times 1.111\ldots11$

step (1): Unnormalize Y to get: $2^0 \times 0.111\ldots11\ \boxed{1}\boxed{0}\boxed{0}$.
step (2): Subtract the two magnitudes:

$$1.000\ldots00$$
$$-$$
$$0.111\ldots11\ \boxed{1}\boxed{0}\boxed{0}.$$

$$Z = 2^0 \times \boxed{0}\,0.000\ldots00\ \boxed{1}\boxed{0}\boxed{0}$$

Normalize the result until N $= 1$ to obtain:

$$Z = 2^{-24} \times \boxed{0}\, 1.000\ldots 00\, \boxed{0}\boxed{0}\boxed{0},$$

whose packed 32-bit single format is: 33800000.

Multiplication/Division

The multiplication/division operations are straightforward, since the significands can be multiplied/divided regardless of the exponents which are added/subtracted.

Procedure 3.15   (Floating-Point Multiplication/Division)

(1)   Generate sign according to convention.
(2a) Multiplication: add the two exponents according to convention.
(2b) Division: subtract the two exponents according to convention.
(3a) Multiplication: multiply the significands.
(3b) Division: divide the significands.
(4a) Multiplication: IF V $= 1$ then right-shift the significand one bit and increment the exponent.
(4b) Division: If N $= 0$, then left-shift the significand one bit and decrement the exponent. The sticky bit S need not participate in the left shift; a 0 or S may be shifted into round bit R from the right.
(5)   Round the result and check for overflow and other floating-point exceptions.

There exist the following special cases:

(a) $Z = \pm 0$, if either operand is ± 0.
(b) $Z = \infty$ with sign equal to the exclusive-or of the operands' signs, if either operand is extremely large (close to $\pm\infty$).

Example 3.21

Multiply the two floating-point numbers whose packed 32-bit single formats are $X = 40C00000$ and $Y = 40C00000$.

Solution

	Packed Format	Unpacked Format 24 Bits
	$X = 40C00000$	$2^1 \times 1.100\ldots 00$
$\times$		$\times$
	$Y = 40C00000$	$2^1 \times 1.100\ldots 00$

step (1):   Sign of result is 0.
step (2a):   Add exponents to get 2^2 .
step (3a):   Multiply the significands:

$$1.1000\ldots00$$
$$\times$$
$$\underline{1.1000\ldots00}$$
$$Z = 2^2 \times \boxed{1}\,0.0100\ldots00\,\boxed{0}\boxed{0}\boxed{0}$$

step (4a):   Since $V = 1$, the significand is right-shifted one bit and the exponent is incremented to get:

$$Z = 2^3 \times \boxed{0}\,1.00100\ldots00\,\boxed{0}\boxed{0}\boxed{0},$$

whose packed 32-bit single format is: 41100000.

Exceptions

Floating-point operations that produce results beyond the range of normalized numbers generate exceptions. The IEEE standard classifies the exceptions as: invalid operation, underflow, overflow, division-by-zero and inexact result. The occurrence of any exception sets a corresponding "sticky" flag associated with that exception. These flags may be tested and cleared by the program. The default response to any exception is to deliver a specified result and proceed.

- *Invalid operation:* This appears when either an invalid operand is used for the operation to be performed or an invalid result arises for the destination. Examples of invalid operations are addition or subtraction ($\infty \pm \infty$), multiplication ($0 \times \infty$), and division ($0/0$). The standard suggests that an invalid result occurs when the result destined for a single or double format is unnormalized but not denormalized.
- *Underflow:* Underflow occurs whenever a nonzero result has an exponent that lies below the exponent range of the destination, i.e., this exponent cannot be represented in the destination's format without further denormalizing. In this case, the result should be first denormalized, then rounded, and then delivered to its destination.
- *Overflow:* An overflow occurs when the exponent of a rounded result is too large to be represented in the destination format. In this case the exponent is adjusted by subtracting a constant A from it, where $A = 192$ in single-precision and $A = 1536$ in double-precision operation.
- *Division-by-zero:* This exception arises in a division operation when the divisor is normal zero and the dividend is a finite nonzero number. The default result is ∞ with the proper sign.

- *Inexact result:* This exception arises when the rounded result of an operation is not exact or it overflows. The default result is the correctly rounded number.

3.4.4 Other Considerations

Precision

The precision of representing a number in floating-point format is increased by increasing the length of its fraction. For example, a binary fraction of twenty-four bits gives a precision of 24 x log2 (i.e., one part in 2^{24} or one part in 16,000,000), or 7.22 decimal digits of accuracy. An easy way to increase precision by increasing the number of significand bits is to use double-precision floating-point arithmetic. For a given length of a fraction, precision is also improved by maintaining as many significant bits as possible in the fraction.

Precision violations are very difficult to handle, and mechanisms of recording loss of precision are very expensive. Precision is limited by the given precision that the input operands have, and also by the required precision of the target destination to which the result is delivered. An improvement is made possible by including some extra "guard bits" to the right end of the operands' fraction, performing the arithmetic operation using these extended operands, and then stripping off these guard bits from the preliminary result and rounding it to fit into the destination. The IEEE standard suggests that floating-point arithmetic operations are presumed to deliver their results to destinations having no less exponent range than their input operands. Loss of precision in floating-point operations is produced by the combination and interaction of significance loss and round-off error.

Significance Loss

As mentioned earlier, unnormalizing of an operand may create accuracy problems in a fixed word length processor, since, if the magnitude of two operands differs by a large amount, their sum will be equal to the larger operand.

What is even more important is the significance loss introduced by such unnormalizing operation on an operand. When the smallest operand's significand is shifted right during this unnormalizing step, say by k places, because of the limited length, the shifted significand loses k of its rightmost bits. Also, any floating-point operation on two n-bit normalized significands will give a result significand with from n to $2n$ bits (in multiplication the product significand is always $2n$ bits long).

After the operation, a renormalization may be performed on the result to normalize its significand. When this renormalization involves j left shifts of the result significand to eliminate all leading 0's, then j 0's are inserted at the right, thus introducing false significance at the j rightmost positions of the significand. (Note that if this renormalizing is done with software, then appropriate instructions should be used to normalize the *whole* $2n$ result significand. The programmer should be especially careful of this, when double-precision lengths are used for the operands' significands).

Various methods have been used in larger machines to deal with this significance loss problem. In microprocessor applications, the easiest thing to do to increase precision is to increase the number of the significand bits. When floating-point arithmetic is performed in software, this results in increases of programming difficulties, memory space requirements, and execution time. In some microprocessor binary floating-point arithmetic packages, a "guard byte" is used as an 8-bit extension to the right end of the significand. This temporarily creates a longer significand, and by keeping track of the increased number of bits of accuracy throughout the operation, significance loss can be minimized. Before it is stored, the result of the operation is rounded back to the normal length of the operands. In such implementations, during the unnormalizing operation that proceeds the arithmetic calculation, the least significant bits shifted out of the smaller significand are saved in the guard byte in order to maintain accuracy. During the renormalization of the result of the calculation, in which the significand is shifted left, the guard byte is used to perform round-off operations.

As an example, consider the subtraction $X - Y$ of two almost equal numbers, where $X = 3F80000 (= 2^0 \times 1.000\ldots00)$ and $Y = 3F7FFFFF$ $(= 2^{-1} \times 1.111\ldots11)$, with 24-bit significands. When Y is subtracted from X, the smaller number must be shifted right in order to align the binary points and perform the operation on two numbers of equal exponents. If a guard byte is included, it will receive the shifted-out bits of number Y, as shown below:

	Significand	Guard Byte
$X = 2\} \times 1.000\ldots00$		0000
$- \quad Y = 2\} \times 0.111\ldots11$		1000
$Z = 2\} \times 0.000\ldots00$		1000

After the subtraction operation, the significand result contains 0's, whereas the guard byte contains 1000. When this result Z is renormalized, it will become $2^{-24} \times 1.000\ldots00|0000$ ($= 33800000$). If no guard byte were used in the above operation, then the operation would be performed as:

$$X = 2\} \times 1.000\ldots00$$
$$- \quad Y = 2\} \times 0.111\ldots11$$
$$\overline{\qquad Z = 2\} \times 0.000\ldots01 \qquad}$$

which, when renormalized, would become $2^{-23} \times 1.000\ldots00$, i.e., a result which is in error by a factor of 2.

Actually, only one or two guard bits are sufficient. The whole 8-bit byte has been used in most floating-point packages, because of the programming convenience it offers the 8-bit microprocessors for which these packages are oriented. The IEEE standard proposes for accurate computation of all arithmetic that results be given to within half a unit in the last place of the destination format. Thus, a single guard bit (G) is added to the right of the significand, as shown in Figure 3.4c. This bit and the sticky bit (S) together are sufficient for perfect rounding, while the round bit (R) is used to accommodate renormalization of the results in some operations.

Rounding

Round-off error is another major concern in floating-point arithmetic. Following the renormalization of the result significand, a rounding scheme is usually used to reduce the significand down to the same number of bits possessed by the operands from which the result was produced.

Various rounding schemes exist, the simplest being merely to drop all excess bits to the right of the significand of the preliminary result Z. This is referred to as *downward biased rounding* (the IEEE standard calls it *round toward zero*), since it always produces a consistently smaller value than the true value. When a guard bit (or guard bits) is (are) used to extend the significand, *rounding-up* can be performed on the result as follows: perform the operation and examine the leftmost guard bit; if it is set, increment the low-order byte of the significand and delete the guard bit(s) to reduce the significand to its original size.

However, in order for the floating-point arithmetic to yield results as accurate as possible, *unbiased rounding* is required. Again, various schemes have been used to perform unbiased rounding. One method rounds the result by adding $r^{-n}/2$ to the magnitude of the significand before dropping the excess least significand bits. A second method is to force a 1 into the remaining least significand bit of the shortened result.

Intel Rounding

To take care of these accuracy problems introduced by significance loss and round-off errors, Intel [14] has adopted internally an unbiased rounding scheme called *round to even* (which is part of the more general case of the *round to nearest* suggested by the IEEE standard).

To simplify the explanation of this scheme, assume a number is represented in the form shown in Figure 3.4c. Shifting operations of such a number involve all bits to the right of the exponent e. The sticky bit is set to 1 if any 1's are shifted right of the rounding bit during the unnormalization of an operand. If the sticky bit S becomes set, it remains set throughout the operation. The S bit does not participate in left shifts, but 0's are introduced into V by right shifts.

After a floating-point operation, a renormalization is performed on the preliminary result as follows:

(a) For addition: if the V bit is set, then shift the result right one position.
(b) For subtraction: shift the result left until the N position is set to 1.
(c) For multiplication: a shift by one position may be needed to normalize the product.
(d) For division: the first bits of the normalized quotient are formed.

Then the "round to even" scheme is applied as follows:

(a) For addition: add 1 to the G position, then if $G = R = S = 0$ set L to 0 (zero).
(b) For subtraction: same as above (except no rounding is needed if more than one left shift was required in renormalization).
(c) For multiplication: if the double length product is

$$\boxed{p_{47} \quad | \quad \cdots \quad | \quad p_3 \mid p_2 \mid p_1 \mid p_0} \, ,$$

then set: $G = p_3$, $R = p_2$, and $S = (p_1 \text{ OR } p_0)$, and round as before.
(d) For division: if the first six bits of the normalized quotient are

$$\boxed{q_5 \mid q_4 \mid q_3 \mid q_2 \mid q_1 \mid q_0} \, ,$$

then set $G = q_1$, $R = q_0$, and $S =$ remainder, and round as before.

After this rounding operation, a renormalization may be required again to correct for overflow after the floating-point operation; if V is set, then shift the result right by 1.

IEEE Standard Rounding

The IEEE standard proposes four rounding modes:

RN: Round to Nearest
RZ: Round toward Zero
RP: Round toward $+\infty$
RN: Round toward $-\infty$.

Let Z be the preliminary result to be rounded, viewed as in Figure 3.4c. From Z determine $Z1$ and $Z2$, the numbers most closely bracketing Z, i.e., $Z1 \leq Z \leq Z2$. The numbers $Z1$ and $Z2$ are exactly representable in the precision of the destination. Since overflow is not checked until after rounding, the exponent of $Z1$ or $Z2$ or both may be overflowed. Thus, if $Z1 = Z = Z2$, there is no rounding error and the result is exact. The four standard roundings are implemented as follows:

(a) Round to Nearest = Unbiased Round = the nearest of $Z1$ and $Z2$ to Z. In case of a tie, round to even (i.e., choose between $Z1$ and $Z2$ the one whose least significand bit is 0).
(b) Round toward Zero = Chop Z = the smaller of $Z1$ and $Z2$ in magnitude.
(c) Round toward $+\infty = Z2$
(d) Round toward $-\infty = Z1$

The latter two modes are referred to as "directed rounding." Round to Nearest is suggested to be the default mode for all operations.

3.4.5 Floating-Point versus Fixed-Point Multiple-Precision

If the word size is fixed, the range and precision of a number are functions of each other. The precision issue, however, is quite often confused with that of range. Programmers sometimes use floating-point arithmetic when they actually require fixed-point multiple-precision, and fixed-point multiple-precision when they actually need greater range (given by numbers in floating-point representation). Since floating-point arithmetic allows for a vast range of representable numbers, range is seldom exceeded. Even when it is, however, range is not so serious a problem as precision.

Some of the advantages that floating-point representation exhibits over fixed-point multiple-precision representation are the following:

(a) The extension of the range of numbers that can be represented.
(b) The shorter, two-portion notation of the floating-point numbers requires fewer memory locations than fixed-point multiple-precision numbers of the same range.

(c)   The capability that floating-point notation has to represent fractional numbers (when the exponent is a negative number). The exponent indicates the location of the binary point: a positive exponent locates the binary point in the significand to the right by the number of places indicated by the exponent; a negative exponent shifts the binary point to the left.

Fixed-point programs, on the other hand, are somewhat easier to write. For example, for 8085-based microprocessor systems, instructions such as add (ADD) and add-with-carry (ADC) can be used to add not only 8-bit numbers, but also multiple-precision fixed-point numbers of sixteen bits, twenty-four bits, or larger. The ADC instructions add the carry bit (if generated) from the lower byte to the sum of the two 8-bit bytes in the next higher position. The operands of fixed-point multiple-precision operations are often held in successive memory locations (or in a table), and the result is returned to another set of memory locations. Memory tables, pointers, counters, etc., are thus required for fixed-point multiple-precision arithmetic.

EXERCISES

3.1   Give the floating-point representation of the following positional binary numbers:

(a) 0110110.110
(b) 0.00010101
(c) 10000

3.2   Compare the ranges of two floating-point numbers, where, in one case the exponent is 12-bit binary, and, in the other case the exponent is 12-bit BCD.

3.3   Give some of the limitations and drawbacks of floating-point number representation.

3.4   List the advantages and disadvantages of binary floating-point numbers as compared to decimal BCD floating-point numbers.

3.5   Give the trade-offs between small and large floating-point number radices.

3.6   Give the trade-offs between small and large floating-point exponent radices.

3.7   Give the advantages and disadvantages of a binary exponent in an excess-N notation versus those of a binary exponent in 2's complement notation.

3.8   List all the cases in which a normalized floating-point number has a 0 immediately to the right of the radix point.

3.9   Let $x = (001011)_2$ and $y = (101101)_2$ in S&M notation. Execute the addition operation as done by humans.

3.10 Let $x = (001100)_2$ and $y = (101111)_2$ in S&M notation. Execute the addition operation as done by the computer.

3.11 Let $x = (1010101)_2$ and $y = (0001111)_2$ in S&M notation. Execute the subtraction $d = x - y$ as done by the computer.

3.12 Let $x = (001011)_2$ and $y = (110010)_2$ in 1's complement notation. Compute the sum $s = x + y$.

3.13   Let $x = (110010)_2$ and $y = (110100)_2$ in 1's complement notation. Compute the sum $s = x + y$.

3.14   Let $x = (001011)_2$ and $y = (001101)_2$ in 1's complement notation. Compute the difference $d = x - y$.

3.15   Let $x = (0101)_2$ and $y = (0010)_2$ in 1's complement notation. Compute the difference $d = x - y$.

3.16   Let $x = (01011)_2$ and $y = (10011)_2$ in 1's complement notation. Compute the difference $d = x - y$.

3.17   Let $x = (0101101)_2$ and $y = (1010)_2$ in 1's complement notation. Compute the product $p = x \times y$.

3.18   Given $x = (010010001)_2$ and $y = (01101)_2$ in 2's complement notation. Execute the division operation $x \div y$ with $k = 5$.

3.19   Given the decimal numbers $x = (0786)_{10}$ and $y = (0690)_{10}$ encoded in BCD format. Execute the subtraction $x - y$ in S&M notation.

3.20   Perform the floating-point addition $X + Y$ with rounding to nearest, when these numbers have the following packed 32-bit single formats:

(a) $X = 3F800000$, $Y = 3F800000$
(b) $X = 3F800000$, $Y = 34000000$
(c) $X = 3F800000$, $Y = 33800000$

3.21   Perform the floating-point subtraction $X - Y$ with rounding to nearest, when these numbers have the following packed 32-bit single formats:

(a) $X = 3F800000$, $Y = 3F800000$
(b) $X = 3F800000$, $Y = 33000000$

3.22   Perform the floating-point multiplication $X \times Y$ with rounding to nearest, when these numbers have the following packed 32-bit single formats:

(a) $X = 40000000$, $Y = 40000000$
(b) $X = 3F800001$, $Y = 3F800001$

REFERENCES AND BIBLIOGRAPHY

[1]   Ashenhurst, R. L., and N. Metropolis "Unnormalized Floating-Point Arithmetic," *Journal of the ACM*, vol.6, no.3, July 1959, pp. 415–28.

[2]   Avizienis, A., *Information Processing Systems.* (Class Notes), Los Angeles, CA: Computer Science Department, U.C.L.A., 1968.

[3]   Bartee, T.C., *Digital Computer Fundamentals*, 2d ed., New York: McGraw-Hill, 1966.

[4]   Bonney, J., "Math in the Real World," *BYTE*, September 1978, pp. 114–19.

[5]   Buchholz, W., *Planning a Computer System: Project Stretch*, New York: McGraw-Hill, 1962.

[6]   Carr, III, W., "Error Analysis in Floating-Point Arithmetic," *Communications of the ACM,* vol.2, no.5, May 1959, pp. 10–15.

[7]   Coonen, J.T., "An Implementation Guide to a Proposed Standard for Floating-Point Arithmetic," *Computer*, January 1980, pp. 68–79.

[8]   Crowder, N.A., *The Arithmetic of Computers*, New York: Doubleday & Co., 1960.

[9]   Flores, I., *The Logic of Computer Arithmetic*, Englewood Cliffs, NJ: Prentice-Hall Inc., 1963.

[10] Hashizume, B., "Floating-Point Arithmetic," *BYTE*, November 1977, p.76–78, 180–88.

[11] IEEE Task P754, Draft 8.0, "A Proposed Standard for Binary Floating-Point Arithmetic," *Computer*, March 1981, pp. 51–62.

[12] Linker, S., "What's in a Floating-Point Package?" *BYTE*, vol.2, no.5, May 1977, pp.62–66.

[13] Memurray, M.W., *Programming Microprocessors*, Blue Ridge Summit, PA: TAB Books, 1977.

[14] Palmer, J.F., "The Intel Standard for Floating-Point Arithmetic." *Proceedings of IEEE COMPSAC 77*, (Computer Software and Applications Conference), Chicago, November 8–11, 1977, pp. 107–12.

[15] Richards, R.K., *Arithmetic Operations in Digital Computers*, New York: D. Van Nostrand Co., 1955.

[16] Robertson, J.E., "Two's Complement Multiplication in Binary Parallel Digital Computers," *IRE Transactions on Electronic Computers*, September 1955, pp. 118–19.

Chapter 4

MICROPROCESSOR (CPU) ARCHITECTURE AND OPERATION

4.1 INTRODUCTION

As already mentioned, the microprocessor is the heart of a microcomputer system, corresponding to its CPU module. It is the most complex component of the system, and synchronizes and coordinates the operation of the other system modules by fetching, decoding, and executing instructions.

Microprocessor architecture refers to the characteristics of the microprocessor visible to the machine language programmer [3]. It is concerned more with the CPU's conceptual and functional behavior rather than with its detailed physical aspects. Microprocessor architectural features covered in this chapter include the microprocessor's internal organization, its register structure, and its operation in terms of machine cycles and states required to sequence and execute instructions. Discussed in subsequent chapters are the external behavior of the microprocessor (i.e., the signals issued on the CPU bus and the ways of interfacing CPU with other system modules), as well as other microprocessor features having to do with instruction formats and ways of accessing memory and I/O devices.

Although the other system modules (memory modules, I/O modules, etc.) have already been standardized to a satisfactory degree, existing microprocessor CPUs differ widely in structure, function, and capabilities. A unified approach is used here to present the architecture and operation of 8-, 16-, and 32-bit microprocessors. More details on the representative products discussed here are given in the Appendices of this book.

4.2 BASIC CHARACTERISTICS AND FEATURES

An overview of some of the architectural features of a microprocessor are given below.

Word Length

The word length of a microprocessor is usually defined according to the number of bits that its ALU can process in parallel. The most common microprocessor word lengths are four, eight, and sixteen bits. Usually, the microprocessor word length also defines the width of the CPU data bus, through which the microprocessor exchanges information with the rest of the system modules and with the outside world. Thus, an 8-bit microprocessor will have an 8-bit wide data bus, a 16-bit microprocessor will have a 16-bit wide data bus, etc.

All microprocessors handle two types of information: *instructions* and *data (or operands)*. The word length is usually independent of the instruction length or the length of the operands that the microprocessor can handle. Microprocessor instruction formats are discussed in chapter 7.

Data Types

The basic data element of the microprocessor is the *word*.[1] The word is the basic addressable element in memory. All other data elements are referenced by specifying their first word address and their length in words. The required number of words for manipulating a data element is either implied by the operation or explicitly provided by the programmer.

The microprocessor architecture supports several data (operand) types: BCD digits (represented as two 4-bit digits—sometimes referred to as *nibbles*—in one byte), bytes (eight bits), words (sixteen or thirty-two bits), double words (thirty-two or sixty-four bits supported by the 16- and 32-bit microprocessors), and both byte and word strings. Data types are classified as follows:

- *Arithmetic data*, representing fixed-point single-precision and multi-precision integers. They may be integer binary numbers (2's complement notation of signed values is used) of one, two, or more words. They may also be packed BCD decimal numbers (usually in sign and magnitude notation) of variable length. The 32-bit microprocessors may also handle floating-point arithmetic data.
- *Logical data*, used by operations such as AND, OR, COMPARE, SHIFT, etc., of one, two, or more words.

---

[1] Unless explicitly stated otherwise, the term "word" will always refer throughout this book to the basic word length of the corresponding microprocessor. Thus, the word of an 8-bit microprocessor is eight bits long (a byte), the word of a 16-bit microprocessor is sixteen bits long, etc.

- *Boolean data,* used by operations that set condition codes or test condtions (for the conditional branch instructions).
- *Bit data,* individually addressable and used by operations such as SET, CLEAR, TEST, etc.
- *Character data* (alphanumeric), where each character is represented by one byte. These data have variable length and are used for string manipulation by MOVE, SEARCH, and TRANSLATE type instructions.

Consider, for example, the various complex data types supported by the new 32-bit Intel APX 432 microprocessor [11]. There are eight "primitive" data types as shown in Figure 4.1. *Characters* are 8-bit quantities representing

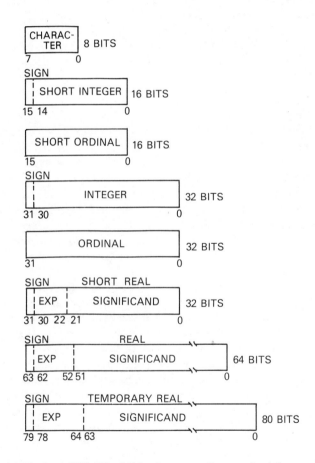

Figure 4.1 The Intel APX 432 primitive data types. *Courtesy Intel Corporation* [11].

unsigned *integers*, ASCII characters, or logical (Boolean) values. *Integers* are signed numerical quantities and may be either sixteen bits (short integers) or thirty-two bits (integers). *Ordinals* are unsigned integers of either sixteen bits (short ordinals) or thirty-two bits (ordinals), and are used commonly as indices into vectors and arrays. *Reals* are three-component real numbers composed of an exponent, a significand (mantissa), and a sign bit. Reals are available in three sizes: 32-bit (short reals), 64-bit (reals), and 80-bit (temporary reals), the last intended for use as intermediate results of floating-point operations. Besides the above primitive data elements, the APX 432 also facilitates access to two "structured" data types (ordered aggregates of primitives): *arrays* (a number of components, each of the same data type) and *records* (a number of components, called "fields," that can be of different data types).

Of course, not all of the above mentioned data types are found in all microprocessors. For example, the 8-bit microprocessors do not have string manipulation instructions.

Speed

The speed with which the microprocessor executes its programs does, of course, constitute a basic criterion for deciding whether to use the microprocessor in a particular application. Speed is usually measured by the time required to execute a basic instruction (e.g., ADD). This, however, does not give a complete picture as far as the microprocessor's throughput or the speed with which it performs input/output are concerned. Decisions may be totally erroneous if they are based solely on the times the manufacturer provides in its manuals for the execution of each individual instruction, and do not take into account the width of the registers and buses or other architectural characteristics of the microprocessor.

Another factor influencing microprocessor speed is clock frequency. Again, however, clock speed by itself reveals little about instruction execution times and does not necessarily constitute a measure of the system's throughput (especially when slower memory modules are connected to a fast microprocessor, and cause the initiation of CPU "wait" states).

Regarding the manufacture of a microprocessor, the smaller the instruction's cycle time, the faster the microprocessor. However, reducing the cycle time quite often is the most expensive way of manufacturing a microprocessor, mainly because this leads to using a faster—and therefore more expensive—technology. The microprocessor's effective speed may be increased by incorporating several architectural characteristics, such as more internal registers, internal parallel buses, fast arithmetic/logic units, pipeline structures, etc. An increase in speed may also be achieved by overlapping the fetch cycle with the execution cycle of the instruction, i.e., by initiating the instruction fetch cycle ahead of time (instruction look-ahead). Finally, another method for increasing the system's speed is to provide special ways of accessing memory, such as through a hardware stack that contains successive memory addresses. Instruction look-ahead and pipelining are discussed in the last section of this chapter.

Processing Capabilities

The operations that can be carried out by the microprocessor's ALU and the total number and type of instructions in the microprocessor's instruction set are referred to as processing capabilities. The operations carried out by the ALU determine whether the microprocessor can perform binary or decimal arithmetic or both, whether it has double precision capability or only single, whether the CPU contains multiply/divide hardware, whether the microprocessor has optional floating-point hardware capability, etc. The number and type of instructions give a measure of the microprocessor's power and flexibility of programming. Furthermore, the instruction set may be fixed, or the microprocessor may be microprogrammable, thus allowing the system designer to define his or her own instructions.

Memory Management

Recent 16- and 32-bit microprocessors can access and manage efficiently much larger memories through a segmentation technique not found in previous microprocessor generations. Memory management through segment relocation and protection is performed by hardware (hardware is used for the address translation to reduce memory and execution time overhead), and implemented either on the same microprocessor chip or on a separate companion chip. Furthermore, most of these 16- and 32-bit devices can also be used in a minimum non-segmented mode (using shorter and more efficient addresses) for those simpler applications that do not require such large amounts of memory.

Interrupt Handling

The microcomputer that can handle external interrupts efficiently is in a position, on the one hand, to execute concurrently more than one function, and on the other hand, to exchange data with external devices faster, since it can overlap the CPU operation with that of I/O.

One of the ways for initiating an I/O operation is with an appropriate interrupt signal, sent by a peripheral device to the microprocessor. This interrupt signal will cause suspension of the program currently being executed, and transfer of control to the routine that will handle this interrupt. To process interrupts efficiently, the microprocessor must include special circuitry that automatically saves the CPU state (the contents of its basic registers) so that, after having satisfied the interrupt, it may return back to the point where it was interrupted. Advanced microprocessor interrupt handling features: (1) allow the programmer to mask interrupts, making the program non-interruptable; (2) provide ways through which the programmer can control the addresses to which the program will branch after each interrupt; and (3) dedicate more than one pin to receiving interrupt signals, and contain the necessary priority resolution circuitry to handle interrupts when more than one appear simultaneously.

Interfacing Capabilities

The interface characteristic refers to the ways that the microprocessor CPU interfaces and communicates with other system modules (memory modules, I/O modules), its flexibility in performing input and output, the number of I/O ports and channels that the microprocessor supports, whether it can support DMA channels for high-speed data transfers directly between main memory and fast peripheral devices, and whether it can support satellite processing and multiprocessor configurations. Interfacing the CPU with memory is discussed in chapter 6, and interrupts, DMA operation, and multiprocessor configuration are covered in chapter 9.

4.3 MICROPROCESSOR INTERNAL ORGANIZATION

The basic architectural components of a microprocessor CPU are: (1) internal registers with appropriate selection circuitry, (2) the ALU section along with its associated input and output circuitry, and (3) the control section that includes instruction decoding, and timing and control circuitry. One or more internal buses are also provided to facilitate data movements within the microprocessor chip itself, while buffers/latches are used for the data transfers on the outside buses. Figure 4.2 shows the simplified functional block diagrams of typical 8-bit medium-level and 16-bit high-level single-chip microprocessors.

4.3.1   Internal Register Structure

General-Purpose Registers

One of the basic architectural components of any microprocessor is its internal general-purpose register file. Quite often, this register file is used as a common resource to be allocated as desired between data and address functions. A general-purpose register can be used by an instruction as a source or destination data register or as an accumulator, and can participate interchangeably in the arithmetic and logic operations of the microprocessor. Such a register may also be used as an address register to contain a memory pointer or an index value. Not imposing any special restrictions in the use of these registers simplifies block moves, enhances indexed addressing, and permits stacking. Other microprocessors, however, have assigned specialized functions to some of these registers (determined through a statistical analysis of their usage). In this case, some of the registers are used only as data registers, while others are used only for memory address purposes (i.e., as index registers, stack pointer registers, etc.). Specializing the functions of some of these registers has the advantage that it may lead to more compact instruction formats. The penalty paid, however, is that in order to use such a register for another function, one is required to temporarily store away its contents, thereby limiting programming flexibility.

Experience seems to confirm that an optimum number of registers is between eight and thirty-two [13]. Some microprocessors (e.g., the 8-bit Zilog Z80) have two alternate sets of general-purpose registers; at any one time the Z80 programmer can elect to work with either set with a single "exchange" instruction. The length of the general-purpose registers conforms with the basic word length of the microprocessor. In 8-bit microprocessors, a general-purpose register is eight bits long (symbolized by an alphabetic letter), and two such registers may also be used together as a pair (symbolized by the pair of the respective alphabetic letters) to hold 16-bit quantities. In 16-bit microprocessors, the length of a general-purpose register is sixteen bits. Accessing an 8-bit quantity is possible by addressing the left half (the HIGH portion) or the right half (the LOW portion) of a register. Quite often a pair or quadruple of registers may also be used together to hold 32- and 64-bit quantities. Finally, 32-bit microprocessors have 32-bit registers, with capabilities of addressing an 8- or 16-bit quantity within a register, or concatenating two registers to hold 64-bit quantities. In both 16- and 32-bit microprocessors a general-purpose register is symbolized by a proper combination of alphabetic letter(s) and numerical digit(s). To hold an address, the proper combination of registers must be used to conform with the address length requirements.

Figure 4.3 shows the general-purpose registers and their symbolic names for some representative microprocessors.

Common Special-Purpose Registers

In addition to the general-purpose registers, all microprocessors include special-purpose registers, each register dedicated to a specific function. Most are directly or indirectly affected by program instructions.

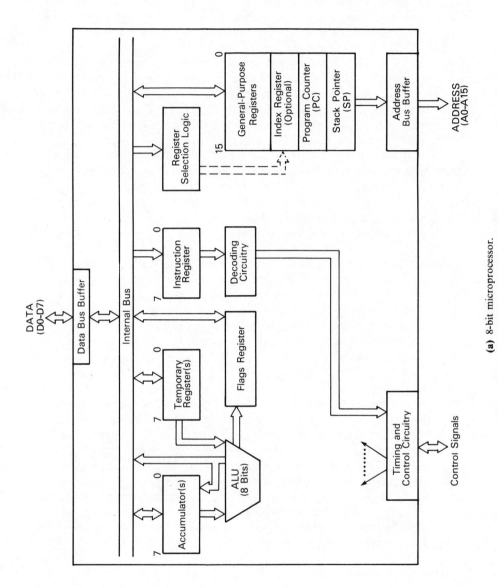

(a) 8-bit microprocessor.

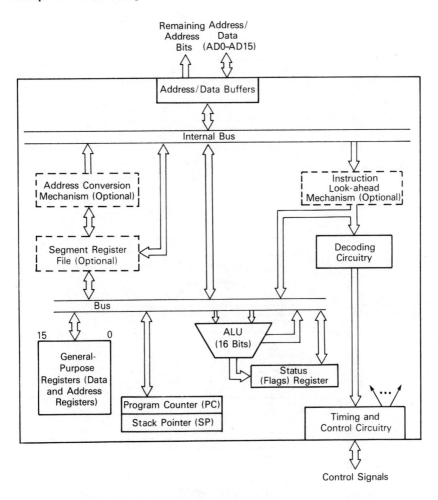

(b) 16-bit microprocessor.

Figure 4.2   The simplified functional block diagrams of typical 8- and 16-bit single-chip microprocessors.

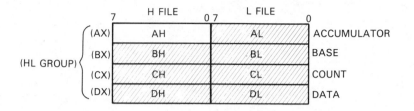

(a) Intel 8086 general-purpose registers (8080/8085 general-purpose registers shown shaded).

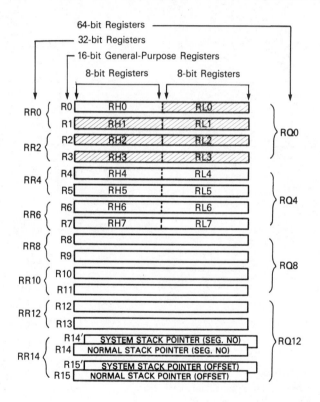

(b) Zilog Z8001 (the 48-pin segmented version) general-purpose registers (Z80 main general-purpose register set shown shaded). *Reproduced by permission . © 1982 Zilog, Inc.* [25]

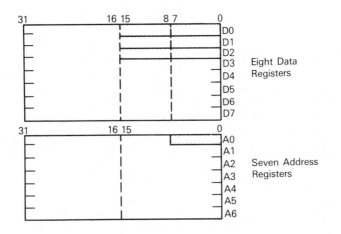

(c) Motorola 68000 general-purpose registers (6809 general-purpose registers shown shaded)[15].

Figure 4.3 General-purpose registers and their symbolic names for some representative microprocessors.

Program Counter (or Instruction Pointer)

The program counter usually contains the memory address from which the next instruction word will be fetched. (In the Motorola 6800 it contains the address of the current instruction byte.) Since instruction words that make up a program are stored in consecutive memory locations, the microprocessor updates the program counter by adding 1 to it each time it fetches one "word" of the instruction so that the program counter always remains current. The only time this normal incrementing of the program counter is violated is when an unconditional jump instruction, or a conditional jump instruction with its condition satisfied, is executed. In this case the program counter is replaced by the address that the jump instruction specifies. The same thing happens during the execution of a "call a subroutine" instruction or in handling "exceptional conditions" (such as external interrupts or software traps). In these cases, however, the previous contents of the program counter are not destroyed (as is done in jump instructions), but instead are "remembered" (usually in a stack), so that the microprocessor can later continue the execution of the main program after returning from the subroutine or the exceptional condition handling routine.

Instruction Register

The instruction register is used to hold the instruction op code, which, when decoded in the associated decoding circuitry, will direct specific processing activities during the remainder of the instruction cycle. The control signals that the decoding circuitry emits are combined with timing signals issued by the timing and control circuitry in order to synchronize the sequence of basic activities required for the execution of the decoded instruction. The length of the instruction register equals the basic word length of the microprocessor. New 16- and 32-bit microprocessors contain more than one such register to queue a number of instructions in an instruction look-ahead mechanism.

Accumulators

Most microprocessors include one or more separate accumulators, each of whose length equals the basic word length of the system. The accumulator is a register that usually holds one of the operands to be operated upon by the ALU, and receives the result of the ALU operation. Microprocessors which do not have separate accumulators usually allow any of their general-purpose registers to be used as accumulators.

Index Registers

Index registers are used to hold constant values which are required in calculating the effective memory address for the indexed addressing mode of operation. The length of an index register usually equals the width of the CPU address bus.

Stack Pointer Registers

Stack pointer registers contain the address of the most recent stack entry in memory (therefore, their lengths must be at least equal to the width of the CPU address bus). The "stack" is a specially reserved area in memory that mitigates some weaknesses of the microprocessor. It operates in last-in-first-out (LIFO) form; each time data is written into the stack (referred to as being "pushed onto" the stack), the stack is moved downward, and the most recently entered data occupies the position on the top of the stack. Data are read from the stack (referred to as being "popped off" the stack) in the opposite direction in which they are written. For each data item being pushed onto or popped off the stack, the stack pointer is decremented or incremented, respectively, to remain always current. In other words, the stack grows "downward," from the highest to the lowest address reserved for it.

Stacks are used mainly during subroutine or exceptional conditions handling. The stack is the place used to store the previous contents of the program counter, which must be "remembered" automatically by the system before branching to a subroutine or an exceptional condition handling routine. When successive branches of this type are performed (e.g., for nested subroutines or multi-level interrupts), the corresponding addresses in the program counter are "remembered" automatically by being pushed one on top of the other onto the stack. When consecutive returns from these routines are executed, stored addresses are popped off the stack and back into the program counter, with the address most recently pushed onto the stack being the first to be popped off. The user may also use the stack to store or read the accumulator or other general-purpose registers of the microprocessor by executing PUSH or POP instructions.

For example, consider the situation of nested subroutines as shown in Figure 4.4. Assume that memory locations $A000_{16}$ through $A010_{16}$ have been reserved to implement a 16-word stack, with the CPU stack pointer initially pointing to location $A010_{16}$ of the most recent stack entry. With the execution of instruction CALL SUB1, the stack pointer will be decremented to become $A00F_{16}$, and the contents of the program counter (4001_{16}) will be saved in this stack location $A00F_{16}$, and the program counter will be replaced by the value 4300_{16} (the absolute location of SUB1). Subroutine SUB1 will start executing. With the execution of CALL SUB2, the contents of the stack pointer will be decremented to become $A00E_{16}$, the current contents of the program counter (5001_{16}) will be saved in the stack location $A00E_{16}$, and the program counter will be replaced by the value 5700_{16}. Subroutine SUB2 will now start executing. The execution of subroutine SUB2's RET instruction will first pop off the stack, placing the value 5001_{16} back into the program counter, and will then increment the stack pointer (it becomes $A00F_{16}$). Finally, the execution of subroutine SUB1's RET instruction will first pop off the stack, placing the value 4001_{16} back into the program counter, and will then increment the stack pointer (it becomes $A010_{16}$). Execution of the main program will now resume from location 4001_{16}.

Microprocessor CPUs may contain one or more stack pointer registers. The 8-bit microprocessors usually have only one stack pointer register. The 16-bit microprocessors usually have two stack pointer registers; for those microprocessors that provide both supervisor and user modes of operation, one register is used for the "supervisor stack pointer," while the other is used for the "user stack pointer." Distinguishing between supervisor and user stacks separates the system software information from application program information. Finally, the 32-bit microprocessors provide more stack pointer registers (e.g., the Intel APX 432 has four).

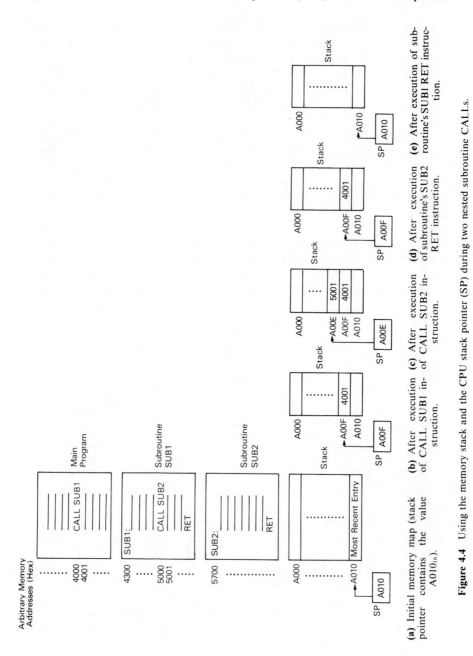

Figure 4.4 Using the memory stack and the CPU stack pointer (SP) during two nested subroutine CALLs.

(a) Initial memory map (stack pointer contains the value A010₁₆).

(b) After execution of CALL SUB1 instruction.

(c) After execution of CALL SUB2 instruction.

(d) After execution of subroutine's SUB2 RET instruction.

(e) After execution of subroutine's SUB1 RET instruction.

Temporary Registers

Most microprocessors include a number of temporary registers to hold the (usually immediate) operands or results of operations. These registers are not user-accessible.

Flags or Status Register

All microprocessors include another special-purpose register, called the flags or status register. In 8-bit microprocessors, the accumulator and the flags register are usually referred to together as the *program status word* (*PSW*). The 16-bit Intel 8086, calls only its flags register PSW, while the Zilog Z8000 and Motorola 68000 use the term to refer to the program counter along with the flags register. The latter contains several 1-bit condition flags affected by some (not all) microprocessor instructions. Other instructions may test these flags to perform conditional jumps in the program. Common flags found in microprocessors include the following:

- *Sign or negative:* This flag has the value of the highest-order bit of the result. It is usually used to test for positive (sign = 0) or negative (sign = 1) arithmetic operation results. This flag is also affected by logical operations.
- *Zero:* This flag is set to 1 when the result of an operation is 0; otherwise, it is reset to 0.
- *Carry:* If an operation resulted in a carry (from addition) or a borrow (from subtraction or a comparison) out of the high-order bit, this flag is set to 1; otherwise, it is reset to 0. It is usually used when multibyte arithmetic or multiword operations are performed.
- *Parity:* This flag is used to form odd parity on the result; i.e., it is set to 1 if the result of a logical, rotate, shift, or input instruction has even parity; otherwise, it is reset to 0.
- *Parity/overflow:* Some microprocessors allocate a flag that, in addition to the above parity check, is also used to indicate overflow as a result of 2's complement arithmetic. If the addition of two positive numbers results in a negative number, or the addition of two negative numbers yields a positive result, this flag is set to 1. If no overflow occurs, this flag is reset to 0. There is a difference between the carry flag and the overflow flag, and the two are not interchangeable.
- *Auxiliary or half-carry:* As mentioned in chapter 3, in order to perform decimal BCD arithmetic, it is necessary to record any carry from the low-order four bits (the rightmost decimal digit) of an 8-bit unit. This flag has the value of the carry from bit 3 into bit 4 of the result. It is principally used with additions and increments preceding a decimal adjust accumulator (DAA) instruction. This flag is not used in connection with branching, i.e.,

it cannot be tested with any of the conditional jump instructions. The Zilog Z8000 calls this carry "decimal adjust."

- *Subtract:* Some microprocessors have this flag which is set to 1 for all operations related to subtractions, and reset to 0 for all operations related to addition. This flag is also important for the DAA instruction. Like the previous auxiliary or half-carry flag, this flag is also not used in connection with branching.

- *Interrupt enable/disable:* When this flag is 1, interrupts are disabled; when it is 0, interrupts are enabled.

- *Trace or trap:* Some 16- and 32-bit microprocessors have this flag, which puts the microprocessor into a single-step mode for program debugging. When this flag is set, the microprocessor generates an interrupt after the execution of each instruction. No instructions are provided for setting or clearing this flag directly. Rather, it is cleared during interrupt transfer sequences after that step of the interrupt sequence which pushes flags. To restore this flag set by the subsequent interrupt return operation, it must be modified in the stack where it was saved by the previous interrupt operation.

- *Direction:* This flag is found in the 16-bit 8086, to control the direction of the string manipulation instruction (auto-incrementing or auto-decrementing). The operand pointers are incremented or decremented (depending on the setting of this flag) after each operation, once for 8-bit byte operations and twice for 16-bit word operations.

- *Supervisor:* The Zilog Z8000 and Motorola 68000 have this bit in their status register to indicate when the processor is in the supervisor mode. (The Zilog Z8000 calls it the System/$\overline{\text{Normal}}$ flag).[2]

Other Special-Purpose Registers

Finally, there exists a third category of special-purpose registers which are found only in some microprocessors.

Segment Registers

Most 16- and 32-bit microprocessors use some kind of segment registers (forming a segment table) when accessing main memory. The segment table along with a special adder form the "mapping mechanism," which translates logical program addresses into physical addresses transmitted to memory, as

---

[2]Bars over words represent signals which are "active low." Thus, $\overline{\text{Normal}}$ indicates that the signal is active low as shown: $\overline{\text{Normal}}$ = asserted (or true) at 0 volts.

will be explained in detail in chapter 10. Usually, this mapping mechanism is implemented on the separate memory management unit (MMU) support chip. One exception to this is the 16-bit Intel 8086 in which both the segment table and the address conversion mechanism have been placed on the same microprocessor CPU chip (the left two dashed boxes of Figure 4.2b). An Intel 8086 segment register may be user-accessible and contains the starting physical address (the base address) of a special memory area referred to as the "segment." The physical address transmitted to the memory is formed by adding the contents of a properly specified segment register and an offset (displacement) specified in the executed instruction. If four such segment registers exist, they may be pointing to four different segments in memory; for example, one segment may be used to hold program instructions, the second, data, the third may be used as a stack, while the fourth is used for additional data (Figure 4.5). These four segments pointed at by the four segment registers

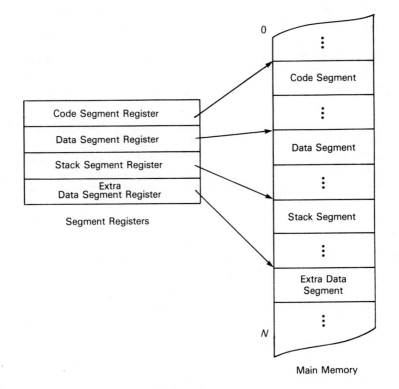

Figure 4.5 Four segment registers containing the physical base (starting) addresses of four special memory areas (called "segments").

need not be unique and, indeed, they may overlap in memory. In the degenerate case in which all four segment registers contain the same starting address, namely address 0, we have the memory structure of a usual 8-bit microprocessor whose CPU has no segment registers.

Page Register

The 8-bit Motorola 6809 has an additional 8-bit direct page register that defines the upper eight bits of a 16-bit address for all direct addressing instructions.

Interrupt Vector Register

The 8-bit Zilog Z80 includes an 8-bit interrupt vector register (I) used in one of the chip's three different programmable interrupt response modes. It holds the upper eight bits of a memory pointer (or "vector address"). The lower eight bits of this pointer are supplied (as a vector number) by the interrupting device that requests service. The CPU then uses this 16-bit vector address to make an indirect call to a memory location that holds the first instruction of the interrupt service routine. This feature allows the vector table to be located *anywhere* in memory.

Memory Refresh Register

The Zilog Z80 also contains an 8-bit memory refresh register (R) that contains the 7-bit current memory refresh address, thus providing for automatic, totally transparent refresh of external dynamic RAM memories. Although the programmer can load this register for testing purposes, the R register is not normally used by the programmer. The 16-bit Zilog Z8000 also contains an analogous 16-bit memory refresh register.

4.3.2   Arithmetic Logic Unit (ALU)

The ALU is the circuitry within the microprocessor that performs arithmetic and logical operations. Quite often the ALU is also used for effective address computations. In almost all microprocessors the 2's complement notation is used to represent negative numbers. The width of the ALU corresponds to the basic word length of the system. Usually, inputs to the ALU come from one or more accumulators or temporary registers, and the result of the operation returns to the accumulator. In general, however, inputs may come from any general-purpose register within the microprocessor or from main memory, and results of the operation may be gated either to internal general-purpose registers or to properly specified main memory locations. Some of the ALU operations affect the value of one or more flag bits in the flags register.

In the 8-bit microprocessors, the arithmetic operations performed on 8-bit operands are only binary addition and subtraction. New 16-bit microprocessors have added capabilities that provide for signed and unsigned 8- and 16-bit arithmetic that also includes multiply and divide, improved bit manipulation, and byte- and word-string handling. Decimal arithmetic (addition and subtraction) is allowed on packed (BCD) decimal representation, as well as on unpacked representation of decimal digits (e.g., ASCII). The Motorola 68000 and National NS16032 can handle 32-bit arithmetic as well. Finally, the latest 32-bit microprocessors, Intel APX-432, Bellmac-32, and National NS16032, have also incorporated floating-point hardware.

A rather unique implementation is found in the execution unit of the Motorola 68000 microprocessor (Figure 4.6). The ALU is powerful and capable of both 16-bit and 32-bit operations. The CPU has three independent arithmetic units on the same chip, which simultaneously interleave arithmetic and memory addressing computations. All words in the CPU registers are connected through two internal 16-bit buses. The register file is divided into three sections, which are either isolated or concatenated using bi-directional bus switches [2,20]. The microcoded control section of the CPU can dynamically reconfigure the two internal buses into three independent sections (carrying the high 16-bit address/data, or the low 16-bit address/data, or 16-bit data). Two limited 16-bit arithmetic units (with a carry from the low to the high unit) are available for the register sections containing 32-bit address register words or the 16-bit high data word, while a general 16-bit ALU is located in the 16-bit data register low word section. This allows address and data calculations to occur simultaneously. Also, in the data register low word section, special function units are provided to perform bit manipulation, packing and unpacking of data, long shifts, etc.

4.3.3   Control Section

This section of the microprocessor includes the instruction decoding, timing, and control circuitry. Its function is to issue properly timed signals in order to control the data handling operations within the microprocessor itself *and* coordinate the operations in all other modules of the system *as well as* synchronize the intermodule communications and data transfers. After the instruction has been fetched and decoded, the output of the decoder, combined with various timing signals, provides the intramodule control signals (to units internal to the CPU, such as ALU, registers, etc.) and intermodule control signals (to external devices such as memories, I/O ports, etc.), which maintain the proper sequence of events required for any processing task. This control circuitry also responds to external signals (such as wait or interrupt requests) issued by a memory or I/O device, to force

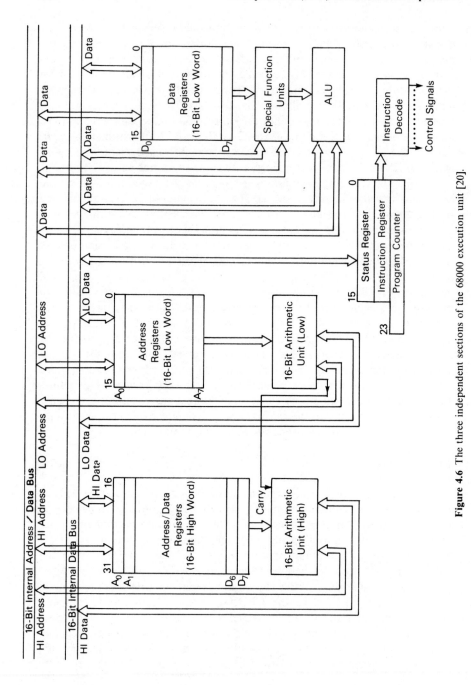

Figure 4.6 The three independent sections of the 68000 execution unit [20].

special activities to be carried out by the microprocessor. (Intermodule control signals are discussed in detail in the next chapter).

During the fetch cycle of the microcomputer's operation, the control section of the CPU interprets the operation code of the instruction which has arrived from main memory. This usually results in a change of the microprocessor's state and causes stimuli to be sent to the other modules of the system. Actually, a sequence of such control signal groups has to be issued, since the execution of a single instruction causes more than one change of state. Each such group of signals causes a specific basic operation (called a *microoperation*) to be performed, such as a data transfer between two internal registers, shifting the contents of a register, placing information on the bus, or latching data from the data bus. The *next* control signals may or may not depend upon the results of the present microoperation or on the value of certain status signals which are generated. Thus, the interpretation and execution of a (macro) instruction involves a sequence of basic machine operations (microoperations), each controlled by a specific group of control signals.

Therefore, to carry out its tasks properly, the control section circuitry must provide for at least the following four capabilities: (1) Establish the state during each machine cycle. (2) Provide logic for determining the correct next state; this next state selection is done through a proper combination of the present state information, the microprocessor's external inputs, and certain feedback lines, either from within the microprocessor module (e.g., flags from the ALU) or from other modules of the system (system status signals). (3) Provide a facility to store the information that identifies the current state. (4) Finally, provide some means for translating this state into proper intramodule and intermodule control signals to be issued by the CPU. Since all microprocessors synchronize their events with single or multiple-phase clocks, these control signals are issued in synchronism with precise clock pulses. The clock source, therefore, synchronizes all system control state transitions.

To implement the control section, either random logic (hardwired) or microprogrammed techniques, or some proper combination of the two have been used. Figure 4.7a shows the simplified structure of a hardwired control unit. It is usually composed of combinations of SSI elements (e.g., gates) and MSI elements (e.g., counters, registers, decoders), all interconnected in a somewhat random fashion, involving complicated clocking and special-purpose data paths or discretional wiring. The instruction code is decoded to identify the specific operation to be performed. Since each such operation is carried out as a sequence of microoperations, multiple control steps are required to process an instruction. The next control state generator is used to time the sequencing of these steps. The hardwired control matrix combines the output signals from the next control state generator along with the decoded instruction code signal to identify the particular microoperation at each instant of the instruction cycle. Accordingly, it generates the proper intramodule and intermodule control signals. The control section of most 8-bit microprocessors is hardwired. The 16-bit Zilog Z8000 has also implemented its control section entirely with random logic.

Most 16- and 32-bit microprocessors, however, have adopted the microprogrammed approach for the design of their control section. Figure 4.7b shows the simplified structure of a microprogrammed control unit. Now the current state is identified by the current control store address, while the contents of this location (called the *microinstruction*) provide the information required to establish the control signal groups and choose the proper next state (or microinstruction address). The control store sequencer generates this next address, based on information it receives from the current microinstruction, on current inputs from the instruction register, and on status signals and condition inputs it receives from the rest of the system modules. Various groups of microinstructions, forming microroutines, are usually incorporated into a complex system. The machine instruction, when properly decoded (mapped) in the control section, points to the appropriate microroutine in the control store. Execution of the microroutine results in control of all fundamental operations such as data transfers and elementary data transformations.

For a well-defined application, the hardwired implementation approach results in a somewhat smaller control section than that of the microprogrammed approach. However, such a control section is inflexible and presents design difficulties which lead to non-structured, quite complex configurations. As the complexity of the system increases, it becomes more expensive than the microprogrammed approach, primarily in terms of development cost, and, with the dramatic reduction in prices of control stores, also in terms of hardware component cost. Modifications are also very difficult, since changing the visible machine requires rewiring, new layouts, etc. On the other hand, the microprogrammed approach has the advantage of leading to a more "regular" design and providing enhanced instruction flexibility. Future changes and improvements are much easier, since this now requires only changing the microroutines or substituting another control store.

Microcoding, however, is slower than random logic. To increase microcode execution speeds, very wide microinstruction words are required, and this results in wasteful use of on-chip control storage space. To reduce large control store area requirements, the Motorola 68000 microprocessor uses a two-level control store structure (Figure 4.8). The first level (the "micro control store") contains the microroutines whose microinstructions have short "vertical" formats of ten bits. Each microinstruction contains an address which is used to reference a nanoinstruction in the lower level (the "nano control store"). Nanoinstructions have wide "horizontal" formats of sixty-eight bits; they are field-encoded such that, with two to three levels of decoding, each will drive control points in the system directly. One-eighth of the Motorola 68000 chip's op code space is still available for future instruction expansion [7].

Finally, the 16-bit Intel 8086 uses a combination of microprogrammed[3] and hardwired designs: a short 21-bit microcode word is used mostly for calling several key control functions directly (for deciding internal data paths and guiding ALU operations common to many instructions) which are designed through random logic techniques.

In the 32-bit category, the APX 432 uses a separate chip, the APX 43201, to implement the instruction decoding. This instruction decoder chip contains a microprogram ROM, which allows many instructions to be executed by just a single microinstruction.

4.4 MICROPROCESSOR INTERNAL OPERATION

This section covers the microprocessor CPU internal operation and the basic steps involved in executing a program. The first part of the section describes the classical way a microprocessor fetches one instruction at a time and fully completes its execution before it fetches the next one. The second part discusses various other possible microprocessor operating modes. The third part describes the way advanced microprocessors perform instruction look-ahead and pipelining to increase the system's throughput.

4.4.1 Fetching and Executing One Instruction at a Time

Microcomputer operation is basically the same as that of larger computers. Since a microcomputer executes a stored program, one usually distinguishes four different modes of sequencing the program's instructions. These modes define the manner in which the control may pass from an original instruction sequence A, to a new sequence B [6].

(a) Sequential (normal) execution: Sequence A keeps control.
(b) Transfer of control (branching): Sequence A gives control to sequence B.

---

[3]Actually, instead of ROM, Intel uses a PLA with some redundancy in the first stage, because there are more op code combinations than starting microstore addresses for the leading byte of the instruction.

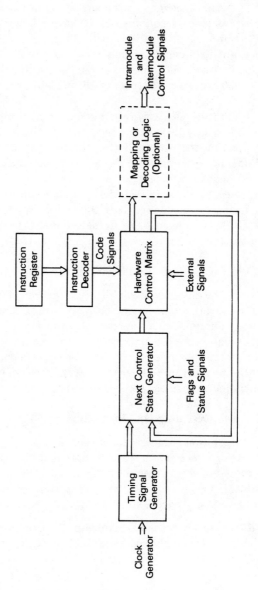

(a)

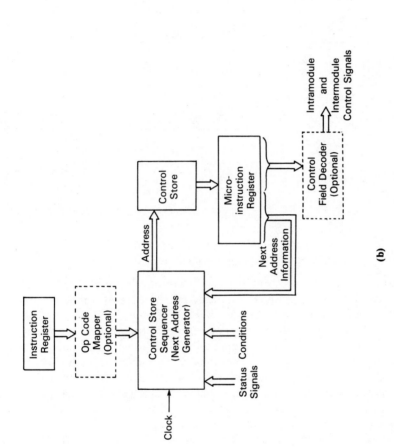

(b)

Figure 4.7 The simplified structure of the microprocessor's control section: **(a)** hardwired implementation; **(b)** microprogrammed implementation.

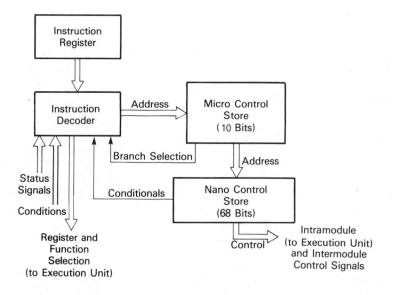

Figure 4.8 Block diagram of the Motorola 68000 microprogrammed control section [21].

(c) Interruption: Sequence B takes control from sequence A.

(d) Lending control: Sequence A lends control to sequence B.

In the first mode, sequential (normal) execution, the next program instruction is specified by a program counter within the microprocessor. In the second mode, transfer of control (or branching within the program), a new instruction sequence B is chosen. The point to which branching will transfer control is specified by the original sequence A. Such transfers of control to a new sequence may be done either "conditionally" or "unconditionally." There are also situations in which an automatic interruption of the executing program may appear, which alters the sequence of executing its instructions. Such modes appear at arbitrary times, at least as far as the executing program is concerned. Therefore, it would be difficult and awkward to have the program itself continuously checking the possible appearance of such random cases of interruption. For that reason, the identification of interrupts is done by the microprocessor automatically. When the microprocessor recognizes the occurrence of such an interrupt, it interrupts the execution of the current sequence A and automatically transfers control to a new instruction sequence B. Since neither the programmer nor the program being executed knows that this transfer of control to a new sequence was done automatically by the system, it is said that sequence B took control from sequence A. The new sequence is always predefined and different for each cause of interruption.

Finally, the mode of lending control usually occurs when program A calls another instruction sequence B, e.g., when it calls a subroutine, in which, when the execution of sequence B finishes, control automatically returns to the instruction immediately following the call in the calling program A.

CPU Sequence Flowchart

The automatic program execution by a microcomputer is performed by the repetitive use of certain system operations, the most important ones being:

- Instruction fetch: Fetching from memory the next program instruction op code.
- Decode: Decoding the fetched instruction's op code.
- Fetch the rest of the instruction: Fetching, for example, immediate operands, an offset, etc., if required.
- Instruction execute: Executing the operation as specified by each decoded instruction (which includes operand fetching, if required).

The sequence of these operations is shown in the flowchart of Figure 4.9. The first two operations are usually required for the execution of any program. They correspond to the system initialization, preparing it and setting its initial conditions for the automatic execution of the program. Thus, before the execution starts, the program instructions (having been properly converted to machine language) are placed in consecutive locations in main memory. For special microprocessor applications in which the program remains fixed and nonalterable, program instructions are usually placed in ROM-type memories; otherwise, RAM memories may be used. Also, the data to be used by the program are placed in memory (usually in RAM). The program counter is initially set to point to the memory location where the first program instruction has been placed. The rest of the sequence flowchart in Figure 4.9 describes the basic microcomputer operations that are repeated continuously during the automatic execution of the program.

The next box in Figure 4.9 shows the contents of the program counter being placed on the address bus and transferred to main memory to access the next instruction word. Immediately thereafter, the program counter is incremented by 1 within the microprocessor to point to the next consecutive word in memory. In the succeeding step, the memory location specified by the program counter address is identified, and the contents of this location (corresponding to the instruction's op code) are read out of memory, and, through the data bus, go to the instruction register within the microprocessor. Thus, as far as external logic is concerned, this is simply a *memory read operation*. Appropriate control circuitry within the microprocessor will then decode the op code to identify the specific instruction and determine its length. If this is a one-word instruction, then the system will advance to the instruction execute

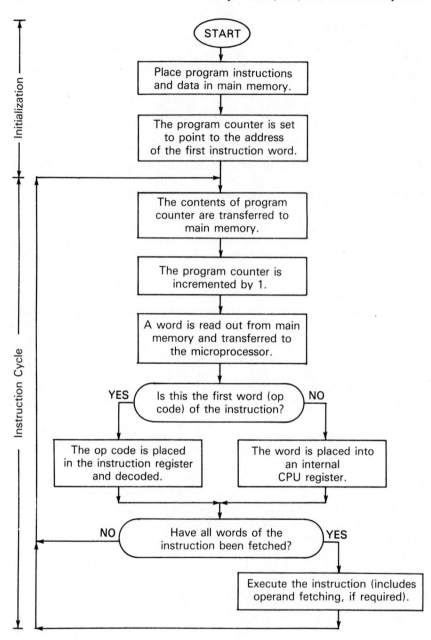

Figure 4.9 The sequence flowchart for the operations carried out by the microprocessor system for each program instruction.

operation. If the instruction is more than one word long, then the contents of the program counter will again be placed on the address bus to perform memory accesses and reads which fetch the rest of the instruction words until the whole instruction has been assembled in the CPU. Since these other words of the instruction usually represent either an immediate operand or an address, when fetched from memory they will be placed into temporary registers within the microprocessor. The instruction execution does not start until all words of the instruction have been fetched and placed inside the microprocessor.

The steps taken during execution vary according to the specific instruction being decoded. Executing an instruction may be either a completely internal operation within the microprocessor CPU, requiring no further memory references (e.g., performing an arithmetic, logical, or data transfer operation on data contained in the microprocessor's registers), or it may require additional memory reference(s) to fetch or store data. In this second case, the microprocessor must first place the effective memory address (having calculated it properly) on the address bus, and then either receive from the data bus the accessed data, or place on the data bus the data to be stored in memory.

Clock Signals

It is imperative that all operations carried out during instruction sequencing take place at well-coordinated times. Almost all modern digital systems synchronize their events with single- or multiple-phase clocks. This coordination is performed by timing signals distributed throughout the microprocessor system.

All microprocessor CPU chips are driven by an external crystal. The logic which generates the clock signals may or may not be on the same chip with the microprocessor CPU. Furthermore, this clock may be either a single-phase clock or a two-phase clock, as shown in Figure 4.10. In the second case, the duty cycle of the two alternating positive pulses of the clock need not be symmetrical (e.g., the Intel 8080A uses an asymmetrical two-phase clock). Although some 8-bit microprocessors (e.g., the Intel 8080A and Motorola 6800) have used the two-phase clock implementation, almost all newer microprocessors (e.g., the 8-bit Intel 8085 and Zilog Z80, and all 16- and 32-bit microprocessors) have adopted the single-phase clock implementation. The single-phase clock implementation will be referred to throughout this book.

The type and number of operations that can be carried out within one clock cycle time depend upon the cycle's duration and the timing exercised by the specific microprocessor.

Machine Cycles and States

"Instruction time" or "instruction cycle" is defined as the time required to fetch and execute an instruction; i.e., the time required for one complete traversal of the outside loop in Figure 4.9.

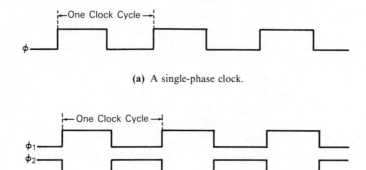

(a) A single-phase clock.

(b) A two-phase clock.

Figure 4.10 Single- and two-phase clocks.

All microprocessors subdivide the instruction cycle into one or more *machine cycles*, M_1, M_2, M_3, ..., i.e., they execute a program by initiating a sequence of such machine cycle types. A machine cycle is required each time the CPU accesses memory or an I/O port. Thus, the simplest possible instruction, a 1-word instruction, will require only the first or M_1 machine cycle (the instruction fetch cycle). Longer instructions will require additional machine cycles in order to fetch the remaining instruction words. Once the instruction has been fetched, its execution may or may not require additional machine cycles. There are various machine cycle types, the most common being: the *instruction fetch* cycle, *memory read* and *write* cycles, *I/O read* and *write* cycles, and the *interrupt acknowledge* cycle.[4] At the beginning of each machine cycle, the microprocessor CPU issues appropriate status and/or control signals which identify to the rest of the system modules of the specific cycle type currently being executed. Figure 4.11 shows in tabular form the identifying status and/or control signals emitted by various representative microprocessors. These status signals are available for the rest of the machine cycle. (Two exceptions are the Intel 8080A and 8086, which multiplex some status signals with other information. As a result, status signals are available only for the first part of the machine cycle). The microprocessor processes an instruction according to the flowchart in Figure 4.9 by simply concatenating a number of these machine cycle types.

---

[4]In most microprocessors, a machine cycle is the same as a "bus cycle," to be discussed in the next chapter.

Most microprocessors subdivide each machine cycle further to a number of *states*, $T_1, T_2, \ldots$ All states are identical in length, their duration equaling that of the microprocessor's clock period. However, the length of the various machine cycle types is not constant; i.e., not all machine cycles have the same number of states.[5] Figure 4.12 shows schematically these subdivisions of the instruction cycle.

A state corresponds to the smallest unit of processing activity, i.e., it defines the execution of one or more simultaneous "microoperations." Since in order to access a memory or I/O device for read or write operations the three basic CPU activities—sending out an address, preparing the data bus to transfer information, and reading the data bus or placing data on it—must always be carried out, most microprocessors require a minimum of three states per machine cycle. Table 4.1 lists the number of machine cycles per instruction cycle and the number of states per machine cycle for several representative microprocessors.

Table 4.1   The number of machine cycles per instruction cycle and the number of states per machine cycle for several representative microprocessors.

Microprocessor	Number of Machine Cycles per Instruction Cycle	Number of States per Machine Cycle
Intel 8080A	From 1 to 5	From 3 to 5 (referred to as "T states").
Intel 8085	From 1 to 5	From 3 to 6 (referred to as "T states").
Zilog Z80	From 1 to 6	From 3 to 4 (referred to as "clock states").
Motorola 6800	From 2 to 12	1 clock cycle per machine cycle (i.e., clock cycles and machine cycles are one and the same thing).
Intel 8086	At least 1	At least 4 (referred to as "T states").
Zilog Z8000	At least 1	From 3 to 39 (for long words) or to max $11 + 14n$ (for n consecutive words). Divide operations of long words may take up to 728 clock cycles.
Motorola 68000	From 1 to $5 + 2n$, where n is the number of registers to move.	From 1 to $20 + 8n$, where n is the number of registers to move. Divide operations may take up to 158 clock periods.

[5]One exception to this is found in the 8-bit Motorola 6800, whose machine cycles and states are one and the same thing.

Type of Machine Cycle	CPU Status Signals / Control Signals		
	Intel 8080A	Intel 8085	Zilog Z80
INSTRUCTION FETCH	Status: D7-D0 = 10100010 Control: $\overline{\text{MEMR}}$ = 0	Status: IO/$\overline{\text{M}}$, S_1,S_0 = 011 Control: $\overline{\text{RD}}$ = 0, $\overline{\text{WR}}$ = 1, $\overline{\text{INTA}}$ = 1	Control: $\overline{\text{M}_1}$=0, $\overline{\text{MREQ}}$ = 0, $\overline{\text{IORQ}}$ = 1, $\overline{\text{RD}}$ = 0, $\overline{\text{WR}}$ = 1
MEMORY READ	Status: D7-D0 = $\begin{cases} 10000010 \\ 10000110 \text{ for stack read} \end{cases}$ Control: $\overline{\text{MEMR}}$ = 0	Status: IO/$\overline{\text{M}}$, S_1,S_0 = 010 Control: $\overline{\text{RD}}$ = 0, $\overline{\text{WR}}$ = 1, $\overline{\text{INTA}}$ = 1	Control: $\overline{\text{M}_1}$ = 1, $\overline{\text{MREQ}}$ = 0, $\overline{\text{IORQ}}$ = 1, $\overline{\text{RD}}$ = 0, $\overline{\text{WR}}$ = 1
MEMORY WRITE	Status: D7-D0 = $\begin{cases} 00000000 \\ 00000100 \text{ for stack write} \end{cases}$ Control: $\overline{\text{MEMW}}$ = 0	Status: IO/$\overline{\text{M}}$, S_1,S_0 = 001 Control: $\overline{\text{RD}}$ = 1, $\overline{\text{WR}}$ = 0, $\overline{\text{INTA}}$ = 1	Control: $\overline{\text{M}_1}$ = 1, $\overline{\text{MREQ}}$ = 0, $\overline{\text{IORQ}}$ = 1, $\overline{\text{RD}}$ = 1, $\overline{\text{WR}}$ = 0
I/O READ	Status: D7-D0 = 01000010 Control: I/OR = 0	Status: IO/$\overline{\text{M}}$, S_1,S_0 = 110 Control: $\overline{\text{RD}}$ = 0, $\overline{\text{WR}}$ = 1, $\overline{\text{INTA}}$ = 1	Control: $\overline{\text{M}_1}$ = 1, $\overline{\text{MREQ}}$ = 1, $\overline{\text{IORQ}}$ = 0, $\overline{\text{RD}}$ = 0, $\overline{\text{WR}}$ = 1
I/O WRITE	Status: D7-D0 = 00010000 Control: I/OW = 0	Status: IO/$\overline{\text{M}}$, S_1,S_0 = 101 Control: $\overline{\text{RD}}$ = 1, $\overline{\text{WR}}$ = 0, $\overline{\text{INTA}}$ = 1	Control: $\overline{\text{M}_1}$ = 1, $\overline{\text{MREQ}}$ = 1, $\overline{\text{IORQ}}$ = 0, $\overline{\text{RD}}$ = 1, $\overline{\text{WR}}$ = 0
INTERRUPT ACKNOWLEDGE	Status: D7-D0 = $\begin{cases} 00100011 \\ 00101011 \text{ (int. ackn. while halt)} \end{cases}$ Control: $\overline{\text{INTA}}$ = 0	Status: IO/$\overline{\text{M}}$, S_1,S_0 = 111 Control: $\overline{\text{RD}}$ = 1, $\overline{\text{WR}}$ = 1, $\overline{\text{INTA}}$ = 0	Control: $\overline{\text{M}_1}$ = 0, $\overline{\text{MREQ}}$ = 1, $\overline{\text{IORQ}}$ = 0, $\overline{\text{RD}}$ = 0, $\overline{\text{WR}}$ = 1
HALT	Status: D7-D0 = 10001010 Control: (None)		Control: $\overline{\text{M}_1}$ = 1, $\overline{\text{HALT}}$ = 0
OTHERS		Status: IO/$\overline{\text{M}}$, S_1,S_0 = XXX Control: $\overline{\text{RD}}$ = 1, $\overline{\text{WR}}$ = 1, $\overline{\text{INTA}}$ = 1 (BUS IDLE CYCLE)	

Continued on next page

Figure 4.11   The status and/or control signals issued by various microprocessors to identify the respective machine cycle type. (Refer to Appendices for the pin layouts of these microprocessors.)

Figure 4.11—*Continued*

Motorola 6800	Intel 8086	Zilog Z8000	Motorola 68000
Control: $R/\overline{W} = 1$, BA = 0, VMA = 1	Status: $\overline{S_2},\overline{S_1},\overline{S_0} = 100$	Status: $ST_3\text{-}ST_0 = \begin{cases} 1101 \text{ (first word)} \\ 1100 \text{ (nth word)} \end{cases}$	Status: $FC_2\text{-}FC_0 = \begin{cases} 010 \text{ (user program)} \\ 110 \text{ (supervisor program)} \end{cases}$
	Control: $\overline{RD} = 0$, $M/\overline{IO} = 1$	Control: $\overline{MREQ} = 0$, $W/\overline{R} = 0$	Control: $R/\overline{W} = 1$
Control: $R/\overline{W} = 1$, BA = 0, VMA = 1	Status: $\overline{S_2},\overline{S_1},\overline{S_0} = 101$	Status: $ST_3\text{-}ST_0 = \begin{cases} 1000 \\ 1001 \text{ (stack read)} \end{cases}$	Status: $FC_2\text{-}FC_0 = \begin{cases} 001 \text{ (user data)} \\ 101 \text{ (supervisor data)} \end{cases}$
	Control: $\overline{RD} = 0$, $M/\overline{IO} = 1$	Control: $\overline{MREQ} = 0$, $W/\overline{R} = 0$	Control: $R/\overline{W} = 1$
Control: $R/\overline{W} = 0$, BA = 0, VMA = 1	Status: $\overline{S_2},\overline{S_1},\overline{S_0} = 110$	Status: $ST_3\text{-}ST_0 = \begin{cases} 1000 \\ 1001 \text{ (stack write)} \end{cases}$	Status: (as for Memory Read)
	Control: $\overline{WR} = 0$, $M/\overline{IO} = 1$	Control: $\overline{MREQ} = 0$, $W/\overline{R} = 1$	Control: $R/\overline{W} = 0$
Same as Memory Read (Memory-Mapped I/O)	Status: $\overline{S_2},\overline{S_1},\overline{S_0} = 001$	Status: $ST_3\text{-}ST_0 = \begin{cases} 0010 \\ 0011 \text{ (special, e.g., from MMU)} \end{cases}$	Same as Memory Read (Memory-Mapped I/O)
	Control: $\overline{RD} = 0$, $M/\overline{IO} = 0$	Control: $\overline{MREQ} = 1$, $W/\overline{R} = 0$	
Same as Memory **Write** (Memory-Mapped I/O)	Status: $\overline{S_2},\overline{S_1},\overline{S_0} = 010$	Status: $ST_3\text{-}ST_0 = \begin{cases} 0010 \\ 0011 \text{ (special, e.g. to MMU)} \end{cases}$	Same as Memory Write (Memory-Mapped I/O)
	Control: $\overline{WR} = 0$, $M/\overline{IO} = 0$	Control: $\overline{MREQ} = 1$, $W/\overline{R} = 1$	
Control: $R/\overline{W} = 1$. BA = 0, VMA = 1 (Sets internal flag)	Status: $\overline{S_2},\overline{S_1},\overline{S_0} = 000$	Status: $ST_3\text{-}ST_0 = \begin{cases} 0101 \text{ (non- maskable)} \\ 0110 \text{ (non-vectored)} \\ 0111 \text{ (vectored)} \end{cases}$	Status: $FC_2\text{-}FC_0 = 111$
	Control: $\overline{INTA} = 0$, **$M/\overline{IO} = 0$**	Control: $\overline{MREQ} = 1$, $W/\overline{R} = 0$	Control: $R/\overline{W} = 1$
Control: $R/\overline{W} = $ OFF, BA = 1, VMA = 0	Status: $\overline{S_2},\overline{S_1},\overline{S_0} = 011$		Control: $\overline{HALT} = 0$
	Status: $\overline{S_2},\overline{S_1},\overline{S_0} = 111$ (PASSIVE: NO BUS CYCLE)	Status: $ST_3\text{-}ST_0 = \begin{cases} 0100 \text{ (segment trap acknowledge)} \\ 0000 \text{ (internal operation)} \end{cases}$	

Note: The overbar indicator over the signal name indicates that the signal is active low as shown: $\overline{MEMR} =$ active or asserted at 0 volts. For example, $\overline{MEMR} = 0$ means active or asserted (i.e., logical 1 or true). The proposed microcomputer system IEEE 796 Bus Standard uses a nathan (asterisk) following the signal name instead of the overbar indicator.

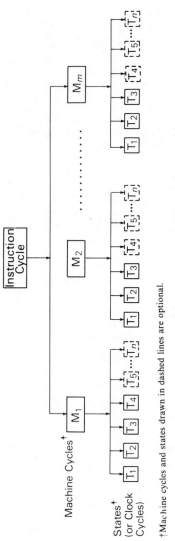

†Machine cycles and states drawn in dashed lines are optional.

Figure 4.12   Subdividing an instruction cycle into machine cycles and states.

CPU State Transition Diagram

Each instruction, then, is processed by the execution of one or more machine cycles, each such cycle composed of a number of states. During each state one or more simultaneous microoperations are carried out. This internal operation can be represented by the simplified[6] state transition diagram shown in Figure 4.13. Each state is represented graphically by a circle, and a mnemonic name T_i is used within the circle to identify the state. All permissible transitions between states are presented graphically by arrows between them. Each transition may be qualified by an expression whose value must be either true

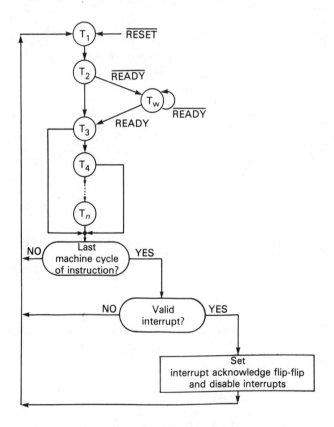

Figure 4.13   The simplified CPU state transition diagram.

---

[6]Other possible states, such as halt and hold states, are not shown in this state transition diagram. They will be discussed in later chapters.

or false. A transition from one state to another occurs if and only if this driving expression becomes true. There exist, however, some time-dependent transitions. In these cases a transition from one state to another occurs after a minimum time period (as indicated in the manufacturer's timing specifications). Such a state transition is not qualified by an expression in the state diagram. Figure 4.14 shows the CPU activities commonly carried out during the first three states of a machine cycle.

State T_1

The start of a new machine cycle is indicated by a proper control signal issued by the microprocessor CPU to synchronize memory and I/O devices. The initial state T_1 is the state during which the microprocessor issues appropriate status signals to identify the specific machine cycle type, and places an address

State	Basic CPU Activities
T_1	a) CPU issues status and/or control signals to identify machine cycle type. b) CPU places a *memory address* or *I/O device number* on the address bus.
T_2	a) If the address or status are placed on a multiplexed bus, the CPU removes them from the bus. b) For a *read cycle*: the CPU issues a READ control signal, and the memory or I/O places its data on the data bus. c) For a *write cycle*: the CPU places data on the data bus and properly notifies the memory or I/O with a WRITE control signal. d) If the read cycle is an *instruction fetch* (i.e., it fetches one word of an instruction), the CPU increments the program counter internally. e) CPU samples its READY input.
T_w (option- al)	The CPU enters this state if the memory or I/O are not ready. (Data output, address, and status are held stable during wait states.)
T_3	a) For an *instruction fetch cycle*: the CPU reads an instruction word from the data bus, and moves it into the instruction register (if at machine cycle M_1; otherwise, it moves it into an internal temporary register). b) For a *read cycle*: the CPU reads a data word from the data bus and moves it into an internal register. c) For an *interrupt acknowledge cycle*: the CPU reads "interrupt information" from the data bus and stores it internally on a temporary basis. d) For a *write cycle*: The memory or I/O reads the data from the data bus. e) The memory and I/O control lines are disabled and the selected device disconnects itself from the bus.

Figure 4.14 Common CPU activities carried out during the first states of a microprocessor machine cycle.

on the address bus. For example, the Intel 8080A issues the SYNC signal, and shortly after its beginning, the address and status are guaranteed to be stable on the bus, and a status valid strobe[7] ($\overline{STSTB}$) is issued by the 8224 clock generator. Other microprocessors issue an address latch enable (ALE), valid memory address (VMA), or address strobe ($\overline{AS}$) while a valid address is present on the bus. Whenever a $\overline{RESET}$ signal appears on the respective microprocessor input line (for example, from a reset button provided on the system front panel for operator use), the microprocessor CPU is reset[8] to its initial state T_1. A detailed description of all CPU input and output signals is given in the next chapter.

State T_2

If the address or status issued during T_1 are placed on a multiplexed bus, then the CPU removes them from the bus during state T_2. For example, the 8-bit Intel 8080A issues during T_1 an 8-bit status word on the multiplexed status/data bus, while the 16-bit Intel 8086 issues the least significant sixteen address bits on the multiplexed address/data bus. As we will see in chapter 6, since this information remains valid on the multiplexed bus for only one clock period, external circuitry can use the ALE-type strobe to latch the information and hold it valid during the entire machine cycle for those system modules which require that such information be stable for the duration of the whole cycle.

For a read cycle, the CPU properly notifies the memory or I/O device, which in turn decodes the address and status/control signals (sometimes uses the status valid strobe as well) in order to condition chip select functions. The addressed device sets up a data transfer with the microprocessor CPU, gates its data onto the data bus, and notifies the CPU (by issuing a signal to the CPU's READY[9] input pin). To indicate that the addressed device is not ready for data transfer, this READY signal is not issued until data is placed on the data bus.

For a write cycle, the CPU places the data on the data bus and properly notifies the memory or I/O device to accept it.

If the read cycle fetches from memory one word of an instruction, the CPU increments internally the program counter, and, as a last step of state T_2, samples its READY input. If this line indicates that the addressed device has

---

[7] The IEEE proposed standard for the S-100 bus denotes this signal PSTVAL* [9].

[8] This $\overline{RESET}$ signal usually zeros at least the program counter and flags register. Exceptions to this, however, also exist, as in the Motorola 6800 in which the $\overline{RESET}$ signal sets into the program counter the value $FFFE_{16}$.

[9] The Intel microprocessors call it the READY pin, the Zilog microprocessors call it the WAIT pin, while the Motorola 68000 calls it the DTACK (data transfer acknowledge) pin.

not completed the requested operation (i.e., placed data on the data bus or read data off it), the CPU enters a "wait state" T_w. The READY line is sampled once every clock period until a ready condition is indicated.[10] The CPU can then be advanced to the next state T_3. State T_w is thus used to synchronize bus cycles generated by the CPU with the response speeds of the memory and I/O devices.

State T_3

State T_3 is the state during which the data transfer actually takes place between the CPU and the addressed device. The operations during T_3 are as shown in Figure 4.14, and depend upon the specific machine cycle type being executed. After completion of state T_3, the CPU may enter one or more additional states (as shown in the state transition diagram of Figure 4.13). These additional states, T_4 and T_5, are present, as required, for operations which are completely internal to the CPU. (For example, T_4 of cycle M_1 is used for instruction decoding.) If this is not the last machine cycle of the instruction, the CPU returns to state T_1 and starts all over again for the new machine cycle. During the last machine cycle of every instruction, however, the CPU examines whether there is a valid interrupt.[11] If there is no valid interrupt, the CPU returns to state T_1 to start the first machine (op code fetch) cycle for the next instruction. If there is a valid interrupt, the CPU usually sets an internal interrupt flip-flop, disables further interrupts, and returns to state T_1 of a new machine cycle. This cycle is the interrupt acknowledge machine cycle.

4.4.2   Other Microprocessor Operating Modes

User versus Supervisor Operating Modes

Most of the 16- and 32-bit microprocessors (e.g., the Zilog Z8000, National NS16032, Motorola 68000, Intel APX 432) can operate in one of two modes: the "user" mode or the "supervisor" mode.[12] Each mode determines which

---

[10]Some CPUs proceed to state T_3 after a fixed number of T_w states, irrespective of the value of the READY signal.

[11]Interrupts will be discussed in detail in chapter 9. For the moment, it suffices to say that a valid interrupt corresponds to an interrupt request signal applied to a respective input pin of the CPU and that interrupts are enabled or disabled by the CPU.

[12]The Motorola 68000 calls them "user state" and "supervisor state," while the Zilog Z8000 calls them "normal" and "system" operating modes. The Intel APX 432 uses the concept of "objects" which work to remove the traditional barriers between the operating system and the application environment.

operations are legal, it is used by certain external devices (such as the memory management unit to control and translate memory accesses), and during instruction processing differentiates use of certain special CPU resources (such as choosing between the user stack pointer and the supervisor stack pointer). Each operating mode is identified by the value of a certain bit in the CPU flags register: in the Zilog Z8000 this flag bit is designated the $S/\overline{N}$ in its "flag and control word" register, while in the Motorola 68000 it is called the S bit in the "status" register. During any bus transaction, the microprocessor identifies to the rest of the system the mode under which it is operating by issuing certain control signals on its output pins: e.g., the Zilog Z8000 issues a Normal/$\overline{System}$ signal on its corresponding output pin, while the Motorola 68000 uses its three function code output pins FC_0–FC_2 (=101 for supervisor data references, =011 for supervisor program references, =100 for user data references, =010 for user program references).

This two-mode mechanism provides security in a computer system. Most user programs execute in the user mode only. In this mode, accesses are controlled; programs are allowed to access only their own code and data areas, and are thus restricted from accessing information which they do not need and need not modify. The operating system, on the other hand, executes in the supervisor mode and has access to all system resources. For example, the handling of exceptional conditions discussed below is always done in the supervisor mode. Most instructions execute the same in user and supervisor mode. However, some instructions which have important system effects are made *privileged*. Privileged instructions are executed only in the supervisor mode (i.e., by system programs), and are therefore not allowed to be used by the normal programmer. Such privileged instructions include: instructions which modify the CPU flags register, input and output instructions, enable and disable interrupt instructions, and other special instructions. Instructions are also provided to allow a user program to enter the supervisor mode in a controlled manner (for example, the Z8000 has the system call or SC instruction, and the 68000 has the TRAP instruction). Switching from the supervisor mode to the user mode can be done by executing privileged instructions that properly modify the specific identification bit in the CPU status register.

Context Switching

Switching from the user mode to the supervisor mode, and vice versa, is called *context switching*.[13] Context switching is usually the responsibility of the system hardware, since the user cannot anticipate the appearance of excep-

---

[13] Also called *task switching* or *process switching*.

tional conditions, and is accomplished using the *processor context* (or program status word). The processor context includes at least the program counter and the status (flags) register.

Context switching is performed by the following four-step procedure:

Procedure 4.1   (Context Switching)

(1) The CPU copies the status register internally, does not update the program counter, sets the value of the respective status bit to put the processor into the proper new operating mode (user or supervisor), and updates the corresponding (user or supervisor) stack pointer.

(2) The CPU identifies the reason for this context switching and generates a "vector address" internally, which points to a location in an appropriate area in main memory referred to as the "vector table."

(3) The current program counter value and the saved copy of the status register are automatically pushed onto the proper memory stack (user or supervisor stack, depending upon the new operating mode). The current memory stack location is identified by the contents of the respective CPU stack pointer (user or supervisor). Neither the stack nor the stack pointer of the previous operating mode is affected by such recursive pushings. This step is referred to as saving the current processor context or "CPU state."

(4) Finally, depending upon the specific cause of this context switching, a new context is obtained (i.e., new values are placed into the program counter and status register). These new values come from the location in the vector table pointed to by the "vector address" which was generated during step (2).

Thus, context switching involves the automatic replacement of the current processor context by a new processor context.

Stopped Processing State

The microprocessor CPU may also be in another state called "stopped processing state." This state is an indication of a catastrophic system failure, such as power failure, double bus faults (in the Motorola 68000), etc. Almost all 16- and 32-bit microprocessors have dedicated a specific input pin to this purpose: in the Intel 8086 and the Zilog Z8000 it is called the "non-maskable interrupt" (NMI) pin; the Motorola 68000 calls it the "HALT" pin. When a signal is detected on this pin, the microprocessor first completes the current machine cycle, and then performs a context switch to the supervisor mode and transfers to the appropriate location in memory to activate the failure routine. Usually, the function of this routine is simply to stop the microprocessor (the system becomes unusable). When the microprocessor is stopped this way, it inactivates all control signals and puts its address and data buses in their high-impedance state (in other words, it "disconnects" itself from the buses). To restart the stopped processor usually requires the application of an external RESET signal. It should be pointed out that a microprocessor in the stopped state is not the same as one in the halted state (which it enters when a HALT instruction is executed), and vice versa.[14]

Processing Exceptional Conditions

Finally, another possible microprocessor state found in 16- and 32-bit CPUs is that of "processing exceptional conditions."[15] Exceptional conditions may be either interrupts or traps. (Microprocessors with eight bits have no traps.) *Interrupts* are externally forced asynchronous events; *traps* are synchronous events, generated internally by an instruction or occurring as an unusual result of its execution. For example, the Zilog Z8000 has the following internal traps: system call, illegal instruction, privileged I/O instruction, and other privileged instructions. A trap occurs when privileged instructions are used in the user mode, or as a result of the system call instruction, or for an unimplemented instruction. The Z8000 also has a segmentation trap ($\overline{\text{SEGT}}$), which is an external trap, and internal traps have higher priority than the external segmentation trap and all interrupts. In the Motorola 68000, internally generated traps come from instructions (e.g., executing trap generating instructions, illegal instructions, or abnormal conditions arising during the execution of an instruction), from address errors (e.g., word fetches from odd addresses), from privilege violations (attempts to execute a privileged instruction while the computer is in the user mode), or from tracing.

Exceptional conditions are sampled by the CPU in the last stage of the currently executing instruction. The processor context often contains a mask indicating the current processor priority. If the priority of the exceptional condition occurring is greater than the current processor priority, then the hardware carries out the following procedure for processing exceptional conditions (during which further interrupts are disabled):

Procedure 4.2 (Processing Exceptional Conditions)

(1) Carry out step (1) of context switching Procedure 4.1 to enter the CPU into the supervisor operating mode. For those microprocessors that do not have both user and supervisor operating modes, this step is carried out in the user mode by implementing a (user) stack pointer.

---

[14]The Motorola 68000 uses the reverse notation for halt and stop; it calls the stopped processing state the "halted processing state," and it enters its "stopped state" by executing a STOP instruction.

[15]In the Motorola 68000 it is called the "exception processing state."

(2) Step (2) of context switching Procedure 4.1 is carried out, during which the CPU identifies the cause of the exceptional condition:

  (a) In the case of external vectored interrupts, the cause is identified by executing an "interrupt acknowledge" machine cycle. During this cycle, the CPU reads information from the data bus and stores it internally on a temporary basis. This information is the "vector number"[16] that the interrupting device transmits to identify the source of the interrupt. The CPU translates this "vector number" internally into a "vector address," which points to a certain location in the vector table in memory.[17] The vector table allocates a separate location for each type of exceptional condition. In most microprocessors (except the Zilog Z8000 and mode 2 interrupt of the Z80) the vector table occupies a designated, fixed location in memory. Also in some microprocessors the "vector number" and the "vector address" are one and the same thing.

  (b) In the case of internal traps, internal CPU logic provides the "vector number" used to generate the "vector address."

(3) Carry out step (3) of context switching Procedure 4.1. (During this step, the Zilog Z8000 also saves the "reason word.")

(4) Carry out step (4) of context switching Procedure 4.1, during which a new "vector"[18] (containing at least the new values for the program counter and the status register) is loaded into the program counter and status registers of the CPU. This vector comes from the location of the vector table pointed to by the "vector address" which was generated during step (2).

Details of generating vector addresses and using the vector tables are given in chapter 9.

After this procedure, the processor resumes normal instruction processing. The instruction at the address pointed to by the new program counter is fetched, and instruction decoding and execution are started. This instruction is the first instruction of the corresponding "exception handling routine." Information that was not automatically saved in the supervisor stack during step (3) of the context switching procedure, but which may be required to

---

[16] In the Zilog Z8000 it is called the "reason word."

[17] In the Zilog Z8000 the vector address is called the "new program status area pointer" (NPSAP), and the vector table, the "new program status area." In the Motorola 68000 the vector address is called the "exception vector address," and the vector table, the "exception vector table."

[18] In the Intel 8086 it is called "interrupt pointer," in the Zilog Z8000, "new program status," and in the Motorola 68000, "exception vector."

handle the exceptional condition, must be saved by this exception handling routine.

In the 8-bit Intel 8080A/8085 microprocessors, the above steps (2)-(4) are carried out by the execution of a "restart" instruction which is jammed externally onto the data bus at the beginning of the interrupt acknowledge cycle.

4.4.3   Instruction Look-ahead and Pipelining

Another advanced architectural feature found in 16- and 32-bit micro-processors is some kind of mechanism to implement instruction look-ahead and pipelined execution.

Pipelining is a well-known technique for using several pieces of hardware concurrently, and thus increasing significantly the performance and overall throughput capability of a system by increasing the number of instructions that may be completed per second [2,4,5]. The intention behind this technique is to subdivide a computational task into several subtasks, each one handled by a separate hardware stage. A series of such hardware stages is called a *pipeline*. All stages operate simultaneously with independent inputs. Temporary storage buffers may exist between stages. A computational task advances from one stage to the next, and comes closer to completion as the end of the pipeline is approached. The pipeline accepts new inputs before previously accepted inputs have been completely processed and output from it. Also, when one subtask result leaves a stage, the logic associated with that stage becomes free and can accept new results from the previous stage. Thus, the rate at which inputs are fed to the pipeline is chosen in relation to the time required to get an input through one stage, with the main goal of keeping all portions of the pipeline fully utilized. Once the pipeline is full, the output rate will match the input rate.

Consider, for example, the simplified two-stage pipeline of Figure 4.15. Figure 4.16 shows the timing diagram of the operations performed by this two-stage pipeline, for every time period T_i.

In this example each computational task is assumed to be composed of two subtasks.[19] During T_1, stage 1 performs the first subtask of computational task j, and places the results in its output buffers. During the next time period T_2, stage 2 receives the results of stage 1, and performs the second subtask of computational task j. At the same time, since stage 1 of the pipeline becomes available, it receives new inputs and performs the first subtask of the next

---

[19]It is also assumed here that the two subtasks require the same time, and that each T_i period is sufficiently long to perform the subtask and place its results on the output buffers of the stage.

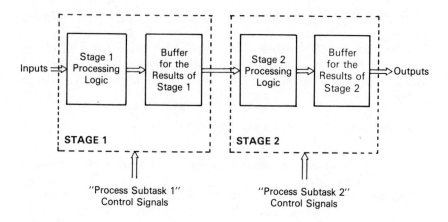

Figure 4.15   A simplified two-stage data flow.

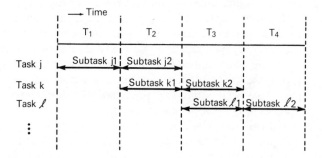

Figure 4.16   Timing diagram of the operations performed by a two-stage pipeline during every T_i time period [2].

computational task k. From that point on, the pipeline is full. At any one time period it overlaps processing portions of two computational tasks, and after every time period, it produces the final result of one task. As can be seen from Figure 4.16, the three computational tasks, j, k, and l, are completed in only four time periods instead of the six time periods that a non-pipelined implementation would require.

In general, if a computational task is subdivided into n subtasks, an n-stage pipeline is used. It takes n time periods to fill the pipeline completely; from that point on, portions of n computational tasks will be processed by the pipeline in parallel form, producing the final result of one computational task after each time period.

The processing of any instruction can be subdivided into the following five subtasks: instruction fetch (F), decode (D),[20] form effective address (A), operand fetch (O), and instruction execute (E). A true pipeline implementation establishes a series of five hardware stages, in which each stage operates concurrently with the others on one of these subtasks of several instructions, as shown in Figure 4.17.[21] It is seen here that four instructions are processed in fifteen time periods, as compared to twenty time periods that a non-pipelined implementation would require.

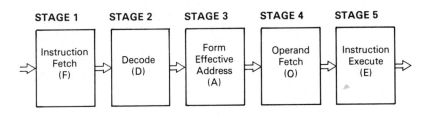

(a)

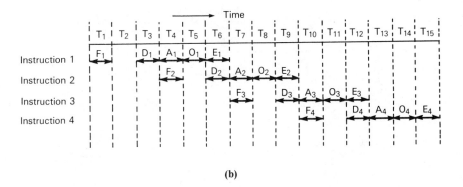

(b)

Figure 4.17 Instruction processing through a true five-stage pipeline: **(a)** functional representation of the pipeline; **(b)** timing diagram of the operations performed [12].

---

[20]This simultaneously fetches the rest of the instruction (immediate data, offset, etc.), if required.

[21]Since during the op code decode subtask (D) a memory fetch may also be performed for the rest of the instruction, the D subtask should not be performed at the same time period as the fetch subtask (F) of the next instruction op code (for example see D_1 and F_2 in Figure 4.17b). Similarly, the D subtask of an instruction should not be performed at the same time period as the operand fetch subtask (O) of the previous instruction (for example, see D_2 and O_1 in Figure 4.17b).

However, cost/performance trade-offs very rarely lead to such true pipeline implementations. One commonly adopted variation is the classic approach of *instruction fetch overlap*, implemented by a two-stage pipeline. A separate processing element is provided for stage 1 of the pipeline to perform the instruction fetch subtask, while the remaining four subtasks are grouped together in a second stage (see Figure 4.18).

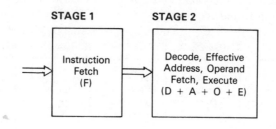

(a)

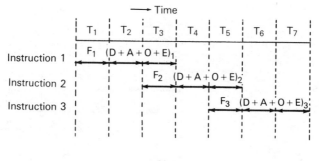

(b)

Figure 4.18 The classic two-stage approach of instruction fetch overlap: **(a)** functional representation of the pipeline; **(b)** timing diagram of the operations performed [14].

Instead of prefetching only one instruction, advanced computers have allocated more buffers in the CPU to implement a multiple *instruction look-ahead* mechanism [8,14,23]. Since the delay involved between the initiation of a memory read and the arrival of the word at its destination (memory access time delay, delay when memory is busy servicing a higher priority request, delay in the word transfer path, etc.,) is usually relatively long, look-ahead mechanisms fetch a number of instructions and operands from main memory in advance of execution by the ALU section of the CPU. This technique "looks" several instructions ahead of the one currently being executed. Buffers or scratch registers are used within the CPU as speed-matching devices: (1) in the control section of the CPU to keep these instructions fetched in advance or to hold several instructions in order to improve performance for small loops, and (2) interposed between the ALU and memory to hold the pre-fetched operands and avoid storing and refetching data used by successive instructions. Through this look-ahead technique, various references are initiated early, and the operands are usually available in the ALU buffer by the time the ALU is ready for them.

The look-ahead concept attempts to have instructions and operands arrive from memory at a rate approximately equal to the rate the CPU can utilize them. However, some interlock problems may arise [23]. First, if an instruction depends on previous ALU results, then it should not be started before these results are available. Second, if a conditional branch-type instruction is encountered, and the previous instruction that sets its conditions has not been completed yet, then the control section will not know whether to prefetch the instruction immediately following the conditional branch instruction or the instruction at the target of the branch. Third, problems also arise when an attempt is made to fetch operands that have not reached storage yet, or when an attempt is made to modify an instruction by a preceding store operation (i.e., instructions are treated as data). Several techniques discussed below have been used to take care of such deadlocks [8].

There are three basic ways for handling the problem of conditional branching on ALU results: (1) The control section can stop the flow of instructions before fetching the next instruction, until the ALU has completed the preceding operation and the result is known. No matter whether the branch is taken or not, this always causes a delay. (2) Based on past experience on the program, make a "guess" as to which way the branch is going to go before it is taken, follow this path, and continue to prepare instructions; if the guess later proves to be wrong, then the prepared instructions must be discarded and the correct path taken instead. (3) The control section can fetch the instructions immediately following the conditional branch as well as instructions at the target of the branch simultaneously, and when the ALU generates the conditions, then determine which of the two groups of prepared instructions to use.

Problems similar to that of treating instructions as if they were data can be handled by the control section, if the control section tests the instruction as soon as it is loaded to see whether it is a store-type instruction. If it is, the fetch sequence must wait until the effective address has been prepared to see whether it is going to modify a successive instruction.

Finally, the problems of fetching operands that have not yet reached storage can be handled if the result of the ALU can return first to an internal operand buffer before being sent to storage.

Unfortunately, multiple instruction look-ahead and true pipelining have a tremendous impact on the microprocessor CPU design: (1) the control function of the CPU becomes very complex, since it must implement these techniques and also take care of all deadlocks that may arise during system operation; and (2) incorporating additional scratch registers, buffers and control gates increases costs and die area requirements. The percentage of performance rise that could be achieved with these techniques does not justify their full implementation on single-chip, low-cost, and limited-real estate microprocessor CPUs.

For that reason Intel decided [12,14,16] to implement in their 16-bit, single-chip 8086 microprocessor, a technique that is halfway between the classic approach of instruction fetch overlap (Figure 4.18) and true pipelining (Figure 4.17). A two-stage (or two-level) architecture was chosen, enhanced by a FIFO buffer (queue) between the two stages (Figure 4.19). The first of these two independently controlled stages is called the *bus interface unit (BIU)*. It keeps the memory busy by fetching instructions one 16-bit word at a time from sequential locations in memory and storing them in the queue. Simulations with "typical" instruction sequences have indicated that the optimum length of the queue should be six bytes [14]. Other related functions provided by this BIU are operand fetch and store. The second stage is called the *execution unit (EU)*, which takes instructions from the queue and executes them. Time-overlapping the decoding of each instruction with the last portions of the execution of the prior instruction is performed in the EU. As can be seen in the timing diagram of Figure 4.19b, the 6-byte queue allows the 8086 to overlap the long fetch time of instruction 4 with the long execution time of instruction 2. Other related functions provided by the EU are receiving memory operands from the BIU and passing to it results for storage.

The 16-bit Zilog Z8000 does not use such an internal instruction queue. However, it provides a form of pipelining, having a look-ahead memory prefetch, but for a single instruction. For most instructions, the data manipulation time is fully overlapped with the fetching of the first word of the next instruction. The Z8000 CPU uses an internal "look-ahead instruction decoder

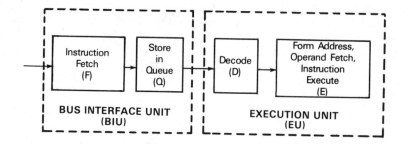

(a)

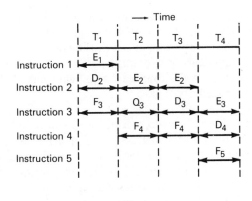

(b)

Figure 4.19 The Intel pipeline architecture adopted for the 16-bit single-chip 8086 microprocessor: **(a)** the two-stage pipeline; **(b)** example of a timing diagram [14].

and accelerator," which is tied to the internal bus, and actually allows an
instruction to begin execution while it is being stored in the instruction
register. In most common addressing modes, the CPU does not require any
additional clock cycles to decode the instruction in deciding whether it is a
short (16-bit) or full offset (32-bit) instruction [19]. The Z8000 also pipelines
memory row addresses some 100 nsec before column addresses, because
typical memory chip row access is 100 nsec faster than column access [22].

The Motorola 68000 CPU is also a pipelined processor in the sense that it
overlaps instruction fetching with execution; one half of the device performs
instruction fetches, while the other half executes the instructions (it allows
address and data calculations to occur simultaneously).

Finally, most 32-bit microprocessors have separate fetch and execution
units. In some of them, the two operations of instruction fetching and executing overlap. In others, the execution is pipelined in three stages: instruction
fetching, decoding, and finally, execution. The three-stage pipeline approach
was adopted by the 32-bit Intel APX 432. The first stage (instruction decoder)
and the second stage (microinstruction sequencer) are physically located on
the APX 43201 chip; the third-stage (execution unit) is on the APX 43202
chip.

EXERCISES

4.1   Describe a way of increasing the instruction processing speed of a
      microprocessor without increasing its clock frequency. (For example,
      by changing its architecture and including some special-purpose
      registers).

4.2   Consider a hypothetical 8-bit microprocessor that uses a 4-bit data bus. Assume that the 2's complement representation of signed values is used. Describe the effect on binary arithmetic operations: (a) when the four most significant bits of the operand are fetched from memory first, and (b) when the four least significant bits of the operand are fetched from memory first.

4.3   Suggest how the microprocessor structure shown in Figure 4.2a might be modified to allow the instruction, "Replace the *next* instruction op code with the contents of the location whose address is specified in the instruction" to be executed. Describe the various machine cycles required and the basic activities carried out during each state. (The *next* instruction is not altered in memory).

4.4   Examine the internal register structure of the 16-bit microprocessors, Intel 8086, Motorola 68000, and Zilog Z8000, and list their similarities and differences.

4.5   In a single-address microprocessor which employs sixty instructions, how many bits are required in the instruction so that all 1024 locations in the memory can be directly addressed?

4.6   For Exercise 4.5, discuss some of the differences which would occur if the word length of the system were eight or sixteen bits.

4.7   Consider an 8-bit microprocessor (8-bit data bus, 8-bit ALU, byte-addressing, etc.). Draw a detailed sequence flowchart (analogous to that of Figure 4.9) for the processing (i.e., fetch and execute) of a 3-byte ADD instruction of which the second and third bytes indicate the location of one operand. (One of the operands is assumed to be in the accumulator. The accumulator receives the result of the addition).

4.8   For Exercise 4.7, describe the CPU activities carried out during each state (in a tabular form analogous to that of Figure 4.14).

4.9   Assume that the program counter of a microprocessor contains 0734_{16}. What are the contents of the program counter and the stack immediately following a CALL to the subroutine at location $A032_{16}$? What is the content of the program counter when the RETURN instruction is executed?

4.10 Consider a 16-bit microprocessor CPU, having instructions composed of two 8-bit fields, where the first byte represents the operation code and the second the operand or address field.

    (a) What is the maximum directly addressable memory capacity (in number of bits)?

    (b) Discuss the impact on the system speed if the system has (1) an 8-bit address bus and an 8-bit data bus, or (2) an 8-bit address bus and a 4-bit data bus.

    (c) How many bits are needed for the program counter and the instruction register?

4.11 Consider the nested subroutines of Figure 4.4. If SUB1 is located in memory location 5000_{16} and SUB2 in memory location 7000_{16}, redraw the figure to correspond to this new situation.

4.12 Examine the internal register structure of the Intel 8085 and Motorola 6800 microprocessors by reference to the manufacturers' literature, and list their similarities and differences.

4.13 Repeat Exercise 4.12 above, and compare the flags of the two microprocessors.

REFERENCES AND BIBLIOGRAPHY

[1] Alexandridis, N.A., "Bit-sliced Microprocessor Architecture," *Computer*, June 1978, pp. 56–80.

[2] Alexandridis, N.A., "Control, Timing, and System Signals," *Fundamentals Handbook of Electrical and Computer Engineering, Volume III: Computer Hardware, Software and Applications,* ed. S.S.L. Chang, New York: John Wiley & Sons, Inc., 1983, pp. 78–119.

[3] Amdahl, G.M., G.A. Blaauw, and F.P. Brooks, Jr., "Architecture of the IBM System/360," *IBM Journal of Research and Development*, 8, no.2, April 1964, pp.87–101.

[4] Anderson, S.F., et al, "The IBM System/360 Model 91: Floating-Point Execution Unit," *IBM Journal*, January 1967, pp.34–53.

[5] Bloch, E. and D. Galage, "Component Progress: Its Effect on High-Speed Computer Architecture and Machine Organization," *Computer*, April 1978, pp.64–76.

[6]   Brooks, F.P., Jr., "Instruction Sequencing," *Planning a Computer System*, ed. W.Buchholz, New York: McGraw-Hill, 1962.

[7]   Bryce, H., "Microprogramming Makes the MC68000 a Processor Ready for the Future," *Electronic Design*, October 25, 1979, pp.98–99.

[8]   Buchholz, W., ed., *Planning a Computer System*, New York: McGraw-Hill, 1962.

[9]   IEEE Task 696.1/D2, "Standard Specification for S-100 Bus Interface Devices," *Computer*, July 1979, pp.28–52.

[10] Intel Corporation, *The 8086 Family User's Manual*, (9800722-03), Santa Clara, CA, 1979.

[11] Intel Corporation, *Introduction to the iAPX 432 Architecture*, (171821-001), Santa Clara, CA, 1981.

[12] Katz, B.J., et al, "8086 Microcomputer Bridges the Gap Between 8- and 16-bit Designs," *Electronics*, February 16, 1978, pp.99–104.

[13] Lunde, A., "Empirical Evaluation of Some Features of Instruction Set Processor Architectures," *CACM*, vol.20, no.3, March 1977, pp.143–52.

[14] McKevitt, J. and J. Bayliss, "New Options from Big Chips," *IEEE Spectrum*, March 1979, pp.28–34.

[15] Motorola, Incorporated, *16-Bit Microprocessing Unit*, (ADI-814-R1), Austin, TX, 1980.

[16] Ogdin, C.A., "Sixteen-Bit Micros," *Mini-Micro Systems*, January 1979, pp.64–72.

[17] Peuto, B., "Architecture of a New Microprocessor," *Computer*, February 1979, pp. 10–21.

[18] Rector, R. and G. Alexy, *The 8086 Book*, Berkeley, CA: Osborne/McGraw-Hill, 1980.

[19] Shima, M., "Two Versions of 16-bit Chip Span Microprocessor, Mini-computer Needs," *Electronics*, December 21, 1978, pp.81–88.

[20] Stritter, E. and T. Gunter, "A Microprocessor Architecture for a Changing World: The Motorola 68000," *Computer*, February 1979, pp. 43–51.

[21] Stritter, E. and N. Tredennick, "Microprogrammed Implementation of a Single Chip Microprocessor," *Proceedings of the 11th Annual Microprogramming Workshop*, November 1978, pp.8–16.

[22] Sugarman, R., "Computers: Our Microuniverse Expands," *IEEE Spectrum*, January 1979, pp.32–37.

[23] Tanenbaum, A.S., *Structured Computer Organization*, Englewood Cliffs, N.J.: Prentice-Hall, Inc., 1976.

[24] Zilog, Incorporated, *Z8000 Technical Manual*, Cupertino, CA, 1979.

[25] Zilog, Incorporated, *1982/83 Data Book*, Campbell, CA, 1982.

Chapter 5

BUSES AND SYSTEM CONCEPTS

5.1 INTRODUCTION

In chapter 4 we covered the internal architecture and operation of the micro-processor CPU. In order to form a working microprocessor system, additional modules are required, such as memory and I/O modules, all properly interconnected and communicating with each other. Before we describe the individual design and operation of these modules, we must explain the communication paths used to enable each module to talk and listen to its neighbors and exchange data with them.

High-speed module-to-module communication is accomplished via *parallel buses* which transfer all bits of information across separate wires at the same time. We distinguish between two types of buses: the "CPU bus" and the "system bus." The *CPU bus* is formed by all lines connected directly to the microprocessor CPU pins. Because of the limited number of available pins, some of the CPU bus lines are multiplexed in time to carry several types of information. The *system bus* is the bus formed after the CPU lines are demultiplexed; thus, functionally separate, non-multiplexed, groups of lines are provided to carry addresses, data, and control signals. In most implementations, memory and I/O components are connected to the system rather than the CPU bus.

CPU buses vary widely from one microprocessor to another. The function, lines, and control signals of the CPU bus are treated in this chapter using a unified approach. Detailed pins and signals of representative 8-, 16-, and 32-bit microprocessor CPUs are given in the Appendices. There are a number of system buses on the market, including the Intel MULTIBUS [13], the hobbyist's S-100 [2,8], the Zilog Z-bus [1,14], etc. Throughout the remainder of this book system bus lines will be referred to following the symbology and notation of the IEEE "Proposed Microcomputer System 796 Bus Standard [3]," which is very similar to Intel's MULTIBUS.

In section 5.2, after an explanation of the need for buses, the CPU bus and the system bus are contrasted, bus masters and slaves are defined, and alternative bus organizations are offered. The next two sections, 5.3 and 5.4, define the address, data, status and control lines, and signals of the IEEE 796 system bus and the CPU bus, respectively, to be used throughout the remainder of this book. (System and CPU bus interrupt lines, bus exchange lines, and bus arbitration lines are covered in chapter 9.) Differentiations on the CPU signals and symbology among representative microprocessors are also discussed. Finally, section 5.4 explains the operation of both CPU and system buses, the information placed on them, and the respective bus timing diagrams for the basic memory-I/O read and write bus cycles.

5.2 ALTERNATIVE SYSTEM CONFIGURATIONS

5.2.1 The Need for Buses

The concurrent manufacture of microprocessors by various companies resulted in the appearance of many and different kinds of "microprocessor system architectures" (i.e., various ways of configuring and interconnecting CPUs, memory modules, I/O modules, etc.). Moreover, it led to different methods of transferring information from one module to another, and generating control and timing signals. Thus, one architecture, for example, may place more emphasis on the ability to perform fast arithmetic operations (an architecture oriented towards the solution of complex mathematical problems), while another architecture may provide greater flexibility for I/O operations (an architecture more suitable for control applications and monitoring the function of external devices).

Consider for example Figure 5.1, which presents a diagram of a medium-level microprocessor system with all possible physical interconnections shown explicitly [9]. The respective numbers in parentheses indicate representative widths of the information transferred. Each of the three basic modules of the figure has the necessary pins for its interconnection and the formation of respective information transfer paths.

The microprocessor CPU controls and synchronizes the functions of other system modules by issuing the proper signals, some of which are shown in Figure 5.1. For example, to access memory the microprocessor must issue a memory address (for data this address is implicitly or explicitly specified by the executed instruction, whereas for instructions this address comes from the program counter) and the respective read or write control signal. The input/output transfer with peripheral devices is initiated either by the instruction's execution, or by way of a DMA controller. In the first case, the executed instruction chooses the peripheral device and specifies whether input or output is to be performed, and the CPU synchronizes the information flow between the peripheral device and the storage registers within the microprocessor. In the second case, the DMA controller accomplishes a high rate of exchange of information directly between the peripheral device and memory, which is concurrent with, and independent of, the normal program execution in the CPU. Finally, another type of signal exchanged between the CPU and the I/O module is the interrupt request/acknowledge signal.

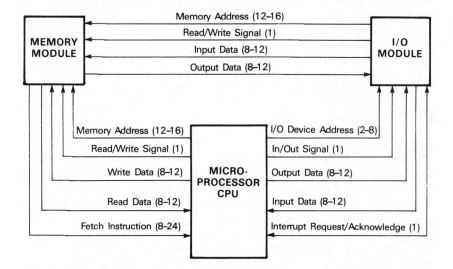

Figure 5.1   Basic microprocessor system diagram with all possible physical interconnections [9]. (Numbers in parentheses denote representative widths of information being transferred.)

As can be seen in Figure 5.1, it is not possible to use a separate group of pins for every information path. For example, representative 8-bit microprocessors are manufactured on a single chip which has a total of forty pins (some exceptions exist with larger numbers of pins). If from these forty pins one subtracts six pins used for power supply, clock, reset signal, and some other initial condition signals, then the chip is left with only thirty-four pins to be allocated to all necessary information transfer paths. These are much less than the required total number of CPU pins suggested by Figure 5.1.

Because of this limitation in the total number of available pins, two other alternative solutions are usually used: (1) the *serial information transfer*, or (2) *multiplexing the information paths*. Both solutions, however, have the drawback that they require the incorporation, both on the microprocessor chip and on the other system modules, of additional control gates and storage elements, which, of course, would not be necessary if separate parallel paths existed. The serial transfer of information is seldom used because, although it requires a minimal number of pins, it does make the whole system rather slow.

A serial transfer of n bits, accomplished within t time units, requires n/t pins. Consequently, on the one hand, the number of pins used is minimized, while on the other hand the information transfer time is increased. The most common solution is to multiplex the information path, if it is possible to realize two or more transfers of information that do not collide with each other. The communications path between the modules that make up the microcomputer system is referred to as the *bus*. Physically, a bus is a collection of wires, over which all signals travel to allow the various modules to interact with each other. Functionally, a bus refers to a set of signals grouped together because of the similarity of their functions. A bus is called a (time-division) *multiplexed bus,* when it is used for transferring different information at different, well-defined, times. In a multiplexed bus, each transmitter and receiver has one or more than one designated time slot. The result of multiplexing is that fewer pins are required.

Because of pin number limitation, most microprocessors cannot provide simultaneously separate buses for all groups of functionally similar lines (such as address, data, status signals, etc.). Multiplexing one or more of these buses is performed. Most often, data lines are multiplexed with some or all address lines to form an "address/data bus." The status signals emitted by the microprocessor CPU sometimes are multiplexed as well, either with the data lines (as done in the Intel 8080A) or with some of the address lines (as done in the Intel 8086).

Whenever multiplexing is used, the CPU interface system must include the necessary hardware to demultiplex those lines to produce the separate address, data, and control buses required for the system. Demultiplexing of a multiplexed bus can be handled either at the CPU interface or locally at appropriate points in the system. Besides a slower system operation, a multiplexed bus also results in additional interface hardware requirements.

Since buses are used to interconnect various components, the bus structure is one of the most important elements in a microprocessor system. The three separate groups of functionally similar signals we will be discussing throughout this chapter constitute the address, data, and control buses. The *address bus* is used to transfer addresses to memory or I/O devices; the *data bus* is used to transfer data from the microprocessor CPU to memory or I/O devices, and vice versa; the *control bus* carries the intermodule timing, status, and control signals.

5.2.2 CPU and System Buses

In most microprocessor systems one may distinguish between two physically different buses: a CPU bus and a system bus. Both buses may be shared by multiple processors.

The CPU Bus

The CPU bus (or local bus) is formed by all lines connected directly to the microprocessor CPU pins. Most often, the CPU bus multiplexes address with data on the same lines. Figure 5.2 shows several examples of multiplexed CPU buses.

The lines of a multiplexed address/data bus contain the address bits (or a low-order portion of the address) during the first clock period or "state" of the bus cycle, while, during the remaining states of the cycle these lines are used to carry data. For example, both the 16-bit Intel 8086 and Zilog Z8000 CPUs (Figure 5.2) provide such a 16-bit address/data bus that multiplexes the low-order sixteen address bits with the 16-bit data word. (The 8086 CPU multiplexes the remaining four address bits, A16–A19, with the four status

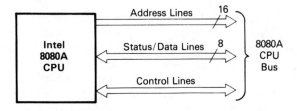

(a) Intel 8080A

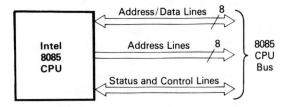

(b) Intel 8085

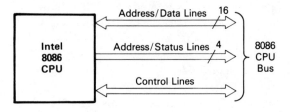

(c) Intel 8086

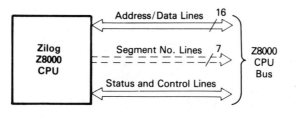

(d) Zilog Z8000

Figure 5.2 Examples of microprocessors with multiplexed CPU buses (Interrupt and bus arbitration lines are not included).

signals S3–S6 on four separate lines). The 8-bit Intel 8085 CPU has an 8-bit address/data bus that multiplexes the lower half of a 16-bit address with the 8-bit data byte. The early design of the 8-bit Intel 8080A of Figure 5.2 provides instead an 8-bit status/data bus that multiplexes an 8-bit status word (issued during the first state T_1) with the 8-bit data (occupying this bus during the remaining states of the cycle). Since the address on a multiplexed address/data bus is not stable for the entire bus cycle,[1] only limited types of memory and I/O devices can be connected directly to the CPU bus. In such connections, however, the designer must guarantee that during a read from memory (or input from I/O) operation no such device corrupts the information (address or status) present on the address/data bus during the first state T_1. There are various ways of protecting against such corruptions, some of which are discussed in chapter 6, where we present ways of interfacing devices to the microprocessor CPU.

In more complex configurations, the CPU bus may also be shared by additional processors directly connected to it, as shown in Figure 5.3. These devices are capable of acting as bus masters (i.e., they can take control of the CPU bus lines), and include independent I/O processors (such as DMA controllers) or special function processors (such as "co-processors" that execute extensions to the CPU instruction set and operate in parallel with the CPU). These processors may also use the CPU status signals on the CPU bus to monitor CPU bus activity. In such multiprocessor configurations, on-chip arbitration logic (implemented via HOLD/HOLDA or bus request/bus grant handshake signals) determines which processor drives the shared CPU bus. Multiple processors connected to the same CPU bus are said to be "local" to each other.

---

[1] Or the status word on the multiplexed status/data bus of the Intel 8080A.

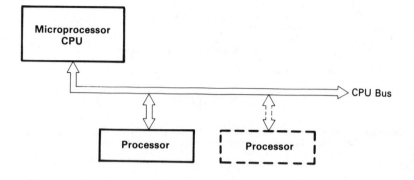

Figure 5.3 A multiprocessor configuration sharing the CPU bus.

The System Bus

Although certain types of memory and I/O components can be connected directly to the CPU bus, most implementations usually require some interface circuitry (*CPU interface*) to demultiplex, buffer, and decode the information on the CPU bus (Figure 5.4a). The new bus thus formed, referred to as the *private system bus*, consists now of three functionally separate, non-multiplexed buses (address, data, and control buses). The group of CPU interface components transforms the signals of a CPU bus into a private system bus. Local (or private) memory and I/O are interconnected to the microprocessor via this private system bus (Figure 5.4b). Such a configuration is representative of small, one- or two-printed circuit board, single-CPU systems, in which the private system bus provides the CPU with a private address space that is not accessible by other CPUs.

However, in large single-CPU designs (systems that contain two or more printed circuit boards) or in multiple-microprocessor (multiple-CPU) systems, a "global system bus" is used as shown in Figure 5.4c. The "system bus interface" circuitry transforms the signals of a CPU bus into a global system bus. The complexity of the interface circuitry (i.e., the number of interface components) that is required to generate the global system bus depends on the size and complexity of the system (e.g., the address space size, which determines the number of interface latches, the data bus width, which determines

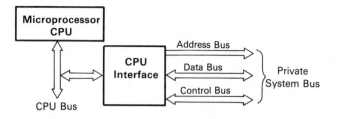

(a) Generating the private system bus.

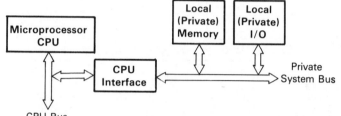

(b) A single-microprocessor system with local (private) memory and I/O.

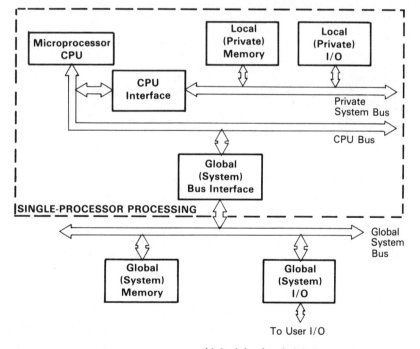

(c) A single-microprocessor system with both local and global memory and I/O.

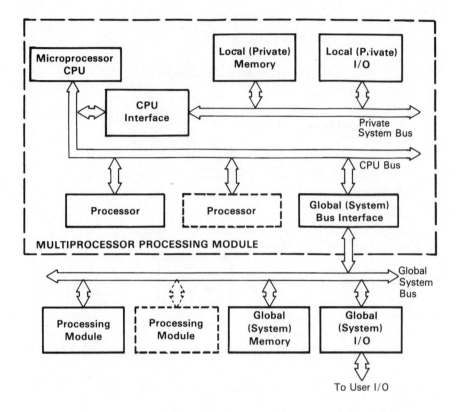

(d) A multi-microprocessor system.

Figure 5.4 Various configurations using the (private and global) system bus.

the number of transceivers, etc.). As with the private system bus, all information lines of the global system bus are demultiplexed to form three functionally separate buses: global system address bus, global system data bus, and global system control bus. If there are multiple processing modules in the system (as in Figure 5.4d), all global memory and I/O connected to this bus are accessible to all processing modules. In this case, the system bus interface of each processing module includes a separate component, called a "bus arbiter" (or "bus exchange"), to take control of the shared bus as it needs to effect data transfers and control the access of the global memory and I/O. The processing modules request system bus control through a bus arbitration (or bus exchange) sequence.

Since both the private system bus and the global system bus are demultiplexed buses providing for separate address, data, and control lines, from now on, they will be referred to collectively as the "system bus."

5.2.3 Bus Masters and Bus Slaves

Functional devices of a system interconnected via the bus are divided into two broad classifications: bus masters and bus slaves. Masters obtain use of the bus and initiate data transfers, while slaves merely perform data transfers. As we will see later, the system bus allows both 8-bit and 16-bit masters and slaves to be intermixed in the system. All data transfer communications between a bus master and a slave are carried out in terms of "bus cycles."

Bus Masters

A device acting as a master has control of the bus and is responsible for the initiation of all bus cycles; i.e., it generates all signals necessary to address all bus slaves (or some portion of them), and transfers data to or from the addressed slave. To perform these tasks, the master is equipped with either a microprocessor CPU or logic dedicated to transferring data over the bus to and from other destinations. The master identifies the nature of the bus cycle in progress and qualifies the nature of the address on the address bus by issuing proper status and control signals over the control bus. Data are transmitted and received on the bidirectional data bus. The processing modules shown in Figures 5.4c and 5.4d represent the general configuration of a master.

Bus masters are further subdivided into two classifications: permanent masters and temporary masters. A *permanent bus master* is usually a CPU, and has the highest priority in the microprocessor system. A *temporary master* may request control of the bus from the permanent master for an arbitrary number of bus cycles. This transfer of bus control from a permanent to a temporary master is termed a "DMA cycle." If the bus is granted, the temporary master is responsible for the generation and timing of the bus cycles until it returns control of the bus to the permanent master. The temporary master differs from the permanent master in that it need not generate all possible bus cycles. In this chapter we discuss microprocessor system configurations having a single permanent master[2].

Bus Slaves

A device acting as a bus slave monitors all bus cycles, and is capable of being addressed by a bus master. If addressed during a particular bus cycle, it accepts or sends the data on the data bus lines. A slave module is not capable of controlling the bus; it simply decodes the address lines and acts upon the control signals from the master. Therefore, a slave always responds to a bus cycle initiated by a master. Examples of bus slaves include memory and I/O modules. An I/O slave module, however, may also request service by a bus master by generating an interrupt request signal.

5.2.4 Bus Organization

Single-Bus Systems

Microprocessor systems can be configured using one or more buses. Figure 5.5a shows the basic diagram of a microprocessor system which has only one bus (a *single-bus microprocessor system*). All its modules are directly connected to this bus for exchanging data. The bus control is distributed, thereby permitting other modules as well to interconnect easily to the bus. In this example, the microprocessor CPU has forty pins, thirty-three of which are allocated to the various interconnections as shown by the respective numbers in parentheses. It is assumed here that the data bus is eight bits wide and that the system uses 16-bit addresses (thus directly accessing up to 64K memory locations). However, since only eight CPU pins have been allocated for memory addressing purposes, two time units are now required to transmit both the upper and lower 8-bit halves of the 16-bit address. Although this brings about a delay in accessing memory, it has the advantage that it leaves a larger number of unused CPU pins. These unused pins may be used for interconnecting the CPU with I/O modules, and thus permitting a more efficient and faster information exchange between the microprocessor CPU and its external environment.

One drawback of the single-bus architecture is that additional control circuitry is required to keep all the system modules properly synchronized.

---

[2]Multi-master or multiprocessor configurations are discussed in chapter 9.

The second drawback is the significant reduction in the total speed of the system, since the small width of the bus does not allow the simultaneous transfer of both addresses and data. In spite of these disadvantages, the single-bus architecture has been used quite satisfactorily, in a number of small-scale applications (e.g., pocket calculators). Figure 5.5b shows a microprocessor system composed of six chips. By adding a keyboard for inputting information, a cassette, and a CRT for displaying the results, it is converted to an autonomous and programmable system that can be used in a large spectrum of educational and commercial applications.

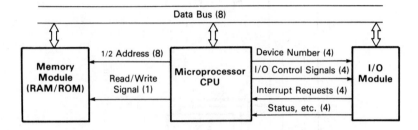

(a) Single-bus configuration.

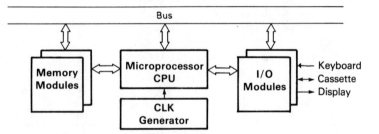

(b) An autonomous 6-chip system.

Figure 5.5   A single-bus microprocessor system [9].

Multiple-Bus Systems

When more processing power is required, two or more functionally separate buses are used (a *multiple-bus microprocessor system*). In this case, one bus is used to transfer addresses to memory and I/O modules, while a second bidirectional bus is used to transfer data, as shown in Figure 5.6. The necessary control signals are issued by the CPU and applied to the other system modules. Quite often, the control lines are also grouped together to form a third "control bus."

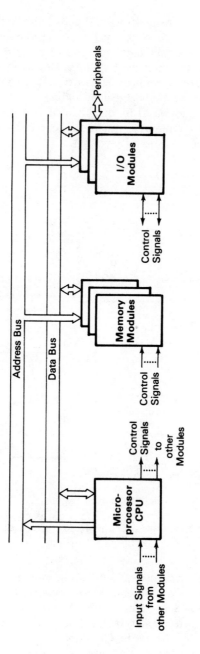

Figure 5.6 A 2-bus microprocessor system.

Finally, microprocessor systems also exist whose architectures contain more buses. For example, one bus may be the address bus, a second bus may be a bidirectional data bus for transferring data between the CPU and memory, a third bus may be an output bus for transferring data from the CPU to the output module(s), while a fourth bus may be an input bus for transferring data from the input module(s) to the CPU.

5.3 BUS LINES AND SIGNALS

This section presents both the system bus and the CPU bus lines and signals.

5.3.1 The System Bus

The model we will be using for the microprocessor system has the configuration shown in Figure 5.7. The system bus will have separate, non-mulitplexed lines.

The term *assert* will be used to mean driving a signal line to the true state. The true state is either a high or low state, as specified for each signal. The term *active* will be synonymous with the true logic state.

Whenever system signals are "active low signals," they are represented with a nathan (asterisk) following the signal name. For example, the memory write command MWTC* indicates that the signal is active low as shown:

$$MWTC* = \text{asserted at 0 volts.}$$

The following is used to explain further the notation used:

Function	Electrical	Definition Logic	State
MWTC	H	1 true	active, asserted
	L	0 false	inactive, not asserted
MWTC*	L	1 true	active, asserted
	H	0 false	inactive, not asserted

All components or modules connected to the system bus operate asynchronously in a master-slave relationship, in which all transfers on the bus are controlled by handshake signals. This allows memory slaves with different access times and I/O slaves with various response times to be connected efficiently to these lines.

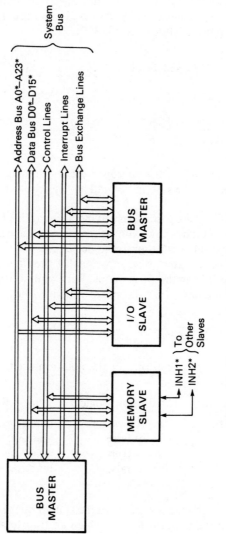

Figure 5.7 The general configuration of a microprocessor system.

As shown in Figure 5.7, the signals transferred over the system bus are functionally divided into the following five groups:

(a) Address (and inhibit) lines
(b) Data lines
(c) Control lines
(d) Interrupt lines
(e) Bus exchange lines

In this chapter we discuss only the first three groups (address, data, and control lines) of the system bus. Figure 5.8 depicts the lines required for a master module to interconnect to the system bus. The last two groups (interrupt and bus exchange lines) will be discussed in chapter 9 along with input/output and multi-master configuration concepts.

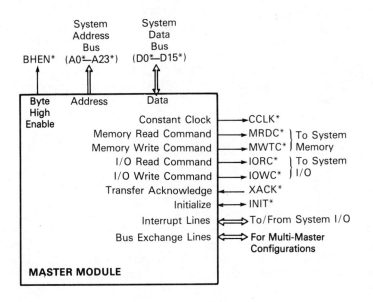

Figure 5.8 Master module signals on the IEEE 796 system bus [3]. (Interrupt lines and bus exchange lines are covered in chapter 9.)

It must be noted here that the system bus design is modular, and that subsets of these signals may be implemented according to the needs of the specific application. For example, the bus exchange lines are not needed in single-processor systems or in multiple-processor systems for which all processors are connected to (and share) the CPU bus (as in Figure 5.3).

The signals shown in Figure 5.8 are discussed below.

Address and Inhibit Lines

Address Lines (AO–A23*)*

These twenty-four lines are denoted as A0*–A23* (where A23* is the most significant), they constitute the system address bus, and are used to transfer either memory addresses or I/O device addresses. They are driven by three-state drivers and are always controlled by the current system bus master.

A 16-bit master in control of the system bus may either use all these twenty-four lines A0*–A23* to transmit a 24-bit address to memory, or use only the first sixteen lines A0*–A15* to transmit a 16-bit I/O device address. Therefore, a 16-bit master can directly access up to $2^{24} = 16,777,216$ locations (bytes) of memory, or up to $2^{16} = 64K$ I/O devices.

An 8-bit master in control of the system bus may either use the first sixteen lines A0*–A15* to transmit a 16-bit address to memory, or use only the first eight lines A0*–A7* to transmit an 8-bit I/O device address. Therefore, an 8-bit master can directly access up to $2^{16} = 64K$ locations (bytes) of memory or up to $2^{8} = 256$ I/O devices.[3]

The above I/O addressing means that, in general, any I/O slave connected to the system bus must be able to be configured also to decode only the eight lower address lines A0*–A7* and ignore[4] the next eight address lines A8*–A15*.

Inhibit Lines (INH1 and INH2*)*

The signals INH1* and INH2* are used to prevent memory slaves from responding to the address on the address bus (i.e., they can be invoked for any memory read or memory write operation). An inhibit line signal is generated by the inhibiting slave (identified by decoding the memory address lines) to inhibit another slave's bus activity. When inhibited in this way, the slave disables its drivers from driving all data, address, and acknowledge bus lines (although it may actually perform internal operations).

The inhibit line signal INH1* is used to inhibit RAM memory devices, whereas INH2* is used to inhibit ROM memory devices. INH1* allows ROM

---

[3]Some 8-bit microprocessors may also use some of the remaining address lines for "extended addressing": for "extended memory addressing" they may use lines A16*–A23*, while for "extended I/O device addressing" they may use lines A8*–A15*.

[4]In some early 8-bit microprocessors (like the Intel 8080A), the 8-bit I/O device address is duplicated onto the next high-order address byte A8*–A15*. While this is considered an acceptable procedure, it is not recommended for new designs.

memory devices to override RAM devices when ROM and RAM memory are assigned the same memory space. INH2* allows auxiliary ROM to override ROM devices when ROM and auxiliary ROM memory are assigned the same memory space.

These two signals INH1* and INH2* may also be used to allow memory-mapped I/O devices to override RAM and ROM devices, respectively.

Thus, a RAM device is considered a bottom priority slave. A ROM device or memory-mapped I/O device is considered a middle priority slave, which may assert INH1* to inhibit the bus activity of a bottom priority slave. An auxiliary or "bootstrap" ROM device is considered a top priority slave. It may assert INH2* to inhibit the bus activity of a middle priority slave or INH1* to inhibit a bottom priority slave as well. When both a middle priority inhibiting slave and a top priority inhibiting slave are activated, INH1* will be asserted by (usually open collector) drivers on both devices.

Data Lines (D0*–D15*)

Sixteen bidirectional data lines (denoted as D0*–D15*, with D15* the most significant), constitute the system data bus, and are used to exchange 8- and 16-bit data with memory and I/O slaves. Data read and data write are always specified relative to the current master. Data transmitted by the current master to a slave is called "data write." Data received by the current master from a slave is called "data read." The data lines are driven by the current master on write operations, and by the addressed slave (memory or I/O) on read operations. Data bus lines are always driven by three-state drivers.

Both memory and I/O cycles can support 8-bit (byte operation) or 16-bit (word operation) data transfers. This allows both 8-bit masters and slaves and 16-bit masters and slaves to co-exist in a single system. In 8-bit masters, only lines D0*–D7* are valid. The details of the 8- and 16-bit data transfer operation are given in the next chapter after methods of organizing and accessing memory are discussed.

Control Lines

Constant Clock Line (CCLK★)

The constant clock provides a clock signal at constant frequency which may be used by masters or slaves as a master clock. It is driven by one and only one source within the system and provides a timing source for any or all modules on the bus. The control and timing for all bus cycles, whether they are cycles of the permanent master or cycles of the temporary master in control of the bus, must be derived from this clock. In a multi-master system, only one of the masters shall have its clock connected to the bus. (Therefore, each bus master must have the capability of generating an acceptable clock that optionally can be connected to, or disconnected from, the system bus.)

Byte High Enable Line (BHEN★)

This signal is used to specify that data will be transferred on the high-order eight data lines D8*–D15*; i.e., it enables the upper byte of a 16-bit word to drive the data bus lines. This signal is used only on systems that incorporate 16-bit memory or I/O slaves. Thus, 8-bit microprocessor CPUs do not issue this type of signal. In the proposed IEEE S-100 bus standard two signal lines control the 16-bit transfers: sixteen request (sXTRQ*) and sixteen acknowledge (SIXTN*).

Read Command Lines (MRDC★ and IORC★)

The two read commands, memory read command (MRDC*) and I/O read command (IORC*), initiate the same basic type of operation. An active read command line indicates to the slave that the address lines are carrying a valid address; MRDC* indicates that a memory address is valid on the address lines, while IORC* indicates that an I/O device address is valid on the address lines. A read command additionally indicates that the slave is to place its data on the data bus.

Write Command Lines (MWTC★ and IOWC★)

The two write commands, memory write command (MWTC*) and I/O write command (IOWC*), also initiate the same basic type of operation. Similar to the read commands, an active write command line indicates to the slave that the address lines are carrying a valid address: MWTC* indicates that a memory address is valid on the address lines, while IOWC* indicates that an I/O device address is valid on the address lines. A write command additionally indicates that the master data on the data lines is stable and can be accepted by the addressed slave.

Transfer Acknowledge Line (XACK★)

Since all exchanges on the system bus are asynchronous, they involve handshaking. Therefore, the addressed (memory or I/O) slave must provide the master with an acknowledge signal in response to the transfer control (read or write) command. The transfer acknowledge (XACK*) signal is issued by the addressed slave to indicate that the commanded read or write operation is complete, and that the data has been placed on, or accepted from, the data lines. This XACK* allows the master to complete the current bus cycle. If such an XACK* signal is not returned to the master, the bus master normally enters a "wait state" which it leaves when the slave asserts XACK*. While in a wait state, the master still has control of the system bus.

To avoid the possibility of an indefinite wait by the master (if a bus master addresses a nonexistent or malfunctioning slave, in which case an acknowledge will not be returned to the master), an optional bus time-out function may be implemented on the master to terminate a bus cycle after a preset interval, even if no acknowledge has been received.

The XACK* line may also be used as a special line commonly used by front panel devices to stop or single-step a bus master. It is also used in multi-microprocessor systems to force a master to wait for access to the system bus. As we will see later, the XACK* system signal is usually converted to the READY or WAIT signal (of the CPU bus) and applied directly to the respective microprocessor CPU input pin.

Initialize Line (INIT)*

Finally, the last system control signal of Figure 5.8 is the initialize (INIT*) signal, generated to reset the entire system to a known internal state. This signal may be generated by an external source or by any or all of the masters.

External Source

The INIT* may be initiated by the following two external sources:

(a) A power-on clear circuit (RC network) generates an INIT* signal which is held low until the power supplies reach their specific voltage outputs;
(b) A (debounced) reset button, which is sometimes provided on the system front panel for operator use.

In multi-master configurations, this externally generated INIT* signal resets all bus masters.

Master

Sometimes a software command can be implemented by a master to assert the INIT* line in order to reset external devices. The internal state of the master processor is not affected by such an internally generated INIT* signal.

This initialize INIT* system signal corresponds to the RESET signal (of the CPU bus) applied to the respective microprocessor CPU input pin.

5.3.2 The CPU Bus

As already mentioned, CPU bus signals vary from one microprocessor to another. In general, they may be divided functionally into the following groups:

(a) Address and data lines
(b) Status lines
(c) Control lines
(d) Interrupt lines
(e) Bus arbitration lines

As was done with the system bus, in this chapter only the first three of the above groups of the CPU bus lines are discussed. The other two groups (interrupt and bus arbitration lines) will be discussed in chapter 9. Figure 5.9 shows these lines of a representative microprocessor CPU, which are presented next.

Address and Data Lines

Address lines are used to carry memory and I/O device addresses. The 8-bit microprocessor CPUs provide 16-bit memory addresses and 8-bit I/O device addresses. The 16-bit microprocessor CPUs provide up to 16-bit I/O device addresses and memory addresses varying from twenty (Intel 8086) to twenty-four (National NS16032) bits.

As already mentioned, most microprocessor CPUs use the same lines to multiplex address bits with data bits (one exception being the Motorola 68000 CPU, which provides twenty-three address lines[5] and sixteen separate data lines) to form what is called the multiplexed "address/data bus." In some cases, the remaining CPU address lines or some or all of the data lines may be multiplexed to carry status signals as well (e.g., the Intel 8086 multiplexes the remaining four address lines A16–A19 with four status signals S3–S6; the Intel 8080A multiplexes the 8-bit status word with the 8-bit data).

Status Lines

Most microprocessor CPUs issue status signals at the start of every machine cycle. These status signals identify the nature of the (bus) cycle in progress, and qualify the nature of the address on the address bus. Figure 5.10 shows the symbolic names used for these status signal outputs for several representative microprocessor CPUs, and the cycle type that their respective binary combinations represent. (The IO/M of 8085 may be thought of as a control signal.)

Status signals can be used by external logic for various purposes, one being to expand the microprocessor's memory space, another being to monitor the status lines and detect a CPU bus cycle request by another master in multi-master configurations, and a third being to allow external devices (e.g., an in-circuit emulator or a special co-processor) to track the CPU instruction execution.

Some microprocessors multiplex their status output signals and others do not. Non-multiplexed status signals are issued by the Intel 8085, the Zilog Z8000, and the Motorola 68000 CPUs; each provides separate output pins for

---

[5]In 68000-based implementations, a 24-bit address actually is transferred to memory. The additional 24th address bit is generated by combining the address strobe ($\overline{AS}$) signal with the two data strobe lines ($\overline{UDS}$ and the $\overline{LDS}$) by means of external gating.

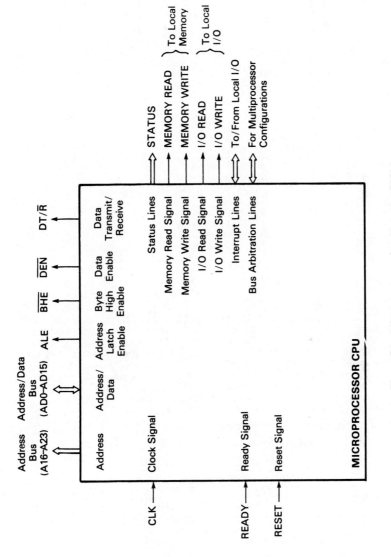

Figure 5.9 Microprocessor signals on the CPU bus.

D0-D7	Cycle Type
01000101	Instruction fetch
01000001	Memory read
00000000	Memory write
01100001	Stack read
00100000	Stack write
01000010	Input read
00001000	Output write
11000100	Interrupt acknowledge
01010001	Halt acknowledge
11010100	Interrupt acknowledge while halt

(a) Intel 8080A

IO/$\overline{M}$		S0	Cycle Type
0	1	1	Opcode fetch (OF)
0	1	0	Memory read (MR)
0	0	1	Memory write (MW)
1	1	0	I/O read (IOR)
1	0	1	I/O write (IOW)
1	1	1	Interrupt acknowledge (INA)
X	X	X	Bus idle (BI)

X = unspecified

(b)   Intel 8085.

$\overline{S2}$	$\overline{S1}$	$\overline{S0}$	Cycle Type
0	0	0	Interrupt acknowledge
0	0	1	Read I/O port
0	1	0	Write I/O port
0	1	1	Halt
1	0	0	Code access
1	0	1	Read memory
1	1	0	Write memory
1	1	1	Inactive

(c)   Intel 8086. *Courtesy Intel Corporation* [9]

ST_3–ST_0	Cycle Type	ST_3–ST_0	Cycle Type
0000	Internal operation	1000	Data memory request (Read/Write)
0001	Memory refresh	1001	Stack memory request (Read/Write)
0010	I/O reference (Input/Output)	1010	Stack memory request (EPU)
0011	Special I/O reference (e.g., to an MMU)	1011	Data memory request (EPU)
0100	Segment trap acknowledge	1100	Program reference, nth word
0101	Non-maskable interrupt acknowledge	1101	Instruction fetch, first word
0110	Non-vectored interrupt acknowledge	1110	Extension processor transfer
0111	Vectored interrupt acknowledge	1111	(Reserved)

(d)   Zilog Z8000. *Reproduced by permission.* © *1982 Zilog, Inc.* [15]

FC_2	FC_1	FC_0	Cycle Type
Low	Low	Low	(Unassigned)
Low	Low	High	User data
Low	High	Low	User program
Low	High	High	(Unassigned)
High	Low	Low	(Unassigned)
High	Low	High	Supervisor data
High	High	Low	Supervisor program
High	High	High	Interrupt acknowledge

(e)   Motorola 68000. *Courtesy of Motorola, Inc.* [10].

Figure 5.10   Status line outputs for several microprocessor CPUs.

these signals. Other microprocessor CPUs (like the Intel 8080A and 8086) multiplex their status signals with other output signals; in these cases, appropriate circuitry is required in the CPU interface to demultiplex the signals. Finally, there are also microprocessor CPUs (like the Zilog Z80 and Motorola 6800) that have no status signals at all.

Control Lines

Clock Line (CLK)

All microprocessor CPUs require a clock signal (CLK) for their operation. For some microprocessors this clock signal is generated by an external clock generator chip; for others, this clock generator is implemented on the same CPU chip, thus requiring only an external RC circuit. Furthermore, some microprocessor CPUs require a single-phase clock (the most common situation), whereas others require a two-phase clock. Examples of the latter case include the 8-bit Intel 8080A and Motorola 6800. In both products, the CLK signal corresponds to the φ_2 signal issued by their external clock generators.

The CLK signal establishes the CPU bus cycle time (i.e., controls timing for all bus cycles), and timing of the control signals bears a specified relationship to the master system clock. The CLK may be either (1) applied directly to the clock input of a slave module or (2) used in conjunction with the address latch enable (ALE) strobe issued by the CPU, or with the address lines, to generate "device select" signals for memory or I/O slaves.

Address Latch Enable Line (ALE)

Since the address is valid on the multiplexed address/data bus for (usually) only the first clock period, external CPU interface circuitry is required to latch this address and maintain it as valid for those memory and I/O devices that require a stable address for the entire bus cycle. The details of such CPU interfacing circuitry will be discussed in the next chapter. It suffices to say here that most microprocessor CPUs output an additional pulse (called address latch enable or ALE by the Intel 8085 and 8086, address strobe or $\overline{AS}$ by the Zilog Z8000 and Motorola 68000, or valid memory address or VMA by the Motorola 6800) which they assert while a valid memory address is present on the address/data bus.

Data Enable $(\overline{DEN})$ and Data Transmit/Receive Lines $(DT/\overline{R})$

In an analogous fashion, to satisfy the capacitive loading and drive requirements of larger systems, the data must be bufferred from the address/data bus by external circuitry. Again, most microprocessor CPUs provide one or more additional output pulses that may be used for this purpose: the Intel 8086 uses the data enable ($\overline{DEN}$) and data transmit/receive (DT/$\overline{R}$) to enable external transceivers and control the direction of data on the bus; the Zilog Z8000 uses the data strobe ($\overline{DS}$); the Motorola 68000 uses the lower data strobe ($\overline{LDS}$) and upper data strobe ($\overline{UDS}$). The Intel 8080A outputs the data bus in (DBIN) signal to indicate that its data bus is in the input state. This signal may be connected to the direction control input of external bidirectional bus drivers so that the correct flow of data on the bus is maintained.

The above-mentioned output CPU pulses provide the appropriate timing to guarantee isolation of the multiplexed CPU address/data bus from the system during the first clock period in which the CPU bus carries the address, and to eliminate bus contention with the CPU during read and write bus cycles.

Byte High Enable Line ($\overline{BHE}$)

The 16-bit microprocessor CPUs also issue the $\overline{BHE}$ signal, which corresponds to the earlier-mentioned BHEN* system bus signal. The Intel 8086 calls the signal byte high enable ($\overline{BHE}$); the Zilog Z8000 calls it byte/$\overline{word}$ (B/$\overline{W}$); the Motorola 68000 calls it upper data strobe ($\overline{UDS}$). The $\overline{BHE}$ signal is issued during the first clock period of a bus cycle and used in conjunction with the A0 (least significant address) line to generate select logic for memory banks (discussed in the next chapter).

READ and WRITE Lines

The various microprocessor products use different names for the read and write control signals transmitted to memory and to the I/O devices. These are shown in Figure 5.11, which is a subset of Figure 4.11 of chapter 4. Usually, these control signals are directly available from the microprocessor CPU itself. An exception to this is the Intel 8080A whose read and write signals are generated instead from an external system controller, which provides separate read/write signals for memory ($\overline{MEMR}$ and $\overline{MEMW}$) and for I/O ($\overline{I/OR}$ and $\overline{I/OW}$) devices.

The distinction between read or write to memory address space or to I/O address space is made differently by the various microprocessors:

(a) The Motorola products (6800 and 68000) perform "memory-mapped I/O," (in which both memory and I/O are mapped on the same address space), and, therefore, no additional control signal is required to distinguish between the two spaces.
(b) Other microprocessor CPUs (e.g., the Intel 8085, Zilog Z80 and Intel 8086) provide two separate output pins for the direct generation of these read ($\overline{RD}$) and write ($\overline{WR}$) control signals.

Distinguishing between memory address space and I/O address space references is also done differently. The Intel 8085 and 8086 provide one

Microprocessor CPU Signals

Operation	Intel 8080A†	Intel 8085 and 8086	Zilog Z80	Zilog Z8000	Motorola 6800 and 68000
MEMORY READ	$\overline{\text{MEMR}}$ = Low	$\overline{\text{RD}}$ = Low, IO/$\overline{\text{M}}$ = Low	$\overline{\text{RD}}$ = Low, $\overline{\text{MREQ}}$ = Low	W/$\overline{\text{R}}$ = Low, $\overline{\text{MREQ}}$ = Low	R/$\overline{\text{W}}$ = High
MEMORY WRITE	$\overline{\text{MEMW}}$ = Low	$\overline{\text{WR}}$ = Low, IO/$\overline{\text{M}}$ = Low	$\overline{\text{WR}}$ = Low, $\overline{\text{MREQ}}$ = Low	W/$\overline{\text{R}}$ = High, $\overline{\text{MREQ}}$ = Low	R/$\overline{\text{W}}$ = Low
I/O READ	$\overline{\text{I/OR}}$ = Low	$\overline{\text{RD}}$ = Low, IO/$\overline{\text{M}}$ = High	$\overline{\text{RD}}$ = Low, $\overline{\text{IORQ}}$ = Low	W/$\overline{\text{R}}$ = Low, $\overline{\text{MREQ}}$ = High	R/$\overline{\text{W}}$ = High (Memory-Mapped I/O)
I/O WRITE	$\overline{\text{I/OW}}$ = Low	$\overline{\text{WR}}$ = Low, IO/$\overline{\text{M}}$ = High	$\overline{\text{WR}}$ = Low, $\overline{\text{IORQ}}$ = Low	W/$\overline{\text{R}}$ = High, $\overline{\text{MREQ}}$ = High	R/$\overline{\text{W}}$ = Low (Memory-Mapped I/O)

† Not directly available from the microprocessor CPU itself.

Figure 5.11 The control signals issued by various microprocessors to perform read and write to/from memory and I/O devices.

additional output line IO/$\overline{M}$ (IO/$\overline{M}$ = low for memory and IO/$\overline{M}$ = high for I/O references) while the Zilog Z80 has two additional control lines ($\overline{MREQ}$ = low for memory and $\overline{IORQ}$ = low for I/O references).

(c) Finally, the Zilog Z8000 has a single output pin W/$\overline{R}$ whose value defines a read (W/$\overline{R}$ = low) and write (W/$\overline{R}$ = high) operation. The distinction between memory address space and I/O address space is made via a second output signal $\overline{MREQ}$ ($\overline{MREQ}$ = low for memory and $\overline{MREQ}$ = high for I/O references).

To generate the system command signals MRDC* and MWTC* discussed earlier, the above output CPU signals must be encoded properly by external circuitry.

READY Line

The READY input signal is used by most microprocessors to accommodate memory and I/O devices that cannot transfer information at the maximum CPU bus bandwidth. When the CPU receives the READY signal, it knows that the requested action has been completed and that the addressed memory or I/O device has placed data on, or accepted data from, the data lines. This allows the CPU to complete the current bus cycle. If it does not receive a READY signal, the CPU will normally enter a wait state. At the same time, it will issue appropriate control signals to inform the other system modules that the CPU is now in a wait state (e.g., the Intel 8080A issues a WAIT signal, whereas the Intel 8086 maintains status lines output $\overline{S0}$, $\overline{S1}$ and $\overline{S2}$ levels active during wait states). While the CPU is in a wait state, it still has control of the CPU bus.

When a system bus exists, the XACK* signal issued by a slave becomes the READY signal applied to the microprocessor. In some microprocessors, READY is applied directly to a respective input pin of the CPU (e.g., to the READY pin of the Intel 8085, the WAIT pin of the Zilog Z80 and Z8000, or the $\overline{DTACK}$ pin of the Motorola 68000). In others, READY is applied to the external clock generator, as is done with the RDYIN signal applied to the 8224 clock generator of the Intel 8080A (Figure 6.9 in chapter 6), or with the RDY signal applied to the 8284 clock generator of the Intel 8086 (Figure 6.8 in chapter 6). In the latter case, the clock generator synchronizes the CPU READY input with the clock.

Depending upon the size and characteristics of the system, READY logic may take one of two approaches: "normally ready" and "normally not ready."

"Normally Ready" Technique

This technique is used for small, single-CPU microcomputer systems. In these, the system is "normally ready," and all slave modules are assumed to operate at the maximum CPU bus bandwidth. If the addressed memory or I/O slave is not able to perform the data transfer at this maximum CPU bus transfer rate, it will not assert the READY signal. This will ensure that wait state clock periods will be inserted.

"Normally Not Ready" Technique

This is the classical implementation that keeps the system "normally not ready." It is used for large multiprocessor systems, or systems with slow devices and large propagation delays. When the selected slave has sufficient time to respond to a (read, write, or interrupt acknowledge) signal it received from the master, it asserts the READY signal to tell the CPU that the slave is ready to receive or transmit data, and to allow it to advance the bus cycle. If a slave does not respond in time, wait clock periods will be inserted in the bus cycle.

RESET Line

Almost all microprocessors provide a RESET input pin which resets the processor to a known internal state. The earlier-mentioned initialize system signal INIT* becomes the RESET signal when applied to the microprocessor CPU. For the Intel 8080A or the 8086 CPU, the RESET is applied to the external clock generator, which synchronizes it and re-transmits it to the CPU. (See Figures 6.8 and 6.9 in chapter 6).

The RESET input signal has different effects on the various microprocessor CPUs, as shown in the representative examples of Figure 5.12. In almost all cases, if a RESET occurs, the CPU address and data buses go to a high impedance state, all CPU control output signals go to the inactive state, the interrupt system is disabled, and the bus cycle ends. For those CPUs that have both user and supervisor modes of operation, the supervisor mode is entered and the appropriate vector is loaded into the program counter (PC) from the corresponding "reset location" of the vector table in memory.

5.4 BUS OPERATION

In this section we analyze the bus timing and the ways in which a master communicates with memory or I/O slave modules and exchanges data with them over the data bus.

Bus operation and timing are important factors in memory and peripheral device interfacing; they identify the type of information placed on the various buses and the time required to carry out bus transactions. This is very useful information to the system designer, in single-stepping and instruction-by-instruction debugging of the system under development, and in interfacing the microprocessor with memories and peripherals that have vastly different access times.

Intel 8080A/8085	Intel 8086	Zilog Z80	Zilog Z8000	Motorola 6800	Motorola 68000
• Resets INTE and HLDA internal flip-flops.	• Flags register is cleared and interrupts and single-stepping mode are disabled.	• Resets INTE flip-flop.	• Processor is forced to supervisor mode.	• Interrupts are disabled.	• Processor is forced to supervisor mode.
• Flags, accumulator, stack pointer, and registers are not cleared.	• DS, SS, ES and PC registers are cleared.	• Registers I and R are cleared.	• Non-segmented Z8002: a 2-word new program status is fetched from address 0.	• PC is loaded with $FFFE_{16}$ to begin the restart sequence.	• Processor interrupt priority mask is set at level 7.
• Program counter (PC) is cleared and program starts at location 0 in memory.	• CS register is set to $FFFF_{16}$. Execution starts from memory location $FFFF0_{16}$.	• PC is cleared and program starts at location 0 in memory.	• Segmented Z8001: a 4-word new program status is fetched from segment 0, offset 0 (from the new program status area.)		• Reset exception vector is referenced at location 0 in the supervisor program space.
					• The address contained in the first two words of the reset exception vector is fetched as the initial supervisor stack pointer.
					• The address contained in the last two words of the reset exception vector is fetched as the initial PC.

Figure 5.12 The effect of the RESET input on various microprocessors.

5.4.1 Definitions

Synchronous Versus Asynchronous Operation

Memory and input-output synchronization are essentially analogous. In a *synchronous* operation, all events take place within a specified time period. Timing and control signals are used to synchronize the master with memory and I/O slaves.

The *asynchronous* operation is based on a handshake process, in which an acknowledge signal (the XACK*) must be generated by the addressed slave in response to the (read or write) command it received from the master. In a read operation, when the addressed (memory or I/O) slave has fetched the data and placed it on the data bus it will assert the XACK* signal to indicate to the master that the slave has completed its operation. In a write operation (an I/O device's readiness is verified through a status-bit or signal), when the addressed slave has accepted the data from the data bus, it will again assert this XACK* signal to indicate to the master that the slave has completed its operation. The XACK* signal allows bus slaves to synchronize the operations of bus masters with conditions internal to the bus slave (e.g., data not ready). As already mentioned, the XACK* is applied (directly or indirectly) to a corresponding input pin of the master CPU.

A synchronous design may yield a higher speed and a lower number of control lines, but it imposes speed constraints on the external devices. An asynchronous design requires the additional acknowledge signal and somewhat more complex interface logic, but allows the use of devices of varying speeds in the same system.

Finally, an improved form of asynchronous bus operation has been introduced by the 32-bit Intel APX-432 microprocessor. This is the *packet-based* operation, which makes a more efficient use of the bus, as discussed in section 5.4.4.

Bus Cycles

All data transfer communications between a bus master and a slave are carried out in terms of a generalized bus cycle. The *bus cycle* is defined as the process whereby digital signals effect the transfer of data between the system modules by means of a fixed sequence of events initiated by a corresponding sequence of control signals. The bus cycle is generated by the bus master interface and responded to by the addressed slave interface.

Thus, bus cycles are an interface system phenomenon and may or may not be independent of the CPU machine cycles. In some microprocessors (like the Intel 8080A), machine cycles correspond to bus cycles. In others (like the Intel 8086) they operate asynchronously. The execution unit (EU) of the 8086 CPU executes the instruction using clock periods that have nothing to do with bus cycles. Bus cycles (mainly instruction fetch cycles) are carried out by the bus interface unit (BIU), and so far as the EU logic is concerned bus cycles do not exist.

In the 32-bit Intel APX-432 the two operations, instruction fetching and execution, have been implemented on separate chips: the APX-43201 instruction decoding unit (which decodes fetched instructions), and the APX-43202 microexecution unit (which executes decoded instructions from the 43201 and generates addresses for accessing memory).

The CPU interface circuitry provides the capability of generating and timing all possible bus cycles to transfer data to and from all bus slaves. The permanent master normally has control of the bus, which it relinquishes to a temporary bus master via a HOLD operation.

5.4.2   System Bus Operation

The system bus provides separate non-multiplexed address, data, and control lines, and its operation is asynchronous. Bus masters and slaves operate in a master-slave relationship, in which all transfers on the bus are controlled by handshake signals.

A permanent master executes a program by initiating a sequence of several bus cycle types. The specific type is signified by status (or function) signals issued by the master CPU. The three most important bus cycles are the *read* and *write* (from and to memory or I/O devices) and the *interrupt acknowledge*.

The asynchronous data transfer operation of the system bus[6] is shown in flowchart form in Figure 5.13, and has the following characteristics:

(a) First, the bus master places the memory or I/O device address on the address bus. If the operation is a write, the data is also placed on the data lines at this time.

(b) The master then generates a command (memory read or write, or I/O read or write), to activate the appropriate bus slave. It may also issue appropriate status signals.

For a read operation, the slave (memory or I/O device) address must be valid on the bus a few nanoseconds prior to the activation of the read command, and must remain valid on the bus for a few nanoseconds after the removal of the read command. The transition of the read command from active to inactive indicates that the master has received the data from the addressed slave.

---

[6]Asynchronous operation has also been implemented on the CPU bus of the Motorola 68000.

BUS MASTER   SLAVE

Address Slave Device
- Place address on address bus.
- Assert read (MRDC* or IORC*) or
  write (MWTC* or IOWC*) command.
- For a write: place data on data bus.
- Issue any other status signals.

Accept or Issue Data
- Decode address.
- For a read: place data on data bus.
- For a write: accept data from data bus.
- Assert Transfer Acknowledge XACK*.

Acquire Data or Terminate Transfer
- For a read: latch data.
- For a write: remove data from data bus.
- Negate read (MRDC* or IORC*) or
  write (MWTC* or IOWC*) command.
- Remove address from address bus.

Terminate Cycle
- Negate Transfer Acknowledge XACK*.
- For a read: remove data from data bus.

Start Next Cycle

Figure 5.13 The flowchart for a read or write operation on the asynchronous system bus.

For a write operation, both address and data must be valid on the respective lines a few nanoseconds prior to the activation of the write command (thus, data may be latched on either the leading or trailing edge of the command). The write command, the address, and the data are not removed by the master from the bus until the master is properly notified by the slave (through a transfer acknowledge signal) that data has been accepted.

(c) The slave then decodes the address. If it is a read operation, the slave places the data on the data lines. If it is a write operation, the slave accepts the data from the data lines. In either case, the slave asserts the transfer acknowledge signal, indicating to the master that it has completed its operation.

(d) If it is a read operation, after having received the transfer acknowledge signal, the bus master will latch the data from the data lines, and terminate the read cycle by removing the read command from the bus. If it is a write operation, after having received the transfer acknowledge signal, the bus master will remove data from the data lines and terminate the write cycle by removing the write command from the bus. In either case, the master also removes the address from the address lines.

(e) The slave terminates its cycle by negating the transfer acknowledge signal,[7] and, for a read operation, also by removing the data from the bus.

Figure 5.14 shows the basic timing for the read and write data transfer operations on the system bus.

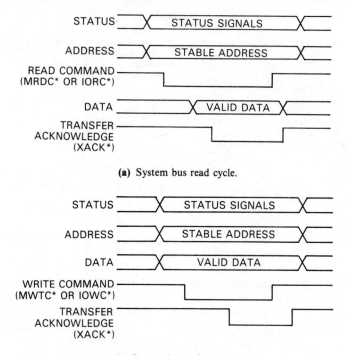

(a) System bus read cycle.

(b) System bus write cycle.

Figure 5.14   Basic timing for the system bus read and write cycles [3]. (Note: Since the cycles are asynchronous, the time scale is not necessarily linear.)

5.4.3   CPU Bus Operation

Information exchange on the CPU bus is also based on the execution of CPU bus cycles, and it is a synchronous operation coordinated by the CLK signal of the clock generator. The CLK signal also determines the duration of each state T_i.

---

[7]The transfer acknowledge signal may also be removed from the bus within a specified time interval after the (read or write) command has been removed from the bus.

Non-multiplexed CPU Bus Lines

Let us first consider those CPUs that provide separate lines for the address
and data buses (e.g., the Intel 8080A, Zilog Z80, Motorola 6800 and Motorola
68000). In this case, the CPU bus basic read and write cycles have the timing
shown in Figure 5.15. The activities carried out during the first three states, T_1,
T_2, and T_3, of the bus cycle were discussed in section 4.4.1 of chapter 4 (also see
Figure 4.14 of that chapter). In Figure 5.15 it is assumed READY is asserted,
and so no wait state intervenes between states T_2 and T_3. Also included here is
the ALE (or $\overline{AS}$, or VMA) signal that most microprocessor CPUs issue to
indicate the placing of a valid address on the address bus. The READ and
WRITE control signals shown here should be replaced by the proper combination of signals used by the specific CPU to distinguish between read and
write operations to memory or I/O address space, as discussed in section 5.3.2
(Figure 5.11).

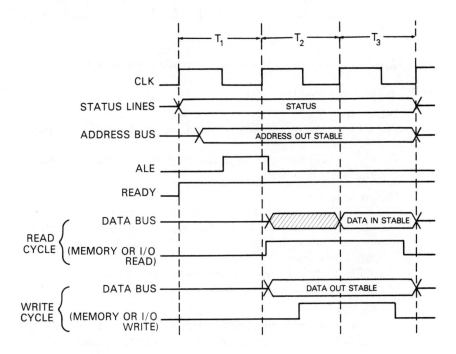

Figure 5.15 Basic timing for the CPU bus read and write cycles (*non-multiplexed* address and
data buses, synchronous operation).

The execution of an instruction is carried out by concatenating a number of
such CPU bus cycles. Two examples follow.

Example 5.1

Consider a simple 2-word *add immediate* instruction, the first word of which is the op code and the second, the immediate operand. Also assume that the data bus width equals that of a word and the address bus width equals that of an address. Therefore, two bus cycles will be required to fetch and execute this instruction from memory. The first cycle will be an "instruction fetch" cycle, and the second will be a "memory read" cycle. The corresponding timing relatonships are shown in Figure 5.16.

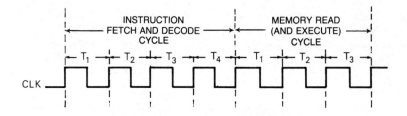

Figure 5.16 Timing relationships for the 2-word "add immediate" instruction.

(1) *Instruction Fetch (and Decode) Cycle*

- During state T_1:
  The CPU issues appropriate status to identify the cycle type (here, instruction fetch status).
  The CPU places the contents of the program counter on the address bus and issues the ALE.

- During state T_2:
  The CPU asserts the MEMORY READ signal, thus causing the selected memory module to fetch data and place it on the data bus. (It is assumed that the duration of the clock period is greater than the memory's maximum access time.)
  The CPU increments the program counter internally.
  (READY is assumed to be valid here).

- During state T_3:
  Since this is an instruction fetch cycle, the CPU reads the op code off the data bus and places it into the CPU's instruction register.

- During state T_4:
  The instruction is decoded and identified as a 2-word instruction, and, therefore, a new bus cycle must start to fetch the second word (the immediate operand). Thus, the CPU starts a memory read bus cycle.

(2) *Memory Read Cycle*

The activities carried out during the three new states, T_1, T_2, and T_3, are similar to those of the instruction fetch cycle, with the following differences:

- The CPU issues appropriate status information to identify this cycle now as a "memory read cycle."
- The data read by the CPU from the data bus will now be placed in another internal register and not in the instruction register.
- The internal immediate add operation is carried out during the last portion of this second machine cycle.[8]

Thus, the execution of this 2-word immediate instruction requires two CPU bus cycles and a total of seven clock periods or states. If the microprocessor operates from a 2 MHz clock (clock period = state = 500 nsec), then it will process this instruction in 7×500 nsec = 3.5 μsec time.

Figure 5.17 shows the complete timing of events on the non-multiplexed CPU bus for the execution of this immediate instruction.

Some new information, however, has now been included in Figure 5.17: the arrows indicating the cause-effect relationship among the various signals on the CPU bus lines (the "tail" designates the cause and the "head" designates the effect), and the control signal READY. During the *instruction fetch* cycle, arrow ① indicates that after having placed the address on the address bus, the CPU issues the MEMORY READ signal to the selected memory module. At the start of state T_2, memory places the fetched word on the data bus, and informs the CPU that the data requested is valid on the bus by issuing the READY signal (arrow ②). As soon as the CPU has read the data from the data bus, it acknowledges this by restoring the MEMORY READ signal (arrow ③). After awhile, the CPU terminates the holding of a valid address on the address bus, and memory terminates the holding of data on the data bus. Finally, the READY signal is restored to its inactive state (arrow ④), before the next MEMORY READ signal is issued.

Rather similar cause-effect relationships exist for signals on CPU bus lines during the *memory read* cycle (these relationships are not redrawn in Figure 5.17), since memory will be accessed again to read a data word.

Example 5.2

As a second example, consider the steps taken by an 8-bit microprocessor system in executing the 3-byte *direct instruction*

---

[8]For some instructions, the execute time is hidden by overlaping the CPU internal operations for the current instruction being executed with the fetch of the next instruction.

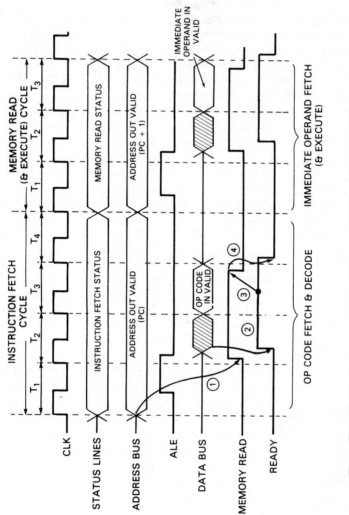

Figure 5.17 Timing of events on the *non-multiplexed* CPU bus for the execution of the 2-word *add immediate* instruction. (Two machine cycles or seven clock periods).

STA addr (store accumulator to memory location whose address is specified in byte 2 and byte 3 of the instruction).

It is assumed that this instruction is stored in three consecutive 8-bit memory locations, the first location containing the op code byte.

An instruction fetch cycle starts, T_1, T_2, and T_3 are used, and the op code byte is fetched from the first location. A fourth state, T_4, is used for internal instruction decoding. The steps and signals are similar to those of the instruction fetch cycle of the previous example.

A memory read cycle then starts, three new states, T_1, T_2, and T_3, are used, and the second byte is fetched from the second location (the updated value PC + 1 is now used as address). Since this second byte is not an immediate operand, but constitutes part of an address, it is now placed in an 8-bit address register X of the CPU. The steps and signals are similar to those of the first three states, T_1, T_2, and T_3, of the memory read cycle of the previous example.

Since this is a 3-byte instruction, another memory read bus cycle starts, three more states, T_1, T_2, and T_3, are used, and the third byte is fetched from the third location (again using another updated value of the program counter) and placed in an 8-bit address register,[9] Y, of the CPU.

The 3-byte instruction has been fetched from memory thus far. Since this is a store instruction, a memory write cycle will start to store the accumulator in memory. During the first state of this cycle, T_1, the CPU places a data address (the contents of its two address registers X and Y together) on the address bus. During the second state, T_2, the CPU places the data (the contents of its accumulator) on the data bus, and, instead of a MEMORY READ, it now issues a MEMORY WRITE control signal. Finally, the third state, T_3, is utilized to execute the write operation itself.[10]

Therefore, this instruction requires a total of four machine cycles or thirteen states. The timing of events on the non-multiplexed CPU bus for this example instruction "STA addr" is shown in Figure 5.18.

Multiplexed CPU Bus Lines

The basic CPU bus cycles of Figure 5.15 show the emitted status signals as valid for the duration of the whole bus cycle and applied on separate bus lines. Similarly, the address issued by the CPU is also shown as valid for the whole bus cycle, and placed on separate bus lines.

---

[9]In some microrpocessors, the general registers may be used as address registers, too. For example, the Intel 8080A usually uses the two general registers H and L as address registers.

[10]It was assumed here that the duration of the third state, T_3, is sufficiently long to include the write operation also. If it is not, a fourth state, T_4, is used for the write operation (which will increase the total number of states required to fourteen).

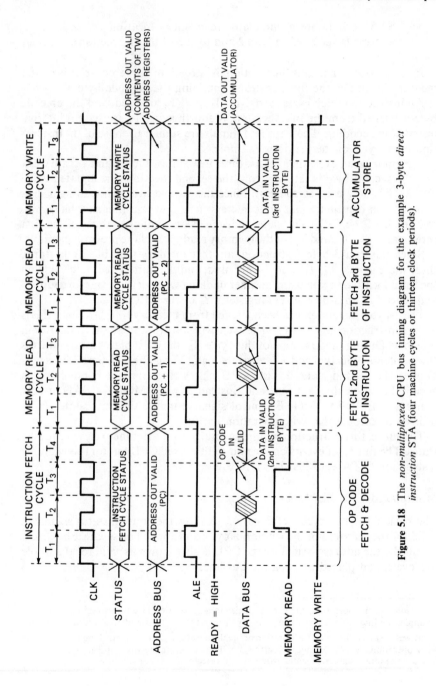

Figure 5.18 The *non-multiplexed* CPU bus timing diagram for the example 3-byte *direct instruction* STA (four machine cycles or thirteen clock periods).

However, this is not always the case. In many microprocessor CPUs, the status and/or address bits are placed on multiplexed CPU bus lines as shown in Figure 5.2.

The Intel 8080A Bus

The timing and synchronization of the 8-bit Intel 8080A CPU represents an example of early design. It is mentioned here because the 8080A influenced the structure of the S-100 bus and is still a widely used product. The operation is a "pseudo-synchronous" operation, that is, the timing of the control signals bears a specified relationship to the clock signal φ_2 (corresponding to the CLK signal discussed earlier).

As was previously mentioned, the Intel 8080A 8-bit data bus is used during state T_1 to transfer an 8-bit status word emitted by the CPU. The beginning of a new bus cycle is indicated by the rising edge of the SYNC signal, which closely follows the rising edge of the φ_2 clock pulse (see Figure 5.19). The SYNC signal is issued by the CPU and applied to the external clock generator chip. During the beginning of the SYNC signal, the address bus and the status lines (on the data bus) are changing to their values for the new cycle. Shortly after they are guaranteed stable, the clock generator asserts the $\overline{STSTB}$ status strobe. The $\overline{STSTB}$ corresponds to the ALE discussed earlier, and may be used as a latching signal to sample the address and status from the 8080A CPU in the current cycle. When the 8228 system controller is used, the $\overline{STSTB}$ signal is applied directly to it, which in turn generates the control signals ($\overline{MEMR}$, $\overline{MEMW}$, $\overline{I/OR}$, and $\overline{I/OW}$ of Figure 5.11) applied to the slave modules.

There are several ways to synchronize slave modules. One is to apply φ_2 output of the clock generator to the clock input of the slave. The other is to have their "device select signals" generated by decoding the CPU address and status lines in conjunction with the $\overline{STSTB}$ strobe. When the 8228 system controller is used, synchronization is accomplished by having the "device select signal" of each slave generated by combining address signals with either the φ_2 clock or with the control signals ($\overline{MEMR}$, $\overline{MEMW}$, $\overline{I/OR}$, $\overline{I/OW}$) issued by the 8228 system controller.

The READY input line is first sampled by the CPU on the rising edge of φ_2 during state T_2, and, if inactive, the CPU enters a wait state (not shown in Figure 5.19), sampling the READY line once every clock cycle on the rising edge of φ_2 until the slave is ready for data transfer.

The DBIN output is a generalized read strobe used to gate data from an addressed slave onto the data bus during a read (or input) operation. The DBIN read strobe is asserted by the CPU after a minimum specified time from the assertion of the $\overline{STSTB}$. The generalized $\overline{WR}$ strobe is used to write data from the data bus into the addressed slave (either the leading or the trailing

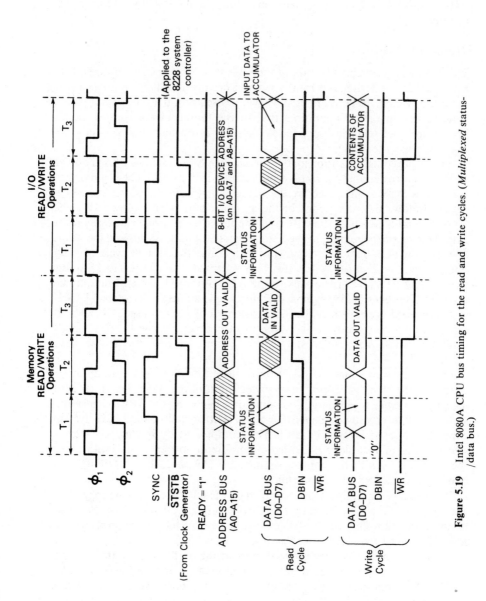

Figure 5.19 Intel 8080A CPU bus timing for the read and write cycles. (*Multiplexed* status-/data bus.)

edge of WR may be used). The write strobe $\overline{\text{WR}}$ may be asserted by the CPU after the completion of the interval during which the SYNC signal is active. Usually, both the DBIN and $\overline{\text{WR}}$ are applied to the 8228 system controller.

Memory read and write cycles are similar to input and output cycles with respect to timing, but they make different use of the status bits and the address bus. (For I/O operations, the 8-bit I/O device address is repeated on both the eight upper and eight lower address lines of the 16-bit address bus.)

Multiplexed Address/Data Lines

Most microprocessor CPUs, however, multiplex either part of or the whole address with the data on the same bus lines (address/data bus). Again, the address is valid on the multiplexed address/data bus during only the first state, T_1, of the bus cycle. These microprocessors also issue the ALE (or VMA or $\overline{\text{AS}}$) signal.

Figure 5.20 shows the timing of the basic read and write CPU bus cycles for a microprocessor (for example, the Intel 8085) that multiplexes the lower half of the 16-bit address with the 8-bit data on the same bus lines.

It is noticed that status signals which identify read or write cycles are issued on separate lines. In the timing diagram shown, a read operation is signified by the control signal $\overline{\text{RD}}$ = low, and a write operation, by the control signal $\overline{\text{WR}}$ = low. The value of the output signal $\text{IO}/\overline{\text{M}}$ distinguishes between memory and I/O operation: $\text{IO}/\overline{\text{M}}$ = low for memory operation and $\text{IO}/\overline{\text{M}}$ = high for I/O operation.

The basic CPU bus cycles for the 16-bit Zilog Z8000 (Figure 5.21) are quite similar to those of the Z80, with the following differences: the Z8000 has a 16-bit address/data bus that multiplexes the sixteen lower address bits with the 16-bit data; instead of two separate read and write control lines, it provides only one, called $\text{R}/\overline{\text{W}}$; the previous $\text{IO}/\overline{\text{M}}$ signal is now called $\overline{\text{MREQ}}$; and finally, it includes a data strobe ($\overline{\text{DS}}$) which indicates the time duration for valid data in and out of the CPU.

Finally, Figure 5.22 shows the basic CPU bus cycles for the 16-bit Intel 8086 microprocessor. It is evident here that the higher four address bits A16–A19 are multiplexed with the four status bits S3–S6, and that the CPU issues an additional signal, $\text{DT}/\overline{\text{R}}$, to control data bus transceivers (or buffers) signaling the direction of the data transfer ($\text{DT}/\overline{\text{R}}$ = low for read, $\text{DT}/\overline{\text{R}}$ = high for write operations). Like the Z8000, the 8086 also has a multiplexed 16-bit address/data bus.

As already mentioned, the 8086 includes the two independent units EU and BIU. All bus cycles are executed by the BIU, and only when a bus cycle is requested by the EU, or when it must fill the instruction queue. Thus, besides the wait states T_W that may be inserted between states T_3 and T_4, the BIU may also have additional "idle states (T_I)." These are clock periods in which there is no BIU activity occurring between bus cycles. They can occur when bus access is granted to a co-processor or in the case of executing "long" instructions (like multiply) in the EU.

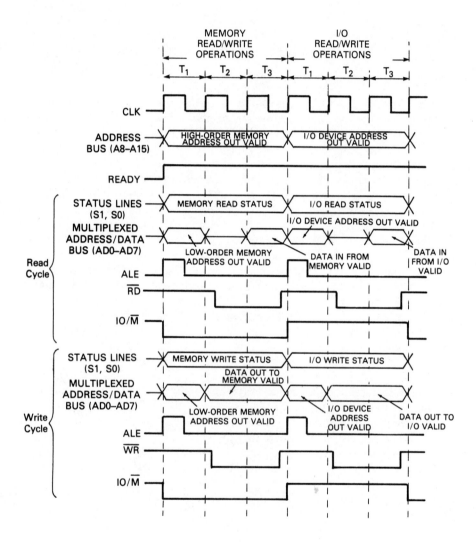

Figure 5.20   Intel 8085 CPU bus timing for read and write cycles. (*Multiplexed* address/data bus.)

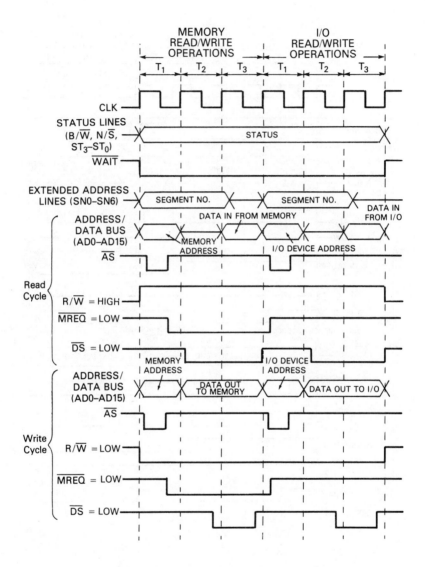

Figure 5.21 Zilog Z8000 CPU bus timing for the read and write cycles. (*Multiplexed* address/data bus.)

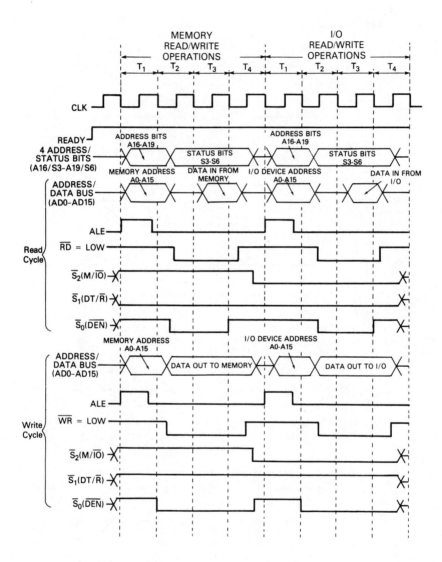

Figure 5.22 Intel 8086 CPU bus timing for the read and write cycles. (*Multiplexed* 16-bit address/data bus and *multiplexed* four address bits with four status bits.)

5.4.4 The 32-bit Intel APX 432 Bus Operation

The operation of the 32-bit Intel APX 432 bus (called the "interconnect bus") is based on the transmission of "packets" [4,5,12]. This is the standard way for processors to communicate with memory and each other. Processors include the 2-chip general data processor (GDP) and the interface processor (IP), which handles all communication with peripheral devices as shown in Figure 5.23.

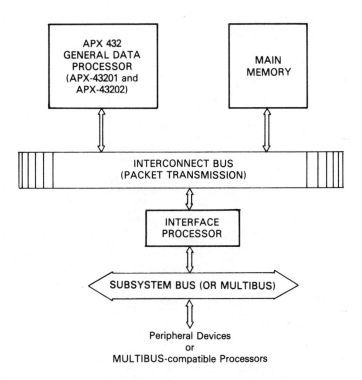

Figure 5.23 The configuration of a simple Intel APX 432 system.

Information exchange is done by putting requests and replies on separate packets. For example, in order for a processor to access a slave, it generates a request packet (which may include the address, byte count, request type, etc.) and places it on the interconnect bus. It expects a reply packet from the slave only if the request specified a read cycle (Figure 5.24). The packets are variable in length; a single request or reply may transmit from one to sixteen bytes of information. This makes more efficient use of the interconnect bus, since the processor ties up the bus only for the time required to transmit the packet.

(Remember that in previous bus implementations, the bus is tied up by the processor while waiting for an XACK* or READY* signal to be returned by the addressed slave). For a read operation, when the slave is ready, it will respond by returning a reply packet to the processor. In the interval, other processors may be using the interconnect bus.

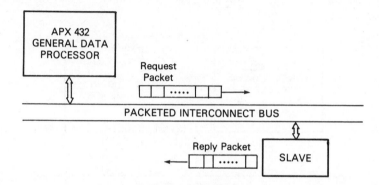

Figure 5.24 Requests and replies are quantized into packets. *Reprinted from* Electronics, *February 24, 1981. Copyright © 1981. McGraw-Hill, Inc. All rights reserved.*

Besides this efficient use of the bus, the designer can further improve system performance by widening the interconnect bus. Finally, a number of processors can be tied easily to the interconnect bus to form a multiprocessor system. Because of the packet format, a processor can send a message to one specific processor or broadcast it to several processors simultaneously (i.e., it can direct either one processor or a set of processors to start, stop, and redispatch).

EXERCISES

5.1 Describe the impact upon the instruction sequencing speed of multiplexed versus non-multiplexed data buses.

5.2 Consider two different microprocessors, one having an 8-bit address bus and the other, a 4-bit address bus. Compare the way each one performs direct access to a memory of 64K bytes capacity and the time each requires for this access.

5.3 Given the Intel 8080A operating with a 2 MHz clock. During execution of instruction IN 10,

(a) What is the information on the address bus, and how long does it last?

(b) What is the control signal issued by the 8080A CPU, and how long does it last?

5.4 Draw the necessary interface circuit to convert the Intel 8085 CPU bus into an Intel 8080A CPU bus.

5.5 Draw the necessary interface circuit to convert the Zilog Z8000 CPU bus control signals to the IEEE 796 system bus MRDC* and MWTC* commands.

5.6 Repeat Exercise 5.5 for the IEEE 796 system bus IORC* and IOWC* commands.

5.7 Draw the CPU bus timing diagram (analogous to that shown in Figure 5.18) for executing the 3-byte direct instruction of Example 5.2 on the Intel 8085 microprocessor.

5.8 Assume a hypothetical simple computer having sixteen different instructions, a maximum addressable memory space of 256 4-bit locations, and a CPU driven by a 2 MHz clock (CLK). How many machine cycles are required and how many μsec does it take to process:

(a) A 4-bit instruction?

(b) An immediate instruction whose operand is four bits long?

(c) A one-address direct STA instruction?

For each of the above, (a), (b), and (c), draw the possible respective bus timing diagrams showing the most important information traveling on the CPU buses.

5.9 Draw the CPU bus timing diagram for the instruction cycle of the "LHLD addr" instruction for

(a) the Intel 8080

(b) the Intel 8085.

5.10 Consider the main program and two nested subroutines, SUB1 and SUB2, located in memory as shown below. Assume that the SP register initially contains $FFFF_{16}$. Draw the CPU bus timing diagram with the most important signals of the Intel 8085 for the instruction cycle (fetch and execute) of the two CALL and two RET instructions.

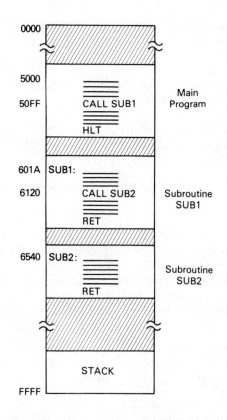

REFERENCES AND BIBLIOGRAPHY

[1] Banning, J., "Z-Bus and Peripheral Support Packages Tie Distributed Computer Systems Together," *Electronic Design,* November 22, 1979, pp. 144–50.

[2] IEEE Task 696.1/D2, "Standard Specification for S-100 Bus Interface Devices," *Computer*, July 1979, pp. 28–52.

[3] IEEE Task P796/D2, "Proposed Microcomputer System 796 Bus Standard," *Computer,* October 1980, pp. 89–105.

[4] Intel Corporation, *Introduction to the iAPX 432 Architecture,* (171821–001), Santa Clara, CA., 1981.

[5] Intel Corporation, *iAPX 432 General Data Processor Architecture Reference Manual,* (171860–001), Santa Clara, CA, 1981.

[6] Intel Corporation, *MCS-80/85 Family User's Manual*, (121506-001), Santa Clara, CA, October 1979.

[7] Intel Corporation, *The 8086 Family User's Manual*, (9800722-03), Santa Clara, CA, October 1979.

[8] Lesea, A. and R. Zaks, *Microprocessor Interfacing Techniques*, Berkeley, CA: SYBEX, Inc., 1977.

[9] Lewin, M.H., "Integrated Microprocessors," *IEEE Transactions on Circuits and Systems,* vol. CAS-22, no. 7, July 1975, pp. 57 7–85.

[10] Motorola, Incorporated, *16-Bit Microprocessing Unit*, (ADI-814-R1), Austin, TX, 1980.

[11] Ogdin, C.A., "Microcomputer Buses," *Mini-Micro Systems,* June–July 1978.

[12] Rattner, J. and W.W. Lattin, "Ada Determines Architecture of 32-bit Microprocessor," *Electronics,* February 24, 1981, pp. 119–26.

[13] Russell, R. and G. Alexy, *The 8086 Book,* New York: Osborne/McGraw-Hill, 1980.

[14] Zilog, Incorporated, *Z-bus Specification,* Cupertino, CA, 1979.

[15] Zilog, Incorporated, *1982/83 Data Book*, Cupertino, CA, 1982.

Chapter 6

CPU INTERFACE AND MEMORY SYSTEM DESIGN

6.1 INTRODUCTION

Section 6.2 of this chapter covers the CPU supporting circuitry (referred to as the "CPU interface") required to convert the CPU bus signals to the non-multiplexed signals of the system bus. Sections 6.3 and 6.4 discuss the organization, design, and operation of the memory system. The chapter concludes with a discussion on byte and word accessing for 16-bit memory (and I/O) slaves and the transfer of both 8- and 16-bit data on the system bus for configurations that allow both 8-bit masters and slaves and 16-bit masters and slaves to coexist in a single system.

6.2 CPU INTERFACE CIRCUITRY

As already mentioned, not all microprocessor CPUs provide the separate, non-multiplexed, address and data buses that are required by the system slaves. Furthermore, the required control and timing signals are not always directly available to the slaves from the microprocessor CPU itself. Similarly, not all control signals generated at various points in the system and transmitted to the bus master are applied directly to the microprocessor CPU input pins; in some cases they are applied instead to a support device external to the CPU chip. Finally, some early microprocessor designs multiplexed the CPU data lines to carry status information as well.

In general, an *interface* is a shared boundary between parts of a microcomputer system, through which information is conveyed. The *interface system* consists of the device-dependent elements (which include all driving and receiving circuits, connectors, and timing and control protocols) of an interface necessary to effect unambiguous data transfer between devices [7]. Information is communicated between devices via the bus, and each device conforms to the interface system definition. CPU interfacing circuitry may be required for several reasons: to demultiplex and/or buffer the CPU address and data lines, to interface CPU with other system modules by providing them with appropriate system control signals, or to receive from them system control signals and apply them in turn to the CPU. The complexity of this circuitry (i.e., the number of interface components) depends upon the specific microprocessor CPU, and the size and complexity of the final system.

Figure 6.1 shows the general configuration of a bus master with all the CPU interface circuitry essential for converting the multiplexed CPU bus to the non-multiplexed system bus. Like the previous chapter, this chapter covers the interfaces to generate system address, data, and control lines. Again, the top two interface boxes of Figure 6.1 required for multi-master configurations and I/O interrupt operation, are left to be discussed in chapter 9.

6.2.1 Clock Generator

The clock generator is an external CPU support circuit necessary for microprocessors to synchronize their operation. Figure 6.2 shows the input and output signals of the clock generator. Every microprocessor is specified to operate with a given minimum frequency.

A clock generator is driven by either a series resonant crystal or an external frequency source; the selection is done according to the logic value that the clock's "driving source" input pin has. The clock generator's CLK output corresponds to the master clock, and provides a timing source for any or all modules on the CPU bus. For those microprocessors that require two phases (e.g., the Intel 8080A and Motorola 6800), the clock generator used provides two output signals, φ_1 and φ_2. A clock generator may also receive a SYNC signal from the CPU that identifies the beginning of a new bus cycle. Two other input pins of the clock generator are the RESET and READY (the 8284 clock generator used with the Intel 8086 CPU has two such ready input pins, RDY1 and RDY2). When a RESET or READY signal is applied (the corresponding system bus signals are the INIT* and XACK*) to these pins, the clock generator synchronizes it and re-transmits it to the respective input pin of the microprocessor CPU. Finally, another output signal may be the status strobe (the $\overline{\text{STSTB}}$ of the 8224 clock generator used with the Intel 8080A), which is asserted by the clock generator shortly after the beginning of the received SYNC to indicate that the CPU address and status output lines are guaranteed to be stable.

6.2.2 Bus Receivers and Drivers

To exchange information over the bus, each module must include bus receivers and drivers. *Bus Receivers* are usually composed of latching flip-flops or "D-latches" to hold the information as long as required. Bus information is latched up by the flip-flops when an appropriate strobe control signal is applied to them [13]. This latching strobe should be applied after the information has been placed on the bus and enough time has elapsed for the informa-

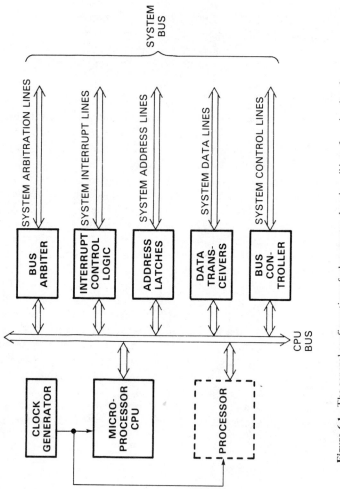

Figure 6.1   The general configuration of a bus master showing all interface circuitry for converting the CPU bus to the system bus.

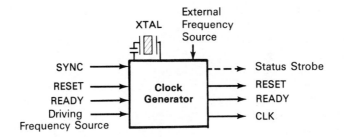

Figure 6.2 Input and output signals of the clock generator.

tion to reach a stable state (i.e., "information valid"). This is shown in the following diagram [13], where the arrows indicate the instances at which the latching flip-flops are loaded. More than one receiver may be connected to the same bus.

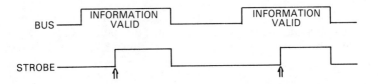

Bus drivers or *buffers* are required to place information on the bus. Furthermore, a bus may be driven by more than one source. A semiconductor device driving the bus may have either open-collector or three-state (tri-state) outputs. Devices with *open-collector* outputs have only two output states: logic 0 (zero), i.e., the gate pulls the output line to logic 0 (zero), using an active circuit element (the gate's internal output transistor); logic 1 (one), i.e., the output line is pulled back to logic 1 (one) by a passive circuit element (an external pull-up resistor). Devices that have open collector outputs allow the logical AND among their outputs by simply tying these outputs together. For this reason, this connection is also called *wire-ANDed* or *AND-tied.* The opposite holds for the *tri-state* devices, which offer better performance in bus-structured designs when used as bus drivers. A tri-state device has both an active pull-up transistor and an active pull-down transistor in its output (to define the logic 1 (one) and logic 0 (zero) states), but a third, extra terminal is used to disable the output. When the output is disabled, it is said that the output *floats.* This third state is often called the *high-Z* or *high-impedance state.* When a device is placed in its high-impedance state, it is considered to be electrically disconnected from the bus. Thus, many tri-state devices (drivers) may be connected to the same bus, with their respective outputs forming the logical OR with each other. For this reason this connection is also called *wire-ORed, OR-tied,* or *bus configuration.* Appropriate control (or select) signals must be applied to select one of them, while holding all other drivers "disconnected" from the bus.

Figure 6.3a shows a tri-state data bus driver transmitting information on the bus for the D-latch data bus receiver, in synchronism with a timing control circuitry. The 8-bit input information is placed on the bus with the beginning of the ENABLE signal (arrows A in Figure 6.3b), and latched by the receiver with the beginning of the STROBE signal (arrows B in Figure 6.3b). The specific receiver has been selected by placing its address on the address bus.

Finally, a *bidirectional* bus employs more than one set of drivers and more than one set of receivers. A circuit that is used both as transmitter and receiver is called a *transceiver.*

6.2.3   Demultiplexing the Address/Data Bus

Multiplexed Address/Data Bus

It was said in the previous chapter (see Figure 5.2) that most microprocessor CPUs issue the address (or a portion of it) on a multiplexed "address/data bus." Since the address is valid on these lines only for the first clock period of the bus cycle, and since most memory and I/O slaves require a stable address for the entire bus cycle, an external latch circuit is needed to latch the address. This is shown in Figure 6.4 for the 8-bit address/data bus of the Intel 8085 and the 16-bit address/data bus of the Zilog Z8000. Most microprocessor CPUs issue a control signal (the ALE of the Intel 8085 and Intel 8086, the $\overline{AS}$ of the Zilog Z8000 and Motorola 68000, or the VMA of the Motorola 6800) at the beginning of a new bus cycle to indicate that a valid address has been placed on the output lines. This signal may be used by the external address latch circuit to demultiplex the bus by latching the address. Although demultiplexing of the multiplexed address/data bus can be done locally at appropriate points in the system, the remainder of this chapter will assume that the bus is demultiplexed at the CPU. Thus, a separate "system address bus" will distribute the address throughout the system.

Figure 6.5 shows the demultiplexing of the 8086 CPU 20-bit bus. Functionally, these twenty lines are divided as follows: (1) sixteen bidirectional lines constitute the address/data bus (denoted as AD0–AD15), which is multiplexed to carry either the sixteen least significant bits of an address or 16-bit data: (2) the remaining four lines constitute an address/status bus (denoted as A16/S3–A19/S6) which is multiplexed to carry either the remaining four most significant bits of an address (A16–A19) or four status bits (S3–S6). Demultiplexing of these lines is done via the ALE signal in order to capture the address bits in external latches (such as the 8-bit 8282's) and generate the 20-bit system address A0–A19.

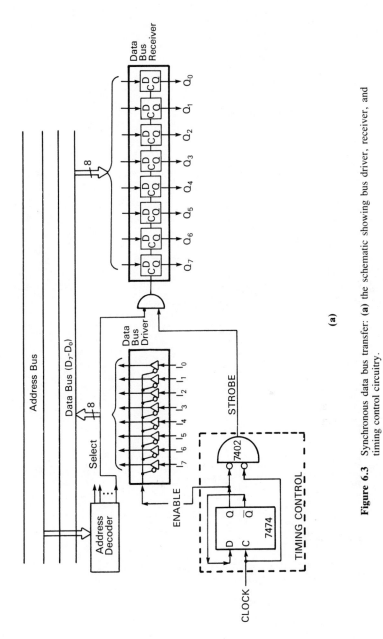

Figure 6.3 Synchronous data bus transfer: **(a)** the schematic showing bus driver, receiver, and timing control circuitry.

(a)

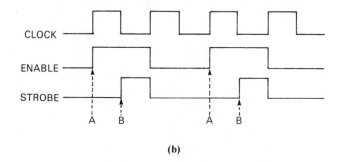

(b)

Figure 6.3 Synchronous data bus transfer: **(a)** the schematic showing bus driver, receiver, and timing control circuitry; **(b)** the corresponding timing diagram [13].

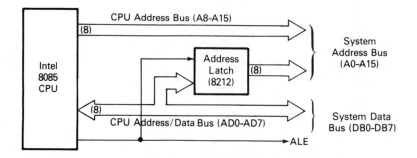

(a) Demultiplexing the Intel 8085 address/data bus.

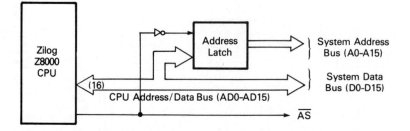

(b) Demultiplexing the Zilog Z8000 address/data bus.

Figure 6.4 Demultiplexing the address/data bus.

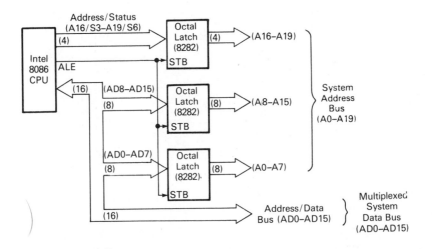

Figure 6.5 Demultiplexing the address from the Intel 8086 address/data bus (system data bus remains multiplexed) [11].

Logical to Physical Address Conversion Mechanism

"Logical" and "physical" addresses and the conversion mechanism required to translate from one to the other type are explained in detail in chapter 10. However, in this discussion of support circuitry to handle the CPU addresses, a few introductory comments are appropriate.

All addresses generated by a program are considered "logical addresses," whereas those applied to memory (or I/O devices) are considered "physical addresses." For those microprocessors that do not support both logical and physical address space (i.e., all 8-bit and smaller microprocessors), the two addresses are one and the same thing; the address issued by the microprocessor CPU is the address applied to memory or I/O slaves.

Advanced 16- and 32-bit microprocessors, however, support both spaces, and an "address conversion mechanism" is now required to translate logical into physical addresses. In this case, the address issued by the microprocessor CPU may or may not be the same as that applied to a slave. For example, the Intel 8086 contains this address conversion mechanism on the CPU chip (see Figure 4.2b in chapter 4); here, the address issued by the CPU is the same as that transmitted to the slave. Most of the other microprocessors, however (e.g., the Zilog Z8000, Motorola 68000, National NS16032, etc.), implement this mechanism on a separate external chip, the "memory management unit" (Figure 6.6). In this case, the logical address issued by the CPU is not the same as the physical address transmitted to memory or I/O slaves.

Unless explicitly specified otherwise, the term "address" by itself will refer for the remainder of this book to the "physical address."

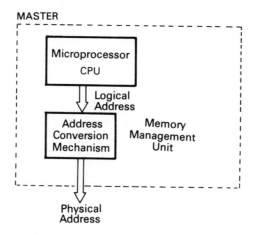

Figure 6.6 Logical addresses issued by the microprocessor CPU are not the same as physical addresses transmitted to memory or I/O slaves.

6.2.4 Buffering the Data Bus

If a microprocessor CPU multiplexes data with other information, this multiplexed data bus can either be used directly or be buffered. When memory or I/O devices are connected directly to the multiplexed CPU data bus, it is essential that they be prevented from corrupting the information (usually an address) present on this bus during the first state, T_1, of the bus cycle. Ways of preventing this are discussed in section 6.4.3. Most often, interfacing requirements become simpler if the alternative of buffering the data bus is followed. Buffering the multiplexed data bus also offers both increased drive current capability and capacitive load immunity. For the bidirectional data bus, this buffering is accomplished by using external bidirectional bus drivers, or *transceivers*. One or more special control signal is issued by the CPU, in order to control these transceivers, such as the $\overline{\text{DEN}}$ and $\text{DT}/\overline{\text{R}}$ signals discussed in section 5.3.2. Figure 6.7 shows an expanded version of Figure 6.5. In addition to demultiplexing the address from the address/data bus, the Intel 8086 $\overline{\text{DEN}}$ and $\text{DT}/\overline{\text{R}}$ signals control the two 8286 transceivers to provide a buffered system data bus D0–D15.

6.2.5 Redefining the CPU Control Signals as System Commands

The third and final CPU interface circuit of Figure 6.1 discussed here is the *bus controller* (or system controller), which is required to convert the control signals of the CPU bus to those of the system bus, and vice versa.

For small system configurations (one or two printed circuit boards) the CPU control signals may be used directly as system commands to interface

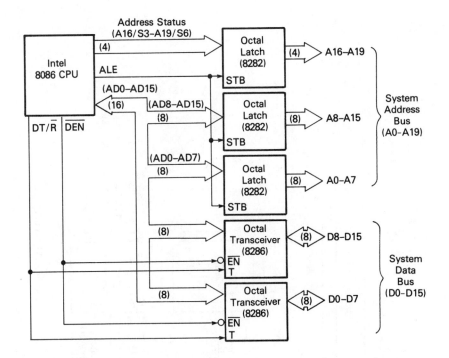

Figure 6.7 Demultiplexing the address from the Intel 8086 address/data bus and providing a buffered system data bus.

with memory and I/O devices. In larger configurations (two or more printed circuit boards or multi-microprocessor configurations), however, an external bus controller is usually required to redefine the CPU control signals and convert them to system commands.

Figure 6.8a shows the Intel 8086 "minimum mode" configuration for small systems without the bus controller, where the CPU itself issues the signals for the system command bus. Figure 6.8b shows the Intel 8086 "maximum mode" configuration for larger systems. In this configuration the bus controller generates the signals for the system command bus. Operating in synchronism with the CPU, the external bus controller also demultiplexes the three CPU status signals $\overline{S}_2$, $\overline{S}_1$, and $\overline{S}_0$, which are multiplexed with the $M/\overline{IO}$, $DT/\overline{R}$, and $\overline{DEN}$, respectively.

Figure 6.9 presents the Intel 8080A CPU interfacing. The 8080A multiplexes the 8-bit data bus to carry also the 8-bit status word emitted during state T_1 at the beginning of each machine cycle. As shown in Figure 6.9a, appropriate circuitry must be used to demultiplex the status information; the external latch latches the status word and then directs it to the gating array to

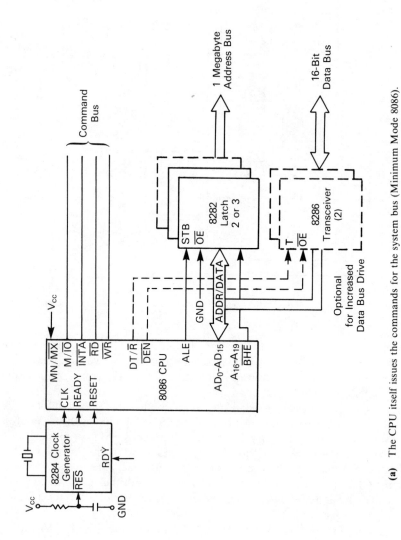

(a) The CPU itself issues the commands for the system bus (Minimum Mode 8086).

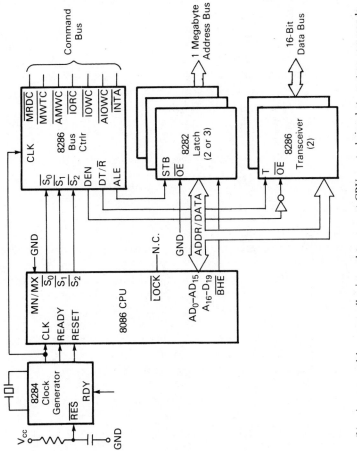

(b) An external bus controller is used to convert CPU control signals to system commands (Maximum Mode 8086).

Figure 6.8 Generating the system commands of an Intel 8086-based system. *Courtesy Intel Corporation)* [11].

produce the system signals required by slaves. Alternatively, the 8228 system controller may be used (Figure 6.9b). The 8228 includes the above status latch and gating array circuitry, along with a bidirectional bus driver. It demultiplexes the 8080A data bus, decodes the status word, and produces the system control signals. The 8228 and the CPU operate synchronously via the common 8224 clock generator (through the $\overline{STSTB}$). The status byte is latched for use at the beginning of each bus cycle (at the time SYNC is applied to the clock generator, which in turn issues the $\overline{STSTB}$ signal).

Figure 6.10 shows some CPU interface circuits for the Zilog Z8000. The status decoder is required to decode the four CPU status output lines (ST_3–ST_0) into all sixteen possible combinations to generate system control signals. The bidirectional buffers are controlled by data strobe ($\overline{DS}$) and read/write ($R/\overline{W}$) signals to provide buffered address/data lines. In systems that use DMA access, three-state buffers must be used (put in their high-Z state by $\overline{BUSACK}$). Finally, the address latches are controlled by the address strobe ($\overline{AS}$) to provide the 16-bit latched address bus.

6.3 MEMORY SYSTEM DESIGN

6.3.1 Introduction

After the CPU, memory represents the most important module of the microprocessor system. A memory slave communicates with the bus master under a master-slave protocol. It continuously monitors the bus, and, when addressed (or selected) by a master during a particular bus cycle, acts upon the control signals provided by the master (i.e., accepts or sends the data on the data bus lines).

The development of high-density, high-speed semiconductor memory has been the prime cause of the accelerated use of microprocessors. The great variety of memory types and manufacturing technologies forces the designer to know more details and take a more careful look before reaching final decisions. One should always keep in mind that the use of microprocessors results in money savings only with regard to the CPU of the system. Memory and peripherals most often constitute the major system expense.

Besides capacity, another basic memory characteristic is speed. A number of different times are usually used to characterize memory speed. One is the *access time,* which corresponds to the time required from the instant the control signal READ[1] and the address bits are applied to memory until its output data start being valid (i.e., reach a stable state and are ready to be used by the rest of the system). As far as ROMs are concerned, this time constitutes the sole criterion for their speed. Another is the *write time,* which is the time required from the instant the control signal WRITE is sent to memory until

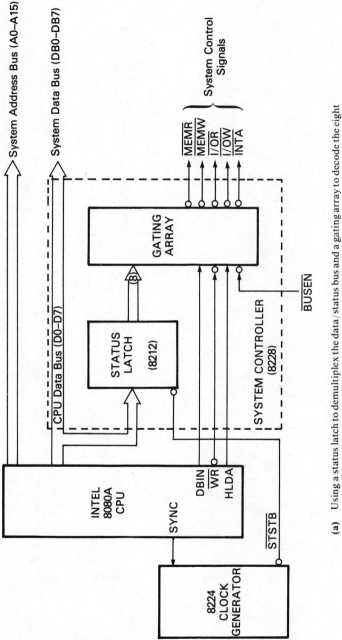

(a) Using a status latch to demultiplex the data/status bus and a gating array to decode the eight status lines and produce the system control signals.

Figure 6.9 (a) Demultiplexing the 8080A data bus [19]. *Courtesy Intel Corporation.*

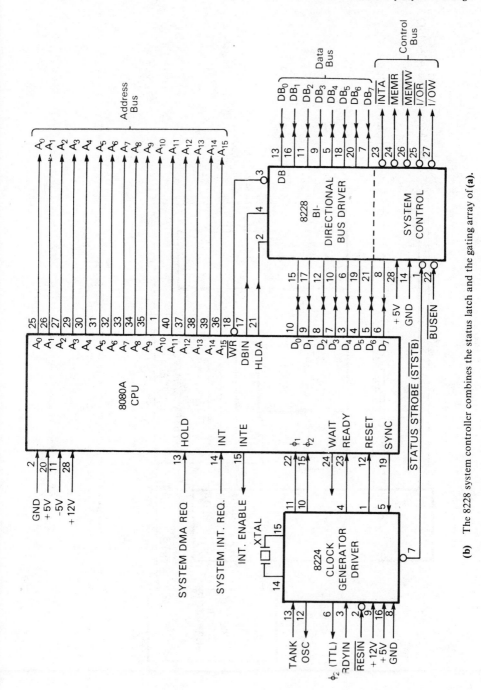

(b)   The 8228 system controller combines the status latch and the gating array of **(a)**.

Figure 6.9 **(a)** Demultiplexing the 8080A data bus; **(b)** the 8080A CPU standard interface. Courtesy Intel Corporation [10].

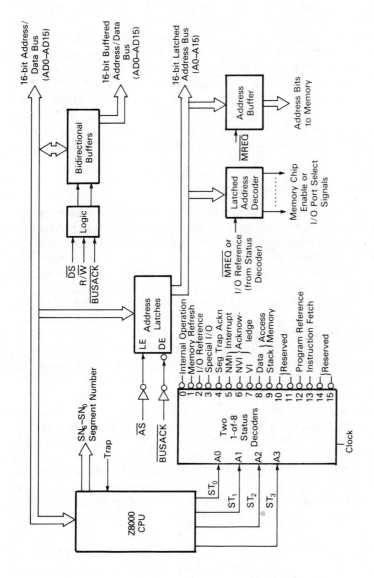

Figure 6.10 Some basic supporting circuitry required to interface the Zilog Z8000 CPU with memory and peripherals.

the new data have been written into it. It is assumed, of course, that the instant the signal WRITE is supplied, the address has already been decoded and now points to a specific memory location, and that the data to be stored have become valid. Finally, the *memory cycle time* is the basic time period that memory requires to complete a specific function, whether this is a read followed by a write (read/write), or a read/read, or a write/write or a write/read. This memory cycle time should last at least as long as the longer of the access or write times. In certain situations the memory cycle time may be even longer, especially when the system has added capabilities, such as performing parity checking on the bits of the data being read, or using some other method to perform error detection and correction. The terms *full cycle* or *read-modify-write cycle* are also used to denote the memory cycle time for dynamic semiconductor memories which require periodic refreshing of their contents.

6.3.2   Memory System Organization

The two most common memory organizations for microprocessors are the *byte* (eight bits) and *word* (sixteen bits) *organizations*. In byte organizations, memory is treated as a sequence of 8-bit bytes, reading and writing refers to a single byte, and multiple memory references are required to fetch multibyte informations. In word organizations, memory is again byte addressable, but the basic data type movement involves a 16-bit word. Words or double words are usually aligned in memory using even addresses (i.e., the address of their first byte is an integral multiple of 2). Figure 6.11 shows the boundaries and word alignment for the first addresses between (hexadecimal) 0 and B. As far as the high-level language programmer is concerned, this boundary alignment is automatically performed by the system. The programmer who codes his programs in assembly or machine language must always be aware of and conform to these boundary alignment rules.

In the 8-bit microprocessors, memory is byte organized; i.e., memory is a sequence of 8-bit bytes, and a byte element is addressed by the specifying of its address (usually ranging between 0 and 65,535). Thus, the byte is the basic addressable element and the smallest unit of information accessed out of memory. Data elements or instructions of sixteen bits or longer may be placed in memory starting at any byte address, and referenced using an address that designates their leftmost (high-order) byte and an implicit or explicit indica-

---

[1] In this section, the read and write control signals applied to memory are denoted by the general names READ and WRITE. It must be remembered that for global (system) memory these names should be replaced by MRDC* and MWTC*, respectively, while for local (private) memory they must take the respective names shown in the first two lines of Figure 5.11 in chapter 5.

Address (Hexadecimal)	0	1	2	3	4	5	6	7	8	9	A	B	...
Address (Binary)	0000	0001	0010	0011	0100	0101	0110	0111	1000	1001	1010	1011	...

Byte · Byte · Byte · Byte · Byte · Byte · Byte · Byte · Byte · Byte · Byte · Byte

Word · Word · Word · Word · Word · Word

Double Word · Double Word · Double Word

Double Word · Double Word · Double Word

Figure 6.11 Boundaries and word alignment for the first twelve locations of a microprocessor memory. *Courtesy of International Business Machines Corporation* [6].

tion of their length. In the case of multibyte elements, two or more successive addresses must be sent by the microprocessor CPU to memory. Individual bits are usually not uniquely addressable in the 8-bit microprocessors; they must be treated as part of the byte accessed out of memory (the Z80, however, does have three bit-manipulation instructions, the SET, RES, and BIT).

In the 16-bit microprocessors, memory is byte addressable, but it is now word organized. Although the byte is still the basic addressable element, any two consecutive bytes may be paired together to form a (16-bit) word. Most 16-bit microprocessor chips provide extra output control signals to indicate whether byte or word memory reference is being performed. In the case of instructions or data elements of sixteen bits or longer, the address designates the leftmost byte. Instructions having sixteen bits are fetched from memory as words, and they are word aligned using even addresses. The 16-bit micropro-cessors, however, have chosen different ways of aligning 16-bit data elements in memory. In the Intel 8086, word (16-bit) operands can be located on even or odd address boundaries, while in both the Zilog Z8000 and Motorola 68000, word or long word (32-bit) operands are always word aligned. Word align-ment is used to avoid the time penalty that results from two successive fetches of the high and low byte of a word when the word crosses the alignment boundary (i.e., when its starting byte is on an odd address). Therefore, if the 8086 programmer wishes to optimize performance and maximize efficiency, he or she must locate word data on even boundaries as well.

6.3.3 Memory Chip Internal Structure

Figure 6.12 gives the general block diagram of a memory chip, with its basic components and input/output signals. The basic input signals to the memory chip are: the address, the READ and WRITE control signals, the data input, and the control signal chip select (CS) that activates this specific memory chip. (Ways of generating chip select signals are discussed later.) The REFRESH signal is used only for dynamic memories whose contents require periodic refreshing. The basic output signals from the memory chip constitute the data output. Usually some of the address bits, $A_0, A_1, \ldots, A_{i-1}$, are supplied internally to a full decoder (for example, a 4-input, 16-output, or a 6-input, 64-output decoder) that selects the reading of only one row of the memory array. The remainder of the address bits, $A_i, \ldots A_{n-1}$, are used internally to control the column select decoder. This internal splitting of the address is done so that the memory array can be manufactured with a shape as close to square as possible, in order to minimize chip area. Minimum chip area is obtained when the row select and column select decoders are of the same size. For example, a 512 word by eight bits per word (or 512×8 bits) memory can be manufactured as a 64×64 square memory cell array. In this case, six of the nine total address bits will be decoded to select one of the sixty-four rows. The remaining three address bits control the column select decoder, which selects one of the eight 8-bit groups of the activated row.

groups of the activated row.

To form a *memory module* for reading or writing 8-bit words, eight such RAM chips will be required, all of them used simultaneously by receiving the same signal in their chip select input pins.

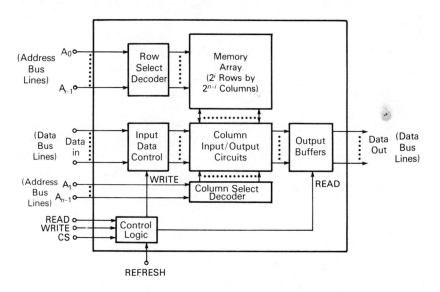

Figure 6.12 The general block diagram of a memory chip with its input and output signals.

6.3.4 Designing the Memory System

Splitting an Address between Word Address Bits and Chip Select Signals

In the design of a microprocessor-based system, usually a mixture of RAM and ROM (or PROM) memories is used. Often ROM (or PROM) is used to hold the bootstrap and permanent programs, while RAM is used for other user programs and data. In these cases, the designer must allocate the addresses (and their corresponding address bus lines) between ROM and RAM chips in such a way that each location will have a unique address, while keeping any address decoding circuits to a minimum. Quite often, however, the microprocessor CPU used is capable of accessing more memory locations than those required by the specific application. The surplus address bits can be used very easily as chip select signals. Thus, one must also split the total address bits between word address bits and chip select signals (to select the appropriate chips that constitute a memory module).

Addresses are usually allocated in such a way that one region of addresses belongs to ROM memory, and a separate region, to RAM memory. The specific allocation is determined by two basic characteristics of the microprocessor CPU: (1) the memory location to which control is transferred when the input RESET signal is applied, and (2) the memory location to which control is transferred after an external interrupt signal is received (when this transfer of control is done using "vectored interrupts").[2] For example, the RESET signal for the Intel 8080A resets its program counter to address 0 (zero) (therefore, the first program instruction should be in ROM memory location 0), whereas, the RESET signal for the Motorola 6800 sets its program counter to address FFFE and $FFFE_{16}$ (locations $FFFE_{16}$ and $FFFF_{16}$ contain the first address of the routine to handle the RESET signal). Corresponding interrupt addresses have also been dedicated to the various interrupt signals.

It is observed, therefore, that the memory regions one allocates to ROM and RAM depend upon the specific microprocessor being used. For the Intel 8080A one should allocate to ROM memory the addresses that start from 0 (zero) up to a required maximum. The RAM addresses may start either immediately after the maximum ROM address, or after leaving some blank addresses (to allow for possible future ROM expansions). With the Motorola 6800, one has the exact opposite situation. Here, addresses that start from 0 (zero) should be allocated to RAM memory. ROM memory should be placed so that its highest address is $FFFF_{16}$ (the maximum accessible memory location) and decreasing, according to the required ROM size.

---

[2]Vectored interrupts provide a way in which an interrupt signal causes an indirect branch to that point in memory where the respective interrupt handling routine is stored.

Figure 6.13 shows an example of a typical memory configuration with its basic interface to the bus structure of an Intel 8080A-based system. This memory is made up of 8K bytes of ROM storage immediately followed by 512 bytes of RAM storage. Each 8316A is a 2K × 8-bit ROM chip. Each 8111 is a 256 × 4 static RAM chip and, therefore, two chips constitute an 8-bit RAM memory module. The $\overline{\text{MEMW}}$ is the memory write control signal (connected to the $\overline{\text{R/W}}$ pin of the RAM chips) and the $\overline{\text{MEMR}}$ is the memory read control signal (connected to the output disable (OD) pin of the RAM chips and to the chip select pin $\overline{\text{CS1}}$ of the ROM chips). Since ROM storage occupies the lower 8K bytes of memory, it is accessed with address bit A13 = 0, while the thirteen lower address bits A0–A12 are used to access a location within this ROM space. Since RAM storage occupies the next 512 bytes, it is reached with A13 = 1, while the nine lower address bits A0–A8 are used to access a location within RAM space. (A13 signal is not shown in Figure 6.12. A13 = 0 may be combined properly with the $\overline{\text{MEMR}}$ signal to select a ROM, whereas A13 = 1 may be combined properly with the $\overline{\text{MEMR}}$ and $\overline{\text{MEMW}}$ to select a RAM module.)

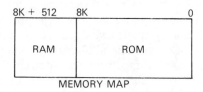

MEMORY MAP

Figure 6.13   A typical memory configuration (8K-byte ROM and 512-byte RAM) with its basic interface to the bus structure of an 8080-based system. *Courtesy Intel Corporation* [8].

As already mentioned, when the system under design requires a total memory space which is smaller than the maximum address space that the microprocessor can access, the designer can split the address into *chip select bits* and *word bits,* the latter being used to access a word within the selected memory module. Such splitting is shown in Figure 6.13. Since 2K × 8-bit ROM chips are used, eleven bits (A0–A10) are sufficient as word bits to access a location within each ROM module. The extra two bits (A11, A12) of the address are now used as chip select bits to select one of the four ROMs. Thus, for each ROM module, the sixteen address bits have the values shown in Table 6.1. ROM module #1 has real addresses ranging from 0000_{16}–$07FF_{16}$ (or 0000_{10}–2047_{10}); ROM module #2 has addresses ranging from 0800_{16}–$0FFF_{16}$ (or 2048_{10}–4095_{10}); ROM module #3 has addresses ranging from 1000_{16}–$17FF_{16}$ (or 4096_{10}–6143_{10}); and ROM module #4 has addresses ranging from 1800_{16}–$1FFF_{16}$ (or 6144_{10}–8191_{10}).

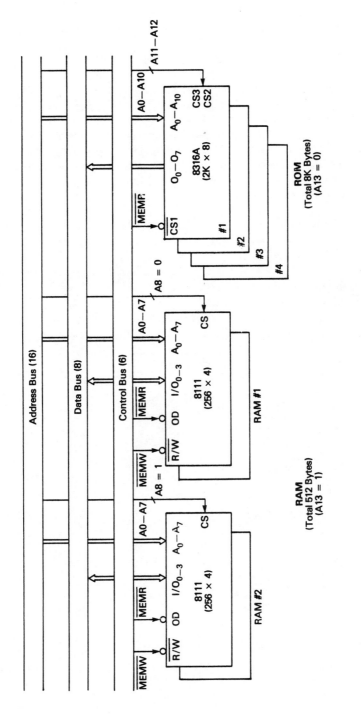

Figure 6.13 A typical memory configuration (8K-byte ROM and 512-byte RAM) with its basic interface to the bus structure of an 8080-based system. *Courtesy: Intel Corporation* [8].

The RAM memory of Figure 6.13 consists of two RAM modules, each one implemented using a pair of 8111 RAM chips. Since RAM address space occupies locations immediately following those of ROM address space, a RAM location is reached when address bit A13 = 1. Since each RAM module is 256×8 bits, eight bits (A0–A7) are sufficient as word bits to access a location within each RAM module. The extra bit A8 is used as a chip select bit to select one of the two RAM modules. Thus, to access RAM memory space, the sixteen address bits will have the values shown in Table 6.2. RAM module #1 has real addresses ranging from 2000_{16}–$20FF_{16}$ (or 8192_{10}–8447_{10}) and RAM module #2 has addresses ranging from 2100_{16}–$21FF_{16}$ (or 8448_{10}–8703_{10}).

Figure 6.14 shows another example in which the address bits A0–A7 are used as word bits to access locations within each 256×8 memory RAM chip, while each of the three extra address bits, A8, A9 and A10, is applied to the CS input of each chip.[3] When A8 = 1, then the RAM_0 chip is selected, whose internal addresses range from 100_{16}–$1FF_{16}$; when A9 = 1, then the RAM_1 chip is selected, whose addresses range from 200_{16}–$2FF_{16}$; when A10 = 1, then the RAM_2 chip is selected, whose addresses range from 400_{16}–$4FF_{16}$.

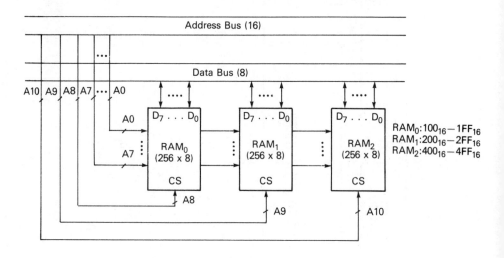

Figure 6.14   Three of the address bits are used as chip select signals.

---

[3]The use of each individual address bit as the exclusive select for a specific memory chip is also called *linear select*.

Table 6.1 The real addresses for the ROM modules of Figure 6.13.

First Address

	Chip Select Bits A15 A14 A13 A12 A11	Word Address Bits A10 A9 A8 A7 A6 A5 A4 A3 A2 A1 A0	(hex)
ROM Module #1	0 0 0 0 0	0 0 0 0 0 0 0 0 0 0 0	0000_{16}
ROM Module #2	0 0 0 0 1	0 0 0 0 0 0 0 0 0 0 0	0800_{16}
ROM Module #3	0 0 0 1 0	0 0 0 0 0 0 0 0 0 0 0	1000_{16}
ROM Module #4	0 0 0 1 1	0 0 0 0 0 0 0 0 0 0 0	1800_{16}

Last Address

	Chip Select Bits A15 A14 A13 A12 A11	Word Address Bits A10 A9 A8 A7 A6 A5 A4 A3 A2 A1 A0	(hex)
ROM Module #1	0 0 0 0 0	1 1 1 1 1 1 1 1 1 1 1	$07FF_{16}$
ROM Module #2	0 0 0 0 1	1 1 1 1 1 1 1 1 1 1 1	$0FFF_{16}$
ROM Module #3	0 0 0 1 0	1 1 1 1 1 1 1 1 1 1 1	$17FF_{16}$
ROM Module #4	0 0 0 1 1	1 1 1 1 1 1 1 1 1 1 1	$1FFF_{16}$

Table 6.2 The real addresses for the RAM modules of Figure 6.13.

First Address

	Chip Select Bits A15 A14 A13 A12 A11 A10 A9 A8	Word Address Bits A7 A6 A5 A4 A3 A2 A1 A0	(hex)
RAM Module #1	0 0 1 0 0 0 0 0	0 0 0 0 0 0 0 0	2000_{16}
RAM Module #2	0 0 1 0 0 0 0 1	0 0 0 0 0 0 0 0	2100_{16}

Last Address

	Chip Select Bits A15 A14 A13 A12 A11 A10 A9 A8	Word Address Bits A7 A6 A5 A4 A3 A2 A1 A0	(hex)
RAM Module #1	0 0 1 0 0 0 0 0	1 1 1 1 1 1 1 1	$20FF_{16}$
RAM Module #2	0 0 1 0 0 0 0 1	1 1 1 1 1 1 1 1	$21FF_{16}$

The main drawback of the configuration of Figure 6.14—one which the programmer must notice—is that RAM addresses are not contiguous. The configuration does, however, have the advantage that with a single write instruction one can store data simultaneously into all three memory chips; for example, a single store instruction with address 760_{16} will store data simultaneously into locations 160_{16}, 260_{16}, and 460_{16}. Furthermore, if these RAMs are of the open collector type, then the execution of a "read from location 760_{16}" instruction will perform the logical AND among the three bytes read out from locations 160_{16}, 260_{16}, and 460_{16}.[4]

In the case of Figure 6.14, the chip select address bits are applied directly to the chip select inputs of the memory chips. Therefore, the three chip select bits can specify only up to three different memory chips. Furthermore, as shown, the real addresses allocated to these chips are not contiguous. Alternatively, an external decoder can be used to allow these three chip select address bits to specify a larger number of memory chips. Passing the three bits A8, A9, and A10 through a 1-of-8 decoder allows the specification of up to eight different memory chips. Furthermore, the real addresses allocated to these chips will become contiguous.

An example of this decoder implementation is shown in Figure 6.15 [16]. Here, eight 256 × 8-bit RAM chips are connected to accommodate a total contiguous address space of 2048 bytes (such a space is sometimes also called a *page*). If the system address is sixteen bits wide (total memory as large as 64K bytes), there may be a total of thirty-two such pages. Addressing within a 2K-byte memory page requires the first eleven address bits, A0–A10. Individual pages will be addressed by the remaining five most significant address bits, A11–A15, after they pass through a 1-of-32 decoder. The selected 2K-byte page in the configuration of Figure 6.15 is page #3; i.e., it is accessed by the combination: $A15A14A13A12A11 = 00011_2 = 03_{16}$. Therefore, the real addresses allocated to this page vary from 1800_{16}–$1FFF_{16}$ (or 6144_{10}–8191_{10}). Within this range, each of the eight RAM chips has the real addresses shown in Table 6.3.

Table **6.3** The real addresses for the eight RAM chips in the configuration of Figure 6.15.

	Hexadecimal	Decimal
RAM_0	1800 to 18FF	G144 to 6399
RAM_1	1900 to 19FF	6400 to 6655
RAM_2	1A00 to 1AFF	6656 to 6911
RAM_3	1B00 to 1BFF	6912 to 7167
RAM_4	1C00 to 1CFF	7168 to 7423
RAM_5	1D00 to 1DFF	7424 to 7679
RAM_6	1E00 to 1EFF	7680 to 7935
RAM_7	1F00 to 1FFF	7936 to 8191

---

[4]Such operations are very useful, for example, for masking operations on data.

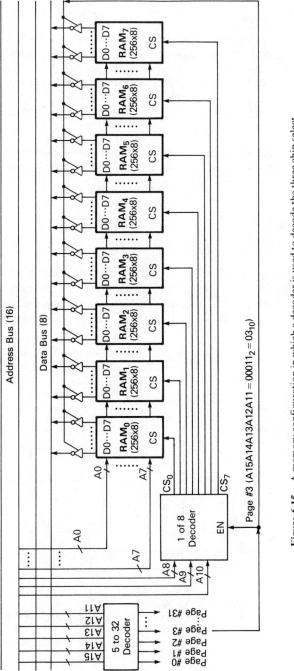

Figure 6.15 A memory configuration in which a decoder is used to decode the three chip select address bits A_8, A_9, A_{10}.

Memory Array Configurations

Since a great variety of memory sizes exist, the architect is usually faced with the problem of properly connecting a number of these memory chips to form a memory array that will provide the required bits per word and the required words of memory [17]. Sometimes, he or she may also want to provide memory expansion capability for the microcomputer.

Bits per Word (or Word Expansion)

To increase the number of bits per word, a number of memory chips are required to be paralleled according to the following simple formula:

$$\text{No. of chips} = \frac{\text{No. of bits per word of the system}}{\text{No. of bits per word of the chip}}$$

This is also known as "word expansion," and has already been used in Figure 6.13. Figure 6.16 shows the paralleling of two 256×4 memory chips to produce a 256×8-bit memory module. To obtain more bits, each individual address and chip select input is parallel connected (i.e., tied together).

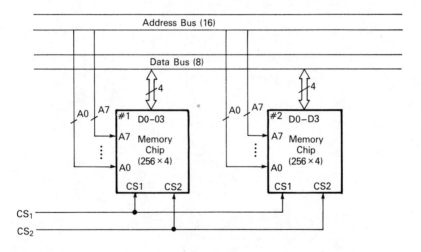

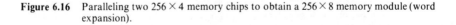

Figure 6.16 Paralleling two 256×4 memory chips to obtain a 256×8 memory module (word expansion).

Words per Memory (or Memory Expansion)

In an analogous scheme, outputs of the memory chips can be wire-ORed to obtain more words per memory according to the following formula:

$$\text{No. of chips} = \frac{\text{No. of words required in the system}}{\text{No. of words in the chip}}$$

This is also known as "address expansion" or "memory expansion," and has also been used in Figure 6.13. Figure 6.17 shows this wire-ORing of the outputs for four $2\text{K} \times 8$ ROM chips (four 8316As) to produce an $8\text{K} \times 8$ ROM memory. When wire-ORing outputs, it is necessary to select only one ROM chip at a time to insure that the correct data is accessed. For each 8316A ROM of Figure 6.17, three programmable chip select inputs exist, denoted as $\overline{\text{CS1}}$, CS2, and CS3. Any combination of active high- or low-level chip select inputs can be defined, and the desired chip select code is fixed during the masking process. Figure 6.17 shows the corresponding programmed levels for the two address bit inputs A11 and A12. In other cases (e.g., for memory chips having only two chip select inputs), additional external logic may be required to decode the two address bits A11 and A12, and activate the chip select for a single memory chip.

Array Configurations

Assume that memory chips of size $2^{\rho} \times r$ bits (i.e., having 2^{ρ} words and r bits per word) are being used to construct an N words by M bits per word (an $N \times M$-bit) memory, where $N = 2^{\kappa}$, and κ is the number of address bits. Since N should be a multiple of 2^{ρ}, and M a multiple of r, this memory can be realized by placing the memory chips in a two-dimensional array configuration having $N/2^{\rho}$ number of rows and M/r number of columns. Since $N = 2$, this configuration will have $2^{(\kappa - \rho)}$ rows, each row containing M/r chips. From the total κ address lines, ρ of them will be common to all chips. The remaining $\kappa - \rho$ address lines, when decoded, will be used to select one of the $2^{(\kappa - \rho)}$ rows at a time (i.e., each decoded signal will be applied simultaneously to the chip select inputs of all chips lying on the corresponding row).

Figure 6.18 shows such an example. Here, it is desired that an $N \times M = 256 \times 8 = 2^{\kappa} \times 8$ memory be constructed, where $\kappa = 8$ equals the total number of address bits required. Assume that memory chips of size $64 \times 4 = 2^{\rho} \times r$ bits

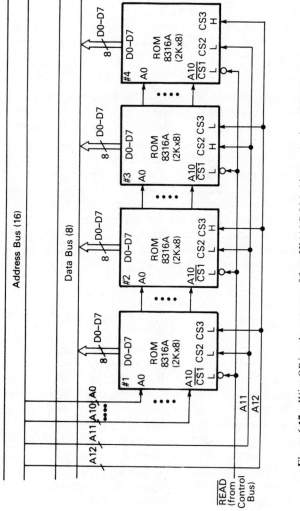

Figure 6.17 Wire-ORing the outputs of four 2K × 8 ROM chips to obtain an 8K × 8 memory. (Address or memory expansion).

are used, where $\rho = 6$ equals the word address bits for each chip. Then from the above, the number of rows and chips is given by:

- No. of rows: $2^{(\kappa - \rho)} = 2^{(8-6)} = 4$ rows
- No. of chips per row: $M/r = 8/4 = 2$ chips

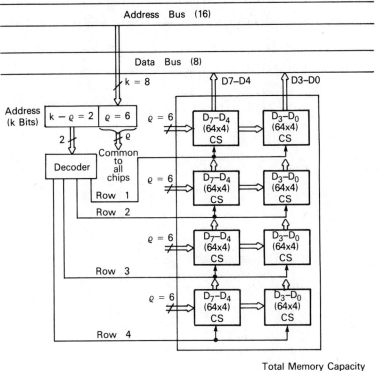

Total Memory Capacity
$2^k \times M = 2^8 \times 8 = 256 \times 8$

Figure 6.18 Configuring a 256 × 8 memory out of 64 × 4 memory chips.

Figure 6.19 below shows an example of a 16K × 8-bit memory circuit for an Intel 8080/8080A-based design. Device decoding is done with the chip enable (CE) input. All devices are unselected during the refresh with CS input. The 8107B is a 4096 × 1-bit dynamic MOS RAM, the 8210 is a dynamic RAM driver, the 8205 is a 1-of-8 decoder (only half of it used here), and the 8212 is an 8-bit I/O port. This configuration has:

- No. of rows: $2^{(\kappa - \rho)} = 2^{(14-12)} = 4$ rows
- No. of chips per row: $M/r = 8/1 = 8$ chips

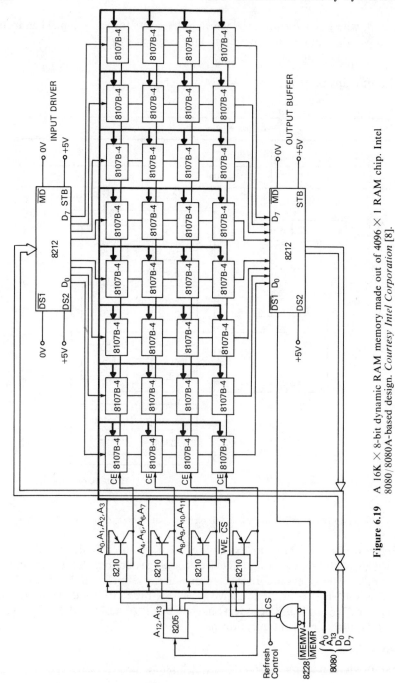

Figure 6.19 A 16K × 8-bit dynamic RAM memory made out of 4096 × 1 RAM chip. Intel 8080/8080A-based design. *Courtesy Intel Corporation* [8].

Memory Refresh

As already mentioned, dynamic RAM memories require periodic refreshing of their contents. Memory refreshing may be done either by the CPU, which contains a special refresh counter, or by an external refresh controller. Memory refreshing can be either *completely transparent* (i.e., done during the gaps in the CPU timing without disturbing the flow of microprocessor instructions) or *partially transparent* (i.e., by inserting a refresh cycle, usually after the next instruction fetch cycle). For example, in the Intel 8080A, the external refresh controller requests a hold from the CPU during the instruction fetch cycle. The 8080A acknowledges this request, floats its address and control buses, and allows the refresh controller to address memory and perform refreshing, while the CPU continues with internal operations.

Refreshing is accomplished by applying a special current to the memory cell capacitors. Common refresh frequency (for operations in temperatures from 0°C to 70°C) is every 2 msec. Consequently, if memory has a capacity of 1024 bits in a 32×32 form, then all thirty-two rows must be refreshed at least every 2 msec, in other words, the refresh cycle will be 62.4 μsec per row. During memory refresh cycles, the respective address originates from a 5-bit "address refresh counter" (either inside the CPU or in the external refresh controller), and not from the normal address source. These five bits define the thirty-two rows, and the counter sequentially passes through all its thirty-two binary states. Figure 6.20 shows a way of generating these addresses. Only the five bits that control the address lines A0–A4 are required to be supplied to memory during the refresh cycles.

In the new 16-bit microprocessors, the refresh period is sometimes programmable. For example, the Zilog Z8000 includes a "rate counter" which consists of a programmable 6-bit modulo-n prescaler ($n = 1$ to 64), driven at one-fourth the CPU clock rate. The refresh period can be programmed from 1 to 64 μsec with a 4 MHz clock, and refresh can also be disabled under software control. When this 6-bit prescaler in the refresh counter has been decremented to 0 (zero), a refresh cycle starts. The CPU uses a 9-bit refresh counter to allow up to 256 consecutive refresh addresses or rows (and since the Z8000 memory is word organized, this refresh counter is always incremented by 2) for higher density memories.

6.3.5 Increasing the Size of the Physical Memory Space

There is no doubt that the requirement of providing increased microprocessor storage space always exists. The size of the physical memory space the microprocessor can handle can expand by various techniques, some of which affect the microprocessor (CPU) architecture and others of which do not. Some of these techniques are examined next.

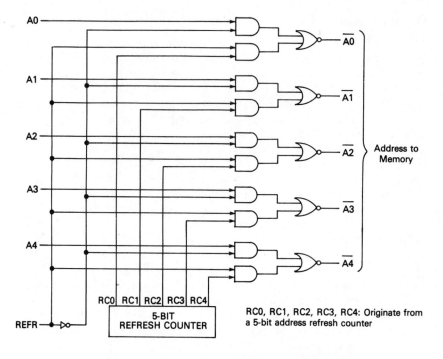

Figure 6.20 Supplying (to memory) the refresh address.

By Providing Wider Instruction Addresses

The easiest way to extend the range of the microprocessor's physical memory is to add more bits to the address field of instructions. However, this technique has a significant impact on microprocessor architecture. It usually involves an increase in the number of pins, since a wider address bus is required to carry the address to the memory system. This is exactly what happened when industry introduced wider word length microprocessors. When the move was made from 8- to 16-bit microprocessors, their CPU architecture was modified; the wider addresses provided in instructions resulted in systems capable of supporting larger physical memory spaces; and the increased number of pins required resulted in the appearance of larger microprocessor chips (chips with forty-eight pins, like the Zilog Z8001 and National NS16032, and chips with sixty-four pins, like the Motorola 68000).

Through Overlay Techniques

When a specific microprocessor CPU is given, there is nothing one can do to change its architecture. Methods must be devised for expanding the range of its physical memory space without interfering with the basic design of the CPU.

An expanded physical memory space can be simulated by the user, thus leading to the *overlaying* technique. With this technique, an auxiliary mass storage device is usually available and used by the programmer to overcome main memory size limitation. The programmer breaks up program and data into small parts or *overlays*, and brings an overlay from mass storage into main memory, when required by the computation. When its use is finished, the overlay may return to mass storage (if it has been modified during execution), or new data may be brought into the same memory locations (without copying the original overlay back into mass storage if it has remained unchanged after execution).

Besides increasing the programmer's effort (one must carefully plan the program's main memory requirements so that no two procedures or data structures which are to be used concurrently occupy the same position in physical memory), time penalties also incur when main memory is loaded with new data from mass storage, and when old data is restored back into mass storage device.

By Increasing the Number of Address Lines Applied to Memory

Another way to expand the range of physical memory space is by somehow providing more address lines to be applied to the memory system. In the context of microprocessor systems, the maximum size of the physical memory space is determined by the number of lines used to access a physical location in main memory. Increasing the range of the physical memory space, therefore, results in the application of more address lines to the memory system. For example, if the address field in the instruction is n bits long, then an "expansion mechanism" placed between the microprocessor CPU and memory takes in n microprocessor address lines and generates m memory system address lines, where $m > n$. In this way, the range of the system's physical memory may expand from 2^n to 2^m bytes as shown diagrammatically in Figure 6.21.

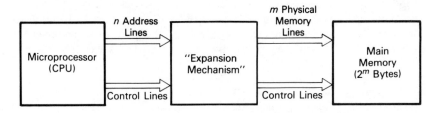

Figure 6.21   Conceptual way of increasing the physical address space by increasing (from n to m, where $m > n$) the number of lines carrying an address to main memory.

Again, several variations have been used to implement this concept of increasing the address lines from n to m; two of them, bank switching and indexed mapping, are outlined here [12].

Bank Switching

In bank switching, main memory consists of a number of separate physical blocks or banks; if the microprocessor CPU issues an n-bit address, then each memory bank consists of 2^n contiguously addressed physical locations numbered from 0 to $2^n - 1$. Since this is the range of the microprocessor's address space, a program and its associated data should reside in one bank. With the bank switching technique, one bank of memory is enabled while all other banks remain disabled.[5] The "expansion mechanism" now consists of a bank selector logic, which, under the control of an appropriate supervisor program, selects one of the memory banks to which it directs the CPU address (Figure 6.22). The concatenation of the bank selector with the n-bit CPU address, in effect, increases the number of address lines used by the memory system. A further increase in physical main memory can be accommodated by additional memory banks (and by appropriately upgrading both the bank selection logic in the expansion mechanism and the supervisor program); the n-bit address issued by the microprocessor is used as an offset within the enabled bank. (Also see section 10.2.1 of chapter 10.)

Indexed Mapping

Indexed mapping is another method for extending the physical addressing range. For example, it is used by Motorola to extend the physical addressing range of the 6809 from 64K bytes to 2M bytes, organized as 1024 pages of memory, with each page containing 2K bytes. The concept is similar to that of paging, the details of which will be presented later, in chapter 10.

The general idea of indexed mapping to extend the physical memory space for a given microprocessor is represented in Figure 6.23. The microprocessor issues a 16-bit address that can directly address a maximum address space of 64K bytes. For the system to be able to access the larger 2M-byte physical memory space, the sixteen address lines must increase to twenty-one. As shown in Figure 6.23, the 16-bit address is divided into two parts. Its leftmost five bits select one of the thirty-two registers in the "expansion mechanism." If each register is ten bits wide and the content of the selected register is

---

[5]Bank switching should not be confused with the two-way memory interleaving technique to be discussed in section 6.4.2, in which all even addresses are in one memory bank, and all odd addresses in the other. Also, notice here conceptual similarity with overlay.

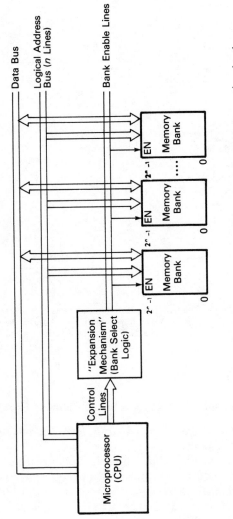

Figure 6.22 Bank switching. One memory bank (2^n locations) is enabled at a time by the expansion mechanism.

concatenated with the low-order 11-bit offset field of the address, then the 21-bit physical address required to access the 2M-byte memory is formed.

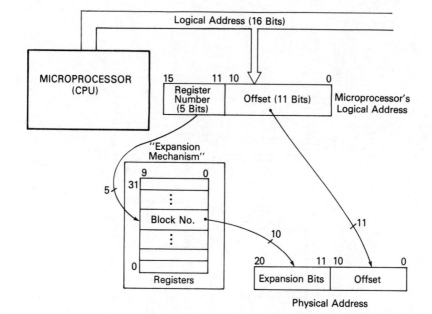

Figure 6.23 Indexed mapping. Concatenating the 10-bit contents of a selected register in the expansion mechanism with the low-order eleven bits of the logical address increases the 16-bit address to a 21-bit physical address transmitted to memory.

6.4 MEMORY OPERATION

6.4.1 Reading From and Writing Data Into a Memory Chip

The memory operation can be deduced easily from the bus operation discussed in the previous chapter.

Reading data from a memory chip is done as follows: the CS and READ control signals and the address bits must be applied to memory. As can be observed from Figure 6.12, these signals should stay valid long enough to compensate for possible delay differences that may result from the fact that they propagate within the chip through different paths, and thus have different delay stages. The READ signal, for example, is routed to the chip's output buffers, passing through only the delay involved in the control logic section. On the other hand, the address signals propagate through a path of greater delay, and the data being read arrive at the chip's output buffers after the arrival of the READ signal. For this reason, the address is placed first onto the address bus along with the CS signal, and after some short time has elapsed for the address to reach the memory chip and to stabilize there, the READ signal is applied to memory. The result of this reading operation is that the contents of the addressed memory location are placed in the memory chip's output buffers ("data out valid"). The timing of events is shown in Figure 6.24a.

Writing new data into memory requires the following sequence of events: first, the address bits and the CS signal are applied to the memory chip to identify the specific memory location where data is to be stored. Immediately thereafter, the CPU issues the data to be applied to the memory chip's input data control section. After a short time has elapsed for the address to reach the selected memory chip and stabilize there, the WRITE signal is applied. The result of this writing operation is that the input data are stored in the addressed memory location. The timing of events during this write operation is shown in Figure 6.24b.

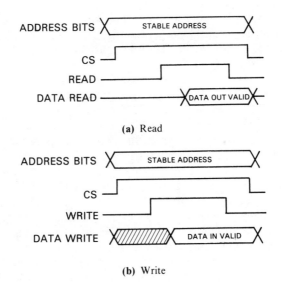

(a) Read

(b) Write

Figure 6.24 Timing of events for a memory operation: **(a)** read operation; **(b)** write operation.

The two popular read/write clocking arrangements discussed in the previous chapter (see Figure 5.11) also should be mentioned here. In one of them (used, for example, by Intel 8085 and 8086) there are two mutually exclusive control pulses $\overline{RD}$ and $\overline{WR}$ that indicate a read or write operation similar to that shown in Figure 6.24 (also see Figure 5.20 of chapter 5). In the second arrangement (used, for example, by Zilog Z80 and Z8000) there is a single control pulse $\overline{\text{MREQ}}$ and a level signal READ or WRITE (from two output pins in the Z80 and from a single output pin in the Z8000) that indicates which type of operation is to take place (also see Figure 5.21 of chapter 5).

6.4.2 Byte (8-Bit) and Word (16-Bit) Accessing

So far, mostly 8-bit oriented memory organizations have been presented; i.e., byte organized and byte addressable memories.

On the other hand, the 16-bit microprocessor oriented memories are byte addressable but word organized. Both 8- and 16-bit operations and data transfers are permitted in the same system. As already mentioned, 16-bit CPUs provide an additional output control signal to identify whether a byte or word access is performed (Figure 6.25); the Intel 8086 calls it byte high enable ($\overline{\text{BHE}}$), the Zilog Z8000 calls it byte/word ($\text{B}/\overline{\text{W}}$), whereas the Motorola 68000 provides two separate signals called upper data strobe ($\overline{\text{UDS}}$) and lower data strobe ($\overline{\text{LDS}}$).

To allow for both 8- and 16-bit data operations in the same system, the memory is organized physically into two 8-bit data banks, which form a single 16-bit word. One bank, called the "upper byte bank," contains the most significant byte of the 16-bit word, and is connected to the upper half lines D8–D15 of the data bus; the other bank, called the "lower byte bank," contains the least significant byte of the 16-bit word, and is connected to the lower half lines D0–D7 of the data bus. This way of organizing memory is also referred to as two-way *memory interleaving.*[6] Figure 6.26 shows the way memory is physically organized for the Intel 8086 and Zilog Z8000 microprocessors [11,23]. The upper byte bank stores the most significant byte transferred on D8–D15 data lines, and the lower byte bank stores the least significant byte transferred on D0–D7 data lines. However, the upper byte bank of the 8086 contains all odd-addressed memory locations, while that of the Z8000 contains all even-addressed locations. Similarly, the lower byte bank of the 8086 contains all even-addressed memory locations, while that of the Z8000 contains all odd-addressed locations.

Accessing a word (sixteen bits) is analogous to the byte access of the 8-bit microprocessors: a memory location is accessed, and a word is placed onto/accepted from the 16-bit data bus. The respective output control signals for word access activate together both the upper and lower byte banks and are: $\overline{\text{BHE}}$ = low for the 8086, $\text{B}/\overline{\text{W}}$ = low for the Z8000, and $\overline{\text{UDS}} = \overline{\text{LDS}}$ = low for the 68000. Since 16-bit words are usually located on even-byte boundaries,

---

[6]The memory interleaving technique may also be used when the necessary bandwidth exceeds the bandwidth of a single memory module.

	Word (16-Bit) Transfers	Byte (8-Bit) Transfers	
	A0 = 0 (Always)	A0 = 0	A0 = 1
INTEL 8086	$\overline{BHE}$ = Low	$\overline{BHE}$ = High Least significant byte (located on an even address) is transferred on lines D0–D7.	$\overline{BHE}$ = Low Most significant byte (located on an odd address) is transferred on lines D8–D15.
Zilog Z8000	$B/\overline{W}$ = Low	$B/\overline{W}$ = High Most significant byte (located on an even address) is transferred on lines D8–D15.	$B/\overline{W}$ = High Least significant byte (located on an odd address) is transferred on lines D0–D7.
Motorola 68000	$\overline{UDS}$ = $\overline{LDS}$ = Low	$\overline{UDS}$ = Low Most significant byte (located on an even address) is transferred on lines D8–D15.	$\overline{LDS}$ = Low Least significant byte (located on an odd address) is transferred on lines D0–D7.

Figure 6.25 The output control signal(s) issued by the 16-bit microprocessor CPUs to identify byte or word access.

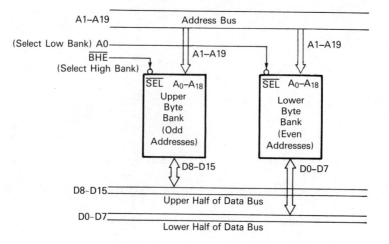

(a) Intel 8086 memory organization.

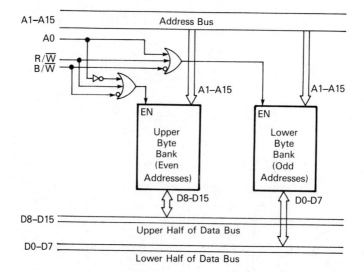

(b) Zilog Z8000 memory organization.

Figure 6.26   Byte/word memory access for the Intel 8086 and Zilog Z8000 [11,8].

the least significant address bit A0 is not really part of the word address (it is always 0 (zero)).

Accessing a byte (8-bits), however, requires the use of bit A0 along with the above output control signals to specify the unique byte. Both the Z8000 and 68000 have similar ways of accessing a byte:

(a) With A0 = 0, the most significant byte—located on an even address—is transferred via the upper half of the data bus D8–D15, and the respective control signals are $B/\overline{W}$= high (for the Z8000) and $\overline{UDS}$ = low (for the 68000).

(b) With A0 = 1, the least significant byte—located on an odd address—is transferred via the lower half of the data bus D0–D7, and the respective control signals are $B/\overline{W}$ = high (for the Z8000) and $\overline{LDS}$ = low (for the 68000).

For the 8086 this order is reversed:

(a) With A0 = 0, the least significant byte—which is now located on an even address—is transferred via the lower half of the data bus D0–D7, and the control signal is $\overline{BHE}$ = high.

(b) With A0 = 1, the most significant byte—which is now located on an odd address—is transferred via the upper half of the data bus D8–D15, and the control signal is $\overline{BHE}$ = low.

If all 8086 word operations occur on an even byte address boundary with $\overline{BHE}$ = low (i.e., the starting byte of the word operand is on an even byte boundary), then one memory access per word is required, thus optimizing performance (A0 = 0 for all even addresses). Word operations on odd byte boundaries will be converted to 2-byte operations by the 8086, one for the least significant byte and one for the most significant byte. In this case, the BIU of the 8086 CPU will perform these two memory accesses automatically.

It should be mentioned here that accessing I/O slave devices is performed in an analogous fashion.

6.4.3 Generating the Chip Select Signals

It was mentioned earlier that some of the address bits may be used directly as chip select signals.[7] Chip select signals may also be generated by one of the following ways: (1) using the clock signal CLK in conjunction with the address latch enable (ALE) strobe issued by the CPU; (2) using the clock signal CLK in conjunction with the address lines; for Intel 8080A-based

---

[7]Sometimes referred to also as "device select signals."

designs, the chip select signals may be generated by decoding the CPU address and status lines in conjunction with the $\overline{\text{STSTB}}$ strobe.

When memory or I/O devices are directly connected to the multiplexed CPU bus, the designer must guarantee that during a read cycle no such device corrupts the information (usually an address) present on the bus during the first state, T_1, of the bus cycle. This can be accomplished in two ways.

Connecting Devices Having Output Enables

In configurations of devices which have output enables, the device output drivers should not be enabled by the chip select signal, but instead, these outputs should be controlled by the READ (or WRITE) signal applied to the device (Figure 6.27a). Most microprocessors with multiplexed address/data buses have timing which guarantees that the READ signal is not valid until after the one state during which the address was valid on the CPU bus, and that the multiplexed address/data bus is floated (i.e., after the address is latched by ALE). Although the $\overline{\text{DEN}}$ and DT/$\overline{\text{R}}$ signals of the CPU discussed in the previous chapter isolate (memory and I/O) devices from the CPU (Figure 6.27b), bus contention may still exist in the system if the devices do not have an output enable (OE) control other than chip select.

Figure 6.28 gives selection techniques for memory devices (the 2142 1024 × 4-bit static RAM) with chip selects and output enables for Intel 8086-based implementations [11]. In Figure 6.28a, write may be gated with $\overline{\text{BHE}}$ and A0 to provide upper and lower byte bank write strobes. This simplifies chip select decoding by eliminating $\overline{\text{BHE}}$ and A0 as conditions of decode. Although during a byte write operation both banks receive the chip select signal, only one will receive a write strobe. During this write operation, no bus contention exists, since, to enable the memory output drivers, a read signal must be issued.

Figure 6.28b shows memory chips with multiple chip select pins for which the $\overline{\text{BHE}}$ and A0 lines now directly control bank selection. (This figure represents the detailed implementation of Figure 6.26a.) The CS is generated by decoding the address bits normally, and the configuration allows direct connection of the read and write signals to the devices.

Finally, Figure 6.28c presents an alternative configuration in which address bits are used directly as chip select signals (linear select), while the logic for $\overline{\text{RD}}$, A0, $\overline{\text{WR}}$ and $\overline{\text{BHE}}$ remains the same as in Figure 6.28a.

However, the designer must be careful of certain restrictions. For example, for a memory device of the type shown in Figure 6.27, which provides separate

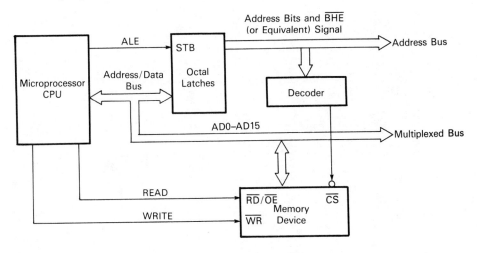

(a)

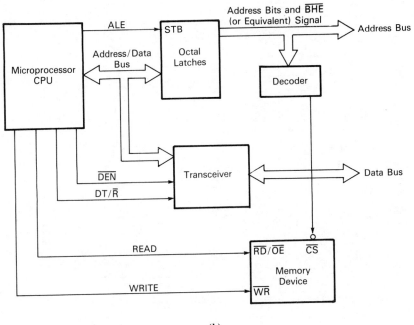

(b)

Figure 6.27 Connecting memory devices with output enables: **(a)** on the CPU multiplexed bus and **(b)** on the buffered system bus.

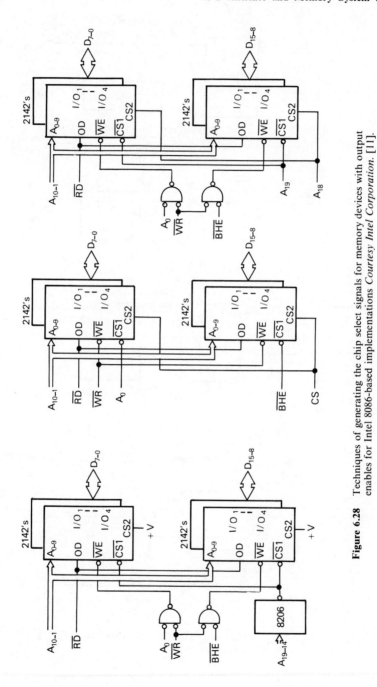

Figure 6.28 Techniques of generating the chip select signals for memory devices with output enables for Intel 8086-based implementations *Courtesy Intel Corporation.* [11].

$\overline{CS}$ and $\overline{RD}/\overline{OE}$ inputs, one should keep in mind that the access actually starts from $\overline{CS}$ internally, but the output drivers onto the data bus are not enabled until $\overline{RD}/\overline{OE}$ is enabled.

Connecting Devices Having No Output Enables

Several techniques exist for cases in which connecting devices have no output enables. One technique usually used is to have the chip select signal externally gated with the READ or WRITE control signal as follows:

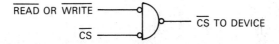

The detailed configuration of such an implemetation is shown in Figure 6.29. Two problems are present in this technique. The first problem arising is that the chip select access time is reduced to the read access time (which may force the use of an otherwise unnecessarily fast support device). The second problem is that the designer must verify that $\overline{CS}$ is not valid prior to the appearance of $\overline{WRITE}$, and that $\overline{CS}$ remains valid for one or two gate delays following the end of $\overline{WRITE}$.

In general, the best solution is obtained using devices having output enables.

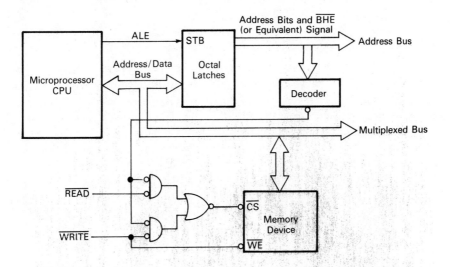

Figure 6.29 Connecting memory devices without output enables on the multiplexed bus.

6.5   DATA TRANSFERS OF 8 AND 16 BITS ON THE IEEE 796 SYSTEM BUS

The IEEE 796 is a demultiplexed system bus with separate address and data lines [7]. It supports two independent address spaces: memory and I/O. The sixteen bidirectional data lines are used to transmit data to and receive it from a memory location or I/O port. Since the IEEE 796 bus allows both 8-bit masters and slaves and 16-bit masters and slaves to co-exist in a single system, it allows both 8-bit and 16-bit data transfers. Two signals control the data transfers: BHEN* active indicates that the bus is operating in the 16-bit mode, and the address bit (A0*) defines an even-byte or odd-byte transfer. For existing devices which only maintain an 8-bit data bus, all 8-bit transfers on the IEEE 796 bus are performed over the lower half of the 16-bit data bus, regardless of the address. The full sixteen data lines are used only for 16-bit transfers. To maintain compatibility, a byte-swapping buffer is required in all 16-bit masters and 16-bit slaves. The 8-bit and 16-bit master alternatives are discussed next. In both cases, 16-bit memory (or I/O slaves) are considered.[8]

Eight-Bit Masters

The two alternatives are shown in Figure 6.30. For a low (even) byte transfer, BHEN* and A0* are inactive, thus indicating an 8-bit even byte operation. The data byte is transferred across on data lines D0*–D7* (Figure 6.30a). For a high (odd) byte transfer, BHEN* is inactive and A0* is active. Again, the data byte is transferred across on data lines D0*–D7* but the swap byte buffer is now used in the 16-bit slave device (Figure 6.30b).

Sixteen-Bit Masters

Three alternative configurations are shown in Figure 6.31. For a low (even) byte transfer, BHEN* and A0* are inactive, thus indicating an 8-bit even byte operation. The data byte is transferred across on data lines D0*–D7* (Figure 6.31a). For a high byte transfer, BHEN* is inactive and A0* is active, thus indicating an 8-bit odd byte operation. The data byte again is transferred across on data lines D0*–D7*, but the swap byte buffer is now used in both the 16-bit master and 16-bit slave devices (Figure 6.31b). Finally, for 16-bit data transfers, BHEN* is active and A0* is inactive. In this type of transfer, the low byte is transferred on D0*–D7*, and the high (odd) byte is transferred across the bus on D8*–D15* lines (the swap byte buffers in the master and slave are not involved).

---

[8]Byte transfers to 8-bit slave devices are independent of the CPU.

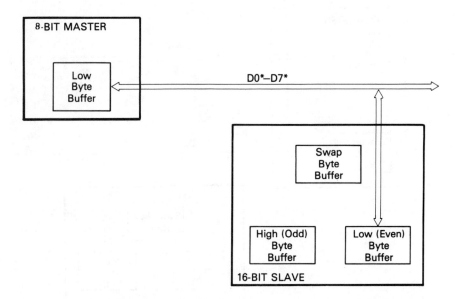

(a) Low (even) byte transfer (BHEN* = inactive, A0* = inactive).

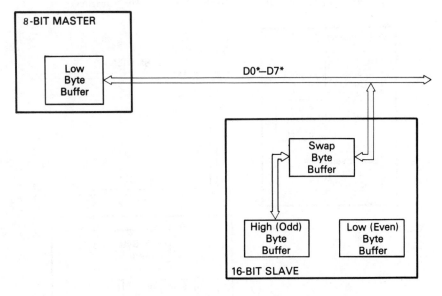

(b) High (odd) byte transfer (BHEN* = inactive, A0* = active).

Figure 6.30   Alternative IEEE 796 data transfers for 8-bit masters [7].

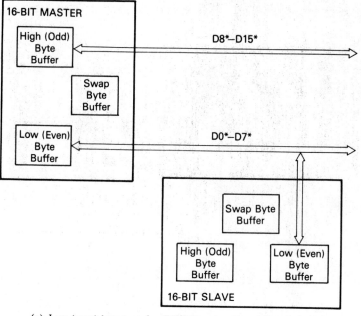

(a) Low (even) byte transfer (BHEN* = inactive, A0* = inactive).

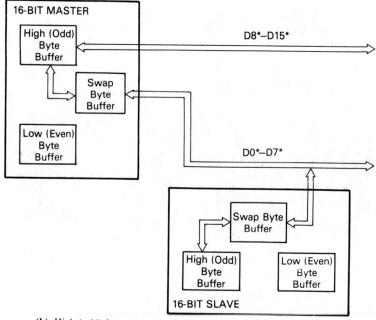

(b) High (odd) byte transfer (BHEN* = inactive, A0* = active).

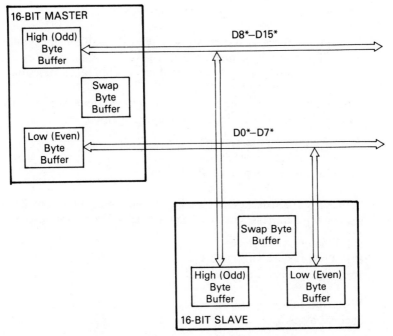

(c) 16-bit transfer (BHEN* = active, A0* = active).

Figure 6.31 Alternative IEEE 796 data transfers for 16-bit masters [7].

EXERCISES

6.1 Consider a memory composed of one 2048 × 8-bit ROM chip and two 256 × 4-bit RAM chips. ROM uses a chip select of A11 = 1, and the RAM module uses a select of A12A13 − 11_2. What are the respective ROM and RAM modules' real address spaces? (Use hexadecimal notation.)

6.2 What is the minimum number of address bits required for a memory module composed of two 256 × 8-bit memory chips?

6.3 What is the minimum number of address bits required for a memory made up of four 256 × 8-bit memory chips? How many of these address bits may be allocated a chip select function, and how many a word address function?

6.4 In Exercise 6.3, how can the external hardware required to access a memory word be minimized (or eliminated)?

6.5 For a microprocessor system whose highest allowable memory address is $FFFF_{16}$, and whose memory consists of $2_K \times 8$-bit memory chips, how many address bits are allocated to the chip select function?

6.6 How many data bus receivers can be selected *directly* with a 16-bit address? Give the hexadecimal value of the 16-bit address:

(a) When it selects receiver # 1
(b) When it selects receiver # 5
(c) When it selects receiver # 15

6.7 Using an 8 to 256 decoder, how many data bus receivers can be selected with an 8-bit address? Give the hexadecimal value of the 8-bit address:

(a) When it selects receiver # 1
(b) When it selects receiver # 5
(c) When it selects receiver # 15

6.8 Write the following 16-bit memory addresses as HI and LO hexadecimal bytes:

(a) 0010001010110111
(b) 0000000100000000
(c) 1111000000000000
(d) 0000100011111111

6.9 In terms of the HI and LO memory address bytes, write the address range (in hexadecimal addresses) for the following memory groups of an 8-bit microcomputer:

(a) The first (lowest) 4K bytes of memory
(b) The last (highest) 8K bytes of memory
(c) The last (highest) 16K bytes of memory

6.10 It is required that a memory of total capacity 4096 bits be constructed, with word lengths of sixteen bits, using RAM chips of size 32×4 bits. Give the array configuration of this memory on one card showing all required input and output signals.

6.11 It is required that a memory of sixty-four words be constructed, eight bits/word, using RAM chips of size 32 × 2 bits. Give the array configuration of this memory on one printed circuit board, showing all required input and output signals.

6.12 Draw the memory organization (analogous to that of Figure 6.26) of the Motorola 68000 for byte and word accessing.

6.13 If the RAM chips of page #3 in Figure 6.15 were of size 128 × 8 bits, what would be the respective real (hexadecimal) addresses assigned to each chip? (Hint: Address bit A7 is not used.)

6.14 Consider a microcomputer memory composed of one 1024 × 8-bit ROM chip and two 512 × 4-bit RAM chips. Accessing the ROM is done using (as chip select) A10 = 1, while accessing the RAM is done using A12 = A13 = 1. If the address bus is sixteen bits wide, list the real addresses (in hexadecimal notation) occupied by the ROM and RAM (assume A14 = A15 = 0). Draw the detailed interfacing of these chips to the Intel 8080A buses.

6.15 Following the circuit shown in Figure 6.15 design a memory system composed of sixteen 4096-byte pages, using RAM chips of size 512 × 8 bits. Show the detailed memory configuration for page # 4, and list the real addresses (in hexadecimal) occupied by each RAM chip within this page.

REFERENCES AND BIBLIOGRAPHY

[1] Bal, S., G. Chao, and Z. Soha, "Bilingual, 16-bit μP Summons Large-Scale Computer Power," *Electronic Design*, January 18, 1980, pp. 66–70.

[2] Banning, J., "Z-bus and Peripheral Support Packages Tie Distributed Computer Systems Together," *Electronic Design,* 24, November 22, 1979, pp. 144–50.

[3] Davis, H.A., "Comparing Architectures of Three 16-bit Microprocessors," *Computer Design*, July 1979, pp. 91–100.

[4] Hartman, B., "16-bit 68000 Microprocessor Camps on 32-bit Frontier," *Electronics*, October 11, 1979, pp. 118–25.

[5] Horody, R. and P. Alfke, "Learn to Apply the Power of the Z8002 by Studying a Small 16-Bit Computer," *Electronic Design*, 22, October 25, 1979.

[6] IBM Corporation, *Introduction to System/360 Architecture*, (C20-1667-1), Data Processing Division, White Plains, NY, 1968.

[7] IEEE Task P796/D2, "Proposed Microcomputer System 796 Bus Standard," *Computer*, October 1980, pp. 89–105.

[8] Intel Corporation, *Intel 8080 Microcomputer Systems User's Manual*, (98-153C), Santa Clara, CA, September 1975.

[9] Intel Corporation, *MCS-80 User's Manual (With Introduction to MCS-85)*, (98-153D), Santa Clara, CA, October 1977.

[10] Intel Corporation, *MCS-80/85 Family User's Manual*, (121506-001), Santa Clara, CA, October 1979.

[11] Intel Corporation, *The 8086 Family User's Manual*, (9800722–03), Santa Clara, CA, October 1979.

[12] Le Mair, I., "Indexed Mapping Extends Microprocessor Addressing Range," *Computer Design*, August 1980, pp. 111–18.

[13] Martin, D.P., *Microcomputer Design*, Northbrook, IL: Martin Research (now Quint Systems, Inc.), 1976.

[14] McKevitt, J., and J. Bayliss, "New Options from Big Chips," *IEEE Spectrum*, March 1979, pp. 28–34.

[15] Morse, S.P., W.B. Pohlman, and B.W. Ravenel, "The Intel 8086 Microprocessor: a 16-bit Evolution of the 8080," *Computer*, June 1978, pp. 18–26.

[16] Ogdin, C.A., "Microcomputer Components," *Mini-Micro Systems*, November-December 1977, pp. 50–58.

[17] Ogdin, C.A., "Reconfigurable Memory Scheme Suits 8- or 16-bit Words," *EDN*, September 20, 1978, pp. 89–93.

[18] Osborne, A., *An Introduction to Microcomputers, Volume I, Basic Concepts*, Berkeley, CA: Adam Osborne and Associates, Inc., 1975.

[19] Osborne, A., *An Introduction to Microcomputers, Volume II, Some Real Products*, Berkeley, CA: Adam Osborne and Associates, Inc., 1976.

[20] Peuto, B.L., "Architecture of a New Microprocessor," *Computer*, February 1979, pp. 10–21.

[21] Rector R., and G. Alexy, *The 8086 Book*, Berkeley, CA: Osborne, McGraw-Hill, 1980.

[22] Stritter, E. and T. Gunter, "A Microprocessor Architecture for a Changing World: The Motorola 68000," *Computer*, February 1979, pp. 43–51.

[23] Zilog, Incorporated, *1982/83 Data Book*, Cupertino, CA, 1982.

Chapter 7

SOFTWARE AND PROGRAMMING ASPECTS

7.1 INTRODUCTION

Before the discussion of microprocessor I/O techniques is continued in chapter 8, some software and programming issues needed to convert the microprocessor hardware into a usable system are presented in this chapter.

One can never say enough about this extensive and important topic. It is assumed here that the reader already has some knowledge of assembly language programming. Therefore, this chapter presents only the highlights and the rules for writing assembly language programs for microprocessors.

Microprocessor software and programming may range from the very simple to the very complex. Towards the low end of the spectrum lies the widely used software that replaces hardwired logic in device and instrument control functions. This type of software was the first to be used, because low-level microprocessors or single-chip microcomputers had limited capabilities and a restricted spectrum of applications. However, with the already available 16- and 32-bit microprocessors that have advanced features and offer increased capabilities, software is moving towards the high end of the spectrum, resembling traditional minicomputer applications programs. The latest microcomputers may have advanced operating systems, a number of high-level languages, and sophisticated software support. Developing such software will require a considerable team effort, which may approach that used for the development of software on larger machines.

The first two sections of this chapter mention briefly the software components usually provided in a microcomputer system,[1] and cover machine and

---

[1]The term "microcomputer system" is used in this chapter to refer primarily to a fully developed system that also includes the basic system software and tools allowing easy programming.

assembly language programming issues. The discussion mainly concentrates on highlighting the format of executable assembly language instructions and representative assembler directives. A very large number of assembly level languages exist for microprocessors, each having its own mnemonics, addressing mode definitions, and operand specifications. In order to establish a uniform basis for microprocessor assembler design, IEEE has proposed a Microprocessor Assembly Language Draft Standard [3]. Section 7.4 outlines instruction formats and lengths. (Instruction formats for several representative microprocessors are given in the Appendices). The last section, 7.5, presents the addressing modes and structures found in microprocessors.

7.2 SOFTWARE AND PROGRAMMING

Software is divided into systems software and applications software. Systems software controls the operation of the computer system, manages and allocates system resources, and provides the programmer with the necessary tools to write applications programs.

7.2.1 Software Tools of a Microcomputer System

There are several types of software components provided in a microcomputer system [10,20]. A discussion of them follows.

Monitor

The monitor is also called the "supervisor," the "executive," or the "operating system." It is the heart of the microcomputer software, allowing the user to communicate with the system, calling (activating) other system software when necessary, scheduling the execution of programs, and managing and allocating resources efficiently. The word "monitor" usually refers to a rather restricted microcomputer system. However, with today's powerful microprocessors, even complex time-sharing operating systems can be designed. More details on that part of the operating system which is responsible for managing and allocating main memory (the major system resource) is given later, in chapter 10. In small microcomputer systems that do not have memory allocation software, this task is usually undertaken by the user.

I/O Driver

The I/O driver consists of one or more routines that handle the interface procedures between the microcomputer and external devices, and control the operation of these devices. The complexity of the driver depends on the configuration of the overall system and the type of I/O interface chips (e.g.,

DMA controllers, I/O processors, etc.) used. In 16- and 32-bit microprocessors that have both user and supervisor mode, these routines execute in supervisor mode.

Data Management or File System

The data management or file system component manages the use of auxiliary (secondary) memory, i.e., the organization, storage, retrieval, updating of auxiliary memory, and its allocation to files. Again, a microcomputer system may or may not have such a software component.

Editor

To prepare, modify and store programs, the editor is used. It allows a user to access a stored program on an instruction-by-instruction basis and modify it properly. Or, while inputting a program or data, the user can utilize the editor to display, delete, change, insert, or modify the input information.

Language Translators

Language translators are system programs that translate user source programs from one form to another. The most common system programs are: macro-assemblers, loaders and compilers/interpreters.

Assembler

The assembler allows the user to write programs in symbolic assembly language using mnemonic abbreviations for the processor's operation codes (op codes) and free symbolic names for program and data addresses. The assembler accepts as input the source program written in assembly language, processes it, and produces the object program. In order to translate the source program, the assembler must do the following: (1) Replace each mnemonic op code with its corresponding binary representation. Upon encountering an executable instruction, the assembler looks it up in its "op code table," and replaces the mnemonic code with its binary equivalent. (2) Replace each symbolic name (label or operand) by a relative numeric value.

The assembler carries out its tasks usually in two "passes" of the source program (a "two-pass assembler"). During the first pass the assembler maintains a counter, called the *location counter*, which increments each time it encounters an executable instruction. The location counter starts with the numeric value specified by the "origin directive" ORG (the default value is usually 0 (zero)) and incremented by a variable number which depends upon the length of the instruction being translated. At the same time, the assembler also constructs the symbol table, by examining the label field of each instruction on the source program. In this table it places the symbolic name found in the label field, along with the running relative numeric value of the location counter. (To reduce the symbol table length, the assembler actually searches the table to see whether this name has already been placed in it.) During pass one, the assembler also performs syntax analysis on the source program to discover any programming errors.

After the symbol table for the whole source program is constructed, the second pass starts. During this pass, the assembler first re-initializes the location counter and again examines each instruction in the source program. Using its op code table, the assembler translates each mnemonic op code to its binary equivalent. It also inspects the operand field of each instruction, and for every symbolic name found there, the assembler replaces it by its corresponding relative numeric value from the symbol table. In this way, the source program is converted into an object binary program. During pass two, the assembler also performs global error analysis and prints the source listing (usually with diagnostic messages for any errors discovered), and, optionally, its corresponding object code. Each of the above two passes is complete when the assembler reaches the directive END.

A *macro assembler* has the additional capability to translate user-defined macros. When a macro is encountered during pass one, the macro assembler replaces it by its respective group of symbolic instructions. (Macros are discussed in section 7.3.1.)

Loader

The object code produced by the assembler may be "absolute" or "relocatable," and is usually input to another system program called the "loader," which places the object code program in free memory locations in main memory.

In the simplest case, the assembler translates the source program into an absolute object code, which is placed directly in memory ready to be executed. The first absolute address of the program is the one specified by the directive ORG (i.e., the initial value placed in the assembler's "location counter"). In this case, the loader is called an *absolute loader* and is really nothing more than an instruction that transfers control to the first executable instruction of the assembled program. An absolute loader presents the following disadvantages:

- The programmer is required to specify the first absolute location in main memory where his or her program actually is to be loaded.
- When the program uses subroutines, the programmer is forced to know the lengths of the program and of all subroutines, so that he or she may specify

their respective first absolute addresses. Thus, the layout of the total program in memory must be preplanned completely by the programmer.

* The result generated by the assembler is an absolute binary code; i.e., all absolute addresses are assigned at assembly time. Thus, with absolute loaders, *addresses are bound at assembly time*. This makes extremely difficult the effective use of subroutine libraries. Furthermore, after assembly, program relocation is impossible.

* It is very difficult for the programmer to make modifications, improvements, and expansions in the program.

* An absolute loader is unaware of any division of the program into smaller modules.

* Sharing of a program module by more than one programmer requires that each programmer obtain a copy of the module and assemble it together along with his or her main program.

An improvement on the above is the situation in which the programmer is not required to specify the first absolute location of a program module. This means that address binding is not done at assembly time; instead, *address binding is delayed until the program is loaded* in preparation for execution.[2] The assembler now generates an object code as though the first instruction were to be loaded into location 0 (zero). It also indicates to the loader all the addresses in the program that would require a modification, should the loading of the program start from a different point in main memory. These addresses are called "relative addresses," and the result of the assembly is called the "relocatable object code." The output of the assembler is taken by the *relocatable loader*, which now places it in any memory area that is free at the time of loading, and properly adjusts all the relative addresses. This adjustment involves the adding to—or subtracting from—each relative address the amount of program relocation.

With an absolute loader, program relocation is done by modifying the directive ORG and reassembling the source program. Using a relocatable loader, however, does away with the requirement of a new assembly each time the program is to be relocated.

Another advantage of the relocatable loader is that a number of separately assembled programs (or program modules) can be linked and loaded into main memory to form one executable unit (without overlapping each other). In this case, a symbol in the object code module may be a "local symbol" (when it refers to a location within the same module, i.e., "intramodule

---

[2]An even more general case of further delaying binding of addresses until the program is actually executed is discussed in chapter 10.

reference"), or a "global symbol" (when it refers to a location in another module, i.e., "intermodule reference"). The additional problem that arises is that, since neither the programmer nor the assembler knows where the various object modules are going to be loaded, intermodule references cannot be resolved before loading. There are several schemes for handling this problem: one method is the *transfer vector technique*; a second method employs a *linking loader* (also called a linkage editor), which allocates free memory areas to the various modules and links them together. With either method, the programmer uses specific directives to pass information regarding global symbols on to the loader. The symbol table generated by the assembler becomes properly modified to include (besides the intramodule relative addresses) additional information regarding each module's external symbols (intermodule references).

Compilers and Interpreters

Compilers and interpreters are high-level language processors. A *compiler* receives and translates the entire source program at once into an entire object code. An *interpreter* translates each source statement as it is encountered during program execution. Although slower in executing a source program, interpreters are preferred for small systems because they are easier to implement. High-level language processors have the following advantages: they make programming easy; the programmer is not required to be familiar with the details of the internal structure of the system; the number of programmer instructions is smaller, and programs written in high-level language are easier to debug; high-level languages are easy to learn and use; and finally, programs written in high-level language are machine-independent (and, therefore, portable). Their major disadvantages, however, are that the programs run slower and occupy more memory space than "equivalent" programs written in assembly language. A survey of microprocessor languages is given in [4].

Cross-Software

Some other software tools provided to the microprocessor programmer should also be mentioned here. They are generally called cross-software because they are not resident in the microcomputer itself; instead, they run on another (usually larger) machine. One such type is the *cross-assembler*. It is written (usually) in FORTRAN and executed on a large- or medium-scale computer. For example, a user can use an Intel 8086 cross-assembler which is executed on a large machine to develop 8086 assembly language programs and produce the respective object codes to be transferred directly to an 8086 based microcomputer. Similarly, *cross-compilers* allow the user to write a program in a microprocessor high-level language. The cross-compiler is again executed on a larger machine to produce the respective microprocessor object code. Finally, microprocessor *simulators* also exist. They receive the object code created by the assembler and execute it in the larger machine, producing conventional results. However, simulators have limitations in simulating real-time operations using interrupts and I/O devices.

7.2.2   Machine and Assembly Language Programming

Each basic instruction of a microprocessor is represented as a pattern of bits. For example, the Intel 8080A/8085 instruction, "add contents of a memory location to the accumulator," has a binary representation of 10000110; similarly, the instruction, "compare the contents of a memory location with accumulator," has a binary representation of 10111110, etc. The set of all the binary instructions of the microprocessor constitutes its *machine language*. Writing a program using these binary instructions is called *machine language programming*. Programming in machine language is a time-consuming process, prone to errors which are difficult to debug; all program and data locations are referenced by their absolute address in memory. Machine language is unique with each microprocessor.

Assembly language programming allows the programmer to use mnemonics for each of the processor's operation codes. For example, the two instructions mentioned above have the mnemonics ADD M and CMP M, respectively. The programmer is also allowed to assign symbolic names freely for referencing program and data addresses. However, since the microprocessor understands only binary patterns, before such an assembly language program can be executed, it must first be translated into machine language. There is always a one-to-one correspondence between symbolic instructions used by the programmer and the translated machine language instructions. This translation is performed automatically by the *assembler*. Writing programs in assembly language permits the programmer to access many of the microprocessor's features directly, such as registers, flags, etc.

Assembly Language Instruction Formats

Before continuing with machine and assembly language programming, let us examine the rules to which an assembly language instruction must adhere, as proposed by the IEEE standard [3].

An assembly language instruction must have the following format, made out of four types of fields:

Label Mnemonic Operand(s)   ; Comments

Label Field

The label field is an optional field used to reference an instruction by a symbolic name. All labels must begin with an alphabetic character in the first position of a line. Labels are not allowed to be duplicated. A label may be terminated by a colon (:), but the colon is not mandatory. At least one blank must separate the rest of the line from the label.

Mnemonic Field

The mnemonic field contains the mnemonic name for an instruction or a directive (defined below). Instruction mnemonics shall not start in the first column of a line, and must always be followed by at least one blank. A mnemonic has a first character which is the first letter of the instruction name (for example, ADD for "add," ADDC for "add with carry," DIV for "divide," MUL for "multiply," LD for "load," etc.). Conditions are embedded in the mnemonic by concatenating the generic instruction name with the condition name (for example, BNE for "branch if not equal," SKLT for "ship if less than," CALLNC for "call if no carry," RETPE for "return if parity even," etc.). Finally, where appropriate, the operand type may be indicated by the last character of the mnemonic as shown below (the default operand type is word):

B:	Byte
H:	Halfword
D:	Decimal
F:	Floating-point
1:	Bit
4:	Nibble or digit
M:	Multiple

For example, ROR4 stands for "rotate right decimal," SET1 for "set bit," MULL for "multiply long," CMPM for "compare multiple," LBD for "load byte," etc.

Operand Field

Depending upon the mnemonic, the operand field may be absent, or may consist of one or more items separated by a comma. The operand sequence is specified using the terms "primary" (the first operand) and "secondary" (the second operand). When more than one secondary operand is specified in the instruction, the operands are sequenced in decreasing order of importance. For "move" operands, their sequence is "source, destination"; for "load and store" operands, their sequence is "register, memory"; and for "arithmetic" operands, two cases exist: (1) in two-operand instructions the primary operand is both the source and destination, and the secondary operand is the second source; (2) in three-operand instructions the primary operand is the destination, followed by the "first" source, then by the "second" source.

Operand Specification

All operands are designated by either a number or a symbolic representation of that number, for both memory and register operands (i.e., the address of the data to be operated on). When multiple registers are addressable, they are assigned numbers consistent with the architecture of the hardware.

To specify the base of a number, an alphabetic character is placed in front of it, followed by an apostrophe (the default base is decimal): B stands for binary, Q for octal, D for decimal, and H for hexadecimal. Examples of numeric constants are:

> B'1101101
> Q'732
> D'9635
> H'1ABF

Character strings are enclosed within quotation marks. The operand may also denote location counter reference. This is specified by the special symbol * which refers to the address of the current instruction. For example, * + 4 indicates the value which is 4 greater than that of the current location counter value. Finally, arithmetic and logical expressions may also be placed in the operand field. The expressions operators are designated by the following infix special symbols:

Symbol(s)	Operation
+	Add
−	Subtract
*	Multiply
/	Divide (signed)
/ /	Divide (unsigned)
AND.	AND
OR.	OR
XOR.	Exclusive OR
NOT.	NOT
SHL.	Left shift
SHR.	Right shift
MOD.	Modulo

**	Exponentiate
<:>	Bit alignment

Comments Field

Comments may be placed after a statement on the same line, or on a separate line. The only rule governing comments is that they must start with a semi-colon (;).

Addressing Mode Specification

To specify the addressing mode, special characters are used which precede the address expression (addr), where pre or post specification implies an operational sequence. The addr may refer to either a memory location or a register. The IEEE standard suggests the following prefix and postfix characters to define the specified address modes (microprocessor address modes are explained in section 7.5):

Mode	Symbol	Example
Absolute	prefix /	/addr
Base page	prefix !	!addr
Indirect	prefix @	@addr
Relative	prefix $	$addr
Immediate	prefix #	#value
Index	enclosing parenthesis ( )	addr(index)
Register	prefix .	.addr
Auto-pre-increment	prefix +	+addr
Auto-post-increment	postfix+	addr+
Auto-pre-decrement	prefix −	−addr
Auto-post-decrement	postfix −	addr−
Indirect-pre-indexed	prefix ( ) @	addr(index)@
Indirect-post-indexed	prefix @, postfix ( )	@addr(index)

Figure 7.1 shows a simple example of an Intel 8080A/8085 assembly language program. Assuming that its first instruction is loaded in memory location 0300_{16}, the leftmost column lists the absolute memory addresses occupied by the program, the second and third colums show the contents of each location in binary and hexadecimal notation, and the fourth column lists the assembly language program. The same program is rewritten in the right column using conventions proposed by the IEEE assembly language standard.

Software and Programming Aspects

Intel 8080/8085

Memory Location (Hex)	Contents		Assembly Language Program	IEEE Assembly Language Standard Convention
	Binary	Hex		
0300	01111110	3E	MVI A, 1	MOV 1, #A
0301	00000001	01		
0302	11010011	D3	OUT 0	OUT 0
0303	00000000	00		
0304	11010011	D3	OUT 1	OUT 1
0305	00000001	01		
0306	11010011	D3	OUT 2	OUT 2
0307	00000010	02		
0308	00000110	06	MVI B, 068H	MOV H'68, #B
0309	01101000	68		
030A	00001110	0E	MVI C, 0FFH	MOV H'0FFH, #C
030B	11111111	FF		
030C	00001101	0D	DCR C	DEC C
030D	11000010	C2	JNZ 030CH	BNZ H'30C
030E	00001100	0C		
030F	00000011	03		
0310	00000101	05	DCR B	DEC B
0311	11000010	C2	JNZ 030AH	BNZ H'30A
0312	00001010	0A		
0313	00000011	03		
0314	00000111	07	RLC	ROLC
0315	11010010	D2	JNC 0302H	BNZ H'302
0316	00000010	02		
0317	00000011	03		

Figure 7.1 An 8080A/8085 assembly language program, assumed to be loaded in memory starting from location 0300₁₆. (Contents of each memory location are shown explicitly in binary and hexadecimal format, and correspond to the program in machine language. The next column shows the program in assembly language and the rightmost column shows the same program following the proposed IEEE standard convention.)

The instructions in this example use absolute addresses in their operand fields. If symbolic names are used in the label and operand fields, and comments inserted, then the assembly language program of Figure 7.1 may look like the program shown in Figure 7.2. If the microprocessor operates with a 2 MHz clock (i.e., each state or clock period equals 500 nsec), then the execution of the two instructions in the inner loop, LOOP1, would require fourteen states (i.e., four states for instruction DCR and ten states for instruction JNZ), which equals 14×500 ns $= 7$ μsec. Since the previous instruction MVI initializes register C with the value $FF_{16} = 255_{10}$, this inner loop, LOOP1. will be executed 255 times, thus providing a time delay of 255×7 μsec $= 1.785$ msec. Since the outside loop is executed 104 times, the overall delay is approximately 185.7 msec.

The simple program of Figures 7.1 and 7.2 distributes a 185.7-msec positive pulse to each of eight 3-wire groups every 185.7 msecs.

Assembler Directives

Besides executable instructions, an assembler also recognizes a number of directives.[3] A directive is written in the same fashion as the assembly language instructions described earlier. As with mnemonics, assembler directives should not start in the first column of a line. Although they are part of the assembly language, directives are not translated into machine language instructions, i.e., they are not executable and, therefore, do not occupy any locations when the program is loaded in main memory. They simply appear in the assembly language source program to provide the assembler with information to be used subsequently while generating the object code.

Figure 7.3 gives an example 8080A/8085 assembly language program which performs a multibyte addition of the two unsigned data quantities 32AF8A and 84BA90 [5]. The leftmost column numbers each line. The second column gives the absolute hexadecimal memory locations where the object program is stored. The third column shows the contents of these locations (representing the machine language instructions in hexadecimal notation). The next three columns list the assembly language source program, and the rightmost column contains comments.

Given below are some of the most common directives used to program microcomputers in assembly language.

The ORG Directive
The origin or ORG assembler directive is used to specify the absolute memory location at which the first executable instruction of the program will be placed

---

[3]Directives are also called *nongenerative instructions, declaratives*, or *pseudo-instructions*.

Label	Mnemonic Op Code	Operand	Comments
	ORG	3ØØH	
	MVI	A,1	; SET LOW BIT OF A TO 1
LOOP3:	OUT	Ø	; OUTPUT ACCUMULATOR TO ; PORT Ø
	OUT	1	; OUTPUT ACCUMULATOR TO ; PORT 1
	OUT	2	; OUTPUT ACCUMULATOR TO ; PORT 2
	MVI	B,Ø68H	; INITIALIZE REGISTER B
LOOP2:	MVI	C,Ø OFFH	; INITIALIZE REGISTER C
LOOP1:	DCR	C	; DECREMENT REGISTER C
	JNZ	LOOP1	; BRANCH TO LOOP1 IF NON ; ZERO
	DCR	B	; DECREMENT REGISTER B
	JNZ	LOOP2	; BRANCH TO LOOP2 IF NON ; ZERO
	RLC		; ROTATE ACCUMULATOR LEFT
	JNC	LOOP3	; BRANCH BACK TO LOOP3, IF ; NO CARRY
	HLT		
	END		

Figure 7.2 The assembly language program of Figure 7.1, using symbolic names in the label and operand fields, and adding comments to each instruction.

```
 1              ;
 2              ; AN 8Ø8Ø/8Ø85 ASSEMBLY LANGUAGE PROGRAM
 3              ;
 4              ; MULTIBYTE ADDITION
 5              ;
 6              ; ASSUMPTIONS: REGISTER E HOLDS LENGTH OF
 7              ; EACH NUMBER (IN BYTES) TO BE ADDED; NUMBERS TO BE
 8              ; ADDED ARE STORED FROM LOW-ORDER BYTE TO
 9              ; HIGH-ORDER BYTE BEGINNING AT MEMORY LOCATIONS
1Ø              ; ''FIRST'' AND ''SECND,'' RESPECTIVELY; RESULT IS STORED
11              ; FROM LOW-ORDER BYTE TO HIGH-ORDER BYTE BEGINNING
12              ; AT MEMORY LOCATION ''FIRST'', REPLACING THE ORIGINAL
13              ; CONTENTS OF THESE LOCATIONS.
14              ;
15              ; START PROGRAM CODE AT LOCATION 2ØØH
16              ;
17                          ORG     2ØØH
18              ;
19  Ø2ØØ 3A1EØ2            LDA     LENTH       ; INITIALIZE COUNT
2Ø  Ø2Ø3 5F               MOV     E,A
21  Ø2Ø4 Ø118Ø2 MADD:     LXI     B,FIRST     ; B AND C ADDRESS FIRST
22  Ø2Ø7 211BØ2           LXI     H,SECND     ; H AND L ADDRESS SECND
23  Ø2ØA AF               XRA     A           ; CLEAR CARRY FLAG
24              ; START LOOP TO ADD BYTE BY BYTE
25  Ø2ØB ØA    LOOP:      LDAX    B           ; LOAD BYTE OF FIRST
26                                            ; NUMBER
27  Ø2ØC 8E               ADC     M           ; ADD BYTE OF SECND WITH
28                                            ; CARRY
29  Ø2ØD Ø2               STAX    B           ; STORE RESULT IN FIRST
3Ø  Ø2ØE 1D               DCR     E           ; DECREMENT E
31  Ø2ØF CA17Ø2           JZ      DONE        ; DONE IF E=Ø
32              ;
33              ; PREPARE TO ADD NEXT TWO BYTES
34              ;
35  Ø212 Ø3               INX     B           ; POINT TO NEXT BYTE OF
36                                            ; FIRST NUMBER
37  Ø213 23               INX     H           ; POINT TO NEXT BYTE OF
38                                            ; SECND NUMBER
39  Ø214 C3ØBØ2           JMP     LOOP        ; JUMP TO LOOP TO ADD
4Ø                                            ; NEXT TWO BYTES
41              ;
42  Ø217 76    DONE:      HLT                 ; END OF EXECUTION
43              ;
44              ; DEFINE FIRST NUMBER
45  Ø218 8A    FIRST:     DB      8AH         ; FIRST NUMBER=32AF8A
46  Ø219 AF               DB      ØAFH
47  Ø21A 32               DB      32H
48              ;
49              ; DEFINE SECOND NUMBER
5Ø              ;
51  Ø21B 9Ø    SECND:     DB      9ØH         ; SECOND NUMBER=84BA9Ø
52  Ø21C BA               DB      ØBAH
53  Ø21D 84               DB      84H
54              ;
55              ; SET LENGTH OF TWO NUMBERS
56  Ø21E Ø3    LENTH:     DB      3           ; HERE EACH NUMBER IS
57                                            ; 3 BYTES LONG
58              ;
59  Ø21F                  END                 ; END OF PROGRAM
```

Figure 7.3   An 8080/8085 assembly language program and its equivalent machine code. (Multibyte addition). *Courtesy Intel Corporation* [5].

when the program is loaded in memory. (In reality, it sets the current "location counter" to the value specified by the operand.) For example, ORG 200H specifies that the first instruction byte will be placed in hexadecimal location 200, and succeeding executable instructions will be placed in contiguous locations 201, 202, 203, etc. Thus, in the example program of Figure 7.3, the first byte of instruction LDA (corresponding to the op code having a hexadecimal value 3A) will be placed in hexadecimal memory location 200. Multiple ORGs may also be used in a program, not necessarily listed in ascending order.

The END Directive

The end of the source program is identified and the assembler is terminated by the END directive. There must be only one END directive in each assembly language source file, and it must be the (physically) last statement of the source. It signifies to the assembler that the physical end of the source program has been reached, and that generation of the object program and (possibly) listing of the source program should now begin. The operand field of this statement may contain an expression specifying the program's starting address (typically saved in the object code) from which it will start executing.

The DB, DW, DD Directive

The define byte (DB), define word or 2-byte (DW), and define double word or 4-byte (DD) directives can be used to cause the assembler to fill one or more memory location(s) with the specified value(s). Locations can be initialized in units of bytes (eight bits), words (sixteen bits), and double words (thirty-two bits), respectively. For example, statement "FIRST: DB 8AH" in line 45 of Figure 7.3 initializes symbolic location FIRST (which corresponds here to absolute hexadecimal location 0218) with the hexadecimal byte 8A. Thus, the three DB statements in lines 45, 46, and 47 result in placing the first of the two added hexadecimal numbers (the 32AF8A) in hexadecimal locations 0218, 0219, and 021A.

The IEEE assembly language standard suggests replacing all the above names with the single *DATA* assembler directive. The data type to be used may be specified by appending a letter to the DATA mnemonic, as explained in section 7.2.2. Thus, the statement in line 45, of Figure 7.3 will be written as "FIRST: DATAB H'8A," while the two statements in lines 46 and 47 can be written as "DATAH H'AF32."

The EQU Directive

The equate or EQU directive equates a symbol with a constant (or an address or an expression). Thus, whenever this symbol is encountered subsequently in the source program, its equivalant constant will be used.

Besides the assembler directives discussed above, the IEEE standard also proposes the PAGE, TITLE, RES, and BASE directives.

A number of other directives exist also: For example, the Intel 8086 SEGMENT/ENDS directives (to name segments), the ASSUME directive, the GROUP directive (to specify that certain segments lie within the same 64K bytes of memory), the LABEL directive (which creates a name for the current location of assembly), the PROC/ENDP directives (to define procedures for implementing the concept of subroutines), etc. [6], or the listing control directives (PAGE, LIST, NOPAGE, NOOBJ, etc.) of the Motorola 68000 macro assembler [11]. These directives are specific to a given assembler, differ from one product to another, and therefore, are not discussed any further.

7.3 MACROS, SUBROUTINES, AND STACKS

So far it has been demonstrated how the programmer can use given mnemonic operation codes of the assembly language, symbolic names and addresses of his or her choice, and assembler directives in the source program.

The fact that many programmers were writing commonly used programs led to the construction of "ready" programs. These programs are constructed in such a way that they are readily available to be used by any programmer. Thus, the programmer can now write a *main program* which in turn can use one or more ready programs, generally called "subprograms," which are composed of an independent group of instructions, and constructed in such a way as to execute a specific work. The programmer may also break up a large program into a number of subprograms.

There are two types of subprograms: macros and subroutines:

- A *macro* (also called open subprogram) is a subprogram whose instructions— after the assembly process—are incorporated (embedded) into the main program, at the point from which the macro was called. Therefore, if the main program calls this macro, say, three times, then the macro's object code will appear in three different places of the object main program. A macro is referenced by its name.
- In contrast, a *subroutine* (or closed subprogram), after being assembled, will be placed in an area of memory which is outside the assembled main program. When during the execution of the main program this subroutine is called, the computer will automatically interrupt the execution of the main program and transfer control to the first instruction of the subroutine.[4] When the subroutine execution is finished (the last executable instruction of a subroutine is always a RETURN), the control automati-

---

[4]This transfer of control from the main program to the subroutine assumes that they have been properly "linked." Their linking is performed either when they are assembled together to form one program, or when they are loaded into the main memory.

cally returns to the place where the main program was interrupted. There-fore, calling a subroutine, say, three times, does not mean that the subroutine's instructions will be inserted in these three calling points of the object main program in memory.

The difference between macros and subroutines can also be expressed in terms of the "binding time" of their parameters: calling a macro results in embedding its instructions into the main program *before* execution time; calling a subroutine results in a "virtual" embedding of its instruction *during execution* of the program. The early binding of the macros yields an increased throughput during execution time. On the other hand, however, the fact that subroutine binding is delayed until program execution allows a much greater flexibility during execution, specifically with regard to the easy handling of the subroutine parameters [4, 19, 22].

7.3.1 Macros

There are many instances in which the programmer discovers that in writing a program he or she is repeating the same group of instructions many times. The job would be much easier, and the length of the program to be assembled smaller, if the programmer took advantage of the capability that the assembly language provides of using macros, by giving a name to this group of instructions, and, instead of repeating the group of instructions each time in the program, simply using its name.

For example, suppose the following group of four instructions appears in a program many times:

```
LOOP:        RRC                 ; ROTATE A RIGHT ONCE
             ANI  7FH            ; CLEAR THE HIGH-ORDER BIT OF A
             DCR  D              ; DECREMENT SHIFT COUNTER IN D
             JNZ  LOOP           ; JUMP BACK FOR ANOTHER SHIFT
```

This instruction sequence shifts the accumulator right a variable number of bit positions specified by the D register (shift counter) contents. It is possible to "define" the above a macro with the name SHV, and use the name SHV instead of repeating its four instructions. The "definition" of the macro is done by the programmer as follows:

```
Label        Code     Operand
SHV          MACRO    ←──────────────BEGIN THE MACRO DEFINITION
LOOP:        RRC
             ANI      7FH        ⎫
             DCR      D          ⎬ MACRO BODY
             JNZ      LOOP       ⎭
             ENDM     ←──────────────END THE MACRO DEFINITION
```

where SHV is the name given to this macro. Each macro ends with the instruction ENDM. This macro definition is (usually) placed before the main program, and both of them are supplied for assembly. The assembler accepts the statements between MACRO and ENDM as the "body" of the macro.

The programmer can call a macro from anywhere in the main program by placing in the code field of an instruction the name of the macro. Upon encountering a macro name in the code field, the assembler treats it as a macro-instruction, and substitutes it with the instructions that make up the body of the macro. This replacement is called *macro expansion*. The assembler then assembles (translates into object code) the expanded version of the main program.

Consider the previous example of the macro SHV that shifts the accumulator right by a variable number of bits. Figure 7.4a shows the macro SHV, and the main program that uses it, before assembly; Figure 7.4b shows the memory map (after assembly) where the macro's object code has been inserted in the object code of the main program, in the position of the two SHV statements of the source main program.

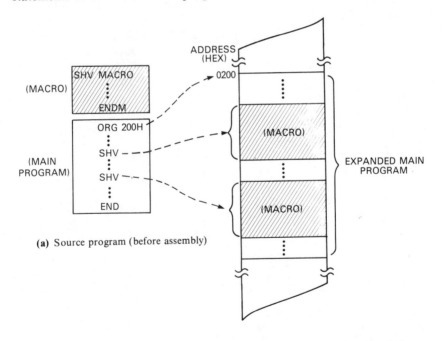

(a) Source program (before assembly)

(b) Main memory (after assembly)

Figure 7.4 (a) Macro SHV is called in two places in the main program; (b) after assembly, the object code of SHV has been inserted in the two places in the main program's object code from where the macro was called.

In Figure 7.5, the source program on the left is equivalent to the expanded program on the right. It is noticed that, although the programmer has been relieved from repeating in his source program the four instructions, nevertheless, the required memory space of the object program has not been reduced. Both versions of the program, at the left and at the right of Figure 7.5, occupy the same amount of main memory.

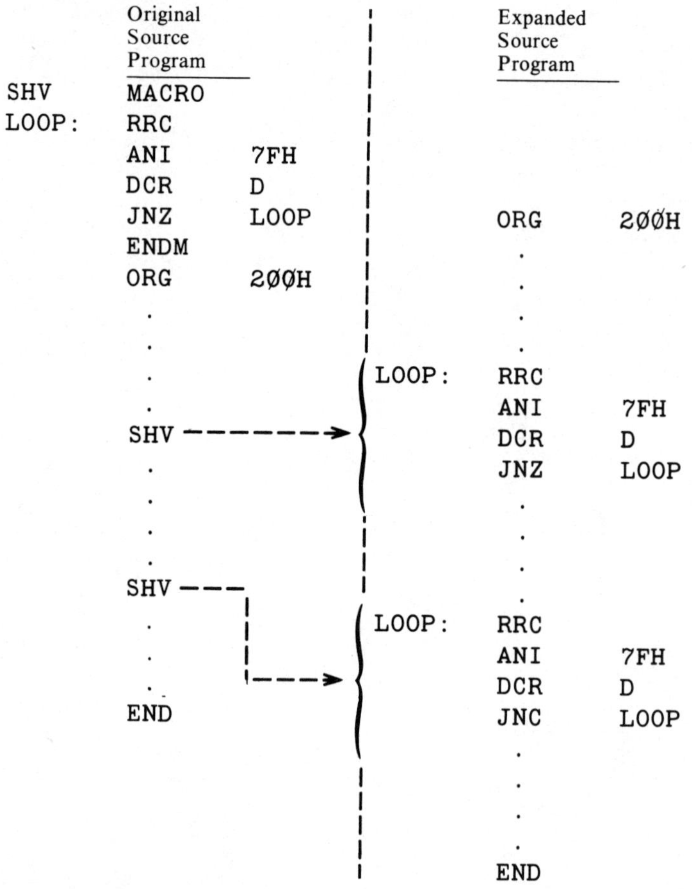

```
              Original                          Expanded
              Source                            Source
              Program                           Program
SHV       MACRO
LOOP:     RRC
          ANI      7FH
          DCR      D
          JNZ      LOOP                ORG      200H
          ENDM                          .
          ORG      200H                 .
            .                           .
            .                           .
            .                 LOOP:     RRC
            .                           ANI      7FH
SHV ------------->                      DCR      D
            .                           JNZ      LOOP
            .                           .
            .                           .
            .                           .
SHV ---                        LOOP:    RRC
            .                           ANI      7FH
            .                           DCR      D
            . .        '--->            JNC      LOOP
          END                           .
                                        .
                                        .
                                        .
                                        END
```

Figure 7.5 Inserting the macro in two different places in the main program.

7.3.2 Subroutines

If a macro becomes too lengthy or must be repeated many times, it is preferable to use subroutines. The use of subroutines in programming has the following advantages:

(a) Similar to macros, a subroutine is written only once. After that, the programmer can call it from any point in a program, by placing the subroutine's symbolic name in the operand field of a CALL instruction. The symbolic name of a subroutine is the label of its first instruction.
(b) A subroutine is considered as a separate program, and thus, can be assembled independently and separately from the main program.
(c) Since the subroutine appears in main memory only once (allocated to a space outside that of the main program's), the total memory space allocated to the assembled main program is smaller when subroutines are used than when macros are used.
(d) Besides the programmer's subroutines, the main program may also use ready subroutines residing in the system's library. The programmer can call these subroutines without necessarily knowing the details of their internal structure or the algorithms they use.
(e) The use of subroutines allows the subdivision of a large program into smaller modules, logically independent from each other, that can be written by different programmers without requiring each programmer to know all the details of the other programmer's program. Thus, a large program becomes modular, with all the advantages that modularity offers.
(f) A subroutine becomes a "general-purpose" subroutine when it can be used by more than one program.

One of the basic problems, however, in modularization of a program using subroutines is to define correctly the interface between modules.

When a subroutine is called, control is transferred to its first instruction. All its instructions are executed, and at the end of execution, control is returned to the instruction in the main program that follows the CALL with which the subroutine was called. To do this, each transfer of control to the subroutine saves in the stack the value of the program counter (which points to the instruction immediately following the CALL instruction in the program). This value must be restored into the program counter after the subroutine has finished executing, so that control can return to the proper place in the calling program.

The use of subroutines is shown schematically in Figure 7.6. The main program calls subroutine A from three different points. With each subroutine call, control is transferred to the first instruction of the subroutine; after each execution of the subroutine, control returns to the instruction following the "CALL A" in the main program. It is also noticed that only one copy of the subroutine resides in main memory.

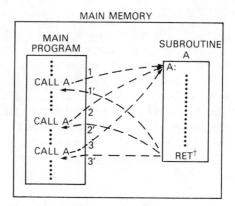

†RET=RETURN

Figure 7.6 The main program calls the subroutine from three different places.

As with macros, subroutine calls can be nested as shown in Figure 7.7. In this case, a subroutine may call one (or more) other subroutines. The main program calls subroutine SUB1, which—during its execution—calls subroutines SUB2 and SUB3, while SUB3 in turn calls SUB4. The figure also shows the ways of returning back from the various subroutines.

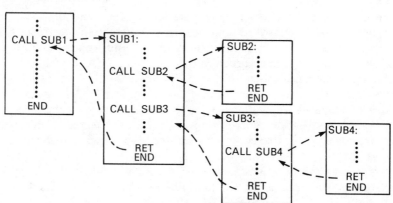

Figure 7.7 Subroutine nesting (three levels).

In the more general case, an executable program is composed of a number of independent smaller modules. Figure 7.8a shows a main program that calls (uses) the three subroutines A, B, and C. These subroutines:

(a) May follow the main source program during input to (and assembly by) the microcomputer system,
(b) May have been constructed by the same or a different programmer, at different times, and may have been stored in the system's auxiliary memory, thus becoming part of the system's user library, or
(c) May be permanent parts of the system library.

Furthermore, these subroutines may be in assembly language form, requiring assembly before execution or—as is the more common case when they are permanently resident in auxiliary memory and are part of the two libraries—they may have already been assembled into machine language, thus becoming object modules.

Figure 7.8b shows the four object modules properly loaded into main memory of the microcomputer as one executable unit. The dashed lines with the arrows denote the linkings between these modules.

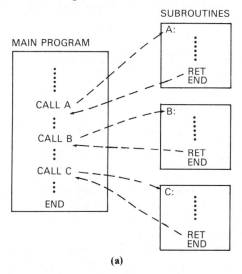

(a)

Figure 7.8 (a) The main program calls the three subroutines A, B, and C.

7.3.3 Stacks

Stacks and stack pointers are discussed in section 4.3.1 of chapter 4. In microcomputer systems, the stack is usually implemented in memory, with the stack pointer register of the CPU pointing to the most recent stack entry in

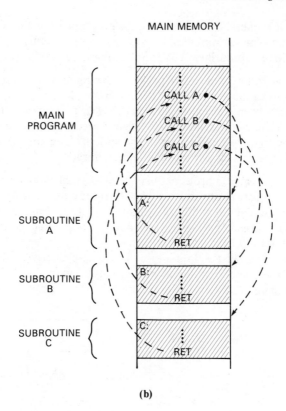

MAIN MEMORY

Figure 7.8 **(b)** The main program and the three subroutines loaded into the system's main memory as one executable unit.

memory. The stack operates in a LIFO concept and usually grows "downward" (i.e., from the highest location reserved for it to the lowest address). Stacks are used mainly to handle subroutines and exceptional conditions (see section 4.4.2 in chapter 4).

In handling subroutines, when a CALL to a subroutine is executed, the stack is used as the place for saving the value of the program counter. This value is automatically placed on the top of the stack, and the stack pointer is properly adjusted. Upon exit from the subroutine, the stack is "popped," and the program counter is reloaded with its old saved address (i.e., the address of the instruction following the CALL to the subroutine). Most microprocessor assembly languages also include PUSH and POP instructions to allow the programmer to save other CPU registers in the stack.

7.4   MICROPROCESSOR INSTRUCTION FORMATS AND LENGTHS

The length of the microprocessor instructions is not fixed. An instruction may be one, two, or more "words" long, thus requiring one, two, or more memory references, respectively, to fetch these instructions over a data bus having a width equal to that of the "word." Each microprocessor usually supports a number of instruction types, and the instruction formats used vary from microprocessor to microprocessor. The design of the instruction format requires decisions on how to allocate a limited number of bits to the op code field, and on the way address mode and other instruction fields are specified. Decisions are usually influenced by instruction usage statistics; this means that instruction formats are usually designed according to the range of applications for which the system is planned to be used.

Commonly instructions may have one, two, or more operands. In the single-operand instruction, the operand may be in memory or any CPU register, or it may be an immediate constant within the instruction. The result of the operation may be directed to memory or register. The two- and three-operand instructions were discussed in section 7.2.2.

Instruction formats for specific 8- and 16-bit microprocessors are discussed in the Appendices. Mentioned here are some of their common features.

For the 8-bit microprocessors, the instruction length may vary from one to four bytes. The first byte (the leftmost byte) of an instruction usually represents the op code. (In some of the Zilog Z80 instructions the second byte may also be part of the op code.) Some of the op code bits may indicate the length of the instruction, others may indicate the category of the instruction or the addressing mode used to access the operand(s), while others may specify a register or a pair of registers to be used during execution. Additional bytes in the instruction may be used to specify an immediate operand, a memory address, an I/O device address, operand source and destination, or a displacement or offset value.

The 16-bit microprocessor instructions may require from one to three 16-bit words. These microprocessors usually include the basic instructions of their 8-bit predecessors, along with instructions for handling program flow and ways of transferring both within the current segment as well as to any other segment. A special group of 1-byte instructions has also been included to manipulate byte and word strings. The 16-bit microprocessors may sometimes include new additional instructions: privileged instructions executing only in supervisor mode (for those microprocessors that allow both user and supervisor modes), multiply and divide instructions, multiple register saving instructions, specialized instructions to facilitate compiler and high-level language support (such as the Motorola 68000's LINK, UNLINK, TRAP, CHK, etc.), instructions to move data rapidly to/from peripheral devices (such as the Motorola 68000's MOVEP), instructions to support multiprocessor configurations, etc.

7.5 ADDRESSING MODES AND STRUCTURES

7.5.1 Introduction

Microprocessor instructions can access main memory in various ways. *Addressing modes* refer to the effective address EA (the final address used to access an element in main memory) formation mechanisms and *addressing structures* refer to the effective address presentation mechanisms. Addressing modes are either explicitly specified or implied by the instruction. The variety of addressing modes provided by a microprocessor is a measure of the richness of its instruction set, the efficiency in programming it and handling various data structures, and is critical for the fast compilation of high-level languages and the development of efficient memory management mechanisms. An addressing specification is said to be *orthogonal* to the operation specification of the instruction, when any addressing mode can be used in any instruction that uses addressing. Thus, understanding the addressing modes provided is very important in enabling the programmer to use the microprocessor instructions efficiently in coding his programs [13,14,15,23].

Described in this section are the major addressing modes and structures found in most microprocessors. Not all of them are provided on all microprocessors. Furthermore, different microprocessors may refer to an addressing mode using different names. The various names used by these microprocessors are given in parentheses in Table 7.1.

7.5.2 Immediate Addressing

Immediate addressing is not really an addressing mode in the formal definition of the term, since no effective address is generated and no further memory accesses are necessary during instruction execution. Immediate addressing refers to the fact that the operand (or data) value is stored along with the instruction; the instruction is a multiword instruction, where the operand(s) immediately follow the op code (Figure 7.9). Both the op code and the operand, therefore, are fetched from memory using the program counter.

Two common uses of the immediate address mode are to load internal registers with initial values or to add the immediate operand to the contents of an internal register.

For the 8-bit microprocessors the immediate operand may be either an 8-bit quantity (the instruction is two bytes long) or a 16-bit quantity (the instruction is three bytes long). When a 16-bit quantity is specified, the Zilog Z80 calls this

Table 7.1 The addressing modes provided by several microprocessors (the specific names used by each microprocessor are given in parentheses).

Addressing Mode	INTEL 8080A/8085	ZILOG Z80	MOTOROLA 6800	INTEL 8086	ZILOG Z8000	MOTOROLA 68000
Immediate	X	X	X	X	X	X
Direct	X	(Modified page zero)	X	X	X	(Absolute short address), (Absolute long address)
Extended	(Direct)	X	X			
Register	X	X	(Accumulator ACCX)	X	X	(Data register direct), (Address register direct)
Indirect						
Register Indirect	X	X			X	(Address register indirect), (Address register indirect with post increment), (Address register indirect with predecrement)
Base				X	X	(Register indirect with displacement)
Indexed		X	X	X	X	X
Base index				X	X	(Address register indirect with index)
Relative		X	X	X	X	(Program counter with displacement), (Program counter with index)
Implied		X	(Inherent)			X
Bit		X				X

mode *immediate extended addressing.* For some systems (e.g., the Intel 8080A/8085 and Zilog Z80), the least significant byte of the 16-bit operand is stored in the second byte of the instruction, while the most significant byte of the operand is stored in the third byte of the instruction.

In the 16-bit microprocessors, the immediate operand may be an 8-bit quantity, a 16-bit quantity, or a 32-bit quantity. When an 8-bit quantity is to be used in a 16-bit operation (e.g., add a byte-immediate value to a word register), the system automatically sign-extends the 8-bit immediate value to sixteen bits. The Motorola 68000 also has a *quick immediate* mode that uses inherent data, i.e., the data is a subfield (of four bits) of the instruction word (usually to reference the status register).

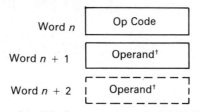

†For a 16-bit operand, in some of the 8-bit microprocessors (e.g., Intel 8080A/8085, Zilog Z80), word $n + 1$ contains the least significant byte, while word $n + 2$ contains the most significant byte of the operand.

Figure 7.9   Immediate addressing.

7.5.3   Direct Addressing

Here, the effective memory address where the operand is to be found is contained within the instruction, immediately following the op code (Figure 7.10). This is a very fast addressing mode, but the number of words directly addressable is limited by the number of address bits.

In most of the 8-bit microprocessors, direct addressing refers to allowing the user to address the lowest 256 bytes of the memory space directly, i.e., locations 0 through 255. A 2-byte instruction is used, where the second byte contains the address. This mode is used when enhanced execution times are required (such as responding to an interrupt). The Intel 8080A/8085 have the capability of directly addressing the first 256 locations but with some restrictions (one example being through the 1-byte RST instruction). The Zilog Z80 also has the 1-byte RST instruction, and since transfer is done to locations whose HI address byte is always 00, it calls this addressing mode *modified page zero addressing.*

In the 16-bit microprocessors, the address is also contained in the instruction. The Intel 8086 performs direct addressing using a 16-bit offset or *displacement* (or a sign-extended 8-bit displacement). The displacements used to calculate an effective address are encoded in the second byte within the *mod* field of the instruction. In the Zilog Z8000, the address used for direct addressing may be one 16-bit word in length (in the nonsegmented mode or in the segmented mode with short offset of eight bits), or it can be two 16-bit words (in the segmented mode with long offset of sixteen bits). In the segmented mode, all addresses within a given segment are relative to the start of the segment, and, since segment base values can be changed within the MMU support device, relocation of code can be achieved. Thus, a relative addressing within the logical address space is allowed. In the non-segmented mode of the Zilog Z8000, an address is absolute within a given address space (code, data, stack, etc.). Finally, the Motorola 68000 calls *absolute short addressing* the direct addressing using an additional 16-bit extension word (the 16-bit address of the operand is sign-extended before it is used) and calls *absolute long addressing* the direct addressing using two extension words, or 32 bits (the first extension word is the high-order part of the address, and the second extension word is the low-order part of the address).

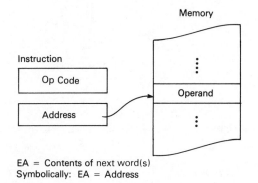

EA = Contents of next word(s)
Symbolically: EA = Address

Figure 7.10   Direct addressing.

7.5.4   Extended Addressing

This terminology is used by the Zilog Z80 and Motorola 6800 8-bit microprocessors to refer to direct addressing using a 2-byte direct address (Figure 7.11). This is generally a slow way of accessing memory, because the instruction is now three bytes long (one byte the op code, and the next two bytes the 16-bit direct address), and requires three memory accesses using the program counter to acquire the instruction. In the Intel 8080A/8085 and Zilog Z80 the address contained in the second byte of the instruction constitutes the eight low-order address bits (LO address) of the operand. The third byte of the instruction contains the higher eight bits of the address (HI address). In the Motorola 6800 this order is reversed.

The Intel 8080A/8085 call this extended addressing mode *direct addressing*.

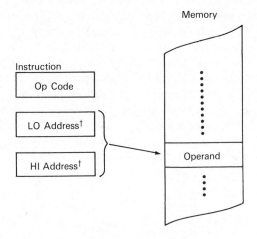

EA = Contents of next two bytes.
Symbolically: EA = Address.

† In the 6800 this order is reversed.

Figure 7.11   Extended addressing for the 8-bit microprocessors. (The 8080 calls this mode *direct addressing*.)

7.5.5   Register Addressing

In this addressing mode the op code of an instruction specifies the CPU register(s) in which the operand(s) is(are) located (Figure 7.12). When two such registers are specified, the most common situation is that in which one of them is the source while the other is the destination register. Designating an operand in an internal register—instead of in memory—reduces instruction length and results in faster execution, since no extra access to memory is required during instruction execution.

In 8-bit microprocessors, the register addressing mode involves single-byte instructions. The Motorola 6800 has a more restricted type of register addressing, called *accumulator (ACCX) addressing* (where either accumulator A or accumulator B is specified as containing the operand).

In the Intel 8086, for 8-bit operations, the eight 8-bit registers of the HL group may be used (except multiply, divide, and the string operations that use AL register implicitly). For 16-bit operations, the four 16-bit general registers and the four 16-bit pointer and index registers may be used (again, except multiply, divide, and the string operations that use AX register implicitly). The registers used to calculate an effective address are encoded in the second byte within the *reg* field of the instruction format.

In the Zilog Z8000, the register type for a source register (byte, word, register pair, or register quadruple) is always implied by the instruction. The destination registers have the same type as the source except for a few cases. The instruction format does not change between nonsegmented and segmented modes, and register addressing requires a single 16-bit register.

Finally, the Motorola 68000 calls it *register direct addressing*, uses an instruction length of one word, and further subdivides it into two different types according to the type of register involved: *data register direct* when the "register field" of the operation word specifies a data register and *address register direct* when it specifies an address register.

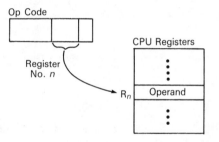

EA = Register R_n.
Symbolically: EA = R_n.

Figure 7.12 Register addressing.

7.5.6 Indirect Addressing

Indirect addressing is quite a sophisticated operation. While a standard mode in minicomputers, true indirect addressing has been very rarely implemented in microprocessors (e.g., in Signetics 2650). None of the six microprocessors of Table 7.1 has true indirect addressing capability, and thus, the corresponding operations have to be simulated to a limited extent. Indirect addressing is discussed here only for completeness purposes and to help understand its variations to be discussed in the following sections.

In the true indirect addressing mode, the instruction contains an (indirect) address that points to a memory location which holds the effective direct address to be used for accessing the operand (Figure 7.13). For a typical 8-bit microprocessor, the address field of the instruction would consist of sixteen bits (a 3-byte instruction), and the effective address in memory would occupy two memory locations as shown in the example of Figure 7.14.

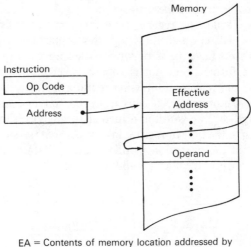

EA = Contents of memory location addressed by
the address field of the instruction.
Symbolically: EA = (Address).

Figure 7.13 True indirect addressing.

In the Intel 8080A/8085, for example, indirect addressing can be somehow implemented using the H and L registers. Consider the following situation in which the effective address required is stored in two memory bytes.

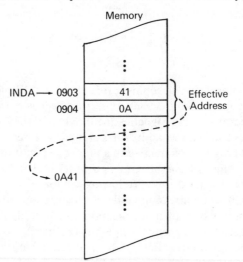

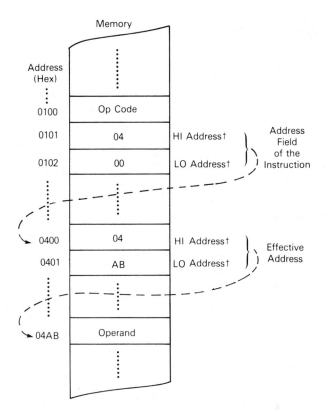

†For the Intel 8080A/8085 and Zilog Z80 the order is reversed.

Figure 7.14 An example of how implied address would be implemented in a typical 8-bit microprocessor.

Here, memory bytes 0903_{16} and 0904_{16} hold the required effective address $0A41_{16}$. (In keeping with the way the 8080A itself handles 16-bit addresses, the LO address byte is shown preceding the HI address byte.) Then the following instruction would simulate indirect addressing:

        LHLD INDA   ;Load effective address into HL

Now access to memory will be done using register indirect addressing, with HL register-pair providing the address.

Indirect addressing is of basic interest in microcomputers for sharing information among several users or several programs in a time-sharing environment. The user does not know the exact address of the shared information during assembly time. When a subroutine or a data structure, such as a data table, occupies a different area of memory the next time the processor attends that program, the only change required (during execution time) is a proper adjustment of the effective address in the indirect address space. Indirect addressing is also a necessity for a paged system, since it presents a means through which a program can access a memory location outside an instruction's own page.

Several variations of indirect memory addressing have been implemented in microprocessors: indirect addressing through a register (called "register indirect addressing"), indirect addressing through an index register (called "indexed addressing"), indirect addressing through a base register (called "base addressing"), and indirect addressing through both a base register and an index register (called "base index addressing"). These are discussed next with the terminology used in microprocessors.

7.5.7 Register Indirect Addressing

In the register indirect addressing mode, the instruction op code specifies an internal register or register pair which contains the effective address to be used for accessing the operand in memory (Figure 7.15). This mode is used to save space and improve speed in situations in which data elements are accessed consecutively.

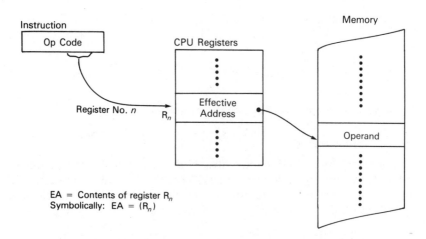

Figure 7.15 Register indirect addressing.

In 8-bit microprocessors, the instruction is one byte long and specifies a register-pair that contains the effective address (Figure 7.16). Usually the register pair HL is used, the first register H containing the HI effective address byte, the second register L containing the LO effective address byte. For some instructions, register indirect addressing is used to specify two bytes to be operated upon by an instruction. For example, the instruction

POP BC

loads the contents of the memory location whose address is specified by the contents of register SP—symbolized as (SP)—into C and loads the contents of the next memory location whose address is specified by (SP + 1) into B.

Of the 16-bit microprocessors, the Intel 8086 does not have register indirect addressing (indirect addressing is done in the 8086 through base and/or index registers discussed below). The Motorola 68000 uses only the address registers (A_n) of the CPU (as specified by the "register field" of the operation word) to hold the effective address, i.e., EA = (A_n). The 68000 also provides two more variations of this mode:

(a) *Address register indirect with postincrement.* Here the effective address is in the specified address register. After the operand is accessed, the effective address in the address register is incremented by the operand size (by 1, 2, or 4, depending upon whether the size of the operand is byte, word, or long word, respectively). If the address register specified is the stack pointer, and the operand size is byte, the address is incremented by 2 rather than 1 to keep the stack pointer on a word boundary. This mode is symbolized as:

$$EA = (A_n); \quad (A_n) \leftarrow (A_n) + N,$$

where $N = 1$ for byte, 2 for word, and 4 for long word operands.

(b) *Address register indirect with predecrement.* Again, the effective address is in the specified address register. Before the operand address is used, the address register is decremented by the operand size (1, 2, or 4). Again, for the stack pointer the address is decremented by 2 rather than 1. This mode is symbolized as:

$$(A_n) \leftarrow (A_n) - N; \quad EA = (A_n)$$

7.5.8 Base Addressing

The mechanics of the base addressing mode are rather similar to those of the indexed addressing mode discussed next. Base addressing has been implemented in some 8-bit microprocessors, and is sometimes called by them "indexed addressing." It is found in most of the larger 16-bit microprocessors. (In the Motorola 68000, this mode may be found under the name *base relative addressing* or *address register indirect with displacement*.)

The instruction op code designates a register (called the base register) that contains an address (called the base address). The instruction also contains an

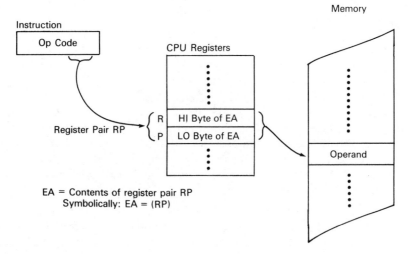

Figure 7.16 Register indirect addressing, as implemented in the 8-bit microprocessors 8080A/ 8085 and Z80.

offset field that contains a displacement D_k (either eight or sixteen bits long, called, respectively, short and long offset). Again, indirect addressing to memory is performed using an effective address to access the operand location, where the effective address is formed by the addition of the base address and the displacement value (Figure 7.17). In other words, in base addressing "the operand value is the content of the location whose address is the address in the (base) register, offset by the displacement in the instruction." In the base addressing mode, the displacement contained in the instruction is fixed at assembly time, while the (base) address contained in the register(s) can change at run time.

In the Intel 8086, the general register BX may serve as base register, the operand by default residing in the current data segment. The pointer register BP may also serve as base register; the operand, however, now resides by default in the current stack segment.

In the non-segmented mode of the Zilog Z8000, the base address mode is logically equivalent to the index mode (discussed next), both the base address in the register and the displacement in the instruction being one word long. In the segmented mode, the displacement in the instruction is still one word long, but a register pair is now required to hold the two-word base address. Therefore, again, the instruction format does not change between non-segmented and segmented modes. In the segmented mode, base addressing allows access to locations whose segment numbers are not known at assembly time.

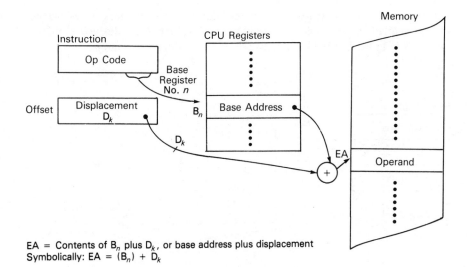

EA = Contents of B_n plus D_k, or base address plus displacement
Symbolically: EA = (B_n) + D_k

Figure 7.17 Base addressing.

Finally, the address register indirect with displacement mode of the Motorola 68000 requires one extension word which contains the sign-extended 16-bit displacement integer, and an address register is used as the base register. For example, instruction

$$\text{MOVE} \quad \#2,10(\text{A2})$$

moves the value 2 to the word whose address is given by adding 10 to the contents of address register A2.

The base register, in effect, is used to extend the limited address of an instruction to a larger address. A base register is used to point to a region of memory where the displacement is effective. For example, the technique may be used to access efficiently a table or vector of data placed in that region. The base register can be loaded with the address of the first entry of the table (the beginning of a region in memory), and all other table entries referred to by their location relative to the first entry. This means that the programmer's instructions specify a displacement relative to the table's base address.

Another major reason for using base registers is that they permit dynamic program (segment) relocation (discussed in detail in chapter 10). In this case, only the operating system uses the base registers (the programmer is not allowed to load or manipulate the base registers).

7.5.9 Indexed Addressing

The instruction op code designates a register (called index register) that contains the offset value or displacement (called index value). The instruction also contains an address field. Indirect addressing to memory is performed through an effective address formed by the addition of the index value and the address (Figure 7.18). The index register value does not change.

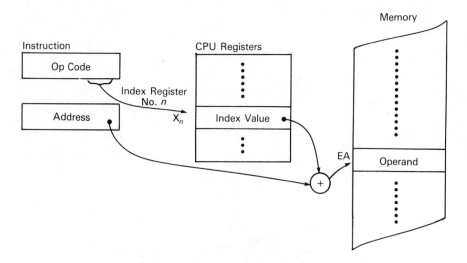

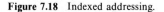

EA = Address plus contents of X_n, or address plus index value
Symbolically: EA = Address + (X_n)

Figure 7.18   Indexed addressing.

In other words, in indexed addressing, "the operand value is the content of the location whose address is the address in the instruction, offset by the displacement in the (index) register." In the indexed addressing mode, the address contained in the instruction is fixed at assembly time, while the displacement contained in the index register(s) can change at run time (the reverse of base addressing).

Indexed addressing is also used for accessing tables of data, especially when these data are accessed in sequential (ascending or descending) order. For example, consider an even number (less than 255) of 8-bit measurement stored sequentially in a source buffer starting at location 0300_{16}. We want to perform a data reduction (or smoothing) on these measurements. The result of this operation is to be placed in a destination buffer starting 255 locations higher in memory. Figure 7.19 shows the flowchart and the corresponding Zilog Z80 assembly language program. The averaging is performed by adding the two measurements (overflow is not considered in this example) and performing a right arithmetic shift on the result.

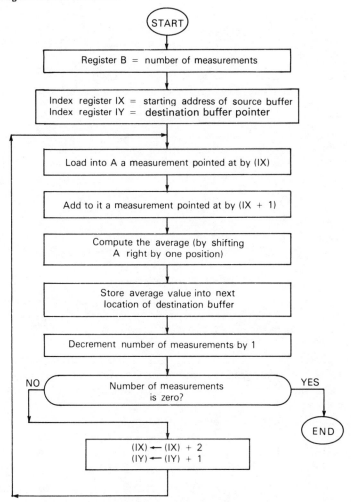

Figure 7.19 (a) Flowchart.

For some special microprocessor applications, it must be remembered that once instructions are placed into ROM, they cannot be changed. Often, the starting address of the table will be fixed (for example, when stored in ROM), whereas an offset will change dynamically. In such cases then, the starting address of the table will be placed in the instruction field, whereas the displacement will be residing in the index register.

Indexed addressing is not provided directly in the Intel 8080A/8085 microprocessors. There are chances that the start address of a table (let's call it "BASE") is a non-varying address, whereas the contents of the index register

Source Listing			Comments
			; DESTINATION BUFFER POINTER
	LD	DE,0002H	; LOAD INTO D,E THE CONSTANT 2
	LD	B,3AH	; LOAD INTO B NUMBER OF MEASUREMENTS
	LD	IX,0300H	; LOAD INTO INDEX REGISTER IX STARTING
			; ADDRESS OF SOURCE BUFFER
	LD	IY,0300H	; LOAD INTO INDEX REGISTER IY
LOOP:	LD	A,(IX)	; LOAD A MEASUREMENT INTO A
	ADD	(IX + 01H)	; ADD TO IT THE NEXT MEASUREMENT
	SRA	A	; ARITHMETIC SHIFT A TO THE RIGHT BY ONE
	LD	IY + FF H,A	; STORE AVERAGE INTO NEXT LOCATION OF DESTINATION
			; BUFFER
	DEC	B	; DECREMENT NUMBER OF MEASUREMENTS BY ONE
	JP	Z,END	; IF ZERO, STOP THE PROCESS
	ADD	IX,DE	; INCREMENT SOURCE BUFFER POINTER BY 2
	INC	IY	; INCREMENT DESTINATION BUFFER POINTER BY 1
	JP	LOOP	; REPEAT ABOVE PROCEDURE
END:	RST	00H	; RETURN TO LOCATION ZERO

(b)

Figure 7.19 Flowchart and Z80 assembly language listing.

(let's call it "INDEX") is constantly changing. Indexed addressing can now be performed in the 8080A/8085 by accessing BASE as an immediate, 16-bit value, but having INDEX assigned two RAM memory bytes with addresses INDX and INDX + 1.

An indexed address can be created as follows:

```
LXI    B,BASE    ; LOAD BASE ADDRESS INTO BC
LHLD   INDX      ; LOAD INDEX INTO HL
DAD    B         ; ADD BC TO HL
```

In the case in which the current index value changes, when the programmer is done, he or she can *restore* the new index value by subtracting BASE from the contents of HL, as follows:

```
LXI    B,BASE    ; LOAD BASE ADDRESS INTO BC
MOVE   A,L       ; ⎫
SUB    C         ; ⎬ SUBTRACT C FROM L
STA    INDX      ; SAVE IN INDX
MOV    A,H       ; ⎫
SBB    B         ; ⎬ SUBTRACT B FROM H WITH BORROW
STA    INDX+1    : SAVE IN INDX+1
```

For both the Zilog Z80 and the Motorola 6800 8-bit microprocessors, indexed addressing involves a 2-byte instruction. However, they do not implement indexed addressing in exactly the same way. In the Z80, the indexing operation looks more like the base addressing described above. The second byte of the instruction contains an 8-bit 2's complement displacement, added to the eight least significant bits of the 16-bit contents (address) of the specified index register. In the 6800, the second byte is treated as an unsigned 8-bit value added to the index register's lowest 8 bits. The carry is then added to the higher order 8 bits of the index register.

In 16-bit microprocessors, the address in the instruction may be eight, sixteen, or thirty-two bits long (e.g., when a Zilog Z8000 instruction contains a segmented address with long offset).

In the Intel 8086 either SI or DI registers may be used as index registers, the operand by default residing in the current data segment.

In the Zilog Z8000 any one of the 16-bit general registers (except the RO) may be used as an index register to contain the index value or *displacement*. Although both the non-segmented and the segmented modes require a single 16-bit register, since the instruction contains an address, the instruction format changes between these two modes. In the non-segmented mode, both the address field in the instruction and the index value are sixteen bits long. The user can use the index mode as base address mode by loading an address in the index register and using a displacement value in the instruction. Thus, in the non-segmented mode, base and index modes become logically equivalent. In the segmented mode, only one 16-bit (index) register is needed, whereas the address in the instruction is a segmented address (one or two words). In this addressing mode, the base address now contained in the instruction is fixed at assembly time and the index value or displacement in the register can change at run time.

Finally, what the Motorola 68000 calls "address register indirect with index" really behaves more like the base index addressing to be discussed next.

7.5.10   Base Index Addressing

This addressing mode is a combination of the previous two modes, base and indexed, usually found in the 16-bit microprocessors. Here the instruction op code specifies two registers: a base register that contains a base address, and an index register that contains an index value. The operand's effective address is formed by adding the contents of the base and index registers, and— sometimes—optionally an 8- or 16-bit displacement specified in the instruction (Figure 7.20).

The Intel 8086 allows indirect addressing to memory through the sum of a base register (BX or BP) and an index register (SI or DI), optionally with an 8- or 16-bit displacement. In this case, the operand by default resides in the

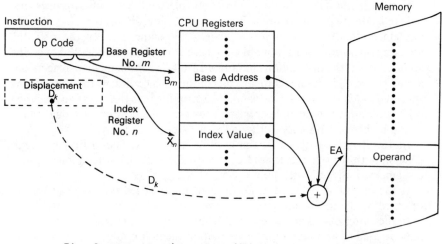

EA = Contents of B_m, plus contents of X_n plus (optionally) displacement D_k, or base address plus index value plus (optionally) displacement
Symbolically: EA = $(B_m + (X_n) + D_k$.

Figure 7.20   Base index addressing (with optional displacement).

segment determined by the base register. The 2-bit mode field (*mod*) and the 3-bit register/mode field (*r/m*) within the second byte of the instruction format together specify the different ways of calculating the effective address shown in Table 7.2 [9].

Table 7.2   The *mod* and *r/m* fields together specify different ways of calculating the effective address. *Courtesy Intel Corporation* [7].

mod ＼ *r/m*	00	01	10	11 (W = 0/W = 1)
000	(BX) + (SI)	(BX) + (SI) + D8	(BX) + (SI) + D16	AL/AX
001	(BX) + (DI)	(BX) + (DI) + D8	(BX) + (DI) + D16	CL/CX
010	(BP) + (SI)	(BP) + (SI) + D8	(BP) + (SI) + D16	DL/DX
011	(BP) + (DI)	(BP) + (DI) + D8	(BP) + (DI) + D16	BL/BX
100	(SI)	(SI) + D8	(SI) + D16	AH/SP
101	(DI)	(DI) + D8	(DI) + D16	CH/BP
110	D16	(BP) + D8	(BP) + D16	DH/SI
111	(BX)	(BX) + D8	(BX) + D16	BH/DI

In the Zilog Z8000, any 16-bit general register or register pair (depending on segmentation mode) can be used to hold the base address, except RO and RRO. Any 16-bit general register can be used to hold the index value, except RO. Since the instruction does not contain a memory address, the instruction format does not change between nonsegmented and segmented modes.

Finally, the *address register indirect with index* addressing mode of the Motorola 68000 requires one extension word. The address of the operand is the sum of the address in the address register (which is again specified by the "register field" in the operation word of the instruction), the contents of the index register (which are specified by the four high-order bits of the extension word and may be either an address or a data register), and the sign-extended offset integer in the eight low-order bits of the extension word. For example, instruction

$$\text{ADD} \qquad \$20(\text{A1}, \quad \text{D2.W}), \text{D5}$$

adds to the low order word of register D5 the word whose address is given by the addition of the contents of base register A1, the low-order word of the index register D2, and the displacement hexadecimal 20.

7.5.11 Relative Addressing

Another addressing mode found in most 8- and 16-bit microprocessors is the relative addressing mode. In this mode, the operand comes from a location relative to the executed instruction's position, i.e., the operand's effective address is generated by the sum of the contents of the program counter (pointing to the next instruction in the program) and the signed value (2's complement) specified by the instruction in its address (or displacement) field (Figure 7.21).

Relative addressing usually applies to jump instructions which facilitate short loops. It also allows the writing of a relocatable code, if only relative jumps are utilized. (Since a normal jump specifies an absolute address, any program that includes normal jump instructions is not relocatable.[5])

Relative addressing is found in the Zilog Z80 and Motorola 6800 8-bit microprocessors. A 2-byte relative instruction is used, the second byte specifying the displacement value in 2's complement. This displacement is added to the program counter's lowest eight bits. Since the PC value used points to the instruction following the relative instruction, the relative addressing mode allows the user to address data within a range of ±127 bytes of the present

---

[5]The topic of program relocation is treated in detail in chapter 10.

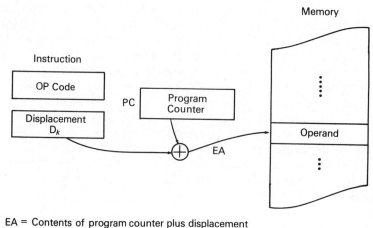

EA = Contents of program counter plus displacement
Symbolically: EA = (PC) + D_k

Figure 7.21 Relative addressing.

instruction. Coding density is improved, since a relative jump requires only a 2-byte instruction, whereas the generalized jump requires three bytes.

Most 16-bit microprocessors have relative addressing, using either a short (8-bit) or long (16-bit) displacement. Where the displacement is a sign-extended 16-bit integer in the extension word, the Motorola 68000 calls this addressing mode *program counter with displacement*. (The program counter points to the address of this extension word.) The 68000 also includes an additional relative addressing mode, called *program counter with index*, which utilizes the address in the program counter, the contents of the index (address or data) register, and the sign-extended displacement integer in the low-order eight bits of the extension word. This is given symbolically as:

$$EA = (PC) + (X_n) + D_8$$

7.5.12   Implied Addressing

Implied addressing (sometimes called *implicit addressing*) is found in some 8-bit microprocessors (Zilog Z80, Motorola 6800). In such cases, the instruction op code automatically implies one particular register (i.e., they are 1-byte instructions, and the code of the register being used by the instruction does not appear explicitly in the op code field). The Z80 has, for example, one such implied instruction, the "ADD A,B," which adds the contents of the B register to the accumulator and loads the sum into the accumulator.The Motorola 6800 also calls this *inherent* addressing, and there are two types of implied addressing instructions: those which do not require an address, and those which do require an address. An example of an instruction which does not require an address is ABA, which specifies the contents of accumulator A to be added to accumulator B, and the result placed in accumulator A. For those instructions which do require an address, the address is held by an internal MPU register such as the stack pointer. Thus, no data is required to develop an address. An example of this type of instruction is PSH. (This second type behaves like the register addressing described in section 7.5.5.)

The Intel 8080A/8085 include this implied addressing mode in their register addressing mode. Compared to the register addressing discussed in section 7.5.5 (where explicit addressing uses 3-bit codes for the eight registers), implied addressing results in a higher complexity at the level of the internal decoder.

The Motorola 68000 also has this addressing mode. The instructions may be only one word long, or they may require an additional "extension" word. For example, one type of a branch conditionally instruction is one word long, with its eight low-order bits specifying an 8-bit offset. Another type of branch conditionally instruction requires the additional "extension" word to specify a 16-bit offset (the eight low-order bits of the first word are 0's (zeros)). Branch conditionally instructions imply use of the program counter (PC). Besides the program counter, other instructions make implicit reference to the status register (SR), the supervisor stack pointer (SSP), or the user stack pointer (USP).

7.5.13   Bit Addressing

Finally, some microprocessors also have some instructions that address individual bits within words stored in memory or registers. The Zilog Z80 has a number of instructions that address individual bits using a combination of addressing modes [13]. Register, register indirect, or indexed addressing specifies the memory location or CPU register of the byte involved; a 3-bit code within the instruction op code specifies the bit number within the byte (numbered from 0 to 7, from right to left). For example, the instruction "SET 3,B" sets to logic 1 the bit number 3 of the B register. Besides SET, instructions RESET and BIT are provided also for bit addressing and manipulation.

Individual bits within a word may also be addressed in the Motorola 68000 with bit manipulation instructions. Bits are numbered from 15 to 0, with 15 being the most significant bit position. For example:

$$\text{BCLR} \quad = 3, \text{xyz(A3)}$$

clears bit number 3 in the byte whose address is given by the address in address register A3 plus a displacement of XYZ.

EXERCISES

7.1   Write an assembly language delay routine to provide a time delay of
       4.5465 msec for an Intel 8085 operating from a 2 MHz clock.

7.2   Repeat Exercise 7.1 for a time delay of 9.0975 msec.

7.3   For each of the following instructions, give the Zilog Z80 addressing
       modes used and the associated hexadecimal code:

       (a) LD A,B   (e) LD   SP,HL
       (b) LD A,(IX+Ø6H)   (f) LD   BC,Ø1Ø9H
       (c) LD (1234H),A   (g) PUSH BC
       (d) LD (IX+Ø9H),33   (h) POP IX

7.4   Consider the assembly language program of Figure 7.19. If this
       program is loaded starting at location 0100_{16}, then list at the left of each
       instruction (in hexadecimal notation) the memory locations along
       with their contents.

7.5   Using the Intel 8085, write a macro to transfer a data byte from one
       location in memory to another.

7.6   Given two 16-bit numbers in 2's complement notation, write the
       assembly language programs for the Intel 8085 and Motorola 6800 to
       perform multiplication using Robertson's second method.

7.7   Write an Intel 8085 assembly language program to extract the most
       significant bit of the data stored in location 500_{16}. Store this bit in
       location 601_{16}.

7.8   Write subroutine to copy an array of N bytes into an N-byte array B,
       where array A starts with address 0750_{16} and array B starts with
       address 0100_{16}.

       a) In the Intel 8085 assembly language
       b) In the Zilog Z80 assembly language
       c) In the Motorola 6800 assembly language.

7.9   Given the following two instructions of an Intel 8080A assembly
       language program:

                          ORA A
                          RM

If the microprocessor, instead of the RM, now includes only the normal RET instruction, what instruction sequence must be used to perform the same operation with the above two instructions?

7.10   Write the Intel 8085 assembly language program to perform a BCD to Gray code conversion.

7.11   Write an Intel 8085 assembly language subroutine to perform Hamming encoding on 8-bit data quantities parallel-fed to the 8-bit input port 40, and output the encoded message serially to output port 50, least significant bit first.

7.12   Write an Intel assembly language program to simulate the logic function:

$$F(A,B,C,D,E,F) = A \, \overline{B} \, C \, D + A \, \overline{B} \, \overline{C} \, D \, \overline{E} \, F.$$

The input variables appear at the rightmost bits of input port 10, and the result of the function sets bit 5 of output port 20.

7.13   Given the Intel 8085 operating at 2 MHz. For each instruction of the following program segment, list the respective clock cycles (or number of states). Also, properly complete the instructions for which a question mark ("?") appears in their operand field, so that this code results in a time delay of 20.4925 msec.

```
START:   LXI    D,?H
ABC:     DCR    E
         JNZ    ?
         DCR    D
         JNZ    ?
         RET
```

7.14   Given the following Intel 8080A assembly language instructions (Assume there is a 2 MHz clock):

```
         MVI    A,DELAY
LOOP:    DCR    A        ⎫
         JNZ    LOOP     ⎬   ''loop''
                         ⎭
```

(a) What is the minimum time delay achieved by "loop?"
(b) What is the maximum?
(c) Without changing the above instructions, how can you complete the above program segment so that the "loop" will result in a time delay of 15 μsec?

7.15 Write an Intel 8080A assembly language program to read twenty-five numbers from input port 10 and store them in consecutive memory locations starting from 300_{16}.

7.16 Write an Intel 8085 assembly language subroutine to convert an ASCII character 0 through F to its corresponding hexadecimal value. When returning from the subroutine, this hexadecimal value should be located in the rightmost four bits of the accumulator (its four leftmost bits should be 0 (zero)), and flag SIGN should be 1. If the examined ASCII character is outside the range 0 through F, the subroutine ends with the unconverted ASCII character in the accumulator and with the flag SIGN having the value 0.

REFERENCES AND BIBLIOGRAPHY

[1] Crespi-Reghizzi, S., P. Corti, and A. Dapra, "A Survey of Microprocessor Languages," *Computer*, January 1980, pp. 48–66.

[2] Donovan, J., *Systems Programming*, New York: McGraw-Hill, 1972.

[3] Fisher, W.P., "Microprocessor Assembly Language Draft Standard," (IEEE Task P694/D11), *Computer,* December 1979, pp. 96–109.

[4] Gear, W., *Computer Organization and Programming*, New York: McGraw-Hill, 1969.

[5] Intel Corporation, *8080/8085 Assembly Language Programming Manual*, Santa Clar, CA, 1977.

[6] Intel Corporation, *MCS-86 Macro Assembly Language Reference Manual*, (9800640-02), Santa Clara, CA, 1979.

[7] Intel Corporation, *The 8086 Family User's Manual,* (9800722-03), Santa Clara, CA, 1979.

[8] Katzan, H., *"Advanced Programming: Programming and Operating Systems,* New York: Van Nostrand Reinhold, 1970.

[9] Lapham, S.A., and H.M. Kop, "The 8086 μP has the Architecture to Handle High-Level Languages Efficiently," *Electronic Design*, 5, March 1, 1980.

[10] Martinez, R., "A Look at Trends in Microprocessor/Microcomputer Software Systems," *Computer Design*, June 1975, pp. 51–57.

[11] Motorola, Incorporated, *MC68000 Systems Cross Macro Assembler Reference Manual*, M68KXASM(D3), Austin, TX, September 1979.

[12] Motorola Incorporated, *16-Bit Microprocessing Unit*, (ADI-814-R1), Austin, TX, 1980.

[13] Nichols, E.A., J.C. Nichols, and P.R. Rony, *Z-80 Microprocessor, Book 1 Programming,* Indianapolis, IN: Howard W. Sams and Co., Inc., 1979.

[14] Osborne, A., *An Introduction to Microcomputers, Volume I, Basic Concepts*, Berkeley, CA: Adam Osborne and Associates, Inc., 1976.

[15] Osborne, A., *An Introduction to Microcomputers, Volume II, Some Real Products*, Berkeley, CA: Adam Osborne and Associates, Inc., 1976.

[16] Presser, L., and J.P. White. "Linkers and Loaders," *Computing Surveys,* vol. 4, no. 3, September 1972.

[17] Rauscher, T.G., "A Unified Approach to Microcomputer Software Development," *Computer,* June 1978, pp. 44–54.

[18] Shima, M., "Two versions of 16-bit Chip Span Microprocessor, Microcomputer Needs," *Electronics,* December 21, 1978, pp. 81–88.

[19] Stone, W., *Introduction to Computer Organization and Data Structures*, New York: McGraw-Hill, 1972.

[20] Ulrickson, R.W., "Software for Microprocessors: Part 1," *Electronic Design,* 1, January 4, 1977, pp. 90–96.

[21] Wegner, P., ed., *Introduction to System Programming,* New York: Academic Press, 1964.

[22] Wegner, P., *Programming Languages, Information Structures and Machine Organization,* New York: McGraw-Hill, 1971.

[23] Zaks, R., *Microprocessors from Chips to Systems,* Berkeley, CA: SYBEX, Inc., 1977.

Chapter 8

PROGRAM-DRIVEN I/O

8.1 INTRODUCTION

This chapter covers techniques and implementations for interfacing external (peripheral) devices to perform the program-driven I/O operation efficiently.

Interfacing an I/O slave device is similar to interfacing a memory slave, a process discussed in chapter 6. An I/O slave device responds to a bus cycle initiated by a bus master. (The bus timing diagrams for I/O read (input) and I/O write (output) are discussed in chapter 5.) An I/O slave device, however, may also request service by a bus master by generating an interrupt request, as is discussed in the next chapter.

This chapter begins by defining input and output ports. Section 8.3 covers the program-driven I/O technique, the two ways of implementing it ("accumulator I/O" and "memory-mapped I/O"), and gives some simple examples. Section 8.4 presents various ways of generating the device select pulses using the I/O read/write control signals and/or the device address bits, and accessing 8- and 16-bit I/O devices. Implementing the I/O interface system using MSI and LSI devices is discussed in section 8.5, while the last section presents an application of the program-driven I/O technique to poll a number of external devices.

8.2 GENERAL CONCEPTS

8.2.1 I/O Interfacing

Microcomputer interfaces may be classified in the following three general categories: (1) *human-oriented*, to provide interfacing for external devices such as switches, keyboards, teletypes, lights, LEDs, alphanumeric displays, etc.; (2) *computer-oriented*, to provide interfacing for external devices such as paper tapes, cassettes, cartridges, floppy disks, modems, etc.; and (3) *external-environment-oriented*, to provide interfacing for devices such as analog-to-digital converters (ADC), digital-to-analog converters (DAC), relays, stepping motors, etc. The I/O interface performs the following tasks:

- Ensures that the microprocessor output will be directed to the destination peripheral device.
- Provides ways through which each external device's data will be transferred properly to the microprocessor, without causing interference to other devices connected to the system's buses.
- Resolves any differences that may exist regarding the timing between the microprocessor and the peripheral device. The microprocessor CPU runs on its own internal clock, while the peripherals may or may not have their own internal clocks.
- When required, converts the format of the data produced by the microprocessor to the format they must have to become acceptable to the peripherals, and vice versa.
- Interrupts. The interface may also produce interrupt signals to force the microprocessor to react immediately in case some peripheral demands immediate service.

For those 16- and 32-bit microprocessors that have both "user" and "supervisor" modes of operation, the input and output operations are performed only in the supervisor mode.

The general configuration of a microprocessor system as shown in Figure 5.7 of chapter 5 is used throughout this chapter. Separate, non-multiplexed, lines are used for the address (A0*–A23*), data (D0*–D15*), and control signals. The control signals that a master issues to access an I/O slave device are the I/O read command (IORC*) and I/O write command (IOWC*), as explained in section 5.3.1 of chapter 5.

8.2.2 Input and Output Ports

Each external device is connected to the microcomputer via one or more *ports*. An external device may be as simple as a single switch or flip-flop, or as complex as another (micro)computer. A port is a controlled pathway (usually implemented as a register) that can be selected to exchange data with the microprocessor system. One port belongs to only one peripheral device. However, a peripheral device may require more than one port for its connection with the microprocessor system. Thus, the I/O interface may contain one or more ports, depending upon the number and complexity of the external devices connected.

All ports exchange data with the microprocessor system via its data bus. However, only one port is allowed access to the data bus at any one time. During input, information is transferred from the selected port (referred to as the *input port*) to the data bus; an input port is usually a tri-state buffer. During output, information is transferred from the data bus to the selected port (referred to as the *output port*); an output port is usually a latch. When the same port can accept both control signals to perform either input or output, this port is referred to as an input/output port, or *I/O port*.

Figure 8.1 is a simplified configuration, showing explicitly all three types of ports. Some microprocessors, especially the earlier ones and the single-chip microcomputers, provide input and output ports implemented on the same CPU chip or on the storage chips. In most cases, however, ports must be designed by the engineer, using some combination of signals provided by the bus master to *select* these ports and control the *direction* of data transfers. For this implementation, the designer may use SSI, MSI or LSI components, or combinations thereof, as explained in section 8.5.

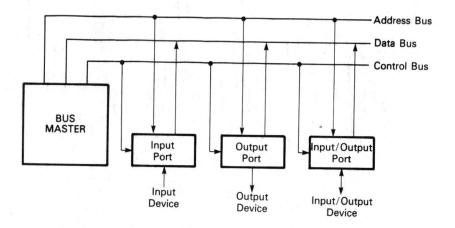

Figure 8.1 A simplified configuration showing the three types of ports.

The exchange of information with a peripheral device may be done either in *parallel* or in *serial* form. Figure 8.2 shows the simplified model of a micropro-cessor system with a parallel output port and a serial output port. In the first case, the parallel output port receives parallel data from the system's data bus and supplies them to its output in parallel form. In the second case, the serial output port supplies its output information in serial form, bit-by-bit. In its simplest implementation, the serial output port may also be receiving data from the microprocessor serially. In a more complex implementation, an LSI interface device may receive parallel data from the microprocessor, serialize them, add start and stop bits, and transmit them serially on its output line. The analogous situations hold for parallel input and serial input ports.

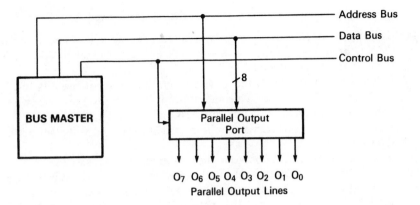

(a)

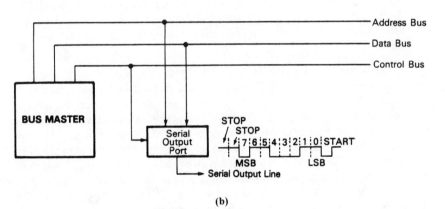

(b)

Figure 8.2 Parallel and serial output ports.

8.3 PROGRAM-DRIVEN I/O

Program-driven I/O is the most common way for exchanging data with peripheral devices. With program-driven I/O, transferring data between the master and a peripheral slave device is done via a port and under the control of the executed program in the master. Access to peripheral devices is done with the execution of either an "I/O-type" instruction or a "memory-type" instruction.

To perform this data transfer, three activities are carried out:

(a) The master must select the specific device—which will either transmit (input) or receive (output) data—and determine whether this device is "ready" to exchange data.

(b) The master must inform this device when the bidirectional data bus is available for the transfer. During output, it indicates to the device when valid data exist on the data bus; during input, it indicates when the CPU is ready to accept from the device the data that the device will place on the data bus.

(c) The actual data transfer between the master and the I/O slave device lasts a very short time. During output, the external device must latch the data transmitted to it on the data bus within a very short time interval (e.g., for the Intel 8080A/8085 operating with a 2 MHz clock this interval is 500 nsec); during input, the master must capture the data that the external device has placed on the data bus. The above is necessary because an I/O device can not communicate with the data bus continuously, since this bus is also used to transfer information between the master and memory slaves.

The input and output operations over the system bus are carried out in terms of read and write bus cycles discussed in section 5.4.2 of chapter 5. During any I/O transaction between the microprocessor and peripherals, the control signals involved inherently provide all the necessary timing, allowing asynchronous operation so that the peripheral devices can be independent of the microprocessor's speed and clock frequencies. The microprocessor is considered the "bus master," the peripherals are considered "slaves," and their asynchronous transactions obey the "master/slave protocol" shown in Figures 5.13 and 5.14 of chapter 5. The respective CPU bus timing diagrams for the input and output operations for representative microprocessors were given in Figure 5.20 (for the Intel 8085), Figure 5.21 (for the Zilog Z8000), and Figure 5.22 (for the Intel 8086) of chapter 5.

With the program-driven I/O method the microprocessor is said to be "I/O-bound," i.e., it spends a lot of time waiting in loops. The data transfers are coordinated by a "handshake" process, whereby the microprocessor examines a "status flag" on the peripheral device indicating "device ready" (i.e., "buffer full" for an input device, or "buffer empty" for an output device) to determine if an I/O operation is needed or possible. When more I/O peripherals than one are connected, the microprocessor must interrogate them sequentially or "poll" their status flags. (For this reason, the program-driven I/O method is also referred to as the "polling" method.) When it finds "device ready," the microprocessor stops the polling, and calls a software driver routine to service the peripheral. Polling is a useful technique in the case of relatively slow peripherals that do not require frequent service, do not demand the microprocessor's attention for long intervals of time, and can wait to be serviced. Polling can be done by taking advantage of the difference in speeds between the microprocessor operation and the I/O device. For example, within 100 msec (the response time of a teletype), the Intel 8080A microprocessor with 2 MHz clock can execute approximately 20,000 instructions! Section 8.6 gives an example case study of using the microprocessor to poll eight peripheral devices.

There are two ways to implement this program-driven I/O: "accumulator I/O" and "memory-mapped I/O."

8.3.1 Accumulator I/O

With the accumulator I/O technique, the data exchange is carried out between the external device and a microprocessor CPU register (usually the accumulator). The data transfer is performed with the execution of input (IN) and output (OUT) instructions, which initiate I/O read and write bus cycles.

The specification of the external device is done via the operand (or address) field of the executed IN or OUT instruction, which contains the device address placed on the address bus. At the same time, an IORC* or IOWC* signal appears on the control bus to indicate the direction of the data transfer.

The accumulator I/O technique has the following *advantages*: (1) Programming becomes easier, since different instructions are used for input (IN) and output (OUT). (2) These I/O-type instructions are usually shorter than the memory-type instructions used in the memory-mapped I/O technique to be discussed in section 8.3.2. (3) The I/O instructions isolate memory and I/O areas so that memory address space is not affected by the I/O structure. (4) The complexity of the device address decoder used depends on the length of the device address field in the I/O-type instruction. (For the 8-bit microprocessors the device address field[1] is eight bits long).

However, the accumulator technique also presents a number of *disadvantages*: (1) Only a few microprocessor registers (usually only the accumulator) are used to exchange information with an I/O device. (2) This technique requires separate instructions for input and output. (3) It is a less powerful, less flexible way of performing input/output as compared to the memory-mapped technique. (4) Two additional control lines are required (which are not necessary in the memory-mapped technique) for issuing the IORC* and IOWC* control signals.

---

[1] Or "device number" field.

Example 8.1

Read the state of an input flip-flop and set the state of an output flip-flop.

Figure 8.3a shows an Intel 8080A-based configuration, connected to an RS input flip-flop A and to a JK output flip-flop B. Flip-flop A is connected to bits 1 and 2 of the 8-bit input port 40, while flip-flop B is connected to bits 1 and 3 of the 8-bit output port 30. Selection of the two ports is done using the 8080A $\overline{I/OR}$ and $\overline{I/OW}$ control signals along with the decoded "device address" bits A0–A7. When the RS flip-flop is set to 1, then the microprocessor resets the JK; otherwise, it sets the JK. Figure 8.3b shows the flowchart and Figure 8.3c, the respective program code.

Example 8.2

Read a character from an encoded keyboard and output a character to an output device.

Figure 8.4a shows the Intel 8085-based hardware configuration. The keyboard[2] is connected to the microprocessor through an interface composed of two 8-bit registers (or input ports): a status register STAT assigned to input port 2 and a data input register DATAI assigned to input port 1. An 8-bit key code is generated and submitted to the DATAI input port by pressing a key on the keyboard. Bit 1 of the STAT input port is used to monitor the "key-pressed" signal (logic 1 if the key is pressed).

The output device also uses two interface registers: the previous status register STAT, and a new data output register DATAO assigned to output port 8. When the output device is "ready," the microprocessor sends a character to it by outputting an 8-bit data to the DATAO port. The "ready" signal of the output device (logic 1 if device is ready, logic 0 if device is busy) is now connected to bit 2 of the STAT input port.

Accumulator I/O is used, and port selection performed using the address bits A3, A1, and A0 directly (i.e., there is no decoding of the device address).

Figure 8.4b shows the input operation, including the polled keyboard flowchart and the respective assembly program portion. Figure 8.4c shows the output operation, including the polled output device flowchart and the respective assembly program portion.

If the output device of this example is a teletype, it has been assumed implicitly that it also includes all the necessary interface hardware to receive the eight parallel bits output by the microprocessor, serialize them, and then transmit them to the teletype to be printed. One such common LSI interface hardware is the universal asynchronous receiver/transmitter (UART).

---

[2]It is assumed that the keyboard contains an LSI keyboard encoder which provides the 8-bit data corresponding to the key pressed, and a "key-pressed" line to flag the processor when a keystroke is ready to be read.

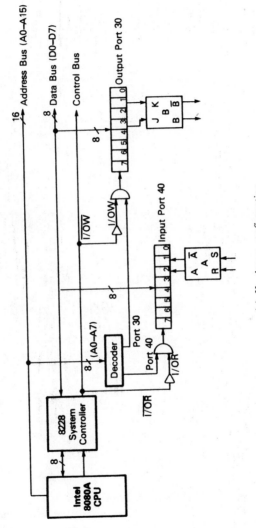

(a) Hardware configuration.

Figure 8.3 Read the state of an input flip-flop and set the state of an output flip-flop (accumulator I/O).

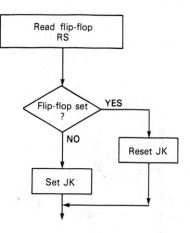

(b) Flowchart.

```
INPUT:  IN    4Ø    ; INPUT PORT 4Ø INTO A
        ANI   Ø4H   ; MASK OUT ALL BITS EXCEPT BIT IN
                    ; POSITION 2
        JNZ   RSET  ; IF RS FLIP-FLOP SET, JUMP TO
                    ; RSET
SET:    MVI   A,8   ; PLACE AN 1 IN BIT 3 OF A
        OUT   3Ø    ; OUTPUT A TO PORT 3Ø (J=1, K=Ø,
                    ; AND JK FLIP-FLOP IS SET)
        JMP   END   ;
RSET:   MVI   A,2   ; PLACE AN 1 IN BIT 1 OF A
        OUT   3Ø    ; OUTPUT A TO PORT 3Ø(J=Ø, K=1,
                    ; AND JK FLIP-FLOP IS RESET)
END:    HLT         ;
```

(c) Program code.

Figure 8.3 Read the state of an input flip-flop and set the state of an output flip-flop (accumulator I/O).

Example 8.3

Read sixty measurements from an external device.

An analog-to-digital converter (ADC) chip is used which has eight bits of output data, a 1-bit START conversion input and a 1-bit DONE (end-of-conversion) output. The START may be activated by the microprocessor (from an output port bit), or it may be tied to the DONE signal. In the second

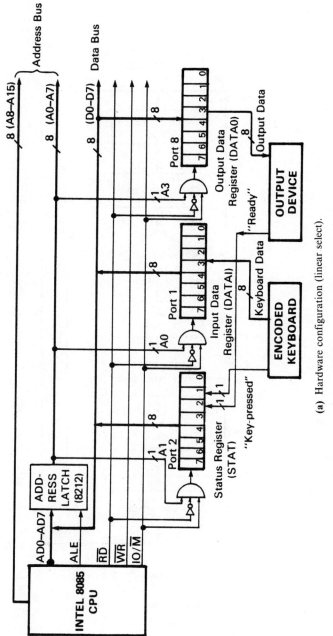

(a) Hardware configuration (linear select).

Figure 8.4 Input from an encoded keyboard and output to an output device (accumulator I/O).

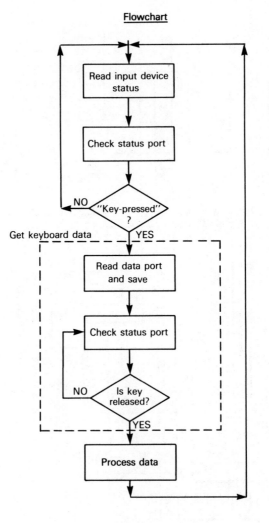

Flowchart

(b)

Figure 8.4   (continued)

Program Code

```
DATAI: EQU  1       ; ASSIGN DATA REGISTER
STAT:  EQU  2       ; ASSIGN STATUS REGISTER
INPUT: IN   STAT    ; INPUT STATUS
       ANI  Ø2H     ; CHECK STATUS BIT ''KEY-PRESSED''
       JZ   INPUT   ; GO BACK TO INPUT, IF BIT 1 IS ZERO
       IN   DATA    ; READ CHARACTER
       (PROCESS CHARACTER)
       JMP  INPUT   ; GO BACK AND CHECK FOR NEW
                    ; CHARACTER
```

(b) Read an 8-bit character from an encoded keyboard.

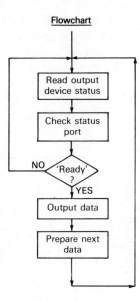

Figure 8.4 (continued)

Program Code

```
DATAO:  EQU     8         ; ASSIGN DATA REGISTER
STAT:   EQU     2         ; ASSIGN STATUS REGISTER
READY:  IN      STAT      ; INPUT STATUS
        ANI     Ø4H       ; CHECK STATUS BIT ''READY''
        JZ      READY     ; GO BACK TO READY, IF BIT 2 IS ZERO
OUT:    OUT     DATAO     ; OUTPUT CHARACTER
        (PREPARE NEXT CHARACTER)
        JMP     READY     ; GO BACK AND CHECK WHETHER
                          ; DEVICE IS READY TO ACCEPT
                          ; NEXT CHARACTER
```

(c) Output an 8-bit character to an output device (continued).

Figure 8.4 Input from an encoded keyboard and output to an output device (accumulator I/O).

case, as soon as a conversion is finished and the 8-bit digital data is output by the ADC, a new conversion will begin immediately. This example uses a configuration in which the microprocessor itself initiates the analog-to-digital conversion. The DONE signal is connected to an input port bit (so that the microprocessor may examine it).

Figure 8.5 shows the simplified configuration of the system. A sensor is used to make the analog measurement, followed by a sample-and-hold circuit. The

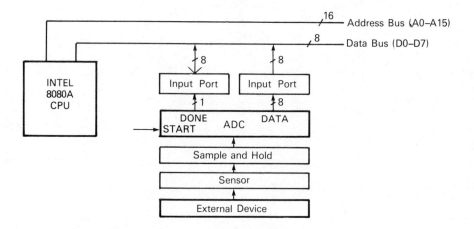

Figure 8.5 Simplified diagram of the system connected to one external input device.

analog output from the sample-and-hold is fed into an analog-to-digital converter to convert the measurement into an 8-bit data. Assume that this conversion from analog to digital requires $20\,\mu$sec; thus, the microprocessor is dedicated to monitoring this single device.

After the microprocessor executes some initialization steps, it calls a subroutine ENADC to enable the analog-to-digital conversion and read the 8-bit data. The flowchart of the ENADC subroutine is shown in Figure 8.6, and the detailed hardware implemention in Figure 8.7.

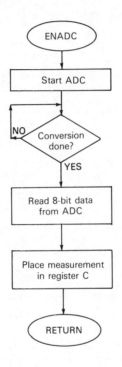

Figure 8.6 Simplified flowchart of the subroutine ENADC, which starts the ADC, reads the 8-bit output of ADC, and places it in register C.

The ADC is enabled with the START signal properly issued by the microprocessor CPU. In this example, it is assumed that the ADC chip has been assigned output port 30, so its starting is done by executing the instruction OUT 30. After that, the microprocessor enters a loop to examine the status flag DONE of the ADC (assumed here to be applied to the most significant bit of input port 40) and determine when the conversion is finished. When the conversion is completed, the ADC issues the signal DONE and places its 8-bit

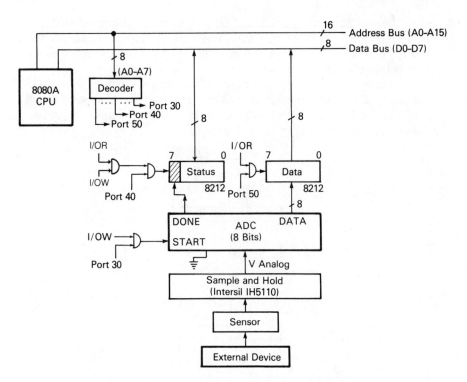

Figure 8.7 The detailed hardware implementation of the data acquisition system from one external device.

output digital data into port 50. When the microprocessor detects this DONE signal, it reads the 8-bit digital data from its input port 50 into the accumulator, transfers it into register C, and exits the subroutine ENADC. Figure 8.8 shows the Intel 8080A assembly language listing of the subroutine ENADC.

Now assume that the microprocessor performs sixty such readings, approximately one reading (or measurement) per 450 msec. A 450 msec software delay routine is now used in the program. The microprocessor places every measurement that it reads in the next available free location in a 60-byte buffer in main memory. Assume that the program starts at location 0300_{16}, the buffer at location 0400_{16}, and the memory stack at location 0500_{16}, as shown in the memory map of Figure 8.9. Figure 8.10 shows the flowchart for reading sixty measurements and storing them in the buffer in main memory. The corresponding program listing for an Intel 8080A operating at 2 MHz is shown in Figure 8.11. A software counter is used by the program for these sixty measurements, implemented as follows: the program examines whether the address in registers H and L is the same as the final one (i.e., sixty bytes higher than the starting address); an equality indicates the end of the loop for the sixty measurements.

```
;
; ASSIGN ADC STATUS AND DATA REGISTERS TO INPUT PORTS
; 4Ø AND 5Ø
; ASSIGN START INPUT OF ADC TO OUTPUT PORT 3Ø
STUS  EQU   4Ø
DATA  EQU   5Ø
START EQU   3Ø
;
;
; SUBROUTINE ENADC TO START ANALOG-TO-DIGITAL CONVERTER
; AND READ ITS 8-BIT OUTPUT DATA
;
; START SUBROUTINE ENADC AT LOCATION ØØ38H.
        ORG   38H
ENADC:PUSH  PSW   ; SAVE ACCUMULATOR AND FLAGS
      OUT   START ; APPLY SIGNAL TO START THE
                  ; ANALOG-TO-DIGITAL CONVERSION
CHECK:IN    STUS  ; READ STATUS BIT (DONE)
      ANI   80H   ; CHECK IF STATUS BIT = 1
      JZ    CHECK ; IF CONVERSION NOT COMPLETE,
                  ; EXECUTE WAIT LOOP
INPUT:MVI   A,Ø   ; CLEAR ACCUMULATOR
      OUT   STUS  ; CLEAR STATUS BIT
      IN    DATA  ; READ 8-BIT OUTPUT OF ADC
      MOV   C,A   ; PLACE IT IN REGISTER C
      POP   PSW   ; RESTORE ACCUMULATOR AND FLAGS
      RET         ; RETURN TO CALLING PROGRAM
```

Figure 8.8 Subroutine ENADC to input 8-bit data from an analog-to-digital converter.

8.3.2 Memory-mapped I/O

Providing separate distinct input and output instructions is not always necessary. Instead, the microprocessor instructions used to exchange information between CPU and memory may also be used for I/O purposes. In this case, the I/O ports are constructed so that they behave exactly like memory locations, and, therefore, are accessed via the MRDC* and MWTC* control signals. This technique of using memory-type instructions to perform I/O is called "memory I/O" or "memory-mapped I/O." Systems configured this way allow the programmer to use all capabilities of the microprocessor instructions for

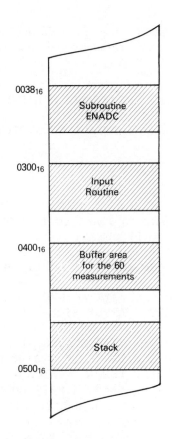

Figure 8.9 Memory map.

both memory data as well as data of the I/O ports. If the contents of memory locations can be increased, compared, and shifted directly, etc., then the microprocessor can also handle the I/O data with the same flexibility.

Furthermore, it was said that in the previous technique, usually only the accumulator is used to exchange information with the peripheral device. Besides the accumulator, however, a microprocessor also has other general registers that are used to exchange information with memory. It would be very useful to the programmer, if these CPU registers could be used equally well (like the accumulator) for the data exchange with external devices.

Thus, the memory-mapped I/O technique refers to using memory-type instructions for accessing peripheral devices, that is, the microprocessor can use the same instructions to exchange information with both memory and peripheral devices. Each port now behaves as a memory location.

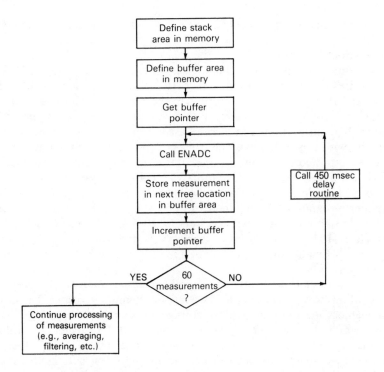

Figure 8.10 Flowchart for reading sixty measurements (one measurement per 450 msec) from one external device. Store them in a 60-byte buffer in memory, and then process them.

Consider the following Intel 8080A example for outputting data from CPU registers:

Octal Contents	Symbolic Instruction		Comments
Ø41 ⎫ Ø00 ⎬ 200 ⎭	LXI	2,2ØØ	; SET THE 16-BIT MEMORY ADDRESS POINTER ; REGISTER (H,L) WITHIN 8Ø8ØA CPU TO ; MEMORY ADDRESS OF PORT A (MEMORY ; ADDRESS OF PORT = 8000_{16})
16Ø	MOV	M,B	; MOVE CONTENTS OF REGISTER B TO PORT A
161	MOV	M,C	; MOVE CONTENTS OF REGISTER C TO PORT A
162	MOV	M,D	; MOVE CONTENTS OF REGISTER D TO PORT A
163	MOV	M,E	; MOVE CONTENTS OF REGISTER E TO PORT A
164	MOV	M,A	; MOVE CONTENTS OF REGISTER A TO PORT A

Every data transfer requires only 2 μsec execution time, which is much faster than the 5 μsec that successive OUT instructions would require (in the accumulator I/O technique).

The memory-mapped I/O technique has the following *advantages*: (1) The port addresses are now 16-bits wide (for microprocessors with 16-bit addresses), thus providing for more than the maximum 256 input and 256 output ports of the accumulator I/O technique. (2) The same powerful memory-type instructions can also be used to perform input/output. (For example, with this technique, one can perform arithmetic directly with an input or output port, without the need of reading out the contents or placing them in temporary registers). (3) More CPU registers may exchange information with I/O devices. (4) For some applications, memory-mapped I/O simplifies programming and increases the speed of I/O transfers. This increase in speed, although not necessary for slow-speed devices (such as, for example, a 110 bps teletype), is nevertheless very useful for interfacing to CRT displays. (5) Finally, there may also be a reduction on the required CPU I/O control pins.

However, this technique also has a number of *disadvantages*: (1) Every I/O port used this way reduces by one the available memory locations. Therefore, if all memory locations are used for storage, the memory-mapped I/O technique cannot be used. (2) The memory-mapped I/O technique utilizes memory-type instructions which are usually longer than I/O-type instructions. (For example, in the Intel 8080A, memory-type instructions are usually three bytes long, while the special I/O-type instructions are only two bytes long). The length of the program, therefore, increases. (3) Because of the wider port address, the interface hardware required is also increased.

8.4   GENERATING THE DEVICE SELECT PULSES

Interfacing I/O devices is rather similar to interfacing memory devices. The selection of one port out of many is done by applying to it a *device select pulse* or *port select pulse*.

8.4.1   Using the I/O Read/Write Control Signals

In the simplest configuration in which only one input port and one output port exist, the only control signals needed are one to strobe the input port and a second to latch the output port. When accumulator I/O is performed, the signals IORC* and IOWC* can be applied directly to the respective ports. When memory-mapped I/O is performed, the signals MRDC* and MWTC* may be used instead. These signals indicate the *direction* of the data transfer: IORC* and MRDC* for input; IOWC* and MWTC* for output. In either case, the device address bits on the address bus are not used.

```
; 8Ø8ØA AT 2 MHZ
;
; ROUTINE TO READ 6Ø MEASUREMENTS FROM ONE DEVICE AND STORE
; THEM IN A BUFFER IN MAIN MEMORY
;
; MEASUREMENTS ARE DONE EVERY 45Ø MSEC
; THE ENADC SUBROUTINE OF FIG. 8.8 IS USED
;
; START INPUT ROUTINE AT LOCATION Ø3ØØH
            ORG     Ø3ØØH
            LXI     SP,Ø5ØØH  ; STACK AREA STARTS FROM LOCATION Ø5ØØH
                              ; (IT GROWS DOWNWARD)
            LXI     H,Ø4ØØH   ; STARTING LOCATION OF BUFFER AREA
ADC:        CALL    ENADC     ; CALL SUBROUTINE ENADC. (THE MEASURE-
                              ; MENT IS PLACED IN REGISTER C)
            MOV     M,C       ; STORE MEASUREMENT IN NEXT FREE
                              ; LOCATION IN BUFFER AREA
            INX     H         ; INCREMENT BUFFER POINTER
            MOV     A,L       ; LEAST SIGNIFICANT BYTE OF BUFFER
                              ; POINTER PLACED IN A
            CPI     6Ø        ; CHECK IF 6Ø MEASUREMENTS HAVE
                              ; BEEN DONE
            JZ      PROCSS    ; IF YES, GO TO PROCESS THEM
            CALL    DELAY     ; OTHERWISE, CALL A 45Ø MSEC
                              ; DELAY ROUTINE
            JMP     ADC       ; AFTER 45Ø MSEC, GO TO READ
                              ; NEW MEASUREMENT
;
; THE 45Ø MSEC DELAY ROUTINE (APPROXIMATELY)
DELAY:      PUSH    PSW       ; SAVE ACCUMULATOR AND FLAGS
            PUSH    D         ; SAVE REGISTERS D AND E
            MVI     D,E9H     ; PLACE DELAY CONSTANT (COUNTER)
LOOP2:      MVI     E,FFH     ; IN D,E
LOOP1:      DCR     E         ; COUNT DOWN DELAY CONSTANT
            JNZ     LOOP1
            DCR     D
            JNZ     LOOP2
            POP     D         ; RESTORE REGISTERS D,E
            POP     PSW       ; RESTORE ACCUMULATOR AND FLAGS
            RET               ; RETURN TO CALLING POINT
;
; ROUTINE TO PROCESS THE 6Ø MEASUREMENTS
PROCSS:
```

Figure 8.11 Reading sixty measurements (one every 450 msec) from one external device and storing them in a buffer area in main memory.

As already mentioned in chapter 5, to generate the above system commands a CPU interface may be required to combine the CPU output control and status signals properly. When an I/O device is connected to the CPU bus, the CPU control signals of Figure 5.11 must be used. In this case, all restrictions mentioned in section 6.4.3 of chapter 6 also apply here for I/O devices.

8.4.2   Linear Select

When more than one input and more than one output port exist, then simply using the above direction signals is not sufficient. For each direction (input or output), the proper one out of many ports must be selected. In this case, the control signal must be combined properly with the device address bits on the address bus.

The *linear select* technique refers to assigning each individual device address bit as the exclusive select for a specific port. This technique is of course limited to designs in which the total number of input and output ports required does not exceed the number of bits allocated for the device address. For example, in 8-bit microprocessors having 8-bit device addresses, this technique limits the accumulator I/O to configurations not having more than eight input and eight output ports. For the memory-mapped I/O (where the address bits increase to sixteen), allocating more address bits for the direct selection of an I/O port limits accordingly the total memory space left for the design. Figure 8.12 shows the maximum configuration of eight 8-bit input ports and eight 8-bit output ports using the accumulator I/O technique for an 8-bit microprocessor with linear select. The linear select technique was used in Example 8.2.

Figure 8.13 shows the linear select technique for an Intel 8080A-based configuration using the 8212 8-bit output latch, the 8255 8-bit programmable peripheral interface and the 8251 programmable communication interface devices. Each device is selected by using the device address bits directly off the address bus (no address decoding is performed). Thus, addressing the 8212s is performed using the following format (in the second byte of the OUT instruction):

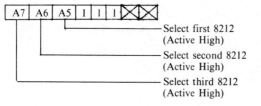

Courtesy Intel Corporation [10].

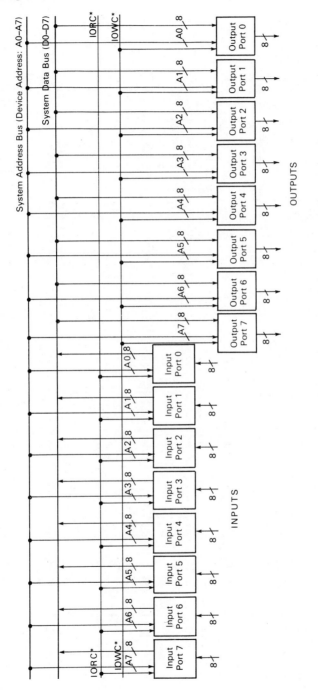

Figure 8.12 Linear select of eight 8-bit input and eight 8-bit output ports using the device address A0–A7.

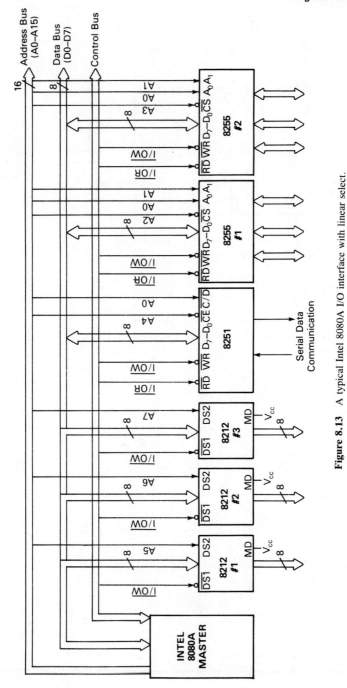

Figure 8.13   A typical Intel 8080A I/O interface with linear select.

Addressing the 8251 is performed using the following format:

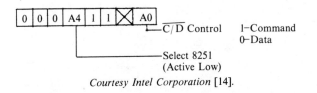

Courtesy Intel Corporation [14].

Finally, addressing the 8255's is performed using the following format:

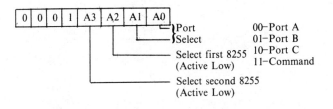

Courtesy Intel Corporation [5].

8.4.3 Decoding the Device Address Bits

When larger configurations require a greater number of ports, then a decoder may be used to decode the device address bits. Thus, the 8-bit device addresses of 8-bit microprocessors, when decoded, can specify up to 256 input and 256 output ports; similarly, the 16-bit device addresses of 16-bit microprocessors, when decoded, can specify up to 64K input and 64K output ports. Selection of the appropriate port is done by combining the output of the device address decoder with the proper control signal on the control bus. This technique was used in Example 8.1. Of course, decoding may be performed on only few of the total device address bits.

Figure 8.14 shows an implementation for an 8-bit microprocessor-based interface to generate the 256 possible maximun different device select pulses for input ports. Seventeen 4-to-16 decoders are used to decode the 8-bit device address carried on the lower half of the 16-bit address bus. For the 256 device select pulses for output ports, seventeen more such decoders will be required, along with the control signal IOWC* (or its equivalent).

8.4.4 Accessing 8- and 16-bit I/O Devices

Most of the 16-bit microprocessors are capable of interfacing with both 8-bit (byte) and 16-bit (word) I/O devices. Transfers of sixteen bits are carried out via the 16-bit data bus, and accessing a 16-bit device may be done using the 16-

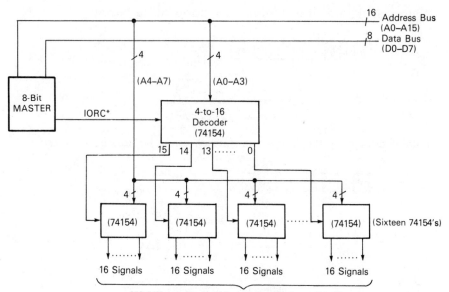

Figure 8.14 Using seventeen 74154's to generate the 256 input device select pulses (accumulator I/O).

bit device address. In this case, 16-bit I/O devices are usually assigned even addresses (e.g., bit A0 = 0), and word addressing is used. Besides A0, the BHEN* system command (or the CPU signal $\overline{BHE}$, B/$\overline{W}$, or $\overline{UDS}$/$\overline{LDS}$) is also decoded to generate the device select signal as discussed in sections 6.4.2 and 6.4.3 of chapter 6.

In the Intel 8086, unlike memory, the I/O space is addressed as if it were a single segment, without the use of segment registers. (I/O physical addresses are in fact twenty bits in length; they appear in the same format as memory address on bus lines A0–A15, but the high-order four bits A16–A19 are always 0 (zero).) An 8-bit I/O device may be connected to either the upper half of the data bus (in which case all I/O addresses assigned to the device must be odd, i.e., A0 = 1), or the lower half of the data bus (in which case all I/O addresses assigned to the device must be even, i.e., A0=0). Subsequently, 8-bit data transfers take place on the upper or lower half of the 16-bit data bus. Since A0 will always be a 0 (zero) or 1 for a specific device, A0 cannot be used as an address input to select registers within the device.

Figure 8.15a shows an Intel 8086-based configuration that uses separate 1-of-8 decoders to generate device select pulses for odd and even addressed byte peripherals. The $\overline{BHE}$ is used to select odd addressed byte peripherals. If a word transfer is performed to an even addressed peripheral, the adjacent odd addressed peripheral is also selected. This allows the peripherals to be accessed individually with byte transfers or simultaneously as a 16-bit peripheral with word transfers.

Figure 8.15b uses a single 1-of-8 decoder to generate odd and even device select pulses for byte transfers, and will only select the even addressed byte peripheral on a word transfer to an even address.

In the Zilog Z8000, when byte I/O is used, only the eight low lines of the address/data bus are involved on the input or output, regardless of the lowest bit of the device address (in contrast with memory addresses).

The high-order byte (on data bus lines D8–D15) of the Motorola 68000 (which performs memory-mapped I/O) has an even address when addressing 8-bit ports, whereas the low-order byte (on data bus lines D0–D7) has an odd address.

The 8- and 16-bit data transfers for I/O devices connected to the IEEE 796 system bus were discussed in section 6.5 of chapter 6.

8.5 I/O PORT IMPLEMENTATION

I/O ports may be implemented using SSI, MSI, or LSI components. The simplest SSI implementation of an input port consists of a 1-bit three-state buffer, whereas the simplest SSI implementation of an output port is a 1-bit D-type latching flip-flop. In Examples 8.1 and 8.2, 8-bit registers are used to implement input and output ports.

8.5.1 Using MSI Components

An I/O port may also be implemented using MSI components. Figure 8.16 shows an implementation using the 8-input three-state multiplexer 74251 as an addressable input port. Eight 74251's are used here to select one of eight ports; each port is "distributed" among the eight multiplexer chips. The ith bit from all eight 8-bit input devices is connected to MUX i. The eight outputs from these multiplexers constitute the byte placed onto the data bus. Address decoding is handled entirely within the multiplexer chips. The three address bits A0–A2 select one of the eight inputs to each multiplexer. Wider-input multiplexers may also be used, if more than eight input ports are required. Multiplexers also may be stacked up in series.

Similarly, Figure 8.17 shows an example of using the 4-bit 74175 latches as addressable output ports. Each 8-bit output port is made up of a pair of 74175's, selected by decoding the three address bits A0–A2.

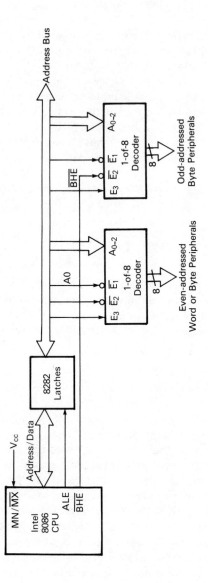

(a)

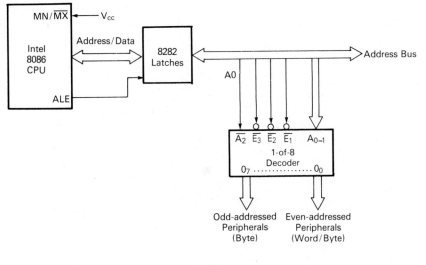

(b)

Figure 8.15 Generating device select pulses for odd and even addressed Intel 8086 byte peripherals.

Figure 8.18 shows an Intel 8080A-based example of using the 6-bit Intel 3404 latches as addressable output ports. It is shown how the 8-bit data byte is split and input to more than one 3404 chip.

8.5.2 LSI Interface Chips

One-chip LSI interfaces are also available to handle complex I/O tasks such as handshaking, parallel/serial and serial/parallel conversion, formatting, parity checking/generation, etc. Both parallel and serial LSI interface chips exist that may perform both the input and output operations. These chips are usually general-purpose programmable devices, in the sense that they can be "configured" as input, output, or bidirectional (I/O) ports, or they may be special-purpose interfaces designed to handle common peripherals such as floppy disks, cassettes, telephone lines, data transmission sets, etc. Use of these interface support chips simplifies design, reduces chip count, and gives flexibility. Since they are programmable, they usually require initialization programs to define a function (or specific "configuration").

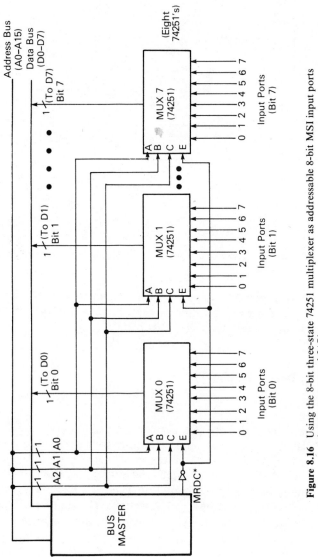

Figure 8.16 Using the 8-bit three-state 74251 multiplexer as addressable 8-bit MSI input ports (memory-mapped I/O).

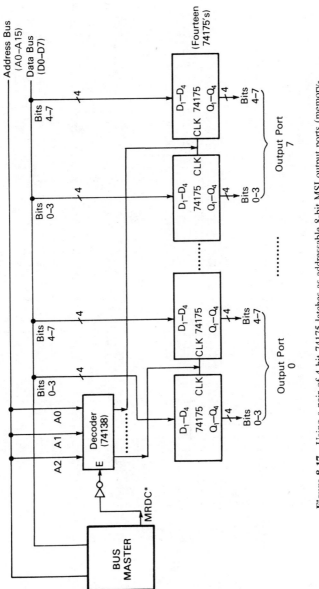

Figure 8.17 Using a pair of 4-bit 74175 latches as addressable 8-bit MSI output ports (memory-mapped I/O) [12].

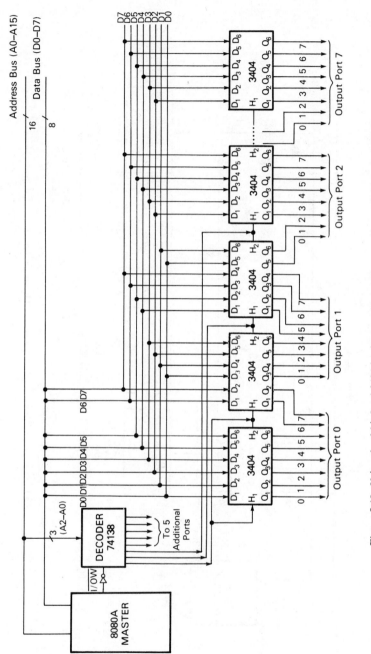

Figure 8.18 Using the 6-bit Intel 3404 latches as addressable output ports (accumulator I/O).

In its most general form, an LSI interface chip is composed of four registers (Figure 8.19). When connected to the microprocessor system, each register is assigned a unique device address (or port number). Thus, as far as the programmer is concerned, these interface registers appear as I/O ports. One register may operate as a data input port, which latches input data from a peripheral device and holds them until the microprocessor reads them. The second register may operate as a data output port, which latches microprocessor data and holds them until they are output to the peripheral device. Thus, these two ports provide two parallel input/output channels. Additional registers may also exist to allow programming of the channels' I/O directions under microprocessor control. Usually, another separate register is provided, referred to as "control register" or "direction register," which can be programmed to define the detailed function of the data input and output registers. Finally, LSI interface chips may include a "status register" indicating if there are data to be read, or whether the data has been output.

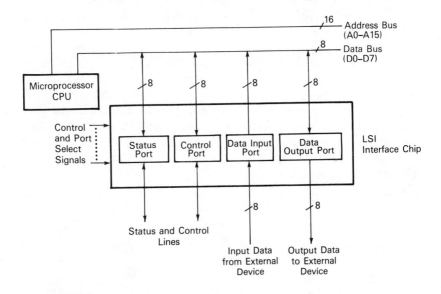

Figure 8.19 The simplified configuration of a programmable LSI interface chip composed of four registers.

The Intel 8355/8755 and 8155 are such LSI interface chips. Presented below are examples of interconnecting them to the Intel 8085 CPU [6,15].

Interfacing the 8355/8755

Figure 8.20 shows the necessary interconnections for the accumulator I/O and memory-mapped I/O implementations. The 8355 and 8755 are equivalent as far as the user is concerned, their only difference being that the former includes a 2K-byte ROM memory, whereas the latter contains a 2K-byte EPROM memory.[3] Since these LSI devices contain 2K bytes of memory, eleven address bits should be used for accessing any of their memory locations. In addition to the 11-bit address, the two chip enable inputs, CE and $\overline{CE}$, must also be utilized; to access the EPROM section of the chip, both chip enables must be active (i.e., CE = 1 and $\overline{CE}$ = 0). If CE · $\overline{CE}$ = 0 and IO/$\overline{M}$ = 0), then when the $\overline{RD}$ goes low, then the eight bits addressed by the 11-bit address are read from the EPROM through the AD0–AD7 output lines. Therefore, using the 8755 as a memory device presents no difficulty, because, since it is directly compatible with the 8085 CPU, the low address and data bus signals are multiplexed on the bidirectional address/data bus lines AD0–AD7. Demultiplexing is performed by the 8755 internally, and is controlled by the ALE signal it receives from the Intel 8085 CPU.

What is of more interest, however, is the utilization of the two 8-bit I/O ports A and B contained in the 8755 chip. The I/O section of the chip is addressed by the two bits AD1 and AD0, and the two chip enable inputs CE = 1 and $\overline{CE}$ = 0. The two low-order bits of the address specify selection of either port A or port B, or their respective status registers, called data direction registers (DDR). Table 8.1 shows the respective values of the two bits for these selections and the corresponding device addresses for the I/O ports and their status registers. The Xs represent "don't care" bits, since their values are irrelevant to the selection of one of the four functions.

Table 8.1 I/O port selection by the two low-order address bits AD1 and AD0 *Courtesy Intel Corporation* [15].

AD1 AD0	Selection	Device address
0 0	Port A	XXXXXX00
0 1	Port B	XXXXXX01
1 0	Port A data direction register (DDR A)	XXXXXX10
1 1	Port B data direction register (DDR B)	XXXXXX11

---

[3]We will refer to the two devices collectively as the "8355/8755," since they are nearly identical as far as their use is concerned.

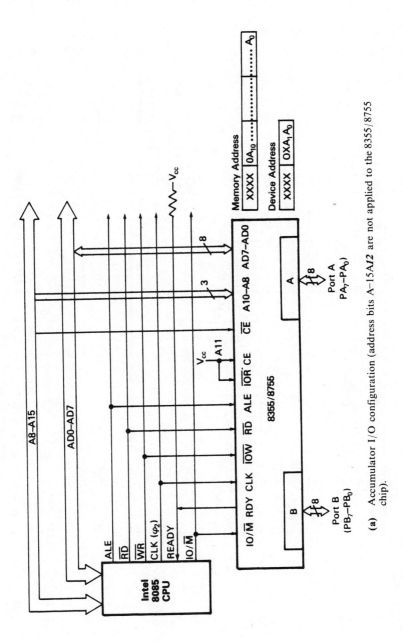

(a) Accumulator I/O configuration (address bits A–15A12 are not applied to the 8355/8755 chip).

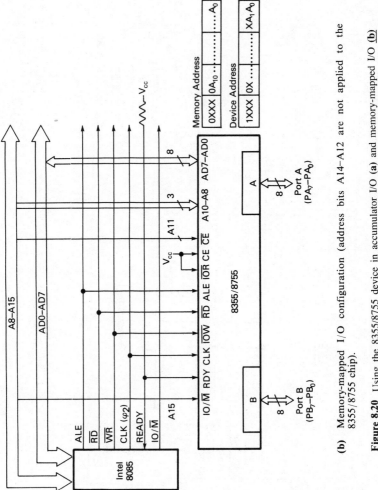

(b) Memory-mapped I/O configuration (address bits A14–A12 are not applied to the 8355/8755 chip).

Figure 8.20 Using the 8355/8755 device in accumulator I/O **(a)** and memory-mapped I/O **(b)** configurations (X's denote "don't care" bits, and bit A11 must be zero to make $\overline{CE}$ = 0).

When the 8755's $\overline{IOW}$ input goes low and CE $\times$ $\overline{CE}$ = 0, the data on the AD0–AD7 pins is written into the I/O port selected by the two bits AD1 and AD0. A selected I/O port can be read out on lines AD0–AD7 when CE$\times\overline{CE}$ = 0 and $\overline{RD}$ goes low with IO/$\overline{M}$ = 1. The I/O ports can be accessed only by use of the IN and OUT instructions, since these are the only instructions that cause IO/$\overline{M}$ to go high.

Recall that the 8085 CPU can perform either *accumulator I/O* (the 8755 is connected as an I/O device and accessed only by use of the IN and OUT instructions) or *memory-mapped I/O* (the 8755 is connected as a memory device and addressed using any of the memory reference instructions). As can be noticed in Figure 8.20, the only difference is that, for the accumulator I/O implementation, the IO/$\overline{M}$ signal from the 8085 is directly connected to the IO/$\overline{M}$ pin of the 8755, while for the memory-mapped I/O implementation, an address bit (say bit A15) is connected to the IO/$\overline{M}$ pin of the 8755. In both implementations   CE is tied to V_{cc}, the 8085 microprocessor control signals $\overline{RD}$ and $\overline{WR}$ are directly applied to the 8755 chip's $\overline{RD}$ and $\overline{IOW}$ pins to coordinate the input or output operation, and input pin $\overline{CE}$ is connected to address bit A11. (The eleven rightmost address bits A10–A0 are used to access a location within the 2K-byte EPROM.) A normal way of connecting the first 8755 in the system is to assign its EPROM (which normally contains the program) to the lowest values of the address space.[4] Therefore, in the accumulator I/O implementation of Figure 8.20a, the 8755 EPROM occupies addresses 0000_{16} through $07FF_{16}$; the I/O ports have 8-bit device addresses 00_{16} and 01_{16}, and their respective status registers have addresses 02_{16} and 03_{16}. The boxes to the right of the configuration in Figure 8.20a indicate the memory and device addresses required to access the 8755 chip.

Since in the memory-mapped I/O implementation on Figure 8.20b the IO/$\overline{M}$ pin of the 8755 is connected to address bit A15, the I/O ports will be accessed (accessed only by memory instructions) whenever A15 = 1. A memory location is accessed whenever A15 = 0. The EPROM again occupies the lowest 2K locations (0000_{16} through $07FF_{16}$), but with this particular scheme the maximum amount of memory that can be used is reduced to 32K bytes. The I/O ports occupy the four memory locations 8000_{16} through 8003_{16}. These addresses are shown in the boxes to the right of Figure 8.20b.

Interfacing the 8155

The 8155 chip contains 256 bytes of R/W memory and the two 8-bit I/O ports A and B (neither the 6-bit I/O port C nor the 14-bit programmable counter of

---

[4]Remember that after RESET, the 8085 microprocessor always starts executing at location 0 (zero).

the 8155 is discussed here). The corresponding accumulator I/O and memory-mapped I/O configurations are shown in Figure 8.21. (For simplicity, only the chip enable and IO/$\overline{M}$ lines are shown; the other lines can be assumed to be connected as in Figure 8.20.) The IO/$\overline{M}$ pin selects the I/O (when IO/$\overline{M}$ = 1) or the RAM memory portion (when IO/$\overline{M}$ = 0). Port A is accessed by the combination A2A1A0 = 001, while port B is accessed by the combination A2A1A0 = 010. The 8155's CE input must be at logic 1 for the memory or I/O ports to operate properly. The boxes at the right of Figure 8.21 indicate the memory and device addresses required to access the 8155 chip.

Finally, Figure 8.22 shows an 8085-based minimum system configuration using the 8155 and 8355/8755 chips in an accumulator I/O configuration. Notice that the 8155 chip is selected by address bit A12.

8.6 CASE STUDY: POLLING EIGHT PERIPHERAL DEVICES

This case study examines the implementation of a microprocessor system connected to eight external devices (such as teletypes and/or analog-digital converters). The system monitors the operation of these devices by going through a polling procedure. The data input operation—done on a byte-by-byte basis—is examined here, and the memory-mapped I/O technique is used.

The simplified configuration of the system is shown in Figure 8.23a. Each peripheral device interface consists of two input ports. One input port (the DATA register) is used to hold the 8-bit data issued by the peripheral device. A second separate input port (the STATUS register) is provided for use by the microprocessor to obtain status information periodically about new data submitted from the peripheral device to its interface. The interface units shown in the figure may be located physically in the peripheral devices.

The microprocessor executes a programmed loop that repeatedly examines or polls the STATUS registers of each peripheral device. If the status bit (bit 0 of the STATUS register) is not set, the program advances to examine the next device; when it finds the status bit set, it realizes that the respective peripheral device has placed an 8-bit data into the DATA register of its interface. The microprocessor then jumps to the proper routine to read new data, store it in the respective buffer in main memory, clear the device's status register and reset the device's status bit, and then the microprocessor returns to the polling loop. The flowchart of this software polling loop is shown in Figure 8.23b. Furthermore, it is assumed that the microprocessor polls all eight peripheral devices fifty times, and places the data read into eight separate buffers (one buffer per device, each buffer up to fifty bytes long).

Each peripheral device is connected to (or contains) one STATUS register and one DATA register. Since memory-mapped I/O is used, each register is treated as a memory location having its own "address" (or I/O port number).

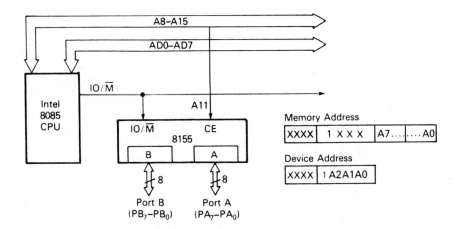

(a) Accumulator I/O configuration.

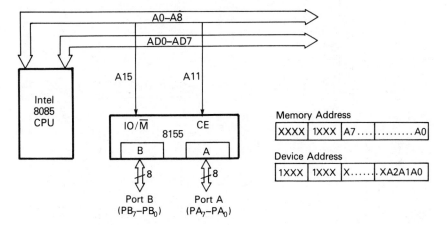

(b) Memory-mapped I/O configuration.

Figure 8.21 Using the 8155 device in accumulator I/O **(a)** and memory-mapped I/O **(b)** configurations. (All other connections are assumed to be connected as in Figure 8.20.) (X's denote "don't care" bits, and bit A11 must be one.)

The microprocessor issues an address to select the STATUS or DATA register of a peripheral device, and the control signals MRDC* and MWTC* to distinguish between input and output operation. (Only the MRDC* is

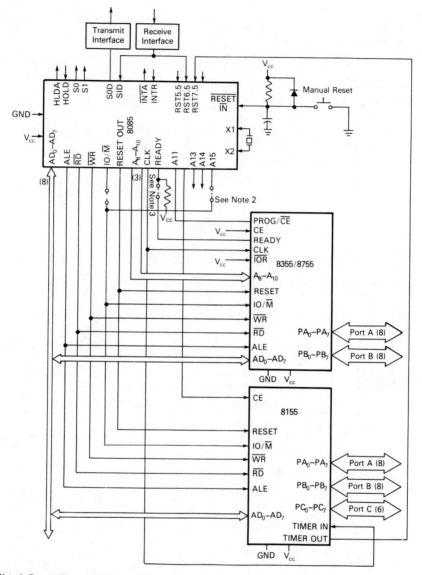

Figure 8.22 Intel 8085-based minimum system configuration (accumulator I/O) *Courtesy Intel Corporation* [7].

shown here, since only the input operation is examined.) The two registers of each device occupy successive memory locations as shown below:

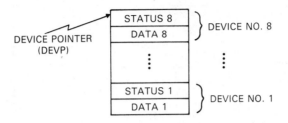

If the directive

```
DEVP    EQU    100H
```

is placed at the beginning of the program, then the sixteen memory locations 0100_{16} through $010F_{16}$ represent the STATUS and DATA ports of the eight peripheral devices. The value of the device pointer DEVP points to the specific peripheral being polled.

The microprocessor examines these eight peripheral devices in sequence. If a peripheral device has data to send (i.e., its STATUS $\neq$ 0), then the microprocessor reads the byte from the device's DATA register and stores it in the next free location of the respective buffer. The flowchart for reading data and storing it in the device's buffer is shown in Figure 8.24.

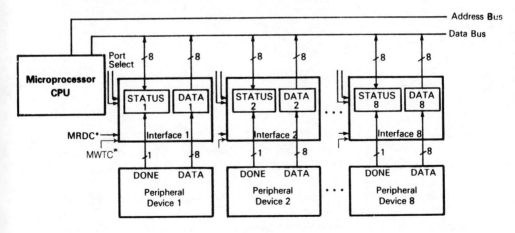

(a)

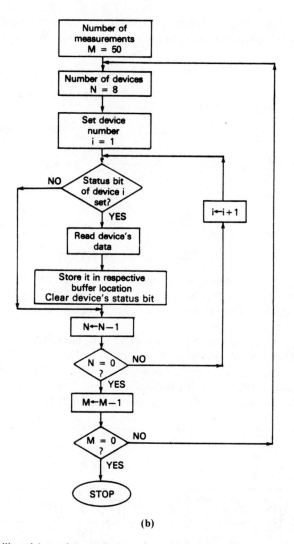

(b)

Figure 8.23 Polling eight peripheral devices to read fifty measurements from each: **(a)** the simplified configuration with memory-mapped I/O; **(b)** the flowchart of the software polling loop.

It is assumed that the program is stored in PROM, so that self-modifying of its instructions is not allowed. A table containing eight 16-bit pointers is required to point to the respective buffers of the peripheral devices, i.e., to those RAM locations where the incoming data are to be stored. This table is not considered part of the final program (assembled in machine language). Let us call this table "data pointer table" (DPT):

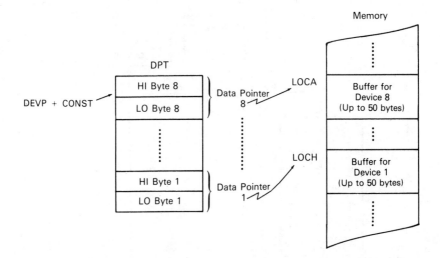

The CONST equals a relocation constant, i.e., a memory location where the table will be loaded after program assembly. (In this example the directive ORG 0200H is used and, therefore, this data pointer table starts from absolute location 0200_{16}.)

The construction of this table is done as follows:

```
            ORG    0200H
DPT:        DW     LOCA
            DW     LOCB
            DW     LOCC
            DW     LOCD
            DW     LOCE
            DW     LOCF
            DW     LOCG
            DW     LOCH
```

This reserves sixteen memory locations, each pair of locations containing the pointer-address (always properly updated) of the respective buffer's free memory location where the incoming data will be stored. It is assumed that these eight buffers start from locations 0300_{16}, 0400_{16}, ..., and $0A00_{16}$ as shown in the memory map of Figure 8.25.

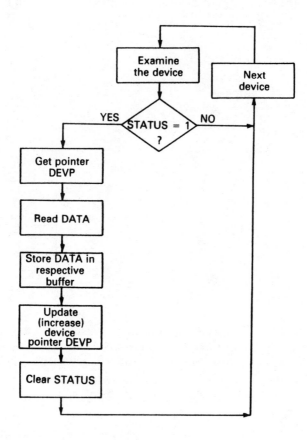

Figure 8.24 Reading data and storing it in the device's buffer in memory.

The detailed flowchart of the polling program is shown in Figure 8.26. Finally, Figure 8.27 shows the respective Intel 8085 assembly language program listing. This program reads a datum (if there is one) from each peripheral device and stores it into the next free location of the respective buffer. It does this fifty times and then stops.

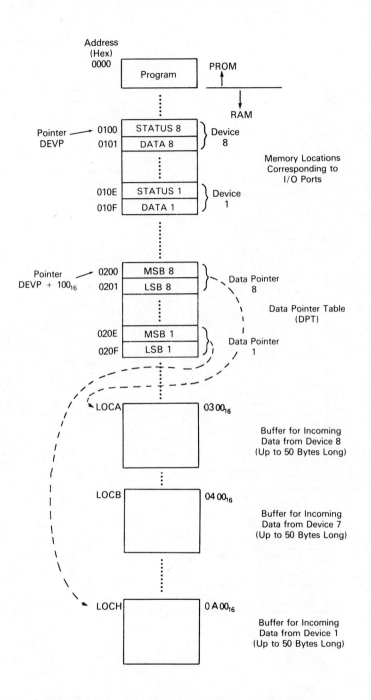

Figure 8.25 Memory map containing the program, the I/O ports, the data pointer table, and the eight buffers for the eight peripheral devices.

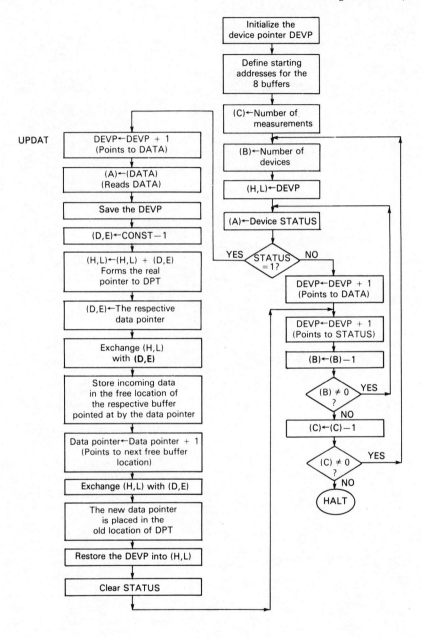

Figure 8.26 The detailed flowchart of the polling program.

```
; PROGRAM FOR POLLING 8 PERIPHERAL DEVICES (MEMORY-MAPPED
; I/O TECHNIQUE IS USED).
;
; INITIALIZE DEVICE POINTER ''DEVP''
DEVP    EQU   Ø1ØØH
;
; DEFINE STARTING ADDRESS OF THE 8 BUFFERS
LOCA    EQU   Ø3ØØH   ; STARTING ADDRESS OF DEVICE 8 BUFFER
LOCB    EQU   Ø4ØØH   ; STARTING ADDRESS OF DEVICE 7 BUFFER
LOCC    EQU   Ø5ØØH   ; STARTING ADDRESS OF DEVICE 6 BUFFER
LOCD    EQU   Ø6ØØH   ; STARTING ADDRESS OF DEVICE 5 BUFFER
LOCE    EQU   Ø7ØØH   ; STARTING ADDRESS OF DEVICE 4 BUFFER
LOCF    EQU   Ø8ØØH   ; STARTING ADDRESS OF DEVICE 3 BUFFER
LOCG    EQU   Ø9ØØH   ; STARTING ADDRESS OF DEVICE 2 BUFFER
LOCH    EQU   ØAØØH   ; STARTING ADDRESS OF DEVICE 1 BUFFER
;
; PROGRAM STARTS AT PROM LOCATION Ø
PROGR: ORG   Ø
        MVI   C,5Ø    ; NUMBER OF MEASUREMENTS PLACED INTO C
POLL:   MVI   B,8     ; NUMBER OF DEVICES PLACED INTO B
        LXI   H,DEVP  ; DEVICE POINTER (DEVP) PLACED IN
                      ; H,L REGISTERS. POINTS TO STATUS
                      ; REGISTER
LOOP:   MOV   A,M     ; READ STATUS (PLACES INTO A CONTENTS
                      ; OF MEMORY LOCATION POINTED AT BY
                      ; (H, L))
        ANI   Ø1H     ; CHECK IF STATUS IS ONE
        JNZ   UPDAT   ; IF STATUS = 1, GO TO UPDAT
        INX   H       ; OTHERWISE, INCREASE POINTER DEVP BY 1
                      ; (H,L) = (H,L) + 1. POINTS TO DATA
                      ; REGISTER
;
; ADVANCE TO EXAMINE NEXT DEVICE
NDEV:   INX   H       ; INCREASE DEVP. IT NOW POINTS TO
                      ; STATUS REGISTER OF NEXT DEVICE
        DCR   B       ; DECREMENT DEVICE COUNT
        JNZ   LOOP    ; BRANCH TO LOOP IF THERE IS A DEVICE
                      ; TO BE EXAMINED
        DCR   C       ; DECREMENT MEASUREMENTS COUNT
        JNZ   POLL    ; JUMP TO POLL IF THERE ARE MORE
                      ; MEASUREMENTS TO BE DONE
        JMP   FIN     ;
;
; READ AND STORE INCOMING DATA
UPDAT: INX   H       ; INCREASE DEVICE POINTER (DEVP). IT
                      ; NOW POINTS TO DATA REGISTER
        MOV   A,M     ; READ DATA. (PLACES INTO A CONTENTS
                      ; OF MEMORY LOCATION POINTED AT BY
                      ; (H,L))
```

Continued on next page

Figure 8.27 Intel 8085 program listing to poll the eight devices and read their data fifty times.

```
        PUSH H      ; SAVE POINTER DEVP (CONTENTS OF H,L)
        LXI  D,ØFFH ; RELOCATION CONSTANT MINUS ONE OF DATA
                    ; POINTER TABLE (DPT) IS PLACED INTO
                    ; (D,E)
        DAD  D      ; (H,L)=(H,L)+(D,E). FORMS REAL
                    ; POINTER TO TABLE DPT
;
; PLACE DATA POINTER INTO D,E
        MOV  D,M    ; MSB OF DATA POINTER PLACED IN D
        INX  H      ; INCREASE POINTER (TO TABLE DPT)
        MOV  E,M    ; LSB OF DATA POINTER PLACED IN E
        XCHG        ; EXCHANGE (H,L) AND (D,E). DATA
                    ; POINTER IS PLACED IN H,L
        MOV  M,A    ; STORE DATA INTO RESPECTIVE BUFFER
        INX  H      ; DEVICE DATA POINTER POINTS TO NEXT
                    ; FREE LOCATION OF RESPECTIVE BUFFER
        XCHG        ; POINTER (TO TABLE DPT) PLACED IN H,L
;
; IN TABLE DPT, IN THE OLD LOCATION OF DEVICE'S DATA POINTER,
; IT NOW PLACES THE NEW, UPDATED, DATA POINTER
        MOV  M,E    ; LSB OF NEW DATA POINTER IS PLACED
                    ; IN THE PROPER LOCATION OF TABLE DPT
        DCX  H      ; DECREMENT (H,L). POINTER TO TABLE DPT
                    ; IS DECREMENTED
        MOV  M,D    ; MSB OF NEW DATA POINTER IS PLACED
                    ; IN THE NEXT LOCATION OF TABLE DPT
;
; RESTORE THE DEVP INTO H,L AND CLEAR DEVICE'S
; STATUS REGISTER
        POP  H
        DCX  H      ; DECREMENT H,L TO POINT TO STATUS
        MVI  M,Ø    ; CLEAR STATUS
        INX  H      ; INCREMENT H,L TO POINT TO DATA
        JMP  NDEV   ; BRANCH TO EXAMINE NEXT DEVICE
FIN:    HLT
;
; DEFINE THE DATA POINTER TABLE (DPT)
        ORG  2ØØH   ; TABLE DPT STARTS AT LOCATION 2ØØH
DPT:    DW   LOCA
        DW   LOCB
        DW   LOCC
        DW   LOCD
        DW   LOCE
        DW   LOCF
        DW   LOCG
        DW   LOCH
;
; END OF PROGRAM
        END
```

Figure 8.27 *Continued*

EXERCISES

8.1 Using the accumulator I/O technique and an 8-bit output port (port address $= 00_{16}$), show the Intel 8080A-based hardware configuration and give the assembly language program for generating a single output control pulse of 12 μsec duration applied to an output device. (Assume the operation is with a 2 MHz clock.)

8.2 Expand Exercise 8.1 to produce a total of 100 such 12-μsec pulses, each pulse issued every 1 sec.

8.3 Consider an Intel 8085-based implementation in which the status flags of eight peripheral devices are connected to the individual bits of input port 40 as follows:

> bit 0: status flag of a pressure measuring device
> bit 1: status flag of a temperature measuring device
> bit 2: status flag of a velocity measuring device
> bit 3: status flag of a flow measuring device
> bit 4: status flag of a voltage measuring device
> bit 5: status flag of a current measuring device
> bit 6: status flag of a liquid-level measuring device
> bit 7: status flag of a frequency measuring device

Status flag logic value 1 indicates that the device is ON; logic value 0 indicates that the device is OFF.

The microprocessor is required to determine which devices have changed state from ON to OFF and which have changed state from OFF to ON, and display that information on two 8-bit display panels (by lighting the respective LEDs) connected to output ports 50 and 60, respectively.

Give the required hardware configuration, the flowchart, and the respective assembly language program code. Use the accumulator I/O technique.

8.4 Show the input and output 16-bit port configuration (and all appropriate control signals) for the accumulator I/O operation of an Intel 8086-based system (minimum mode 8086) with linear select, using the four rightmost device address bits.

8.5 Show the Z80-based configuration (and all appropriate control signals) for the accumulator I/O, using four 8-bit input and four 8-bit output ports. Port selection is done by decoding the two least significant bits of the device address. Ports are assumed to be connected to the CPU bus.

8.6 Repeat Exercise 8.5 using the Intel 8085 microprocessor.

8.7 Using the memory-mapped I/O technique for an 8-bit microprocessor, design the I/O interface with the minimum number of 74154 decoders to produce device select pulses for thirty-two input and thirty-two output ports. Give the respective hexadecimal address for each port.

8.8 Using the accumulator I/O technique for a 16-bit bus master (word transfers on the data bus), design the I/O interface using the minimum number of 8-input 74251 multiplexers to implement four 16-bit input and four 16-bit output ports.

8.9 Using the accumulator I/O technique, show the Intel 8085-based hardware configuration and give the assembly language subroutine for generating a continuous square wave having a period of 24 μsec. The value passed to the subroutine is to be used for terminating the square wave.

8.10 Given the Intel 8085 microprocessor and an 8-bit memory-mapped I/O port. Accessing this port is done by using directly address bits 14 and 15, whose values must be 0 and 1, respectively. Answer the following questions using hexadecimal notation:

(a) With how many different addresses is this port accessed?
(b) What are the respective values of the highest and lowest of these addresses?
(c) How many addresses are left for accessing memory?

8.11 Repeat Exercise 8.9 to produce two square waves on two output lines, one wave lagging behind the other by 12 μsec.

REFERENCES AND BIBLIOGRAPHY

[1] Artwick, B.A., *Microcomputer Interfacing*, Englewood Cliffs, NJ: Prentice-Hall, Inc., 1980.

[2] Guzeman, D.J., *Microprocessor Applications Handbook*, Sunnyvale, CA: Iasis Inc., 1976.

[3] Hilburn, J.L., and P.M. Julich, *Microcomputers/Microprocessors: Hardware, Software, and Applications*, Englewood Cliffs, NJ: Prentice-Hall, Inc., 1976.

[4] IEEE Task P796/D2, "Proposed Microcomputer System 796 Bus Standard," *Computer*, October 1980, pp. 89–105.

[5] Intel Corporation, *Intel 8080 Microcomputer Systems User's Manual*, (98-153C), Santa Clara, CA, September 1975.

[6] Intel Corporation, *MCS 85 User's Manual*, Santa Clara, CA, 1977.

[7] Intel Corporation, *MCS-80/85 Family User's Manual*, (121506-001), Santa Clara, CA, October 1979.

[8] Intel Corporation, *The 8086 Family User's Manual*, (9800722-03), Santa Clara, CA, 1979.

[9] Klingman, E.E., *Microprocessor Systems Design*, Englewood Cliffs, NJ: Prentice-Hall, Inc., 1977.

[10] Larsen, D.G., *The Bugbook I–V*, Derby, CT: E & L Instruments, Inc., 1976.

[11] Lesea, A., and R. Zaks, *Microprocessor Interfacing Techniques*, Berkeley, CA: SYBEX, Inc., 1977.

[12] Martin, D.P., *Microcomputer Design*, Northbrook, IL: Martin Research (now Quint Systems, Inc.), 1976.

[13] NEC Microcomputers, Incorporated, "Illustrate a 10 CPS Teletype I/O Subroutine," *The µCOM-8 Software Manual, Programming Problem No. 8*, 1975.

[14] Peatman, J.B., *Microcomputer-Based Design*, New York: McGraw-Hill, 1977.

[15] Titus, C., et al, "Interfacing Fundamentals: The 8085 Family of Memory Devices," *Computer Design*, August 1978, pp. 122–28.

Chapter 9

INTERRUPTS, DMA, AND MULTIPROCESSOR CONFIGURATIONS

9.1 INTRODUCTION

The program-driven I/O technique discussed in the previous chapter has the following major drawbacks: (1) it cannot handle asynchronous, unpredictably occurring, external events efficiently; (2) it cannot provide an acceptable solution to real-time type applications which require the microprocessor to respond instantly to external events, because of the technique's intrinsically slow characteristic of having to poll the status of all external devices before coming back to any specific one; and (3) it does not utilize to the maximum the microprocessor's processing power, because the CPU may become I/O-bound in checking (polling) the status of all devices, and thus, has little free time to do useful work.

Another input/output method refers to data transfers initiated by an interrupt signal issued by a peripheral device requesting to exchange information with the master CPU. *Interrupt signals* or *interrupt request signals* are the means by which one or more external slave devices notify the bus master that they require its immediate attention (or service), for example, need to send or receive data from it. The interrupt lines used for both the system bus and the CPU bus are examined in section 9.2. Section 9.3 explains how the microprocessor, in general, services an interrupt request from an external device, while section 9.4 outlines the peculiarities of interrupt handling for a number of representative microprocessors. Finally, the interrupts sections of this chapter conclude by explaining single-line (section 9.5) and multi-line (section 9.6) interrupt configurations.

In both the program-driven and interrupt-driven I/O methods, the microprocessor CPU intervenes in the data transfer path between central memory and peripheral devices. Section 9.7 describes another method of performing

I/O (the DMA-I/O), in which an external DMA controller is used to allow peripherals to access main memory directly so that I/O transfers do not go through the microprocessor. The DMA controller has some processor-like features, in that it requests and gains control of the bus and initiates memory read and memory write bus cycles.

Carrying the DMA controller concept one step further, one may consider incorporating in the system even more intelligent processors (e.g., I/O processors or other microprocessor CPUs). This leads to multiprocessor system configurations discussed in section 9.8 of this chapter.

9.2 INTERRUPT LINES

The general description of handling interrupts was covered in section 4.4.2 (under the title of "Processing Exceptional Conditions") in chapter 4. As soon as the interrupt request signal[1] from the external interrupting slave device is recognized, the bus master will suspend execution of the program, put the microprocessor in the supervisor mode (when such a mode exists), identify the reason for the interrupt, save the CPU state in the (supervisor) stack, and finally, transfer control to the respective interrupt handling routine to service the device. When the routine finishes servicing the interrupting device, the saved processor "state" is restored, and program execution resumes from where it was interrupted.

This method represents an improvement over the program-driven I/O in that it allows a better utilization of the fast CPU. The CPU operates normally, executing the main processing program. Its operation is temporarily interrupted in order to service a peripheral device only when the device sends an interrupt signal to the CPU. In addition, it makes the application programmer's work easier, since he or she is not required to bother with all the details of the external requests for I/O. When the peripheral device requires attention, it will send the proper interrupt signal to the CPU.

This method, however, makes the central system more complex. Because these interrupts can appear at any time, the central system must be capable of "saving" or "remembering" the point at which the execution of the main program was interrupted, so that it can return to it later, when it will have finished servicing the peripheral device. Furthermore, when more than one peripheral slave device is connected to the bus master, each with its own interrupt signal, the following additional problems arise: (1) the specific device requesting service must be properly identified; and (2) when service is

---

[1]The INIT* or (RESET) signal is also treated as an external interrupt.

requested by more than one device at precisely the same time, a way must exist to prioritize the interrupts, so that the devices can be serviced in some logical sequence.

Figures 5.8 and 5.9 of chapter 5 show that another set of lines, called "interrupt lines," are now required to connect a master module or a microprocessor CPU with external I/O slave devices. Interrupt lines for both the system bus and the CPU bus are discussed next.

9.2.1 System Bus Interrupt Lines

System bus interrupt lines are differentiated as "interrupt request lines" and an "interrupt acknowledge line."

System Interrupt Request Lines (INT0*–INT7*)

For interrupt-driven I/O, the IEEE 796 system bus allocates eight interrupt request lines INT0*–INT7*. If a slave I/O module requires service by a bus master, it will have to generate an interrupt request by activating one of these lines. INT0* has the highest priority, and INT7* has the lowest priority.

System Interrupt Acknowledge Line (INTA*)

The system interrupt acknowledge signal INTA* is generated by a bus master with vectored interrupt capability (explained later) in response to a received external interrupt signal, indicating to the slaves that the master requests them to place interrupt information on the data bus lines. The type of interrupt information that will be placed on the data bus depends on the specific implementation of the interrupt scheme. (Usually, this information is the interrupt "vector number" placed by the interrupting slave device.) The leading edge of INTA* indicates that the system address bus is active; the trailing edge indicates that data is present on the data lines. (The IEEE 796 system bus can support masters that generate either two or three INTA* commands.)

Thus, the system configuration with an interrupting I/O slave connected to the system bus will be that shown in Figure 9.1. The box labeled "CPU interface" may contain any of the interfacing circuitry (discussed in section 6.2 of chapter 6) to convert the CPU bus to the system bus. However, the "interrupt control logic" box (also see Figure 6.1 of chapter 6) has now been included here; it accepts interrupt requests from I/O slaves over the eight system interrupt lines INT0*–INT7*, converts them to the appropriate interrupt request input signals for the master CPU, and issues the interrupt acknowledge signal on the output system line INTA*. The optional dashed lines included in Figure 9.1 are used for those interrupting I/O slaves that

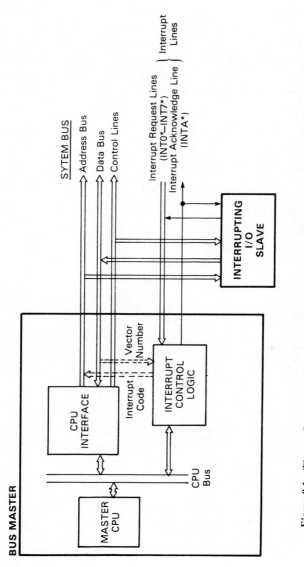

Figure 9.1 The configuration of a system with one interrupting I/O slave connected to the system bus.

transfer an interrupt vector number over the system data bus to the bus master. As will be explained later, the bus master's interrupt control logic puts an "interrupt code" on the system address lines, which forces the highest priority slave to place its vector number on the data bus. The complexity of this interrupt control logic depends on the specific master CPU used and the complexity of the interrupt system. Generally, it may be placed anywhere in the system (i.e, not necessarily on the bus master module). In some microprocessors, most of the functions carried out by the interrupt control logic interface box have been implemented on the same microprocessor CPU chip (e.g., the Motorola 68000).

9.2.2   CPU Bus Interrupt Lines

CPU Interrupt Request Lines

Microprocessor CPUs allocate one or more input pins to receive interrupt request signals as shown in the representative examples of Table 9.1. Interrupt lines used to request service from the CPU may be of two general types: non-maskable and maskable.

Non-maskable Interrupt Lines

Non-maskable lines[2] are: the 8085 TRAP line; the Z80, 6800, and Z8000 $\overline{\text{NMI}}$ lines; the 8086 NMI line; and priority level 7 interrupt ($\overline{\text{IPL0}}$ to $\overline{\text{IPL2}}$ asserted) of the 68000. A non-maskable interrupt cannot be masked off or disabled by the CPU (it is always enabled) and takes priority over other maskable interrupts. It is usually intended for "catastrophic events," such as imminent loss of power, memory error detection, etc. Accepting an interrupt request on this line need not generate any interrupt acknowledge cycles. The response is usually a transfer to a predetermined location in memory as shown in the right column of Table 9.1. For the Intel 8085 and Zilog Z80, this location contains the first instruction of the interrupt handling routine. For the remaining microprocessors of Table 9.1, this location contains a pointer which, when loaded into the program counter, will point to another location where the first instruction of the interrupt handling routine resides. (As will be seen next, the above pointer is called the "auto-vector," and the indirect transfer to the interrupt handling routine is called "auto-vectoring.") A non-maskable interrupt can override the maskable interrupts even if they are in progress.

---

[2]Although the RESET signal is not mentioned here explicitly, it is also treated as a non-maskable interrupt of the highest priority. The way the various microprocessors handle the RESET signal is discussed in section 5.3.2 of Chapter 5.

Maskable Interrupt Lines

For the remainder of this chapter, only maskable interrupt lines are considered. Maskable interrupt lines include: the 8080A INT line; the 8085 INTR, RST 5.5, RST 6.5, and RST 7.5 lines; the Z80 $\overline{\text{INT}}$ line; the 6800 $\overline{\text{IRQ}}$ line; the 8086 INTR line; the Z8000 $\overline{\text{VI}}$ (vectored interrupt) and $\overline{\text{NVI}}$ (non-vectored interrupt) lines; and the three encoded input lines $\overline{\text{IPL0}}$–$\overline{\text{IPL2}}$ of the 68000 that provide the six levels (levels 1 to 6) of maskable interrupt priorities. A maskable interrupt can be masked off by the CPU via internal software operation. If the master CPU accepts the interrupt request on the INTR* line, it may respond with an interrupt acknowledge bus sequence.

To avoid confusion caused by the various names used by these microprocessors, a maskable interrupt request input line will be denoted from now on by the generalized signal INTR*. This generalized INTR* line of the master CPU may be asserted either directly by the I/O slave or by the interrupt control logic.

In the system configuration of Figure 9.1, this INTR* line is implemented as a "group interrupt" line in conjunction with the system bus interrupt lines INT0*–INT7*. In this case, INTR* indicates the presence of one or more interrupt signals on these system bus interrupt lines.

CPU Interrupt Acknowledge Line

When the master CPU accepts an interrupt request on the INTR* input line and if this interrupt is enabled, the CPU will then respond with an interrupt acknowledge sequence (issuing a corresponding interrupt acknowledge signal), accept "interrupt information" from its data bus,[3] load a new value into the program counter, and transfer control to the appropriate interrupt handling routine. There are two general ways of loading a new value into the program counter: by executing a RESTART instruction, or by fetching a vector from a specialized area in memory referred to as the "vector table."

Like the interrupt request lines, the various microprocessor CPUs have different ways of generating the interrupt acknowledge signal; they also use different names for it, as shown in Table 9.2. When the Intel 8080A acknowledges an interrupt, it issues a status bit D0 = high on the CPU data bus; CPU interface support circuitry may be used (e.g., the 8228 system controller of Figure 6.9 in chapter 6) to generate the $\overline{\text{INTA}}$ signal corresponding to the system signal INTA*. The Intel 8085 has an output pin $\overline{\text{INTA}}$ which may also be tied directly to the INTA* system line. The Zilog Z80 and Motorola 6800

---

[3]It is assumed that if an interrupt acknowledge sequence occurs, an interrupt control logic somewhere in the system will respond appropriately with the "interrupt information."

Table 9.1 The response of several microprocessors to interrupt request signals applied to their interrupt input pins. (The RESET input pin is not included here.)

MICROPRO-CESSOR	Types of Interrupts			
	Maskable			Non-Maskable
	NON-VECTORED (Interrupt information on data bus is a RESTART instruction)	VECTORED (Interrupt information on data bus is a vector number)	AUTO-VECTORED (No vector number on the data bus)	(No vector number on the data bus)
INTEL 8080A	**INT:** To handling routines in eight fixed locations 0_{16}, 8_{16}, 10_{16}, 18_{16}, 20_{16}, 28_{16}, 30_{16}, 38_{16}	—	—	—
INTEL 8085	**INTR:** Like INT of 8080A **RST 5.5:** To handling routine in fixed location $2C_{16}$ **RST 6.5:** To handling routine in fixed location 34_{16} **RST 7.5:** To handling routine in fixed location $3C_{16}$	—	—	**TRAP:** To handling routine in *fixed* location 24_{16}
ZILOG Z80	$\overline{\text{INT}}$ **(Mode 0):** Like INT of 8080A. $\overline{\text{INT}}$ **(Mode 1):** To handling routine in fixed location 56_{16}	$\overline{\text{INT}}$ **(Mode 2):** To *variable* vector locations in a vector table placed *anywhere* in memory	—	**NMI:** To handling routine in *fixed* location 66_{16}

Table 9.1 (Continued)

MOTOROLA 6800	—	—	**IRQ:** To a vector in *fixed* location FFF8$_{16}$.	$\overline{\textbf{NMI}}$**:** To a vector in *fixed* location FFFC$_{16}$. (Autovectored)
INTEL 8086	—	**INTR:** To *variable* vector locations in a vector table that occupies *fixed* memory locations	—	**NMI:** To a vector in *fixed* location 08$_{16}$. (Autovectored)
ZILOG Z8000	—	$\overline{\textbf{VI}}$**:** To *variable* vector locations in a vector table that occupies *fixed* locations within a segment	$\overline{\textbf{NVI}}$**:** To a vector in *fixed* location within a segment (To location Segment 0, Offset 24 & 26$_{10}$ bytes for non-segmented Z8000; to any Segment, Offset 48, 50, 52, 54$_{10}$ bytes for segmented Z8000)	$\overline{\textbf{NMI}}$**:** To a vector in *fixed* location within a segment (to Segment 0, Offset 20 & 22$_{10}$ bytes for non-segmented Z8000; to any Segment, Offset 40, 42, 44, 46$_{10}$ bytes for segmented Z8000) (Autovectored)
MOTOROLA 68000	—	**Level 1 to level 6:** To *variable* vector locations in a vector table that occupies *fixed* memory locations	**Level 1:** To a vector in *fixed* location 064$_{16}$. **Level 2:** To a vector in *fixed* location 068$_{16}$. **Level 3:** To a vector in *fixed* location 06C$_{16}$. **Level 4:** To a vector in *fixed* location 070$_{16}$. **Level 5:** To a vector in *fixed* location 074$_{16}$. **Level 6:** To a vector in *fixed* location 078$_{16}$.	**Level 7:** To a vector in *fixed* location 07C$_{16}$. (Autovectored).

378

Table 9.2 Generating of the interrupt acknowledge signal by several microprocessor CPUs.

INTEL 8080A	INTEL 8085	ZILOG Z80	MOTOROLA 6800	INTEL 8086	ZILOG Z8000	MOTOROLA 68000
Status D0 (on the CPU data lines) or $\overline{\text{INTA}}$ (generated by the 8228 system controller)	$\overline{\text{INTA}}$	$\overline{\text{IORQ}}$	R/$\mathbf{W}$= read (high)	a) Max mode: $\overline{\text{S0}}$, $\overline{\text{S1}}$, $\overline{\text{S2}}$ = 000 decoded by 8288 bus controller to produce $\overline{\text{INTA}}$ b) Min mode: $\overline{\text{INTA}}$	Status bits ST3–ST0: = 0100 for SEGT trap acknowledge ($\overline{\text{SEGTACK}}$) = 0101 for $\overline{\text{NMI}}$ acknowledge ($\overline{\text{NMIACK}}$) = 0110 for $\overline{\text{NVI}}$ acknowledge ($\overline{\text{NVIACK}}$) = 0111 for $\overline{\text{VI}}$ acknowledge ($\overline{\text{VIACK}}$)	Status FC0–FC2 = 111 for interrupt acknowledge (interrupt level is placed on address lines A1, A2, A3)

CPUs do not have separate interrupt acknowledge output pins; instead they assert signals $\overline{IORQ}$ and R/W, respectively. The Intel 8086 in its "minimum mode" configuration has an output pin for the $\overline{INTA}$ signal; in its "maximum mode," it issues a 3-bit status code ($\overline{S0}$, $\overline{S1}$, $\overline{S2}$ = 000) on the respective three output pins, and an external status decoder is required to convert it to the system signal INTA*. The Zilog Z8000 places a 4-bit status code on its respective ST3–ST0 output lines, which identifies acknowledgment to the corresponding one of four interrupt request inputs activated; as with the 8086, an external status decoder is required to convert the status code to the system signal INTA*. Finally, the Motorola 68000 CPU acknowledges an interrupt by issuing the 3-bit code 111 on its function lines FC0–FC2, which must again be decoded externally to produce the INTA*. In addition, the 68000 CPU places on its address lines A1, A2, and A3 the "level number" of the interrupt being acknowledged.

Again, to avoid using different names, the interrupt acknowledge signal will be denoted from now on by the generalized signal INTA*.

9.3 SERVICING THE INTERRUPT

The interrupt processing activities carried out by the permanent bus master are summarized in the chart of Figure 9.2 and explained next.

9.3.1 Finish Current Instruction

Interrupt requests arriving at the bus master do not force immediate interrupt processing but are made pending. Pending interrupts are detected between instruction executions. Since virtually all microprocessors complete the current instruction before taking action on the interrupt, this wait period before start processing of the interrupt request may equal the time required to execute the most complex instruction of the microprocessor. As soon as an interrupt is accepted, the system disables all I/O interrupts.

9.3.2 Masks

It is possible that at any given time all external interrupt request signals will be disabled, or that the interrupt request signals of some of these devices will be masked off to prevent them from interrupting the CPU (for example, during the period of executing some critical process). One or more microprocessor input pins are allocated for maskable-type interrupts, and these interrupts can be masked internally by software. For microprocessors with multiple-level interrupt inputs, the priority level of the pending interrupt must be compared with the current priority of the bus master. This comparison is usually done by external interface support circuitry (e.g., an interrupt controller) in the master module or inside the master CPU itself (as done in the Motorola 68000 CPU).

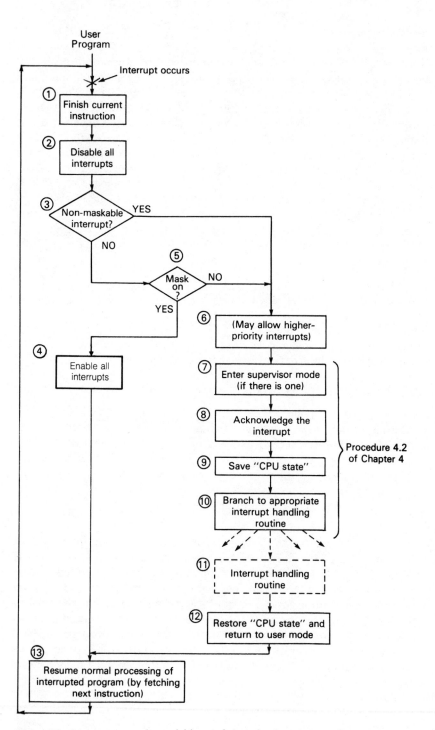

Figure 9.2 Interrupt processing activities carried out by the permanent bus master.

If the priority of the pending interrupt is lower than or equal to the current master CPU priority, then processing of this interrupt is postponed. Either a special interrupt queue routine is executed to store information for the new interrupt in a queue by priority, or external circuitry latches them and also gives them an order of priority. If the priority is greater, then processing advances to the next step below.

9.3.3 Enter Supervisor Mode

For 16- and 32-bit microprocessors that have both user and supervisor modes, the CPU enters into the supervisor mode. All interrupt servicing activities are carried out in the supervisor mode.

9.3.4 Acknowledge the Interrupt

The CPU then initiates an interrupt acknowledge sequence. As a first step of this sequence, the CPU floats its address bus, does not update the program counter, and asserts the interrupt acknowledge (INTA*) signal which requests gating of the "interrupt information" on the data bus. (As discussed in section 9.6 for multi-level interrupts, the interrupt control logic[4] of the bus master puts an "interrupt code" on the system bus address lines which is the address of the highest priority active interrupt request line). The interrupt information (which for some microprocessors is a RESTART instruction, and for others, a vector number) will be used by the CPU to generate the starting address of the respective interrupt handling routine. The interrupt acknowledge sequence is executed differently by the various microprocessors as discussed in detail in section 9.4.

9.3.5 Save "CPU State"

What we call "state saving activity" and "CPU state" are referred to by the 16- and 32-bit microprocessors as "context switching" and "current processor context," respectively.

Before calling the appropriate interrupt handling routine, the processor enters the state saving activity, whereby it automatically saves the CPU state by pushing it into the (supervisor) stack area in memory via one or more memory write bus cycles. The current memory stack location is identified by the contents of the (supervisor) stack pointer register in the CPU. This activity is necessary to allow a later return to the interrupted program.

---

[4] For the Motorola 68000, this 3-bit interrupt code (called "interrupt level") is issued by the CPU itself.

9.3.6 Transfer to Interrupt Handling Routine

Once the interrupt request has been received, accepted, and identified by the master CPU, then the interrupting slave device must be serviced. This is done by executing an interrupt handling routine for that device. (The last four steps, 7 through 10, of Figure 9.2 correspond to the four steps of Procedure 4.2 in chapter 4). It is the responsibility of the interrupt handling routine to save in the stack the rest of the CPU registers that were not automatically saved during the previous step, and to re-enable interrupts (if required). Figure 9.3 shows the simplified flowchart of the activities carried out by an interrupt handling routine.

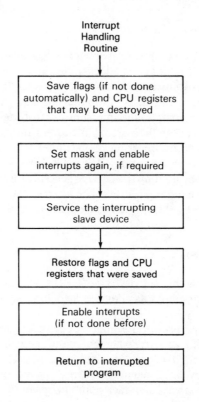

Figure 9.3   Simplified flowchart of an interrupt handling routine activities.

As already mentioned, depending upon the specific microprocessor CPU and the interrupt system implementation, branching to the interrupt handling routine may be done either by executing a RESTART instruction or by loading a vector into the program counter.

Executing a RESTART Instruction

The interrupt information mentioned earlier, which is jammed onto the data bus at the beginning of the interrupt acknowledge sequence, is automatically routed into the instruction register of the CPU and interpreted as a RESTART instruction. The execution of this instruction carries out steps seven through ten of Figure 9.2 (the 8-bit microprocessors which execute a RESTART instruction have no supervisor mode of operation), i.e., it saves the unincremented program counter in the stack and places a new address into the program counter, thus forcing an automatic program branch to the starting address of the interrupt handling routine. This technique has been implemented in the Intel 8080A and 8085 microprocessors and is discussed in more detail in section 9.4.

Loading a Vector into the Program Counter

A second and more flexible way of branching to an interrupt handling routine is via the use of vectors. Such interrupts are called "vectored interrupts."

The interrupt information placed on the data bus (by either the interrupting slave device directly or the interrupt control logic) is called the "vector number." In a vectored interrupt implementation, when an interrupt request is accepted and acknowledged, the master CPU reads the vector number off its data bus and converts it internally into a "vector address," pointing to a location in memory that holds a vector. This vector is another address which is fetched and loaded into the program counter, thus forcing a branch to the beginning of the appropriate interrupt handling routine (Figure 9.4). When more than one vector type exists, vectors are usually placed in the specialized memory area[5] called the vector table. In some microprocessors (e.g., the Intel 8086) this vector table occupies fixed locations in memory, whereas in others (e.g., the Zilog Z80 Mode 2 and Zilog Z8000), it occupies variable locations in memory. (The specific vectors used by individual microprocessors are discussed in section 9.4.)

With the previous restart instruction technique, vectors could take on only predetermined fixed values specified via the execution of a RESTART instruction. Therefore, *fixed* starting locations had to be used for placing the respective interrupt handling routines. In the more flexible vectored interrupt implementation, these vectors may take on variable values. Since these values are assigned by the programmer, he or she is allowed to place the interrupt handling routines *anywhere* in memory.

---

[5]All vectors lie in the supervisor data space (if the microprocessor has a supervisor mode of operation).

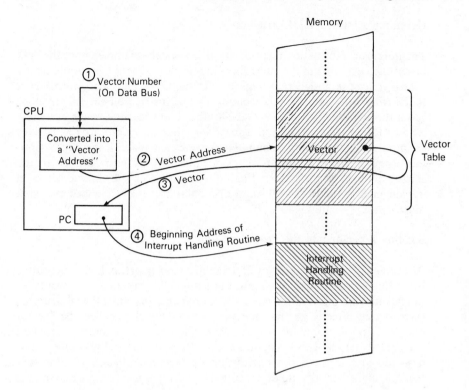

Figure 9.4   Using the vector number to branch to the interrupt handling routine.

Auto-vectoring is a special case referring to those interrupt request input signals for which no external vector number is placed on the data bus. Instead, depending upon the specific input pin asserted, the CPU generates internally the corresponding vector number and then converts it to a vector address pointing to the location in memory where an auto-vector resides. For example, auto-vectoring (see third column of Table 9.1) is performed when the Motorola 6800 IRQ, the Intel 8086 NMI, and the Zilog Z8000 NVI input pins are being asserted. For the Motorola 68000, each individual priority level, from level 1 to level 7 (level 7 is treated as a non-maskable interrupt) may also be used for auto-vectoring. Auto-vectored input pins are commonly used by peripheral devices not equipped to respond with vector numbers.

9.3.7   Return from Interrupt Handling Routine

The last steps of Figure 9.2 involve activities taking place when program control is returning from the interrupt handling routine. The CPU state is automatically restored (when the CPU executes the interrupt handling routine's RETURN instruction), the CPU returns to the user mode of operation, and normal processing resumes from the point at which the program was interrupted.

Interrupt processing, therefore, provides a means by which the microprocessor can make very rapid response to external events occurring at arbitrary times and perform a maximum amount of useful work while waiting for such events. The time between the interrupt request issued by an external device and the first instruction of the software that services it is known as the *interrupt response time*.

With regard to *interrupt response time*, the following things must always be kept in mind:

(a) There are several critical time periods in the processing, during which the system should not be interrupted by an external event. In the simple (single-level) interrupt structures, "enable interrupts" and "disable interrupts" instructions are provided to set a software-controlled flag to turn the interrupt system on or off. In more complex situations (in which several interrupt levels are available), an appropriate interrupt mask should be used to disable interrupt levels selectively.

(b) The interrupting slave device must recognize the CPU acceptance of the interrupt and deactivate its interrupt request to allow processing of the next event (e.g., start assembling the next character into its input buffer).

(c) The single-line interrupt system cannot handle a second or subsequent interrupt that occurs before a pending interrupt has been acknowledged by the processor.This means that some sort of external hardware logic is required to queue multiple interrupts arriving in chronological order.

(d) In single-line interrupt implementations, if a high-level interrupt is to be allowed to interrupt a lower-level interrupt handling routine once it is in progress, an "enable interrupts" instruction must be included early in the interrupt handling routine. In multi-line interrupt implementations, a higher-priority interrupt can interrupt the processing of a lower priority interrupt.

9.4   INTERRUPTS OF REPRESENTATIVE MICROPROCESSORS

The interrupt acknowledge sequence of section 9.3.4 and the interpretation of the interrupt information on the data bus are performed differently by the various microprocessors. For vectored interrupts, the interrupt acknowledge cycle is a standard bus read cycle, which requests a vector number from the interrupting slave or the interrupt control logic to be asserted on the data bus.

9.4.1   Intel 8080A

An interrupt request appearing on its single input line INT will be acknowledged if interrupts have been enabled through the enable interrupts (EI)
instruction. Acknowledging an interrupt automatically disables further interrupts; the program counter is not updated, and signal $\overline{\text{INTA}}$ is asserted (by the
8228 system controller). This $\overline{\text{INTA}}$ causes interface logic to jam an 8-bit
RESTART instruction RST N onto the CPU's data bus[6] during state T_3 and
route it into the instruction register of the CPU. The object code of instruction
RST is

$$11 \; \textbf{xxx} \; 111,$$

where xxx is the 3-bit representation of N, supplied by external logic. Execution of the RST saves only the current (unincremented) program counter
contents onto the stack (by executing two memory write cycles using the stack
pointer[7]), and then loads a new starting address into the program counter.
This address is a vector, whose decimal value is eight times N, and which
points to one of the eight locations of Figure 9.5 that holds the first instruction
of the respective interrupt handling routine for this device. Since the space
allocated to each individual interrupt handling routine is limited to only eight
bytes, a branch instruction may be placed there to continue a longer routine
from somewhere else in memory. Furthermore, if a configuration is to use all
eight classes of interrupts, no program section should occupy any of these
reserved memory locations. If fewer than eight classes of interrupts are to be
used, then the programs should be written around the corresponding critical
interrupt locations in low memory addresses.

It is the responsibility of the programmer to use the interrupt handling
routine, and first push onto the stack any other information required (such as
accumulator and flags by executing a PUSH PSW instruction, and any other
CPU registers), which must again be restored before the end of the routine (by
executing respective POP instructions). If interrupts are kept disabled for the
duration of the interrupt handling routine, the programmer must enable them
by executing the EI instruction.[8] The last instruction of the interrupt service
routine is a return (RET) to restore the program counter from the stack.

---

[6]In a typical 8080A-based system, this means that the data-in bus from memory must be
disconnected temporarily from the CPU's main data bus, so that the interrupting device can
command the bus without interference.

[7]The SP-1 to store PC_H, followed by the SP-2 to store PC_L.

[8]Interrupts actually are enabled after the execution of the *next* instruction to allow a return
from the interrupt handling routine before enable.

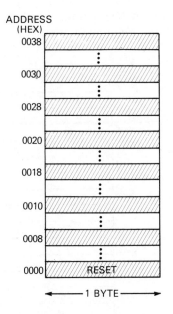

ADDRESS
(HEX)

0038

0030

0028

0020

0018

0010

0008

0000   RESET

←——— 1 BYTE ———→

Figure 9.5 Fixed starting addreses of Intel 8080A interrupt handling routines.

9.4.2 Intel 8085

Compared to the one level of the 8080A, the 8085 CPU provides *five* priority levels of interrupt, which are, in overall priority from highest to lowest: TRAP, RST 7.5, RST 6.5, RST 5.5 and INTR. The INTR is identical in function to the 8080A INT. The TRAP is the highest priority interrupt, and it is non-maskable (i.e., is always "on"). It causes the internal execution of a RESTART instruction, which forces an automatic program branch to fixed memory location 0024_{16} (i.e., 0024_{16} is the vector loaded into the program counter) independent of the state of the interrupt enable or masks. The three RST interrupts 5.5, 6.5, and 7.5 can interrupt the 8085 CPU (and cause the internal execution of a respective RESTART instruction) if the interrupts are enabled and if the interrupt mask is not set. Each of these three RST interrupts has a programmable mask, i.e., it can be individually masked and thus prevented from interrupting the 8085 CPU. However, there are two different types of inputs to these RST pins. RST 5.5 and RST 6.5 are *high-level sensitive* (or logic 1 sensitive) like INTR. The third RST 7.5 is *rising-edge sensitive* (or positive edge sensitive), i.e., only a pulse is required to set the interrupt request. The RST 7.5 will be remembered until the request is serviced, or reset by $\overline{\text{RESET}}$ input (pin 36) or by the SIM instruction. RST 5.5, RST 6.5, and RST 7.5 force an automatic program branch to fixed memory locations $002C_{16}$, 0034_{16} and $003C_{16}$ (Figure 9.6), where the respective interrupt handling routines reside.

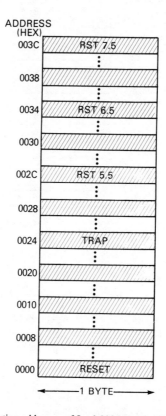

ADDRESS
(HEX)

003C	RST 7.5
0038	
0034	RST 6.5
0030	
002C	RST 5.5
0028	
0024	TRAP
0020	
0010	
0008	
0000	RESET

◄——1 BYTE——►

Figure 9.6 Fixed starting addresses of Intel 8085 interrupt handling routines (unlabeled shaded locations are for INTR as in Figure 9.5).

Two new, 1-byte instructions are implemented in the 8085 for management of interrupts: SIM (set interrupt mask) and RIM (read interrupt mask), where the accumulator or A register is used as the source or destination of the data bytes of each operation (see Figure 9.7). For the SIM instruction, the contents of the accumulator are used to program the RST interrupt masks. Bits 0–2 will set/reset the mask bit for RST 5.5, 6.5, and 7.5 of the interrupt mask register, if bit 3 is 1 ("set"). Setting the mask bit to 1, *disables* the corresponding interrupt. RST 7.5, whether masked or not, will be *reset* if bit 4 is 1. RESET input pin 36, will set all three RST masks, and reset/disable all interrupts. For the RIM instruction, the accumulator is loaded with the status

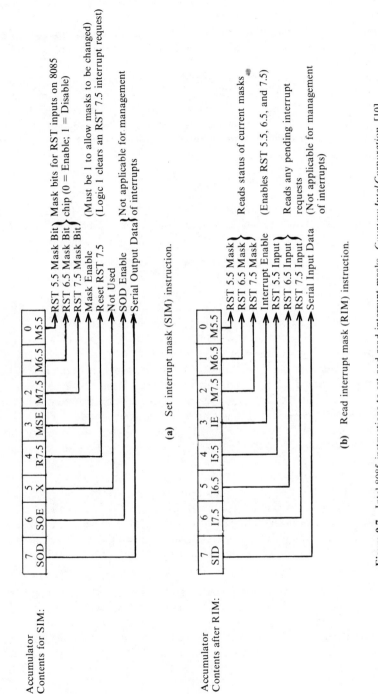

Accumulator Contents for SIM:

7	6	5	4	3	2	1	0
SOD	SOE	X	R7.5	MSE	M7.5	M6.5	M5.5

→ RST 5.5 Mask Bit ⎫ Mask bits for RST inputs on 8085
→ RST 6.5 Mask Bit ⎬ chip (0 = Enable; 1 = Disable)
→ RST 7.5 Mask Bit ⎭
→ Mask Enable (Must be 1 to allow masks to be changed)
→ Reset RST 7.5 (Logic 1 clears an RST 7.5 interrupt request)
→ Not Used
→ SOD Enable ⎫ Not applicable for management
→ Serial Output Data ⎬ of interrupts

(a) Set interrupt mask (SIM) instruction.

Accumulator Contents after RIM:

7	6	5	4	3	2	1	0
SID	I7.5	I6.5	I5.5	IE	M7.5	M6.5	M5.5

→ RST 5.5 Mask ⎫ Reads status of current masks
→ RST 6.5 Mask ⎬
→ RST 7.5 Mask ⎭
→ Interrupt Enable (Enables RST 5.5, 6.5, and 7.5)
→ RST 5.5 Input ⎫ Reads any pending interrupt
→ RST 6.5 Input ⎬ requests
→ RST 7.5 Input ⎭
→ Serial Input Data (Not applicable for management of interrupts)

(b) Read interrupt mask (RIM) instruction.

Figure 9.7 Intel 8085 instructions to set and read interrupt masks. *Courtesy Intel Corporation* [10].

of the three RST interrupt masks and any pending interrupt requests (the contents of the serial input data line (SID) are also read into the accumulator bit 7).

The state-saving activities of the 8085 are the same as those of the 8080A, and the 8085 interrupts have *fixed* vectors pointing within the address space 0000_{16} and 0040_{16}, shown in Figure 9.6. However, some of the 8085 vectors point to addresses that are placed between the 8080A corresponding addresses, thus leaving only four bytes of storage space between successive interrupt handling routine starting addresses.

9.4.3   Zilog Z80

The Z80 acknowledges an interrupt request by issuing an $\overline{IORQ}$ = low. Depending on which of the three modes the programmer has selected for the Z80, the vector is calculated differently and can take one of three forms:

Mode 0: The interrupt information on the data bus is a RESTART instruction treated exactly as done in the Intel 8080A (i.e., specific vectors are computed and loaded into the program counter, branching to interrupt handling routines that are in *fixed* memory locations).

Mode 1: No interrupt information is placed on the data bus. The Z80 CPU places the fixed vector 0056_{16} into the program counter and branches to the interrupt handling routine in location 0056_{16}.

Mode 2: Here, variable vectors are used to branch to interrupt handling routines residing *anywhere* in memory. The interrupting device places an 8-bit vector number on the data bus; only the first seven bits are used; the low-order bit is always set to 0 (zero) to permit 16-bit vector addresses to point to even memory locations. The Z80 CPU concatenates in front of this vector number the 8-bit contents of internal register I, thus forming a 16-bit vector address which points to a memory location containing the 16-bit vector to be loaded into the program counter. Mode 2 vectors can be placed in consecutive memory locations to form the vector table (assumed to have been constructed in memory prior to the occurrence of interrupts), with the value placed in register I corresponding to the high-order byte of the 16-bit base (or starting) address of the table. Thus, in this mode, not only the interrupt handling routines, but *also* the vector table itself can be placed *anywhere* in memory (Figure 9.8).

Finally, the non-maskable interrupt ($\overline{NMI}$) has priority over the maskable interrupt ($\overline{INT}$) and operates in Mode 1 only, placing into the program counter the fixed vector 0066_{16}.

The Z80 has two sets of registers, main and alternate. When an interrupt occurs, instead of being forced to save the CPU state (which includes the accumulator, flags, and general-purpose registers) in the external stack, one

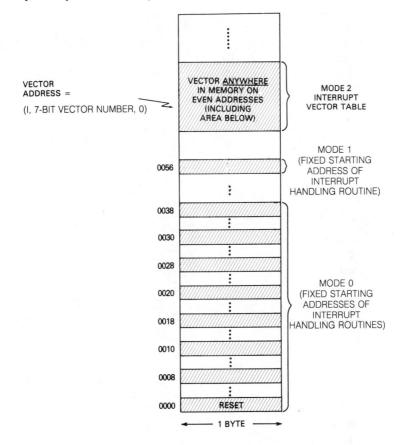

Figure 9.8 Memory locations used by the Zilog Z80 interrupt system.

set of registers is deactivated (without destroying the contents), and the second set is activated. Servicing the interrupt is done using the alternate set of registers.

9.4.4 Motorola 6800

The 6800 does not have memory addresses set aside for vectoring purposes. Each of its two interrupt inputs has its own auto-vector address: $FFF8_{16}$ for an $\overline{IRQ}$ interrupt, and $FFFC_{16}$ for an $\overline{NMI}$ interrupt (Figure 9.9). These two auto-vector addresses contain the 16-bit auto-vectors ($\overline{IRQ}$ auto-vector and $\overline{NMI}$ auto-vector) pointing to the starting address of the respective interrupt handling routine located anywhere in memory. The lower half of each auto-vector address (i.e.,

FFF8$_{16}$ and FFFC$_{16}$) holds the HI byte of the respective auto-vector. The CPU state automatically saved onto the stack when acknowledging an interrupt, includes all CPU registers, i.e., the program counter (low and high), the index register (low and high), accumulators A and B, and condition flags, in that order.[9]

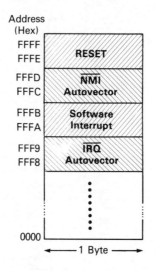

Figure 9.9   Auto-vectors for the Motorola 6800 interrupt system.

9.4.5   Intel 8086

In the 8086, the higher memory locations from FFFF0$_{16}$ through FFFFF$_{16}$ are reserved for operations including a jump to the initial program loading routine. Following a RESET, the CPU will always begin execution at absolute location FFFF0$_{16}$ (an appropriate jump instruction may be placed in that location). The lowest 1024 locations from 00000$_{16}$ through 003FF$_{16}$ are reserved for interrupt operations (Figure 9.10).

The *non-maskable interrupt* (NMI) has higher priority and is a type 2 interrupt, i.e., it performs an indirect call to the interrupt handling routine through vector (referred to by the 8086 as "pointer") 2 in fixed vector address 00008$_{16}$). The *maskable interrupt* (INTR) can be masked internally by software (by resetting the interrupt enable (I) bit in the flag register). Individual

---

[9]Since the 6800 stack grows downward, the flags are placed in the lowest stack address; after saving the state vector, the stack pointer points to flags address minus 1.

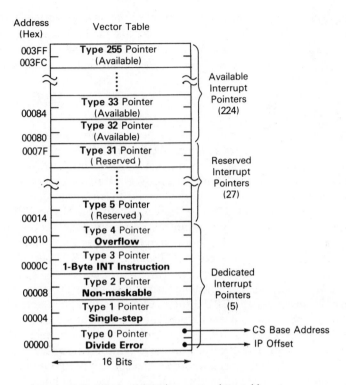

Figure 9.10 The Intel 8086 interrupt pointer table.

devices on this INTR input can be distinguished by different vector numbers and the software has full control over the placement and execution of the interrupt handling routines. A 256-element vector table occupying *fixed* locations in memory is used to perform indirect calls to these routines, according to the vector number issued by the interrupting device. Each vector is a 4-byte pointer consisting of a 16-bit segment address[10] and a 16-bit offset address. Each vector points to one of the 256 maximum possible interrupt handling routines.

Upon receipt of a signal on the INTR pin, the 8086 CPU disables further interrupts and issues two successive INTA signals; the interrupt interface must respond with a vector number (or vector type) on the second signal. This vector number is eight bits long and is placed on bus lines D0-D7. This byte is multiplied

---

[10]That is, the high-order sixteen bits of the starting physical address (or base address) of a segment.

internally by four to generate the vector address pointing to the vector table. Then, the 8086 pushes the current instruction pointer and the flags onto the stack and performs the indirect call (of the inter-segment type) to the corresponding interrupt handling routine through the designated vector in the table.

9.4.6   Zilog Z8000

The Z8000 calls the vector table the "new program status area," and this table occupies the first positions of a segment[11] (Figure 9.11). Each entry in the table contains either a trap or an interrupt vector, called by the Z8000 the "new program status," to be loaded into the program status registers of the CPU. The program status may consist of two or four 16-bit words, depending upon whether the non-segmented or the segmented version of the CPU is used. Thus, each vector in the new program status area may consist of two or four words. Each entry in the table is pointed to by a proper vector address, called by Z8000 the "new program status area pointer," or NPSAP, which resides in the respective register(s) of the CPU.

Processing of internal traps is done through the following steps: (1) When an internal trap occurs, the CPU disables further interrupts, enters the supervisor mode, and copies internally the flag and control word. The program counter is not updated, but the system stack pointer is decremented. (2) The cause or the vector number for the corresponding trap that occurred is identified. Z8000 calls this vector number "reason." It is one word long and is the first word of the trapped instruction. This "reason" will be used later for generating an address pointing to the new program status area in memory. (3) The updated value of the system (or supervisor) stack pointer (in the CPU) is used, and the old program status is pushed onto the supervisor stack with one more word that typically indicates the "reason" for the occurrence, as shown in Figure 9.12. The user stack is not affected by such recursive context switches. (4) A new program status is fetched from the new program status area, specified by the new program area status pointer. This pointer is the most significant byte in the new program status area pointer (NPSAP) register. In the case of the segmented Z8001, the pointer is two words; the segment number is specified by the seven most significant bits of its first word. (5) The processor then resumes instruction execution. The instruction at the address pointed to by the (new) program counter is fetched, and instruction decoding and execution are started. This instruction is the first instruction of the corresponding routine that will service that trap.

---

[11]As explained in chapter 10, each Z8000 segment starts in a physical address which is always evenly divisible by 256.

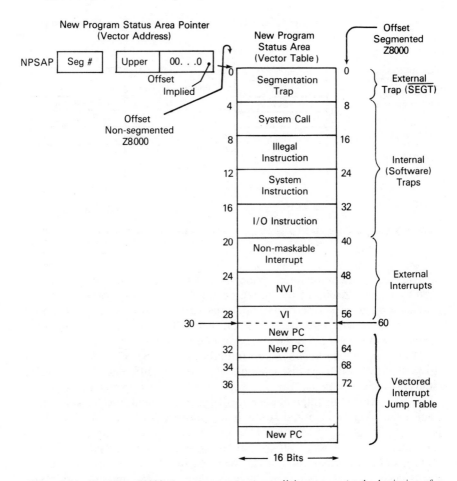

Figure 9.11   The Zilog Z8000 "new program status area" in memory (at the beginning of a segment) [26]. *Reproduced by permission. ©1979 Zilog, Inc. This material shall not be reproduced without the written consent of Zilog, Inc.*

Compared to the two levels of the 8086, the Z8000 provides three priority levels of external interrupts. The highest priority interrupt is the non-maskable interrupt ($\overline{\text{NMI}}$), which represents a catastrophic event. The other two are maskable interrupts: the non-vectored interrupt ($\overline{\text{NVI}}$) and the vectored interrupt ($\overline{\text{VI}}$). Both the non-maskable $\overline{\text{NMI}}$ and the non-vectored $\overline{\text{NVI}}$ interrupts transfer control to fixed locations in the new program status area in memory.[12] The vectored interrupt $\overline{\text{VI}}$ transfers control to variable locations in

---

[12]For that reason they are called "auto-vectored interrupts."

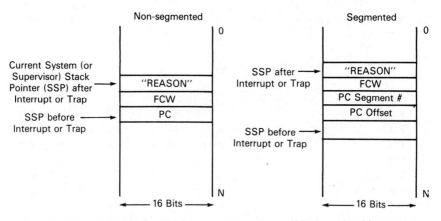

Figure 9.12   The Zilog Z8000 program status saving sequence [26]. *Reproduced by permission.*
©1979 Zilog, Inc. This material shall not be reproduced without the written consent of Zilog, Inc.

the new program status area in memory, depending on the vector number (referred to by Z8000 as the "jump vector") presented to the CPU by the interrupting device. Interrupts and traps have the following priorities (in descending order): internal traps, non-maskable interrupts, segmentation traps (SEGT), vectored interrupts, and non-vectored interrupts.

Processing of external interrupts (and the external SEGT) is done similarly to that of internal traps discussed above. The only difference occurs during step (2) in identifying the "reason" word. For a SEGT trap and all interrupts, the CPU—during its interrupt acknowledge cycle—reads the "reason" information on AD0–AD15 and stores it temporarily, to be saved later on the supervisor stack along with the old program status. For the non-vectored and non-maskable interrupts, all sixteen "reason" bits can represent peripheral device status information. For the vectored interrupt, the low byte of the "reason" is the vector number (which also determines a jump table address—in the vectored interrupt jump table of Figure 9.11—pointing to the respective interrupt handling routine) and the high byte can be extra user status. For the segmentation trap SEGT, the high byte is the memory management unit (MMU) identifier and the low byte is undefined. After that, the remaining processing steps are the same: the old program status and the "reason" word are saved in the supervisor stack, and a new program status is then fetched from the new program status area location designated by the NPSAP (i.e., the flag and control word will be fetched from offset 28 or 56,[13] while the new

---

[13]Depending on whether the non-segmented or segmented mode is used.

program counter value will be fetched from a location in the vectored interrupt jump table pointed to by the vector address).

9.4.7 Motorola 68000

The Motorola 68000 calls the vector table, which resides in the reserved lower 1024 words of memory (Figure 9.13), the "exception vector table"; each vector is called an "exception vector," to be loaded into the program counter. All vectors are two words in length and lie in the supervisor data space, except for the reset vector, which is four words long and lies in the supervisor program space. Thus, 256 unique vectors are provided (in this 512-word vector table), 192 of which are reserved for user interrupt vectors (locations 100_{16} through $3FF_{16}$).

Processing of internal exceptions is done in the following steps:

(1) When an internal exception occurs, the CPU masks off (disables) further interrupts, enters the supervisor mode and copies internally the status register.

(2) An 8-bit vector number of the exception is generated by internal logic. This number, when multiplied by 4, generates the address of the corresponding vector in the vector table.

(3) The supervisor stack pointer (in the CPU) is used, and the old program counter value (usually pointing to the next unexecuted instruction) and the copied status register are pushed onto the supervisor stack.

(4) The previously generated (in step 2) vector address points to an entry in the vector table from which a new program counter value is fetched.

(5) The processor then resumes instruction execution. The instruction at the address pointed to by the (new) program counter is fetched, and instruction decoding and execution are started. This instruction is the first instruction of the corresponding routine that will service the internal exception.

We should mention here the capability of the 68000 for *emulating new instructions* which have not yet been implemented in the processor. Usually, if the user uses a bit pattern which is not the bit pattern of the first word of a legal instruction, an "illegal instruction" exception occurs (sending the processor to location 10_{16} for the address of a routine). However, two such patterns (instructions with bits 15 through 12 equaling 1010 or 1111) have special meaning, sending the processor to either location 28_{16} or $2C_{16}$. The user now can emulate any unimplemented instruction by specifying one of the operation codes 1010 or 1111, and placing in address 28_{16} or $2C_{16}$, a vector (pointer) to a user-written routine that emulates the desired unimplemented instruction in software.

Address (Dec)	Address (Hex)	Vector Number	Vector
0	000	0	Reset (initial SSP)
4	004		Reset (initial PC)
8	008	2	Bus error
12	00C	3	Address error
16	010	4	Illegal instruction
20	014	5	Zero divide
24	018	6	CHK instruction
28	01C	7	TRAPV instruction
32	020	8	Privilege violation
36	024	9	Trace
40	028	10	Line 1010 emulator
44	02C	11	Line 1111 emulator
48	030	12	(Unassigned, reserved)
52	034	13	
56	038	14	

16 bits

Address (Dec)	Address (Hex)	Vector Number	Vector
60	03C	15	Uninitialized interrupt vector
64	04C	16	(Unassigned, reserved)
95	05F	23	
96	060	24	Spurious interrupt
100	064	25	Level 1 interrupt auto-vector
104	068	26	Level 2 interrupt auto-vector
108	06C	27	Level 3 interrupt auto-vector
112	070	28	Level 4 interrupt auto-vector
116	074	29	Level 5 interrupt auto-vector
120	078	30	Level 6 interrupt auto-vector
124	07C	31	Level 7 interrupt auto-vector
128	080	32	16 TRAP instruction vectors
191	0BF	47	
192	0C0	48	(Unassigned, reserved)
255	0FF	63	
256	100	64	192 User interrupt vectors (Vectored interrupt jump table)
1023	3FF	255	

16 bits

Figure 9.13 The lower 1024 bytes of memory are reserved for the vector table (or "exception vector table" as it is called by the Motorola 68000). *Courtesy of Motorola, Inc.* [15]

To borrow an example from H. Bryce [5], assume that you want to add floating-point math operations to the basic 68000 instruction set. Then you can specify an instruction of the form:

15	12	11	10	9	8	3	2	1	0
1010		Reg. 1			Operation		Reg. 2		

where bits 15–12 indicate unimplemented instruction, and fields Reg. 1 and Reg. 2 specify the particular registers to be used in the floating-point operations. Bits 8–3 will have to be decoded further by the emulating routine to specify the desired operation: floating-point add, subtract, multiply, etc. When the program reaches this instruction, the processor initiates an internal exception handling procedure. If location 28_{16} has the address of the emulating routine (FLTP), since this address will be loaded into the program counter during the context switching process, the processor will jump to this routine and start executing it. This routine must decode the above instruction further to determine the desired operation. Since six bits have been assigned to the operation, the FLTP routine may contain a total of sixty-four possible different math operations.

The 68000 far surpasses the other two 16-bit microprocessors by providing both vectored and auto-vectored external interrupts [21]. Besides the spurious interrupt (which performs an indirect call to the interrupt handling routine through a vector in fixed address 60_{16}, as shown in Figure 9.13), the 68000 provides seven more priority levels of external interrupts. Interrupt priority levels are numbered from 1 to 7 (level 7 being the highest priority), and referred to as auto-vectored interrupts. These levels transfer control to *fixed* locations 64_{16}–$7C_{16}$ in the vector table. This is a set of default vector numbers implemented by the processor (one for each priority level), so that peripheral devices, not equipped to respond with vector numbers, can be used.[14] However, peripheral devices that can respond with a vector number still can be chained externally on the same priority level, thus increasing the total number of devices that can interrupt the processor. With such vectored interrupts, the peripheral device puts a vector number on the data bus. The vector number is used by the processor to index into the "user interrupt vector table" in low memory to find which vector should be used for an indirect jump to the appropriate interrupt handling routine. There are 192 such fixed locations (100_{16}–$3FF_{16}$ in Figure 9.13) allocated for these user interrupt vectors.

---

[14] A peripheral identifies itself as one that cannot generate a vector number by asserting $\overline{\text{VPA}}$ instead of $\overline{\text{DTACK}}$.

The operating system can manipulate the vector table as necessary, so that software has full control over the placement and execution of interrupt handling routines.

A peripheral device sends an interrupt request to the processor by asserting the three interrupt priority inputs ($\overline{IPL0}$, $\overline{IPL1}$, $\overline{IPL2}$); level 0 (zero) indicates no interrupt request. The current priority level of the processor is kept in its status register. If the arriving interrupt request has a priority level lower than or equal to that of the current processor priority, it is inhibited (its processing is postponed). If the interrupt request has a higher priority than the current processor level in the status register, the processor acknowledges it and automatically sets the interrupt mask in the status register equal to the new, higher priority level. Since the processor always monitors the three interrupt pins for a request that has a higher priority than the current level in the status register, interrupt handling may be nested.

Processing of external interrupts follows the same sequence as does processing of internal exceptions (sequence (1) through (5), discussed above), with the following differences:

(a) During step (1) the interrupt priority mask is updated in the status register.

(b) During step (2), if the external device does not respond with a vector number, an auto-vector number is generated internally, according to the interrupt level number; otherwise, the processor reads the 8-bit vector number provided by the interrupting device on data bus lines D0–D7 (Figure 9.14a). The processor translates the vector number into a full 24-bit address, as shown in Figure 9.14b.

Priority level 7, however, is a special case, providing a non-maskable interrupt capability. A level 7 interrupt is always taken, irrespective of the

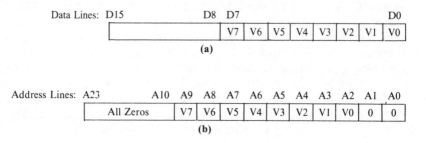

Figure 9.14 Computing the Motorola 68000 vector address: **(a)** the 8-bit vector number on lines D0–D7; **(b)** the 24-bit address generated from the 8-bit vector number [15]. *Courtesy of Motorola, Inc.*

current processor level in its status register. An interrupt is generated each time the interrupt request level changes from some lower level to level 7. In any case, the processor's level can be restored by executing the "return from exception" (RTE) privileged instruction, or it can be restored earlier if desired, by executing a privileged or a status register instruction to manipulate the status register directly.

We should mention here that the RESET input provides the highest exception level, by setting the processor interrupt priority mask at level 7. Neither program counter nor status register is saved, and the reset vector (at location 0) contains the initial supervisor stack pointer and initial program counter (the reset vector is four words).

9.5 SINGLE-LINE OR SINGLE-LEVEL INTERRUPT SYSTEMS

This implementation involves a number of interrupting I/O slaves, all connecting their individual interrupt request lines to the same interrupt line of the bus (wire-ORed interrupt requests), as shown in Figure 9.15. The signal on this bus line is applied to a single interrupt input pin of the master CPU. These interrupts are also called "single-priority-level interrupts."

Two distinct problems arise in such configurations. One is to identify which slave has triggered the interrupt request so that the master CPU will branch to the appropriate interrupt handling routine to service that slave. The second is to determine the priority with which interrupting slaves will be serviced if two or more of them trigger the interrupt request at precisely the same instant. The solution to these problems can be done in software, in hardware, or by a combination of both methods.

9.5.1 Polling Devices Not Equipped to Respond with Vector Numbers

A pure software solution to these problems involves polling the peripheral slaves. For example, consider the configuration shown in Figure 9.16, where the individual interrupt request lines (REQ) of eight peripheral slaves all trigger the same interrupt line INTR*. These interrupt requests are also directed to respective latches of an interrupt requests latching port. An activated latch of this port will remain active until cleared via the respective interrupt handling routine for that device.

Once an interrupt request signal is issued from a slave device and recognized by the master CPU, the processor disables further interrupts, asserts the INTA* output signal and saves the "CPU state." After that, the processor diverts control to a "polling routine" in memory to poll the latched requests of each external device in sequence in order to identify which device caused the

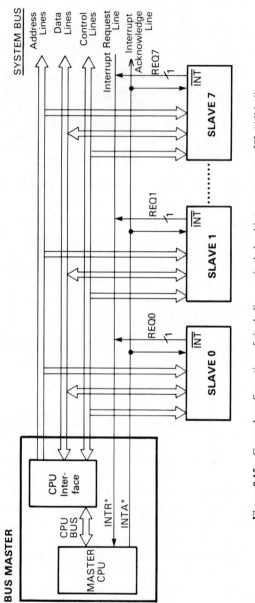

Figure 9.15   General configuration of single-line or single-level interrupt system [8]. (All individual interrupt request signals are wire-ORed together.)

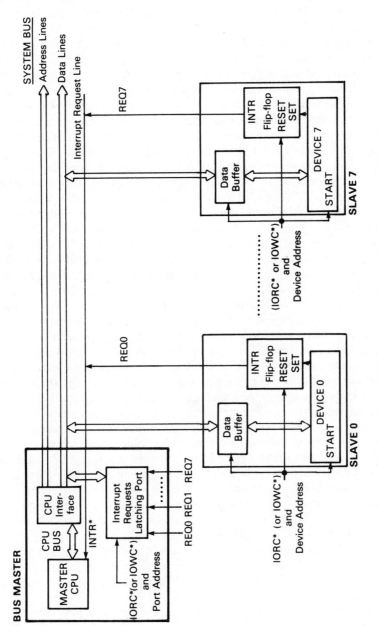

Figure 9.16   Polling eight interrupting I/O slave devices not equipped to respond with vector numbers in a single-level interrupt configuration [8].

Interrupts, DMA, and Multiprocessor Configurations

interrupt. The polling routine is shown in Figure 9.17. After saving any other CPU registers in the stack, the polling routine then inputs the interrupt requests latching port into the accumulator (strobing the port with a device select pulse generated by combining the IORC* signal and the port address), and starts examining the accumulator bits one after the other. When the interrupting device is identified, the polling routine branches to the respective interrupt handling routine for that device. (Different interrupt handling routines are required if each device is to be serviced in a different way.)

The first thing the interrupt handling routine does is clear the interrupt request flag for that device in the interrupt requests latching port, for example, by executing a proper output instruction. (This port will now be enabled with a device select pulse generated by combining the IOWC* signal and the port address.) It then services the interrupting device (e.g., reads its data buffer or writes data into it). The control signal applied to the device's data buffer also clears its interrupt flip-flop and may be applied to the START input pin of the device as well, notifying it that it may now begin assembling the next data into its data buffer (for input operation) or read the data placed in its data buffer (for output operation). This way, the device is being prevented from issuing another REQ signal before it has received the START signal from the master. Each of the eight interrupt handling routines will (as a last step) return control to the same point in the polling routine (point ABC in Figure 9.17), which concludes by restoring the saved CPU registers and enabling interrupts. Since re-enabling of interrupts is done at the end of the polling routine, this routine itself will not be interrupted. If another REQ (of higher or lower priority) occurs while the polling routine is executing, it will set an appropriate flag in the interrupt requests latching port and remain pending, waiting to be serviced when interrupts are again enabled at the end of the polling routine.

Through the above polling procedure, device priorities are said to be assigned by software: if two or more devices request service at precisely the same instant, the one encountered first in the polling sequence will receive service first. In this example, device 7 has the highest priority and device 0, the lowest (since the interrupt requests latching port is scanned from right to left). A slave device will not be serviced again until all other devices are polled, and, if necessary, also serviced. For this reason, single-line polled interrupts are slow, and this technique is most useful with relatively slow devices that do not require very "immediate" and frequent service.

One last question not answered yet, however, is how the microprocessor gets the starting address of the polling routine. The answer to this question depends upon the specific microprocessor CPU used and the specific interrupt input pin it uses to apply the INTR* signal.

For example, if the INTR* is applied to any of the input pins of the Intel 8085, RST 5.5, RST 6.5, or RST 7.5, or INT (Mode 1) of the Zilog Z80, then

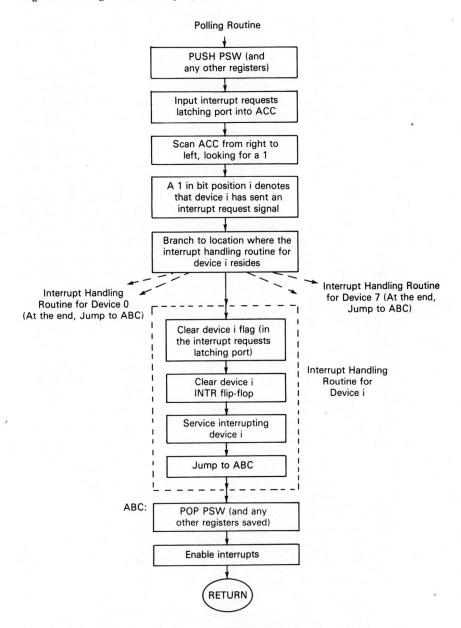

Figure 9.17   The flowchart of the polling routine to identify and service interrupting devices in a single-line configuration.

(see Table 9.1) the microprocessor will automatically branch to the predetermined locations $2C_{16}$, 34_{16}, $3C_{16}$, and 56_{16}, respectively, where the polling routine must have been placed.

If the INTR* is applied to a maskable auto-vectored interrupt pin of a processor (column 3 of Table 9.1), then a branch will be taken automatically to a fixed location in memory. In that location, a proper vector should have been placed by the programmer to point to the beginning of the polling routine.

Finally, if INTR* is applied to input pin INT of the Intel 8080A, or INTR of the Intel 8085, or $\overline{INT}$ (Mode 0) of the Zilog Z80, then, when acknowledging the interrupt, the CPU will expect a RESTART instruction to have been jammed onto its data bus. Figure 9.18 shows an implementation based on the Intel 8080A for jamming the RST 7 instruction. When the 8080A CPU accepts the interrupt input, the CPU acknowledges it by issuing the $\overline{INTA}$ signal. This $\overline{INTA}$ gates the restart instruction port onto the data bus. Since all inputs of this port are tied to 5v, the RESTART instruction will have the format FF_{16} (i.e., RST 7), which, when executed, will force a jump to the polling routine residing in location 38_{16}.[15]

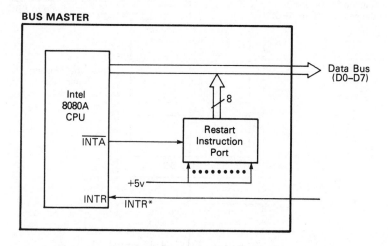

BUS MASTER

Data Bus (D0–D7)

Intel 8080A CPU

$\overline{INTA}$

Restart Instruction Port

8

+5v

INTR   INTR*

Figure 9.18   An Intel 8080A-based implementation for jamming the RST 7 instruction onto the data bus.

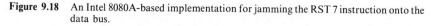

[15]In an Intel 8080A-based implementation, if the $\overline{INTA}$ output of the 8228 system controller (pin 23) is tied to the +12 volt supply (through a series 1K ohms resistor), then, when the DBIN is asserted, it will cause an RST 7 instruction to be gated onto the data bus when the interrupt is acknowledged, and jammed into the CPU's instruction register.

Figure 9.19 shows a more general case, in which an additional output port (say, port 40) may be used to provide *priority masking*. This port holds a priority mask, which allows or disallows interrupts from peripherals. A 0(zero) in any bit position of this output prevents the respective request line from initiating an interrupt. Each time an interrupt is recognized, the previous polling routine of Figure 9.17 is executed. However, when the corresponding interrupt handling routine for this device is entered, it will first output the proper priority mask into output port 40 in order to reflect the new situation (e.g., allow higher-priority REQs to cause interrupts) and then re-enable interrupts at that instant (instead of at the end of the polling routine). The last step of the polling routine now must set the interrupt mask to all 1's (thus, again allowing all REQs to cause interrupts).

9.5.2   Executing an RST N Instruction to Branch Directly to Individual Handling Routines (No Polling)

Slave devices not equipped to respond with vector numbers in configurations in which no polling is required may use the interrupt input pins INT of the Intel 8080A, INTR of the Intel 8085, and $\overline{\text{INT}}$ (Mode 0) of the Zilog Z80. In these cases, an RST N instruction, with variable N, must be jammed onto the data bus to branch directly to the respective interrupt handling routine for the interrupting device. Figure 9.20 shows two alternative configurations.

In Figure 9.20a only three external devices are used to form the 3-bit code N. Depending upon the specific device causing the interrupt, the system will branch to three different interrupt handling routines (to location 08_{16} for the interrupt handling routine of device 0, to location 10_{16} for the interrupt handling routine of device 1, and to location 20_{16} for the interrupt handling routine of device 2).

When more than one device issues an interrupt request signal at precisely the same instant, then a different 3-bit code $A_2 A_1 A_0$ will be inserted into the RST instruction, thus forcing a branch to one of the other fixed locations allocated in memory (to location 18_{16} when REQ0 and REQ1 appear simultaneously, to location 28_{16} when REQ0 and REQ2 appear simultaneously, to location 30_{16} when REQ1 and REQ2 appear simultaneously, and to location 38_{16} when all three requests appear simultaneously).

If more than three external devices are to be connected to the system, then one or more than one external priority encoder chip must be used. Figure 9.20b shows one priority encoder that is used to connect up to eight external devices. The 8-line-to-3-line priority encoder (assumed to be enabled) receives the eight interrupt request signals. Device 0 has the lowest priority and device 7, the highest. The encoder provides the three output bits A_2, A_1, A_0 which

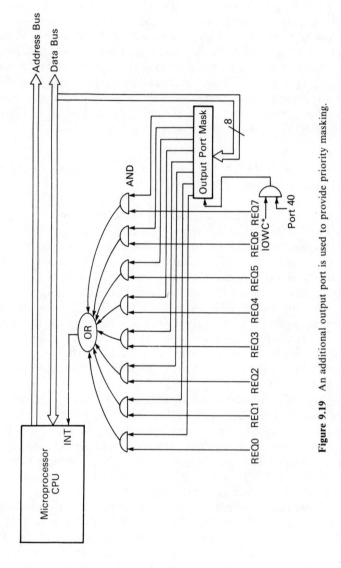

Figure 9.19 An additional output port is used to provide priority masking.

correspond to the encoded code of the highest priority input present. Any interrupt request input signal will cause a logic 1 output to appear at the enable output (EO) (pin 15) of the priority encoder chip, which is inverted and applied to the interrupt input line INTR*, thus causing an interrupt. The EO signal is also applied as input to the interrupt disable latch to set its output HIGH. The HIGH output of the interrupt disable latch disables the AND gate, blocks further interrupt request signals, and latches the 3-bit priority code into the 8212. The output of the AND gate goes low, and the next system clock pulse will return the interrupt request latch output to its original state. The bus master's response to the interrupt is the INTA* signal applied to the 8212, which jams an RST instruction ($11A_2A_1A_0111$) corresponding to the highest-priority interrupt request onto the data bus. The INTA* response also clears the interrupt request latch. No polling is necessary here. Furthermore, before servicing of this device is started, interrupts are also enabled by the execution of an enable interrupts instruction in the interrupt handling routine, so that a higher-priority interrupt may interrupt the servicing of a lower-priority device. (Note: interrupts must be disabled during pushing and popping activities and then enabled again.)

A technique similar to that shown in Figure 9.16 can be used to clear the individual request latch (in an interrupt requests latching port, not shown in Figure 9.20) under program control (e.g., by executing an output instruction in the device's interrupt handling routine).

Figure 9.21 shows an extension to the previous design, in which the interrupt request signals are first latched into the interrupt requests latching port (port 40) before being applied to the priority encoder. In addition, output port 50 is used to hold the 8-bit mask. Thus, the various interrupt priorities are enabled and disabled under the control of the program.

Finally, Figure 9.22 shows the tasks carried out by such an interrupt handling routine (here for device N) in a system configuration of Figure 9.20 that does not require polling. The routine allows the acceptance of higher-level interrupts while servicing device N, but lower-level interrupts will remain pending. The interrupt system is disabled during the critical period of popping the accumulator and flags and other registers, and is then re-enabled. When program control returns from routine N, if any lower priority interrupts are pending, a similar interrupt handling routine will be executed to honor the highest pending interrupt.

It is noticed here that each interrupt handling routine becomes longer, because it must now execute some of the operations that were previously carried out by the polling routine. On the other hand, however, this technique provides a faster method of responding to an interrupt.

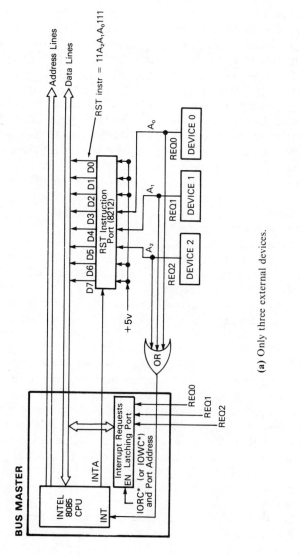

Figure 9.20 An Intel 8085-based implementation for jamming a variable RST N instruction onto the data bus. (No polling is required.)

(a) Only three external devices.

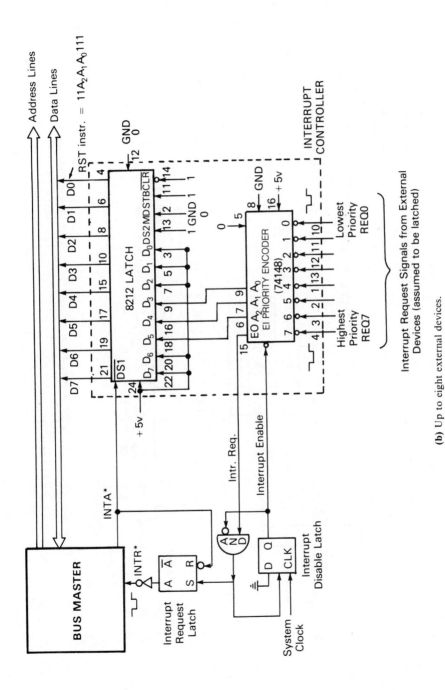

(b) Up to eight external devices.

Figure 9.20 (Continued)

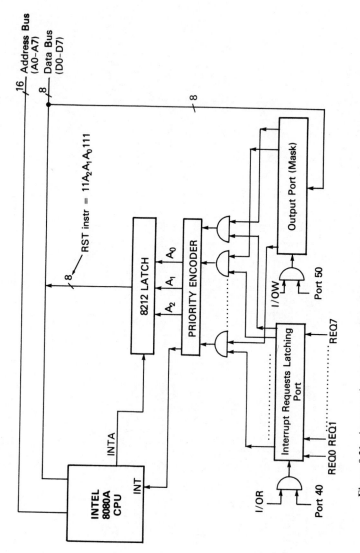

Figure 9.21 An extension to the previous design of Figure 9.16, in which the interrupt request signals are first latched into an input port. An additional output port is used for masking purposes.

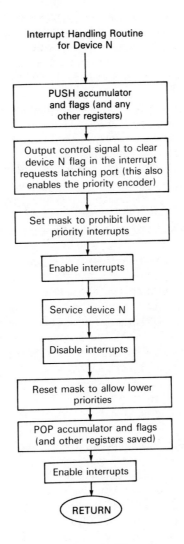

Figure 9.22 An interrupt handling routine for device N in a system configuration which does not require polling.

9.5.3   Vectored Interrupts

This technique is used for interconnecting external devices equipped to respond with vector numbers. The configuration is similar to that of Figure 9.16, in which all external devices are triggering the same interrupt request line. However, when the bus master acknowledges the interrupt, the INTA* signal applied to the slave forces it to place its identifying vector number on the data bus. This vector number will be received by the master CPU during the interrupt acknowledge sequence and converted to a vector address pointing to a location that holds the vector to be loaded into the program counter of the CPU. Control will then be transferred to the respective interrupt handling routine for the interrupting device.

Thus, when more than one external slave utilizes this single line, identification of the specific device causing the interrupt is done via the vector number each issues. However, the problem of servicing devices when the single interrupt line is triggered by more than one at precisely the same instant still remains. This can be solved either by having the bus master poll the devices (as already discussed) or by "daisy-chaining" these devices to avoid possible bus conflicts (discussed next).

In the single-line vectored interrupt system, the *daisy chain* configuration provides another method for implementing priority arbitration logic. The external devices are configured in a chain as shown in Figure 9.23. Any number of devices may request interrupt simultaneously. The device that is physically closer to the CPU (here device 1) has the highest priority and is serviced first, after having given the proper interrupt acknowledge signal (INTA*). All lower-priority devices down the chain are inhibited from interrupting the master, while all higher-priority devices are left free to interrupt the microprocessor.

As soon as the microprocessor recognizes an interrupt from a device, it issues the INTA* signal to the first device in the daisy chain. This device must have logic so that, if it causes the interrupt, it will prevent the INTA* signal from being passed on to the next device down the chain; otherwise, it will pass on this INTA* to the next device. The first interrupting device in the chain will place its vector number on the data bus, to be read by the microprocessor.

Figure 9.24 shows another example of a Zilog Z8000-based daisy chain configuration for three peripheral devices [3]. A separate set of interrupt protocol signals—INTR*, INTA*, IEI, and IEO—is used for each type of interrupt. The INTR* line of the system bus shown may be connected to one of the $\overline{NMI}$, $\overline{VI}$, or $\overline{NVI}$ CPU input pins, and the corresponding one of the three interrupt acknowledge signals (non-maskable interrupt acknowledge, non-vectored interrupt acknowledge, or vectored interrupt acknowledge) will be formed by decoding the four signals on the status line outputs ST3-ST0 and then applied to the INTA* output line of the bus.

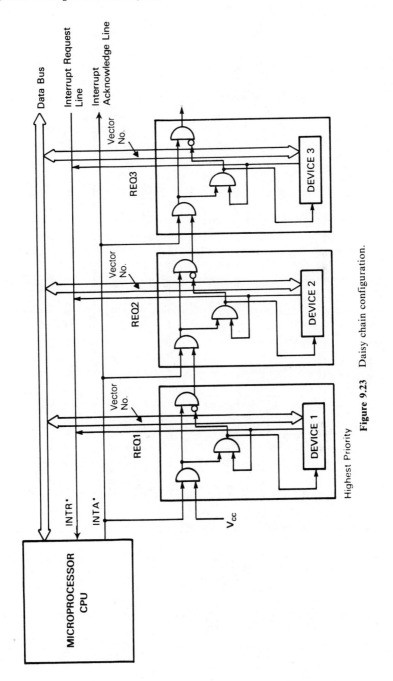

Figure 9.23   Daisy chain configuration.

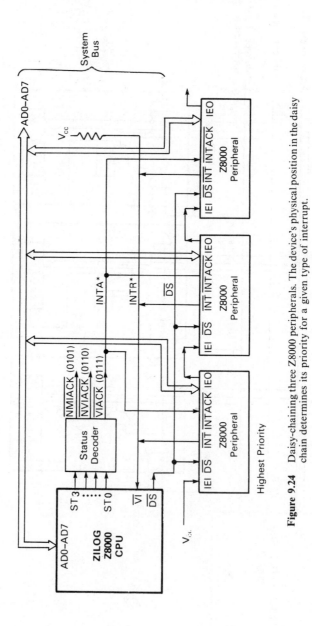

Figure 9.24 Daisy-chaining three Z8000 peripherals. The device's physical position in the daisy chain determines its priority for a given type of interrupt.

In the daisy chain configuration of Figure 9.24, the three peripherals are assumed to be using the vectored interrupt ($\overline{\text{VI}}$) type. To interrupt the CPU, a peripheral must issue an interrupt request signal, $\overline{\text{INT}}$ low. When there are more than one peripheral, all their $\overline{\text{INT}}$ output lines for one of the processor's interrupt types (here the $\overline{\text{VI}}$) are wire-ORed together to the INTR* line of the bus. The INTR* is sampled by the CPU in the last cycle of the current instruction; it then issues status signals ST3–ST0, and starts the interrupt acknowledge cycle. The ST3–ST0 are decoded, and the appropriate interrupt acknowledgement returns via the INTA* bus line to all the daisy-chained peripherals. The V_{cc} = high applied to the interrupt enable input (IEI) pin of the first peripheral is output at its interrupt enable output (IEO) pin and propagates through the daisy chain network (in at the next IEI and out at IEO) among the peripherals. The peripheral that issued the $\overline{\text{INT}}$ will be served; but the peripheral's IEO remains low, propagating down the chain and preventing lower-priority peripherals from interrupting the CPU. Then the $\overline{\text{DS}}$ issued by the CPU stimulates this interrupting peripheral to place its vector number on the data bus. After the completion of the interrupt transaction, INTA* returns high and is applied to all daisy-chained peripherals; any requestor on the daisy chain can now issue an interrupt request.

When interrupt requests are issued simultaneously by more than one device, the highest-priority device (determined by the device's physical position in the daisy chain) will be served first; its IEO remains low, thus aborting any other interrupt requests further down the chain, until INTA* returns high.

9.6   MULTI-LINE OR MULTI-LEVEL INTERRUPT SYSTEMS

9.6.1   Introductory Remarks

In multi-line or multi-level interrupt systems, the individual request lines from I/O slaves are connected to different interrupt request lines of the bus. Figure 9.25 shows eight such I/O slave devices, each one connecting its REQ output line to a separate INTx* line of the bus. In this configuration, slave 0 has the highest priority and slave 7, the lowest.

If the master CPU has only one general-purpose interrupt input, the interrupt control logic (e.g., an interrupt controller) generates the generalized INTR* signal. If slaves are not equipped to respond with vector numbers, the vector number is generated by the interrupt control logic on the master and transferred to the processor over its CPU data bus; when slaves respond with vector numbers, the interrupt control logic (e.g., a programmable interrupt controller) resolves priority, issues to the slaves an interrupt code (the address of the highest priority active interrupt line) on the system bus address lines,

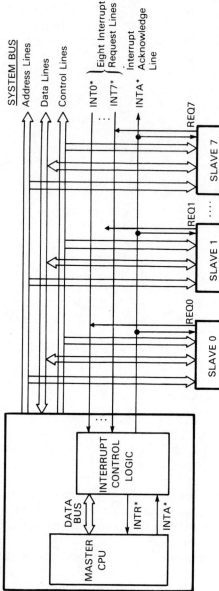

Figure 9.25 The general configuration of a system with multi-line or multi-level interrupts [8]. (There is also a "CPU interface" on the Bus Master module to connect the CPU to the System Bus, not shown in the figure).

receives the vector number from the addressed interrupting slave via the system bus data lines, and then transmits the vector number to the master CPU to service the interrupt.

If the master CPU has more than one interrupt input, several configuration alternatives exist.

(a) In the simplest case, each interrupt input pin of the CPU can be tied to a separate slave device interrupt request signal, as shown in the simplified diagram of Figure 9.26a. In this configuration, each interrupt input line corresponds to a separate interrupt level (priority resolution is done inside the CPU). Most microprocessors have at least two such interrupt lines, one maskable and one non-maskable.

(b) In more advanced interrupt structures, however, there may be n such interrupt input pins on the master CPU which, when decoded internally, will generate the corresponding one out of $2^n - 1$ priority levels (level 0 (zero) indicates no interrupt request). This group of n input lines indicates the encoded priority level of the device requesting an interrupt; therefore, an external interrupt encoder is required (Figure 9.26b). For example, the Motorola 68000 has three such interrupt input pins, $\overline{IPL0}$, $\overline{IPL1}$, and $\overline{IPL2}$, to receive the encoded interrupt requests. Encoded request signals applied to these pins are decoded internally within the microprocessor to provide seven priority levels of external interrupts. These seven levels are also referred to as *auto-vectored interrupts* (see third column of Table 9.1), because each level automatically transfers control to a unique location in the vector table in memory (so that the external device need not send its vector number).

Furthermore, in multi-level interrupt systems, each INT $_x$* line of the bus of Figure 9.25 can be used to connect to it more than one device (where the REQ lines of all these devices are wired-ORed together to this INT$_x$* line through any of the techniques discussed in section 9.5), thus further increasing the total number of devices that can interrupt the master CPU.

9.6.2 Connecting Devices Not Equipped to Respond with Vector Numbers

This section examines (using the IEEE 796 system bus of Figure 9.25) the connection of slave devices not equipped to respond with vector numbers and devices equipped to respond with vector numbers [8].

Figure 9.27 shows the corresponding configuration. The slave devices being connected do not use the system data bus to transfer a vector number. The interrupt controller on the bus master resolves priorities and interrupts the master CPU. When acknowledging the interrupt with the INTA* signal, the interrupt controller generates the proper vector number and transfers it to the

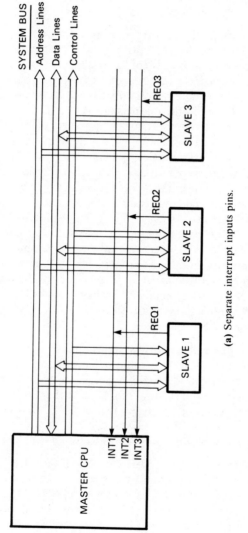

(a) Separate interrupt inputs pins.

Figure 9.26   Connecting slave devices to a master CPU that has more than one interrupt input pin: (a) non-encoded input pins; (b) encoded input pins.

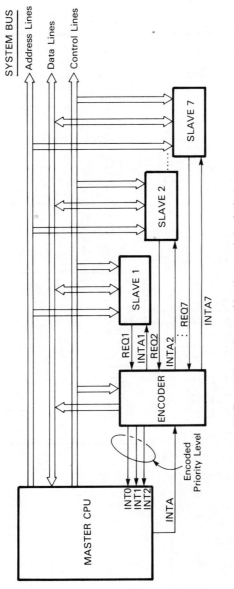

(b) External encoder provides the encoded priority level.

Figure 9.26 (*Continued*)

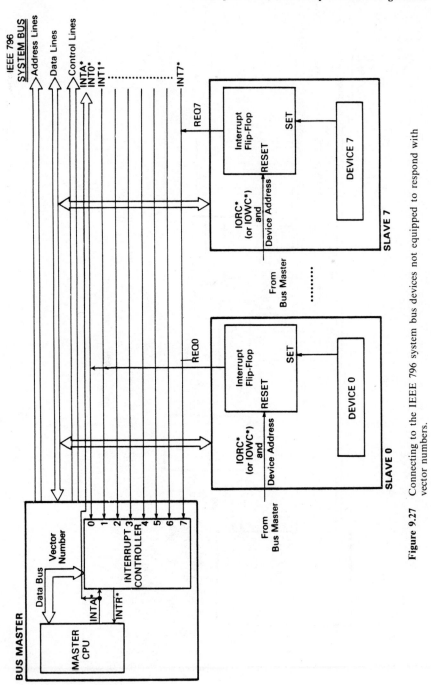

Figure 9.27 Connecting to the IEEE 796 system bus devices not equipped to respond with vector numbers.

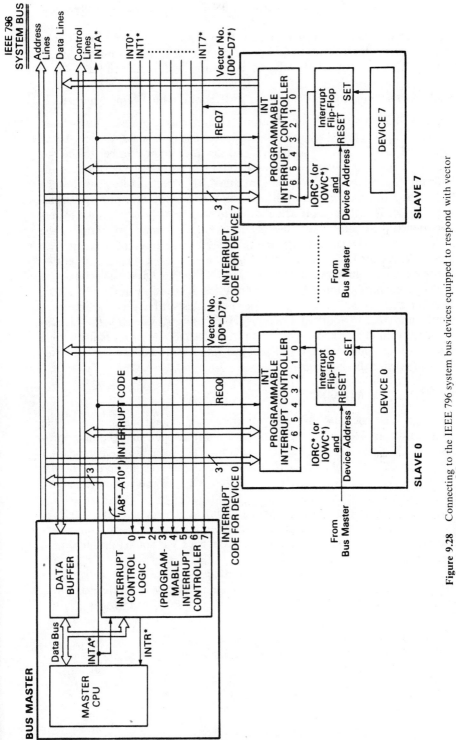

Figure 9.28 Connecting to the IEEE 796 system bus devices equipped to respond with vector numbers [8].

CPU over its data bus. The master CPU then processes the interrupt. The bus master removes the interrupting slave's respective REQ signal from the system bus by issuing a command to the slave, as discussed in section 9.5.1.

9.6.3   Connecting Devices Equipped to Respond with Vector Numbers

Figure 9.28 shows the configuration of the connecting of devices which are equipped to respond with vector numbers. The I/O slave devices being connected use the INTA* signal and transfer the vector number to the bus master via the system data bus. When an interrupt request occurs, the master's interrupt control logic interrupts the master CPU, which in turn generates the INTA* and freezes the state of the interrupt control logic for priority resolution. Higher-level interrupts are allowed to interrupt the service of a lower-level interrupt. Figure 9.29 shows the flowchart and timing diagram for the interrupt acknowledge sequence (in Figure 9.29b, two different sequences can occur because the IEEE 796 bus can support masters that generate either two or three INTA* commands). After the first INTA*, the bus master's interrupt control logic puts an interrupt code[16] on system bus address lines A8*–A10*. The interrupt code is the address of the highest-priority active interrupt request line (INT x* address). The second INTA* signal will cause the slaves to decode this interrupt code, and the addressed slave's interrupt control logic places its vector number on the system bus data lines to be used by the master CPU to service the interrupt.

9.7   DIRECT MEMORY ACCESS (DMA)

Although the interrupt driven I/O presents an improvement over the program-driven I/O, both methods have the drawback that the microprocessor CPU intervenes in the data transfer path between central memory and peripheral devices. If the data transfer speed is high (as in the case of fast peripheral devices), then most, if not all, of the CPU time is spent in handling the input/output operation.

An improvement was first presented by introducing single-chip interface controllers between the CPU and peripheral devices. These controllers remove the lowest level of device control from the CPU and let the microprocessor transfer whole words at once.

The next step was to replace these interface controllers and the software routine performing the transfer between memory and peripheral devices by a direct memory access (DMA) controller.[17] The DMA controller has the

---

[16]In the Motorola 68000, the interrupt level is placed on address lines A1, A2, and A3.

[17]Also referred to as a "temporary master."

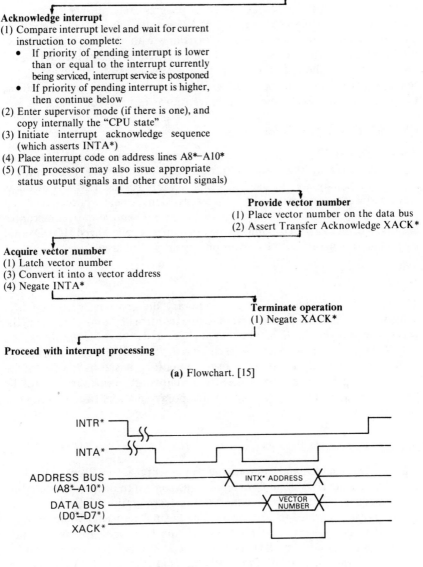

BUS MASTER   INTERRUPTING SLAVE
                                                Request interrupt

Acknowledge interrupt
(1) Compare interrupt level and wait for current
    instruction to complete:
    • If priority of pending interrupt is lower
      than or equal to the interrupt currently
      being serviced, interrupt service is postponed
    • If priority of pending interrupt is higher,
      then continue below
(2) Enter supervisor mode (if there is one), and
    copy internally the "CPU state"
(3) Initiate interrupt acknowledge sequence
    (which asserts INTA*)
(4) Place interrupt code on address lines A8*–A10*
(5) (The processor may also issue appropriate
    status output signals and other control signals)

                                                Provide vector number
                                                (1) Place vector number on the data bus
                                                (2) Assert Transfer Acknowledge XACK*

Acquire vector number
(1) Latch vector number
(3) Convert it into a vector address
(4) Negate INTA*

                                                Terminate operation
                                                (1) Negate XACK*

Proceed with interrupt processing

(a) Flowchart. [15]

INTR*

INTA*

ADDRESS BUS
(A8*–A10*)   INTX* ADDRESS

DATA BUS
(D0*–D7*)   VECTOR
                                                NUMBER
XACK*

(b) Timing diagram.

Figure 9.29 Interrupt acknowledge sequence for multi-line vectored interrupts on the IEEE 796
          system bus.

ability to request use of the CPU bus for direct transfer of whole blocks of data between an I/O device and memory without CPU intervention. The CPU completes the current bus cycle, if one is in progress, relinquishes the bus, and then grants control of the bus to the DMA controller. This data transfer does not go through the microprocessor (as done with the previous two I/O methods), and is thus transparent to the CPU. No program intervention is required during the transfer. Even with DMA controllers, however, the microprocessor's normal operation is still interrupted, since it cannot itself use the memory space each time a DMA transfer is in progress.

9.7.1 CPU Bus Arbitration Lines

The last set of CPU signals in Figure 5.9 of chapter 5 not discussed so far are those that make up the "bus arbitration lines" used for DMA operations. These signals may also be used by other masters besides DMA controllers which request control of the CPU bus (discussed in the next section). Table 9.3 shows the names used for these signals by various representative microprocessors. Again, to avoid this multiplicity of names, a generalized HOLD input signal and a generalized HLDA output signal will be used here.

HOLD

The HOLD input line is used by temporary bus masters (such as DMA controllers or multiple processors) to request control of the CPU bus from the permanent bus master. This line may only be asserted at certain times, i.e., only if (1) HLDA is not asserted (the permanent master has the bus), and (2) HOLD is not already asserted (no other temporary master has requested the bus). The HOLD line may be masked (under hardware or software control) by the permanent bus master to prevent temporary masters from gaining bus control.

HLDA

If a HOLD is enabled and asserted, the permanent master will enter the "hold state," assert the HLDA, and relinquish bus control to the (highest-priority) temporary master, thus enabling the bus transfer operation for that requestor. If the bus is not granted to a requestor, this "losing" requestor will usually try again. The permanent master remains in the hold state for an arbitrary number of cycles until the HOLD signal becomes false. Upon completion of the hold operation, control of the CPU bus is always returned to the permanent master.

Hold operations always take priority over interrupt operations.

Table 9.3   The bus arbitration signals of several microprocessors.

INTEL 8080A/8085	ZILOG Z80/Z8000	MOTOROLA 6800	INTEL 8086	MOTOROLA 68000
HOLD (input) HLDA (output)	$\overline{\text{BUSRQ}}$ (input) $\overline{\text{BUSAK}}$ (output)	DBE (input) BA (output)	(1) Minimum Mode: HOLD (input) HLDA (output) (2) Maximum Mode: $\overline{\text{RQ}}/\overline{\text{GT}}_0$ (bidirectional) $\overline{\text{RQ}}/\overline{\text{GT}}_1$ (bidirectional)	$\overline{\text{BR}}$ (input) $\overline{\text{BG}}$ (output) $\overline{\text{BGACK}}$ (input)

9.7.2 DMA Transfer Methods

Several DMA transfer methods and bus-access techniques exist: the "halt," "suspend," or "idle" the microprocessor method; the "cycle stealing" method; and the "multiplex DMA/CPU" or "slow-the-processor" method. A fourth method, that of using "dual port memories," is not that common with microprocessor systems. Discussed below are the first two methods most commonly found in microprocessors.

The Halt Method

The halt method is the simplest approach and the one used most often: the operation of the microprocessor is suspended while a DMA transfer occurs. The DMA controller has control of the CPU bus to manage the transfer, while the CPU is idled and thus no longer has control of its bus. The CPU becomes "disconnected" from its bus by forcing its bus drivers to their high-impedance state. Therefore, either the CPU or the DMA controller is using the bus at any given time.

Consider the simplified configuration of Figure 9.30, in which a peripheral device is connected to one channel of the DMA controller. When the device requires service, it sends a DMA channel request signal (DREQ) to the DMA controller rather than to the CPU. The DMA controller in turn asserts the HOLD signal to the microprocessor. The microprocessor completes its current bus cycle, floats its address and data lines, and indicates that the bus is floated by asserting the acknowledge signal HLDA. (The contents of the microprocessor registers are not altered when the microprocessor is "disconnected" from the bus.) Priority assertions on the arbitration bus are also settled in the interval between the assertion of a HOLD and a HLDA. With the HLDA signal, the bus is granted to the highest-priority requestor, thus enabling the bus transfer operation for that requestor. This scheme usually results in the first requestor's winning the bus. Only if simultaneous bus requests occur will the bus arbitration (discussed below) have any effect.

Upon receiving the HLDA, the successful DMA requestor asserts its DMA channel acknowledge (DACK output) to allow the requesting peripheral to access memory. The peripheral device is now prepared to place—or accept—data for memory transfer. In this way, the external device is synchronized so that it will not attempt a transfer until it receives the DACK from the DMA controller. The DMA controller conducts a number of standard bus cycles (bus control is never transferred between cycles). Upon issuing the DACK, the DMA controller will place an address on the address lines automatically, to specify the memory location at which the data transfer is to take place. It then generates a memory read or memory write signal and lets the peripheral device

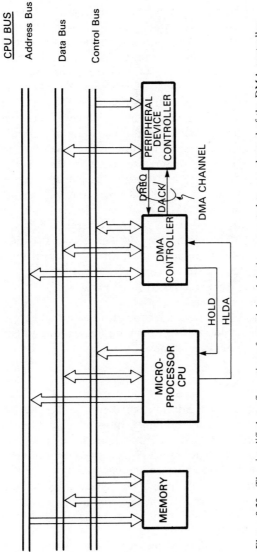

Figure 9.30 The simplified configuration of a peripheral device connected to one channel of the DMA controller.

generate or receive data on the data bus. When the DMA controller is done, it is "disconnected" from the bus (and returns to an idle state); the microprocessor CPU consequently has complete control of the bus and continues its normal processing.

To accommodate block-transfers, the DMA controller contains some kind of counting mechanism (typically an n-bit counter to allow automatic transfers of up to 2^n words). The data transfer stops whenever either the counter goes to 0 or the DREQ from the peripheral device disappears.

It is observed, therefore, that the DMA controller exhibits some processor-like features, including a number of registers and counters. (Some newer DMA controller chips also include RAM memory to facilitate internal buffering.) One such register is the *address register*, which contains the address of the next memory location to be accessed for reading or writing data. Another component is a *counter* that contains the number of words to be transferred to or from memory. Other common registers identify the *direction* of data flow, the *mode* selected for the DMA transfer, etc. Most DMA controllers can accommodate more than one DMA channel, and so some of these registers will be repeated for each DMA channel available. Figure 9.31 shows the simplified diagram of connecting four peripheral devices to the respective channels of a DMA controller. The DMA controller also includes the necessary logic to increment the address register, decrement the word counter, determine when the transfer is complete, "float" the bus, and provide all control and timing signals required for the transfer.

DMA controller registers are initialized by the CPU. To the programmer, the DMA controller registers are thought of as a number of I/O ports (or addressable memory locations), which are loaded and unloaded using I/O-type (or memory-type) instructions.

The Cycle-steal Method

Whereas the halt method is usually used for "burst-type" DMA transfers, (called "halt-burst," "burst," or "block-transfer" mode), in which a block of words is transferred while the CPU is locked out, the cycle-steal method (called "halt-steal" or "byte-transfer" mode) refers to transferring only one word at a time, between CPU cycles. (Some DMA controllers can operate in either of these two modes.) Although the cycle-steal method usually involves a somewhat higher hardware cost when compared to the previous method, it is considered the best on a cost/performance basis. It also presents the lowest single word transfer delay.

With this method, memory cycles are "stolen" from the microprocessor for use by the external device, transferring data with minimal disruption of the CPU program execution. The DMA controller gains immediate access to

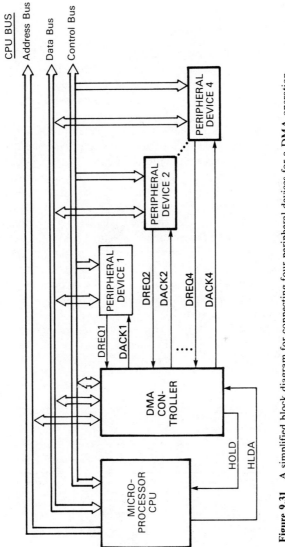

Figure 9.31   A simplified block diagram for connecting four peripheral devices for a DMA operation.

memory, since it "freezes" the processor execution at *any* cycle, even in the middle of a long instruction execution. However, this "freezing" has only limited duration (usually a few μsecs) to allow DMA transferring of one or two words per transfer.

9.7.3 Bus Arbitration Protocol

When many DMA requestors are connected to the CPU bus, then proper arbitration is required to resolve simultaneous requests. One technique is to provide a serial non-preemptive distributed arbitration policy implemented by daisy-chaining all DMA controllers to determine which one will be the bus master device.

Figure 9.32 shows a Zilog Z8000-based implementation, in which three bus requestors are connected in a daisy chain. Their bus request output signals are wire-ORed together via a common line applied to the $\overline{\text{BUSRQ}}$ input pin of the CPU [3,17,20]. To request control of the bus, the requestor asserts its bus request output signal ($\overline{\text{BUSRQ}}$ = low). The CPU samples the $\overline{\text{BUSRQ}}$ after the completion of any bus cycle and asserts $\overline{\text{BUSAK}}$ output signal ($\overline{\text{BUSAK}}$ = low) to acknowledge release of the bus. This $\overline{\text{BUSAK}}$ propagates through the daisy chain network; it enters each requestor's $\overline{\text{BAI}}$ input and leaves via its $\overline{\text{BAO}}$ output. The device that requested control of the bus becomes the bus master and begins to use it; but the requestor's $\overline{\text{BAO}}$ remains high, is propagated down the chain, and prevents lower priority devices from using the bus. When the requestor completes its use of the bus, $\overline{\text{BUSRQ}}$ returns to high. One cycle later, the processor asserts $\overline{\text{BUSAK}}$ ($\overline{\text{BUSAK}}$ = high to indicate that the processor again controls the bus), which is propagated among the bus requestors; any requestor in the daisy chain can now request control of the bus. Thus, the Z8000 CPU is the default bus master.

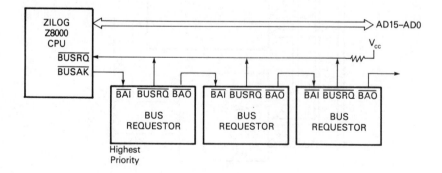

Figure 9.32   Daisy-chaining three Zilog Z8000 bus requestors [14].

As with interrupts, when bus requests are issued simultaneously by more than one bus requestor, the one with the highest priority (determined by the requestor's physical position in the chain) will become the bus master; its $\overline{BAO}$ remains high, aborting any other bus requests further down the chain, until $\overline{BUSAK}$ returns high. If a bus requestor goes through an unsuccessful bus request attempt, it will usually have to try again after a few cycles.

A second technique is a parallel arbitration technique, in which, similar to interrupts, an external priority encoder may be used to supply the DMA request signal of the higher priority bus requestor. The more general parallel arbitration technique (using the bus arbiter) among a number of processors is discussed in section 9.8.3.

9.7.4 I/O Processors

Recent microprocessors perform the I/O operation using separate, more complex, "I/O processors." The capability of an I/O processor approaches that of a microprocessor and removes another level of control from the CPU. I/O processors contain a number of DMA channels, have their own instruction sets, execute their own channel programs in parallel with the CPU (which performs other processing), and notify the CPU when they have completed their program. Furthermore, an I/O processor can support multiple peripheral devices on a single channel (with all DREQ lines wire-ORed together), provided that only one device is in the active transfer mode at any one time. Each device is assigned a unique port address so that an individual acknowledge DACK signal (properly decoded) is returned to only the active device. Unlike simple DMA controllers, an I/O processor can service peripheral devices directly, thus eliminating this task from the CPU. Finally, an I/O processor can share the CPU bus or the system bus via a bus arbiter. An I/O processor is an independent processor, acts like any other CPU master, and is connected in a similar fashion. This leads to multiprocessor configurations discussed next.

9.8 MULTIPROCESSOR CONFIGURATIONS

9.8.1 Introduction

The introduction of low-cost microprocessors is pushing towards distributed processing, multiprocessor configurations, and parallel processing. Almost all microprocessors have the capability and the standard interfaces to be interconnected into *distributed processing systems*. In such systems, processors may be installed at remote sites, near where processing is needed; redundancy may also be employed in critical applications, and intercommunication among processors is usually done using *serial transmission* techniques.

The 16- and 32-bit microprocessors, however, contain both hardware and software interlocks that provide the capability for *multiprocessor system configurations* [12,25]. Such configurations can be done either by satellite processing (i.e., using special co-processors), or by using I/O processors that free the CPU from complex tasks that formerly required considerable CPU time. These external intelligent requestors cooperate (and compete) for mastership not only of the common shared bus, but also of other shared resources of the system (e.g., memory and I/O space, a peripheral, etc). In such cases, a management protocol is required in order to make the relationship more equitable than a common master-slave relationship in which the resource-request line is dominated by a single system component. In the most general case, external intelligent requestors may all be CPUs, and thus form a multiprocessor system in which each resource requestor has equal importance and capability. In this way, functions may be distributed fully among those CPUs sharing common system resources. The system designer can thus partition the problem into separate tasks that each of several processors can handle individually and in parallel, increasing system performance and throughput [4,19]. In such configurations, these complete and self-contained systems intercommunicate using *parallel transmission* techniques, usually via the system bus. Appropriate connection links among processors are provided to free the system designer from having to define which is the master and which the slave. Furthermore, the system bus allows each processor to work asynchronously and, therefore, both fast and slow microprocessors can be incorporated in the same system.

The most important considerations in multiprocessor systems are: (1) the processors should be able to interact properly without mangling the data; (2) they should be able to share system resources; and (3) synchronization among the processors should be ensured. Usually mechanisms for ensuring these requisites are provided by software operating systems, but they do require proper hardware support. All 16- and 32-bit microprocessors have appropriate control pins and special instructions for semaphore signaling, which temporarily render one CPU the "system master" that controls a certain critical shared resource and excludes all other processors from using this resource. Such hardware support allows the development of operating systems to provide the mechanisms for multiprocessing implementations.

9.8.2 System Bus Exchange Signals

Although multiple processors can share the local CPU bus, a more general and flexible design is the one that allows independent CPUs to share the global system bus in multi-master (or multiprocessing module) configurations (see Figure 5.4 in chapter 5). Each master module now makes use of the bus exchange lines of the system bus (Figure 5.8 in chapter 5) and has the general configuration shown in Figure 6.1 of chapter 6. The bus masters request bus control through a "bus exchange sequence."[18] When a "parallel" bus exchange priority resolution technique (to be discussed below) is implemented, the bus arbiter interface circuit must be used. Before the details of the bus exchange operation are examined, the bus arbiter signals to/from the IEEE 796 system bus (shown in Figure 9.33) are explained.

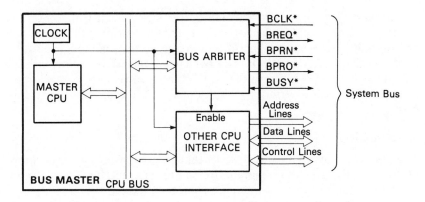

Figure 9.33 A bus master module equipped with a bus arbiter.

Bus Clock (BCLK★)

The bus clock is a periodic clock signal used to synchronize the bus exchange logic; it may be slowed, stopped, or single-stepped. Each bus master must have the capability of generating an acceptable clock that optionally can be connected to, or disconnected from, the system bus. In a multi-master system, only one of the masters must have its clock connected to the bus.

Bus Request (BREQ★)

When a master requests system bus control, it asserts the BREQ* line. This line is used with the parallel priority resolution scheme through the bus arbiter. The highest-priority request enables the BPRN* input of that master, thus allowing it to gain control of the bus.

---

[18]Again, the proposed IEEE 796 standard bus terminology is used here. The Motorola 68000, for example, calls it "bus arbitration sequence."

Bus Priority In (BPRN*)

The "bus priority in" input signal and the next output signal BPRO* are "non-bused" signals. The BPRN* input signal indicates to a master that no master of higher priority is requesting control of the bus. This signal is daisy-chained when serial priority arbitration is used. When using parallel priority arbitration, a bus arbiter generates the BPRN*.

Bus Priority Out (BPRO*)

When the "bus priority out"—a "non-bused" signal—is activated by a bus master, it indicates to the bus master of the next lower priority that it may gain control of the bus (i.e., no higher-priority requests are pending for control of the bus). Like BPRN*, BPRO* is daisy-chained when serial priority arbitration is used; BPRO* is fed to the BPRN* input of the next lower priority master. When parallel priority arbitration is used, the BPRO* signal is not used.

Bus Busy (BUSY*)

The bus busy signal is a bidirectional signal asserted by the master in control of the bus. All other masters monitor BUSY* to determine the state of the bus, i.e., whether or not they may acquire control of the bus.

9.8.3 System Bus Arbitration and Priority Resolution Techniques (Bus Arbiter)

To initiate a system bus cycle, the master CPU issues appropriate status and/or control signals, irrespective of bus arbiter presence. The master's bus arbiter and the box labeled "other CPU interface" monitor these lines to detect a bus cycle request. If the bus arbiter does not have control of the system bus (is not driving BUSY* low), it will issue a control signal to the "other CPU interface," to force all bus-driven outputs into the high impedance state. Thus, the bus master is "disconnected" from the system bus and the CPU enters into wait states. When the bus arbiter acquires access to the system bus, it enables all bus drivers, thus allowing the bus master to access the system bus and the master CPU to complete its transfer cycle. At the same time, the bus arbiter asserts BUSY* to other bus masters.

Multiple masters connected via the system bus require priority resolution when the bus is requested simultaneously by more than one master, so that the master with higher priority will take control of the system bus. The synchronization of master requests and the arbitration function are integrated into the bus arbiter. Two bus exchange priority resolution techniques are used, serial and parallel. Since they are compatible, the two schemes can be combined and used together on the same bus.

Daisy Chain or Serial Priority Resolution Technique

In this scheme, all master requestors are arranged in a configuration of daisy-chaining their bus arbiters, as shown in Figure 9.34. The bus request lines BREQ* are not used in this configuration. The technique is analogous to the daisy chain priority resolution technique discussed in section 9.7.3 for DMA requestors; here, however, a bus arbiter is included and BPRN* is the master's input from the priority chain. The BPRO* output signal of each master's bus arbiter is connected to the BPRN* input of the next lower priority master's bus arbiter. The BPRN* of the highest-priority master in the daisy chain will always be active (grounded), signifying to the other bus arbiters that it always has highest priority when requesting the bus.

Serial priority resolution is accomplished as follows: all masters monitor BUSY* to determine the state of the bus. When a master requests control of the bus (when no other master has control of the bus), it sets its BPRO* high. This signal in turn disables the BPRN* of all lower-priority masters. The BPRO* output for a particular master is asserted if and only if its BPRN* input is active and that master is not requesting control of the bus. The BUSY* line, which indicates an idle or "not busy" status of the system bus, is common to all bus masters. Through this line, a higher-priority master will wait until the current bus master has completed any bus cycles already in progress. Upon completing its transfer cycle, the master in control of the bus determines that it no longer has priority, and surrenders the bus, releasing BUSY*.

The major drawback of this technique is that it can accommodate only a limited number of masters, because of gate delays through the daisy chain. When a parallel-serial priority structure is to be used, the BPRN* of the highest-priority master in the chain should be connected to a priority resolution circuit, which is described next.

Parallel Priority Resolution Technique

In this scheme, the BPRO* lines are not utilized [16]. An external parallel priority resolving circuit is used to resolve the priorities of the bus request BREQ* from each master (Figure 9.35). Each BREQ* line enters the priority encoder of this external circuit, which generates, as output, the binary address of the highest-priority BREQ* line asserted at its inputs. This address, after being decoded inside the priority resolving circuit, selects the corresponding bus priority in line (BPRN*) to be returned to the highest priority requesting bus master. The bus arbiter receiving this BPRN* signal then allows its associated bus master to access the system bus as soon as the bus becomes available. Thus, the highest-priority request enables the BPRN* input of that master, allowing it to gain control of the bus. The BUSY* line functions in the same way as it does for the serial technique.

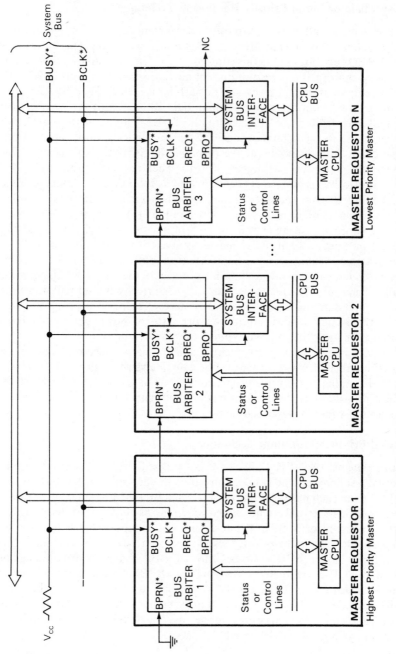

Figure 9.34 Daisy chain or serial bus exchange priority resolution technique. (Note: BREQ* is not used.)

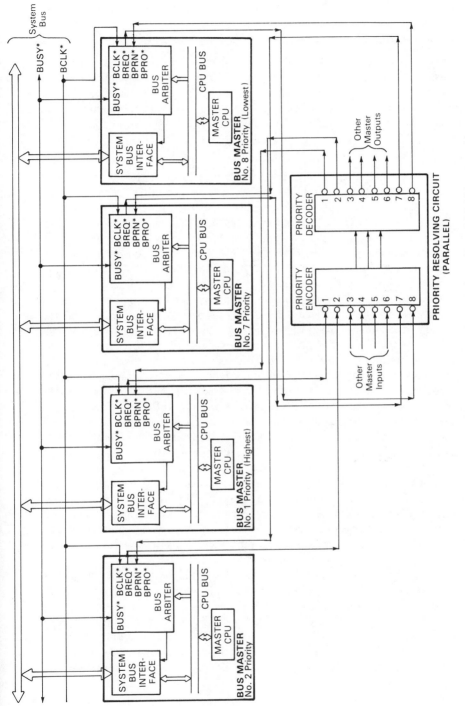

Figure 9.35 Parallel bus exchange priority resolution technique. (Note: BPRO* is not used.)

9.8.4 Multiprocessor Capabilities of Various Microprocessors

Early microprocessors of the Intel 8080A/8085, Motorola 6800, or Zilog Z80 class were not designed for multiprocessor applications, although the 8080A and 8085 have an extra hold state to accommodate slow memories; this state was used to create a multiple-processor board. Discussed below in more detail are the newer Intel 8086, Zilog Z8000 and Motorola 68000 [3,6,11,15,16,17,22].

Intel 8086

The 8086 uses a "master-slave bus architecture." In this architecture when a master accesses the system bus, it does not allow any other master to obtain the bus. The master processor enables a bus-lock function (usually by a software 1-byte "LOCK" prefix that can be attached to any 8086 instruction) and maintains control of the system bus until the lock is disabled by program control. Satellite processing is also available—in which a co-processor, such as the Intel 8087 math co-processor, is used to perform specialized operations (e.g., exponentiation)—through the WAIT and ESCAPE instructions.

For transfer to satellite processing—in which an external processor or co-processor can be utilized—the 8086 uses a software-driven escape and lockout mechanism. When the external processor is ready, it asserts its bus request on the "event test" input pin of the CPU ($\overline{\text{TEST}}$ = low); from there on the requestor continuously monitors the 8086 system bus, thus staying aware of the current instruction being executed. However, software must be used to render this requestor the bus master. The 8086 CPU has to execute a WAIT (wait for test) instruction, which tests the $\overline{\text{TEST}}$ pin. If the pin is low, it means that the requestor is ready and execution continues; otherwise, the WAIT instruction holds up the CPU in an "idle" state, until the $\overline{\text{TEST}}$ pin is reset. In this way, synchronization is ensured between the CPU and the requestor. After that, in order to grant control to the requestor and have its operations commence, the 8086 CPU must execute the special ESCAPE instruction. The ESCAPE instruction simply makes a "dummy read." In other words, it places the 20-bit address of the operand for the instruction (which corresponds to the programmed address of a subroutine) on the address bus, to perform a read, for which it will ignore the result. This in effect allows the external requesting processor to see the address on the bus.

In multiprocessor systems, mechanisms should be provided so that all processors are able to share resources and control their access to these resources. Instead of using the code-waster ESCAPE instruction, the 8086 provides a special code-saving 1-byte "LOCK" prefix that can be attached to any instruction. When the instruction is executed by a processor, the prefix causes the processor to lock the bus (i.e., the processor maintains control of the system bus) for the consecutive bus cycles required during the execution of the instruction. It does that by issuing a signal on its $\overline{\text{LOCK}}$ output pin, which prohibits all other bus masters from accessing the bus during the period of its assertion. Thus, the processor can be performing read/modify/write operations on memory without the possibility of another processor receiving intervening memory cycles. The $\overline{\text{LOCK}}$ signal is activated (forced low) in the clock cycle following the cycle in which the software "LOCK" prefix instruction is decoded, and it is deactivated at the end of the last bus cycle of the instruction following the "LOCK" prefix instruction.

The instruction most likely to have such a prefix attached to it is "exchange register with memory" (XCHG). A simple software lock may be implemented with the following code sequence [14]:

```
CHECK:  MOV        AL,1      ; SET AL TO 1 (IMPLIES LOCKED)
        LOCK XCHG  SEMA, AL  ; TEST AND SET LOCK
        TEST       AL,AL     ; SET FLAGS BASED ON AL
        JNZ        CHECK     ; TRY AGAIN IF LOCK ALREADY SET
        ⋮                    ; (CRITICAL REGION)
        MOV        SEMA,∅    ; CLEAR THE LOCK WHEN DONE
```

Here the test and set function is performed by exchanging the accumulator with the memory location, preceding the instruction by a "LOCK" prefix.

Zilog Z8000

The multiprocessor configuration is an extension and generalization of the bus-sharing configuration discussed earlier. The complexity of the resource requestor may be approaching that of the CPU. Resources being shared are not limited only to the system bus, but may also include address space, a peripheral, etc. This configuration is also supported by a more equitable management protocol than the bus arbitration protocol of section 9.7.3, in which all resource requestors have equal importance and can use the resource in a non-preemptive manner.

To coordinate multiprocessor systems, the Z8000 CPU provides a pair of control lines used in conjunction with certain privileged instructions. These two pins are the "multi-micro out" ($\overline{\text{M}}_O$), which issues a request for the resource, and the "multi-micro in" ($\overline{\text{M}}_I$), used to recognize the state of the resource (i.e., it recognizes outside requests). Thus, any processor in a multiprocessor configuration can exclude all other asynchronous processors from being able to access a critical resource by using these two pins. Five privileged instructions (executed only in supervisor mode) are provided for semaphore signalling: multi-micro request (MREQ), multi-micro release (MRLSE), test input pin $\overline{\text{M}}_I$ (MBIT), set output pin $\overline{\text{M}}_O$ (MSET), and reset output pin $\overline{\text{M}}_O$ (MRES).

Any requestor may acquire a resource and become the controller of the resource. Before it makes a resource request, the requestor must first check its input pin $\overline{M_I}$ to see if the resource is busy. If busy (indicated by $\overline{M_I}$ = low), additional requests are blocked (no requestor can preempt another). If not busy (indicated by $\overline{M_I}$ = high), the requestor can issue a request signal to its output line ($\overline{M_O}$ = low) to acquire the resource.

Figure 9.36 shows an example of three resource requestor devices sharing a common resource and arranged in a daisy chain configuration [3]. An interface logic box (Figure 9.36b) is provided for each requestor, so that requestors which have only two pins, $\overline{M_I}$ and $\overline{M_O}$, can get into the daisy chain via the four system bus (the Z8000 Z-bus [27]) lines $\overline{MMAI}$, $\overline{MMST}$, $\overline{MMRQ}$ and $\overline{MMAO}$.

To acquire a resource, a requestor must issue an $\overline{M_O}$ = low which passes through the requestor's interface logic and is applied to the $\overline{MMRQ}$ bus line. All $\overline{MMRQ}$ signals for a given resource are wire-ORed to a common bus line. Bus line $\overline{MMST}$ indicates whether the resource is busy or not: a low on the $\overline{MMST}$ bus line indicates that the resource is busy; a high, that it is not busy. When a requestor is not requesting the resource, its $\overline{M_O}$ output is high. This signal opens gate G3 in the requestor's interface logic, thus allowing the value on bus line $\overline{MMST}$ to pass to the requestor's input pin $\overline{M_I}$. A low on the $\overline{MMAI}$ bus line enters the $\overline{MMAI}$ input of each interface logic and exits from its output pin $\overline{MMAO}$ (through gate G4) only when the corresponding requestor is not requesting the resource (i.e., its $\overline{M_O}$ = high). When a requestor requests the resource (i.e., its $\overline{M_O}$ = low), the requestor's interface logic blocks the $\overline{MMAI}$ = low signal from propagating further down the chain and prevents the lower-priority requestors from acquiring the resource. Therefore, when simultaneous requests are made for the same resource, the requestor higher on the daisy chain will seize the resource first. The $\overline{MMAO}$ of this requestor remains high.

When $\overline{MMST}$ bus line is high, the resource is not busy and can be seized by a requestor. A requestor recognizes this $\overline{MMST}$ high (after checking its own input pin $\overline{M_I}$) and issues an $\overline{M_O}$ = low which sets the $\overline{MMRQ}$ bus line to low as well. After a finite delay, if $\overline{MMAI}$ also goes low, the resource has been seized successfully and the intended transaction can begin. This resource master is identified by a low on its $\overline{MMAI}$ and $\overline{MMRQ}$ and a high on its $\overline{MMAO}$. If, however, after issuing an $\overline{M_O}$ = low, the requestor's $\overline{MMAI}$ does not go low, the request is aborted because another device higher on the chain has already seized the resource and is sending to this requestor an $\overline{MMAI}$ = high. A requestor that has been thus preempted by a higher-priority requestor may try again immediately or after some delay.

Like the 8086, the Z8000 can also support satellite processing. These satellite processors or extended processing units (EPUs) free the CPU from

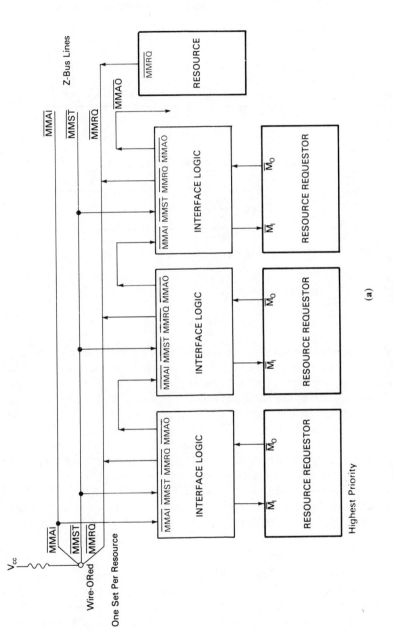

Figure 9.36 Daisy-chaining three resource requestors that share a common resource for a Zilog Z8000 implementation.

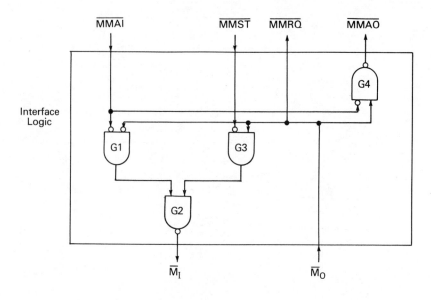

(b)   *Reproduced by permission ©1982 Zilog, Inc.* [28]

Figure 9.36   *(Continued).*

complex tasks that formerly required considerable CPU time (e.g., floating-point arithmetic). The enhanced Z8000 instruction set contains extended instructions to support the EPUs. These instructions specify the activities that must be carried out by the CPU and the EPU, and include [6]: EPU internal operations, data transfers between the memory and EPU, data transfers between the CPU and EPU, and status transfers between the EPU and the CPU status flags. EPUs operate in a way similar to that of the satellite processors or co-processors of the 8086 (i.e., they monitor the bus continuously) and they latch the command if an instruction fetched by the Z8000 is an extended instruction. Since more than one EPU may be connected to a CPU (all of them can operate concurrently and independently), a special ID flag in the extended instruction indicates the specific EPU that will execute it.

Motorola 68000

Finally, the 68000 chip includes both hardware and software interlocks for multiprocessor system configurations. It uses ready and wait semaphores throughout the distributed system through a number of privileged instructions executing in supervisor mode [15,22]. Such privileged instructions include the TEST and SET, TEST and RESET, etc.

The 68000 also provides the bus arbitration logic for a shared system bus and shared memory environment. The 68000 CPU provides three pins for this purpose: the bus request ($\overline{BR}$) pin, which receives an input from a bus requestor asking to use the system bus; the bus grant ($\overline{BG}$) output pin which signals that the processor is granting bus arbitration; and the bus grant acknowledge ($\overline{BGACK}$) input pin, through which the bus requestor notifies the processor that it has become the bus master. Bus mastership is terminated when the requestor negates bus grant acknowledge.

Again, a priority encoded network or a daisy chain configuration may be used when there is more than one bus requestor in the system. The three signals $\overline{BR}$, $\overline{BG}$, and $\overline{BGACK}$, form the on-chip implemented[19] bus arbitration circuit to determine which requestor will be the bus master device.

EXERCISES

9.1 Consider the 8080A vector table of Figure 9.5. Assume that the interrupting device transmits the "vector number" $N = 4$. How can the microprocessor transfer control to the respective interrupt handling routine if the routine's first instruction resides in location 0100_{16}?

9.2 When do we say that the priority of serving the microcomputer's peripheral devices is determined by the software? When by the hardware? Give an example for each case.

9.3 Consider an external device similar to that shown in Figure 8.7 of chapter 8, but in which the DONE signal of the ADC is connected to the interrupt input pin INT of the Intel 8080A. Each time the microprocessor is interrupted, it reads a measurement from the external device. Assume this is repeated 100 times, filling a 100-byte buffer in memory, after which the microprocessor calculates the average of the 100 measurements and outputs the information to output port 200. Show the detailed hardware implementation and write the respective assembly language program.

9.4 Assume that three interrupting devices, numbered 50, 60, and 70, are connected to an Intel 8085 microprocessor. Each time a device interrupts the microprocessor, its data is stored in one of the three respective lists X,

---

[19]A specialized bus arbitrator support circuit introduced by Motorola for the 68000 system helps resolve disputes between various processors and peripherals seeking to use the system bus in multiprocessing applications.

Y, and Z. Each list is fifty locations long, and when any of the lists receives fifty items, further processing is stopped. Assuming that the three devices have vectoring capability, design the interface and write the corresponding assembly language program.

9.5 Assume that in one installation there are eight sensors, $S_0, \ldots, S_7$, that monitor eight different physical variables. These sensors are properly interfaced to an Intel 8080A. When a sensor identifies that the variable it monitors exceeds an allowable upper limit, it sends an interrupt signal to the microprocessor. Design the minimum configuration of this system and write the assembly language program which, when it receives an interrupt signal from sensor S_i, lights up the respective lamp L_i on a display panel composed of eight lamps $L_0, \ldots, L_7$. (Assume that only one interrupt signal arrives at a time.)

9.6 The Intel 8085 is used to monitor the operation of a small installation. Assume that ten measuring devices are wire-ORed to the INTR input pin of the CPU and interrupt the processor at random times to supply it with 8-bit measurements. After fifty measurements have been read from any device, the processor disables further interrupts, computes the ten average values, stores them in a proper buffer in memory, and resumes the monitoring operation. Design the hardware configuration showing all the interfacing details and write the appropriate assembly language routine.

REFERENCES AND BIBLIOGRAPHY

[1] Artwick, B.A., *Microcomputer Interfacing*, Englewood Cliffs, NJ: Prentice-Hall, Inc., 1980.

[2] Atkins, R.T., "What is an Interrupt?" *Byte*, March 1979, pp. 230–36.

[3] Banning, J., "Z-Bus and Peripheral Support Packages Tie Distributed Computer Systems Together," *Electronic Design*, November 22, 1979, pp. 144–50.

[4] Bowen, B.A. and R.J.A. Buhr, *The Logical Design of Multi-Microprocessor Systems,* Englewood Cliffs, NJ: Prentice-Hall, Inc., 1980.

[5] Bryce, H., "Microprogramming Makes the MC68000 a Processor Ready for the Future," *Electronic Design*, October 25, 1979, pp. 98–99.

[6] Bursky, D., "Z8000 CPUs Expand Processing Power with New Instructions, Special Processors," *Electronic Design*, 2, January 18, 1980, pp. 32–36.

[7] Field, E.P., et al, "Microcomputer Interfacing: a Software UART," *Computer Design*, October 1976, pp. 118–20.

[8] IEEE Task P796/D2, "Proposed Microcomputer System 796 Bus Standard," *Computer*, October 1980, pp. 89–105.

[9] Intel Corporation, *MCS-80 User's Manual (with Introduction to MCS-85)*, (98-1530), Santa Clara, CA, October 1977.

[10] Intel Corporation, *MCS-80/85 Family User's Manual*, (121506-001), Santa Clara, CA, October 1979.

[11] Intel Corporation, *The 8086 Family User's Manual*, (9800722-03) Santa Clara, CA, 1979.

[12] Kartashev, S.I. and S.P. Kartashev, "LSI Modular Computers, Systems and Networks," *Computer*, July 1978, pp. 7–15.

[13] Lesea, A. and R. Zaks, *Microprocessor Interfacing Techniques*, Berkeley, CA: SYBEX, Inc., 1977.

[14] Morse, S.P., et al, "The Intel 8086 Microprocessor: A 16-bit Evolution of the 8080," *Computer*, June 1978, pp. 18–27.

[15] Motorola, Incorporated, *16-Bit Microprocessing Unit*, (ADI-814-R1), Austin, TX, 1980.

[16] Nadir, J. and B. McCormick, "Bus Arbiter Streamlines Multiprocessor Design," *Computer Design*, June 1980, pp. 103–109.

[17] Peuto, B.L., "Architecture of a New Microprocessor," *Computer*, February 1979, pp. 10–21.

[18] Rony, P.R., *The Bugbook V*, Derby, Connecticut: E & L Instruments, Inc., 1976.

[19] Satyanarayanan, M., *Multi-Processors,* Englewood Cliffs, NJ: Prentice-Hall, Inc., 1980.

[20] Shima, M., "Two versions of 16-bit Chip Span Microprocessor, Minicomputer Needs," *Electronics*, December 21, 1978, pp. 81–88.

[21] Stockton, J. and V. Scherer, "Learn the Timing and Interfacing of MC68000 Peripheral Circuits," *Electronic Design*, November 8, 1979, pp. 58–64.

[22] Stritter, E. and T. Gunter, "A Microprocessor Architecture for a Changing World: The Motorola 68000," *Computer*, February 1979, pp. 43–52.

[23] Titus, J.A., P.R. Rony, and D.G. Larsen, "Microcomputer Interfacing: Microcomputer Interrupts," *Computer Design*, November 1976, pp. 142–43.

[24] Titus, J.A., P.R. Rony, and D.G. Larsen, "Microcomputer Interfacing: The Vectored Interrupt," *Computer Design*, December 1976, pp. 112–14.

[25] Weissberger, A.J., "Analysis of Multiple-Microprocessor System Architectures," *Computer Design*, June 1977, pp. 151–63.

[26] Zilog, Incorporated, *Z8000 Technical Manual*, Cupertino, CA, 1979.

[27] Zilog, Incorporated, *Z-bus Specification*, Cupertino, CA, 1979.

[28] Zilog, Incorporated, *1982/83 Data Book*, Cupertino, CA, 1982.

Chapter 10

SEGMENTATION AND MEMORY MANAGEMENT MECHANISMS

10.1 INTRODUCTION

Main memory is considered the central resource of a microcomputer system that must be dynamically allocated to users, programs, or processes. Today's microprocessors can support very large physical memory spaces, and effective mechanisms must be provided to manage these large amounts of memory.

Another advanced architectural feature found in new 16- and 32-bit microprocessors is that they distinguish the logical address space from the physical memory space, and have the necessary hardware support both to map one space to the other and handle large logical address spaces efficiently through dynamic storage allocation mechanisms. Although the physical organization and access of memory is covered in chapter 6, terms like "segment registers," "logical addresses," and "logical address spaces" are used in several instances throughout chapter 6. All of these directly relate to that aspect of memory architecture having to do with the way memory is "logically" organized.

Most 8-bit microprocessors have a "linear" organization of the logical address space. The addresses start at location 0 (zero) and proceed in linear fashion (without breaks or holes) to the upper limit imposed by the total number of bits in a logical address. The addresses generated by programs are used directly by memory hardware to locate data. This simple organization presents limitations when several programs are to share the system's resources efficiently, and when these programs (and their data) have to be protected from one another. With no memory-management facility available, management of the assigned memory is left to the user program.

The increased use of high-level languages and the trend towards more advanced applications and larger programs demanded new capabilities from microcomputer systems. One new capability was to provide large virtual memory to free users from concern over the size limitations of physical memory and from keeping track of assigned memory spaces. Newer microprocessors have abandoned the simple linear memory organization altogether and use, instead, different forms of logical memory organization: "segmented memory" and/or "paged memory."

This chapter covers the architectural feature of "memory management" found in newer microprocessors and the hardware mechanisms they provide to support it. In order to understand better how they implement it, some related background material and useful definitions are also included early in the chapter. The topics discussed here are useful to the microprocessor system architect, the assembly language programmer, and the system software engineer. The application programmer should also be aware of the *effect* that segmentation and paging hardware may have on his programs.

10.2 LOGICAL ADDRESS SPACE

One major requirement for accomplishing efficient memory management and allocation is to distinguish between the logical and physical address spaces and to make logical addresses independent of physical addresses. This is also a prerequisite to the design of virtual memory systems.

An address used by the programmer or generated by a program (or process) to specify a particular informational item is called a *logical address*.[1] The set of all logical addresses which can be used by a program to refer to informational items is called the *logical address space*.[2] The address used by main memory to access the location in which the item is stored is called a *physical address*.[3] The set of actual physical main memory locations in which informational items may be stored is called the *physical address space* or the *physical memory space* [3,5,14,16,18,21,22].[4] When the above two address spaces are independent, this means that system and user procedures and data are independent of the amount of main memory existing in the system. No physical addresses ever appear in the object code program, which resides in its own logical address space, and any reference it makes to an informational item consists of a logical address.

The above distinction must be made despite the fact that on many microprocessors, particularly the early ones, such logical and physical addresses appeared to be identical. There exist several ways of structuring the logical address space and forming a logical address. Furthermore, it will be shown

---

[1]Also called *name, virtual address,* or *generalized address.*

[2]Also called *name space, logical space, logical memory, virtual address space, virtual space, abstract space, addressing space, personal address space, user address space,* or simply *address space.*

[3]Also called *memory address, real address,* or *absolute address.*

[4]Also called *main memory, working storage, physical space, memory space,* or *real space.*

that logical address contiguity does not necessitate a complete physical address contiguity.

After a distinction has been made between these two address spaces, however, a "mapping mechanism" is required to facilitate going from logical to physical address space (i.e., a mechanism to translate logical addresses used by a program into physical addresses which are used by memory to access its locations). This is conceptually illustrated in Figure 10.1. If one considers two users (or programs or processes),[5] each one having its own logical address space, then Figure 10.1 is modified to become Figure 10.2 in order to reflect the new situation. The sizes of the two users' logical address spaces need not necessarily be equal. Furthermore, the mapping mechanism may be implemented in software, hardware, or some combination of the two.

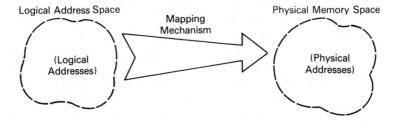

Figure 10.1   An illustration of the mapping of a logical address space into physical memory space.

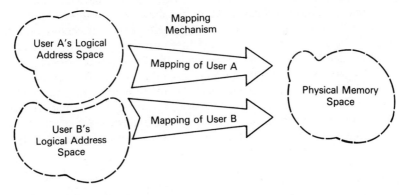

Figure 10.2   An illustration of the mapping of two logical address spaces into one physical memory space.

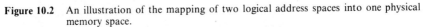

[5]Although strictly speaking the terms "user," "program," "process," or "task" are not exactly equivalent, to simplify our presentation they will be used in this chapter interchangeably to refer to the same thing.

It must be emphasized once more that *logical address space is the only space that the program (or process) is aware of*. Advanced memory management involves developing successful techniques to manage both the physical memory space (i.e., actual main memory) *and* the logical address space dynamically. The first is referred to as the "physical memory space allocation problem" (i.e., that of assigning main memory to a program or process during execution time); the second is referred to as the "logical address space allocation problem" (i.e., that of assigning logical address space to a program or process, again during execution time).

10.2.1 Size of the Logical Address Space

The size of the logical address space can be smaller than, equal to, or larger than that of physical memory. Various techniques exist that allow expanding the maximum size of either one.

In section 6.3.5 of chapter 6, we see ways for expanding the physical memory space of a microprocessor by providing external mechanisms which in effect increase the number of address lines applied to memory. However, expanding the physical memory space by adding more memory chips and providing capabilities for accessing all its locations might not always be economically the best solution. Consider, for example, the actual cost of a microprocessor system having an array of memory chips that form a real capacity of 16M bytes! Furthermore, even if the physical memory space is larger than the logical address space (as in the cases of bank switching and indexed mapping discussed in chapter 6), the microprocessor is still restricted to one section of physical memory at any one time, the addressing range of which equals the microprocessor's maximum possible logical address space. Difficulties also arise in allocating the logical and physical address spaces to a number of concurrently running programs and in supporting the sharing of programs and data with full generality. Finally, in bank switching, identical supervisors must occupy the same physical locations in each memory bank; similarly, in indexed mapping, the supervisor is always active and always occupies the same memory locations regardless of where in main memory the program's logical address space is mapped.

10.2.2 Virtual Memory

For these preceding reasons and others to be discussed next, it is preferable to provide mechanisms through which the microprocessor's logical address space can be made larger than the size of actual memory found in a given system implementation. When the logical address space is larger than the physical memory space, the term *virtual memory* is often used. In this case, the logical address space is implemented in both the actual physical main memory and in less expensive mass storage (auxiliary storage) such as disks. Thus, the user can write large programs without worrying about the physical memory limitations of the system. Furthermore, the user's programming effort is simplified, since the virtual memory scheme frees him or her from worrying about the details of memory management.

Such a virtual memory implementation, however, requires a mechanism to indicate automatically whether the addressed element resides in main memory or in an auxiliary storage device. When an access is attempted to an element not residing in main memory, it must be detected automatically by the system, and the instruction execution held in abeyance until the operating system brings this element from auxiliary into physical main memory. Afterward, the instruction is allowed to proceed with the memory access. In virtual memory systems, the operating system undertakes this movement of information between main and auxiliary memory; this multiplexing of main memory is called *swapping*. Swapping is performed by the operating system during program execution (at run time) to overcome limitations on main memory size.

Although the virtual memory concept offers many advantages to the programmer, the operating system becomes quite complex and difficult and costly to design. Furthermore, its continuous intervention during program execution to perform swapping results in a considerable time overhead.

We will see that, for efficiency purposes, the operating system does not swap individual information elements, but rather, "blocks" of such elements. Two techniques, "segmentation" and "paging," are used to implement a logical address space larger than physical memory space, and the blocks of elements swapped are called "segments" or "pages," respectively. Furthermore, in such virtual memory systems, it is not necessary to place the entire program into main memory at the time its execution begins. Only those segments/pages initially required can be placed into main memory, and as a reference is made to a segment/page not in main memory, the "mapping mechanism" will indicate the fact by generating a call to the operating system, which will then bring in the segment/page. Therefore, there is no reason why a program should not be larger than the physical main memory, since at no point in time are all the segments/pages of the program required to be resident in main memory.

An important architectural characteristic that the microprocessor should exhibit to allow the implementation of a true virtual memory system is that the processor must be able to be interrupted in the middle of an instruction execution to allow memory swapping, and not after the instruction is finished. In other words, the instruction should be able to be aborted and later re-executed once the virtual memory operating system provides the appropriate data. Some of the presently available microprocessors that have this charac-

teristic are the National NS16032, the Motorola 68000, and the Zilog Z8000.[6]
These may operate with an auxiliary support device called a memory management unit or MMU, which receives each address that the processor issues and
examines it to determine if the referenced element resides in main memory.
The MMU does other things, too; i.e., it checks various attributes, such as
whether the processor is trying to access a protected area of memory, etc. If the
element resides in main memory, then the MMU translates the logical (or
virtual) address to a physical address and sends it to memory. If, however, the
MMU identifies that the element does not reside in main memory, it sends an
"abort" signal to the CPU. The CPU in turn immediately stops the executing
of the instruction (i.e., it does not wait until the instruction is completed),
automatically saves the program counter (so that the instruction can be
re-executed later), returns to the state it was in prior to the aborted instruction
(i.e., returns all registers that were altered by the instruction to their condition
before the instruction started), and calls the virtual memory operating system.
The operating system will find and properly place the element from peripheral
to main memory, restore any register required, and then try the aborted
instruction again. In contrast, the Intel 8086 [12] does not exhibit this architectural feature of allowing for interruption in the middle of the instruction
execution.

10.2.3 Structure of the Logical Address Space

A user writes a program in logical address space using logical addresses (we
are not concerned here with the rare case of absolute coding). Therefore, the
structure of the logical address space is of immediate importance to the user of
the system, because it has a direct influence on the way he or she writes
programs.

Linear Memory

The most common structure is that of the *linear* (or *one-dimensional*) logical
address space, in which permissible logical addresses are the integers $0,1...,n$.
The logical address space is an array of contiguous logical locations with
logical addresses numbered in sequence. A program or task accesses an
informational item in its logical address space using a single number (rather
than a pair of numbers, as required by a segmented logical address space, to be
discussed next). The linear logical address space is thus *one homogeneous
unit*. Figure 10.3a shows a 20-bit logical address defining a linear logical

---

[6]In the Zilog Z8003 and Z8004 versions of the CPU, a previously undefined pin is now defined
as the "instruction-abort control," intended for use in virtual memory operations and in the
MMU support circuit.

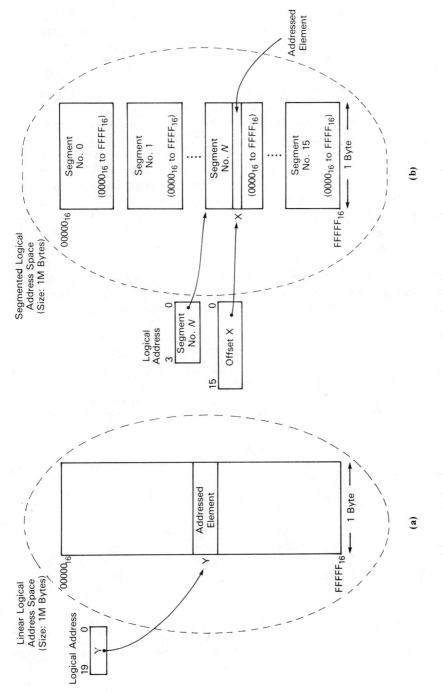

Figure 10.3 1 M-byte logical address spaces: **(a)** a *linear* logical address space addressed by a 20-bit address; **(b)** a *symbolically segmented* logical address space addressed by the pair "segment number–offset."

address space of up to $2^{20} = 1$M bytes (assume addressing is done to the byte). Since such a linear or one-dimensional logical address space allows direct access to it using a single number, address arithmetic may be done on the entire logical address (i.e., logical addresses are manipulated as one of the data types of the same size).

In most 8-bit microprocessors, the maximum size of the logical address space is directly related to the number of bits used to represent real physical memory addresses. Physical and logical addresses for those microprocessors are sixteen bits wide, the maximum size of the logical address space is $2^{16} =$ 64K bytes, and the two address spaces are considered the same. Similarly, the logical address space presently implemented in the National NS16032 and Motorola 68000 microprocessors [7] is linear. These microprocessors use 24-bit logical addresses that can directly access a large 16M-byte linear (uniform) logical address space.

The next level of sophistication is obtained by systems that provide a relocation or *base register* [16]. All logical addresses are added to the content of the base register in order to produce the physical address. The two address spaces are no longer necessarily the same. A linear logical address space whose size is smaller than the maximum physical memory space can be used to access items starting at an arbitrary address in physical memory.

In either of the above two cases, however, the size of the logical address space can never exceed that of the maximum physical memory space. Another technique, called *paging*, can be used to allow a linear logical address space not to have a direct relationship to the set of actual main memory locations and not be limited in size by the physical memory space.

Base registers and paging are discussed at greater length in section 10.3. With either approach, the structure of the logical address space obtained is identical: it is a linear logical address space which is dynamically relocatable. The major limitations of the linear organization are readily apparent when several programs must share the same machine in order to try to use the system's resources efficiently.

Segmented Memory

The second structure is that of the *segmented* (or *non-linear*) logical address space.[8] A segmented logical address space is composed of a number of linear arrays (i.e., a set of separate linear logical address spaces) called *segments*, and all addresses within a given segment are relative to the start of the segment. To

---

[7] The 68000 used by itself (without an external MMU).

[8] More complex structures for the logical address space also exist, but they are not treated in this book because they have not been implemented in microprocessors.

access a particular informational item in such a segmented space requires the specification of two entities: the segment's number and an offset within the segment. For this reason, a segmented logical address space is also called *two-dimensional*. For example, if the logical address space is composed of sixteen segments of up to 64K bytes per segment, then the two parts of the logical address would be a 4-bit segment number and a 16-bit offset. Such a 1M-byte segmented logical address space is shown in Figure 10.3b. In the most general case, the various segments can have different maximum sizes. In the 16-bit microprocessors Intel 8086 and Zilog Z8000 and in the 32-bit Intel APX 432 their maximum size is limited to 64K bytes. In the Motorola 68000 (used with an external MMU), a segment can be as large as 16M bytes.

Segmentation as implemented in the Intel 8086 and Zilog Z8000 is also referred to as *symbolic segmentation*. In symbolic segmentation, the segments are logically independent (i.e., there are no contiguous addresses across segment boundaries) and unordered (i.e., segments need not be in sequential order in the logical address space). There is no relationship between the last address of segment n and the first address of segment $n + 1$. This means that if a program is 68K bytes long and running in a microprocessor whose maximum segment size is 64K bytes, simply allowing the instruction counter to increment past the 64K bytes limit will either cause the program to "jump" to its beginning (as done in the 8086), or—in a more general situation—will bring an error message from the system indicating that the maximum segment size limit was exceeded. Similarly, if the microprocessor system allows the user to specify the size of the segment, and if the size specified for, say, segment n is 32000 bytes, then a reference to byte 32020 of segment n will also bring an error message from the system, indicating that the allocation limit for segment n was exceeded. The system will not respond with byte 20 of segment $n + 1$. There is no way using address modification, through indexing for example, to obtain a logical address in segment $n + 1$ from a logical address in segment n. Thus, a reference to one segment cannot inadvertently access another segment (of the same or different user).

Therefore, a segmented system provides a logical address space of *non-homogeneous units* called segments. A segment is a "block" of contiguous locations in logical address space, representing a package of information which is directly addressable, and, as we will see later, accessible in a controlled fashion. Segments can be named by the programmer, so that he or she may partition the program along logical, rather than physical, boundaries. For example, the programmer may assign logical modules, subtasks, or *objects* (such as main routines, subroutines, data arrays, symbol tables, or pushdown stacks) to individual segments. For those memory management systems that allow variable-sized segments, within limits, the user can also specify the size of each segment according to the size of the logical module it contains.

Two common techniques are used by microprocessors to form the segmented logical address.[9] The first one (implemented in the Zilog Z8000) has the logical address completely contained in the instruction itself. This logical address explicitly specifies both the particular segment and the offset within the segment. With the second technique (implemented in the Intel 8086), access to an item in logical address space is done by a shorter address field in the instruction that explicitly specifies the offset within the segment, while the specification of a particular segment is done implicitly. A further description of each of these techniques follows:

(a) When the whole logical address is contained in the instruction, the address is composed of two parts: the segment number and the offset. Figure 10.4a shows the logical address of the Zilog Z8000. Although each part can be manipulated separately, only the offset part participates in address arithmetic (such as indexing, etc.). The segment number points to the location of a segment in the logical address space, while the offset points to the location of the referenced element relative to the start of the segment. Figure 10.5a shows the way accessing is peformed to a location in the Z8000's segmented logical address space. The 7-bit segment number can select explicitly one of 128 segments, each segment having a maximum size of 64K bytes, and the 16-bit offset specifies a location within the selected segment. Thus, instead of specifying an address as one number, say, 988, the programmer may specify a pair of numbers, such as location 4 in segment 12. (One may also consider the linear logical address of the Motorola 68000 as a segmented space allowing only one segment, and thus, the segment number is implicit. The same holds for paged systems and systems using a base register).

(b) In the Intel 8086 only part of the logical address is contained in the instruction. The instruction contains a 16-bit offset that can access a location directly within a segment having a size of up to 64K bytes. The 8086 logical address is shown in Figure 10.4b. Only four segments (code, data, stack, and extra) can be addressed directly at any one moment. The particular segment is specified implicitly according to predefined rules (i.e., by default according to the specific type of memory operation) and not explicitly under control of the instruction currently executing. Figure 10.5b shows the way accessing is performed to a location in the 8086's segmented logical address space.

---

[9] A segmented logical address may also be paged, but we will ignore this level of detail for the moment.

```
22        16  15                    0
┌──────────┬─────────────────────┐
│ Segment  │      Offset         │
└──────────┴─────────────────────┘
```

The logical address is contained completely in the instruction itself and is composed of two parts.

(a) Z8000 logical address.

(Implicit specification of one of four segment registers).

$+$

The logical address is formed by the 16-bit offset contained in the instruction and an implicit specification of one of four segment registers.

(b) 8086 logical address.

Figure 10.4 Logical addresses for the Zilog Z8000 and the Intel 8086 16-bit microprocessors.

10.3   MEMORY ALLOCATION AND MAPPING

10.3.1   Memory Allocation

So far, we have seen how a program is written and accessed in logical address space. We have also seen that a logical address space can be structured in two different ways, that it may be larger than physical memory space, and that logical addresses are independent of the physical locations that the program occupies when it is placed in main memory.

Before a program is executed, real physical memory space must be allocated to it. In simple cases when only one program runs at a time, the memory allocation problem is easy: a sufficient memory space is required to contain all the program code and data. This placing of the program into main memory is performed by the relocating loader. If several program modules assembled independently are to be executed together, a linking loader links them together and loads them in main memory as one unit. This allocation of main memory, performed when the program is loaded, is called *static memory allocation*; the "mapping mechanism" used to convert logical addresses to physical addresses is the loader itself. The main disadvantage of static memory allocation techniques is that, after being loaded, the program becomes *absolute* or *bounded to physical memory space*; i.e., when the object program is removed to auxiliary memory and then returned to main memory, it must be placed in the same locations as before.

However, in more advanced applications, static techniques are not satisfactory because it is difficult (if not impossible) to meet the following requirements [5,21]:

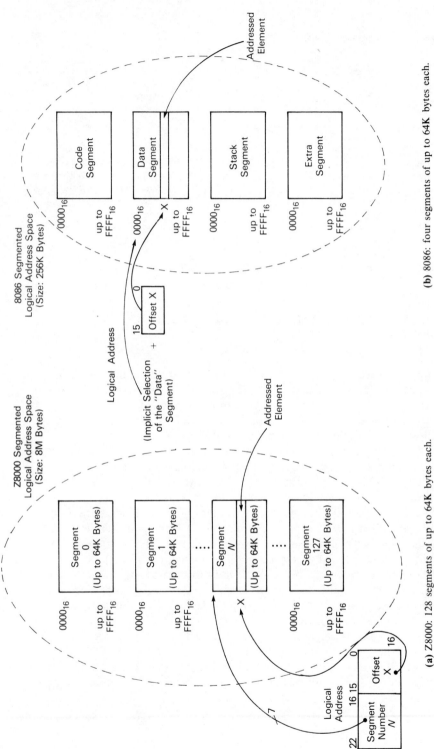

(a) Z8000: 128 segments of up to 64K bytes each.

(b) 8086: four segments of up to 64K bytes each.

Figure 10.5 Accessing an element in the segmented logical address spaces of the Zilog Z8000 and Intel 8086 microprocessors.

- There may be a requirement to have more than one program coexisting in main memory, so that, while one program is being swapped out, another program can start executing.
- A capability may be required to allow easy sharing of software modules (e.g., a compiler, an editor, a questionnaire, a data file, etc.) among concurrently running programs by having only one copy of the particular module in main memory rather than providing separate copies of it to each program. Furthermore, two (or more) users should be able to share the single copy of a module in memory, by not necessarily using the same name for it in their programs.
- Program modularity requires that the separately compiled modules not be linked together to form a complete program until execution time.
- It may be required to allow varying the program size and the size of the data structures it uses *during execution time.*
- If a program's logical address space or the sum of several user's logical address spaces in a multi-user environment exceeds that of available main memory, then the ability should be provided to run a partially loaded program.
- System and user procedures and data should be independent of the amount and type of physical memory, so that the system can be expanded easily by adding more main memory or additional auxiliary memory devices without forcing reprogramming.
- Finally, the ability to relocate a program (or sections of it) anywhere in main memory *during execution time* may be required.

Since all the above requirements arise during execution time, preplanning the memory allocation strategy is not feasible; instead, memory allocation should be performed dynamically by the system, i.e., *at run time.*

To perform dynamic memory allocation, three methods have been used in contemporary systems[5].[10] Each method subdivides the logical address space into *blocks* of contiguous logical addresses. In the first method, *segmentation*, the programmer (or compiler) subdivides the program's *logical address space* into blocks (called *segments*) of arbitrary size, each one addressed separately by its segment name. An individual program module (such as a subroutine) can be assigned to each segment.[11] Segment names are interpreted by the software. The segment is the unit of main memory allocation and of transfer

---

[10]Another simple method using a base register used by earlier systems is examined later.

[11]This breaking up of a program into modules, such as main program, subroutines, and data structures, was of course also done on earlier systems. However, in those cases a fixed amount of main memory was allocated to each program module at the time the module was first loaded into memory. The problem we are trying to solve with dynamic memory allocation refers to activities taking place *after* the initial loading has been done, and the loader is not in the picture any more.

between main and auxiliary memory. The second method, *paging*, organizes the *physical memory space* into uniform-sized blocks (called *page frames*), which serve to accept matching size blocks of logical addresses (called *pages*). The physical subdivision of the program's logical address space into equal-sized pages is done by the system, and page names are interpreted by the hardware. Here the unit of main memory allocation and of transfer between main and auxiliary memory is the page. Thus, in segmentation the unit of main memory allocation is non-uniform, whereas in paging it is uniform. Pages are usually much smaller than segments. The third method combines segmentation with paging, thus allowing both levels of logical address space subdivision: into variable-sized segments, which are in turn subdivided into fixed-sized pages.

As already mentioned, the more general case of memory allocation must solve *both* problems: that of the *physical memory allocation* (i.e., assigning main memory to a program or process during execution time), and that of the *logical address space allocation* (i.e., assigning logical address space to a program or process, again during execution time). In all dynamic memory allocation systems the units of main memory allocation are blocks of contiguous physical locations. The size of these blocks may or may not be fixed and may or may not be apparent to the user, depending upon the memory allocation technique used.

10.3.2 Mapping

In all dynamic memory implementations, some sort of "mapping mechanism" is used to translate (or map) logical addresses to the appropriate physical addresses of main memory where the program actually resides. The translation is performed during execution time. This mechanism includes (among other things) the map that contains the assignments[12] at any given moment of main memory's physical addresses to the program's logical addresses.

In the most general case, this map is a set of registers, called the *mapping table*. Figure 10.6 shows this mapping table conceptually as a mapping mechanism interposed between the processor and main memory. This mechanism receives the logical address X and does one of the following two things: (1) if the addressed element is not in main memory, the Xth register of the mapping table will contain the address in auxiliary storage where the element resides, and the mapping mechanism will notify the operating system to take proper action (e.g., find the missing item in auxiliary storage, bring it to main memory, and insert its physical address in the Xth register of the mapping

---

[12]These main memory assignments are done at run time by the operating system which is also responsible for properly modifying the map.

table); (2) if the addressed element resides in main memory location Y, the Xth register of the mapping table will contain the physical address Y, to be transmitted to main memory. In this way, the mapping mechanism converts each logical address to a physical address.

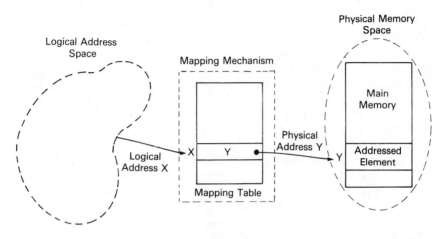

Figure 10.6 Conceptual operation of the mapping mechanism [5].

Such an implementation would be impractical, since the mapping table would require as many registers as the number of locations of the main memory (i.e., a second memory!). However, when one of the above-mentioned subdivision techniques is used (i.e., segmentation or paging), the size of the mapping table is decreased considerably, since the "registers" refer now to blocks of logical addresses (which are far less numerous than individual logical addresses).

The number of registers contained in the mapping table determines the maximum number of program segments or pages that can be mapped (or residing) in main memory at any one time. One register of the mapping table will be required for *each* block of the program's logical address space. Since segments are usually much larger than pages, the length of the mapping table is shorter in segmentation than in paging. To decrease its length further and reduce table lookup or table modification (or update) times, the mapping table can be structured and addressed in an "associative" manner. Then, only one register is required per program block *used*. Such an associative hardware mechanism has been implemented on the 32-bit Intel APX 432 microprocessor.

Finally, this mapping table can be implemented either in software (i.e., composed of main memory locations) or in hardware (i.e., composed of a set of hardware registers).[13] The operating system will have to load to it new values whenever relocation of program information in main memory is performed (i.e., whenever the main memory map changes). If it is implemented in software, the mapping table itself can be relocated. On the other hand, however, to fetch an operand would require an additional memory access first to fetch the contents of the appropriate register of the mapping table.

In multiprogramming systems where many programs may be executing concurrently, several mapping tables will exist, one for each program. Each program runs in its own logical address space, which is independent of the other logical address spaces. Since the mapping table identifies those blocks of the program that reside in main memory at any one time, *the mapping table is regarded as the map of a program's logical address space*. If the mapping tables are implemented in software, then, when the processor is switched from one program to another, the operating system should be activating properly the corresponding mapping table in memory. If they are implemented in hardware, a method similar to bank switching may be used to select (enable) the appropriate table that corresponds to the program in control of the system. Finally, if only one mapping table exists, the operating system will have to load into it new values when the system switches from one program to the other. For a two-user (or two-program) situation, the mappings of linear and segmented logical address spaces are shown diagrammatically in Figure 10.7. In the case of Figure 10.7a, the lengths of the two users' logical address spaces need not necessarily be the same. Similarly, in the case of Figure 10.7b, the total number of segments in the two users' logical address spaces need not necessarily be the same.

10.3.3 Base Registers

In the base register's simplest form, one base register may be used. If the program consists of a number of independently assembled modules, the (linking) loader properly links them all together to form a large contiguous *linear* logical address space prior to execution, and assigns the base register to it. Since during execution, each logical address of the program will have to use the base register, loading binds the program to this base register.

The loader initially places the program into main memory using static allocation techniques, and inserts the program's starting physical address into the base register. Translating or mapping each logical address to a physical address, then, simply means adding the contents of the base register to the logical address for each memory operation (Figure 10.8a). Thus, the mapping table consists of only one register, the base register. During its total execution

---

[13]In the newer 16- and 32-bit microprocessors, the mapping table is implemented in hardware.

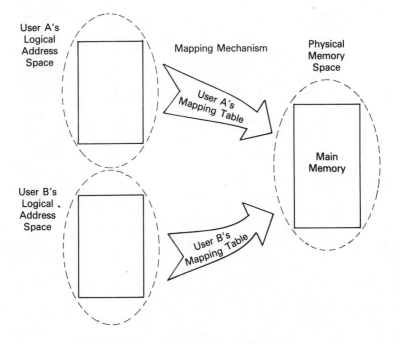

(a) Mapping of linear logical address spaces.

Figure 10.7 Mapping of two users' logical address spaces into the physical memory space.

time, the program can be removed to auxiliary storage and then returned to different main memory locations (without passing through the loader again), by simply having the operating system adjust the contents of the base register to point to the program's new starting physical address. In this way, the whole program can be dynamically relocated anywhere in main memory as one unit (Figure 10.8b). The size of the logical address space obtained with the base register technique can never exceed the size of available physical memory space.

In the base register approach, if the maximum size of any program is very small compared to the size of the available physical memory space, then swapping of complete programs in and out of main memory may be feasible. Even in this case, however, a sufficiently large block of contiguous physical memory locations must be found to contain the program. Furthermore, the unit of main memory allocation is non-uniform; it varies in order to suit the needs of the program to be stored. Therefore, after a few such swappings, the problem of *memory fragmentation* arises; this refers to situations in which, although enough free locations are available in main memory for the program

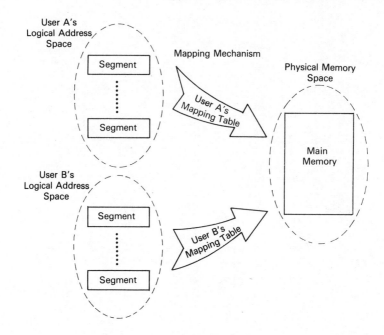

(b) Mapping of segmented logical address spaces.

Figure 10.7   (*Continued*)

being brought in from auxiliary storage, they are not in one large enough contiguous physical block. In this case, the operating system must form such a large free block of contiguous memory locations (for example, by performing a memory compacting operation) into which to place the program.

The memory fragmentation drawback can be reduced somewhat, if more than one base register is used. Then the programmer or compiler can split up the program, for example, into code and data modules,[14] and assign a different base register to each (Figure 10.8c). The units of physical memory allocation are now reduced in size, and it is easier to find two such areas of contiguous main memory locations into which to place the two program modules.

Some systems allow the base register to be addressed directly and modified by the program. Other systems do not allow programs to manipulate the contents of base registers, and a base register is addressed implicitly depending

---

[14]That is, into two blocks of contiguous logical address space locations.

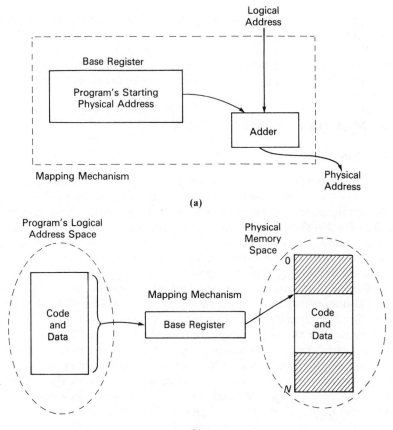

(a)

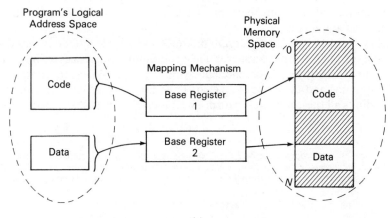

(b)

(c)

Figure 10.8 **(a)** The mapping mechanism using one base register; **(b)** with one base register, the whole program can be dynamically relocated anywhere in memory; **(c)** with two base registers the code and data modules can be relocated independently anywhere in memory.

on the type of memory operation being executed (for example, all instruction fetches use one base register and all data fetches and stores use a second base register). In this case, the base register is used to translate addresses completely independently of the program that generates them. If a program is to be dynamically relocatable, it should not be allowed to load or manipulate the base registers.

10.4   MEMORY SEGMENTATION

10.4.1   Introduction

As pointed out earlier, proper management not only of the physical address space but of the *logical address space as well* is required in order to have a fully dynamic allocation capability at run time; i.e., an efficient mechanism is required for assigning base registers to blocks of contiguous logical address space locations (e.g., program modules) during execution time (not before, during loading). This leads to the segmentation technique.

To reduce the fragmentation problem of the previous base register approach, main memory should be allocated in physical blocks of smaller sizes. This means that the program should also be divided into smaller logical blocks. Segmentation is a scheme whereby the program's logical address space is broken up into blocks of contiguous logical locations, called *segments*, of arbitrary size. All addresses within a segment are relative to the start of the segment. Each segment is placed in its entirety into a main memory area of contiguous physical locations during execution time. A technique similar to that of the base registers is used, in which a separate base register will (eventually) be assigned to each segment containing the starting physical address of that segment in main memory. The set of such base registers forms the mapping table, called *segment table*,[15] whose length determines the maximum number of program segments that can be mapped (residing) in main memory at any one time.

Segments correspond to program modules and have symbolic names usually assigned by the programmer.[16] The programmer references an informational item using a two-component symbolic address which contains a segment name and the name of an element within this segment. The (linking) loader links all these modules to form a *segmented* logical address space, prior

---

[15]The Intel 8086 microprocessor calls these registers *segment registers*, and calls the mapping table the *segment register file*. The Zilog Z8000 calls them *base address registers* and *base address register file*, respectively. Finally, the APX 432 calls them *segment descriptors* and *segment table*, respectively.

[16]Segmenting may also be specified automatically by a compiler.

to execution. But the loader does not assign one register of the segment table to each specific segment. Thus, a segment is not bound to logical address space because all its addresses are relative to the beginning of some segment. Only when the segment is referenced (i.e., at run time), is it placed in main memory; its starting physical address is inserted into the segment table, and the index of that entry is assigned as its segment number.[17] In other words, only when the segment is to be executed does the operating system assign to it a register of the segment table, and only then do the segment's addresses become absolute within the logical address space (i.e., binding to logical address space takes place). The segment number given to a segment is to be used to combine with the offset within the segment to produce the physical address sent to main memory. This is shown conceptually in Figure 10.9a where the logical address (2,345) refers to the 345th location in the second segment. Figure 10.9b shows a simple mapping mechanism. The segment number points to a register of the segment table. The register contains the starting physical address of this segment in memory, or contains its address in auxiliary storage if the addressed segment is not in main memory.[18] The offset is added to the contents of the "register" to produce the physical address of the addressed element.

It is seen, therefore, that segmentation solves the logical address space allocation problem, since loading does not bind the program to positions in logical address space; the registers of the segment table are assigned to segments only at execution time. Thus, on different occasions, a segment can be in different places in the program's logical address space. In addition, a segment may grow up to the maximum segment size without affecting any of the logical addresses that refer to it.

Figure 10.10 shows the mapping of the segmented logical address space of Figure 10.3b into physical memory. We can notice that each segment is mapped into physically contiguous locations in main memory; logically contiguous segments need not necessarily be mapped into physically contiguous areas of main memory;[19] we also see that segments may overlap when placed in main memory. However, it it not necessary to have the entire program placed into main memory at the time execution begins. Only those segments which are required initially can be resident. When a reference is made to a

---

[17]This is done by the operating system and is also referred to as "making a segment known."

[18]Usually, each segment table entry also contains a "segment residence bit", which is zero if the segment is not in main memory and one if the segment is in main memory.

[19]This illusion given the programmer by the mapping mechanism—that segments consecutive in logical address space are stored consecutively in main memory—is known as "artificial contiguity [16]."

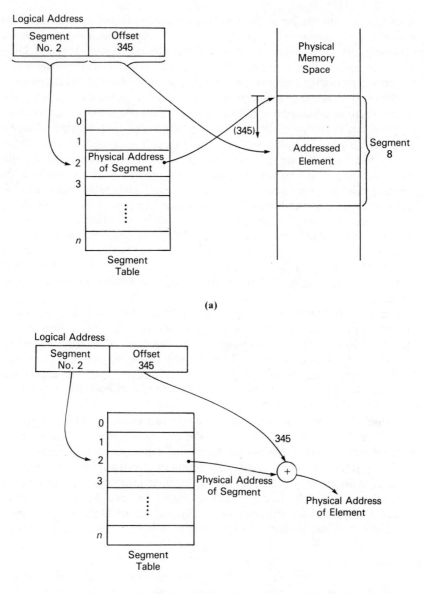

Figure 10.9   (a) Addressing an element in memory through a segmented logical address; (b) the mapping mechanism for converting a segmented logical address into a physical address transmitted to memory. *R.W. Watson,* Timesharing System Design Concepts, *©1970. Adapted by permission of McGraw-Hill, New York.*

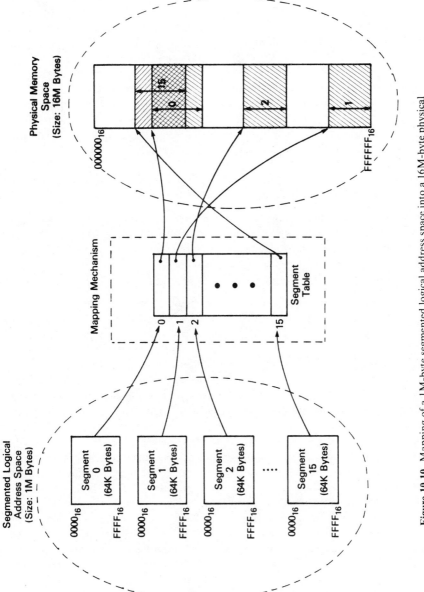

Figure 10.10 Mapping of a 1M-byte segmented logical address space into a 16M-byte physical memory space.

segment not in main memory, the operating system intervenes to bring it into main memory and properly adjust the segment table to reflect the new situation. In the case of more than one concurrent program, one segment table is associated with each program.

The problems of swapping large program modules and of memory fragmentation have not been eliminated completely. These problems become even more serious if the system allows for segments of sufficient maximum size that only a few can be entirely main memory resident at any one time. On the other hand, however, the smaller the maximum allowable segment size, the more segments that can be defined for a logical address space, thus increasing the size of the segment table required to map the logical address space into physical memory.

10.4.2   Segmentation as Done in Several Microprocessors

Having discussed the general concepts of memory management and segmentation, we proceed to describe the mechanisms used to support segmentation in some of the new microprocessors.

Zilog Z8000

The non-segmented Z8002 uses non-segmented 16-bit addresses that can access a logical address space of 64K bytes directly. Since no address translation is performed, the logical address space is the same as the physical memory space. In this case, code written for the 40-pin Z8002 can run in one segment of the 48-pin Z8001. Thus, full software compatibility exists between the two versions of the microprocessor. In either the Z8002 or the non-segmented mode of the Z8001, therefore, an address is—at run time—absolute within the 64K-byte physical memory space. Six separate logical address spaces exist in the Z8002: *code, data*, and *stack*, for both the *supervisor* mode and the *user* mode of operation. Thus, six 64K-byte logical address spaces are provided, which increase the Z8002's *total* logical address space to 384K bytes. The Z8001 version of the CPU can be used in either a non-segmented or a segmented mode. When used in the non-segmented mode, it behaves exactly like the Z8002.

When the Z8001 is used in the segmented mode, however, it can directly address larger amounts of memory. In this case the Z8001 can directly address a segmented logical address space of 8M bytes, composed of 128 segments that can vary in size from 256 to 64K bytes. The technique used by the Z8001 is that of having all addressing information explicitly contained *within the instruction itself*;[20] each logical address in an instruction contains both the segment

---

[20]Or in registers, for some addressing modes.

number (an unsigned 7-bit segment number to identify one of the 128 segments) and the offset within the segment. Only the offset participates in addressing arithmetic. As shown in the hardware representation of segmented addresses of Figure A6.6 of Appendix 6, this offset may be an unsigned 8-bit number, referred to as "short offset," or an unsigned 16-bit number, referred to as "full offset." In our discussions here, we will be using mostly the 16-bit full offset, which corresponds to the maximum addressing capability of the Z8001.[21] The 7-bit segment number points to the beginning of a contiguous area within logical address space (i.e., to a segment), while the offset addresses any location relative to the beginning of the segment. The two parts of the segmented logical address can be manipulated separately. Again, since six separate logical address spaces exist, the segmented Z8001 provides six 8M-byte logical address spaces, thus increasing the system's total logical address space to 48M bytes.

The segmented Z8001 can be used either alone, or together with a number of support memory management units (MMUs). When the segmented Z8001 is used alone, no address translation or mapping is performed, and, therefore, the 8M-byte logical address space is equivalent to the 8M-byte maximum physical memory space. The 23-bit logical address is the physical address transmitted to memory, and, therefore, this address is—at run time—absolute within the 8M-byte physical memory space. Designing a system using the segmented Z8001 without MMUs presents the following shortcommings: (1) No dynamic mapping is performed, and therefore, no distinction exists between logical and physical address spaces. (2) Dynamic program relocation is not supported, and memory protection through the checking of attributes associated with each segment in logical address space is not performed. (3) The maximum possible physical memory space is 8M bytes. (4) Each program entity (subroutine, data set, etc.) is placed in its own separate memory area and has a unique segment name (or number). The same segment name cannot be used by two different users to refer to two different program entities. Neither can two separate users use two different segment names to refer to (i.e., map into) the same program entity (or physical locations) in main memory.

To accomplish effective memory management, mapping of the logical address space into physical memory space and checking of segment attributes must be performed; furthermore, both should be done with each memory request at run time. To do this, the segmented Z8001 must be used along with at least one external MMU, as shown in Figure 10.11. Since the segmented Z8001 and the MMU, operating together, now issue a 24-bit physical address

---

[21] The Z8000 architecture provides a maximum of up to 31-bit addresses for future implementations.

to memory, the maximum capacity of the physical memory increases, from the previous 8M bytes to 16M bytes. The 8M-byte segmented logical address space can now be mapped anywhere in the 16M-byte physical memory space. The mapping mechanism is implemented on the external MMUs (Figure 10.12).

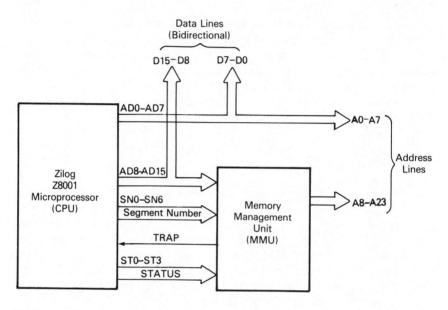

Figure 10.11   The Zilog Z8001 microprocessor CPU with one memory management unit (MMU) [15].

Dynamic mapping of logical into physical address space is done by the MMU. The MMU's management scheme divides physical memory into 256-byte blocks and assigns segments to contiguous blocks. The starting physical address of a segment is always evenly divisible by 256; i.e., its rightmost eight bits are always 0 (zero). The MMU contains the mapping table and the hardware to convert logical addresses into physical addresses. The mapping table in the MMU associates the 7-bit segment number with the starting physical address of the segment in memory, and the 16-bit offset is added to this starting address to obtain the actual 24-bit physical address transmitted to memory. Since each MMU contains a mapping table of only sixty-four entries, it is capable of mapping only a 4M-byte[22] segmented logical address

---

[22] 64 segments of up to 64K bytes each.

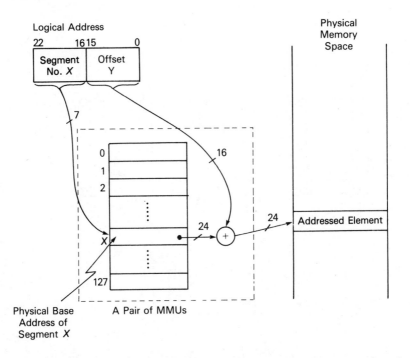

Figure 10.12 Mapping the 8M-byte Zilog Z8001 segmented logical address space into the 16M-byte physical memory space using a pair of external MMUs to convert 23-bit logical addresses into 24-bit physical addresses.

space into the 16M-byte physical memory space. Therefore, to support the mapping of the 8M-byte maximum Z8001 logical address space, two such external MMUs must be used in pair (providing two mapping tables for the total 128 segments), as shown in Figure 10.13. We notice that contiguous (logical) segments need not be mapped into contiguous physical memory (for example, the last segment, 127, has been mapped before segment N) and that segments may also overlap physical memory (for example, segments 1 and 2). The offset is now absolute within a given segment, but since segment base values can be changed within the MMU, relocation of code can be achieved.

Figure 10.14 shows the hardware details of the MMU used to convert 23-bit logical addresses into 24-bit physical addresses. A 24-bit origin or base is associated with each segment. To form a 24-bit physical address, the 16-bit offset is added to the base for the given segment. As seen, the lower half of the 16-bit offset is placed on the address/data bus AD0–AD7 and goes directly to memory. The upper half of the offset AD8–AD15 and the segment number SN0–SN6 both go to the MMU. The MMU uses the 7-bit segment number to

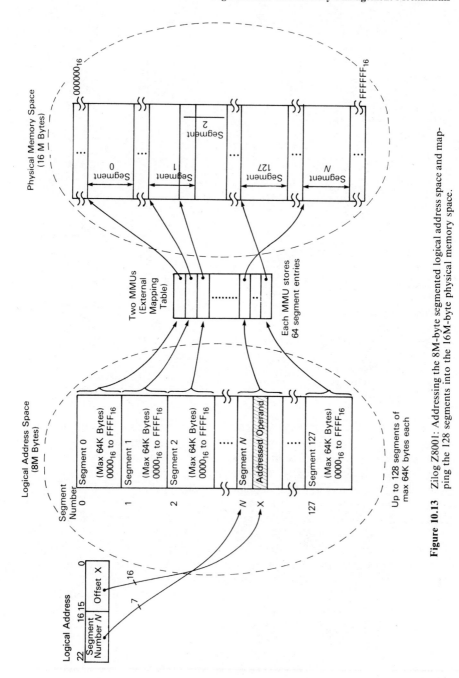

Figure 10.13 Zilog Z8001: Addressing the 8M-byte segmented logical address space and mapping the 128 segments into the 16M-byte physical memory space.

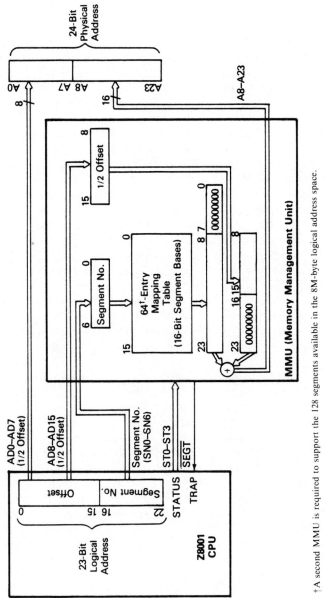

Figure 10.14 Interconnecting a Z8001 with one MMU and the mechanism involved in converting logical to physical addresses.

†A second MMU is required to support the 128 segments available in the 8M-byte logical address space.

point to an entry in its mapping table from which a 16-bit base is extracted. This base is appended at the end with eight 0's (zeros) (because the starting physical address of a segment is always evenly divisible by 256), the upper half of the offset is appended at the beginning with eight 0's (zeros), and the two are added together[23] to form the sixteen most significant bits of the physical address. In operation, since the segment number does not participate in address arithmetic, it is sent out by the Z8001 half a clock cycle ahead of the 16-bit offset address. This compensates for the time delay involved in the use of the MMU; the MMU then functions in parallel with the CPU, having essentially no impact on memory access time.

The MMU also performs *memory protection*. It receives status information[24] from the CPU and outputs to it the segmentation trap signal ($\overline{\text{SEGT}}$). Therefore, besides the mapping table mentioned earlier, each MMU also includes a "protection table" that contains segment attributes (given to each segment when it is initially loaded into the MMU). Segment attributes include: segment size and type (read only, supervisor only, execute only, valid DMA, invalid DMA, etc.). When a memory reference is made, the protection mechanism checks these attributes against the status information it receives from the CPU for the following: user vs supervisor memory areas; code vs data and read/write vs read only; the absence of a valid entry for the segment; and the size of the segment (protecting segments in increments of 256 bytes). When a memory protection violation is detected, a write inhibit line guarantees that memory will not be incorrectly changed, and a trap is generated using the segmentation trap line. The program status is saved automatically on the supervisor stack, and this interrupt to the operating system informs it of the violation.

The MMU is used as an I/O peripheral (i.e., it has chip select, address strobe, data strobe, and read/write lines), and the operating system can set up the MMU tables using twenty-two special I/O instructions executing in the supervisor mode. These privileged instructions use the upper byte of the data bus and allow loading and unloading of the mapping and protection tables of the MMU. Thus, the operating system may dynamically reload the mapping table as tasks are created, suspended, or changed.

Moreover, several MMUs can be used together to accommodate several mapping tables, although only a single pair may be enabled at any one time. When a single pair is used, to choose the correct MMU chip of the pair, the upper-range-select flag in the MMU's mode register is used in connection with bit SN6 of the 7-bit segment number, to indicate that a second MMU is

---

[23]A fast 8-bit adder and eight bits of carry propagation are used.

[24]Using the status information provided with each reference, a number of MMU pairs can be enabled dynamically.

mapping the additional sixty-four segments. The maximum Z8001 configuration can contain six MMU pairs, capable of handling six separate users' 8M-byte logical address spaces. In this case, the multiple-segment-table and normal-mode-select flags in the MMU mode register are used together with the CPU N/$\overline{\text{S}}$ signal (monitored by added special external circuitry) to select the appropriate MMU [17]. Figure 10.15 shows an example of six different programs (or users), each having a separate 8M-byte logical address space, all

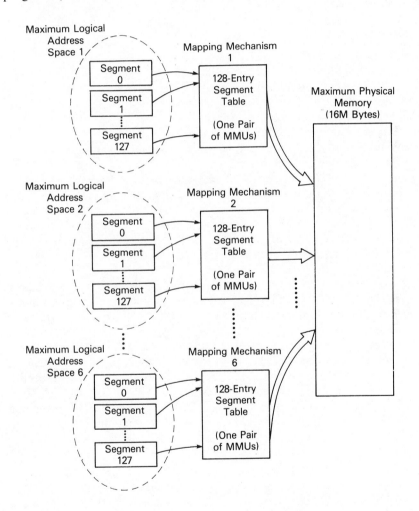

Figure 10.15 Mapping of six separate users into the same 16M-byte physical memory space of the Z8000 [19].

of them mapped into the same physical memory space of size 16M bytes. Only one of these MMU pairs is active at any one time. A method similar to bank switching (utilizing control lines emitted from the CPU) may be used by the operating system to select the appropriate MMU pair[25] (i.e., the appropriate 128-entry segment table that corresponds to the program in control of the system). The operating system can also intervene to load and modify the contents of the segment table of the MMU pair being active, to reflect the current situation.

Intel 8086

In the 8086, the mapping mechanism (segment table and adder) is implemented on the same chip as the CPU. The program instructions do not contain a two-part logical address. As already mentioned, the 8086 processor provides a 20-bit physical address to memory which locates the byte being referenced. Physical addresses range from 00000_{16} to $FFFFF_{16}$. This memory may be considered to be composed of up to sixteen segments, each segment having a *fixed size* of 64K bytes, and beginning at an address which is evenly divisible by 16 (Figure 10.16).

The address objects that the 8086 manipulates (in address arithmetic) are sixteen bits in length. In other words, individual instructions contain a 16-bit *offset address*, that can directly access up to 64K bytes. The 20-bit physical address issued by the CPU is formed by properly combining the 16-bit offset with the 16-bit contents of one of four segment registers contained in the CPU.[26] The four segment registers are the code, data, stack, and extra segment registers.

Before we go further with the 8086 segmentation, let us pause momentarily to describe the function of the four 16-bit CPU segment registers we did not cover in our previous discussions on the 8086 (also see Figure A5.1a in Appendix A5).

The four segment registers that constitute the segment register file (or S group) are called code segment (CS) register, data segment (DS) register, stack segment (SS) register, and extra segment (ES) register. Their respective associated mnemonic words are CODE, DATA, STACK, and EXTRA. Each segment register is used for a specific type of memory operation and contains the *starting physical address*[27] of the corresponding current segment

---

[25]Selecting of only one MMU is also possible.

[26]These four segment registers are in effect used as base or relocation registers.

[27]Actually, since the starting physical address of a segment in memory is always evenly divisible by 16 (which means that its low-order four bits are always 0 (zero)), it is sufficient to have segment registers of only sixteen bits long (instead of twenty bits) and have them contain the high-order sixteen bits of those physical addresses.

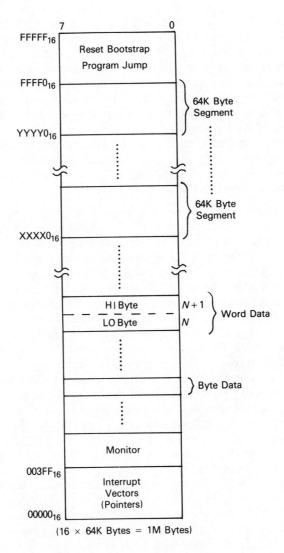

Figure 10.16 Physical memory space of the Intel 8086. *Courtesy Intel Corporation* [6].

type. The contents of the code segment or CS register define the *current code segment* by pointing to its starting physical address in memory; the contents of the data segment or DS register define the *current data segment* by pointing to its starting physical address in memory; the contents of the stack segment of SS register define the *current stack segment* by pointing to its starting physical address in memory; and the contents of the extra segment or ES register define the *current extra segment* by pointing to its starting physical address in memory. The extra segment has no specific use, although it is usually treated as an additional data segment. Assignment of segment space is left to the designer, but for practical systems, the code segment usually begins at location $FFFF0_{16}$ to handle the reset vector (see Figure 5.12, chapter 5). These four segments pointed at by the four segment registers need not be unique, and indeed, they may overlap in memory.

Since a segment register contains a physical pointer to the starting address of a segment, the segment registers are always used in all address calculations. The 8086 uses two ways for specifying which segment register to use in forming the final physical address:

(a) Segment registers are *implicitly addressed* depending on the type of memory operation being executed. All instruction fetches are taken by default to be relative to the CS register, using the instruction pointer (IP) as an offset (indicated by the corresponding arrow at the right side of Figure A5.2 in Appendix 5). All data references except those involving the pointer registers BP or SP are taken by default to be relative to the data segment register DS (indicated by the corresponding arrow at the right side of Figure A5.2 in Appendix 5). Operands in memory may also be addressed indirectly with a base register (the general register BX and the pointer register BP may serve as base registers) and/or index register (the SI or DI serve as index registers) added to an optional 8- or 16-bit displacement constant. When BX is the base, or an index register alone is used, the operand by default resides in the current data segment (i.e., addressing is done relative to the data segment register DS). Those data references which explicitly or implicitly involve the pointer register BP (which may also serve as a base register) or the SP are taken by default to be relative to the stack segment register SS (shown by the corresponding arrow at the right side of Figure A5.2 in Appendix A5), i.e., the operand by default resides in the current stack segment. This includes all PUSH and POP operations, including those caused by CALL operations, interrupts, and RETURN operations. Finally, when both base and index registers are used to address an operand indirectly in memory, the operand by default resides in the segment determined by the base register (BX or BP).

(b) The 8086 also allows a program to *address directly* and access the segment registers. Several 8086 instructions are provided to manipulate the four segment registers. The above-mentioned default segment register for the two types of data references (DS or SS) can be overridden. By preceding the instruction with a special 1-byte prefix, the reference can be forced to be relative to one of the other three segment registers.

Since in any memory reference, both the offset in the instruction and the contents of one of these segment registers are involved, the maximum logical address space that the user sees at any one time is 256K bytes, subdivided into four fixed segments (code, data, stack, and extra) or 64K bytes each. This logical address space is accessed by a logical address composed of an implicit specification of one of the four segment registers and the offset, as shown in Figure 10.5b. The specified segment register contains the starting physical address of the segment; the offset indicates relative location of the addressed element within this segment. Figure 10.17 shows the mapping the 256K-byte logical address space into the 1M-byte physical memory space of the 8086. It can be noticed also that, in this example, the data and stack segments overlap in main memory.

These four segment registers constitute the *segment map* or *mapping table* involved in converting logical addresses into physical addresses. The 8086 provides instructions, so that the programmer can manipulate this mapping table (i.e., load, unload, and modify these segment registers). Therefore, he or she can place a segment anywhere in memory (by modifying its starting address in the corresponding segment register), thus fully utilizing the whole 1M-byte logical address space provided to the programmer.[28]

The 8086 on-chip mapping mechanism combines the 16-bit logical offset from the instruction with the 16-bit contents of a segment register (specified implicitly) to generate the 20-bit physical address required to access any location in the 1M-byte physical memory (Figure 10.18). Figure 10.19 shows the block diagram of the on-chip hardware involved for the logical-to-physical address conversion. This hardware is contained in the upper half of the 8086 CPU in its bus interface unit (BIU). The mapping mechanism uses the 16-bit contents of a segment register, appends to its right end the four 0's (zeros), receives the 16-bit offset-within-segment as specified by the instruction, and adds them properly in a dedicated adder to generate the 20-bit physical address. The delay involved in forming this physical address can be minimized if this segmentation addition for a new memory cycle is performed—when possible—in the last two clock periods of the previous cycle.

Therefore, it is observed that the effective address is a combination of a shorter field in the instruction and other extension bits found in an implied segment register. This approach chosen by the 8086 to implement segmentation results in fewer bits being needed in an instruction to specify addresses. The shorter object code saves memory space and executes faster, since the number of memory references for the program are reduced. On the other

---

[28]Since four segment registers exist, four logical address spaces can be handled, which theoretically increases the total user logical address space to 4M bytes.

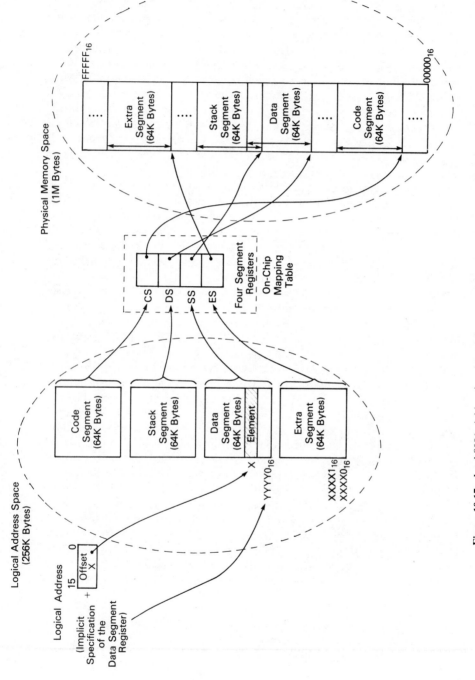

Figure 10.17 Intel 8086: Addressing the maximum 256K-byte segmented logical address space and mapping it into the 1M-byte physical memory space.

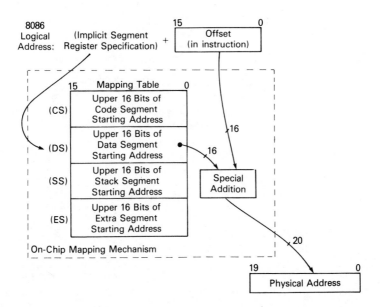

Figure 10.18 Converting an 8086 logical address into a 20-bit physical address.

hand, however, since the mapping table can be under explicit program control and because it has a limited size of only four entries, extra instructions are required to manipulate it (i.e., load and save its registers) when the accessing of more than four segments is needed. These extra instructions will increase the size of the program and the execution time. Furthermore, in the 8086 approach, the four segment registers act as base registers that can have their contents added to the logical offset for each memory operation. This leads to certain inherent problems of physical memory allocation.

Since splitting up the program and data requires assignments of specific segment registers to the various pieces, and since segments start at specific physical memory locations (evenly divisible by 16) and cannot exceed the 64K-bytes limit, any growth or contraction of programs and data structures requires explicit allocation planning by the programmer or compiler. For example, if a program is longer than the maximum segment size of 64K bytes, then crossing this 64K boundary by automatically incrementing the program counter will cause the program to "jump" to its beginning. Instead, software instructions sould be used to change the code segment (CS) register suitably, to get beyond the 64K bytes. The same holds for the data segment (DS) register, which, again, can be under programmer control for accessing data.

Programs that do not load or manipulate segment registers are said to be dynamically relocatable (at run time). If dynamic relocatability is required,

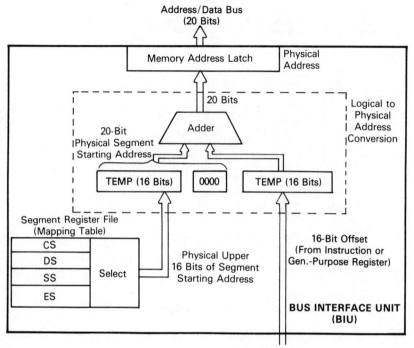

Figure 10.19 The BIU section of the 8086 CPU, containing the logical to physical address conversion mechanism [12].

then the user programs should not be allowed to load or manipulate this mapping table. Since no "privileged" instructions or "supervisor" mode operation are provided in the 8086, dynamic memory allocation to a number of concurrently running programs cannot be undertaken by an operating system that will trap violations and perform context switching in supervisor mode; it is the responsibility of the programmer to trap violations of assigned physical memory space. Instead of performing swapping (a system responsibility), a larger physical memory space can be simulated in the 8086 through overlays (a user responsibility). Thus, the 8086 seems to be aimed primarily at applications in which only one program runs at a time.

Finally, it should be mentioned that the 8086 has no protection mode for memory management.

Motorola 68000

The current implementation of the Motorola 68000 has a maximum directly-accessible logical address space of 16M bytes. This is a large, uniform (non-segmented) logical address space, accessed by a 24-bit single number provided as a logical address within the instruction.[29] If this space is considered as a single 16M-byte segment, then this 24-bit address corresponds to an offset within the segment. The 68000's maximum physical memory space is also 16M bytes.

Motorola is introducing a memory management unit (the MC68451). When the processor is in the user mode, this external memory management unit will manage the large addressing space for the programmer. The memory management unit operates much like the Zilog Z8000's external MMU, i.e., it distinguishes between logical and physical address spaces; its operation is transparent to user software; it can be changed or updated only in the supervisor mode and accessed by any potential bus master; it provides for a variable number of variable sized segments; in addition to segmentation, it supports dynamic memory relocation and protection (through attribute checking) of the 16M-byte 68000 logical address space; and, it supports multi-task operations.

When used with the external MMU, the 68000 can support an efficient true virtual memory system. When the MMU examines a virtual address sent by the CPU and finds that it does not reside in main memory, it sends the bus error ($\overline{\text{BERR}}$) signal to abort to the CPU. This $\overline{\text{BERR}}$ signal causes a very high priority exception, whose processing begins at the next minor cycle (i.e., it does not wait until the instruction is executed as is done, for example, for external interrupts). The processor stacks information needed to determine the system state and, hence, allow recoverability. It then calls the virtual memory operating system routine, which locates the needed data on the auxiliary storage and loads it into main memory. Once the appropriate data has been provided, the system recovers by re-executing the aborted instruction.

The 16-bit offset (logical address within a segment) limitation of both the Intel 8086 and Zilog Z8000, restricts maximum segment size to 64K bytes. A logical module greater than 64K bytes cannot be addressed efficiently, requiring an increased overhead for software development. The large uniform logical address space of the 68000 eliminates this disadvantage of segmentation. Its presently-implemented 24-bit uniform logical address can access up to 16M bytes without segments (or, if considered as offset, it can specify any logical location within one segment whose maximum size is 16M bytes).

---

[29]The Motorola 68000 architecture provides a maximum of up to 32-bit addresses for future implementations.

Intel APX 432

The 32-bit Intel APX 432 also uses a segmented memory, which it calls "structured memory [7]." Each segment can be up to $2^{16} = 64$K bytes long and the system can address up to 2^{24}, or approximately 16 million, segments. It has the necessary hardware-supplied mechanisms to implement a virtual address space whose total size is 2^{40} bytes, that is to say, more than one *trillion* bytes!

An APX 432 instruction may contain up to three logical addesses, each logical address having two parts, a *segment selector* and a *displacement* (see Appendix 8). The segment selector identifies the segment that contains the operand, while the displacement locates the operand within the segment. (This displacement really consists of two subcomponents: a base value and an index value.)

Translating logical to physical addresses is done as before using a segment table containing a *segment descriptor* for each segment. A segment descriptor contains the starting physical address, the length of a segment and the "type" of the segment (data segment or access segment). However, the APX 432 uses a "two-step" mapping process, where *access segments* form the other step (Figure 10.20). Each independently translated program module is supplied at run time with a collection of segment numbers (i.e., values that can be used as pointers to the segment table to select segment descriptors) for all the segments it may need to access during execution (and no others). This collection describes the "access environment" of the module (i.e., the logical address space available to the module), and the entire collection is stored in a set of *access segments*. These access segments contain "access rights" (or access descriptors) only, which are separated from the segment descriptors. Besides access segments, the APX 432 also recognizes data segments (used to contain both instructions and operands). Type information contained in the segment descriptors is checked whenever an attempt is made to access a segment, and, if access is not allowed for that type, a fault occurs.

To avoid the memory access time overhead this two-step mapping procedure (fetch an access descriptor and a segment descriptor) imposes, the APX 432 maintains an internal associative cache to speed up the address translation process. The most recently used segment descriptors, access descriptors, and the addresses of a number of commonly accessed items (e.g., the segment table) are all stored on the chip.

10.5 PAGING

Page-oriented memory systems have also been implemented in some microprocessors (e.g., the National NS16032).

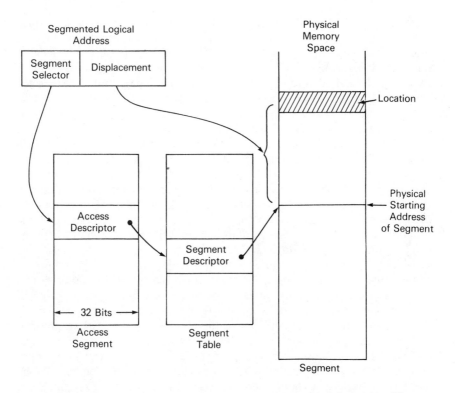

Figure 10.20 Intel APX 432 two-level mapping. *Courtesy Intel Corporation* [7].

To reduce the memory fragmentation problem further, the unit of memory allocation should be reduced further. Paging allows main memory to be allocated in small blocks of equal size, called *page frames*. A *page* (a set of contiguous logical addresses) can fit exactly within a page frame. Since pages are all of equal size, memory space allocation is simplified; while in segmentation enough free memory space is required to fit an incoming large segment of non-uniform size, in paging a much smaller page frame must be found in memory to place an incoming page of fixed size. Like segmentation, paging allows the implementation of a logical address space larger than the installed physical memory. If a referenced page is missing from main memory, it is swapped in from auxiliary storage as a unit [23].

In systems with paging, the subdivision of the program's logical address space into pages is done by the system (not by the programmer or compiler as in segmentation). Again, if the program consists of a number of independently assembled modules, the linking loader properly links them all together to form (as in the base register approach) a large contiguous *linear* logical address space[30] prior to execution, and assigns a specific register of the page table to each page. As in segmentation, the loader cannot do the logical to physical address conversion, since it cannot assume that consecutive program pages will be stored in consecutive main memory page frames. Since the assignment of registers of the page table is done by the loader, the initial program loading is (as in base registers) considered to be a *binding process to logical address space.* Each program page is bound to a specific register of the page table, and once loading is accomplished, every time this program page is executing, it will use the same register; i.e., the page's addresses are now *absolute within the logical address space.*[31] The major drawback of such binding of program pages prior to execution is that it cannot handle efficiently the following cases [11]: (1) the situation in which the set of modules (and therefore, of total pages) required by a program is in part determined by the program itself during the course of execution; (2) the situation in which the length of one or more modules changes radically during execution; and (3) the situation in which two (or more) programs may share a code page in main memory by referring to it using different names (i.e., using different registers in their individual mapping tables). The mapping from logical to physical address space is done during execution using the page table, each page using its assigned register. The contents of the register are the starting physical address of the page frame in main memory containing this program page. Since the program page may be occupying different main memory locations at different instants of the program's total execution time, the *contents* of the register will have to be changed appropriately by the operating system. Since the operating system adjusts the contents of the registers and not the register assignments (as it was done in segmentation), this corresponds to *managing the physical memory space.*

For example, assume that main memory is organized into 2^k page frames, each of 2^d bytes. Also assume that there is a logical address space of 2^n bytes (thus, each byte is addressed with a logical address field of n bits) which is similarly subdivided into pages of 2^d bytes each ($d < n$). In such a paged system, the leftmost $(n - d)$ bits of a logical address are treated as the page number (identifying one of the 2^{n-d} possible pages), and the d rightmost bits as an offset within the indicated page (identifying one of the 2^d bytes in the page). Thus,

---

[30]Since paging is transparent to the programmer, he or she thinks of the logical address as being one number, as contrasted to the two-number logical address of segmentation. Thus, the loader now also allocates logical address space to the various program modules.

[31]Similarly, in the two base register technique discussed earlier, the two program modules are also bound to logical address space, because the particular base register to be used by a module has been assigned before the program has started executing, and this assignment cannot change dynamically at run time.

the page table will consist of 2^{n-d} registers (Figure 10.21a). The translating of a logical address into a physical address is achieved by using the page number as an index to the page table, the contents of which register will either be the address in auxiliary storage[32] (if the page does not presently reside in main memory) or the starting physical address[33] of a page frame of main memory (in which the page resides). In the first case, the operating system will be notified to take the proper action and swap in the page from auxiliary storage; in the second case, the address mapping mechanism will concatenate the contents of the specified register with the d-bit offset of the logical address, to generate the $(k + d)$-bit physical address transmitted to main memory.

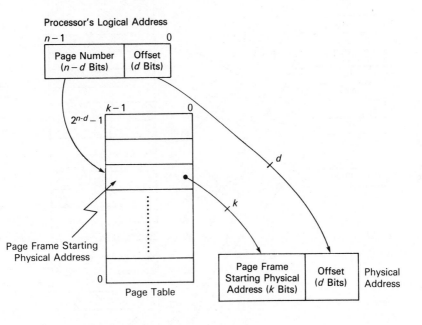

(a)

Figure 10.21 Paging: **(a)** Forming the physical address; **(b)** an example of mapping a 64K-byte paged logical address space (sixteen pages of 4K bytes each) into a 1M-byte physical memory space [9].

---

[32]Similar to the segment tables discussed earlier, each page table entry also contains a "page residence bit," which is zero if the page is not in main memory and one if the page is in main memory.

[33]Actually, it will be the k higher order bits of the address.

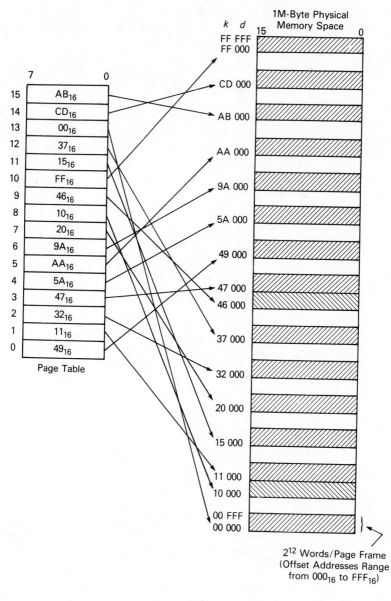

(b)

Figure 10.21   (*Continued*)

The size of the offset field determines the size of each page (in bytes). The size of the page number field determines the number of registers in the page table, and, therefore, the maximum number of pages mapped concurrently. The product of these cannot exceed the system's logical address range. Finally, the number of bits in each register of the page table determines the number of page frames of main memory.

Figure 10.21 b shows an example in which the logical address is sixteen bits long and the linear logical address space is composed of $2^{16} = 64K$ bytes subdivided into $2^4 = 16$ pages of $2^{12} = 4K$ bytes each. This 64K-byte paged logical address space is mapped into a 1M-byte physical memory space which is organized into $2^8 = 256$ page frames of $2^{12} = 4K$ bytes each [9].

The 16-bit NS 16032 microprocessor used in conjunction with the NS 16082 memory management unit, enables the user to construct a page-oriented virtual memory system. The 16M-byte logical address space is divided into 32,768 pages, each page with a fixed size of 512 bytes. The MMU has an on-chip translation buffer that holds the thirty-two most recently referenced logical addresses and their translations.

With paging, the memory fragmentation problem is still not completely eliminated, but its effect is reduced significantly, since it now occurs within the much smaller page frames. As in segmentation, the entire program does not have to be placed into main memory at the time execution begins. Only those pages initially required can be resident. When a reference is made to a page not in main memory, the operating system intervenes to bring it into main memory and properly adjust the page table to reflect the new situation. (This is called *demand paging*.) Again, the page table can, in general, be implemented in hardware or software. However, to have full generality of program and data sharing, and capability of allowing data structures to grow and contract at execution time, paged systems require large logical address spaces, which means having enough address bits in the instruction and a large page table for each program. Finally, as already mentioned, paging does not provide for efficient management of the logical address space.

10.6 SEGMENTATION WITH PAGING

The concepts of paging and segmentation may be combined to have the advantages of both. This combination allows segments to be partitioned further into pages of equal size. Similarly, main memory is partitioned into equal-sized page frames. A segment is placed in main memory by placing each of its pages in a different page frame (not necessarily physically contiguous), and the page is the unit of main memory allocation and of transfer between main and auxiliary memory.

In such implementation, address translation is performed by a two-level table look-up scheme, using both segment tables and page tables. A separate segment table is provided for each program; the table contains an entry for each segment of the program. Since segments are composed of a number of pages, each segment has it own page table. Thus, a separate page table is in turn provided for each entry in the segment table. Figure 10.22a shows the concept of the translation performed using this technique. As in segmentation, the logical address is composed of two numbers: the segment number and the segment offset. The segment offset is subdivided further into a page number and a page offset. The segment number points to a register of the segment table, and the contents of this register point to the page table[34] that

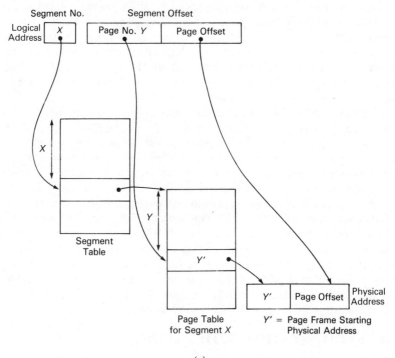

(a)

Figure 10.22   Segmentation with paging: **(a)** A conceptual illustration of translating a logical address to a physical address; **(b)** an example of mapping segment 0 of Figure 10.10 which is now paged into, say, five pages. *From* [21]. *Adapted by permission of McGraw-Hill, New York.*

_____

[34] If this page table is implemented in memory, the register contains the starting physical address of the page table.

corresponds to this segment. The page number field of the logical address identifies the proper register in the selected page table (containing the starting physical address of the page frame in main memory where the page resides, or, if this page is missing, the page's address in auxiliary storage). The contents of this register will in turn be concatenated with the page offset field of the logical address to form the physical address transmitted to memory.

This combination of segmentation with paging provides solutions to both the logical *and* the physical address space allocation problems.

Figure 10.22b shows the mapping of segment 0 of Figure 10.10 which is paged into, say, five pages. The page frames used to store a segment need not be contiguous.

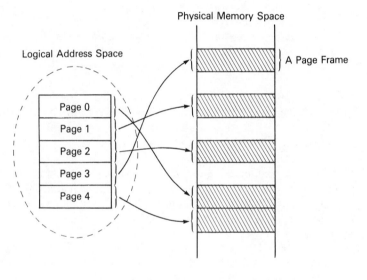

(b)

EXERCISES

10.1 Compare static and dynamic relocation with respect to software properties and required hardware.

10.2 Consider the Zilog Z8000 segmented logical address space of Figure 10.5a. Assume that each segment is 64K bytes long and that the 128 segments are residing in the 8M-byte main memory in an inverse order (i.e., segment 127 in low memory, segment 0 in high memory).

(a) Give the range of real physical addresses (in hexadecimal notation) occupied by segments 0, 50, 100, and 127.
(b) Give the format of the logical address to access main memory location $01AF32_{16}$.
(c) Give the real main memory locations (in hexadecimal notation) accessed by the following logical addresses:
$7F4000_{16}$ $01FFFF_{16}$ $43251A_{16}$

10.3 Assume that the four 64K byte segments code, data, stack and extra, of the Intel 8086 are residing in contiguous areas in the lower portion of main memory:

(a) What are the hexadecimal values contained in the four segment registers of the BIU?
(b) When an instruction accesses directly a data element in location 17320_{16}, what is the value contained in the data segment register, and what is the offset contained in the instruction?

10.4 In Exercise 10.3, what would the contents of the four segment registers of the BIU be if the four 64K-byte segments were placed in contiguous areas in the upper portion of main memory in the order: code segment, stack segment, data segment and extra segment?

10.5 Consider the segmented Zilog Z8000 with a 4M-byte physical main memory and a single MMU. Assume that, at some instant, the first 64 64K-byte segments 0 through 63 are residing in contiguous areas in main memory. Using hexadecimal notation list the contents of the MMU's mapping table.

10.6 Assume that a program is initially loaded into main memory starting at physical location 0100_{16}. At some instant during its execution, the program is removed to auxiliary storage and then returned to main memory (without passing through the loader again), and now occupies memory locations that are FF_{16} higher than those occupied previously. If the system contains only one base register, what are the values contained in the base register before and after this program swapping activity?

10.7 Consider a 16K-byte program composed of a 10K-byte code module and a 6K-byte data module. Also assume that this program is initially loaded into the Intel 8086's main memory starting at physical location 0100_{16}, and that the two modules occupy contiguous areas in memory. At some instant during its execution, the whole 16K-byte program is removed to auxiliary storage and then returned to main memory, the code module occupying memory locations that are 100_{16} higher than those occupied previously, and the data module occupying memory locations that are $3FF_{16}$ higher than those occupied previously.

(a) Which segment registers of the BIU have been affected by the swapping activity?
(b) What are the values contained in these segment registers before and after the swapping activity?
(c) If a dynamic relocation is to be allowed, what are the restrictions imposed on the above program?

10.8 Consider a paged logical address space (composed of thirty-two pages of 2K bytes each) mapped into a 1M-byte physical memory space.

(a) What is the format of the processor's logical address?
(b) What is the length and the width of the page table?
(c) What is the effect on the page table if the physical memory space is reduced by half?

10.9 Repeat Exercise 10.8 where the same logical address space is subdivided into pages of 1K byte each.

REFERENCES AND BIBLIOGRAPHY

[1] Bal, S., et al, "Bilingual 16-bit μP Summons Large-Scale Computer Power," *Electronic Design*, 2, January 18, 1980, pp. 66–70.

[2] Bensoussan, A., et al, "The MULTICS Virtual Memory," *Proceedings of the Second ACM Symposium on Operating Systems Principles*, Princeton, NJ, October 20–22, 1969, pp. 30–42.

[3] Daley, R.C. and J.B. Dennis, "Virtual Memory, Processes, and Sharing in MULTICS," *Communications of the ACM*, vol. 11, no. 5, May 1968, pp. 306–12.

[4] Denning, P.J., "The Working Set Model for Program Behavior," *Communications of the ACM*, vol. 11, no. 5, May 1968.

[5] Denning, P.J., "Virtual Memory," *Computing Surveys*, vol. 2, no. 3, September 1970, pp. 153–89. Copyright 1970, Association for Computing Machinery, Inc.

[6] Intel Corporation, *The 8086 Family User's Manual*, (9800722-03), Santa Clara, CA, 1979.

[7] Intel Corporation, *Introduction to the iAPX 432 Architecture*, (171821-001), Santa Clara, CA 1981.

[8] Lavi, Y., et al, "16-Bit Microprocessor Enters Virtual Memory Domain," *Electronics*, April 24, 1980, pp. 123–29.

[9] Le Mair, I., "Indexed Mapping Extends Microprocessor Addressing Range," *Computer Design*, August 1980, pp. 111–18.

[10] Mateosian, R., "Segmentation Advances μC Memory Addressing," *Electronic Design*, February 19, 1981, pp. 155–61.

[11] McGee, W.C., "On Dynamic Program Relocation," *IBM Systems Journal*, vol. 4, no. 3, 1965, pp. 184–99.

[12] Morse, S.P., W.B. Pohlam, and B.W. Ravenel, "The Intel 8086 Microprocessor: A 16-bit Evolution of the 8080," *Computer*, June 1978, pp. 18–26.

[13] Motorola, Incorporated, *16-Bit Microprocessing Unit*, (ADI-814-R1), Austin, TX, 1980.

[14] Parmelee, R.P., et al, "Virtual Storage and Virtual Machine Concepts," *IBM Systems Journal*. no. 2, 1972, pp. 99–130.

[15] Peuto, B.L., "Architecture of a New Microprocessor," *Computer*, February 1979, pp. 10–21.

[16] Randell, B. and C.J. Kuehner, "Dynamic Storage Allocation Systems," *Communications of the ACM*, vol. 11, no. 5, May 1968, pp. 297–306.

[17] Roloff, J.J., "Managing Memory to Unloose the Full Power of Microprocessors" *Electronics*, April 10, 1980, pp. 130–34.

[18] Sams, B.M., "The Case of Dynamic Storage Allocation," *Communications of the ACM*, vol. 4, no. 10, October 1961, pp. 417–18.

[19] Stevenson, D., "Memory Management Rescues 16-bit μPs from Demands of Multiple Users' Tasks," *Electronic Design*, 1, January 4, 1980, pp. 112–16.

[20] Stritter, E. and T. Gunter, "A Microprocessor Architecture for a Changing World: The Motorola 68000," *Computer*, February 1979, pp. 43–51.

[21] Watson, R.W., *Timesharing System Design Concepts*, New York: McGraw-Hill, 1970.

[22] Wilkes, M.V., *Time-Sharing Computer Systems*, London: McDonald, 1968.

[23] Zaks, R., *Microprocessors from Chips to Systems*, Berkeley, CA: SYBEX, Inc. 1977.

[24] Zilog, Incorporated, *Z8000 Technical Manual*, Cupertino, CA, 1979.

Chapter 11

BIT-SLICED MICROPROCESSOR ARCHITECTURE

11.1 INTRODUCTION

This last chapter covers multiple-chip *bipolar* microprocessors having *bit-sliced architectures.*

Bit-sliced microprocessors differ from conventional MOS microprocessors primarily in the architectural philosophy of constructing the CPU. In most of the conventional microprocessors, both the data processing function and the control function of the CPU are manufactured together on the same chip. In bit-sliced microprocessors, these two functions are realized on a number of separate chips. The data processing function is realized using a number of similar CPU slices, while the control function is realized using (at least) a microprogram memory and a microprogram sequencer. While conventional microprocessors have predefined and unchangeable word lengths, architectures, and instruction sets, this is not true in the bit-sliced microprocessors. These chips can be configured in various ways to provide a wide variety of system architectures with various word lengths and instruction set capabilities. Since they are manufactured with bipolar technology, bit-sliced microprocessor systems have effective speeds that are greater—by at least a factor of 5—than those of systems based on conventional MOS microprocessors. Furthermore, since these microprocessors are *user-microprogrammable*, the system designer can design a flexible system and overcome most of the deficiencies of a conventional MOS microprocessor (such as limited word lengths).

Bit-sliced microprocessors may be used in a number of applications. One is to emulate the machine language (i.e., perform some or all instructions) of other existing computers. In this case, the designer can define a number of microroutines (residing in the microprogram memory), each microroutine realizing one machine language instruction (referred to here as a "macroinstruction") of the target emulated machine. Another application is to implement high-level languages directly. The designer can choose the language to be interpreted by defining a proper instruction set for the system under design. In other cases, bit-sliced microprocessors represent the most appropriate solution for replacing customized rigid hardwired designs with a more flexible system. For some applications in which the special functions and high throughput rates required cannot be met by conventional MOS microprocessors, bipolar bit-sliced designs may represent the only practical alternative. Such noticeable application areas include signal processors (digital filtering, correlation, FFT, etc.), real-time systems, specialized high-speed controllers (in process control or for units such as disks, video, and graphics displays), etc. Finally, another major area where these devices may have a tremendous impact is in the realization of algorithms and designs that are susceptible to parallel processing.

Using bit-sliced devices allows the designer to optimize the system's architecture and processing capabilities for the unique requirements of the application. At the same time, the system becomes much more flexible. Changing some microroutines in the microprogram memory, or substituting another microprogram memory, alters the functional complexity of the machine; it now behaves in an entirely new fashion—i.e., executes a completely different set of macroinstructions, has different architecture, and can be tailored to specific types of applications. Since these devices are also user-microprogrammable, on-site improvements, enhancements or alterations of the system's architecture and capabilities are also possible.

To achieve all these advantages, however, the design engineer must have a proper mixture of hardware *and* software skills required for firmware development, a clear understanding of the tradeoffs among various system architectures, and the ability to function in the microprogramming sphere as well. Within any microprogrammed digital machine, there are at least two levels of control and two levels of programming to be considered: the macro level and the micro level. The bit-sliced system designer quite often has to handle both the definition of the macroinstruction set and its implementation as a set of microprograms. Working with bit-sliced microprocessors is more difficult and time-consuming than working with conventional processors. Microinstructions are more complicated than macroinstructions, and therefore, microcoding takes longer. Furthermore, the microprogramming aids presently available are much poorer than the aids for conventional software. Still, this user-generation of microinstructions is one of the features which enhances the performance aspects of the bit-sliced approach.

Section 11.2 outlines the architecture of a bit-sliced microprocessor. The next three sections, 11.3, 11.4, and 11.5, examine in more detail the major components of this architecture; i.e., the data processing component configured as a cascade of "CPU slices," the microprogram sequencer which controls the execution of microinstructions (defining the control signals of the system), and the microprogram memory that contains these microinstructions. To help understand how to define such microinstructions, section 11.6 presents a simple microprogrammed system and gives an example of the microinstructions required to execute a simple macroinstruction. The chapter concludes by listing a number of design aids available for designing bit-sliced systems and the advantages/disadvantages of microprogrammable bit-sliced microprocessors.

11.2 BIT-SLICED ARCHITECTURE

For the best utilization of microprogrammable bit-sliced devices, the design engineer needs to have a clear understanding of a number of terms and concepts such as "control store," "sequencer," "pipelining," "CPU slices," "microprogramming" (horizontal, encoded, polyphase), and "microinstruction fields." Since the presently available system support software for firmware development is rather poor, the design engineer is also required to have a detailed knowledge of architectural organization and timing requirements. In putting together the microprogram instructions, most of the designer's effort is toward direct control of the specific hardware elements that bind him with timing restrictions, propagation delays, and the like. The techniques needed for programmed logic design with microprogrammable bit-sliced devices usually are implemented in order to extend the level of programmability one level down from that of machine language.

Most microprogrammable bit-sliced systems have the basic functional block diagram shown in Figure 11.1 [6]. Unlike the MOS-type single-chip CPU, the microprogrammable bit-sliced CPU uses bipolar Schottky technology. Because of internal functional complexity and the current limitations on chip complexity, pin numbers, and chip size possible with bipolar technologies, CPU is implemented on a multi-chip basis. Two commonly used commercial microprogrammable bit-sliced microcomputers, the Intel 3000 and AMD 2900 series, are shown in Figure 11.2.

The two major components of the control section are the *microprogram memory* and the *microprogram sequencer.* The microprocessor fetches macroinstructions from the system's main memory under the direction of microinstructions read from its microprogram memory. The operation code of the macroinstruction is interpreted by the microprogram sequencer (i.e., mapped into a microprogram memory address), and then executed as a series of microinstructions. The operand portion of the macroinstruction is routed to the bit-sliced processing section of the microprocessor to be used either in computations or in main memory address manipulation. Thus, while the system's main memory contains macroprograms (application programs), the microprogram memory of the control section contains microprograms that

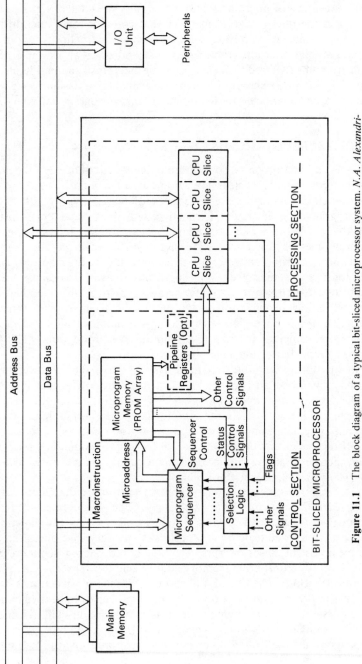

Figure 11.1   The block diagram of a typical bit-sliced microprocessor system. *N.A. Alexandridis, "Bit-sliced Microprocessor Architecture," Computer, June 1978, p. 61. ©1978 IEEE, New York.*

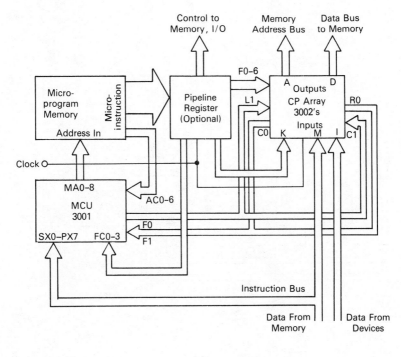

Figure 11.2 Two commercial microprogrammable bit-sliced microcomputers: **(a)** the Intel 3000 series and **(b)** the AMD 2900 series *From* [6], *p. 59. ©1978 IEEE, New York.*

define the realized microprocessor. The microprogram memory, also viewed as a programmable finite-state machine, generates control pulses timed to control the rest of the system. The state of its output control lines is represented by microinstructions stored in it. The microprogram sequencer is the unit that determines the microprogram memory inputs, based on various proper machine status bits, and on some feedback it receives from the microprogram memory itself.

The data processing section is composed of a number of cascaded CPU *slices*.[1] Each slice represents a vertical partition of the data processing section that includes a slice of the ALU and its supporting input and output registers. All these slices operate on their input operands in parallel under proper control of microinstructions.

---

[1]Sometimes called RALUs (register arithmetic logic units).

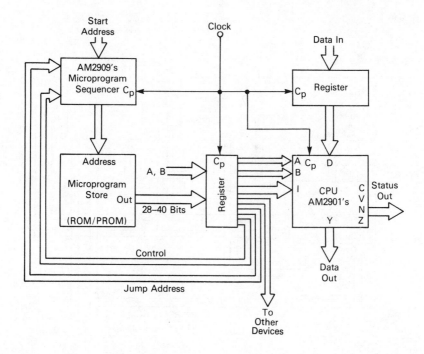

Figure 11.2 Two commercial microprogrammable bit-sliced microcomputers: **(b)** the AMD 2900
series. *From* [6], *p. 59. ©1978 IEEE, New York.*

In some cases *pipelined registers*, shown in Figure 11.1, may also be inserted
between the microprogram memory and the CPU slices to improve overall
system performance and speed by overlapping the microinstruction execution
with the fetching of the next microinstruction(s).

11.3 THE DATA PROCESSING SECTION

Arithmetic (usually including address arithmetic) and logic operations are all
carried out in the data processing section of the CPU.

A past practice of implementing a modular ALU involved cascading a
number of 74181 4-bit parallel adders capable of performing arithmetic and
logic functions at the desired operand length. Some extra signals from the
ALU were also required to perform either the ripple-carry operation or the
improved "carry look-ahead" using the 74182 carry look-ahead device. The
next step of improvement involved using the 74281 ALU, which also contains
an accumulator and a shift matrix.

Today, a vertically partitioned processing section may be implemented by cascading a number of equal-length and functionally equivalent LSI chips, called "CPU slices" (Figure 11.3). Each slice can by itself replace a large number of MSI devices previously used to perform the same functions.

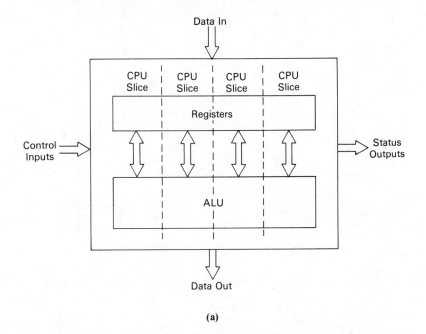

(a)

Figure 11.3 (a) A vertically partitioned processing section made out of a number of cascaded CPU slices and (b) the general block diagram of a slice *From* [6], *p. 73. ©1978 IEEE, New York.*

In general, a typical CPU slice contains some or all of the following: an ALU, a multiple (one to sixteen) word register file with one or two ports[2] (which may hold operands and temporary data, or may receive results of operations), a shifter,[3] attributes for data I/O (either one set of lines for input and one set of lines for output, or multiple sets of input lines internally

---

[2]The two-port structure allows the contents of two registers to be output at once. Input is, of course, allowed to only one register at a time.

[3]The shifter unit may be attached to the output of the ALU, thus providing a postshift capability, or to the input of the ALU to provide a preshift capability, or it may be independent of the ALU to facilitate parallel operation.

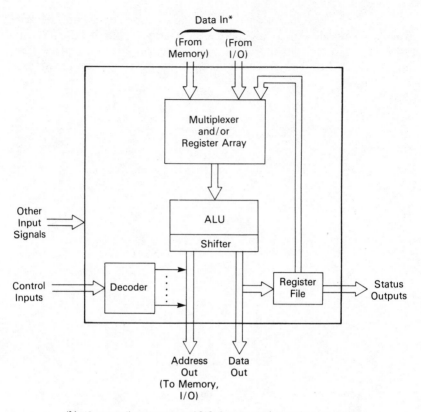

(b)   *In some slices, memory and I/O data are moving on the same data bus.

Figure 11.3   **(b)** The general block diagram of a slice. *From* [6], *p. 73.* ©*1978 IEEE, New York.*

multiplexed and multiple sets of output lines[4]), control inputs (which may be microinstruction control bits decoded internally in the slice), and status-bit outputs. A CPU slice may also allow detection of internal conditions such as overflow, zero, and sign, and contain the necessary function bus decoder logic to control the ALU and register transfers. Use of a vertically sliced instead of a horizontally partitioned processing section requires fewer data movements, fewer and often narrower microinstructions, and less hardware [23,29].

---

[4]In some devices the multiplexing of the output lines is also done by an internal multiplexer on the chip.

Figure 11.4 shows the block diagrams of two common bipolar slices, the 2-bit Intel 3002 and the 4-bit Am2901, and Table 11.1 lists some commercially available bipolar slices.

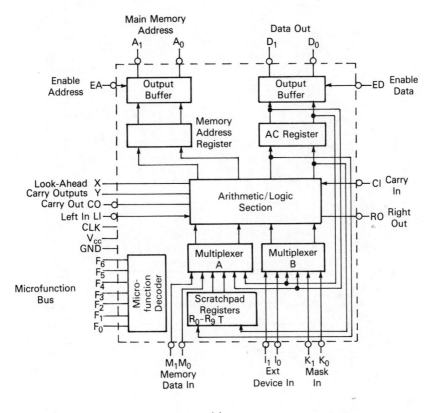

(a)

Figure 11.4 The block diagrams of two commercially available CPU slices: **(a)** the 2-bit Intel 3002 and **(b)** the 4-bit Am2901. *From* [6], *p. 74.* © *1978 IEEE, New York.*

A CPU slice can handle two or four bits (the 4-bit slices are becoming almost a standard), and a number of slices can be cascaded to form a wider processing unit to handle increased word lengths. Thus, microprocessors can be built now that can handle non-conventional word lengths (e.g., 24, 32, 48 bits, etc.). Such a cascaded arrangement usually requires all similar control lines from each slice to connect in parallel and the carry output of one chip to connect to the carry input of the next. The arithmetic or logical operations and the sources and destinations for the ALU are the same for all slices. The input

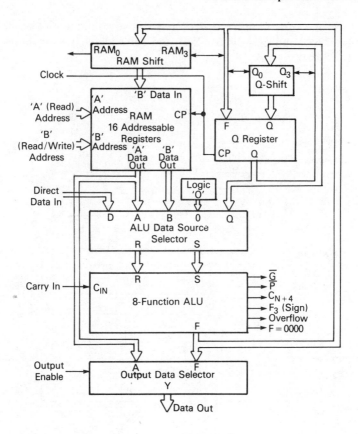

Figure 11.4 The block diagrams of two commercially available CPU slices: **(b)** the 4-bit AM2901.
From [6], *p. 74.* ©*1978 IEEE, New York.*

Table 11.1 Commercially available LSI bipolar slices *From* [6], *p. 74,* © *1978 IEEE, New York.*

- AMD 2901, 2903 (second-sourced by Raytheon, MMI, National, Signetics) (4-bit slice)
- INTEL 3002 (second-sourced by Signetics) (2-bit slice)
- SIGNETICS 2901-1 (4-bit slice), 3002 (2-bit slice)
- MONOLITHIC MEMORIES 6701 (4-bit slice)
- TEXAS INSTRUMENTS 74S481, SBP-0400 (4-bit slice)
- FAIRCHILD 9405A (4-bit slice,) 100220 (8-bit slice)
- MOTOROLA 10800 (4-bit slice)
- RCA 4057 (4-bit slice)
- RAYTHEON 2901/2903, RP16 (4-bit slice)
- NATIONAL GPC/P (4-bit slice)

data bus is divided into sections of the proper width when entering the processor slices, and the output data bus is recombined when exiting the slices. Figure 11.5, shows an implementation using four 4-bit AMD 2903 slices operating in parallel and one AMD 2902 carry lookahead to form a 16-bit processing unit [24].

11.4 MICROPROGRAM SEQUENCERS

Generally, the control section of a microprocessor gives the digital machine its "personality" and presents a rather complex design, since the designer has many alternatives from which to choose for the system's specific implementation. The control section issues appropriate control signals to control the parallel operation of the cascaded CPU slices and is usually implemented using microprogramming techniques.

A simple microprogrammed control section is shown in Figure 11.6. Typically it consists of a microprogram memory (also called microprogram control memory or control store) with its microprogram address register (MMAR) and microinstruction register (MIR), a microprogram sequencer (also called microprogram control unit or controller), and some remaining circuitry such as selection logic and pipeline registers. Each of these components is usually manufactured on a separate chip. The microprogram memory contains the microinstructions, which specify the steps through which the machine sequences and controls the parallel operation of the functionally equivalent slices of the processing section. The microprogram memory is discussed further in section 11.5.

The most important aspect of a control section is the structure of its microprogram sequencer, since this structure is what determines the general characteristics of the control section and the available sequencing mechanisms used for implementing modularity in microprograms. The microprogram sequencer provides the macroinstruction decode logic and determines the "next microaddress" generation scheme for sequencing the microprograms [30,22]. As far as hardware is concerned, the sequencer may be as simple as a single register or as complex as a special LSI device, the latter being the case for bit-sliced microprocessors. Before we continue with alternative implementations for the microprogram sequencer, let us first discuss possible ways of sequencing microinstructions.

11.4.1 Microinstruction Sequencing

The two aspects of microinstruction sequencing have to do with timing of microinstruction fetches (serial or parallel, depending upon the non-overlap or complete overlap between the execution of the current microinstruction and the fetching of the next microinstruction) and with methods used to take

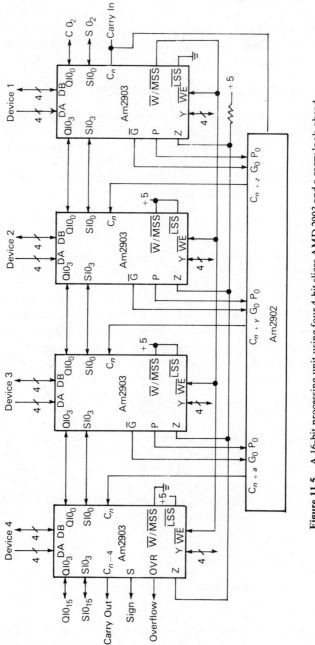

Figure 11.5   A 16-bit processing unit using four 4-bit slices AMD 2903 and a carry look-ahead AMD 2902. *Copyright © 1979 Advanced Micro Devices, Inc. Reprinted with permission of copyright owner. All rights reserved.*

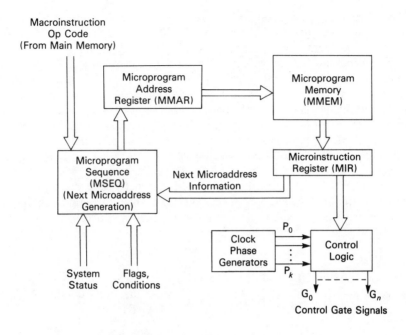

Figure 11.6   Simple microprogrammed implementation of the control function. *N.A. Alexandridis, "Control, Timing, and System Signals,"* Fundamentals Handbook of Electrical and Computer Engineering III: Computer Hardware, Software and Applications, *ed. S.S.L. Chang,* © *1983, p. 93. Reprinted by permission of John Wiley & Sons, Inc., New York.*

care of conditional branch situations in the microprogram and generate next microprogram memory addresses.

Similar to fetching macroinstruction from main memory, using the microprogram memory is also an operation performed on a cycle time, called *control store cycle time* or *control cycle* of the microprogrammed control section. It corresponds to the time required to transfer the next microinstruction address to the microprogram memory address register (MMAR), plus the time required for the microinstruction to be read out into the microinstruction register (MIR), i.e., the access time. During each *microcycle*, a microinstruction is fetched from microprogram memory and the microoperations[5] it specifies are then executed. Under this description, then, a two-phase clock (or two-phase microcycle) would suffice for the microprogrammed control sec-

---

[5]Also called "micro-orders."

tion. During the first phase, the sequencer transfers the address of the next microinstruction to MMAR, and, at the same time, the microoperations activated by the microinstruction control bits in the MIR register are carried out. During the second phase, the next microinstruction is read out of microprogram memory into register MIR. However, since some microoperations may be of the conditional type, and since this condition may not be known to the sequencer until the microoperations are executed in the processing section, the next microinstruction address transfer to MMAR and the execution of the microoperations cannot occur in the same clock phase. Therefore, a third phase is used for the microcycle. During the first phase, the address of the next microinstruction is transferred to MMAR; during the second phase the microinstruction is read into MIR; and during the third phase, the microinstruction is executed (i.e., the respective microoperations are performed). The events involved during each microcycle are shown in Figure 11.7 and are as follows:

Previous Microcycle $\begin{cases}\end{cases}$ Phase P_2: MIR $\leftarrow$ (MMAR)   Fetch next microinstruction, from location pointed at by MMAR.

Current Microcycle $\begin{cases}\end{cases}$ Phase P_0:   Execute microinstruction.

Phase P_1: MMAR $\leftarrow$ Next microinstruction address   (Conditions have been examined.) The microprogram sequencer sends next microinstruction address to MMAR.

This is *serial* microinstruction sequencing, in which the next microinstruction is not fetched from microprogram memory before the current microinstruction has completed its execution. *Parallel* microinstruction sequencing, on the other hand, allows the next microinstruction fetching to be done concurrently with the execution of the current microinstruction (Figure 11.8a). This of course yields speed advantages, and parallel implementation runs almost twice as fast as the serial implementation. The parallel case, however, presents some problems, the most important one having to do with treating conditional branches properly. The microcycle for the next microinstruction cannot start before the current microinstruction has been executed (or its op code decoded) and the correct next microinstruction address has been extracted. To deal with such problems of conditional branches several techniques are available, one of which is the *serial-parallel* implementation shown in Figure 11.8b. Here, the microcycle for the next microinstruction

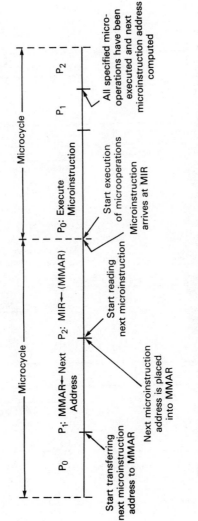

Figure 11.7 Events involved during a microcycle. *From [7], p. 91. Reprinted by permission of John Wiley & Sons, Inc., New York.*

follows the execution of the current microinstruction, if the current microinstruction contains a conditional branch microoperation.

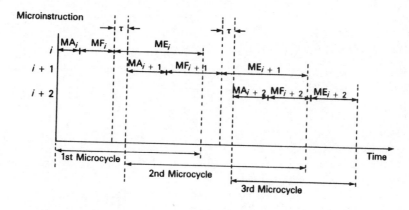

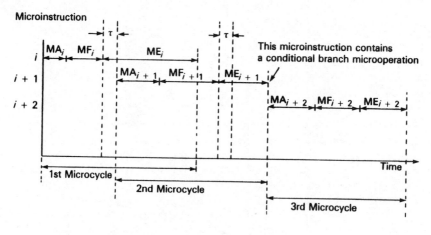

(b)

where: MA = Transfer microinstruction address to MMAR.
         MF = Fetch microinstruction into MIR.
         ME = Execute microinstruction.
         τ — Time to decode microinstruction op code. (to ensure no conditional branches).

Figure 11.8   Microinstruction sequencing: **(a)** Parallel implementation. **(b)** Combined serial-parallel implementation, where microinstruction $i + 1$ contains a conditional branch microoperation. *From* [7], *p. 95. Reprinted by permission of John Wiley & Sons, Inc., New York.*

11.4.2 Microprogram Sequencer Implementations

In this section we present several ways of implementing the microprogram sequencer. We start off using MSI components and then present the LSI sequencers most commonly found in bit-sliced microprocessor inplementations.

Implementations Using MSI Components

Microprogram sequencers may be implemented for simple sequential control with no branching capabilities. In one of the simplest forms of the microprogram sequencer, all that is required to progress successively through the microinstructions is a microprogram address counter (Figure 11.9a). The macroinstruction op code from main memory goes directly into the microprogram address counter. The address of the next microinstruction is selected simply by incrementing the microprogram address counter by one on each clock cycle. The microinstruction itself does not contain a "next address" field. This counter technique permits only sequential microcontrol; it is not very flexible and it provides no means for altering—conditionally or unconditionally—the established flow of control.

Microprogram sequencers can be used for sequencing with branching capabilities, if they may load a new number that is present on their data input lines. For example, for each microinstruction, the counter shown in Figure 11.9a may be loaded with the next address from a field in the microinstruction which is currently executing. The microinstructions now become wider, but they offer additional capability for performing unconditional jumps in the microprogram.

In most situations, however, microprogram sequencers are required also to facilitate conditional branching capabilities in the microprogram. The microprogram sequencer will have more decision-making capability, if it can examine—before branching—condition or status signals which originate from various parts within the system. There are many possible alternative implementations available. Only one of them is shown in Figure 11.9b. This microprogram sequencer is composed of a decoder and a decision logic box. The decoder decodes the condition code field bits of the microinstruction. The decision logic combines the decoder outputs and the condition signals originating from various parts of the system, and decides whether it should advance to the next microinstruction in the microprogram (i.e., it signals the +1 input of the microprogram memory address counter to advance by one), or branch to the address specified by the current microinstruction (by enabling the LD input of the microprogram memory address counter to parallel-load the next address).

For example, if the branch condition code field of the microinstruction is three bits wide, then the decoder specifies eight condition codes. Assume that

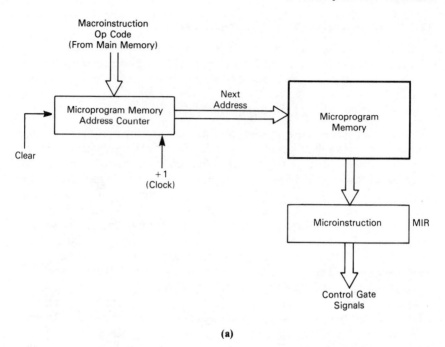

Figure 11.9 Alternative implementations of microprogram sequencers: (a) using a microprogram address counter. *From [7], p. 97. Reprinted by permission of John Wiley & Sons, Inc., New York.*

a branch condition code field having the values of 000, 001, and 010 indicates normal advancing to the next microinstruction; a condition code of 011 indicates a branch if ACC = 0; a code of 100 indicates a branch if B = 0; a 101 indicates branch if PC = 0; and codes 110 or 111 indicate a branch if ACC overflows. Then, the details of the microprogram sequencer would be as shown in Figure 11.9c.

Figure 11.10 shows representative examples of microprogram sequencing involving conditional branching techniques within the same microprogram page. In Figure 11.10a the INC microinstruction executed in location (X) is used to sequence the microprogram address register serially by 1. When the "test" condition examined by BRT is true, the branch is taken. The branch address is supplied via the next address field of the microinstruction in location (X + 1). In this example the branch address is (Y). In its Algol-type equivalent, the /MX notation indicates the microinstruction which is to be performed in parallel with the specified test [22,13]. Thus, in Figure 11.10a

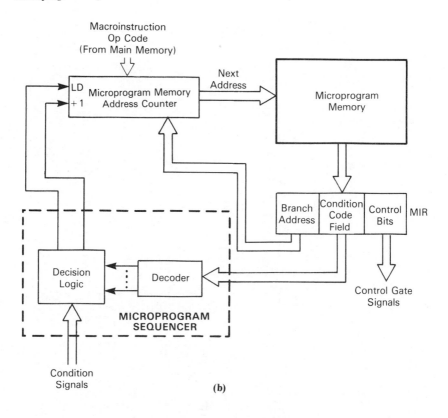

Figure 11.9 Alternative implementations of microprogram sequencers: **(b)** providing conditional branching capability based on external condition signals. *From* [7], *p. 97. Reprinted by permission of John Wiley & Sons, Inc., New York.*

microinstruction M0 must be able to reach M1 (if A is true) or M2 (if not) in the next clock cycle. This can be accomplished by placing the address of M1 (the Y) in the next address field of M0 and placing microinstruction M2 immediately after M0 (in location X + 2). M3 is the successor to the selection sequence (M0 − M2). The analogy holds for Figure 11.10b. For example, microinstruction M1 is in (Y) and, with its next address field, points to address (Z) of microinstruction M2. Similarly, M4 is in (X + 2), while M6 is in (X + 3).

The above examples represent implementations of conditional branching using the so-called "binary branching" technique. This technique is prohibitively expensive for complex conditions, since it requires the use of many successive conditional branches.

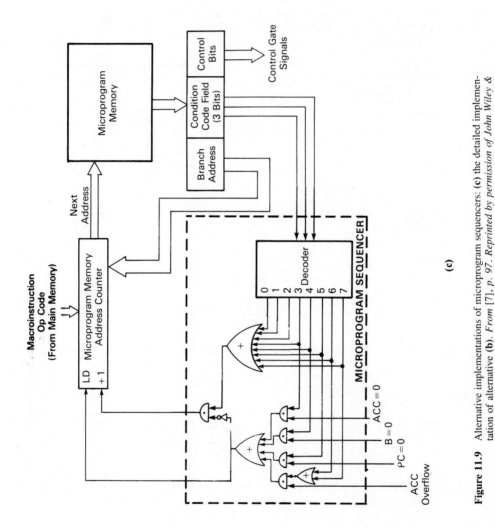

(c)

Figure 11.9 Alternative implementations of microprogram sequencers: **(c)** the detailed implementation of alternative **(b)**. *From [7], p. 97. Reprinted by permission of John Wiley & Sons, Inc., New York.*

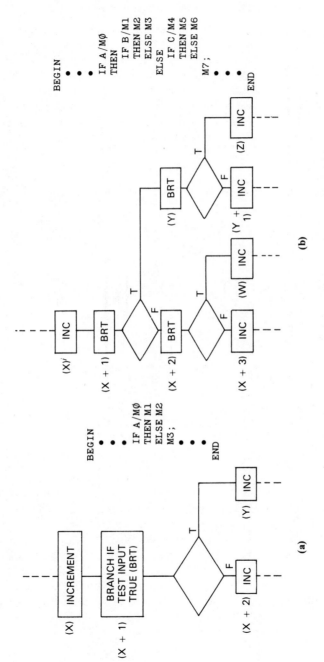

Figure 11.10 The flowcharts and their respective Algol-type structures showing two conditional branching examples: **(a)** single test and conditional branch and **(b)** more complex nested conditional branches. *D. R. Hawk and D. M. Robinson, "A Microinstruction Sequencer and Language Package for Structured Microprogramming,"* Proc. of the MICRO 8. © *1975, IEEE, New York.*

Commercial LSI Microprogram Sequencers

Today's commercial LSI microprogram sequencers have all the above-mentioned capabilities, and much more. They receive many more control signals and system status bits, and they have everything required for address-incrementing functions and complex multi-way conditional microbranching. They also have on-chip loop counters for repeated microprogram loops, and may also include on-chip pushdown stacks and pointers, a useful feature for saving the return-to addresses of nested microsubroutines. A typical block diagram of a commercial sequencer is shown in Figure 11.11.

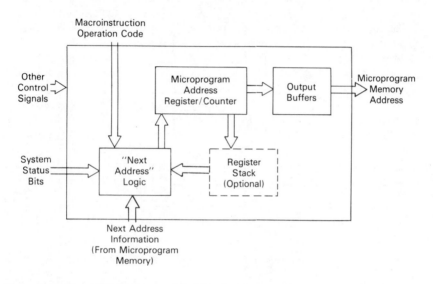

Figure 11.11   General block diagram of the LSI microprogram sequencer *From* [6], *p.71.* © *1978 IEEE, New York.*

The main purpose of any microprogram sequencer is to present an address to the microprogram memory so that a microinstruction may be fetched and executed. The next address logic part of the sequencer determines the specific address source to be loaded into the microprogram address register/counter. The choice of the address source is guided by the next address information bits the sequencer receives, and these bits can generally specify one of the following: increment, conditional skip next instruction, conditional branch to a microsubroutine, push/pop the register stack, and so on. Most of the LSI sequencers include an on-chip register stack (usually four levels deep) operating in a last-in, first-out fashion. This stack is used as a temporary storage of addresses during microprogram looping or microsubroutine branching, operating under PUSH and POP type commands. Finally, an address-output latch lies in the interface region between the microprogram sequencer and the microprogram memory.

Available LSI microprogram sequencers may be divided into two general categories—those with a fixed number of memory locations within their addressing capability, and those which are cascadable bit-sliced devices [12]. Members of the first category are the Intel 3001 (Figure 11.12a, second-sourced by Signetics), the M onolithic Memories 67110, the Signetics 8X02 (Figure 11.12b), and the Fairchild 9408. Bit-sliced microprogram sequencers are usually four bits wide; representative examples are the advanced micro devices 2909 and 2911[6] (Figure 11.12c second-sourced by Raytheon) and the Texas Instruments 74S482. In the fixed-address category, the Intel 3001 and Monolithic Memories 67110 can create a 9-bit address capable of directly accessing 512 words of microprogram memory, whereas the Signetics 8X02 and Fairchild 9408 can generate a 10-bit address capable of accessing 1024 words of microprogram memory. To extend their memory-access range, these fixed-address sequencers require additional circuits and paging techniques. The 4-bit wide bit-sliced sequencers (2909/2911, 74S482) are cascadable, thus allowing two such chips to address up to 256 words of microprogram memory, three chips to address up to 4096 words, and so on. This expandability feature becomes quite important, since microprogram memories (and the control programs they contain) are becoming larger all the time. Newer sequencers from Advanced Micro Devices are the 2910 (12-bit fixed-address) and the 2930/2931 (4-bit slices).

Another difference among the available sequencers is that some of them (3001, 8X02, 67110, 9408, and 74S482) provide on-chip address-output latches, while others (2909/2911) do not have such latches. The 2909/2911 allow more flexibility but require the designer to add his or her own latches. The on-chip address-output latches allow the designer to use a pipelining technique which may lead to faster operation, although it makes microprogramming more difficult.

Some of these devices exhibit unusual addressing schemes. The Intel 3001 microprogram sequencer, for example, works with a microprogram address space organized as an n-dimensional array. Although this may succeed in minimizing the microinstruction width and reducing the next-address logic, it results in some loss of addressing capability and an increase in microprogram-

---

[6]The Am2911 is an identical device to the Am2909, except that the four OR inputs are removed and the D and R inputs are tied together. The Am2911 is in a 20-pin package, whereas the Am2909 is in a 28-pin package.

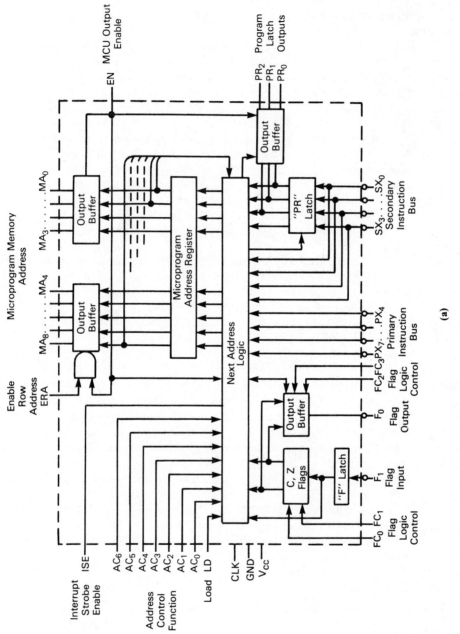

(a)

Figure 11.12 Examples of commercial LSI microprogram sequencers: **(a)** Intel 3001. *From* [6], *p. 72.* ©*1978 IEEE, New York.*

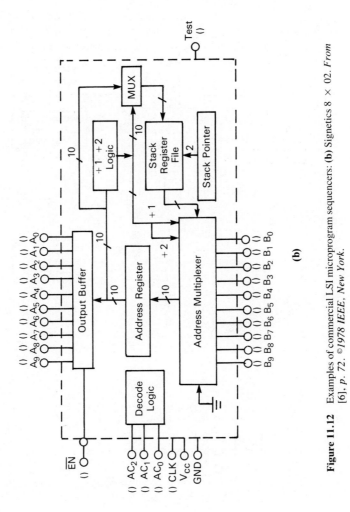

(b)

Figure 11.12 Examples of commercial LSI microprogram sequencers: **(b)** Signetics 8 × 02. *From [6], p. 72. ©1978 IEEE, New York.*

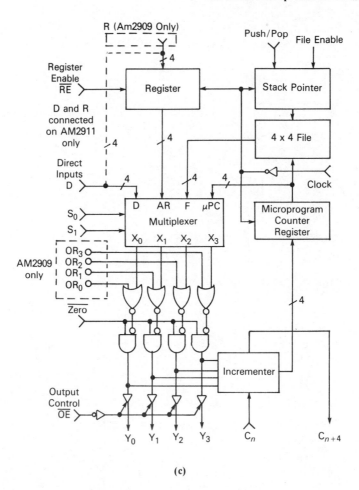

(c)

Figure 11.2   Examples of commercial LSI microprogram sequencers: **(c)** Am 2909/2911. *From [6], p. 72. ©1978 IEEE, New York.*

ming effort, since the programmer must keep in mind the locality exhibited in the microprogram branching.

Approximate cycle times for some of these sequencers are 44 ns for the 8X02; 50 ns for the 3001, 2909, 2911, and 74S482; and 100 ns for the 67110 [12].

Table 11.2 lists commercially available LSI microprogram sequencers, their manufacturers' names, and representative second sources.

Finally, Figure 11.13 shows an actual 16-bit bit-sliced microcomputer constructed using the AMD 2910 microprogram controller sequencing the microprogram memory, a 16-bit processing section made out of four 4-bit AMD 2901A CPU slices, and other AMD devices [2].

Table 11.2   Commercially available LSI microprogram sequencers. *From [6], p. 73. © 1978 IEEE, New York.*

- AMD 2909/2911, 2910, 2930/2931 (second-sourced by Raytheon, Signetics)
- INTEL 3001 MCU (second-sourced by Signetics)
- SIGNETICS 8X02/3, 3001 Control Store Sequencer
- MONOLITHIC MEMORIES 6710, 67110 Controller
- TEXAS INSTRUMENTS 74S482
- FAIRCHILD 9408 Program Controller
- MOTOROLA 10801 Microprogram Control Device
- NATIONAL CROM

11.5   THE MICROPROGRAM MEMORY AND MICROPROGRAM-MING ISSUES

11.5.1   Considerations for Designing the Microprogram Memory

Besides the microprogram sequencers discussed in the previous section, a central issue in the design of a microprogrammed control section is the organization of its microprogram memory, which contains the microinstructions that constitute the microprograms [4,26]. Advances in memory technology have resulted in the availability of large, fast, inexpensive microprogram memories and the appearance of several types of microprogram memory structures. The microprogram memory of bit-sliced microprocessors is implemented using ROMs, PROMs, or PLAs (programmable logic arrays).

Functional Characteristics

One characteristic of the microprogram memory is whether it is writable. ROM based non-alterable microprogram memories are usually provided (written) by the manufacturer, are usually tailor-made, and depend upon the system's architecture. On the other hand, writable control store (WCS), realized using fast random access memories (RAMs), has the advantage that it provides user-microprogrammability, allowing the user to create or modify the system's architecture. Advances in technology will continue to produce larger and faster RAMs, and their utilization in implementing microprogram memories will allow greater freedom and flexibility in system designs. The user can define the instruction set best suited to the specific application. He or she can also implement certain critical routines (e.g., specialized I/O and interrupt handling procedures, floating-point routines, system tables, etc.) as microprograms, thus improving system performance for a given application.

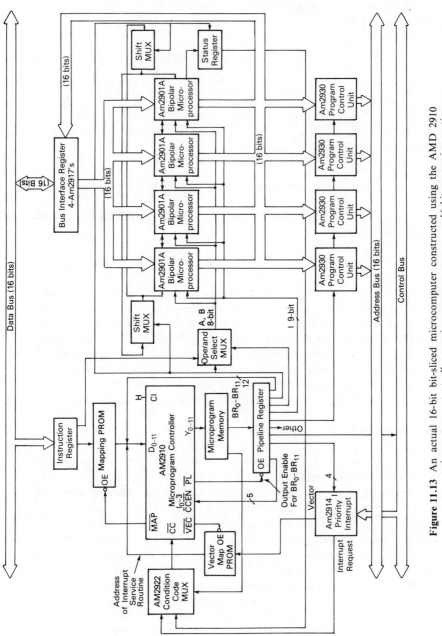

Figure 11.13 An actual 16-bit bit-sliced microcomputer constructed using the AMD 2910 microprogram controller, a microprogram memory, a 16-bit processing section made out of four 4-bit AMD 2901A CPU slices, and other AMD devices. *Copyright © 1978 Advanced Micro Devices, Inc. Reprinted with permission of copyright owner. All rights reserved.*

Dynamically microprogrammable systems can also be implemented with WCS, whose microprograms can be modified electronically during operation. Between these two extremes, various technologies also permit intermediate characteristics, employing, for example, programmable ROMs (PROMs) or the facility to switch from one ROM to another.

Speed

An important characteristic of the microprogram memory is its speed, described by its *access time*, which corresponds to the time required to read a microinstruction from the microprogram memory into the MIR. This speed is very important and is generally the limiting factor in the overall speed of the system. On the other hand, the microprogram memory should be fast enough so that the degradation it may cause (relative to hardwired control) to the system's speed will be compensated by the advantages of microprogramming. If user-microprogrammability is to be allowed in order to make attractive the implementation of functions in firmware rather than in software, then the ratio of main memory cycle time to microprogram memory cycle time is usually of the order of 10:1.

Size

The size of the microprogram memory depends on the number of bits in a microinstruction word and the number of words in the microprogram memory. The size may be a limiting factor to what applications can be microprogrammed on the system.

The number of microinstruction words in the microprogram memory primarily depends upon the macroinstruction repertoire. On contemporary user-microprogrammable machines, the lengths tend to vary from 256 to 4K words of sixteen to sixty-four bits.

Microprogram Memory Organizations

In the simplest and most common structure, there is one microinstruction in each microprogram memory location. A different structure may have two microinstructions per location, thus reducing the number of microprogram memory references. A third alternative divides the microprogram memory into blocks (sometimes called pages), and the specific addressing scheme addresses either within the same block as the current microinstruction or to another block. This shortens the addresses when addressing is done within the same block. Another scheme is the split microprogram memory, which comprises two separate storage units that have different word lengths. The shorter word length unit contains microinstructions that move data or initiate the execution of a microinstruction which resides in the other storage unit. The longer microinstructions that reside in the other unit can exercise more direct control over machine resources. A final scheme involves structuring the microprogram memory into multi-level organizations; in the two-level case, the second level usually contains longer microinstructions called "nanoinstructions" and the unit that contains them is called the "nanostore."

11.5.2 Microinstructions

The size, width, and structure of the microprogram memory are strongly influenced by the format and coding used in designing the microinstructions residing in it. The factors affecting the number of bits and their arrangement within the microinstruction word include: the way of sequencing microinstructions, the total number of different microoperations the system can perform, and the desired degree of parallelism in executing these microoperations.

Microinstruction Formats

In its simpler form a microinstruction usually contains two fields—those bits that correspond to the control signal patterns which define and control all elemental microoperations to be carried out, and those bits that identify and control the address of the next microinstruction to be executed (i.e., identify the source selection of the next microinstruction address or sometimes supply the actual address of the next microinstruction).

In general there is a great variety of possible microinstruction formats, lengths, and timing schemes. When bit-sliced machines are worked with, however, the use of predefined slices of the processing section limits the choices. Formatting usually refers to the definition of the various fields of the microinstruction.

Fixed and Variable Format

The microinstruction's format may be fixed or variable. In the fixed format, each bit in the microinstruction is always interpreted the same way, while in the variable format the meaning of the bits or fields changes according to certain system conditions. Variable format leads to shorter microinstructions, but also requires more complex decoding logic and delay time for format control.

Horizontal and Vertical Microinstructions

Horizontal microinstructions represent several microoperations that in general are executed concurrently. In the extreme, each horizontal microinstruction controls all the hardware resources of the system. Each control bit corresponds to a distinct microoperation: a 1 appearing in a bit position is used solely to activate a separate control line or point in the system, indicating that the corresponding microoperation is to be executed. Because these microinstructions control multiple resources simultaneously, they usually have more control bits than the other implementations we will see next. Lengths of forty-eight bits or more are common. Such an organization utilizes hardware more efficiently, provides flexibility in microprogramming, and requires a smaller number of microinstructions per microprogram. However, it is rarely used in organizing microprogram memories, since, for any reasonably sized machine, the microinstruction lengths become very large. The close association of horizontal microcode with hardware has also been described as *hard, hardview*, or *structural microprogramming*.

The *vertical* microinstruction format resembles the classical macroinstruction format and consists of one microoperation code (mop code), one or more operand, and some other fields (such as a condition code field for conditional branches). Each vertical microinstruction generally represents a single microoperation (e.g., a transfer or a data transformation operation), whereas operands may specify the data sink and source. Since vertical microinstructions resemble macroinstructions in format and operation, it is easier to write vertical microprograms than their horizontal counterparts, and this ability enhances a system's microprogrammability. This scheme also requires relatively short word lengths, in the range of sixteen to sixty-four bits. On the other hand, vertical microinstructions require more complex decoding logic and do not take full advantage of parallelism in the system's microarchitecture. Vertical microprogramming is slower than horizontal, since only one microoperation is done at a time. Vertical microprogram memory organizations are also relatively inflexible, because the addition of a new microinstruction type may require a change in the decoder logic. This format is also referred to as *soft, softview*, or *functional microprogramming*.

With the advances of technology, where a number of simple microoperations can now be combined into one more complex microoperation, it is difficult to define exactly the dividing line between horizontal and vertical microinstructions.

Non-encoded and Encoded Forms

If each bit in the microinstruction is used solely to control a separate control line or point in the system, then the microinstruction is called *non-encoded*, or is said to be of *unpacked* or *exploded form* (Figure 11.14a). This format leads to wider microinstruction words, higher operating speeds, and greater concurrency. Of course, a wider microinstruction also widens the microprogram memory.

An alternate scheme identifies groups of mutually exclusive control lines which are controlled by an encoded single control field in the microinstruction. If, for example, 2^n such lines exist, an n-bit field in the microinstruction is required. The n bits, by means of a decoder, regenerate these 2^n control signals when the microinstruction is executed (Figure 11.14b). Such a microinstruction is called *encoded* or of *packed* form. Two groups of control lines that are not mutually exclusive must be controlled by two separate encoded control fields of the microinstruction. Separate control fields are also provided for each independent functional unit, such as ALU, shifters, etc. This allows simultaneous use of system resources, as long as the functional units do not make conflicting use of a datum. This scheme leads to shorter microinstructions and smaller microprogram memories. It provides a more flexible design at the loss of some concurrency and speed.

Nanoinstructions

In some cases, another mode of operation can be used in which an encoded microinstruction, through a limited number of control fields, addresses yet another, lower level of storage, called the nanostore (Figure 11.14c), which contains *nanoinstructions*. Figure 11.14d shows an alternate two-level memory design used with large horizontal microinstructions. The microstore (microprogram memory) has a large number (1K) of short (8-bit) words, while the nanostore is wide but contains fewer (256) words. Thus a total microprogram memory of 4K words by thirty-two bits can be implemented with only 4K words by eight bits plus 256 words by thirty-two bits.

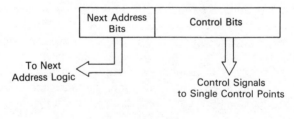

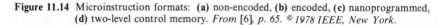

(a)

Figure 11.14 Microinstruction formats: **(a)** non-encoded, **(b)** encoded, **(c)** nanoprogrammed, **(d)** two-level control memory. *From* [6]*, p. 65.* © *1978 IEEE, New York.*

11.5.3 Microinstruction Execution Schemes

Depending upon the way the control bits of the microinstruction activate microoperations, there can be a monophase or a polyphase implementation.

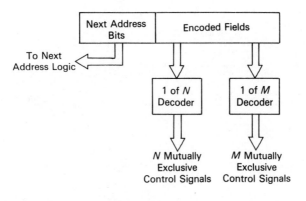

(b)

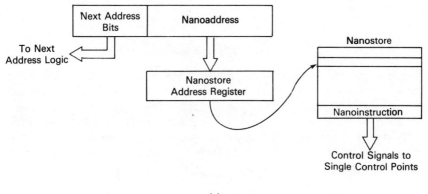

(c)

Figure 11.14 (*Continued*)

In the *monophase* implementation, the execution of each individual microinstruction requires only one clock phase. In other words, all the microoperations that this microinstruction initiates are completed within this clock phase duration P_0 as shown in Figure 11.15a. This requires more microinstructions in the microprogram memory, but their widths are narrower. In the *polyphase* implementation, the execution of each individual microinstruction requires more than a single clock phase. The control signals of a single microinstruction are issued in sequence over a number of clock phases (Figure 11.15b) and sequence accordingly the respective microoperations. Polyphase systems allow microprocessor functions to overlap, permitting an increase in effective operation speeds. Assignment of activities to each time slot increases the

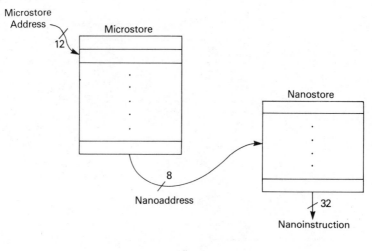

(d)

Figure 11.14 (*Continued*)

pipelined capabilities of bit-sliced microprocessors. Furthermore, polyphase implementations are characterized as synchronous or asynchronous. In the *synchronous polyphase*, the number of clock cycles required for the microinstruction execution remains constant (i.e., same number of clock phases for every microinstruction). In the *asynchronous polyphase*, the number of clock phases required to execute a microinstruction depends upon the complexity of its microoperations.

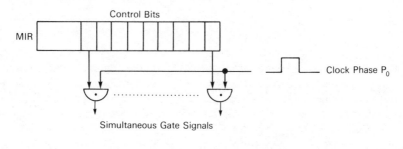

(a)

Figure 11.15 **(a)** Monophase implementation: all microoperations initiated and completed within one clock phase. **(b)** Polyphase implementation: during every clock phase a pair of microoperations is executed; three pairs are executed during three different clock phases P_0, P_1, P_2. *From [7], p. 94. Reprinted by permission of John Wiley & Sons, Inc., New York.*

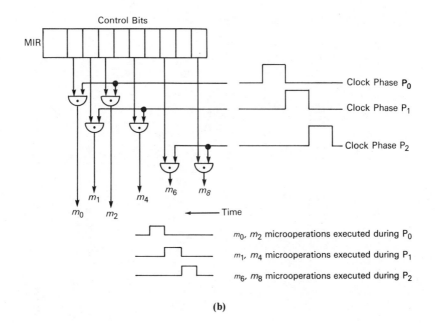

(b)

Figure 11.15 (*Continued*)

In both monophase and polyphase, timing structure can also vary when some control fields in the microinstruction have explicit or implicit timing information associated with them.

11.6 EXAMPLE OF EXECUTING A MACROINSTRUCTION

In order to understand better the design requirements of a microprogrammed control section, we present an example for defining the microoperations and control signals involved in the execution of a simple macroinstruction [7,30].

Consider the microprogrammed system of Figure 11.16, consisting of a control section and a data processing section. Although the data processing section is not of the bit-sliced type, the control section contains both a microprogram memory and a microprogram sequencer, to help us analyze the design procedure.

The processing section contains a parallel adder, an 18-bit accumulator ACC, an 18-bit temporary register B, the program counter (PC) and two internal buses, the left adder bus L and right adder bus R. The adder can add two operands with input carry G_{20} being 0 or 1. The processing section also has a zero detect logic (ZDL) that issues a 1 when the output of the adder is all 0's (zeros); otherwise, it issues a 0 (zero). The system uses the 2's complement notation.

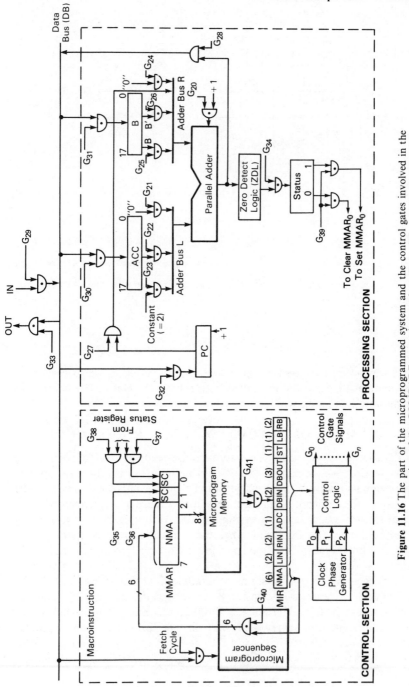

Figure 11.16 The part of the microprogrammed system and the control gates involved in the execution of the COMPARE macroinstruction. *From [7] p. 104. Reprinted by permission of John Wiley & Sons, Inc., New York.*

The control section contains a microprogram memory along with its microprogram address register MMAR and microinstruction register MIR, and a microprogram sequencer which also receives the macroinstruction op code from the system's data bus. A polyphase implementation is used with three clock phases, P_0, P_1, P_2, and a control logic unit which combines the clock phases with the control bits of the microinstruction to generate the control signals G_i applied to respective control points (gates) of the system.

The necessary microoperations are grouped and coded in assigned fields of the microinstruction with one code of the field usually designating one microoperation. The format of the microinstruction is as follows:

(6)	(2)	(2)	(1)	(2)	(3)	(1)	(1)	(2)
NMA	LIN	RIN	ADC	DBIN	DBOUT	ST	LB	RB

The six leftmost bits of the microinstruction make the field NMA, which signifies the next microinstruction address. The next 2-bit field LIN is chosen to designate the left inputs to the adder as shown in Table 11.3. This table also shows the respective control gate signals.

Table 11.3 Field LIN (left input to the adder). *From* [7], *p. 104. Reprinted by permission of John Wiley & Sons, Inc., New York.*

Code	Microoperations	Control Gate Signals
00	Adder ← "0"	G_{21}
01	Adder ← ACC	G_{22}
10	Adder ← "2"	G_{23}
11	Not used	—

The next 2-bit field RIN is used to designate the right inputs to the adder as shown in Table 11.4 (where B′ is the 1's complement of the contents of temporary register B).

Table 11.4 Field RIN (right input to the adder). *From* [7], *p. 104. Reprinted by permission of John Wiley & Sons, Inc., New York.*

Code	Microoperations	Control Gate Signals
00	Adder ← "0"	G_{24}
01	Adder ← B	G_{25}
10	Adder ← B′	G_{26}
11	Adder ← PC	G_{27}

The next 1-bit field ADC is used to designate the microoperations of the parallel adder as follows: when ADC = 0 (i.e., G_{20} = 0) the addition is performed with no carry in; if ADC = 1 (i.e., G_{20} = 1) the addition is performed with carry in (2's complement addition).

The 2-bit field DBIN designates connections to the data bus as shown in Table 11.5, where IN is an external source, such as main memory, placing data on the data bus.

Table 11.5 Field DBIN (data bus in). *From [7], p. 104. Reprinted by permission of John Wiley & Sons, Inc., New York.*

Code	Microoperations	Control Gate Signals
00	Not used	—
01	DB ← Adder	G_{28}
10	DB ← IN	G_{29}
11	Not used	—

The next 3-bit field DBOUT designates the destination of the information on the data bus, as shown in Table 11.6, where OUT is an external destination device, such as main memory, receiving data from the data bus.

Table 11.6 Field DBOUT (data bus out). *From [7], p. 105. Reprinted by permission of John Wiley & Sons, Inc., New York.*

Code	Microoperations	Control Gate Signals
000	Not used	—
001	ACC ← DB	G_{30}
010	B ← DB	G_{31}
011	PC ← DB	G_{32}
100	OUT ← DB	G_{33}
101		—
110	Not used	—
111		—

Storing of the result of the zero detect logic ZDL in the 1-bit register STATUS is designated by the 1-bit field ST as shown in Table 11.7.

Table 11.7 Field ST (STATUS). *From [7], p. 105. Reprinted by permission of John Wiley & Sons, Inc., New York.*

Code	Microoperations	Control Gate Signals
0	No operation	—
1	IF(ZDL = 0)	G_{34}
	THEN(STATUS←0)	
	ELSE(STATUS←1)	

The microprogram memory of Figure 11.16 has an 8-bit microprogram memory address register (MMAR). Its six high-order bits, $MMAR_{7-2}$, are provided by the next microinstruction address field NMA of the microinstruction in MIR. The two low-order bits $MMAR_1$ and $MMAR_0$ are determined by fields LB and RB as shown in Tables 11.8 and 11.9.

Table 11.8 Field LB. *From* [7], *p. 105. Reprinted by permission of John Wiley & Sons, Inc., New York.*

Code	Microoperations	Control Gate Signals
0	$MMAR_1 \leftarrow 0$	G_{35}
1	$MMAR_1 \leftarrow 1$	G_{36}

Table 11.9 Field RB. *From* [7], *p. 105. Reprinted by permission of John Wiley & Sons, Inc., New York.*

Code	Microoperations	Control Gate Signals
00	$MMAR_0 \leftarrow 0$	G_{37}
01	$MMAR_0 \leftarrow 1$	G_{38}
10	$MMAR_0 \leftarrow STATUS$	G_{39}
11	Not used	—

Now consider the execution of the following simple COMPARE macroinstruction [9]:

$$\text{IF ACC} = \text{B} \quad \text{THEN PC} \leftarrow \text{PC} + 2$$
$$\text{ELSE PC} \leftarrow \text{PC} + 1$$

The comparison in this example is performed by subtracting the number in register B from the accumulator, and then, the examination of the value of the zero detection logic will determine whether PC (the program counter) will be incremented by 1 or by 2.

As shown in Figure 11.17 this COMPARE macroinstruction requires three microinstructions. The first microinstruction in location YYYYYYY performs the above comparison; the subtraction is carried out by adding the 2's complement of the number in register B to the number in the accumulator. Either microinstruction in location ZZZZZZ00 (i.e., PC ← PC + 1) or microinstruction in location ZZZZZZ01 (i.e., PC ← PC + 2) will be executed next, depending upon the result of the first microinstruction. Finally, no matter which one of the two is executed, the sequence eventually reaches the microinstruction in location XXXXXX11.

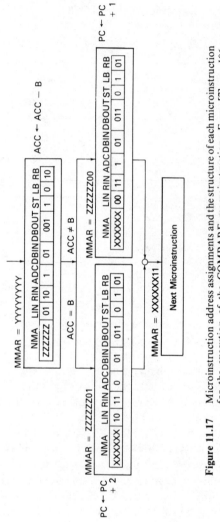

Figure 11.17 Microinstruction address assignments and the structure of each microinstruction for the execution of the COMPARE macroinstruction. *From [7], p. 106. Reprinted by permission of John Wiley & Sons, Inc., New York.*

Each microinstruction in the control store is processed under the control of a three-phase clock, P_0, P_1, P_2. Assume that during the previous microcycle a control signal G is provided to start the sequence with a proper address in MMAR as follows:

$$P_0 \qquad : \quad G \leftarrow 0$$
$$\overline{G} AND P_1 \quad : \quad MMAR \leftarrow YYYYYYYY, \ G \leftarrow 1$$
$$G AND P_2 \quad : \quad MIR \leftarrow (MMAR) \ ,$$

where (MMAR) denotes the contents of location pointed at by MMAR. Then, for the first microinstruction in location YYYYYYYY, which compares the contents of register B and the accumulator, the sequence of microoperations executed and the control gate signals emitted are shown in Table 11.10. The sequence of microoperations executed and the control gate signals emitted for the microinstruction in location ZZZZZZ00 (i.e., PC $\leftarrow$ PC $+$ 1) are shown in Table 11.11,[7] while the microoperations executed and the control gate signals emitted for the microinstruction in location ZZZZZZ01 (i.e., PC $\leftarrow$ PC $+$ 2) are shown in Table 11.12.

Table 11.10 Execution sequence for microinstruction ACC $\leftarrow$ ACC $-$ B from location YYYYYYYY. *From* [7], *p.107. Reprinted by permission of John Wiley & Sons, Inc., New York.*

Timing		Microoperations	Control Gate Signals
(LIN = 1)	AND P_0	Adder $\leftarrow$ ACC	G_{22}
(RIN = 2)	AND P_0	Adder $\leftarrow$ B'	G_{26}
(ADC = 1)	AND P_0	$G_{20} \leftarrow 1$	G_{20}
(DBIN = 1)	AND P_0	DB $\leftarrow$ Adder	G_{28}
(DBOUT = 1)	AND P_0	ACC $\leftarrow$ (DB)	G_{30}
(ST = 1)	AND P_0	IF (ZDL = 0) THEN (STATUS $\leftarrow$ 0)ELSE (STATUS $\leftarrow$ 1)	G_{34}
(LB = 0)	AND P_1	MMAR$_1$ $\leftarrow$ 0	G_{35}
(RB = 2)	AND P_1	MMAR$_0$ $\leftarrow$ STATUS	G_{39}
G	AND P_1	MMAR$_{7-2}$ $\leftarrow$ NMA	G_{40}
G	AND P_2	MIR $\leftarrow$ (MMAR)	G_{41}

---

[7]The ADC field is 1 and gate G_{20} receives the control signal 1, to add 1 to the program counter (PC).

Table 11.11   Execution sequence for microinstruction PC ← PC + 1 from location ZZZZZZ00.
From [7] p. 107. Reprinted by permission of John Wiley & Sons, Inc., New York.

Timing		Microoperations	Control Gate Signals
(LIN = 0)	AND P_0	Adder ← "0"	G_{21}
(RIN = 3)	AND P_0	Adder ← PC	G_{27}
(ADC = 1)	AND P_0	G_{20} ← 1	G_{20}
(DBIN = 1)	AND P_0	DB ← Adder	G_{28}
(DBOUT = 3)	AND P_0	PC ← DB	G_{32}
(ST = 0)	AND P_0	——	—
(LB = 1)	AND P_1	$MMAR_1$ ← 1	G_{36}
(RB = 1)	AND P_1	$MMAR_0$ ← 1	G_{38}
G	AND P_1	$MMAR_{7-2}$ ← NMA	G_{40}
G	AND P_2	MIR ← (MMAR)	G_{41}

Table 11.12   Execution sequence for microinstruction PC ← PC + 2 from location ZZZZZZ01.
From [7] p.107. Reprinted by permission of John Wiley & Sons, Inc., New York.

Timing		Microoperations	Control Gate Signals
(LIN = 2)	AND P_0	Adder ← "2"	G_{23}
(RIN = 3)	AND P_0	Adder ← PC	G_{27}
(ADC = 0)	AND P_0	G_{20} ← 0	—
(DBIN = 1)	AND P_0	DB ← Adder	G_{28}
(DBOUT = 3)	AND P_0	PC ← DB	G_{32}
(ST = 0)	AND P_0	——	—
(LB = 1)	AND P_1	$MMAR_1$ ← 1	G_{36}
(RB = 1)	AND P_1	$MMAR_0$ ← 1	G_{38}
G	AND P_1	$MMAR_{7-2}$ ← NMA	G_{40}
G	AND P_2	MIR ← (MMAR)	G_{41}

11.7   DESIGN SUPPORT FOR BIT-SLICED MICROPROCESSORS

Design aids, software, and debugging support for bit-sliced machines are not as available as the support for user-microprogrammable minicomputers [6]. Quite a few of the available microprocessor design aids are common to both single-chip and bit-sliced microprocessors. Others are specifically applicable to bit-sliced machines and can simplify microprogramming and bit-slice architecture implementation. Some of the most valuable design aids for bit-sliced machines are given below.

Assemblers

- Assemblers translate programs into binary machine code.
- With microassemblers the designer may also specify microprogram memory characteristics, microinstruction formats, microinstruction operation codes, and output formats.
- Some assemblers are available on timesharing systems in a cross-assembler form.
- Examples include [24]:
   RAPID from Scientific Micro Systems;
   CROMIS cross-assembler from Intel;
   AMDASM from Advanced Micro Devices;
   DAPL from Zero Systems;
   MICRO-AID from Monolithic Memories;
   RAYASM from Raytheon;
   Signetics microassembler supporting the Intel 3002 and AMD 2901 central processing elements, and the Signetics 8X02 control store sequencer.

In-circuit Emulators

- In-circuit emulators simulate other microcomputer chips (e.g., microprocessors, microprogram sequencers, CPU slices).
- They determine the exact state of the chip at any instant in time.
- They plug into the socket of the circuit being emulated.
- They make development and real-time debugging easier and faster, allowing system state displaying, modifying, and real-time tracing.

An example is the Intel ICE-30 which emulates the 3001 MCU chip.

ROM Simulators

- ROM simulators are essentially in-circuit emulators for memories.
- They allow the use of RAMs for real-time debugging of microprograms, so that they go "bug free" into their final ROM/PROM locations.
- They are "plug-to-socket" compatible with standard ROMs/PROMs.
- They allow easy changes to the ROM contents during development and debugging, and can provide hard copy of the debugging record.
- Examples are:

   Scientific Micro Systems ROM simulator;
   Intel ROM simulators for the 3601/3604 PROMs.

Others

Work continues on better software support for microprogramming bit-sliced microprocessors:

- A cross-assembler and simulator (the MCR 3000) for the Intel series 3000 microcomputer chip set runs under IBM System/360 OS/MVT [32].
- A microassembler (the MICROBE), built for an AMD 2900-based processor, generates a symbolic commentary for each microinstruction and yields many of the benefits of programming in a high-level language, without the high implementation costs [17].
- A portable compiler, with the language consisting of register-transfer microinstruction descriptions, makes structured microprogramming possible on 4-bit-sliced devices [13].

11.8   ADVANTAGES/DISADVANTAGES

The system designer who uses these LSI bipolar bit-sliced devices is faced with a series of complex tradeoffs that must be evaluated for each application under consideration [6].

The microprogrammable bit-sliced processors have economic application primarily in replacing hardwired logic of the SSI/MSI level with LSI microprogrammed logic; in designing new, flexible, and faster microprocessor-based digital systems and controllers; and in emulating other already existing computers to capture old, tested, operational software. Some of their key advantages are:

- Bipolar LSI bit-sliced devices make microprogrammed design techniques quite feasible for the average user, since they do not require the large development costs only large companies can afford.
- The microprogrammable feature of bit-sliced processors offers the system designer new techniques with which to create well-structured, flexible systems. Such well-structured implementation makes testing and debugging easier. Incorporation of special microinstructions provides in-line software operation checking and real-time fault recovery capabilities.
- Special microcode instructions can be implemented to provide a speed improvement, because microinstructions are generally more efficient than macroinstructions. Certain critical routines (e.g., specialized I/O and interrupt handling procedures, floating-point routines) may be implemented as microprograms. Such microprograms can improve system performance for a given application.
- Microprogrammable digital systems are more flexible and more adaptable to a new application or to the increased requirements of an old application.

This can be done by adding new microinstructions or modifying existing ones.

- Microprogrammable bit-sliced architectures allow the designer to tailor word lengths to the specific application, since non-standard lengths (e.g., fourteen, twenty-four, or thirty-two bits) are possible.
- Bit-sliced devices make tremendous speed increases possible through the use of bipolar technology.
- A dynamically microprogrammable system, whose microprograms can be modified electronically during system operation, can easily respond to a fault and reconfigure the system to bypass the faulty element until it is replaced.
- These bit-sliced devices lead to compact system implementations. They also permit greater flexibility of design because of the greater number of pins available in multi-chip processors. This greatly reduces multiplexing problems.
- From the designer's point of view, the microprogrammable bit-sliced approach offers an advantage in that the same processor components may be used to define various products. The design of a new system simply means the development of a new microprogram, rather than a repetition of the lengthy overall system design cycle. This also helps the designer to meet changing market requirements.

The bit-slice approach, however, has some major drawbacks:

- A microprogrammed control section is generally slower than a specially-made hardwired control unit. Sometimes this disadvantage may be partially overcome by incorporating more parallelism into the system.
- Many bit-sliced microprocessors lack a fixed instruction set at the macroinstruction level, thus making the user's job even more difficult.
- Design and software support presently available for bit-sliced processors is rather limited.
- Multi-chip sets are less reliable than single-chip microprocessors, because of the increased number of interconnections.

Despite these drawbacks, bit-sliced microprocessor architecture is attractive whenever an application demands production of large numbers of high-speed devices.

EXERCISES

11.1 Compare fully hardwired versus microprogrammed control units.

11.2 Describe how a bit-sliced microprocessor can emulate a 16-bit minicomputer.

11.3 List some advantages and disadvantages of encoding a microinstruction.

11.4 Indicate some places within the control section of a bit-sliced microprocessor where a PLA (programmable logic array) can be used. What advantages does the microprocessor have with a PLA present?

11.5 Consider a microinstruction that includes a 4-bit condition code field C_3, C_2, C_1, C_0. Design the microprogrammed control section using a PLA as a microprogram sequencer to take care of the following conditional branches in the microprogram:

- Advance to the next microinstruction when C_3, C_2, C_1, $C_0 = 0101$ or C_3, C_2, C_1, $C_0 = 1101$.
- Jump to the address pointed at by the "branch address" field of the microinstruction when C_3, C_1, $= 11$ or when C_3, C_2, $C_0 = 000$.

11.6 Repeat Exercise 11.5, now using a PROM instead of a PLA.

11.7 Consider a microinstruction that includes a 2-bit condition code field C_1, C_0. Design the microprogrammed control section using a 4-input multiplexer as a microprogram sequencer to take care of the following functions in the microprogram:

Condition Code field C_1 C_0	Function
00	Continue
01	Jump if ACC = 0
10	Jump if ACC overflows
11	Jump unconditionally

11.8 Assume the COMPARE instruction of section 11.6 is now executed as follows:

$$\text{IF ACC} = \text{B} \quad \text{THEN PC} \leftarrow \text{PC} + 1$$
$$\text{ELSE PC} \leftarrow \text{PC} + 3$$

Give the microinstructions required by the respective microprogram to implement this instruction.

11.9 Consider the COMPARE instruction of section 11.6 and the micro-programmed system of Figure 11.16. Assume that the two 2-bit fields LIN and RIN of the microinstruction are now replaced by a single 2-bit field LRI which designates (executes) the following microoperations:

Code	Microoperations	Control Gate Signals
00	Adder ← PC	
01	Adder ← ACC and Adder ← B'	
10	Adder ← ACC and Adder ← B	
11	Adder ← "0"	

List the proper control signals (to the respective control gates) in the right column of the above table.

REFERENCES AND BIBLIOGRAPHY

[1] Advanced Micro Devices, Incorporated, *AM 2901, AM 2909 Technical Data Manual,* Sunnyvale, CA, 1975.

[2] Advanced Micro Devices, Incorporated, *AM 2903 Four-Bit Bipolar Microprocessor Slice, AM 2910 Microprogram Controller Technical Data,* 1978.

[3] Advanced Micro Devices, Incorporated, *Build a Microcomputer,* Sunnyvale, CA, 1978.

[4] Agrawala, A.K. and T.G. Rauscher, *Foundations of Microprogramming,* New York: ACM Monograph Series, Academic Press, 1976.

[5] Alexandridis, N.A., "Bit-Sliced Microprocessors, PLA's and Microprogramming in Replacing Hardwired Logic," *Proceedings of the International Symposium on Wired Logic versus Programmed Logic,* Lausanne, Switzerland, March 1977.

[6] Alexandridis, N.A., "Bit-sliced Microprocessor Architecture," *Computer,* June 1978, pp. 56–80.

[7] Alexandridis, N.A., "Control, Timing, and System Signals," *Fundamentals Handbook of Electrical and Computer Engineering III,* ed. S.S.L. Chang, New York: John Wiley & Sons, 1983, pp. 78–119.

[8] Andrews, M., *Principles of Firmware Engineering,* Rockville, MD: Computer Science Press, Inc., 1980.

[9] Chu, Y., *Computer Organization and Microprogramming*, Englewood Cliffs, N.J.: Prentice-Hall, Inc., 1972.

[10] Davies, P.M., "Readings in Microprogramming," *IBM Systems Journal*, vol. 11, no. 1, 1972, pp. 16–41.

[11] Flynn, M.J., "Microprogramming—Another Look at Internal Computer Control," *Proceedings of IEEE*, vol. 63, no. 11, November 1975, pp. 1554–67.

[12] Gold, J., "Bipolar Controllers—They're Fast, Cheap, and Easy to Use," *Electronic Design*, 22, October 25, 1976, pp. 106–10.

[13] Hawk, D.R., and D.M. Robinson, "A Microinstruction Sequencer and Language Package for Structured Microprogramming," *Proceedings of MICRO 8*, IEEE Catalog no. 75 CH1053-8C, September 1975, pp. 69–75.

[14] Husson, S.S., *Microprogramming: Principles and Practices*, New York: Prentice-Hall, Inc., 1970.

[15] Intel Corporation, INTEL *Series 3000 Microprogramming Manual*, Santa Clara, CA, 1975.

[16] Jones, L.H., "Instructions Sequencing in Microprogrammed Computers," *APIPS Conference Proceedings of NCC*, 1977, pp. 91–98.

[17] Laws, B.A., Jr., "Microbe: A Self Commenting Microassembler," *Proceedings of MICRO 10*, October 1977, pp. 61–65.

[18] McGlynn, D.R., *Modern Microprocessor System Design*, New York: John Wiley & Sons, 1980.

[19] Mick, J.R., "AM 2900 Bipolar Microprocessor Family," *Electronics, Eighth Annual Workshop on Microprogramming*, Chicago, IL, September 1975, pp. 56–63.

[20] Mick, J.R., "Microprogramming for the Hardware Engineer," *Proceedings of the DISE Workshop on Microprocessors and Education*, Fort Collins, CO: Colorado State University, August 16–18, 1976, pp. 6–14.

[21] Myers, J., *Digital System Design with LSI Bit-Slice Logic*, New York: John Wiley & Sons, 1980.

[22] Nemec, J., et al, "A Primer on Bit-Sliced Microprocessors," *Electronic Design*, 3, February 1, 1977, pp. 52–60.

[23] Ogdin, J.L., "Survey of Microprogrammable μP's Reveals Ultimate Flexibility," *EDN*, July 20, 1974, p. 69.

[24] Powers, V.M. and J.H. Hernandez, "Microprogram Assemblers for Bit-sliced Microprocessors," *Computer*, July 1978, pp. 108–20.

[25] Rosin, R.F., "Contemporary Concepts of Microprogramming and Evaluation," *Computing Surveys*, vol. 1, no. 4, December 1969, pp. 197–212.

[26] Salisbury, A.B., *Microprogrammable Computer Architectures*, New York: Elsevier, 1976.

[27] Sawin, D., "Microprogrammable Microprocessors," *New Logic Notebook*, Microcomputer Technique, Inc., vol. I, no. 9, May 1975.

[28] Signetics Corporation, *Signetics Control Store Sequencer 8X02 2-B-2*, Sunnyvale, CA, 1977.

[29] Vahey, M., "Bit-Sliced Architectures for Microcomputers," presented at Microprocessors III Conference, Fullerton, CA, 1976.

[30] Vandling, G.C., and D.E. Waldecker, "The Microprogram Control Technique for Digital Logic Design," *Computer Design*, August 1969, pp. 44–51.

[31] Wilkes, M.V., "The Growth of Interest in Microprogramming," *Computer Surveys*, vol. 1, no. 3, September 1969, pp. 139–45.

[32] Willen, D., "An INTEL 3000 Cross Assembler," *SIGMICRO Newsletter*, vol. 7, no. 4, December 1976, pp. 87–94.

Appendices:
REPRESENTATIVE
MICROPROCESSORS

INTEL 8080A

Figure A1.1a shows the simplified functional block diagram of the 8080A microprocessor; its pins and signals are shown in Figure A1.1b.

The 8080A was the first 8-bit NMOS medium-level microprocessor to appear in the market. It is the most widely known chip, and it usually constitutes a frame of reference in the discussion and comparison of other single-chip 8-bit microprocessors. The 8080A is manufactured in NMOS technology on a 40-pin chip, and was designed to eliminate some of the 8008 limitations (e.g., decrease the number of external TTL interfaces that the 8008 required, overcome the 8008's lack of multiple interrupts, etc.)[10, 12, 22, 25, 33, 35].

The 8080A microprocessor communicates with the other system modules via three separate functional buses. One bus is the 16-bit *address bus* (A0–A15), used for the parallel transfer of 16-bit addresses between the microprocessor and memory or I/O modules. I/O is performed by specific input and output instructions that provide the 8-bit device numbers. These device numbers appear on both the eight upper and eight lower lines of the address bus, and allow the user to select directly up to 256 input or 256 output ports. The second bus is an 8-bit bidirectional *data bus* (D0–D7), used for the transfer of data. This bus is multiplexed by the 8080A to carry also the eight status signals issued at state T_1 of each machine cycle. The 16-bit addresses allow the 8080A to address directly a memory of up to 64K bytes capacity. Data is stored in the form of 8-bit binary integers, and all data transfers on the system data bus are in the same format. Furthermore, the 8080A has DMA capability, a simple way of handling multiple interrupts, and the ability to provide priority vectored interrupts. It has seventy-two basic instructions of one, two, or three bytes, and a basic instruction cycle of 2 μsec. It is driven by a two-phase clock and requires three power supplies (+12v, +5v, −5v). Six output signals (SYNC, DBIN, WAIT, $\overline{WR}$, HLDA and INTE) emanate from the microprocessor, while four inputs (READY, HOLD, INT, and RESET) are accepted by it. External interface logic (e.g., the 8228 system controller) is used to combine the above output signals with the status signals to create an adequate set of control signals, as shown in Figure 6.9b of chapter 6. These control signals functionally constitute the *control bus*.

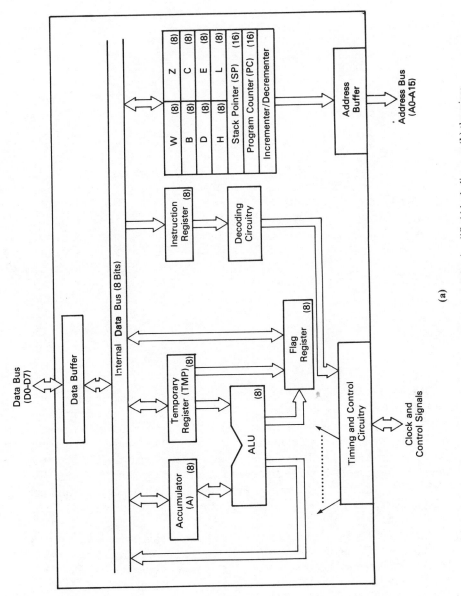

(a)

Figure A1.1   The Intel 8080A microprocessor: **(a)** the simplified block diagram; **(b)** the micro–processor pins and signals.

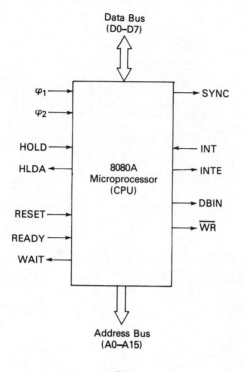

Data Bus
(D0–D7)

φ_1 →

φ_2 →

HOLD →

HLDA ←

8080A
Microprocessor
(CPU)

→ SYNC

← INT

→ INTE

→ DBIN

→ $\overline{\text{WR}}$

RESET →

READY →

WAIT ←

Address Bus
(A0–A15)

(b)

Figure A1.1 (*Continued*)

The 8080A ALU performs 8-bit binary additions and subtractions, and logical and rotate operations on operands it receives from the accumulator and the temporary register TMP. Register TMP receives its input from the internal bus, while the accumulator can be loaded either from the internal bus or from the ALU. The flag register may also be effected directly from the temporary register TMP. The 8080A contains two other temporary registers, W and Z. They are used to store information required for the internal execution of instructions and are not directly addressable by any user instruction.

Figure A1.2 shows the 8080A register structure which includes the registers that may be affected by user instructions. The accumulator register is symbolized by the letter A. There also exist six 8-bit general-purpose registers. They may be used either individually as 8-bit registers (referred to as B, C, D, E, H, and L) or as 16-bit register pairs (referred to as BC, DE, and HL). Registers B, C, D, and E are used to store temporary data or intermediate results of operations. Although registers H and L may be used also in a similar fashion, their actual use is to store memory addresses. When used in pair to store addresses, register H contains the eight most significant bits, while register L contains the eight least significant bits of the address. A limited number of memory reference instructions use the BC and DE register pairs, too, to hold the implied memory address. The 8080A instructions allow easy data transfers from register to register or between a register and memory. In this second case, the transfer will take place between the specified register and a memory location whose address is contained in registers H and L.

Also included in the CPU is a 16-bit stack pointer (SP), which contains an address pointing to the memory location of the most recent stack entry. The program counter (PC) is also sixteen bits wide, contains the memory address of the next instruction byte of the program, and is automatically incremented by 1 with every instruction byte fetch. Finally, the flags register contains the five flags: sign (S), zero (Z), auxiliary carry (AC), parity (P) and carry (CY). The accumulator A and the flag registers are sometimes treated together as a 16-bit unit, corresponding to the program status word (PSW).

The instruction set of 8080A includes five different types of instructions:

- *Data transfer group:* move data between registers or between memory and registers.
- *Arithmetic group:* add, subtract, increment, or decrement data in registers or in memory.
- *Logical group:* AND, OR, exclusive-OR, compare, rotate, or complement data in registers or in memory.
- *Branch group:* conditional and unconditional jump instructions, subroutine call instructions and return instructions.
- *Stack, I/O, and machine control group:* includes I/O instructions, as well as instructions for maintaining the stack and internal control flags.

Instruction lengths are of one, two, or three bytes, as shown in Figure A1.3. The first byte always corresponds to the op code placed in the instruction register of the microprocessor. The contents of the instruction register are in turn available to the op code decoder. The decoder decodes the first instruction byte in order to: (a) determine whether additional bytes exist in the instruction that will require successive memory references to fetch them; (b) produce an output, which, when combined with various timing signals, will provide the CPU intramodule control signals and will generate the machine cycle and state timing signals. When the instruction is a 2-byte instruction, the second byte may either contain an 8-bit *immediate operand* to be used by the instruction or an 8-bit *device number* corresponding to an input or output port (for the I/O instructions). For 3-byte instructions, the second and third

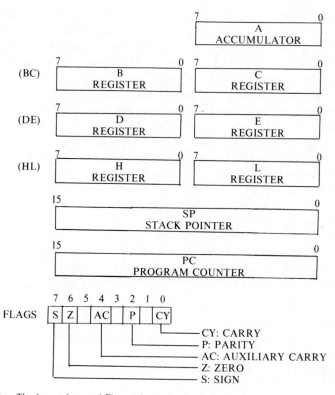

Note: The Accumulator and Flags registers are sometimes treated as a 16-bit unit (PSW).
Figure A1.2   The programming model for the 8080A and 8085 microprocessors.

bytes may either contain a 16-bit *immediate operand* or a 16-bit *memory address* (the second byte containing the low-order part and the third byte the high-order part of the operand or address.)

Every 8080A instruction cycle consists of from one to five machine cycles (M_1, M_2, M_3, M_4, M_5). The CPU indentifies the beginning of every machine cycle by issuing the SYNC signal. Every machine cycle consists of from three to five states (T_1, T_2, T_3, T_4, T_5). The instruction fetch machine cycle must have four or five states, and thus, no instruction can be processed in less than four states. Each state is defined by the rising edge of clock phase φ_1.

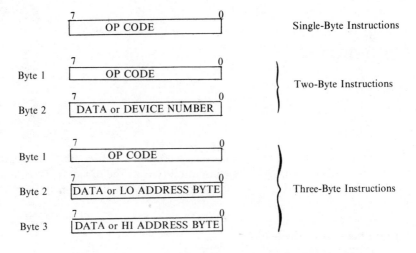

Figure A1.3 The Intel 8080A/8085 instruction formats.

Appendix 2

INTEL 8085

The 8085 represents a new generation of 8080A which is 100% software compatible with the 8080A. The compatibility is at the object or "machine code" level so that existing programs written for 8080A execution will run on the 8085 as is.

Improvements over the 8080A

The simplified functional block diagram of the 8085 is shown in Figure A2.1 and is quite similar to that of the 8080A, with the following improvements [4, 13, 34, 44]:

- The 8085 has higher integration (the result of which is placing both the 8224 clock generator and the 8228 system controller of Figure 6.9 in chapter 6 on the same CPU chip). The 8085 requires externally only a crystal or RC network.
- The data bus buffer drives an 8-bit multiplexed bidirectional address/data bus (AD0–AD7) and the pure address bus is 8-bits wide (A8–A15).
- The address/data bus carries either the 8-bit data or the eight least significant bits of the address, the eight most significant bits of the address being transferred on the 8-bit address bus.
- The 8085 is driven by a single +5v power supply.
- The 8085 has improved speed with a basic clock speed of 3 MHz (1.3 μs basic instruction cycle).
- The 8085 has two extra instructions: RIM (read interrupt mask) and SIM (set interrupt mask).
- The 8085 has four additional vectored interrupt inputs, three of them being maskable and one non-maskable.
- The 8085 also provides serial input data (SID) and serial output data (SOD) lines for simple serial interface.
- The multiplexed address/data bus allows for extra control signals.
- Finally, its instruction and basic system timing has been simplified, when compared to the 8080A.

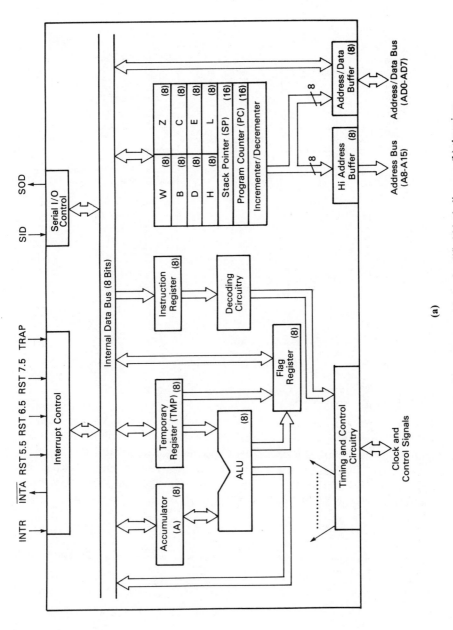

(a)

Figure A2.1 The Intel 8085 microprocessor: **(a)** the simplified block diagram; **(b)** the micro-processor pins and signals.

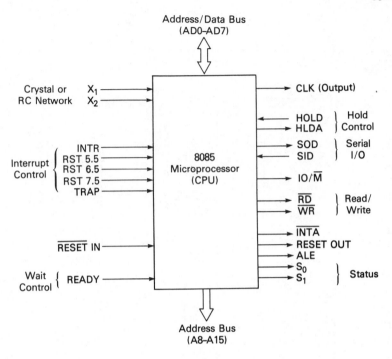

(b)

Figure A2.1 (*Continued*)

Similarities with the 8080A

All other main features of the 8085 are the same as those of the 8080A; i.e., the 8085 ALU operates in a similar way, the 8085 register structure is the same (see Figure A1.2), having the same condition flags, the 8085 instruction formats are the same, the 8085 has the same instructions[1] (with the addition of two new instructions RIM and SIM), and, finally, both the 8085 and 8080A have the same addressing modes.

---

[1]Some differences, however, do exist in the execution of these instructions, specifically in the number of states required and the flags affected.

Appendix 3

ZILOG Z80

Since the Z80 appeared somewhat later than the 8080A, it exhibited architectural enhancements and improvements that established it as the standard 8-bit medium-level microprocessor and it generated multiple second sources. The Z80, too, is manufactured in NMOS technology on one 40-pin chip. It requires a single external RC and a single 5v power supply, and all output signals are fully decoded and timed to control standard memory or peripheral circuits [45]. The Z80 also provides more registers and addressing modes than the 8080A, has an additional non-maskable interrupt input pin, built-in logic to refresh dynamic RAM memories, and a much larger instruction set than the 8080A [31]. The standard Z80 is driven by a 2.5 MHz clock, whereas the Z80A is driven by a 4.0 MHz clock (1.0 μs basic instruction time).

The simplified functional block diagram of the Z80 microprocessor is given in Figure A3.1a, and its pins and signals in Figure A3.1b. Like the 8080A, the Z80 also communicates with the other system modules via three functionally separate buses. One bus is an 8-bit bidirectional *data bus* (D0–D7). The second bus is a 16-bit *address bus* (A0–A15) that provides the address for memory data exchanges (maximum address space, 64K bytes) and for I/O module data exchanges. As in the 8080A, I/O is performed using specific I/O instructions, and the device address (or number) uses the eight lower-order bits[2] of the address bus to allow selection of up to 256 input or 256 output ports. During memory refresh time, the seven lower-order bits of the address bus (A0–A6) contain a valid refresh address.

Functionally, a *control bus* also exists to carry three types of control signals: system control signals ($\overline{M_1}$, $\overline{MREQ}$, $\overline{IORQ}$, $\overline{RD}$, $\overline{WR}$, $\overline{RFSH}$), CPU control signals ($\overline{WAIT}$, $\overline{HALT}$, $\overline{INT}$, $\overline{NMI}$), and bus control signals ($\overline{BUSRQ}$, $\overline{BUSAK}$, $\overline{RESET}$).

The ALU is eight bits wide and performs similar functions to those of the 8080A ALU.

---

[2]It is not duplicated on both the upper and lower eight lines of the address bus.

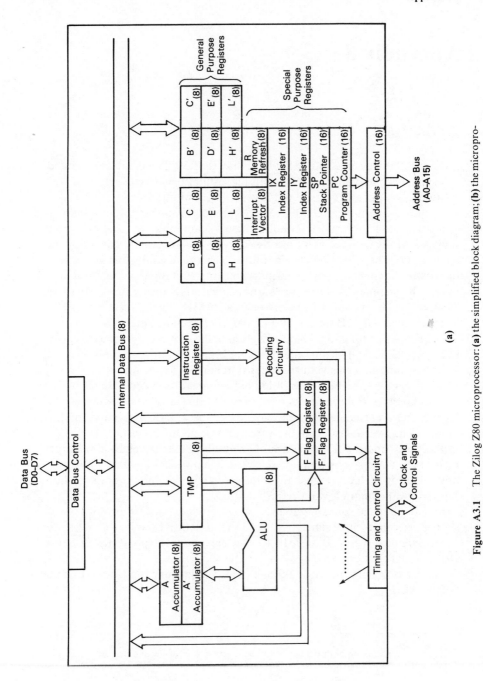

(a)

Figure A3.1   The Zilog Z80 microprocessor: **(a)** the simplified block diagram; **(b)** the microprocessor pins and signals.

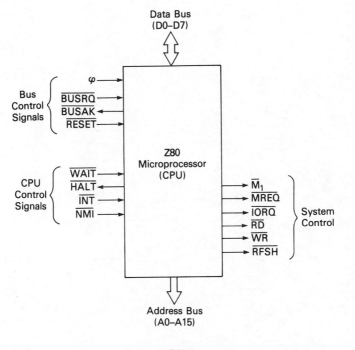

(b)

Figure A3.1 (*Continued*)

Figure A3.2 shows the register structure of the Z80 microprocessor. The chip contains two independent 8-bit accumulators A and A', as well as two alternate sets of six 8-bit general-purpose registers (B, C, D, E, H, L, and B', C', D', E', H', L',). These registers may be used individually as 8-bit registers (referred to as (B, C, D, E, H, and L) or as 16-bit register pairs (referred to as BC, DE, and HL). At any one time the programmer can select to work with either main or alternate register set with a single exchange instruction (EXX) for the entire set. This alternate set allows foreground/background mode of operation or handling fast interrupt response requirements. Instead of being forced to store the contents of the accumulator/flag and general-purpose registers in the external stack, the interrupt handling or subroutine processing times are greatly reduced by simply deactivating one set without destroying its contents and switching to the other set through a group of exchange instructions.

Besides the duplicate accumulators, the Z80 also includes two independent flags registers (F and F'), each containing the six flags: sign (S and S'), zero (Z and Z'), carry (C and C'), parity/overflow (P/V and P/V'), half-carry (H and

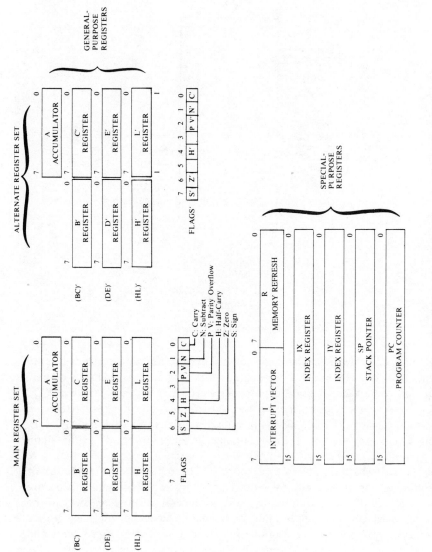

Figure A.3.2   The programming model for the Z80 microprocessor.

Note: The accumulator (A / A') and flags (F / F') registers are sometimes treated as a 16-bit unit (PSW / PSW').

H') and subtract (N and N'). As for the two alternate sets of general-purpose registers, the programmer may select the accumulator and flag register pair with which he or she wishes to work, with a single exchange instruction (EX AF,AF') so that he may work easily with either pair. This makes it very easy to handle single-level interrupts, since the PSW (the accumulator and flag register contents) no longer need to be saved on the external stack; instead, the program may simply switch to the alternate register pair.

The 16-bit program counter (PC) and stack pointer (SP) registers are the same as those of the 8085 microprocessor and operate in exactly the same way. Two other 16-bit registers found in the Z80 microprocessor are the two index registers IX and IY, which allow for two independent index addressing modes.

Finally, the Z80 includes two new 8-bit registers, the interrupt vector register (I) and the memory refresh register (R) whose operation was discussed in section 4.3.1 of chapter 4.

The Z80 can execute 158 instruction types. The microprocessor includes all the instructions of the 8080A microprocessor with total software compatibility at the machine code level. New instructions include 1-, 4-, 8- and 16-bit operations, exchange instructions, block-transfer and block-search instructions, and a full set of rotate-and-shift instructions applicable to any register, rather than just to the accumulator.

The instructions may require only a single byte, or two, three, or even four successive bytes. The 1-byte instructions represent an op code. In 2-byte instructions, the first byte is the op code, while the second byte may be the op code, data byte, device number, or displacement. In 3-byte instructions, the first byte is the op code, the second byte is the op code, data byte, or low address byte, and the third byte is the data byte, high address byte, or displacement. In all but one 4-byte instruction type, the first one or two bytes are op codes and the remaining bytes are information needed to carry out the instruction; the third byte is the data byte, low address byte, or displacement, and the fourth byte is the data byte or high address byte. Again, the first byte determines the way the other bytes of the instruction will be interpreted. A *data byte* is an 8-bit immediate operand (binary, BCD, ASCII, etc.) that can be used in an arithmetic or logical operation or to store in memory. A *device number* is an 8-bit code corresponding to an input or output port (for the I/O instructions). Two consecutive instruction bytes may also contain a 16-bit *address,* the first containing the low-order part of the address, and the second containing the high order part. Finally, a *displacement* byte may also appear in an instruction. The displacement is a signed 2's complement number which is added to a 16-bit number residing in an index register, during indexed addressing.

Every Z80 instruction cycle consists of from one to six machine cycles (M_1, M_2, M_3, M_4, M_5, M_6). All machine cycle types consist of either three or four states (T_1, T_2, T_3, T_4). Some Z80 instructions always insert T_w states between states T_2 and T_3. The low to high transition of the clock signal defines each state. The basic operation of the Z80 is analogous to that of the Intel 8085. The main difference in the timings between memory read/write and I/O operations is that, for the former, the $\overline{\text{MREQ}}$ is activated (output low), while for the latter, the $\overline{\text{IORQ}}$ is activated (output low). For interface purposes, the Z80 has a general read ($\overline{\text{RD}}$) and a general write ($\overline{\text{WR}}$) signal, coupled with the memory request ($\overline{\text{MREQ}}$) and I/O request ($\overline{\text{IORQ}}$) signal (also see third column in Figure 5.11 of chapter 5).

Appendix 4

MOTOROLA 6800

The Motorola 6800 product family was originally introduced in 1974. The 6800 microprocessor CPU is manufactured in NMOS technology on a 40-pin chip, has TTL compatible pins, and was the first 8-bit single-chip microprocessor to exploit a single 5v power supply. The 6800 CPU can drive from seven to ten 6800-family devices without buffering. It is capable of handling two types of interrupts: maskable and non-maskable interrupt inputs. Like the 8080A, the 6800 CPU requires two input clock phases, φ_1 and φ_2. Its architecture represents an improvement over the 8080A and closely resembles that of minicomputers like the PDP-11 [28, 29]. The simplified functional block diagram of the 6800 microprocessor is given in Figure A4.1a and its pins and signals in Figure A4.1b.

The 6800 CPU uses three buses to communicate with the other system modules: a 16-bit *address bus* (A0–A15), an 8-bit non-multiplexed bidirectional *data bus* (D0–D7), and a *control bus* that carries the control bus signals (VMA, R/W, $\overline{\text{IRQ}}$, φ_2, and $\overline{\text{RESET}}$) and the microprocessor (CPU) supervisory signals (BA, $\overline{\text{HALT}}$, TSC, DBE, $\overline{\text{NMI}}$, RESET, φ_1, φ_2, and $\overline{\text{IRQ}}$).

The capability of the 6800's ALU is similar to that of the 8085 ALU.

Figure A4.2 shows the register structure of the 6800 microprocessor. It contains two accumulators, A and B, both being primary accumulators, a 16-bit index register (X), a 16-bit stack pointer (S), and a 16-bit program counter (PC) that points to the current program instruction address. Finally, it includes a condition code register that contains the six flags: half-carry (H), interrupt enable/disable (I), negative (N), zero (Z), overflow (V) and carry (C). The unused bits of the condition code register (bits 6 and 7) are 1's.

Since memory-mapped I/O is exercised by the 6800 (i.e., no I/O instructions as such exist), the seventy-two instructions of the 6800 are classified into three distinct groups:

(a) Accumulator and memory instructions: In many instances the CPU performs the same operation on both its internal accumulators and external memory locations. These instructions can be subdivided further into four categories: arithmetic, logic, data test, and data handling instructions.

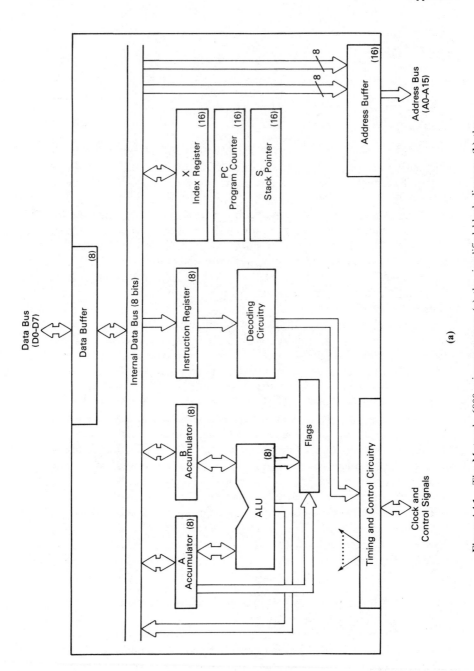

Figure A4.1 The Motorola 6800 microprocessor: **(a)** the simplified block diagram; **(b)** the microprocessor pins and signals.

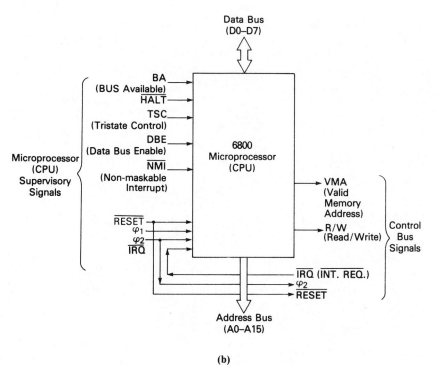

(b)

Figure A4.1 (continued)

(b) Program control instructions: These instructions are used for direct operation on the CPU's index register and stack pointer and for controlling the sequence of executing the program instructions. They may be subdivided further into: index register/stack pointer instructions; jump and branch instructions.

(c) Condition code register manipulation instructions: These instructions are available to the user for direct manipulation of the condition code (or status) register. In addition, appropriate status bits of this register are set or cleared automatically according to the specific instruction being executed. This CPU register is very useful in controlling program flow during system operation.

A 6800 instruction may be one, two, or three bytes long, its length being closely related to the addressing mode used.

Usually every 6800 instruction cycle consists of from two to eight machine cycles, all of which are identical in length (except interrupt instructions, which

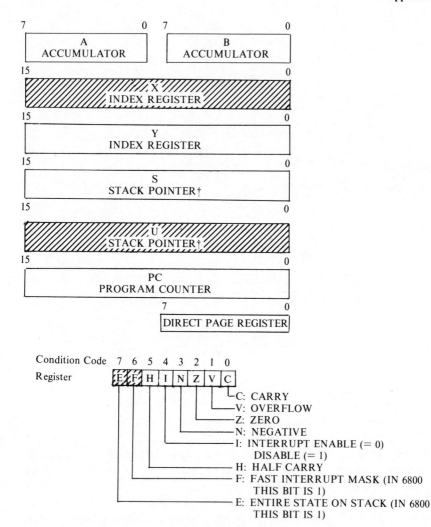

†Both stack pointers can be used as index registers.

Figure A.4.2 The programming model for the Motorola 6800 and 6809 microprocessors. (Shaded registers and flag bits found only in 6809.) [12, 46]

require longer instruction execution cycles). In the 6800, a machine cycle is one and the same thing as a clock cycle (or state). The operation of the 6800 is very simple, since it consists of only three types of machine cycles: a *read machine cycle* (during which a byte of data is input into the CPU[3]), a *write machine cycle* (during which a byte of data is output by the CPU), and an *interrupt operation machine cycle* (during which the CPU is busy and no activity occurs on the system buses). The timing of any 6800 instruction is simply a concatenation of these three basic machine cycle types.

The control signals required to access a memory location are R/W, VMA, and DBE. Under normal circumstances, DBE is identical to φ_2. The signal R/W controls whether reading (R/W = 1) or storing (R/W = 0) will take place.

---

[3]All 6800 I/O ports are treated exactly like memory locations (memory-mapped I/O).

Appendix 5

INTEL 8086

The simplified functional block diagram of the 8086 microprocessor is shown in Figure A5.1a and its pins and signals in Figure A5.1b.

The 8086[4] is manufactured in HMOS technology on a 40-pin chip containing approximately 29K transistors, having a size of 225 × 225 mils and operating at a clock rate of 5 MHz (200 nsec) on standard chips or of 8 MHz (125 nsec) on selected chips. The 8086 is fully software compatible to the 8080A/8085 (at the assembly language level not object code level), and includes a compatible subset of registers. Thus software that was generated for those previous Intel chips (the 8080A/8085) can also run on the new product [2, 5, 6, 7, 9, 14].

The 8086 microprocessor communicates with the other system modules via two buses. One bus is the *control bus*, which carries all control and status signals; it will be discussed later. The second bus is a 20-line time-miltiplexed bus. Functionally these twenty lines are divided as follows: (a) sixteen bidirectional lines constitute the *address/data bus* (denoted as AD0–AD15) that carries either the sixteen least significant bits of an address or 16-bit data; (b) the remaining four lines constitute an *address/status bus* (denoted as A16/S3–A19/S6) that carry either the remaining four most significant bits of an address A16–A19 or four status bits S3–S6. The multiplexing technique used by the 8086 CPU for address and data resembles the one used by the 8085 CPU, where each processor bus cycle consists of at least four clock periods or states T_1, T_2, T_3, T_4. As in the 8085, the 8086 CPU emits the ALE (address latch enable) signal, so that the bus may also be demultiplexed at the processor using a single set of address latches, when a standard non-multiplexed bus is desired for a specific system configuration. Since it transfers a 20-bit physical address to memory, the 8086 can directly access a physical memory of up to

---

[4]The 8088 microprocessor is almost identical to the 8086, the primary difference being that the 8088 is designed with an 8-bit external data path to memory and I/O, while the 8086 can transfer sixteen bits at a time.

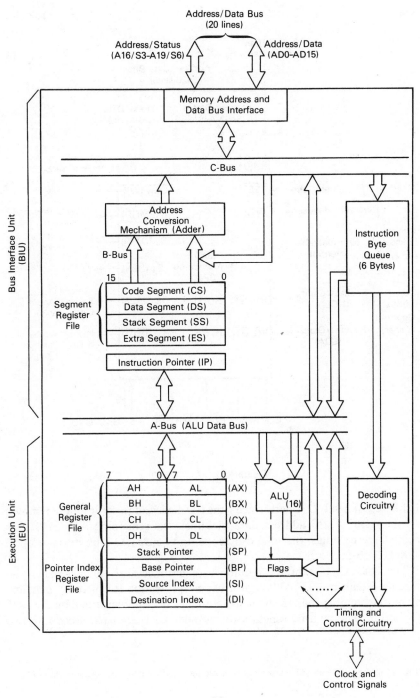

Figure A5.1 The Intel 8086 microprocessor: **(a)** the simplified block diagram; **(b)** the microprocessor pins and signals.

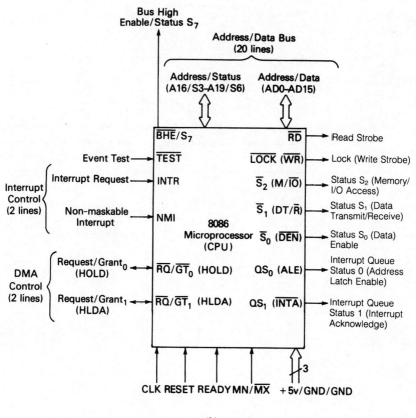

Bus High
Enable/Status S7

Address/Data Bus
(20 lines)

Address/Status   Address/Data
(A16/S3–A19/S6)   (AD0–AD15)

BHE/S7   RD   Read Strobe

Event Test → TEST   LOCK (WR)   Lock (Write Strobe)

Interrupt Request → INTR   S2 (M/IO)   Status S2 (Memory/
Interrupt   I/O Access)
Control
(2 lines)   S1 (DT/R)   Status S1 (Data
Non-maskable → NMI   Transmit/Receive)
Interrupt   8086
                        Microprocessor   S0 (DEN)   Status S0 (Data)
                        (CPU)   Enable

Request/Grant0   Interrupt Queue
(HOLD) → RQ/GT0 (HOLD)   QS0 (ALE)   Status 0 (Address
DMA   Latch Enable)
Control
(2 lines)
Request/Grant1 → RQ/GT1 (HLDA)   QS1 (INTA)   Interrupt Queue
(HLDA)   Status 1 (Interrupt
                                                           Acknowledge)

                                                            3

CLK RESET READY MN/MX   + 5v/GND/GND

(b)

Figure A5.1   *(Continued)*

1M bytes. When I/O is performed,[5] the I/O device address (or number) moves
on the AD0– AD15 address/data bus lines, the remaining A16– A19 lines
being 0 (zero). Thus, the 8086 can access up to 64K I/O 8-bit ports or up to
32K I/O 16-bit ports.

The 8086 CPU exhibits a number of architectural enhancements and
advanced features [1]. Although it has no protection for memory management, the memory management structure has been implemented on the 8086
CPU chip. The internal functions of the 8086 CPU are partitioned into two

---

[5]Like all Intel products, the 8086 provides designated input and output instructions to perform I/O.

independently controlled processing units: the "bus interface unit" (devoted exclusively to updating the 64K-byte segments or logical address subspaces[6] of the 1M-byte physical memory space), and the "execution unit" (used for arithmetic/logic operations). These units can interact directly, but for the most part perform as separate asynchronous operational processors. The bus interface unit handles I/O data transfers and interfaces with memory. The execution unit includes the ALU, executes the instruction stream from a queue, and manipulates the internal registers. This concurrent operation improves bus efficiency by eliminating much of the bus dead-time and, at the same time, the standard 8086 permits a memory access time of 460 nsec.

The *bus interface unit* (BIU) provides the functions related to address relocation, instruction fetching and queuing, operand fetching and storing, and also provides the basic bus control. To perform dynamic address relocation, four special segment registers (in this case not allowed to be accessed by the normal programmer) are included in the BIU, along with an address conversion mechanism. Un-relocated operand addresses are provided to the BIU by the execution unit. The execution unit also passes the processing results to the BIU for storage into the external memory. The use and operation of the segment registers, the address conversion mechanism of the BIU, and the operation of the instruction stream queuing mechanism of the 8086 BIU are discussed in detail in section 10.4.2 of chapter 10. Overlap of instruction fetching and execution is accomplished in the BIU in its 6-byte instruction queue (or FIFO buffer). This queue smooths the random flow of instructions with different byte lengths and speeds up the processor.

The *execution unit* (EU) of the 8086 CPU contains the programmer-accessible general purpose register file, the 16-bit ALU with its flag register, and the instruction decoding circuitry. The EU receives prefetched instructions from the BIU queue and provides un-relocated operand addresses to the BIU. Processing is performed in the EU on operands passed to it from the BIU, and the EU then passes results to the BIU for storage. (Also see section 4.4.3 of chapter 4 for the operation of the EU.)

The 8086 has 135 basic instruction op codes, and each individual instruction can directly access up to 64K bytes in memory. Several of these instructions may manipulate the four segment registers in the BIU. Most of the rest of the 8086's instruction set operates with the general register file in the EU. The 8086 has two priority levels of external interrupts: one higher priority non-maskable interrupt, and one lower priority maskable interrupt, the second

---

[6]The terms "logical address space," "segments," "program relocation," and "dynamic memory allocation" are defined in chapter 10.

being a vectored interrupt which transfers control to a location in a 256-element vector table. This vector table is in *fixed* memory locations.

A stack marker is provided which can shift stack references during the move to a new relocatable code segment. The 8086 provides both signed and unsigned 8- and 16-bit arithmetic (including multiply and divide), both packed and unpacked binary coded representations, efficient byte string operations, improved bit manipulation, re-entrant code, position independent code, and dynamically relocatable programs.

To support either minimum (MN) or maximum (MX) system configuration flexibility, the 8086 is equipped with a strap pin (MN/$\overline{\text{MX}}$) which defines the system configuration. As shown in Figure A5.1b, several processor pins perform dual system functions based on the value of the signal of the MN/$\overline{\text{MX}}$ pin.

The 8086 has the ability to support multiprocessor configurations through a "master-slave bus architecture" and a number of special instructions. When a master accesses the system bus, it does not allow any other master to obtain the bus. Intel also provides co-processor devices (e.g., the 8087) to facilitate satellite processing. The 8086 can support the design of efficient high-level languages and improved operating system implementations. However, the 8086 does not have separate "user" and "supervisor" modes, as do other 16- and 32-bit microprocessors (e.g., Zilog Z8000, National NS16032, Motorola 68000, Intel APX 432).

The 8086 CPU contains one 16-bit ALU, which can execute both 8- and 16-bit signed and unsigned binary arithmetic, including both signed and unsigned multiply and divide, as well as logical operations on 8- and 16- bit operands. Standard 2's complement representation of signed values is used. A general-purpose register file provides operands for the microprocessor's 16-bit arithmetic/logic operations. A multiply operation produces a double length product, while a divide operation returns a single-length quotient and a single-length remainder from a double-length dividend and a single-length divisor. Sign extension operations allow one to construct the double-length dividend needed for signed division.

With the aid of its correction operations, the 8086 can also do arithmetic directly on either packed or unpacked (e.g., ASCII) BCD representations of decimal digits, and the conversion is done in hardware by one instruction. For packed BCD operations two accumulator adjustment instructions are provided, one for addition and one for subtraction. For unpacked BCD operations, four such adjustment instructions are provided, one for addition, one for subtraction, one for multiplication, and one for division (unlike the other three, this last adjustment is performed prior to a division operation). Unlike packed BCD, unpacked BCD byte multiplication does not generate cross terms, and so multiplication and division adjustments are possible.

The system can also handle bit, byte, and block operations. Primitive (1-byte) string instructions exist to operate on a string of bytes or words, for large data handling operations.

Figure A5.2 shows the register structure of the 8086 microprocessor. It contains eight 16-bit registers that make up the general-purpose register file and four 16-bit special registers that make up the segment register file (or S group). The eight general-purpose registers are further divided into two groups: one is the HL group, consisting of four registers that are used for arithmetic and logical operations, and the other is the P & I group, consisting of four registers that are primarily used for memory address calculations, two as pointer registers and two as index registers. Included also is a 16-bit instruction pointer and the 16-bit PSW register that contains the nine 8086 flags. The four segment registers and the instruction pointer are located in the bus interface unit (BIU) of the CPU; the remaining registers are located in the execution unit (EU) (also see Figure A5.1a).

The AX-BX-CX-DX register set is called the *general register file*, or *HL group*. The registers can participate interchangeably in the arithmetic and logical operations of the 8086. Some other operations, however (e.g., string operations), dedicate some of the general registers to specific uses as, for example, "base and count," as indicated by the mnemonic names in Figure A5.2. The upper and lower halves of these registers are separately addressable as 8-bit registers, forming the H and L files, respectively. Upward compatibility with the 8080/8085 is maintained by pairing 8080/8085 registers (BH, BL, CH, CL, DH, DL) to define three 8086 16-bit registers.

The second CPU register file is the *pointer and index register file*, or *P&I group*. Like the HL group, they can also participate interchangeably in the 16-bit arithmetic and logical operations. Generally, they contain offset addresses used for addressing within the segment. The pointer registers SP and BP (or P-group) contain by default offset addresses within the current stack segment, as shown by the arrow at the right side of Figure A5.2. Similarly, the index registers SI and DI (or I-group) contain by default offset addresses within the current data segment. All data manipulation instructions apply to all 16-bit general-purpose registers; certain addressing modes imply specific registers.

The other 8086 set of registers constitute the *segment* (or relocation) *register file*, or *S group*, that handles memory management on-chip by dividing program and data space. The way the 8086 performs memory management through segmentation was discussed in section 10.4.2 of chapter 10. This segment register file extends the chip's direct addressing capability up to 1M bytes of physical memory—in contrast to the 64K-byte capacity of the 8080/8085. In this file, address relocation values for up to four 64K-byte

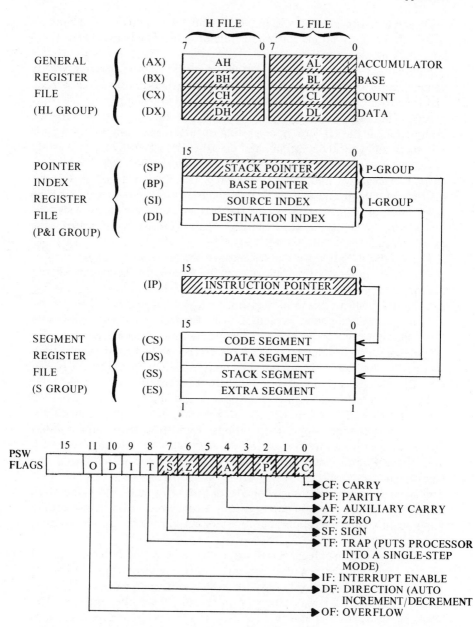

Figure A5.2   The Intel 8086 internal register structure (8080/8085 registers shown shaded).

segments are stored, thus allowing a logical address space of up to 256K bytes to be addressed at any one time as combined code, stack, and data.

The last register found in the 8086 is the 16-bit PSW that contains the nine 1-bit condition flags: overflow (OF), direction (DF), interrupt enable (IF), trap (TF), sign (SF), zero (ZF), auxiliary carry (AF), parity (PF) and carry (CF).

The 8086 includes the basic instructions of its 8-bit predecessors, 8080A/ 8085, along with new additional instructions. Unlike the Zilog Z8000 and Motorola 68000, the 8086 does not have privileged instructions.

The 8086 instruction length varies from one to four bytes. Most commonly an instruction is two bytes long, and nearly all instructions operate on either 8- or 16-bit operands. Both single- and dual-operand instructions are provided. Two-byte instructions are word-aligned in memory using even addresses; the instruction stream is fetched from memory as words, and is addressed internally by the processor to the byte level as necessary.

Several 8086 instructions may manipulate the four segment registers that make up the segment register file. It must be noted that if a program is larger than the maximum segment size of 64K bytes, simply allowing the instruction pointer to increment will cause the program to "jump" to its beginning. To get past the 64K limit, the code segment (CS) register must be changed suitably. In a similar manner, when data are accessed by adding the contents of the data segment (DS) register to the operand address, again the DS register is explicitly under programmer control and is not automatically incremented/decremented by the hardware. Similar control techniques are applicable to the stack segment (SS) and the extra segment (ES) registers.

Most common formats for the 8086 instructions are those of Figure A5.3. The registers and displacements used to calculate an effective address (EA) are encoded in the second byte within two fields of the instruction format. The 2-bit mode field *(mod)* and the 3-bit register/mode field *(r/m)* together specify one operand while the *reg* field specifies the register operand. The direction bit, d, specifies the direction of the operation: $d = 0$ signifies operation from, and $d = 1$ operation to the register. Both 8- and 16-bit registers and memory operands in the 8086 are facilitated with an additional word/byte bit, w, contained within the first byte of the instruction format.

The instruction set of the 8086 includes six different types of instructions:

- *Data transfer group:* Four classes of data transfer operations are distinguised: general-purpose (MOVE, PUSH, POP, and EXCHANGE), accumulator-specific (INPUT, OUTPUT, TRANSLATE), address-object transfers (load effective address and load pointer) and flag transfers (providing access to the collection of flags for such operations as PUSH, POP, load and store).

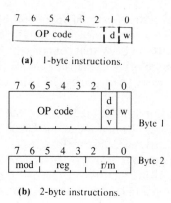

(a) 1-byte instructions.

(b) 2-byte instructions.

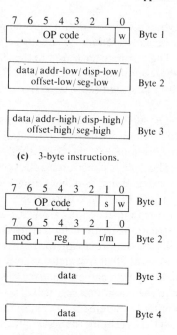

(c) 3-byte instructions.

(d) 4-byte instruction.

where:
if d = 1 then "to" reg; if d = 0 then "from" reg,
if w = 1 then word instruction; if w = 0 then byte instruction

if mode = 11 then r m is treated as a REG field
if mode = 00 then DISP = 0*, disp-low and disp-high are absent
if mode = 01 then DISP = disp-low sign-extended to 16-bits, disp-high is absent
if mode = 10 then DISP = disp-high: disp-low

if r/m = 000 then EA = (BX) + (SI) + DISP
if r/m = 001 then EA = (BX) + (DI) + DISP
if r/m = 010 then EA = (BP) + (SI) + DISP
if r/m = 011 then EA = (BP) + (DI) + DISP
if r/m = 100 then EA = (SI) + DISP
if r/m = 101 then EA = (DI) + DISP
if r/m = 110 then EA = (BP) + DISP*
if r/m = 111 then EA = (BX) + DISP
DISP follows 2nd byte of instruction (before data if required)

*except if mode = 00 and r/m = 110 then EA = disp-high: disp-low

if s : w = 01 then 16 bits of immediate data form the operand
if s : w = 11 then an immediate data byte is sign extended to form the 16-bit operand
if v = 0 then "count" =1; if v = 1 then "count" in (CL)

SEGMENT OVERRIDE PREFIX
0 0 1 reg 1 1 0

REG is assigned according to the following table

16 Bit (w = 1)	8 Bit (w = 0)	Segment
000 AX	000 AL	00 ES
001 CX	001 CL	01 CS
010 DX	010 DL	10 SS
011 BX	011 BL	11 DS
100 SP	100 AH	
101 BP	101 CH	
110 SI	110 DH	
111 DI	111 BH	

Figure A5.3 The most common 8086 instruction formats. *Courtesy Intel Corporation* [14].

- *Arithmetic group:* For 8- and 16-bit binary and decimal (packed and unpacked) add, subtract, multiply, divide, increment, decrement, compare, etc.
- *Logical group:* Includes all standard logical operations, plus an additional logical "TEST for specific bits" that only sets the flags.
- *String manipulation group:* This is a group of 1-byte instructions which perform various primitive operations for manipulating byte and word strings. By preceding the instruction with a special prefix, these primitive operations can be performed repeatedly in hardware, until the operation count in CX is satisfied. There are five primitive string operations (MOVB or MOVW, CMPB or CMPW, SCAB or SCAW, LODB or LODW, and STOB or STOW), all of which use the SI register to address the source operands which are assumed to be in the current data segment. The DI register is used to address the destination operands which reside in the current extra segment.
- *Control transfer group:* Both direct and indirect transfers (such as calls, jumps, and returns) are provided in the 8086 either within the current code segment (intra-segment transfers) or to an arbitrary code segment (inter-segment transfers), which then becomes the current code segment. The 8086 also provides for a self-relative addressing on a conditional branch, but restricts the offset to +128 and −126 bytes. This may pose a problem when a branch to a location outside the range of the conditional jump is required. Included in this group are the interrupt-type instructions and the four iteration-control transfer operations used for string manipulation: LOOP, LOOPZ, LOOPNZ, and JCXZ.
- *Processor control group:* This includes instructions that set and clear CPU flags, halt and wait instructions, and two special instructions: an ESCAPE to an external processor instruction to perform specialized operations, and a lock exchange instruction (LOCK XCHG, also known as test-and-set-lock) to control access to shared resources in a multiprocessor configuration.

Appendix 6

ZILOG Z8000

The simplified functional block diagram of the Z8000 is given in Figure A6.1a; Figure A6.1b shows the microprocessor alternate configuration with the additional memory management unit (MMU) and Figure A6.1c shows the CPU signals.

The Z8000 microprocessor is software compatible to its earlier 8-bit counterpart product, the Z80, and includes a compatible subset of registers. The Z8000 is a 16-bit word length machine, manufactured through HMOS technology, containing approximately 17.5K transistors on a 238x256 mils chip which comes in two versions (a 40-pin non-segmented and a 48-pin segmented version). It uses a single 5v supply and can operate at a clock rate of 4 MHz (250 nsec clock cycle).

The smaller 40-pin chip microprocessor (called the Z8002) can directly address a physical memory space of up to only 64K bytes. The larger 48-pin chip (called the Z8001 and compatible to Z8002) provides a segmented addressing scheme. When used by itself, it issues a 23-bit address to memory capable of directly addressing a physical memory space of 8M bytes. When used with one external MMU however, its current implementation issues a 24-bit address to memory capable of accessing a large 16M bytes physical memory space. In this case, a translation is performed from logical to physical addresses. Logical addresses are still twenty-three bits long, defining a maximum directly addressable logical address space of 8M bytes. (To map this maximum logical address space, two external MMUs are required.) Instead of treating the logical address space as a linear logical space, the Z8000 organizes it into a set of 128 segments of up to 64K bytes each. The MMU also performs dynamic program relocation and memory protection. Using additional MMU chips, the 48-pin Z8001 is capable of handling up to six separate 8M-byte logical address spaces, extending total logical address space up to 48M bytes [37, 46, 47].

The Z8000 provides both *normal* and *system* operating modes. Memory references may be instructions (code), or data or stack accesses, each type of access being possible in either normal or system mode. This defines six possible address spaces, each possibility distinguished by a unique combination of signals on the status lines ST_3-ST_0 and the control line $N/\overline{S}$.

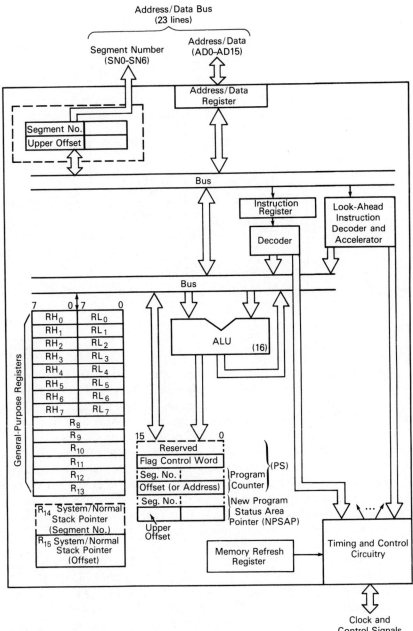

(a)

Figure A6.1   The Zilog Z8000 microprocessor: **(a)** the simplified block diagram; **(b)** the Z8001
with one MMU; **(c)** the microprocessor pins and signals.

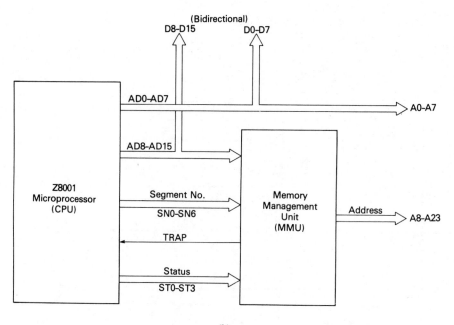

(b)

Figure A6.1 (*Continued*)

The Z8000 has more than 110 basic instructions, capable of appropriately defining up to 418 op codes. It can handle seven data types, from bits to word strings, and offers eight selectable addressing modes. Like 8086, the Z8000 distinguishes between memory and I/O spaces, thus providing specific I/O instructions (memory-mapped I/O is still possible). The Z8000 was designed to accommodate three priority levels of external interrupts: non-maskable, non-vectored, and vectored interrupts, where the vector table (referred to by the Z8000 as "vectored interrupt jump table") can be placed *anywhere* in memory. Regarding stacks, the Z8000 exhibits more than one stack and has the ability to switch groups of stacks simultaneously. Finally, distributed processing or multiprocessor configuration capabilities also exist in the Z8000.

Besides the larger addressing capability, the Z8000 has the following significant differences from the 8086:   (1) Memory management and translation of logical addresses into physical addresses is performed in the *external* memory management unit (MMU). (2) The Z8000 provides a set of *privileged instructions* that may be executed only by system programs operating in the system mode. Thus, the Z8000 can support concurrently running programs in a

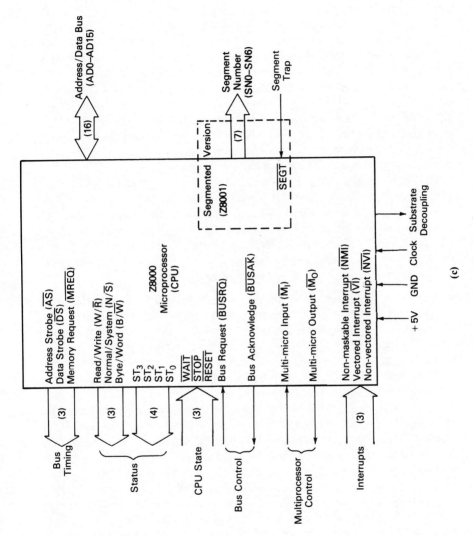

Figure A6.1 (*Continued*)

multi-user environment. (3) The Z8000 does not use an internal instruction queue, but it does use some form of pipelining, having a look-ahead memory prefetch, but only for a single instruction. (4) The Z8000 also exhibits a *memory protection* mechanism for both system and user memory areas, implemented on the external MMU chips.

The smaller 40-pin microprocessor communicates with the other system modules via two buses. One bus is the *control bus*, which carries all control and status signals. The second bus is a time-multiplexed *address/data bus* that carries either 16-bit addresses (memory addresses or I/O port numbers, distinguished by the CPU status outputs) that can access up to 64K bytes of memory (the equivalent of one segment) or 16-bit data. The larger 48-pin Z8001 microprocessor includes additionally one input control line (the "segment trap") and seven output lines SN0–SN6. These output lines provide the 7-bit *segment number* used to address one of 128 segments via external memory management units as shown in Figure A6.1b.

The Z8000 CPU contains one 16-bit ALU, which may execute both signed and unsigned arithmetic (including signed multiply and divide), as well as logical operations on a variety of data types. For negative values the standard 2's complement signed representation is used.

Finally, the Z8000 provides both the necessary hardware and instructions to support an increased number of data types. The seven *basic types of data* are mentioned here in ascending order of their size:

- *Bits:* They are addressed by number within a byte or word, counting from right to left. When a bit is referenced in memory, the memory address designates the byte or word that contains it. Bits can be set, reset, and tested.
- *BCD digits:* They are represented as two 4-bit digits in a byte and used in BCD arithmetic operations. When a digit is referenced in memory, the memory address designates the byte that contains it.
- *Bytes:* They are eight bits long and used for character or small integer values. They are addressed in memory by specifying a byte address that can range between 0 and 8,388,607 (or 65,535, depending on whether segmented or non-segmented mode is used).
- *Words:* They are sixteen bits long and used for larger integer values, instructions, and non-segmented addresses. A word data type can be addressed in memory by specifying the byte address of its left-most byte (the high order byte). Words are always aligned (i.e., the left-most byte of a word has an even-numbered address) to avoid the time penalty resulting from successive fetches of the high and low byte of a word spanning the alignment boundary.

- *Long words:* They are 32 bits long and used for long integer values and segmented addresses. A long word (or double word) data element can be addressed in memory by specifying the leftmost byte of its leftmost (high order) word.
- *Byte strings:* They are composed of $8n + 8$ bits, their length in bytes explicitly provided by the programmer. They may be accessed in either ascending or descending address order.
- *Word strings:* They are composed of $16n + 16$ bits, their length in words explicitly provided by the programmer. They may be accessed in either ascending or descending address order.

All data elements except strings can reside either in registers or memory. A data element in a CPU register is designated by a byte register address for a bit, BCD digit, or byte data type, by a 16-bit register address for a word type, or by a 32-bit register pair address for a long word type. Byte/word strings are stored in memory and designated by the lowest or the highest byte/word address, and length in bytes/words. Their maximum length is 64K bytes.

Figure A6.2 shows the internal register structures of the 48-pin Z8001 and the 40-pin Z8002. The Z8000 CPU contains sixteen 16-bit internal registers, R0–R15, all accessible by the programmer. All of them can be used as accumulators, and the R1–R15 registers can also be used as index registers or as base registers. Pairs of 16-bit registers can be combined when operating on 32-bit (long word) data, while quadruple registers can be combined to accommodate 64-bit data fields for instructions such as multiply and divide.

As shown in Figure A6.2 the flexibility of the registers is afforded by a unique arrangement of the *general registers* file, or by grouping and overlapping its multiple registers. For byte operations, there are sixteen 8-bit registers (RH0–RH7 and RL0–RL7), all of which may be used as accumulators, and which are overlapped with the first eight 16-bit general-purpose registers (R0–R7). Eight more 16-bit general purpose registers (R8–R15) are also available. All of these sixteen 16-bit general registers may be used as word accumulators or source operands, and all but one (the R0) can serve as index registers or memory pointers, including stack pointers (with the aid of PUSH and POP instructions). Thus, the Z8000 has chosen this regularity of register structure instead of dedicating registers to special functions which could possibly lead to some encoding improvements in instruction formats. The sixteen 16-bit registers are grouped in pairs (RR0, RR2, ..., RR14) to form eight 32-bit long word registers. Also, four 64-bit registers (RQ0, RQ4, RQ8, RQ12) used by few instructions such as multiply, divide, and extend sign, may be formed by grouping together quadruples of 16-bit general registers.

Figure A6.2 The Z8000 internal register structure: **(a)** the 48-pin segmented version Z8001; **(b)** the 40-pin non-segmented version Z8002 [46]. *Reproduced by permission.* ©1982

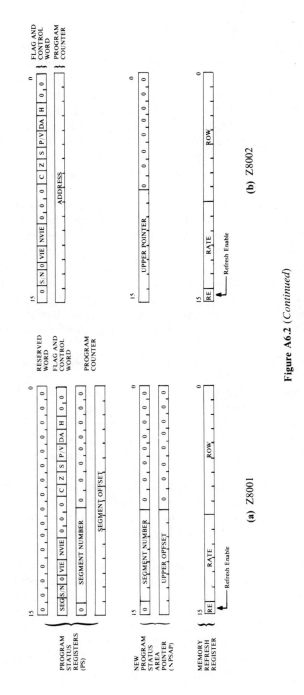

Figure A6.2 (*Continued*)

Both the non-segmented (Z8002) and the segmented version of the chip (Z8001) can use stacks located anywhere in memory. The only instructions that use the *stack pointer* exclusively are call (CALL), call relative (CALR), return (RET), and return from interrupt (IRET); the PUSH and POP instructions can use any register as a stack pointer. However, the user can manipulate the stack pointer with all instructions, since it is in the general register group. In the non-segmented Z8002, the last 16-bit general register, R15, is the stack pointer. In the segmented Z8001, the last two registers, R14 and R15 (or the long word register RR14) are needed to hold the stack pointer; register R14 contains the 7-bit segment number while R15 contains the 16-bit offset. Since the Z8000 has two running modes—normal and system—there are two copies of the stack pointer: one for the normal mode (R15 or R14 and R15) and one for the system mode (R15' or R14' and R15'). This distinction between normal and system stacks separates the application program information from system information. Although the stacks are separated, it is possible to access the normal stack registers while they are in the system mode by using the privileged instruction "load-control-word" (LDCTL). Having two sets of stack pointers facilitates context-switching when interrupts or traps occur. The normal stack never contains system information, since the information saved when interrupts or traps occur is always pushed onto the system stack before the new program status is loaded.

In addition to the above-discussed general registers, there are some other, special registers in the Z8000 CPU.

The *program status (PS) registers* are special registers that contain program status information. The program status is a group of words containing the current state of the CPU (i.e., the flags, the control bits, and the program counter). Upon the occurrence of an interrupt or trap, CPU program status is saved in the system stack (thus preserving the status of the interrupted program), and a new program status is loaded. The loading of this new program status results in branching to the appropriate routine to handle the interrupt or trap. In the non-segmented Z8002, the program status consists of two words (held in two 16-bit registers) containing the following (see Figure A6.2): the first word contains the flag and control bits and is called "flag and control word" (FCW); the second word is the program counter (PC). In the segmented Z8001, the program status consists of four words: one is the "flag and control word" (FCW), two words correspond to the segmented program counter (PC), and the fourth word is reserved for future use. Seven bits of the first PC word designate one of the 128 segments. The second word supplies the 16-bit offset that designates a location within the segment. With the exception of the segment enable bit (SEG) in the Z8001 program status, the flag and control bits are the same for both CPU versions. The abbreviations used for the flag and control bits are given in Table A6.1.

Table A6.1 Abbreviations for the flag and control bits of the Z8000 program status information [46]. *Reproduced by permission. ©1979 Zilog, Inc. This material shall not be reproduced without the written consent of Zilog, Inc.*

Flags	Controls
C: Carry	SEG: Segmentation enable
Z: Zero	S/N̄: System/normal mode
S: Sign	VIE: Vectored interrupt enable
P/V: Parity or overflow	NVIE: Non-vectored interrupt enable
DA: Decimal adjust	
H: Half carry	

Another type of special register is the *new program status area pointer* (NPSAP) that holds the pointer to the new program status area in memory. In the non-segmented Z8002 it comprises one word, while in the segmented Z8001 it comprises two words.

Finally, the Z8000 CPU includes a *refresh register* for automatic refresh of dynamic memories. It consists of a 9-bit row counter, a 6-bit rate counter and an enable bit. A special referesh memory access is made at programmable intervals. The 9-bit row counter is incremented by two each time the rate counter reaches end-of-count; it can address up to 256 rows (16K dynamic RAMs have 128 rows). The rate counter determines the time between successive refreshes. It consists of a programmable 6-bit modulo-n prescaler ($n = 1$ through 64), driven at one-fourth the CPU clock rate. With a 4 MHz clock, the refresh period can be programmed from 1 to 64 μsec. The refresh operation is generated by a privileged load control register (LDCTL) instruction in the microprocessor's refresh register. The rate counter is free-running, but refresh access can be delayed up to one refresh interval without missing a refresh. Refresh can be disabled if necessary by programming the refresh enable/disable bit.

The Z8000 instructions are grouped functionally into nine groups:

- Load and exchange group
- Arithmetic group
- Logical group
- Program control group
- Bit manipulation group
- Rotate and shift group
- Block transfer and string manipulation group
- Input/output group
- CPU control group

The Z8000 instruction length varies from one to five words (Figure A6.3), depending on its type and addressing mode. The Z8000 offers eight addressing modes. Instructions are always addressed as 16-bit words, and the leftmost byte of an instruction word has an even-numbered address.

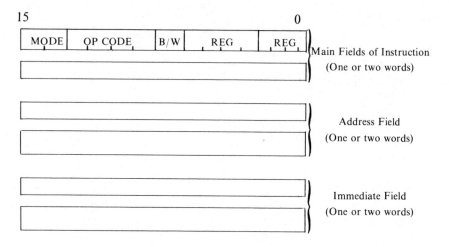

Figure A6.3   Typical Z8000 instruction fields.

The most frequently used instructions in the Z8000 (1- and 2-operand instructions) have been coded as *one word* (referred to as *tight* or *short* instruction format). Among these are load byte register immediate, load word register immediate (for small immediate values), call relative, jump relative, and decrement and jump on non-zero. Less frequent instructions which use more than two operands use *two words*. Depending on the addressing mode, an address follows the instruction if one of the operands resides in memory. There are often additional fields for special elements such as immediate values. Instructions can designate one, two, or three operands explicitly. The instruction translate-and-test is the only instruction with four operands and is also the only instruction with an implied register operand.

A number of powerful instructions which are not usually seen in previous microcomputers have been added to the Z8000 repertoire. These include the extended precision multiply and divide (which manipulate 32-bit long words), translate, and repeat. There are instructions that increment and decrement the contents of any register or memory location by any number from 1 to 6. There are instructions for performing string comparison and block move operations (to compensate somehow for the absence of memory-to-memory instructions). To allow easy communication between the user and system, a "system call" (SC) instruction is provided which performs a software interrupt to the operating system. Finally, the specially privileged instructions test multi-micro bit (MBIT), multi-micro request (MREQ), multi-micro reset (MRES), and multi-micro set (MSET), have been added to govern the two Z8000 pins M_1 and M_0 and allow configuring the microprocessor into efficient multi-processor or network systems.

The formats for the Z8000 instructions are shown in Figure A6.4 [47]. The two most significant bits in the instruction word determine whether the tight

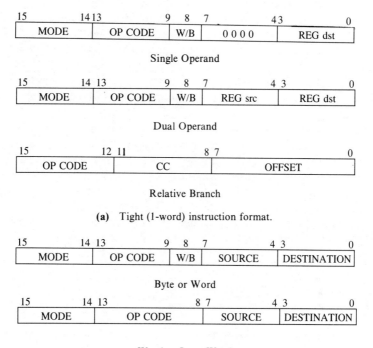

(a) Tight (1-word) instruction format.

Byte or Word

Word or Long Word

(b) General instruction format.

where:

MODE = 11 : Tight instruction format.
MODE = 10 : Register
MODE = 00 : Immediate   }   For SOURCE = 0000
MODE = 01 : Direct
MODE = 00 : Indirect Register }   For SOURCE ≠ 0000
MODE = 01 : Indexed

Figure A6.4   Z8000 instruction formats (not including address or immediate fields shown in Figure A6.3) [47]. *Reproduced by permission.* © *1982 Zilog, Inc.*

(one word) instruction format or the general instruction format is used. As long as these two bits are not both 1's, the general instruction format applies, and this mode field in conjunction with the source-register field specifies the addressing modes (for example, register, direct, etc.). An all-zero source specification distinguishes immediate or direct addressing from indirect and indexed addressing, both of which require a source register. The op code field specifies the type of instruction. Long word instructions use a different op code value from their byte or word counterparts. Field B/W designates the data element type (byte/word). The source and destination fields are four bits wide for addressing the sixteen general registers. Finally, a 4-bit condition code (CC) field may also be used, having the binary values shown in Figure A6.4.

Some implications of instruction formats that the two modes (segmented and non-segmented) and the two versions (40- and 48-pin) have should be discussed here.

The non-segmented Z8002 (or the segmented Z8001 running in non-segmented mode) has only one representation for addresses: *a word*. In contrast, a segmented Z8001 running in the segmented mode has several representations for addresses. In an instruction, they can be one word for the short offset or a long word for the full offset. In a short offset segmented address, the upper eight bits of the full 16-bit offset value used are 0 (zero). A segmented address in registers or memory is always a long word. These are summarized in Figure A6.5.

15   0
```
|                     Non-segmented address                           |
```

(a) Any non-segmented address is one word, whether it is in a register, memory, or an instruction.

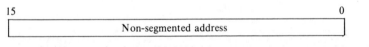

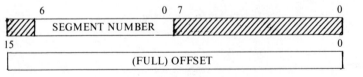

(b) A segmented address in a register pair or memory.

Figure A6.5   Hardware representation of Z8000 segmented addresses [46]. *Reproduced by permission. ©1982 Zilog, Inc. This material shall not be reproduced without the written consent of Zilog, Inc.*

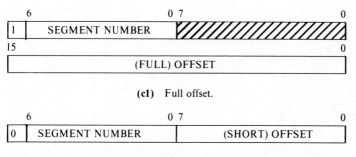

(c1) Full offset.

(c2) Short offset.

(c) A segmented address in an instruction: (c1) when a full offset is used, the address requires two words; (c2) when a short offset is used, the address requires only one word.

Figure A6.5 (*Continued*)

Appendix 7

MOTOROLA 68000

The simplified functional block diagram of the Motorola 68000 CPU[7] is given in Figure A7.1a, and its pins and signals in Figure A7.1b.

Similar to the Zilog Z8000, the Motorola 68000 architecture allows for future expandability. The 68000 is a 16/32-bit word length machine (it is the first microprocessor having 32-bit internal registers), manufactured through HMOS technology, containing approximately 68K transistors on a larger 64-pin chip of size 265x265 mils, and operating at clock rates from 4 MHz (250 nsec clock period) to 8 MHz (125 nsec clock period).

The memory addressing range of the 68000 has increased even further, being the first to implement uniform 16M-byte (16,777,216 bytes) direct physical memory addressing, without segmentation[8] (actually only twenty-three bits are delivered by the CPU's address bus, and they are used in conjunction with the CPU two data strobe outputs, $\overline{UDS}$ and $\overline{LDS}$, to address the 16M-byte range). External chips, called memory management units (MMUs) can be used to support segmented logical address space and provide both management of a variable number of variable sized segments and dynamic multi-task memory relocation and protection.

Like the Z8000, the 68000 provides both *user* and *supervisor* operating modes. The 68000 has sixty-one instruction mnemonics. Although this is eleven fewer than in the earlier 8-bit 6800, the 68000's mnemonics are more powerful and symmetrical; the instruction can use any register for any purpose and every instruction can make use of every relevant addressing mode. Combining instruction types, data types (bits, BCD digits, bytes, words, and long words), and the fourteen addressing modes, provides over 1000 useful instructions. As with all Motorola microprocessors, I/O is done through memory-mapping techniques, where the I/O space is handled similarly to memory space and is serviced by the same memory management facilities. For handling interrupts, three input pins are assigned on the CPU chip, thus

---

[8] Referred to as MC68000.

[9] The 68000 architecture provides for 32-bit addresses to allow a physical memory space of 2^{32} bytes (= 4295M bytes) for future implementations.

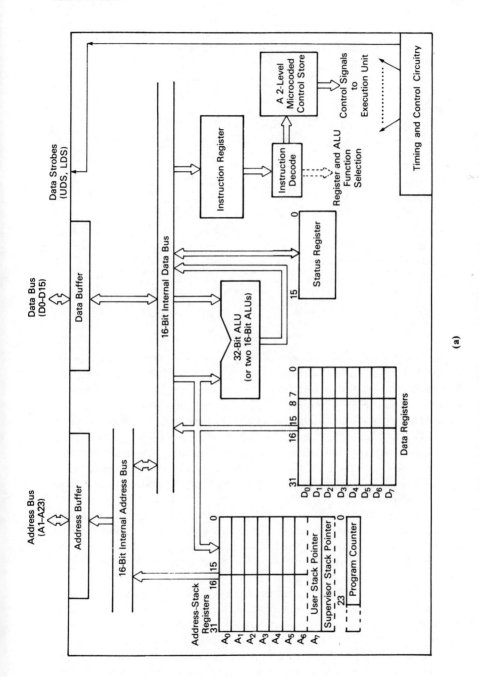

Figure A7.1 The Motorola 68000 microprocessor: (a) the simplified block diagram; (b) the microprocessor pins and signals. *Courtesy of Motorola, INc.* [30].

(a)

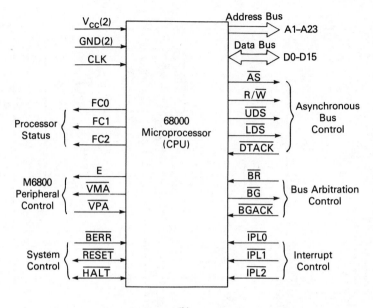

(b)

Figure A7.1 (*Continued*)

providing eight levels of vectored priority interrupts. The maskable levels provide 192 *fixed* vector locations, and software has full control over the placement and execution of interrupt handling routines. Traps are also available. The remaining sixty-four (out of the 256 possible) vector locations are available for software and hardware traps. Like the Z8000, the 68000 provides more than one stack with the ability to switch groups of stacks simultaneously; it has a number of privileged instructions executing in supervisor mode; it includes two stack pointers, one active in user mode and the other active in supervisor mode; and it can facilitate multi-user features and support multiprocessor capabilities.

Besides larger direct addressing capability, wider internal registers, bigger CPU chip size, a greater number of pins, and eight priority levels of external interrupts, the 68000 also has the following differences: (1) While both the 8086 and the Z8000 use a multiplexed address/data bus, the 68000 uses separate address (23-bit) and data (16-bit) buses in an *asynchronous bus structure*. No demultiplexing is required; transfers on the bus are controlled by accompanying handshake signals, and thus devices and memories with large variations in response time may be used on the same bus. (2) The control logic in the 68000 CPU is implemented completely in microcode to enhance instruction flexibility and easy future modifications and expansions. (3) The 68000's symmetrical nature simplifies writing programs in both assembly and high-level languages. No separate special instructions are necessary for operations on byte, word, and long word integers. Thus the programmer needs only to remember one mnemonic for each type of operation and merely specify the appropriate data size and addressing modes for source and destination. (4) User-written routines, which are invoked through the use of the "unimplemented instruction trap," can emulate a desired unavailable instruction [8, 21, 41, 42].

The 68000 ALU can handle six data types: bits, BCD digits, bytes (eight bits), ASCII characters, words (sixteen bits) and double words (thirty-two bits). The ALU is powerful and capable of both 16-bit and 32-bit operations. The operations supported include: integer and multi-precision integer (including signed and unsigned multiply and divide), logical, boolean, bit, decimal (BCD), character, and address operations. It can also handle string data and execute a more flexible MOVE instruction, which allows memory-to-register, register-to-register, register-to-memory, immediate-to-register, immediate-to-memory, and memory-to-memory transfers to be executed efficiently.

Figure A7.2 shows the register structure of the 68000 CPU [30]. The 68000 CPU contains sixteen 32-bit data and address-stack registers, fifteen of which are typically user-accessible *general-purpose* types, that can serve as accumulators or source or destination registers; in some cases, the sixteenth register A7 can also be used in this manner. Although none of these registers is assigned a designated function (as done in the 8086), they all are divided functionally into two classes: the first eight *data registers* (D0–D7) are used primarily as data manipulation registers for byte (8-bit), word (16-bit), and long word (32-bit) data operations. When a data register is used as either a source or destination operand, only the appropriate low-order bits (that correspond to the operand's length) are changed; any remaining high-order bits are neither used nor changed. The eight remaining *address registers* (A0–A7) are used primarily for addressing (i.e., as software stack pointers and base-address registers). Furthermore, address registers can also be used for 16-bit and 32-bit data operations (they do not support byte operands). When used as a source operand, either the sixteen low-order bits or the entire thirty-two bits are used depending upon the operation size. However, unlike data registers, when an address register is used as the destination operand, the entire register is affected regardless of the operation size. If the operation size is sixteen bits, any other operands are sign extended to thirty-two bits before the operation is performed. Finally, all sixteen registers can be used as index registers.

The *stack pointer* is one of these address registers, address register seven (A7). This is either the "user" stack pointer (USP) or the "supervisor" stack pointer (SSP), depending on the state of the S bit in the status register (to be

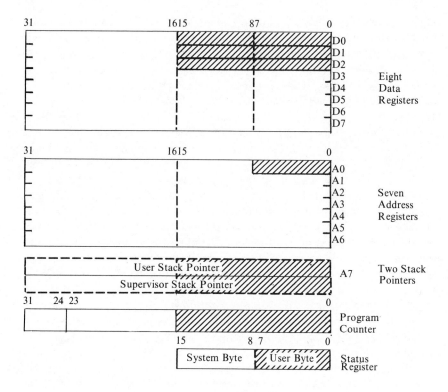

(a)

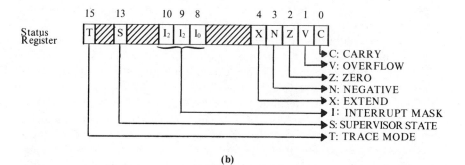

(b)

Figure A7.2 The 68000 CPU internal register structure: **(a)** the internal registers; **(b)** the detailed format of the status register [26]. (The 6809 registers and flag bit are shaded.) *Courtesy of Motorola, Inc.* [30]

described next). If this S bit indicates user mode (S = low), USP is the active stack pointer, and the SSP cannot be referenced as an address register. If the S bit indicates supervisor mode (S = high), SSP is the active stack pointer, and the USP cannot be referenced. Each stack fills from high memory to low memory.

Another register found in the 68000 CPU is the 32-bit *program counter* (twenty-four bits in the initial implementation). The 24-bit program counter permits a direct addressing range of 16M bytes; however, only twenty-three bits are actually delivered by the CPU's address bus. The 24th program counter bit is used to generate the upper ($\overline{\text{UDS}}$) and lower ($\overline{\text{LDS}}$) data-strobe signals that select the high byte, low byte or both bytes of the data bus (see section 6.4.2 of chapter 6).

Finally, a 16-bit *status register* exists, composed of an upper "system byte" and a lower "user byte." At present, the following ten bits are used: carry (C), overflow (V), zero (Z), negative (N), and extend (X). These five bits provide indicators for various ALU operations. There are also three bits (I_2, I_1, I_0) that provide the interrupt mask for the desired priority-interrupt level (eight levels are available). The S bit indicates when the processor is in the supervisor mode, as discussed earlier. Finally, the T bit indicates when the processor is operating in the trace mode. All status bits can be read in either the supervisor or user modes; however, the T and S bits can be set only while in the supervisor mode.

One of the powerful features of the 68000 is its small number of basic instructions (thus, fewer mnemonics for the programmer to memorize), with extensions via the six data types and the addressing modes. Almost all instructions can operate on bytes, words, and double words, and most instructions can use any addressing mode. Furthermore, all data registers and memory locations may be used either for source or destination for most integer-data operations. Thus, the only thing the programmer has to do is specify the type of operation to be performed (the corresponding instruction mnemonic name), the operand size, source addressing mode, and destination addressing mode. The operand size is either explicitly encoded in the instruction or implicitly defined by the instruction operation. All 68000 instructions have the same format of only one word for the "operation word" [28]. Additional "extension words" are required only when the addressing modes use constants (immediate values), absolute addresses, or displacement offsets.

The location of the operand(s) can be specified by the instruction in one of three ways: register specification, effective address, and implicit reference.

Register Specification

In this case, the format of the instruction is very simple. It consists of one word, called the *operation word*, and has the format shown in Figure A7.3a. It uses a 6-bit address specification field, called "effective address field" to specify the location of the operand. Its leftmost three bits are called "mode field" and specify whether the operand is in one of the eight data registers (mode = 000) or in one of the eight address registers (mode = 001); its rightmost three bits are called "register field" and specify the register to be used.

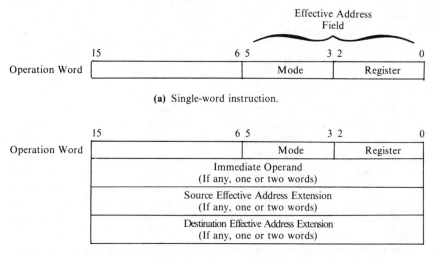

(a) Single-word instruction.

(b) Multiple-word instruction

Figure A7.3 68000 instruction formats: **(a)** the general format of a single-word instruction; **(b)** the general format of a multiple-word instruction. *Courtesy of Motorola, Inc.* [30].

Effective Address

When the operand is an immediate operand or in memory, then the "mode field" of the operation word has one of the binary values 010 to 111. The instructions are now from one to five words in length, as shown in Figure A7.3b. The first word of the instruction, the operation word, specifies the length of the instruction and the operation to be performed and uses its effective address field to specify the mode(s) to be used in accessing the operand. These modes are further classified into memory address modes and special address modes. The last two columns in Table A7.1 give the values of the effective address field. For the special address modes, the mode field always has the value 111, while the register field, instead of specifying a register number, specifies the special addressing mode. The remaining words are either immediate operands or extensions to the effective address mode specified in the first operation word. The second column in Table A7.1 shows the number of extension words required by the various addressing modes. A number of instructions may reference the condition codes or status register by means of the effective address field.

Table A7.1 Encoding of the mode and register fields of the operation word [30].

	Addressing Mode	No. of Extension Words Required	Effective Address Field	
			Mode Field	Register Field
Register Direct Modes	Data register direct	0	000	register number
	Address register direct	0	001	register number
Memory Address Modes	Address register indirect	0	010	register number
	Address register indirect with postincrement	0	011	register number
	Address register indirect with predecrement	0	100	register number
	Register indirect with displacement	1	101	register number
	Address register indirect with index	1	110	register number
Special Address Modes	Absolute short address	1	111	000
	Absolute long address	2	111	001
	Program counter with displacement	1	111	010
	Program counter with index	1	111	011
	Immediate or status register	1 or 2*	111	100

*Depending on the size of the operation.

The definition of certain instructions implies the use of specific registers.

It should also be mentioned here that the *MOVE* instruction provided, which can move eight, sixteen, or thirty-two bits of data from any location to any other location, and its move peripheral data (MOVEP) version, which can move data into or out of a register in 8-bit bursts, have the power to facilitate interfaing to 8-bit peripheral support chips.

Other useful instructions provided are the *exchange (EXG)* instructions that exchange the contents of any two registers, and the *SWAP* instruction that swaps the upper sixteen bits of a register with its lower sixteen bits. Two other powerful instructions, the *link (LINK)* and *unlink (UNLK)*, which are very useful for implementing high-level languages, are also provided.

Finally, the 68000 incorporates instruction-by-instruction tracing of a program and powerful trap capabilities. There are seventeen TRAP instructions, sixteen of which are unconditional, providing sixteen different software interrupts. A user program can use the TRAP instruction for implementing supervisor calls. As already mentioned, the 2-level microprogram structure has permitted leaving one eighth of the op code map unimplemented (to be used for future instructions). Unimplemented instructions cause traps. In addition to the above sixteen software-trap vectors, two other trap vectors have been assigned (in locations 28_{16} and $2C_{16}$) to allow a user-written routine to emulate a desired unavailable instruction.

The 68000 instructions are grouped functionally into eight groups:

- Data movement
- Integer arithmetic
- Logical
- Shift and rotate
- Bit manipulation
- Binary coded decimal
- Program control
- System control

Appendix 8

INTEL APX 432

The Intel APX 432 processing system (or "micromainframe") is a recent 3-chip 32-bit microcomputer [15–19, 38]. Two of these chips (the APX 43201 and APX 43202) make up the general data processor (GDP), while the third chip (the APX 43203) is the interface processor (IP). Each chip is manufactured with the new semiconductor process—high-density MOS, or H-MOS—using a new package with a high pin count—the 64-pin quad in-line package (QUIP)—and operates from a single 5-volt supply. A 2-phase clocking at 8 MHz yields the minimal 125-nsec microcycle time. The APX 43201 is the *instruction decoder/microinstruction sequencer,* containing more than 100,000 devices; it fetches and decodes instructions. The APX 43202 is the *execution unit*, having over 60,000 devices; it executes the decoded instructions from the APX 43201. The third chip, the APX 43203, is the *interface processor*, and includes 65,000 devices; it offloads the general data processor of the tasks involved in communicating with input/output devices. Both the GDP and the IP are microprogrammed, each containing a 4K- $\times$16-bit and a 2K- $\times$ 16-bit ROM, respectively. Communication among the GDP, IP, and memory is provided by a *packet-based interconnect bus*.

The 32-bit GDP can support an extremely large logical address space. The memory architecture of the system is "structured segmented" (2^{24} segments, 2^{16} byte displacement) permitting a virtual memory system address space of up tp 2^{40} bytes (over a trillion bytes). Accessing memory is done via the 2-level addressing architecture discussed in section 10.4.2 of chapter 10. The system can handle eight "primitive" data types and two "structured" data types (see section 4.2 of chapter 4), and has variable length instruction formats that have from 0- to 3-operand references.

The 32-bit APX 432 system has an *object oriented architecture* that can handle several object types, each one identified by a descriptor-type code. Objects present a consistent framework in which both processes and processors may communicate conveniently. An object is a data structure, having a label that tells the object's type, and capable of being referenced (addressed) as one thing. A simple object can be stored in a single memory segment (up to 64K bytes in length), while complex objects may occupy many segments. One type of object is the *data object* which is a linear, logical address space from 1 K to 64K bytes in length. A second group are the "system objects" which include *domain objects* (representing the addressing environment of a program module), *context objects* (to support the dynamic allocation of memory every time they are activated) and *processor objects* (where a data structure exists to represent each individual GDP in an APX 432 system, and contains information such as whether the GDP is running or halted, machine check information, and references for other objects which the processor needs). Finally, other object types include *process objects* (each representing an independent concurrent program or task), *storage resource objects* (each representing a portion of the allocatable or free storage in the system), and *port objects* (used to support the buffered transmission of messages between processes or programs).

An APX 432 instruction varies in length and has from 0 to 3 operand references. The general instruction format consists of four fields arranged in the format shown in Figure A8.1. The first two fields encountered by the processor in the instruction stream are called the *class* field and the *format* field; they specify how many operands are in the instruction and supply information on how they are to be accessed. The *operator code field* corresponds to the normal op code defining the operation to be executed. Finally, the *reference field* contains the logical addresses of up to three operands; each logical address is composed of a segment selector and a displacement (also see the Intel APX 432 segmentation in section 10.4.2 of chapter 10).

Instructions are contained in special hardware-recognized *instruction segments* in memory, may contain a variable number of bits, and may begin at any bit boundaries. The processor views an instruction segment (presently in units of thirty-two bits) as a continuous string of bits called the instruction stream.

The APX 432 instruction set is completely *symmetric* in that all addressing modes exist for every operand and all required operators exist for every data type (see data types in section 4.2 in chapter 4) in the instruction set.

The General Data Processor

The general data processor (GDP) handles all program decoding, address generation, and computation. It is organized internally as a 3-stage microprogram-controlled pipeline (see section 4.4.3 of chapter 4). The first stage is the instruction decoder (ID); the second stage is the microinstruction sequencer (MI); and the third stage is the execution unit (EU). The first two stages of the pipeline are physically located on the APX 43201, and the third stage is located on the APX 43202.

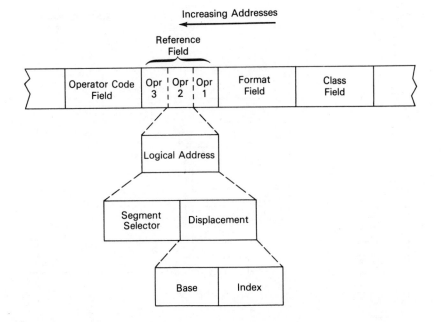

Figure A8.1   The Intel APX 432 instruction format (three operands).*Courtesy Intel Corporation* [15].

The APX 43201 (Instruction Decoder/Microinstruction Sequencer)

The functional block diagram of the APX 43201 is shown in Figure A8.2a, and its pins and signals are shown in Figure A8.2b. The *instruction decoder* of the APX 43201 receives macroinstructions, processes variable-length fields, extracts logical addresses, generates starting addresses for the microinstruction sequences, and generates microinstructions for simple operations. The second stage of the pipeline (the *Microinstruction Sequencer*) issues microinstructions to the execution unit (the APX 43202), executes microinstruction sequences out of its ROM, responds to the bus control signals, invokes macroinstruction fetches, and initiates interprocessor communication and fault-handling sequences.

The APX 43202 (Execution Unit)

The functional block diagram of the APX 43202 is shown in Figure A8.3a, and its pins and signals in Figure A8.3b. This chip is the *execution unit*, corresponding to the third stage of the pipeline. It is made up of two independent subprocessors, each one controlled by a separate sequencer: the data manipulation unit (DMU) and the reference generation unit (RGU).

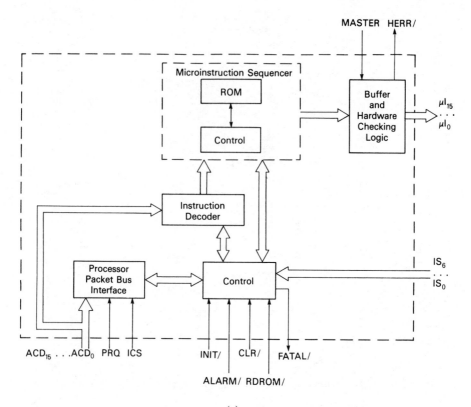

(a)

Figure A8.2   The Intel APX 43201 instruction decoder/microinstruction sequencer: **(a)** the simplified functional block diagram; **(b)** the chip's pins and signals. *Courtesy Intel Corporation* [17].

The reference generation unit handles sequencing of memory accesses and performs memory mapping by translating a 40-bit virtual address into a 24-bit physical address and checking memory (actually, domain) protection attributes. The unit also contains a cache that maintains the physical base address as well as the length of the segment and a hardware-implemented mechanism which uses least-recently-used algorithms for deciding which segment base-length pair to replace in the cache when a new segment is referenced.

The data manipulation unit contains the ALU and all necessary registers for 16-and 32-bit fixed-point arithmetic (including multiply and divide) as well as the 32-, 64-, and 80-bit floating point arithmetic proposed by the IEEE standard [11].

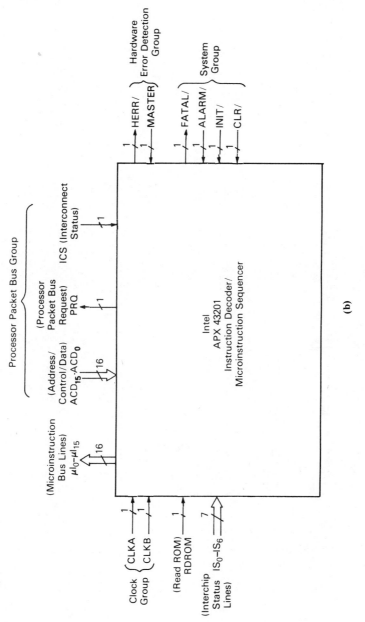

Figure A8.2 (*Continued*)

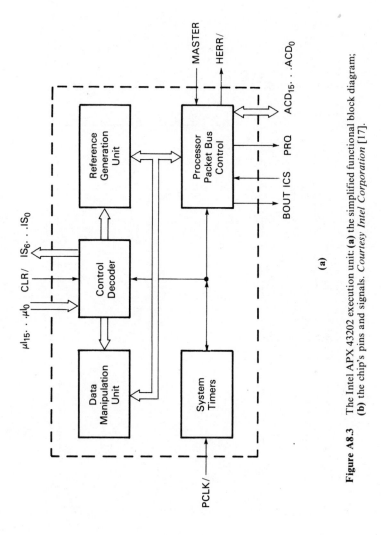

(a)

Figure A8.3 The Intel APX 43202 execution unit: (a) the simplified functional block diagram; (b) the chip's pins and signals. *Courtesy Intel Corporation* [17].

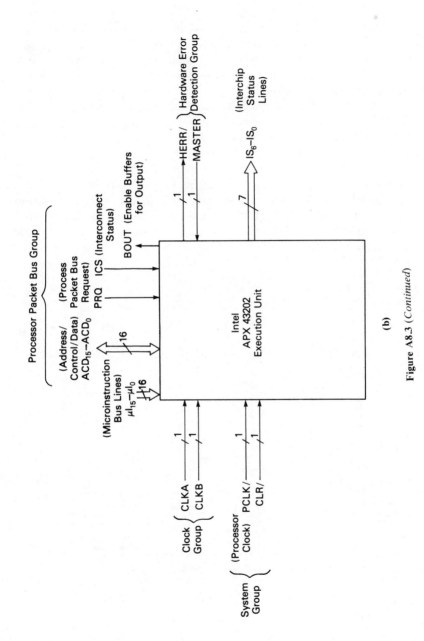

Figure A8.3 *(Continued)*

The APX 43203 (Interface Processor)

The third chip making up an APX 432 system is the interface processor (IP) APX 43203 (Figure A8.4). As any APX 432 processor, the IP operates in an object-oriented, multiprocessing environment, provides fully independent and decentralized I/O facilities, and maps a portion of the peripheral subsystem address space into the APX 432 system memory. A peripheral subsystem is an autonomous microcomputer system with its own local memory, I/O devices and controllers, at least one conventional processor (e.g., the 8086), called an *attached processor* (AP), and software. The IP and the AP form the logical I/O processor of an APX 432 system. All peripherals are interfaced to the interrupt-driven I/O subsystem bus (e.g., the MULTIBUS). The IP communicates with I/O devices by executing various tasks, including device driver execution, device interrupt handling, and DMA channel initialization. The IP also includes capability for hardware error detection and MULTIBUS system compatible interface. More than one IP may be connected to the system, each one attaching one peripheral subsystem to the main APX 432 system.

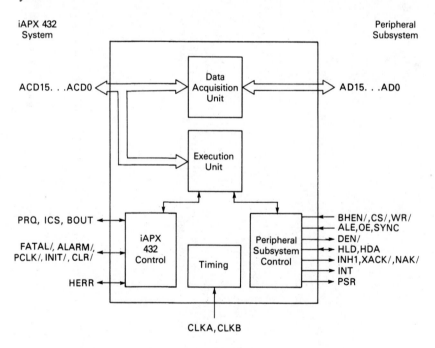

(a)

Figure A8.4 The Intel APX 43203 interface processor: **(a)** the simplified functional block diagram; **(b)** the chip's pins and signals. *Courtesy: Intel Corporation* [18]

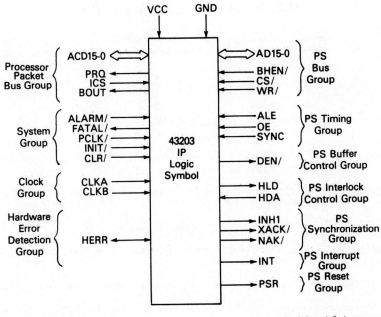

iAPX 432 System

Peripheral Subsystem

(b)

Figure A8.4 (*Continued*)

REFERENCES AND BIBLIOGRAPHY

[1] Alexandridis, N.A., "Microprocessor Systems—Architecture and Engineering," *Infotech State of the Art Report on Microelectronics*, Pergamon Infotech, series 8, no. 2, 1980, pp. 1–41.

[2] Bursky, D., "Microprocessor Data Manual," *Electronic Design*, 24, November 22, 1979, pp. 49–60.

[3] Bursky, D., "Z8000 CPUs Expand Processing Power with New Instructions, Special Processors," *Electronic Design*, 2, January 18, 1980, pp. 33–34.

[4] Crook, C., "Microcomputer Architecture—A Survey Report," *Infotech State of the Art Report on Microelectronics*, Pergamon Infotech, series 8, no. 2, 1980.

[5] Davis, H.A., "Comparing Architectures of Three 16-bit Microprocessors," *Computer Design*, July 1979, pp. 91–100.

[6] Davis, S., "Microprocessors," *EDN*, August 5, 1979, pp. 71–85.

[7] Garrow, R., et al, "16-bit Single-Board Computer Maintains 8-bit Family Ties," *Electronics*, October 12, 1978, pp 105–10.

[8] Halsema, A.I., "A Preview of the Motorola 68000," *BYTE*, August 1979, pp. 170–74.

[9] Hemenway, J., and E. Teja, "As You Get to Know the 8086, Use Your 8-bit Experience," *EDN*, January 20, 1979, pp 81–87.

[10] Hilburn J.L. and P.M. Julich, *Microcomputers/Microprocessors: Hardware, Software and Applications*, Englewood Cliffs, N.J. Prentice-Hall, Inc., 1976.

[11] IEEE Task P754, Draft 8.0, "A Proposed Standard for Binary Floating-Point Arithmetic," *Computer*, March 1981, pp. 51–62.

[12] Intel Corporation, *8080 Microcomputer System User's Manual*, Santa Clara, CA, September 1975.

[13] Intel Corporation, *MCS-80 User's Manual(with Introduction to MCS-85)*, Santa Clara, CA, October 1977.

[14] Intel Corporation, *The 8086 Family User's Manual*, Santa Clara, CA, 1979.

[15] Intel Corporation, *Introduction to the iAPX 432 Architecture*, (171821-001), Santa Clara, CA, 1981.

[16] Intel Corporation, *iAPX 432 Object Primer*, (171858-001, Rev. B), Santa Clara, CA, 1981.

[17] Intel Corporation, *iAPX 43201, iAPX 43202 VLSI General Data Processor*, (171873-001, Rev. A), Santa Clara, CA, 1981.

[18] Intel Corporation, *iAPX 43203 VLSI Interface Processor*, (171874-001 Rev. A), Santa Clara, CA, 1981.

[19] Johnson, R.C., "32-bit Microprocessors Inherit Mainframe Features," *Electronics*, February 24, 1981, pp. 138–41.

[20] Katz, B.J., et al, "8086 Microcomputer Bridges the Gap Between 8- and 16-Bit Designs," *Electronics*, February 16, 1978, pp. 99–104.

[21] Kister, J.E., and R.H. Naugle, "Develop Software for 16-bit μC Without Making Costly Commitments," *Electronic Design*, 19, September 13, 1979, pp. 112–16.

[22] Klingman, E.E., *Microprocessor Systems Design*, Englewood Cliffs, NJ: Prentice-Hall,Inc., 1977.

[23] Lapham, S.A., and H.M. Kop, "The 8086 μP has the Architecture to Handle High-Level Languages Efficiently," *Electronic Design*, 5, March 1, 1980, pp. 97μ99.

[24] LeMair, I., and R. Nobis, "Complex Systems are Simple to Design (with the MC68000)," *Electronic Design*, 18, September 1, 1978, pp. 100–107.

[25] Martin, D.P., *Microcomputer Design*, Martin Research (now Quint Systems, Inc.), Northbrook, IL, 1976.

[26] McKevitt, J., and J. Bayliss, "New Options from Big Chips," *IEEE Spectrum*, March 1979, pp. 28–34.

[27] Morse, S.P., et al, "The Intel 8086 Microprocessor: A 16-bit Evolution of the 8080," *Computer*, June 1978, pp. 18–27.

[28] Motorola, Incorporated, *M6800 Microprocessor Applications Manual*, Austin, TX, 1975.

[29] Motorola, Incorporated, *M6800 Microcomputer, System Design Data*, Austin, TX, 1976.

[30] Motorola, Incorporated, *16-Bit Microprocessing Unit*, Austin, TX, 1980.

[31] Nichols, E.A., J.C. Nichols, and P.R. Rony, *Z80 Microprocessor, Book 1, Programming*, Indianapolis, IN: Howard W. Sams and Co., Inc., 1979.

[32] Ogdin, C.A., "Sixteen-Bit Micros," *Mini-Micro Systems*, January 1979, pp. 64–72.

[33] Osborne, A. *An Introduction to Microcomputers, Volume I, Basic Concepts*, Berkeley, CA: Adam Osborne and Associates, Inc., 1976.

[34] Osborne, A., *An Introduction to Microcomputers, Volume II, Some Real Products*, Berkeley, CA: Adam Osborne and Associates, Inc., 1976.

[35] Peatman, J.B., *Microcomputer Based Design*, New York: McGraw-Hill, 1977.

[36] Peuto, B.L., "Architecture of a New Microprocessor," *Computer*, February, 1979, pp. 10–21.

[37] Rampil, I., "Preview of the Z-8000," *BYTE*, March 1979, pp. 80–91.

[38] Rattner, J., and W.W. Lattin, "Ada Determines Architecture of 32-bit Microprocessor," *Electronics*, February 24, 1981, pp. 119–26.

[39] Ritter, T., "A Microprocessor for the Revolution: The 6809," Part 1, *BYTE*, January 1979, pp. 14–42.

[40] Shima, M, "Two Versions of 16-bit Chip Span Microprocessor, Minicomputer Needs," *Electronics*, December 21, 1978, pp. 81–88.

[41] Starnes, T.W., "Compact Instructions Give the MC68000 Power while Simplifying its Operation," *Electronic Design*, 20, September 27, 1979, pp. 70–74.

[42] Stritter, E., and T. Gunter, "A Microprocessor Architecture for a Changing World: The Motorola 68000," *Computer*, February 1979, pp. 43–51.

[43] Sugarman, R., "Computers: Our Microuniverse Expands," *IEEE Spectrum*, January 1979, pp. 32–37.

[44] Titus, C., et al, "Interfacing Fundamentals: The 8085 Family of Memory Devices," *Computer Design*, August 1978, pp. 122–28.

[45] Zilog, Incorporated, *Z80-CPU, Z80A-CPU Product Specification*, Cupertino, CA, 1977.

[46] Zilog, Incorporated, *Z8001 CPU, Z8002 CPU Product Specification*, (Preliminary), Cupertino, CA, 1979.

[47] Zilog, Incorporated, *Z8000 Technical Manual*, Cupertino, CA, 1979.

Subject Index